"Be Fertile and
Increase, Fill the
Earth and Master It"

ALSO BY JEREMY COHEN

The Friars and the Jews: The Evolution of Medieval Anti-Judaism

"Be Fertile and Increase, Fill the Earth and Master It"

The Ancient and Medieval Career of a Biblical Text

JEREMY COHEN

Cornell University Press

ITHACA AND LONDON

First published 1989 by Cornell University Press.

International Standard Book Number 0-8014-2307-4
Library of Congress Catalog Card Number 89-7149

Printed in the United States of America

*Librarians: Library of Congress cataloging information
appears on the last page of the book.*

*The paper in this book is acid-free and meets the guidelines for
permanence and durability of the Committee on Production
Guidelines for Book Longevity of the Council on Library Resources.*

Any man who has no wife
lives without blessing,
as Scripture states (Gen. 1:28),
"God blessed them"—
them meaning when they are a couple.

Midrash Tᵉhillim 59.2

Contents

Acknowledgments

THIS book has occupied much of my time and thought during the past decade, and I take pleasure in thanking the many individuals and institutions that helped me bring the project to its conclusion. John Burnham, William Childs, Howard Eilberg-Schwartz, Avraham Grossman, David Halivni, Moshe Idel, Joseph Lynch, Sam Meier, David Stern, Michael Twomey, and David Zisenwine read drafts of various chapters and offered valuable criticism and advice. Among countless others, Alan Cooper, Arthur Green, Martha Himmelfarb, Marc Hirshman, Brian Tierney, and Christian Zacher graciously allowed me to exploit their fields of expertise with numerous questions as my work continued. Grants from the Society for the Humanities at Cornell University, the National Endowment for the Humanities, and the Memorial Foundation for Jewish Culture afforded me precious time to pursue my research, as did the particularly generous support of the Dean of Humanities at The Ohio State University. The College of Humanities, the Department of History, the Melton Center for Jewish Studies, and the Center for Medieval and Renaissance Studies at Ohio State kindly bore the costs of my research and of preparing the index, and my colleagues in each of those units took a helpful and supportive interest in this project at every step. I enjoyed the hospitality of many colleagues and librarians at the Hebrew University of Jerusalem during 1984–85; citations from rabbinic responsa were amassed during the same year, in part with the kind help of the computerized Responsa Project at Bar-Ilan University in Ramat-Gan. My student research assistants of the past years, Timothy Crow, Wendy Horowitz, Madelene Kerns, Ken Schurb, and Elizabeth Todd, provided me with loyal and highly competent service. The interlibrary loan office of The Ohio State University Libraries extended itself on my behalf with endless forbearance. And with his friendly patience and mild manner, Michael Szczepanik saved me untold aggravation by making my computer user-friendly.

I do not believe that students of antiquity and the Middle Ages are usually so fortunate as to find in their research the direct, personal relevance that this study of "be fertile and increase" has had for me. My son Raphael was born just as I began work on this project. Ethan was born as the project crystallized into its present form. And Adena and Ariel were born in the final months before its completion. Together they have shown me the joys and rewards of procreation; with them the ideas of this book have assumed life and meaning. My subject also taught me about being a child, and I thank my parents, Gerson and Naomi Cohen, for their constant encouragement and insightful suggestions. Most of all, I am indebted to my wife, Deborah, who has borne much of the burden of this book, just as she has borne our children. In a life of partnership with her, I too have come to appreciate Joseph Karo's dictum, that "the greatness of the commandment to 'be fertile and increase' extends to the heavens, and there is none which compares to it among all the commandments."

JEREMY COHEN

Columbus, Ohio
ʿErev Rosh ha-Shanah 5749

Abbreviations

EcclR	*Ecclesiastes Rabbah*
EH	*'Even ha-'Ezer*
Eruv.	*'Eruvin*
ET	Berlin, Meyer, and Shlomo Josef Zevin, eds. *Talmudic Encyclopedia* (Hebrew). Jerusalem, 1947– .
ExR	*Exodus Rabbah*
GCS	Die griechischen christlichen Schriftsteller
GenR	*Midrash Bereshit Rabba: Critical Edition with Notes and Commentary* (Hebrew). Ed. J. Theodor and C. Albeck. 3 vols. 1903–36; repr., Jerusalem, 1965.
Git.	*Giṭṭin*
Hag.	*Ḥagigah*
HTR	*Harvard Theological Review*
HUCA	*Hebrew Union College Annual*
Hul.	*Ḥullin*
ICC	International Critical Commentary
JBL	*Journal of Biblical Literature*
Jobl. diss.	Jobling, David Kenneth. "'And Have Dominion . . .': The Interpretation of Old Testament Texts Concerning Man's Rule over the Creation (Genesis 1:26, 28, 9:1–2, Psalm 8:7–9) from 200 B.C. to the Time of the Council of Nicea." Th.D. Dissertation, Union Theological Seminary, New York, 1972.
JQR	*Jewish Quarterly Review*
JS	Green, Arthur, ed. *Jewish Spirituality*. 2 vols. World Spirituality: An Encyclopedic History of the Religious Quest 13–14. New York, 1986–87. Vol. 1.
JSOT	*Journal for the Study of the Old Testament*
Ket.	*Kᵉtubbot*
LCL	Loeb Classical Library
LevR	*Midrash Wayyikra Rabbah* (Hebrew). Ed. Mordecai Margulies. 5 vols. Jerusalem, 1953–60.
LOJ	Ginzberg, Louis. *The Legends of the Jews*. Tr. Henrietta Szold and Paul Radin. 7 vols. Philadelphia, Pa., 1909–38.
LXX	Septuagint
M	Mishnah
MAgg	*Midrash 'Aggadah 'al Ḥamishah Ḥumshe Torah*. Ed. Solomon Buber. 1894; repr., Jerusalem, 1972.
Mak.	*Makkot*
MBR	*Midras Beresit Rabbati* (Hebrew). Ed. C. Albeck. Jerusalem, 1940.
Meg.	*Mᵉgillah*
MGWJ	*Monatsschrift für die Geschichte und Wissenschaft des Judentums*
MHG	*Midrash Haggadol on the Pentateuch* (Hebrew). Ed. Mordecai Margulies et al. 5 vols. Jerusalem, 1947–75.

MHZ	Lachover, F., and Isaiah Tishby, eds. *The Wisdom of the Book of Splendour* (Hebrew). 2nd ed. (vol. 1 only). 2 vols. Jerusalem, 1957–61.
MQ	*Moʿed Qaṭan*
MT	Moses b. Maimon. *Mishneh Torah.*
MTad	"*Midrash Tadsheʾ.*" Ed. Abraham Epstein. In *Mi-Qadmoniyyot ha-Yᵉhudim: Meḥqarim u-Rᵉshimot,* pp. 130–75. Ed. A. M. Habermann. Jerusalem, 1957.
MTeh	*Midrash Tᵉhillim.* Ed. Solomon Buber. 1891; repr., Jerusalem, 1966.
Ned.	*Nᵉdarim*
Nid.	*Niddah*
NJPS	*Tanakh: A New Translation of the Holy Scriptures according to the Traditional Hebrew Text.* Philadelphia, Pa., 1985.
NumR	*Numbers Rabbah*
OHG	Lewin, B. M., ed. *Otzar ha-Gaonim: Thesaurus of the Gaonic Responsa and Commentaries* (Hebrew). 15 vols. Haifa and Jerusalem, 1928–43.
OJPS	*The Holy Scriptures according to the Masoretic Text: A New Translation.* 1917; repr. Philadelphia, Pa., 1966.
OP	*Otzar Haposkim* (Hebrew). Ed. Isaac Halevi Herzog et al. 15 vols. to date. Jerusalem, 1962–87.
OTP	*The Old Testament Pseudepigrapha.* Ed. James H. Charlesworth. 2 vols. Garden City, N.Y., 1983–85.
PDRE	"*Pirqe dᵉ-Rabbi ʾEliʿezer.*" Ed. Michael Higger. *Horeb* 8 (1944), 82–119; 9 (1946), 94–166; 10 (1948), 185–294.
Pes.	*Pᵉsaḥim*
PesR	*Pesikta Rabbati: Midrasch für den Fest-Cyclus und die ausgezeichneten Sabbathe* (Hebrew). Ed. Meir Friedmann (Ish-Shalom). 1880; repr., Tel Aviv, 1963.
PG	Patrologia graeca
PL	Patrologia latina
PO	Patrologia orientalis
PRK	*Pesikta de Rav Kahana* (Hebrew). Ed. Bernard Mandelbaum. 2 vols. New York, 1962.
Qid.	*Qiddushin*
RaMba"N	Moses b. Nahman. *Perush ha-Torah.* Ed. Charles B. Chavel. 2 vols. Jerusalem, 1959–60.
RaSh"I	Solomon b. Isaac (Rashi). *RaSh"I ʿal ha-Torah.* Ed. Abraham Berliner and C. B. Chavel. Jerusalem, 1962.
REJ	*Revue des études juives*
RSV	Revised Standard Version
Sab.	*Shabbat*
San.	*Sanhedrin*
SC	Sources chrétiennes

ShA	Joseph b. Efraim Karo. *Shulḥan ʿArukh*.
SHB	Judah b. Samuel the Pious. *Sefer Ḥasidim*. Ed. Reuben Margaliot. Jerusalem, 1970.
Shev.	*Shᵉvuʿot*
SHP	Judah b. Samuel the Pious. *Das Buch der Frommen* (Hebrew). Ed. Jehuda Wistinetzki and J. Freimann. 2nd ed. Frankfurt a.M., 1924.
Shu"T	*Shᵉʾelot u-Tᵉshuvot*
SifD	*Sifre on Deuteronomy* (Hebrew). Ed. Louis Finkelstein. Corpus tannaiticum 3,3,2. 1939; repr., New York, 1969.
SifN	*Siphre ad Numeros adjecto Siphre zutta* (Hebrew). Ed. H. S. Horovitz. Corpus tannaiticum 3,3,1. 1917; repr., Jerusalem, 1966.
SSR	*Midrash Shir Hashirim* (Hebrew). Ed. Eliezer Grünhut and Joseph Chaim Wertheimer. 2nd ed. Jerusalem, 1981.
ST	*Summa theologiae*
T	*Tosefta*
Taan.	*Taʿanit*
Tan.	*Midrash Tanḥumaʾ*. 1563; repr., Jerusalem, 1971.
TanB	*Midrash Tanḥumaʾ he-Qadum wᵉha-Yashan*. Ed. Solomon Buber. 6 pts. in 2 vols. 1885; repr., Jerusalem, 1964.
TB	Babylonian Talmud
TJ	Palestinian Talmud
Tur	Jacob b. Asher. *Ṭurim*.
TZ	*Sefer Tiqqune ha-Zohar*. Ed. Reuben Margaliot. 1948; repr., Jerusalem, 1978 (bound with *Sefer ha-Bahir*).
VT	*Vetus Testamentum*
Yev.	*Yᵉvamot*
Z	*Sefer ha-Zohar*. Ed. Reuben Margaliot. 3 vols. Jerusalem, 1940–47.
ZAW	*Zeitschrift für die alttestamentliche Wissenschaft*
ZH	*Zohar Ḥadash*. Ed. Reuben Margaliot. 1955; repr., Jerusalem, 1978.

"Be Fertile and
Increase, Fill the
Earth and Master It"

Introduction

"GOD blessed them and God said to them, 'Be fertile and increase, fill the earth and master it; and rule the fish of the sea, the birds of the sky, and all the living things that creep on earth'" (Gen. 1:28). The scene is the sixth day of creation. God has finally fashioned man and woman, the last of his creatures, and in this verse he entrusts them with a singular mission in the cosmic order. Thus Scripture culminates its account of the world's genesis, offering a brief but valuable statement of biblical cosmology and anthropology. Of all God's creatures, humans alone bear the image of God. They alone engage in direct conversation with their maker. And they alone receive authority over the natural world: a responsibility to populate it, to control it, and thereby to civilize it.

The ramifications of this charge are numerous and far-reaching, as God lays the basis for his relationship with humans and for his expectations of them. The verse captures the complexity of human nature; men and women must reproduce sexually like other animals, but because humans wield dominion they are somehow superior to other earthly creatures. Situated near the end of the Genesis cosmogony, perhaps the verse suggests that God created the world and its inhabitants expressly

Unless otherwise indicated, all translations from the Hebrew Bible follow NJPS, while those from the New Testament follow the RSV.

for the benefit of human beings. More profoundly still, the verse implies that God fashioned humans to carry on—indeed, to complete—the process his creation began. As noted biblical scholars have observed, here is "a whole programme for the cultural history of mankind,"[1] a rationale for human civilization that reflects and informs much of the theology of the Hebrew Bible. It is not surprising that the divine mandate for human procreation and dominion has weighed heavily on readers of the Bible and that it has figured prominently in the diverse texts and traditions of Judaism and Christianity. Western attitudes toward marriage, sexuality, technology, and even the mysteries of communion with the divine have regularly drawn on this primordial blessing and its interpretation.

Recently, too, Gen. 1:28 has been receiving considerable attention. Feminist theology and innovative trends in literary criticism have fueled new interpretations of the Bible's "primeval history" and of its sexual motifs in particular. Since the awakening of intense public concern for the environment, scholars and laypeople have repeatedly cited the injunction to "fill the earth and master it" in an attempt to identify the ethos that has nurtured our ecological values. Lynn White's seminal essay "The Historic Roots of Our Ecologic Crisis" induced many to attribute Western society's "ruthlessness toward nature" to the biblical foundations of "Judeo-Christian teleology,"[2] while others have since rushed to defend Scripture against this indictment. Students of Gnosticism continue to illuminate the diversity and hermeneutical ingenuity in ancient interpretation of the Genesis cosmogony. And the preceding year has seen the publication of important studies on sexuality in late antique Christianity by Elaine Pagels and Peter Brown.[3]

Yet for all the time and energy expended in these efforts, no one has systematically studied Jewish and Christian interpretation of Gen. 1:28 to determine the meaning and implications of the verse in the history of Western religions. This task has been repeatedly overlooked. For strik-

1. Walter Eichrodt, *Theology of the Old Testament,* tr. J. A. Baker, 2 vols. (Philadelphia, Pa., 1961–67), 2:127, quoting Hermann Gunkel, *Genesis,* Göttinger Handkommentar zum Alten Testament 1,1, 3rd ed. (1910; repr., Göttingen, 1922), p. 113.

2. Lynn White, Jr., "The Historic Roots of Our Ecologic Crisis," *Science* 155 (1967), 1203–7. White has continued to adhere to his position, both in "Continuing the Conversation," in *Western Man and Environmental Ethics: Attitudes towards Nature and Technology,* ed. Ian G. Barbour (Reading, Mass., 1973), pp. 55–65, and in a letter to me dated July 7, 1982.

3. Elaine Pagels, *Adam, Eve, and the Serpent* (New York, 1988); Peter Brown, *The Body and Society: Men, Women, and Sexual Renunciation in Early Christianity* (New York, 1988).

ingly ahistorical reasons, some historians of ideas have excluded the legacy of the Bible from their elaboration of Western thought and values, even in contexts where the themes of the Genesis cosmogony are directly relevant. From this point of view, as espoused by Bruno Snell, "European thinking begins with the Greeks. They have made it what it is: our only way of thinking; its authority, in the Western world, is undisputed."[4] Others have shortchanged the subject, merely assuming that Gen. 1:28 originally intended to convey a license for environmental exploitation, just as they now interpret it. Those, like White, who condemn the Bible in this regard decry a biblical idea of dominion over nature; theologians defending Scripture typically marshal other biblical passages to temper the ostensive message of Gen. 1:28. Even the two doctoral dissertations that undertake to trace the career of the verse let the Bible's presumed meaning—rather than the textual unit of the verse itself—define their interests. One examines the "fruitfulness ideal" in the first half of the verse,[5] the other focuses on the "dominion commandment" in the second half,[6] but neither considers the entire verse, and the resulting bifurcation appears actually to defy the intention of the biblical author. The topical focus of these studies, then, leads them to discover references to Gen. 1:28 in postbiblical discussions of its supposed theme, often with no demonstrable evidence of direct quotation or indirect allusion.

In an article published several years ago, I attempted to establish the importance of Gen. 1:28 as a subject for cultural and intellectual historians, and I set out to pursue the research myself.[7] As my work progressed, the hazards of defining such a project around any predetermined idea—human dominion over nature, for example—quickly became clear to me, for in the case of dominion, despite the prevalent presumption to the contrary, a careful review of Scripture suggests that there is no readily identifiable biblical idea. Certain passages, including

---

4. Bruno Snell, *The Discovery of the Mind: The Greek Origins of European Thought,* tr. T. G. Rosenmeyer (Oxford, 1953), p. v.

5. David Anthony Yegerlehner, "'Be Fruitful and Multiply, and Fill the Earth . . .': A History of the Interpretation of Genesis 1:28a and Related Texts in Selected Periods" (Ph.D. Dissertation, Boston University, Boston, Mass., 1975).

6. Jobl., diss. Despite its methodological shortcomings, Jobling's dissertation is a meticulously indexed, invaluable florilegium of Jewish, Gnostic, classical, and Christian sources on the theme of dominion. Shorter studies, on portions of the exegetical career of Gen. 1:28, will be cited in the footnotes further below.

7. See Jeremy Cohen, "The Bible, Man, and Nature in the History of Western Thought: A Call for Reassessment," *Journal of Religion* 65 (1985), 155–72.

Gen. 1:28, might lend themselves to interpretation as bespeaking this idea, and at times, they have been so interpreted. But one cannot simply postulate the existence of such a notion in the message of Scripture and then reconstruct its history. Such a procedure mistakes one's own understanding of the Bible for the putative intention of the biblical author. Rather, one should be more objective and commence with the text of Scripture itself and study the history of its interpretation, inquiring if, when, and how the presumed idea—or any other idea—was perceived in the words of the Bible. Although the written record of the biblical text also developed and changed over time, at a certain point in history its words became constant while its meaning continued to vary considerably.

Standing clear of contemporary religious concern with the environment, the status of women, patterns of sexual preference, and the like, this book charts the career of Gen. 1:28 in the Jewish and Christian traditions, from biblical antiquity until the Protestant Reformation. (At that point in history, Scripture began to lose the controlling influence on mores and values in Western society that it had wielded previously. The Reformation hardly signaled an end to Jewish and Christian interest in Gen. 1:28, but the nature and substance of the interpretation did change, providing this book with a sensible terminus.) I set out from the premise that the meaning, and hence the legacy, of any sacred text lies in the history of its function, and the ensuing study of Gen. 1:28 and its interpretation construes function in a broad sense. Not only do I examine the literature of Jewish and Christian biblical commentary, but I follow our biblical verse wherever it leads, through texts of sermons, law, theology, mysticism, and even popular poetry. Certain collections of sources are more prone to exhaustive review than others, and there is here no claim to have located every reference to Gen. 1:28 during the period under study. Nor does this book attempt an equally extensive survey of each genre of text. I have sought to analyze the evidence as well as to collect it, and the relative historical significance of the sources has borne heavily on my allocation of space.

To portray the role Gen. 1:28 has played in biblical and Western culture before the onset of modernity, I break with convention and mix genres of scholarly discussion that commonly remain distinct. What follows is not the standard interpretation-history concerned exclusively with postbiblical texts from late antiquity and beyond, nor is it a new, critical exegesis of Scripture. It is neither of the two and yet somehow it is both, as I hope to reconstruct an interpretative tradition that evolved even as the text of the Bible took shape. Chapter 1 thus considers the contents and scriptural context of Gen. 1:28, applying current tendencies in modern biblical scholarship to assess the ancient perceptions of the verse and its message. The book next turns to the traditions of post-biblical Judaism, focusing first on the homiletical and legal texts of the classical rabbinic period in Chapters 2 and 3, and then on medieval Jewish jurisprudence, exegesis, and Kabbalah in Chapter 4. Finally, the book considers the pertinent Christian traditions, which developed contemporaneously with their rabbinic counterparts. Chapter 5 treats patristic and medieval biblical commentary, and Chapter 6 explores a revealing assortment of medieval texts on the subject of nature—ranging from academic lectures on theology and the notes of canon lawyers to Jean de Meun's *Roman de la Rose* and Geoffrey Chaucer's *Canterbury Tales.* Despite the vast expanse of Christian literature during these periods, it contributed less to our story than did the corpus of rabbinic sources, for a number of reasons to be elaborated.

My research on the career of Gen. 1:28 has yielded three kinds of conclusions. First, with regard to Gen. 1:28 itself, the ecologically oriented thesis of Lynn White and others can now be laid to rest. Rarely, if ever, did premodern Jews and Christians construe this verse as a license for the selfish exploitation of the environment. Although most readers of Genesis casually assumed that God had fashioned the physical world for the benefit of human beings, Gen. 1:28 evoked relatively little concern with the issue of dominion over nature. One might, of course, find that other biblical texts did evince such concern, but in the exegesis of Gen. 1:28 other issues so eclipsed the matter of dominion that the little attention it receives in this book might appear to be unfair or perhaps altogether unnecessary. Yet the imbalance accurately reflects the data and itself comprises a significant result of this book.

Second, though dedicated to the career of Gen. 1:28, a verse that has intersected with numerous fascinating chapters in the history of Western religious thought, this book is hardly an anthology of unrelated interpretations. It narrates a story with a striking, albeit unanticipated, thematic unity: If rabbis and churchmen had little interest in dominion when they encountered the text of the primordial blessing, how did they react to the verse? God's initial words to human beings, especially those mandating sexual reproduction, repeatedly raised the theological issue of divine covenant. Jurists, preachers, mystics, and philosophers—in their respective idioms—focused on this verse (1) as an expression of God's relationship with all humanity and (2) as an expression of the tension between that universal commitment and God's election of a single people. In the first instance, the sexual and ruling functions mandated by our verse struck many readers as paradoxical if not contradictory: To reproduce and fill the earth, on the one hand, and yet to master it on the other hand, suggested that humans are situated on a cosmic frontier, between terrestrial and supernal realms of existence. Our verse led exegetes to harp on this puzzling aspect of human nature, which the Bible openly cast as divine blessing. How, they wondered, were humans to confront their sexuality properly, so as to attain divine reward and realize the godliness implicit in their dominion? In the second instance, the universal applicability of our verse troubled Jewish and Christian exegetes. The ostensive election of all human beings challenged their notion of a chosen people, prodding them to address the problem exegetically. Rabbinic lawyers, for example, sought to exclude Gentiles and women (!) from the commandment to "be fertile and increase," the blatant literal meaning of the Bible notwithstanding. (According to Genesis, God had addressed his instructions to both of the first parents, who lived twenty generations before Abraham, the original Hebrew patriarch.) Medieval Jewish kabbalists deemed the commandment of paramount importance, labeling the Jew who fails to have children "a despoiler of the covenant." And a famous monastic preacher of the Middle Ages claimed that Catholics alone enjoy the blessing of "fill the earth and master it," while Jews, infidels, and heretics inherit the curse of Eve (Gen. 3:16), "in pain you shall bear children."

And third, on a methodological level, this book offers a case-study in the history of biblical interpretation. Few works have analyzed the understanding of a single scriptural passage over as long a period of time, with sufficient concern for biblical antiquity, across two religious traditions, and throughout so many different textual genres. Many have studied the history of particular biblical ideas, but we cannot assume that the Bible always contained the ideas we attribute to it and therefore identify as biblical. The purview of this study in the history of ideas has been delimited by the text of the Bible and by its readers, not by the modern historian.

Although religion, chronology, and textual genre afforded the most effective basis for dividing this book into chapters, so that I examine

Jewish and Christian sources successively and not simultaneously, the career of Gen. 1:28 manifests an impressive array of cross–cultural parallels in the history of Judaism and Christianity. Testifying to the depth and significance of the interaction of two biblical religions, these merit considerable attention, often more than this book can accord them. I hope at least to identify some of them here and, especially when they reflect more extensive, recurring phenomena, to return to them on subsequent occasions. One cannot appreciate the history of majority culture and religion in the West without scrutinizing those of minorities, and vice versa to be sure. All too often, the study of this encounter has dealt exclusively with its hostile repercussions, or with isolated instances of more constructive interaction. Yet similarity and symmetry in the evolution of Judaism and Christianity, while more elusive, are equally instructive. Illuminating the career of a sacred text that Jews and Christians shared, the story that follows will, I hope, contribute to an appreciation of this intriguing and underexplored relationship.

Because this study entails the analysis of often obscure Jewish and Christian sources, I have included a Glossary of Names and Terms to ease the burden on readers who are familiar with one tradition but not with the other. As frequently happens, the transliteration of Hebrew terms has presented problems that defy an entirely consistent solution, especially if one seeks to avoid the overly awkward—hence "Kabbalah" and a more Anglicized rendition of personal names (Akiva, Kafah, Kimhi), except when these names themselves appear in Hebrew phrases and titles (*'Otiyyot de-R. 'Aqiva, Y*e*sodot ha-Qabbalah*). When a Semitic work has a romanized title, I have cited it accordingly, noting the language of the text in parentheses. Unless otherwise noted, all translations are my own.

CHAPTER I

Biblical Foundations

THIS history of how Jews and Christians have understood Gen. 1:28 begins in the opening chapter of the Hebrew Bible. Such a statement may seem unnecessary, barely worth the consideration of its readers, but it proceeds from methodological premises that deserve mention—considerations that properly inform the study of biblical interpretation in general as well as our present concern for one verse of Scripture in particular.

On a fundamental level, the Bible itself is an interpreted text. Nowhere in its totality or in its smaller component parts did the Bible record a simple, one-dimensional message so blatant that it reduced the homilies of postbiblical theologians to a secondary status on the grounds that Scripture never intended such interpretation. To be sure, Judaism and Christianity differentiated vociferously between the antique, immutable word of the canonical text and its subsequent, less definitive midrashic interpretation—witness the rabbinic demarcation between written law (*Torah shebbi-khtav*) and oral law (*Torah shebbe-ʿal peh*), and the many ecclesiastical discussions of the authority of tradition relative to the authority of the Bible. Yet within the exegetical systems of both religions, the consistency and rigidity of such a distinction have often broken down. Even a casual familiarity with the magnitude of Jewish and Christian biblical commentary reveals that the supposedly plain, original meaning of Scripture could easily elude its devotees. And the substance of those commentaries demonstrates that the definition of the literal sense of Scripture has itself fluctuated considerably over time.

Biblical interpretation is therefore not a strictly postbiblical phenomenon. While it has long outlived the biblical period, it did not begin after the composition of Scripture; it was endemic to the very process of its composition. Generations of modern scholarship have appropriately focused on the biblical text as a point of culmination—rather than commencement—in the theological history (*Traditionsgeschichte*) of ancient Israel. Recently, investigators have also identified the extensive phenomenon of the conscious invocation and reinterpretation of earlier biblical texts by later biblical authors. As Michael Fishbane suggested in the epilogue to his groundbreaking study of inner-biblical exegesis, "exegetical techniques and traditions developed locally and cumulatively in ancient Israel from monarchic times and continued into the Greco-Roman period, where they served as a major reservoir for the Jewish schools and techniques of exegesis then developing."[1] Even though Fishbane judiciously refrained from asserting a direct historical link between inner-biblical exegesis and that of specific postbiblical schools, the fruits of his research still lend support to the current tendency of literary critics to deemphasize an author's intentions when seeking the meaning that the text communicated to its readers. This is not to deny that the biblical writer had a particular message to impart, that the text did impart a particular message, or that these messages may have been identical. As Robert Alter has responded to the deconstructionist attack on traditional literary criticism, concepts like the "positive," intended meaning of a text "have their notorious ambiguities and fuzzy boundaries, but we would be tongue-tied if we threw them out, and for all their problems, they repeatedly help us to make valuable distinctions and to grasp individual cases better."[2] At the same time, however, one should not assume a generic dissimilarity between the contributions of theologians who lived and wrote during the biblical period and those who lived and wrote centuries later *simply because the canonization of Scripture intervened.* Even in the world of the Bible, as the evidence of inner-biblical exegesis attests, the oral and written words of a tradition continually interacted with readers, listeners, transmitters,

---

1. Michael Fishbane, *Biblical Interpretation in Ancient Israel* (Oxford, 1985), p. 525.
2. Robert Alter, "The Decline and Fall of Literary Criticism," *Commentary* 77 (March 1984), 54.

copyists, and editors to generate new words, new meanings, and new texts.

The analysis of the book of Genesis brings many of these issues to the fore. In the case of Gen. 1:28, which records specific events ("God blessed them and God said to them") as well as direct discourse (" 'Be fertile and increase . . .' "), the Bible not only blends disparate types of material but also clearly embodies narration composed long after these events were to have occurred. Even the staunch fundamentalistic champion of the Bible's literal truth will argue that the narrative process resulting in this verse transpired many centuries after the six days of creation. Where, then, should a modern study of this text commence—with the action or speech it recollects, or with some aspect of the factors that gave rise to its composition? That is, where does the original meaning of a biblical verse reside?

The question is a difficult one, and it has commanded the attention of numerous biblical scholars from diverse backgrounds and methodologies. In his commentary on the first chapters of Genesis, Umberto Cassuto distinguished between action ("intrinsically of no great importance") and speech, concluding: "The doctrines that the Torah wished to inculcate here are not comprised in the *episodes* it relates, but in *the words of the Lord* that it connects therewith."[3] Discussing the institutionalized commemoration of miraculous instances of divine revelation in the ancient Israelite cult, Bertil Albrektson questioned the enduring significance of these events: "Where, then, are we to place the *locus* of revelation: in the original historical occurrence, or in the cultic experience of it?" If the Bible intended to impart revealed truth, does it function as Holy Scripture primarily because of *what* it remembers or because of *how* it remembers—the processes whereby it narrates and inspires? Albrektson asserted that the core of the biblical message "cannot be discovered from the course of events, from the deeds themselves, but has to be revealed in a verbal communication, in words."[4] And Hugh White proposed to consider the stories of Genesis as the self-conscious, autobiographical narrative of a nation. Its meaning, embedded in the relation between signified (event) and signifier (language), is

3. Umberto Cassuto, *A Commentary on the Book of Genesis,* tr. Israel Abrahams, 2 vols. (Jerusalem, 1961–64), 1:184 (italics Cassuto's).

4. Bertil Albrektson, *History and the Gods: An Essay on the Idea of Historical Events as Divine Manifestations in the Ancient Near East and in Israel,* Coniectanea biblica: Old Testament Series 1 (Lund, 1967), pp. 117–18 (italics Albrektson's).

hardly an objective one, but derives from sacred events of "word reception" by the Israelite collective and the traditions or memories that emanated from these events, linking them with a later narrator. For White, the message of biblical narrative stems not from the historical particulars of events but from the thoroughly subjective processes whereby such events affected those who participated in them and were interpreted by those who later came to record them.[5]

A discussion of scholarly concern with these issues might proceed without end, but the role of interpretation in the formation of the biblical text is for this book a methodological premise, not a general hypothesis I shall seek to validate. A historical study of biblical interpretation may not casually presume that at the moment of its composition a scriptural text possessed a clear, indisputable meaning from which all subsequent understanding of that text departed. It is difficult if not impossible to determine whether a text ever had an original, uninterpreted meaning; more often than not, the qualitative distinction between this meaning and later, interpretative expositions is untenable. The extant text of the Bible itself derives from several lengthy processes of transmission, reflection, and revision; it never did have a single, absolute value that the historian can recover.

Commencing with the Bible, therefore, this book on the career of Gen. 1:28 does not advance a single allegedly authentic reading of the verse to the exclusion of all others. Rather, it draws on the conclusions of contemporary investigators in order to confront the biblical canon directly—as the first accessible phase in an evolving interpretative tradition. On the assumption that the typical reader of this book owns a Bible and has read the story of the creation, this chapter surveys a broad range of scholarly assessments of Gen. 1:28 and its meaning and attempts to evaluate the key issues involved in such analysis as well as the implications of varying critical approaches. We begin with the language of the verse itself and then move outward in what might be likened to a series of concentric circles: first to the place of Gen. 1:28 in the immediate context of the cosmogony, next to the relationship of the verse with

---

5. Hugh C. White, "Word Reception as the Matrix of the Structure of the Genesis Narrative," in *The Biblical Mosaic: Changing Perspectives,* ed. Robert Polzin and Eugene Rothman (Philadelphia, Pa., 1972), pp. 61–83. White does not consider Gen. 1 here because it "contains a word event for which there is no human response" (p. 74), yet his treatment of Gen. 2, 12, and 22 proffers potentially valuable suggestions for an appreciation of Gen. 1:28, which constitutes the very first "word event" linking God and human beings. See below, p. 65.

other scriptural passages, and finally to the importance of the verse for
different currents in modern biblical criticism. Although scholars continue to debate numerous questions, we will arrive at a consensus. Even
in this earliest stage of its career, Gen. 1:28 conveyed much the same
message it would continue to impart for centuries thereafter.

THE VERSE

Gen. 1:28 marks a climax in the biblical account of creation in six
days. God has created (*br'*, not *'sh* as with the other land animals) man
and woman in his image and after all other creatures—particulars that
point to the unique and superior station of humans in the natural order.
With his work behind him, the creator now turns to the first parents to
bless them, establishing an avenue for direct discourse between terrestrial and supernal realms. One thus expects Gen. 1:28 to convey a
message of paramount importance in the relationship between God and
his creatures—what has been labeled the initial covenant by Julius
Wellhausen and "the goal of the creation" by Karl Elliger.[6] In marked
contrast with other ancient cosmologies, Gen. 1:28 places humans at the
pinnacle of the world order; they are the partners of God in his ongoing
work of creation.[7] Addressing man and woman, God accordingly un-
leashes the powers that will ensure the survival of his creation in perpetuity, and unlike the ensuing account of human origins in Gen. 2–4,
Gen. 1 thus lays the foundation for an intrinsically valuable human
civilization even before people sin. Our verse surely suggests the dependence of the natural world upon the blessing of God, although, as Claus
Westermann noted, it frees human beings from the constraining, static
world view of ancient Near Eastern mythology by granting them
opportunity, and not a packaged civilization whose limits have been
predetermined.

> Faced with the mythology of the Ancient Near East, the Bible takes the
> same stand as does the modern secular historian: all progress in civiliza-

6. Julius Wellhausen, *Prolegomena to the History of Ancient Israel* (Cleveland, Ohio, 1957),
p. 338; Karl Elliger, "Sinn und Ursprung der priesterlichen Geschichterzählung," *Zeitschrift
für Theologie und Kirche* 49 (1952), 135.

7. Nahum M. Sarna, *Understanding Genesis: The Heritage of Biblical Israel* (1966; repr.,
New York, 1970), pp. 14–16; Bernard Rordorf, "'Dominez la terre' (Gn 1, 28)," *Bulletin du
Centre protestant d'études* 31 (1979), 9–11.

tion is a human achievement. . . . Blessing is concentrated on humanity in the Old Testament; the power and dynamism of the blessing enables people to "fill the earth and subdue it," and to make, discover, and invent. The blessing penetrates far more deeply into the story of humanity; the creator does not bestow ready-made products on people, but gives them the capacity to acquire and to create.[8]

Even in its words of introduction, "God blessed them (*'otam*) and God said to them (*lahem*)," Gen. 1:28 articulates a pointed opinion concerning human nature and responsibility in the world of God's creation. The recipients of the divine blessing can be none other than the first male and female humans similarly labeled *'otam* in the closing word of Gen. 1:27. While postbiblical Jews and Christians frequently asserted the superiority of the male over the female in their interpretation of Gen. 1:28, the Bible makes no such distinction here. Man and woman share equally in the various aspects of the divine charge.

Gen. 1:28a: "Be fertile and increase, fill the earth and master it."

Because the Hebrew word for mastering the earth (*we-khivshuha*) belongs to the first half of God's blessing, the syntax of Gen. 1:28 militates against a neat division between the instructions to procreate and those to rule.[9] Although many modern-day readers harp on its conferral of dominion, which they construe as a wantonly antiecological statement, the verse comprises a coherent entity, not readily susceptible to dissection based upon ideas external to it. Still, the weight of the verse does fall on its opening imperatives (*peru u-revu u-mil'u 'et ha-'arez*), highlighting the call for human reproduction more than the

---

8. Claus Westermann, *Genesis 1–11: A Commentary,* tr. John J. Scullion (Minneapolis, Minn., 1984), pp. 61–62; see also Johannes Pedersen, *Israel: Its Life and Culture,* 2 vols. (London, 1926–40) 1:182, 204.

9. See, for instance, Phyllis A. Bird, " 'Male and Female He Created Them': Gen 1:27b in the Context of the Priestly Account of Creation," *HTR* 74 (1981), 152: "The expression *wekibšuha* forms a bridge in the present text between the word of increase and the word of sovereignty. In subject matter it appears linked to the latter, suggesting that *RDH* might be understood as an elaboration or specification of *KBŠ*. Grammatically, however, it is an extension of the blessing, with an object and function distinct from that of the following verb, and must consequently be distinguished from the theme of dominion articulated by *RDH*." Beginning in the days of the Talmud, rabbinic tradition proposed that the feminine pronominal suffix indicating the object of *we-khivshuhah* ("and master it [lit., her]") referred to woman and not to the land; see below, p. 142.

call for mastery over other creatures, and affording some justification to the prevalent tendency to consider them seriatim.

Acknowledging the wondrous quality of reproduction, Gen. 1:28a views human procreation as a blessing and thereby bequeathes the divine image to posterity even prior to the expulsion from Eden, not merely as a response to the curses that accompanied the fall.[10] The verbs *prh* (to be fertile) and *rbh* (to increase) typically appear together in biblical benedictions, comprising hendiadys and best understood in Gen. 1:28 as "be abundantly fruitful."[11] Offspring and land constitute the hallmarks of promise texts in the Hebrew Bible, and even the imperatives of Gen. 1:28 need not denote a commandment but may bespeak an emphatic good wish for progeny, as in the declaration of Laban and Bethuel to the betrothed Rebekah (Gen. 24:60): "O sister! May you grow (*'at hayi*) into thousands of myriads; may your offspring seize the gates of their foes."[12] Such blessings of fertility and land themselves may have derived from formalized marriage ceremonies, and some scholars discern the motif of a divinely sponsored wedding lurking in the background of Gen. 1:28.[13] Yet in the biblical instance of this motif, marriage and sexuality lie not in the province of the deity but exclusively within that of his creatures, contrasting sharply with their function in the deified natural order of other ancient Near Eastern mythologies. Thus Raymond Collins notes: "The blessing of Gen. 1:28 has effectively separated fertility-oriented sexuality from man's being created in the divine image, has removed fertility from valorization in

---

10. Paul Humbert, "Trois notes sur Genèse 1," in *Interpretationes ad Vetus Testamentum pertinentes Sigmundo Mowinckel septuagenario missae* (Oslo, 1955), pp. 93–94; Henricus Renckens, *Urgeschichte und Heilsgeschichte: Israels Schau in die Vorgangenheit nach Gen. 1–3* (Mainz, 1959), p. 48.

11. Francis I. Andersen, *The Sentence in Biblical Hebrew*, Janua linguarum: Studia memoriae Nicolai van Wijk dedicata, Series practica 231 (Hague, 1974), p. 117.

12. W. Malcolm Clark, "The Animal Series in the Primeval History," *VT* 18 (1968), 436 n. 3; and on promise texts in general, see C. Sant, "The Promise Narratives in Genesis," *Melita theologica* 11 (1959), 1–13; 12 (1960), 14–27. With regard to Gen. 1:28, cf. the alternative suggestion of Christopher Wright Mitchell, *The Meaning of "Brk," "To Bless," in the Old Testament*, Society of Biblical Literature Dissertation Series 95 (Atlanta, Ga., 1987), pp. 62–63. Contrary to the understanding of classical Jewish and Christian traditions, David Daube has argued that Gen. 1:28 connotes no obligation to procreate whatsoever, a suggestion to which we shall return at the end of Chapter 3.

13. Alan Richardson, *Genesis I–XI: Introduction and Commentary* (London, 1953), p. 68; John Van Seters, *Abraham in History and Tradition* (New Haven, Conn., 1975), p. 283, who labels the *prh/rbh* hendiadys "a kind of divine liturgical blessing"; Claus Westermann, *The Promises to the Fathers: Studies on the Patriarchal Narratives*, tr. David E. Green (Philadelphia, Pa., 1980), pp. 149–55. For a similar connection drawn in rabbinic midrash, see below, p. 106, and, on a liturgical *Sitz im Leben* for the entire heptameral cosmogony, see p. 43f.

fertility rites, and has likewise proclaimed that fertility is a secular reality. As such it belongs to the sacral order because all that is of the saeculum is of God's sacrum."[14] According to a number of critics, Gen. 1:28's relegation of sexuality to a singularly human realm further charges people to transform their otherwise instinctive sexual drives into subjects of their rational wills, thereby using sexuality to express the distinctively human freedom of choice.[15] This in turn points to a more figurative interpretation of the verse, namely, that it instructs humans to grow spiritually and to realize their full potential by ruling over their passionate energies.[16]

Gen. 1:28b: "Rule the fish of the sea, the birds of the sky, and all the living things that creep on earth."

Together with its injunction to subdue the earth (*wᵉ-khivshuha*), Gen. 1:28's call upon man and woman to assume dominion (*u-rᵉdu*) over fish, birds, and animals has recently sparked much and often heated discussion of the verse in both nonacademic and scholarly circles.[17] Lynn White's address "The Historic Roots of Our Ecologic Crisis," first published in 1967, prodded numerous readers of the Bible to grapple with the concept of dominion in Gen. 1:28, typically focusing on the

---

14. Raymond F. Collins, *Christian Morality: Biblical Foundations* (Notre Dame, Ind., 1986), pp. 163–64. See also Stephen Sapp, *Sexuality, the Bible, and Science* (Philadelphia, Pa., 1977), pp. 1–12; and cf. Herbert Schmid, "Die 'Mutter Erde' in der Schöpfungsgeschichte der Priesterschrift," *Judaica* 22 (1968), esp. 242, who finds a similar polemical intention in the motif of man's subduing (mother) earth. On the ancient Near Eastern mythological background, see Samuel Noah Kramer, *The Sacred Marriage Rite: Aspects of Faith, Myth, and Ritual in Ancient Sumer* (Bloomington, Ind., 1969), and the additional works cited below, n. 112.

15. David Hartman, *A Living Covenant: The Innovative Spirit in Traditional Judaism* (New York, 1985), p. 23; Walther Zimmerli, *1. Mose 1–11: Die Urgeschichte*, 2nd ed. (Zurich, 1957), p. 319; Michael Fishbane, *Text and Texture: Close Readings of Selected Biblical Texts* (New York, 1979), p. 18.

16. Werner Wolff, *Changing Concepts of the Bible: A Psychological Analysis of Its Words, Symbols, and Beliefs* (New York, 1951), pp. 241–63; Ludwig Köhler, *Hebrew Man*, tr. Peter R. Ackroyd (London, 1956), pp. 126–27. For a similar interpretation in patristic literature, see below, Chapter 5.

17. Claiming the concurrence of the Septuagint and the Samaritan Pentateuch, Westermann, *Genesis 1–11*, p. 79, reinserts *bᵉhemah* into the animal series of Gen. 1:28b, just as it appears in God's plan for human dominion in Gen. 1:26b; cf., however, Abraham Tal, ed., *The Samaritan Targum of the Pentateuch* (Hebrew), 3 vols., Chaim Rosenberg School of Jewish Studies Texts and Studies in the Hebrew Language and Related Subjects 4 (Tel Aviv, 1980–83), 1:4–5. Clark, "Animal Series," pp. 433ff., argues that stylistic considerations prompted an intentional omission. See also Bird, "Male and Female," pp. 151–54, who distinguishes sharply between the role and meaning of these verbs in Gen. 1:28.

implications of these two Hebrew verbs. In the Hebrew Bible, *kbš* usually denotes the enslavement of people[18] or the physical conquest of territory.[19] *Rdh,* often reinforced by terms of harshness,[20] refers in general to the rule over slaves,[21] subjects,[22] or enemies,[23] at times to the vanquishing of an opponent in battle,[24] and perhaps even to the trampling upon grapes in a winepress.[25] As one might expect, the attempt to relate these terms to modern ecological concerns has produced a broad spectrum of opinion.

The apparent severity of the words has led some flatly to agree with White, maintaining that Gen. 1:28 here grants man unlimited power over the rest of creation;[26] the conclusion that the Bible hereby promotes a climate conducive to scientific invention and unreceptive to environmental sensitivity is often not far behind. In the words of Jean Daniélou, "nothing is more biblical than the technical."[27] While acknowledging the aggressiveness of its verbs, some investigators defend the anthropocentrism of Gen. 1:28, affirming the value of the instruction to harness the forces of nature on behalf of human civilization and praising the Western biblical legacy for stimulating the growth of technology. Gen. 1:28 notwithstanding, runs this argument, the violation of nature has resulted primarily from modern avarice and irresponsibility and not from biblical values.[28] Other scholars discern a call for

18. Jer. 34:11, 16; Neh. 5:5; 2 Chr. 28:10.
19. Num. 32:22, 29; Josh. 18:1; 1 Chr. 22:18.
20. As in Lev. 25:43, 46, 53; Is. 14:6; and Ezek. 34:4.
21. In Lev., ibid.; 1 Kings 5:30, 9:23; and 2 Chr. 8:10.
22. 1 Kings 5:4; Ezek. 29:15, 34:4; Ps. 68:28, 72:8.
23. Lev. 26:17, Is. 14:2, Ps. 110:2, Neh. 9:28.
24. Judg. 5:13, Is. 41:2.
25. Joel 4:13, as interpreted by Westermann, *Genesis 1–11,* p. 158.
26. See B. Jacob, *Das erste Buch der Tora: Genesis, übersetzt und erklärt* (Berlin, 1934), p. 61; Arvid S. Kapelrud, "Die Theorie der Schöpfung im Alten Testament," *ZAW* 91 (1979), 166–67; Hans Walter Wolff, *Anthropology of the Old Testament* (Philadelphia, Pa., 1974), pp. 162, 226–27; Manfred H. Vogel, "Man and Creation according to the Religious Tradition of Judaism," *Service internationale de documentation judeo-chrétienne* 12 (1979), 8–9.
27. Jean Daniélou, *In the Beginning . . . : Genesis I–III,* tr. Julien L. Randolf (Baltimore, Md., 1965), p. 40. Those who have reprinted, adopted, exploited, and/or rejected Lynn White's thesis are too numerous to list here; the important perspectives have been amassed in Daniel O'Connor and Francis Oakley, eds., *Creation: The Impact of an Idea* (New York, 1969), and in David and Eileen Spring, eds., *Ecology and Religion in History* (New York, 1974). Recently, White's thesis has even inspired a statistical survey that claims to demonstrate that "non-Judeo-Christians are slightly more likely to evidence greater concern for environmental issues than Judeo-Christians"; see Carl M. Hand, "Religion, Mastery-over-Nature, and Environmental Concern," *Social Forces* 63 (1984), 555–70 (quotation on p. 567).
28. K. Luke, "The Biblical Account of Creation and Terrestrial Realities," *Jeevadhara* 8 (1978), 108–11, 120; Donald E. Gowan, "Does 'Subdue' Mean 'Plunder?' " in Donald E.

human responsibility in our verse, which brings the supreme power implicit in the grant of dominion into balance. Man may stand at the pinnacle of creation, noted Walter Eichrodt, but the dependence of his rule on God remains unmitigated;[29] the exercise of dominion therefore rests conditionally upon human compliance with the divine will.[30] C. F. Whitley and Westermann, among others, have held that because Gen. 1:28 reflects the terminology and ideology of ancient Near Eastern kingship, human rule must entail concern for the welfare of its subjects; kingship without responsibility was universally unacceptable.[31] Drawing an analogy to the shepherd kings of Ezek. 34, Walter Brueggemann thus likened the dominion of Gen. 1:28 to "that of a shepherd who cares for, tends, and feeds the animals."[32] George Coats interpreted *kbš* as "render productive,"[33] arguing that "the subdued earth is a land that serves its master productively. The use of the verb in relation to the Holy Land[34] shows that no denotation of uncontrolled or destructive exploitation appears here." According to Westermann, just as one may not construe the governance of the sun and moon in Gen. 1:16 too literally, so does Gen. 1:29–which ostensibly prescribes a vegetarian diet for the first parents—mandate that human dominion over animals be defined in terms of a hierarchical relationship and not as the un-

---

Gowan and Millard Schumaker, *Subduing the Earth: An Exchange of Views* (Kingston, Ont., 1980), pp. 10–14.

29. Walter Eichrodt, *Man in the Old Testament*, tr. K. and R. Gregor Smith, Studies in Biblical Theology 4 (Chicago, 1951), pp. 29–30. See also Gina Hens-Piazza, "A Theology of Ecology: God's Image and the Natural World," *Biblical Theology Bulletin* 13 (1983), 107–10; and Walter C. Kaiser, Jr., *Toward an Old Testament Theology* (Grand Rapids, Mich., 1978), p. 76.

30. Edmund Jacob, *Theology of the Old Testament*, tr. Arthur W. Heathcote and Philip J. Allcock (London, 1958), p. 171; David J. A. Clines, "The Image of God in Man," *Tyndale Bulletin* 19 (1968), 95ff. True to patristic tradition, David Tobin Asselin, "The Notion of Dominion in Genesis 1–3," *CBQ* 16 (1954), 277–94, thus concludes that human dominion was lost with the fall from Eden.

31. Westermann, *Genesis 1–11*, pp. 157–61, and *Elements of Old Testament Theology*, tr. Douglas W. Stott (Atlanta, Ga., 1982), pp. 98–99; C. F. Whitley, *The Genius of Ancient Israel: The Distinctive Nature of the Basic Concepts of Israel Studied against the Cultures of the Ancient Near East* (Amsterdam, 1969), pp. 157–58. Cf. also Karlfried Froelich, "The Ecology of Creation," *Theology Today* 27 (1971), 270; and Norbert Lohfink, " 'Macht euch die Erde untertan?' " *Orientierung* 38 (1974), 137–42.

32. Walter Brueggemann, *Genesis* (Atlanta, Ga., 1982), p. 32.

33. George W. Coats, "The God of Death: Power and Obedience in the Primeval History," *Interpretation* 29 (1975), 229. Cf. Nehama Leibowitz, *Studies in the Book of Genesis in the Context of Ancient and Modern Jewish Bible Commentary*, tr. Aryeh Newman (Jerusalem, 1972), p. 5.

34. See above, n. 19.

limited power to destroy and exploit.[35] Odil Hannes Steck interpreted the dominion of Gen. 1:28 as a "framework of rule for the benefit of the whole," supporting this notion of stewardship with the strictly agricultural context for filling and subduing the earth supplied by Gen. 1:29–30.[36] And Walther Zimmerli contended that the ensuing climax of the creation in the Sabbath demonstrates that human dominion must be exerted for the sake of a higher, nonhuman objective.[37]

The most forceful response to the indictment of Gen. 1:28 by Lynn White and others is that of James Barr.[38] *Kbš* and *rdh,* Barr has written, do not connote the consumption or exploitation of other creatures; while *kbš* in Gen. 1:28 refers to the land alone, *rdh* may evoke the image of peaceful dominion, as in the description of Solomon's harmonious rule in 1 Kings 5:4. One may profitably compare the blessing of Gen. 1:28b to the instruction of Adam to till and preserve the Garden of Eden in Gen. 2:15,[39] while distinguishing it from God's blessing of Noah in Gen. 9:1–7, which reiterates Gen. 1:28 without *kbš* and *rdh* but speaks of violent, fearful interaction between humans and beasts. According to Barr and J. Donald Hughes, the Bible blatantly lacks a spirit of ecological functionalism and technological inventiveness, which Greco-Roman civilization bequeathed to the Western tradition; biblical Israel, in fact, displayed more environmental sensitivity than its neighbors in the ancient Near East.[40] Richard Hiers concluded that White confronted the text of Scripture in a "critically illiterate" manner.[41] It is significant that both Barr and Steck have conceded that while scholars have studied the biblical text of Gen. 1:28 exhaustively, its postbiblical interpretation, which could validate or disprove White's condemnation, has consistently been neglected by modern scholars.[42]

---

35. Westermann, *Genesis 1–11,* p. 159; see also James Barr, "Man and Nature—The Ecological Controversy and the Old Testament," *BJRL* 55 (1972), 21.

36. Odil Hannes Steck, *World and Environment* (Nashville, Tenn., 1980), pp. 104–107; cf. the similar perceptions of Bernhard W. Anderson, "Creation and Ecology," in *COT,* pp. 157–59.

37. Walther Zimmerli, *Der Mensch und seine Hoffnung im Alten Testament* (Göttingen, 1968), pp. 71–72.

38. Barr, "Man and Nature," pp. 9–32.

39. So too Claus Westermann, "Der Mensch im Urgeschehen," *Kerygma und Dogma* 13 (1976), 239.

40. J. Donald Hughes, *Ecology in Ancient Civilizations* (Albuquerque, N.M., 1975), pp. 45–47, 148ff.

41. Richard H. Hiers, "Ecology, Biblical Theology, and Methodology: Biblical Perspectives on the Environment," *Zygon* 19 (1984), 45.

42. Barr, "Man and Nature," p. 23; Steck, *World and Environment,* p. 198.

THE BIBLICAL CONTEXT

The failure to evaluate the message of Gen. 1:28 as one should characterizes not only the works of intellectual history that improperly disregard the verse, but also the works of many who exploit it for polemical purposes.[43] The verse contributed significantly to the enduring legacy of the Bible in Western culture, but its bequest to posterity proceeded directly from its role and meaning in Scripture itself. We therefore turn to the textual surroundings in which Gen. 1:28 functioned: first to the immediate context of the Genesis cosmogony and then to other related passages throughout the biblical canon.

The Story of Creation

Gen. 1:22. Exploring the connotations of Gen. 1:28 in the neighboring verses of the heptameral cosmogony, one must certainly consider the verse that concludes the creation of marine life and birds on the fifth day: "God blessed them, saying, 'Be fertile (p^eru) and increase (u-r^evu), fill (u-$mil'u$) the waters in the seas, and let the birds increase ($yirev$) on earth.'" This verse confirms the nexus between progeny and blessing encountered in Gen. 1:28, and it emphasizes that while other earthly creatures shared in the capacity to reproduce, only humans received the otherwise heavenly function (as in Gen. 1:18) of dominion. The introduction to the divine statement in Gen. 1:22 appears to precede a public announcement, failing to convey the sense of direct discourse or conversation one finds in the opening words of Gen. 1:28, "God blessed them and God said to them." Naturally, the fish and the birds could not respond in kind to the words of God, but then Scripture records no human response to Gen. 1:28 either. Some scholars regard the difference in wording as yet another indication of the superiority of human beings: Humans not only receive power over other creatures, but from the outset they engage in a closer relationship with God.[44] Phyllis Bird has agreed, but she suggests that the twofold introduction to Gen. 1:28 may also derive from the dual nature of its contents: words of blessing and words of authority. Westermann, moreover, has deemed the

---

43. J. Cohen, "Bible, Man, and Nature."
44. For example, B. Jacob, *Das erste Buch*, pp. 54–56, who adheres to the precedent set by numerous ancient and medieval commentators.

longer phraseology of Gen. 1:28 stylistically awkward; relying on the
example of Gen. 1:22 and the Septuagint's reading of Gen. 1:28, he has
proposed to read "saying" (*le'mor*) for "and God said to them" (*wa-yo'mer lahem 'Elohim*). In this case, the earlier verse reveals that fish and
birds—all animate creatures (*nefesh ḥayyah*), for that matter—shared in
the same fertility blessing bestowed upon humans.[45] This issue of parity
between the two blessings raises another: Why did God not include the
land animals in the commission to be fertile and increase? Although
some critics offer specific reasons for the conscious exclusion of the
animals—for instance, that man would not have benefited from their
unlimited reproduction[46]—most agree that they too enjoyed the blessing of procreation. Perhaps the now awkward Gen. 1:28a originally did
mention them, or at least implied their inclusion. Created on the same
day as humans, perhaps they forfeited a blessing that could be bestowed
only upon one order of being in a single day or in a single physical space
and that might have constituted an unwelcome addition to the neat
series of three blessings now in the creation story (Gen. 1:22, 1:28, 2:3).
Yet the mention of animals in the series of *prh/rbh* blessings after the
flood (Gen. 8:17, 9:1, 9:7) does weigh on behalf of their antediluvian
inclusion as well.[47]

Gen. 1:26–27. If the similarity between the blessing of the fish and
Gen. 1:28 forges a bond between humans and other animate creatures,
the juxtaposition of our verse and its two immediate predecessors
speaks to the singular, superior status of men and women in the biblical
world view. Following the creation of the animals on the sixth day, the
Bible relates: "[26] And God said, 'Let us make man in our image, after
our likeness. They shall rule the fish of the sea, the birds of the sky, the
cattle, the whole earth, and all the creeping things that creep on earth.'
[27] And God created man in his image, in the image of God he created

45. Bird, "Male and Female," pp. 151–52 (with n. 56); Westermann, *Genesis 1–11*, pp. 79,
160.

46. B. Jacob, *Das erste Buch*, pp. 54–56; cf. also the suggestion of Robert Sacks, "The Lion
and the Ass: A Commentary on the Book of Genesis (Chapters 1–10)," *Interpretation: A
Journal of Political Philosophy* 8 (1980), 43, that fish and humans share an openness of direction—i.e., an ability to err—and therefore shared the divine blessing as well.

47. Werner H. Schmidt, *Die Schöpfungsgeschichte der Priesterschrift: Zur Überlieferungsge-
schichte von Genesis 1,1—2,4a und 2,4b—3,24*, Wissenschaftliche Monographien zum Alten und
Neuen Testament 17, 3rd ed. (Neukirchen, 1973), p. 147; Bird, "Male and Female," pp. 145–
46 (with n. 42); Westermann, *Genesis 1–11*, pp. 138–42; Dianne Bergant and Carroll Stuhlmueller, "Creation according to the Old Testament," in *Evolution and Creation*, ed. Ernan
McMullin (Notre Dame, Ind., 1985), pp. 160–61.

him; male and female he created them." These illustrious words, which have consistently overshadowed Gen. 1:28 in both scholarly and popular study of the Bible from antiquity until the present, evoke numerous issues well beyond the purview of this book. The enigmatic use of the plural in Gen. 1:26a, the relationship between image (*ṣelem*) and likeness (*dᵉmut*), and whether they denoted physical or spiritual characteristics need not concern us at present.[48] Yet this passage evidently links the creation of humans in God's image and likeness to both dominion and sexuality, the two human characteristics at the heart of Gen. 1:28. To what extent do sexual differentiation and its procreative purpose manifest the divine image in human beings? Some critics perceive the *imago Dei* and fruitful heterosexual relationships as inseparably intertwined. For Karl Barth, who conceived of human sexuality within the context of an I-Thou relationship, the bond between man and woman bespeaks—and transmits to their posterity—the divine image within them, preserving their station above that of the beasts, just as their dominion does.[49] From an avowedly feminist perspective, Phyllis Trible stressed the tripartite poetic structure of Gen. 1:27, which draws parallels (1) between "the image of God" and "male and female" and (2) between the generic "man" (*ha-'adam*) and the concluding plural "them" (*'otam*).[50] Raymond Collins found support for this view in Gen. 5:1–2, which comments before listing the generations between Adam and Noah, "When God created man, he made him in the likeness (*dᵉmut*) of God; male and female he created them. And when they were created, he blessed them and called them Man."[51] Gen. 1 thus mirrors Gen. 5 in its progression from the creation of humans in God's image (v. 26) to

---

48. Of the plethora of treatments of these biblical concepts, see esp. the valuable excurses of Karl Barth, *The Doctrine of Creation*, Church Dogmatics 3,1, tr. J. W. Edwards et al. (Edinburgh, 1958), pp. 191–206; Schmidt, *Schöpfungsgeschichte*, pp. 132–44; and Westermann, *Genesis 1–11*, pp. 147–55; and the particularly helpful monographic studies of James Barr, "The Image of God in the Book of Genesis: A Study of Terminology," *BJRL* 51 (1968), 11–26; Oswald Loretz, *Die Gottenbildlichkeit des Menschen* (Munich, 1967); and J. Maxwell Miller, "In the 'Image' and 'Likeness' of God," *JBL* 91 (1972), 289–304.

49. Barth, *Doctrine of Creation*, pp. 184–97. See also H. W. Wolff, *Anthropology*, p. 162; Emmanueli Testa, *Genesi: Versione, introduzione, note*, 4th ed. (Rome, 1981), ad loc.; Loretz, *Gottenbildlichkeit*, pp. 68–71; and Paul Jewett, *Man as Male and Female* (Grand Rapids, Mich., 1975), pp. 33ff.

50. Phyllis Trible, *God and the Rhetoric of Sexuality*, Overtures to Biblical Theology 2 (Philadelphia, Pa., 1978), pp. 15–20.

51. Collins, *Christian Morality*, p. 175; at p. 179 n. 24, Collins reaffirms on the basis of Gen. 9:6–7 that "for the Priestly author there is a connection between being in God's image and the procreative capacity." See below, p. 110, where this conclusion was reached by the Tannaitic rabbis. See also Robert R. Wilson, *Genealogy and History in the Biblical World*, Yale Near Eastern Researches 7 (New Haven, Conn., 1977), p. 164.

the sexual differentiation between them (v. 27) to their reception of the divine blessing (v. 28). Bird, on the other hand, echoing an earlier comment of Gerhard von Rad, deemed Gen. 1:27b–28a a striking digression in the Gen. 1 report of God's creative acts (*Tatbericht*). Consistent with her view that Gen. 1:22 and 1:28a reflect an equivalence between humans and other animate creatures, Bird contended that sexual differentiation does not compound the superiority implicit in the notion of God's image, but contrasts with it. "*Unlike* God, but *like* the other creatures, *adam* is characterized by sexual differentiation."[52] Nevertheless, Gen. 1:26–27 in its present form bears heavily on the meaning of Gen. 1:28. "Fertility and dominion belong to two separate themes or concerns: one, the theme of nature with its subtheme of sustainability (fertility), the other, the theme of order with its interest in position and function. The word of sexual distinction pertains only to the first."[53]

Although the connection of the divine image with dominion over nature may appear more certain than the connection of the divine image with sexual differentiation, it too has been questioned and debated by biblical scholars. The importance of dominion in Gen. 1:26b—the divinely stated rationale for the creation of humans in God's image—leads several authorities to define the one in terms of the other: the essence of the image of God in people is their *function* of ruling over nature, or, conversely, when one encounters human rule over other creatures, one perceives nothing less than the *imago Dei*. David Asselin wrote: "Man does not rule over the animal kingdom because he is God's image; rather, he is God's image precisely because he rules over the animal kingdom."[54] If so, then the divine blessing in Gen. 1:28b be-

---

52. Bird, "Male and Female," p. 148 (italics Bird's); see also Eichrodt, *Theology*, 2:128, and Gerhard von Rad, *Genesis: A Commentary*, tr. John H. Marks, 9th ed. (Philadelphia, Pa., 1972), p. 61.

53. Bird, "Male and Female," p. 150. The dispute here seems to echo a similar divergence of opinion among rabbinic homilists. For some, human procreation expressed the *imago Dei* in man; for others, it ranked as one of man's several beastly traits, contrasting against an equal number of heavenly traits. Bird's argument also bears upon the question of whether women shared in the divine image along with men. On p. 151 she contends that Gen. 1 contains no message of sexual equality as far as dominion is concerned. *Kbš* and *rdh* assign tasks to the entire species, but "the social metaphors to which the key verbs point are male, derived from male experience and models, the dominant social models of patriarchal society." When the Priestly writer speaks of the species, he thinks of its male characteristics, as does the writer of Ps. 8. Still, Bird acknowledges that maleness is not the defining characteristic of the species in the Bible. The word of bisexual creation guards against this false assumption, "even if it provides only a minimal base for an anthropology of equality." On this issue of women and the image of God, see esp. Maryanne C. Horowitz, "The Image of God in Man—Is Woman Included?" *HTR* 72 (1979), 175–206.

54. Asselin, "Notion of Dominion," p. 283; cf. also E. Jacob, *Theology*, pp. 166ff.; Luke, "Biblical Account," p. 107; and H. W. Wolff, *Anthropology*, p. 159.

stows upon man and woman nothing they did not already have; it merely *confirms* a fait accompli. But if, as another scholarly camp contends, dominion *results* from the divine image but does not comprise it, then the empowering of humans in Gen. 1:28 *implements* the divine plan of Gen. 1:26 to its logical conclusion. According to von Rad, Gen. 1 "speaks less of the nature of God's image than of its purpose. There is less said about the gift itself than about the task . . . : domination in the world, especially over animals."[55] David Clines hastened to add that such a causal relation in no way trivializes either dominion or the *imago Dei*. In view of the ancient Near Eastern notion of continuity between divine, human, and animal realms, dominion over animals emphatically highlights the godliness of man and woman. "Though man's rulership over the animals is not in itself the image of God, no definition of the image is complete which does not refer to this function of rulership."[56] Still a third opinion construes the conferral of dominion in Gen. 1:28, which makes no mention of the image of God, as intentionally severing any presumed link between the two.[57]

Gen. 1:29–2:3. The divine blessing of humans may bring the first chapter of Genesis to a climax, but the biblical creation story does not end with Gen. 1:28. Before the sixth day draws to a close, God announces to the first man and woman that he has given them all seed-bearing vegetables and fruits for their food, while to other animal creatures he has allotted all the green plants. On the seventh day, God creates no more, but he blesses and sanctifies the Sabbath in commemoration of his primal rest. The apparent restriction of the human diet to flora immediately following the grant of dominion over fauna and the absence of any human role in the concluding scene of the creation story certainly raise questions about Scripture's own appreciation of Gen. 1:28. Both Hermann Gunkel and Werner Schmidt thus inferred that Gen. 1:28 and 1:29 must have derived from different sources and found their way into the same text long-after their composition.[58] As noted above, some have read the dietary instructions as evidence of domin-

55. Von Rad, *Genesis*, p. 59; see also Loretz, *Gottenbildlichkeit*, pp. 21–22, 72; and Barr, "Man and Nature," p. 20.

56. Clines, "Image," pp. 97–98.

57. Gunkel, *Genesis*, p. 112; Eichrodt, *Theology*, 2:127; Schmidt, *Schöpfungsgeschichte*, p. 142. Westermann, *Genesis 1–11*, pp. 155ff., and Rordorf, "'Dominez la terre,'" p. 12, believe that Gen. 1:26 conveys no message concerning the essence of human nature, but rather is concerned with the manner in which God created humans.

58. Gunkel, *Genesis*, pp. 113–14; Schmidt, *Schöpfungsgeschichte*, p. 152.

ion's inherent limitations: Human rule over the natural order did not entail the right to eat the animals, and it properly expressed itself within an agricultural framework.[59] Dequeker, on the other hand, did not equate the right to consume vegetables and fruits with a prohibition against eating meat. Asserting that God's instructions to Noah after the flood (Gen. 9:1–7) restored precisely the primal order established during the six days of creation, he has held against a vegetarian interpretation of Gen. 1 on the basis of Gen. 9:3: "'Every creature that lives shall be yours to eat; as with the green grasses, I give you all these.'" Rather than limiting the superiority of person over beast, the contrast between human and animal diets in Gen. 1:29–30 reinforces and elaborates upon it.[60]

One might also argue that the divine institution of the Sabbath overshadowed human primacy in the natural order, implicitly subordinating the earthly dominion of humans to the achievement of an otherworldly, spiritual objective.[61] Perhaps the failure of humans to assume the role of grammatical subject in any verse of this creation story also manifests their subservience to the realm of the divine.[62] Yet inasmuch as only humans (Gen. 1:28), fish and birds (Gen. 1:22), and the Sabbath (Gen. 2:3) shared in the initial blessings of God, the sanctification of the seventh day may also reinforce the importance of Gen. 1:28. Westermann concluded: "God's blessing bestows on this special, holy, solemn day a power which makes it fruitful for human existence. . . . It is not the day in itself that is blessed, but rather the day in its significance for the community. In the context of creation it is for the world and humankind."[63]

---

59. Westermann and Steck, cited in nn. 35–36 above; Jacob Milgrom, "The Biblical Diet Laws as an Ethical System," *Interpretation* 17 (1963), 288.

60. L. Dequeker, "Green Herbage and Trees Bearing Fruit (Gen. 1:28–30, 9:1–3)," *Bijdragen: Tijdschrift voor filosofie en theologie* 38 (1977), 118–27, and "L'alliance avec Noé (Gen. 9,1–17)," in *Noé, l'homme universel,* by J. Chopineau et al., Publications de l'Institutum iudaicum 3 (Brussels, 1978), pp. 4–9.

61. Thus Zimmerli, above, n. 37; and W. J. Dumbrell, "The Covenant with Noah," *Reformed Theological Review* 38 (1979), 7, and *Covenant and Creation: An Old Testament Covenantal Theology* (Exeter, 1984), p. 34.

62. A. Scult et al., "Genesis and Power: An Analysis of the Biblical Story of Creation," *Quarterly Journal of Speech* 72 (1986), 120.

63. Westermann, *Genesis 1–11,* p. 172. Cf. Ralph W. Klein, *Israel in Exile: A Theological Interpretation* (Philadelphia, Pa., 1979), p. 126; and Gerhard F. Hasel, "The Sabbath in the Pentateuch," in *The Sabbath in Scripture and History,* ed. Kenneth A. Strand (Washington, D.C., 1982), p. 25.

Beyond Creation

Echoes of Gen. 1:28 extend throughout the Hebrew Bible and are hardly confined to its opening chapter. The similar conjunction of creation in God's image, sexual distinction, and divine blessing introducing the genealogy of Gen. 5 was mentioned above, and later in this chapter we explore the overall thematic significance of our verse for the Bible's "primeval history" (Gen. 1–11). For the moment, we proceed to other passages of Scripture that, by revealing the antecedent or subsequent uses of our verse, offer further insight into its meaning.

The Aftermath of the Flood. No particular approach or method in the study of the Bible can obscure the numerous parallels between the story of creation and the story of the flood—whether one focuses on the process of separation of water from land essential to the first story and reversed during the second, on the stories' initiation of new epochs in human history, or on their shared interest in sin, justice, and providence. Granting the importance of Gen. 1:28 in the account of creation, one should confront its reappearance in the story of Noah without surprise but with curiosity. Does the new context lead to departure from our verse's original intention, or does the obviousness of the allusion serve to reassert it?

Upon their disembarkation from the ark, "[Gen. 9:1] God blessed Noah and his sons, and said to them, 'Be fertile (*p^{e}ru*) and increase (*u-r^{e}vu*), and fill (*u-mil'u*) the earth. [9:2] The fear and dread of you shall be upon all the beasts of the earth and upon all the birds of the sky— everything with which the earth is astir—and upon all the fish of the sea; they are given into your hand.'" There follow the aforementioned license to eat the animals (Gen. 9:3), a proviso that their blood not be consumed (9:4), and a ban on the shedding of human blood by any creature (9:5–6), "for in his image did God make man." At this juncture God reiterates (9:7): "'Be fertile (*p^{e}ru*), then, and increase (*u-r^{e}vu*); abound (*shir$\d{z}$u*) on the earth and increase (*u-r^{e}vu*) on it.'" Once again God blesses the first humans of a cosmic epoch with fertility and dominion, using the terminology of Gen. 1:28 to denote procreation. Just as a similar blessing of fish and birds (Gen. 1:22) preceded that of humans in the creation story, so did God first instruct Noah (Gen. 8:17) concerning the animal occupants of the ark, "'Let them swarm (*w^e-shar^e$\d{z}$u*) on the earth and be fertile (*u-faru*) and increase (*w^e-ravu*) on the

earth.'"' The repetition of the instructions for human reproduction in
the first and seventh verses of Gen. 9 signals their singular importance.
And mention of creation in the divine image, situated precisely between
the designation of human (vs. animal) life as of supreme value and the
call to procreate, again suggests the linkage between human godliness,
sexuality, and dominion. Nevertheless, the extent of the similarity
between God's speech to Noah and sons and his words to the first
parents heightens one's sensitivity to the differences between them.
Even though Gen. 9 stresses human superiority over the beasts, *kbš* and
rdh are blatantly absent from the Masoretic Text. Whether or not the
original allotment of fruits and vegetables to humans technically excluded the consumption of meat, its juxtaposition with Gen. 1:28 at
least implied a primarily agricultural outlet for human dominion. In the
wake of the flood, however, God highlights human carnivorousness.
While the concluding verse of Gen. 1 depicted a completely harmonious
interaction among all God's creatures—"and God saw all that he had
made and found it very good"—Gen. 9 reacts to violence and blood-
shed in both interpersonal and interspecific relations. And curiously,
God now proclaims his instructions to procreate only to males—that is,
to Noah and his sons but not to their wives.

Faced with this comparison, some have stressed the symmetry of
Gen. 9:1–7 and 1:28–30, proposing to emend the end of Gen. 9:7 to read
"and rule (*u-rᵉdu*) over it," instead of the duplicated "and increase (*u-
rᵉvu*) on it."[64] Support for this reading derives from the Greek Septuagint, which contains Gen. 1:28's words for *wᵉ-khivshuha*, "and master it" (*katakyrieùsate autês*), both in Gen. 9:1 and in place of the second
u-rᵉvu of 9:7. At the same time, most critics acknowledge that the
opening verses of Gen. 9 entail a conscious reinterpretation of Gen.
1:28, probably insofar as the fall from Eden and its aftermath subverted
the tranquility and extent of human dominion over the animals.[65]

---

64. Thus Gunkel, *Genesis*, p. 149; E. A. Speiser, *The Anchor Bible: Genesis* (Garden City,
N.Y., 1967), p. 57; Zimmerli, *1. Mose 1–11*, p. 319; and Westermann, *Genesis 1–11*, p. 460. On
the symmetry and equivalence of the passages in Gen. 1 and Gen. 9, see also George W. Coats,
Genesis, with an Introduction to Narrative Literature, Forms of the Old Testament Literature 1
(Grand Rapids, Mich., 1983), p. 78; Dequeker, "L'alliance," pp. 4–9; Jack M. Sasson,
"'Tower of Babel' as a Clue to the Redactional Structuring of the Primeval History (Gen. 1–
11:9)," in *The Bible World: Essays in Honor of Cyrus Gordon*, ed. Gary Rendsburg et al. (New
York, 1980), pp. 216–17; and Cassuto, *Commentary*, 2:124–29, who adamantly rejects the
proposed emendation of Gen. 9:7.

65. Thus Barr, "Man and Nature," p. 21; B. Jacob, *Das erste Buch*, p. 241; and von Rad,
Genesis, pp. 131–32.

Michael Fishbane, however, perceived a more subtle reworking of Gen. 1:28 in the aftermath of the flood. He maintained that the license to kill and eat animals in Gen. 9, coupled with the ban on shedding human blood, actually extends the dominion granted humans in Gen. 1:28. The statement that God created humans in his image, now voiced in the third person by an anonymous narrator, is here positioned (Gen. 9:6b) after the description of human superiority clearly in order to justify it.[66] Several investigators also argued that the poetic structure of Gen. 9:7 itself manifests a conscious reworking of the "be fertile and increase" formula in the creation story. Against the emendation of the Septuagint, they contend that the repetition of *u-r^evu* suits the cadence and thrust of the verse, whose four verbs (*prh, rbh, šrṣ,* and *rbh*) correspond almost exactly to a like number in Gen. 1:22.[67]

One can conclude that the opening verses of Gen. 9 respond to the burning theological question of Noah's own day: Did God's initial blessing of humankind survive the flood? Or, as von Rad paraphrased, "Did the creature which had fallen from God's first estate still have God's will on its side?"[68] The obvious allusions to Gen. 1:28 resound affirmatively that the blessing did prevail, although not without modification and refinement. Moreover, the absence of women from Gen. 9:1 and 9:7[69] suggests not that reproduction could ensue without them but that the purpose of the call for procreation had changed. In Gen. 1:28, "be fertile and increase, fill the earth and master it . . . ," had conveyed the divine blessing par excellence, establishing a hierarchical structure for the natural order and the means for its survival in perpetuity; procreation and dominion themselves were of paramount importance. In the wake of the flood, the repeated invocation of Gen. 1:28 reveals that its words had assumed formulaic significance; recalling the primal institution of human sexuality and authority, they now guaranteed to the male leaders of the day that God's commitment to the world had indeed survived his destruction of life and his concomitant demon-

---

66. Fishbane, *Biblical Interpretation,* pp. 318–20, contra Sean E. McEvenue, *The Narrative Style of the Priestly Writer,* Analecta biblica 50 (Rome, 1971), pp. 68–69, who deems Gen. 9:4–6 a later interpolation but does consider Gen. 9:2–3 an extension of dominion; see also the nuanced comments of Steck, *World and Environment,* pp. 110–12.

67. Bezalel Porten and Uriel Rappaport, "Poetic Structure in Gen 9.7," *VT* 21 (1971), 363–69; John S. Kselman, "The Recovery of Poetic Fragments from the Pentateuchal Priestly Source," *JBL* 97 (1978), 167. See also Lloyd M. Barré, "The Poetic Structure of Genesis 9:5," *ZAW* 96 (1984), 101–4.

68. Von Rad, *Genesis,* p. 131.

69. McEvenue, *Narrative Style,* p. 67, notes the exclusion but offers no explanation for it.

stration of human powerlessness. This impression that the terminology of Gen. 1:28 has come to denote a binding compact between God and his creatures finds confirmation in the passage that follows immediately: "And God said to Noah and his sons with him, 'I now establish (*meqim*) my covenant (*bᵉriti*) with you and your offspring to come, and with every living thing that is with you'" (Gen. 9:8–10). In addition, as Fishbane pointed out, the repetition of Gen. 9:1 by Gen. 9:7 parallels the reformulation of Gen. 9:9–10 in Gen. 9:17, where God refers to "the sign of the covenant (*ha-bᵉrit*) that I have established (*haqimoti*) between me and all flesh that is on earth."[70] Literary style thus reinforces the correspondence of the *prh/rbh* formula with the ensuing covenantal agreement—a type of transaction in which ancient Semitic women normally would not have participated. Within several chapters of the initial appearance of Gen. 1:28, the long, evolving history of its reinterpretation had begun.

The Ensuing Career of prh/rbh. As the narrative of Genesis emerges from its primeval history and focuses on Abraham and his Israelite descendants, the blessing of "be fertile and increase" continues to reappear. Raphael Patai quipped that blessings of progeny recur in Genesis "with an insistent and unrelenting monotony that could stem only from the conviction that numerous progeny is the highest of all human aspirations."[71] Yet careful examination of the *prh/rbh* texts reveals a more powerful and nuanced message. When God seals his covenant with Abraham, he promises the patriarch:

> I am *'El Shaddai*. Walk in my ways and be blameless. I will establish my covenant (*bᵉriti*) between me and you, and I will make you exceedingly numerous (*'arbeh 'otᵉkha bi-mᵉod mᵉᵉod*). . . . I will make you exceedingly fertile (*wᵉ-hifreti 'otᵉkha bi-mᵉod mᵉᵉod*), and make nations of you; and kings shall come forth from you. I will maintain (*wa-haqimoti*) my covenant (*bᵉriti*) between me and you, and your offspring to come, as an everlasting covenant throughout the ages, to be God to you and to your offspring to come. I assign the land you sojourn in to you and your

---

70. Cf. von Rad's notice of "the strong legal tone accompanying the gracious Noahic dispensation" of 9:1–7 (*Genesis*, p. 133). On the technical nature of the terminology *haqem bᵉrit*, see McEvenue, *Narrative Style*, p. 74; and Dumbrell, "Covenant with Noah," pp. 5–8.

71. Raphael Patai, *Sex and Family in the Bible and the Middle East* (Garden City, N.Y., 1959), p. 72.

offspring to come, all the land of Canaan, as an everlasting holding. (Gen. 17:1–2, 6–8)

Although now in the causative *hif'il* form and separated by several intervening verses, the verbs *prh* and *rbh* still function as a pair, as their identical pronominal objects and emphatic adverbial modifiers indicate. The repeated reminder that this divine promise comprises a covenant— the word *bᵉrit* occurs ten times in Gen. 17:1–15—supports our inference from the story of Noah that the original blessing of procreation in Gen. 1:28 now conveys the assurance of divine commitment and protection. The causative reformulation of the *prh/rbh* blessing only strengthens this impression, because God himself is the subject of the verbs, and not those involved in the actual reproductive process.[72] Later in the same chapter, God bequeaths his covenant with Abraham to the patriarch's heirs:

> Sarah your wife shall bear you a son, and you shall name him Isaac; and I will maintain (*wa-haqimoti*) my covenant (*bᵉriti*) with him as an everlasting covenant for his offspring to come. As for Ishmael, I have heeded you. I hereby bless him. I will make him fertile (*wᵉ-hifreti 'oto*) and exceedingly numerous (*wᵉ-hirbeti 'oto bi-m'od mᵉ'od*). He shall be the father of twelve chieftains, and I will make of him a great nation. But my covenant (*bᵉriti*) I will maintain ('aqim) with Isaac, whom Sarah shall bear to you at this season next year. (Gen. 17:19–21)

In this passage, God evidently distinguishes between his covenant, to be maintained with Isaac, and the blessing of *prh/rbh,* to be transmitted to Ishmael.[73] Yet the subsequent uses of the *prh/rbh* formula in Genesis demonstrate that the blessing of fertility and increase extended to the line of Isaac as well. Perhaps these verses of Gen. 17, which now express an anti-Ishmaelite polemic, assumed their present form for stylistic reasons: the introduction and conclusion of the divine promise with the technical term for striking a covenant (*haqem bᵉrit*), just as we found in

---

72. Walter Gross, "Jakob, der Mann des Segens," *Biblica* 49 (1968), 321–44, argues that the *hif'il* formulation of *prh/rbh* in Gen. 17 constitutes a later refinement of the earlier *qal* forms in Gen. 28 and 35.

73. See the comments of Walter Brueggemann, "The Kerygma of the Priestly Writers," in *The Vitality of Old Testament Traditions,* by Walter Brueggemann and Hans Walter Wolff, 2nd ed. (Atlanta, Ga., 1982), p. 105.

Gen. 9:9–17), with *prh/rbh* conveying the substance of God's commitment. In any event, the verbs of Gen. 1:28 seem to satisfy Abraham's wish for divine providence for Ishmael; and whether in its symmetrical *haqem b*ᵉ*rit, prh/rbh, haqem b*ᵉ*rit* structure or by their juxtaposition of Isaac's *covenant* and Ishmael's *blessing,* Gen. 17 maintains the association between the two.

In the following generation, Isaac passes along his father's blessing to his son Jacob on the eve of the latter's departure to Haran (Gen. 28:3–4): "May '*El Shaddai* bless you, make you fertile (*w*ᵉ*-yafr*ᵉ*kha*) and numerous (*w*ᵉ*-yarbekha*), so that you become an assembly of peoples. May he grant the blessing of Abraham to you and your offspring, that you may possess the land where you are sojourning, which God assigned to Abraham." When Jacob subsequently returns to Palestine, God himself reaffirms the promise:

> I am '*El Shaddai.* Be fertile (*p*ᵉ*re u-r*ᵉ*ve*) and increase; a nation, yea an assembly of nations, shall descend from you. Kings shall issue from your loins. The land which I assigned to Abraham and Isaac I assign to you; and to your offspring to come will I assign the land. (Gen. 35:11–12)

Both these blessings of Jacob reiterate God's bequest of the land to Abraham in Gen. 17, and like the commitments to Abraham and Ishmael, Gen. 35:11 includes the promise of royal progeny—additional echoes of the conferral of dominion on the sixth day of creation. Yet on the basis of its simple *qal* formulation of *prh* and *rbh,* Walter Gross asserted that the text of Jacob's blessing in Gen. 35 antedated that of Abraham and his sons in Gen. 17, where the key verbs appeared in the causative *hif'il*.[74] Along similar lines, the absence of the term *b*ᵉ*rit* in both speeches may indicate that these passages represent an earlier stage in the Bible's own thinking on the *prh/rbh* formula of Gen. 1:28. Each passage unquestionably serves to transmit the divine election of the patriarchs from one generation to the next, but neither explicitly associates *prh/rbh* with the notion of covenant.

The biblical narrator indicates (Gen. 47:27) that God's promises to the patriarchs remain in force when Jacob moves his family to Egypt, settling in the land of Goshen, where they "were fertile (*wa-yifru*) and

74. W. Gross, "Jakob."

increased (*wa-yirbu*) greatly." Lying on his deathbed in Egypt, Jacob begins his blessing of Ephraim and Manasseh by relating to Joseph (Gen. 48:3–4), "*'El Shaddai* appeared to me at Luz in the land of Canaan, and he blessed me, and said to me, 'I will make you fertile (*mafrᵉkha*) and numerous (*wᵉ-hirbitikha*), making of you a community of peoples; and I will assign this land to your offspring to come for an everlasting possession.'" Willing his special affinity with God to yet another generation, Jacob has here altered the language of Gen. 35:11, to which he refers. But in quoting Jacob's own direct quotation of God's words to him, Scripture removes all doubt of the formulaic importance of Gen. 1:28's key verbs; according to the narrative, the patriarchs themselves recognized their technical significance.

The hendiadys of *prh/rbh* occurs six more times in the remaining books of the Hebrew Bible. As the book of Exodus opens, with its new focus on the collective of Israelite people in Egypt, the narrator reports (Ex. 1:7): "But the Israelites were fertile (*paru*) and prolific (*wa-yishrᵉzu*); they multiplied (*wa-yirbu*) and increased very greatly, so that the land was filled (*wa-timmale'*) with them." The progression of biblical history may have moved to a new book and altered its focus, but Scripture here reminds its readers that even in Egypt, years after the death of Jacob, Joseph, and their children, the divine commitment to Israel's forefathers stood firm. It is interesting that the verb *šrz,* which here stands between *prh* and *rbh,* also appears in conjunction with them in Gen. 8:17 and 9:7; and the verb for filling (*ml'*) the land recalls the language of Gen. 1:28 and 9:1. As Bezalel Porten and Uriel Rappoport pointed out, the sequence of five verbs in Ex. 1:7 also reproduces the poetic rhythm of Gen. 1:28.[75]

At the end of Leviticus (26:9), the explicit linkage of *prh/rbh* and divine covenant returns. Elaborating the reward for obedience to the commandments, God promises the Israelites: "I will look with favor (*u-faniti*) upon you, and make you fertile (*wᵉ-hifreti*) and multiply (*wᵉ-hirbeti*) you; and I will maintain (*wa-haqimoti*) my covenant (*bᵉriti*) with you."[76] The book of Jeremiah similarly foretells a glorious, albeit

---

75. Porten and Rappoport, "Poetic Structure." See the intriguing suggestion of Lohfink, "Macht euch die Erde untertan," p. 138, that this final appearance of *prh/rbh* in the pentateuchal narrative indicates that the Israelite population had reached its desired limit.

76. On Lev. 26:9, see Norbert Lohfink, "Die Abänderung der Theologie des priesterlichen Geschichtswerks im Segen des Heiligkeitsgesetzes," in *Wort und Geschichte: Festschrift für Karl Elliger zum 70. Geburtstag,* Alter Orient und Altes Testament 18 (Kevelaer, 1973), pp. 129–36.

somewhat distant, future (Jer. 3:16): "And when you increase (*tirbu*) and are fertile (*u-feritem*) in the land, in those days—declares the Lord—men shall no longer speak of the ark of the covenant (*berit*) of the Lord, nor shall it come to mind. They shall not mention it, or miss it, or make another." The prophetic writer here describes restoration in terms of the fulfillment of the promise of *prh/rbh* and so perfect an actualization of the divine covenant that its physical representation in the ark would no longer be necessary.[77] Jeremiah later proclaims God's vow to return his flock to pasture (Jer. 23:3), "where they shall be fertile (*u-faru*) and increase (*we-ravu*)," and again evokes a covenantal association by including in each of the next two verses the word *wa-haqimoti:* "I will appoint over them shepherds who will tend them . . . I will raise up a true branch of David's line."[78] The book of Ezekiel transmits the same message more clearly still, this time addressing his words to the promised land (Ezek. 36:9–11a):

[v. 9] For I will care for you; I will turn (*u-faniti*) to you, and you shall be tilled and sown. [v. 10] I will settle a large population (*we-hirbeti* . . .) on you, the whole house of Israel; the towns shall be resettled, and the ruined sites rebuilt. [v. 11] I will multiply (*we-hirbeti*) men and beasts upon you, and they shall increase (*we-ravu*) and be fertile (*u-faru*).

One might speculate that Ezekiel consciously echoed Jeremiah's prophecy, but it appears certain that he had Lev. 26:9 in mind. The language

---

77. John Bright, *The Anchor Bible: Jeremiah* (Garden City, N.Y., 1965), p. 27, maintains that this verse derives from an anonymous editor who followed Jeremiah; so too N. Mendecki, "Die Sammlung und die Hineinführung in das Land in Jer. 23,3," *Kairos* 25 (1983), 99–103. F. Giesebrecht, *Das Buch Jeremia*, 2nd ed., Handkommentar zum Alten Testament 3,2,1 (Göttingen, 1907), p. 20, suggests that the word *berit* itself might be an interpolation. Moshe Weinfeld, "Jeremiah and the Spiritual Metamorphosis of Israel," *ZAW* 88 (1976), 19–26, defends the Josianic provenance and preexilic authenticity of the passage.

78. Much discussion has also transpired concerning the origins and date of this verse, believed by many to have been added by an exilic editor; for a recent review of the literature on all sides of the question, see William McKane, *A Critical and Exegetical Commentary on Jeremiah*, vol. 1 of the International Critical Commentary (Edinburgh, 1986), pp. 553–59. On the midrashic value of *wa-haqimoti*, see Fishbane, *Biblical Interpretation*, pp. 471–72, who deems the term a *Stichwort* linking this oracle and Jer. 33:14–16. The contention of Richard Elliot Friedman, *Who Wrote the Bible?* (New York, 1987), p. 168, that Jer. 3:16 voiced an antagonistic response to the Priestly document (which therefore antedated Jeremiah) by "eschewing the ark in a twist of P's own language"—i.e., by invoking the formula of *prh/rbh*—would apply equally to Jer. 23:3–5. Repeated use of the typically Priestly verb *wa-haqimoti* following immediately upon the *prh/rbh* hendiadys but without the expected object of "my covenant" (*beriti*) might have served the same polemical purpose. On the implications of such debate for our appreciation of *prh/rbh*, see below, pp. 46ff. (on P).

and tone of prophetic admonition, the *prh/rbh* hendiadys, and the verbs at the beginning of each of his three verses, matching those of the Leviticus text, make the allusion difficult to dispute. In light of the close correspondence, it is tempting to conclude that *wᵉ-hirbeti* in Ezek. 36:10 should properly read *wᵉ-hifreti*, thus allowing the prophet to replicate the *u-faniti, wᵉ-hifreti, wᵉ-hirbeti* sequence of the Mosaic passage before him.[79] Ezekiel's intended homily on Lev. 26:9, which itself had constituted a reinterpretation of the blessings of Gen. 1:28, testifies further to the function of *prh/rbh* as an accepted metaphor for divine commitment and promise.

The commonly oriented allusions to Gen. 1:28 in five different books of Scripture raise the issue of whether their authors shared a particular ideological stance, as well as the problem of their chronological sequence, and we shall return to these questions below, in our discussion of the Priestly document and the recurring name of *'El Shaddai*. At the moment our concern lies with the bearing these subsequent passages have on the meaning of *prh/rbh* in its biblical context. In the creation story, these verbs denote the substantive results of God's providence: progeny and, by extension, land. But with each successive occurrence of the phrase, the words of Gen. 1:28 assume an additional function: Comprising the divine blessing of humans par excellence, they become a metaphor, a formularized guarantee of divine protection, divine election, and the divine covenant. No wonder the blessing of *prh/rbh* is repeated for Noah, Abraham, Isaac and Ishmael, Jacob, Joseph and his sons, the children of Israel in Egypt, and those who would ultimately enjoy the future redemption—by which times human procreation and

79. See Karl Marti, "Die Spuren der sogennanten Grundschrift des Hexateuchs in der vorexilischen Propheten des Alten Testaments," *Jahrbucher für protestantische Theologie* 6 (1880), 326, G. A. Cooke, *A Critical and Exegetical Commentary on the Book of Ezekiel,* International Critical Commentary (Edinburgh, 1951), p. 388, and Keith W. Carley, *The Book of the Prophet Ezekiel* (Cambridge, 1974), p. 240, among others, who have suggested a parallel between these passages in Ezekiel and Leviticus, although to my knowledge no one has proposed this emendation of Ezek. 36:10. Walther Zimmerli, *Ezekiel 2: A Commentary on the Book of the Prophet Ezekiel, Chapters 25–48,* tr. James D. Martin (Philadelphia, Pa., 1983), p. 230, rejects the parallel altogether, "since in the present passage, [Ezek.] 36:9–11, the same three verbs certainly occur more than once, but nowhere in the uniform sequence of the statements in Lev. 26." Georg Fohrer, *Ezechiel,* Handbuch zum Alten Testament 1,13 (Tübingen, 1955), p. 201, and Walter Eichrodt, *Ezekiel: A Commentary,* tr. Cosslett Quin (London, 1970), pp. 488–89, call for deleting Ezek. 36:10 as a dittography (Eichrodt: "an inferior variant") of 36:11, but a reading along the lines we have proposed might address the problem of repetition more effectively. Cooke, Eichrodt, and Zimmerli, pp. 230, 238, delete *wᵉ-ravu u-faru* as "an insertion, betrayed by the sudden change of person" (Cooke), and unattested in the Septuagint.

superiority over animals would long have been established facts of life! While the biblical people never lost their concern for fertility and prosperity, the clearly interpretative texts we have considered (e.g., Gen. 9, Gen. 17, Ezek. 36) demonstrate that Gen. 1:28 had come to mean something more. Commenting on Gen. 35:11, B. Jacob aptly reflected that its language "is a promise, a challenge, a blessing, a comfort, and a joyful affirmation of life. It presupposes a nation which enjoys the present and is conscious of its mission."[80]

"What is man . . . ?" Our survey of biblical passages that contribute to an understanding of Gen. 1:28 has rightly concentrated on its key verbs: *prh* and *rbh*. Nevertheless, one additional text, in which many critics find clarification of the dominion God granted the first humans, remains to be considered.

> What is man that you have been mindful of him,
> mortal man (*ben 'adam*) that you have taken note of him,
> that you have made him little less than divine (*me-'elohim*)
> and adorned him (*te'att̄erehu*) with glory (*khavod*) and majesty (*hadar*);
> you have made him master (*tamshilehu*) over your handiwork,
> laying the world at his feet,
> sheep and oxen, all of them,
> and wild beasts, too;
> the birds of the heavens, the fish of the sea,
> whatever travels the paths of the seas. (Ps. 8:5–9)

Recognizing that this passage lavishes more praise on humans than does the hexameral account of creation, Eichrodt concluded that the psalm antedated Gen. 1 because as Israelite thought matured it tended over time to deemphasize human control over nature. Bernhard Anderson concurred regarding the temporal sequence of the two texts, stressing the more primitive cultic imagery of royal investiture pervading Ps. 8, which gives way to a more sophisticated motif of divine blessing in Gen. 1:28.[81] Others, including Patrick Miller, Brevard Childs, and

---

80. B. Jacob, *The First Book of the Bible: Genesis,* ed. Ernest I. Jacob and Walter Jacob (New York, 1974), p. 238; cf. Walther Zimmerli, *The Old Testament and the World,* tr. John J. Scullion (Atlanta, Ga., 1976), ch. 3, and Westermann, *Genesis 1–11,* pp. 139–41.

81. Eichrodt, *Theology,* 2:152–62; Bernhard W. Anderson, "Human Dominion over Nature," in *Biblical Studies in Contemporary Thought,* ed. Miriam Ward (Burlington, Vt., 1975), pp. 34–37.

Gnana Robinson, have considered the Genesis text older and deem Ps. 8 an expanded gloss on the idea of dominion in Gen. 1:26–28.[82] Most, however, would acknowledge that the two passages bespeak an instructively similar message. On the one hand, each depicts the human being as belonging to the natural order of creation and therefore insignificant compared with God himself. On the other hand, each perceives humans as unique among God's creatures because humans somehow bear the divine image (*ʒelem 'elohim,* Gen. 1:27) or stand only slightly below *'elohim* (Ps. 8:6), meaning the deity or perhaps (as in the Septuagint followed by Heb. 2:7) his angelic ministers.[83] In either case, God entrusts humans with the work of his creation, elaborating their superiority over land animals, birds, and fish. And just as the last scene of the Genesis creation story returns to the divine realm for the sanctification of the Sabbath, so Ps. 8 concludes (v. 10) as it too began, with testimony to the incomparable feats and glory of the creator: "O Lord, our Lord, how majestic is your name throughout the earth!"

APPLICATIONS OF BIBLICAL SCHOLARSHIP

Scrutinizing the divine blessing of the first parents and its relationship to other passages in Hebrew Scripture, we have touched upon fundamental aspects of the biblical world view: belief in creation (cosmology), the nature of human beings (anthropology), God's concern for his creatures (providence), and the covenantal bonds between the deity and particular individuals or communities (salvation history). The breadth of its ramifications signals the doctrinal importance of Gen. 1:28, and the passage has appropriately figured in a wide range of modern works on the foundations and history of Israelite religion. Assessing our verse as an expression of ideology, and grappling with the historical background of its biblical career, such critical studies can further illuminate the ancient appreciation of Gen. 1:28, suggesting the uses to which it

---

82. Brevard S. Childs, "Psalm 8 in the Context of the Christian Canon," *Interpretation* 23 (1969), 20–31; Gnana Robinson, "The Biblical View of Man," *Indian Journal of Theology* 27 (1978), 138ff.; Patrick D. Miller, Jr., *Genesis 1–11: Studies in Structure and Theme, JSOT* Supplement Series 8 (Sheffield, 1978), pp. 19–20.

83. On the relation between the thought of Gen. 1 on the divine image and Ps. 8, see Conrad Louis, *The Theology of Psalm VIII: A Study of the Traditions of the Text and the Theological Import,* Catholic University of America Studies in Sacred Theology 99 (Washington, D.C., 1946), pp. 101–9.

was put and the meaning it bore. We therefore move on to evaluate Gen. 1:28 against a spectrum of critical theories and methodologies, some of which may have developed and even originated in opposition to one another but whose valuable applications for this book are seldom mutually exclusive. Having no need or intent to espouse one school of thought over all others, we have amassed, organized, and classified numerous works of modern scholarship to emphasize their significance for our specific concerns. This survey of currents in biblical criticism proceeds in the chronological order of the dimensions of Scripture they investigate. Commencing with the history of the traditions that gave rise to biblical cosmology, and touching briefly on the *Sitz im Leben* of the passages that record it, our survey then examines the relevant trends in pentateuchal source criticism, turning at last to the structural and rhetorical analysis of the final text of the Bible.

The Substance and Setting of Biblical Creation Faith

Much scholarly discussion of the biblical idea of creation has in recent decades revolved around von Rad's pivotal essay of 1936, "Das theologische Problem des alttestamentlichen Schöpfungsglaubens."[84] Von Rad then argued that creation faith was a relatively late addition to ancient Israelite religion, that it was hardly an original or necessary dimension of the "predominating belief in election and redemption."[85] Granted that testimony to God's creation does figure prominently in Genesis, Second Isaiah, and the Psalms, von Rad still affirmed: "In genuinely Yahwistic belief the doctrine of creation never attained to the stature of a relevant, independent doctrine. We found it invariably related, and indeed subordinated to soteriological considerations. . . . Either it remained a cosmic foil against which soteriological pronouncements stood out the more effectively, or it was wholly incorporated into the complex of soteriological thought."[86] Only with the emergence of its later wisdom tradition did ancient Israel begin to counte-

---

84. Translated as Gerhard von Rad, "The Theological Problem of the Old Testament Doctrine of Creation," in *The Problem of the Hexateuch and Other Essays,* tr. E. W. Trueman Dicken (New York, 1966), pp. 131–43, and reprinted in *COT,* pp. 53–64. See also the summary and comments of B. D. Napier, "On Creation-Faith in the Old Testament," *Interpretation* 16 (1962), 21–42.

85. *COT,* p. 53.

86. Ibid., pp. 62–63.

nance rational speculation regarding the natural order and to evince an interest in cosmology for its own sake. By then the biblical scheme of salvation history had acquired sufficient doctrinal fortification to allow "this liberty . . . for an undiluted doctrine of creation."[87]

Some have strenuously disagreed. Douglas Knight maintained that biblical concern with creation is too pervasive to warrant the relegation of cosmogony to the status of the peripheral, while J. W. Rogerson objected to von Rad's use of modern criteria for evaluating an ancient people's conception of nature.[88] H. H. Schmid contended that ancient Israel shared its Near Eastern neighbors' interest in cosmic order and in fact grounded its doctrine of salvation history in creation faith, "plainly the fundamental theme" of biblical theology.[89] And George Landes deemed the biblical notion of God as liberator incomprehensible without the underpinnings of a well-developed creation faith.[90] Others have proposed modifications of von Rad's thesis but have nonetheless found its influence inescapable. Hans-Jürgen Hermission accepted the linkage of creation faith and wisdom but finds evidence for genuine cosmological concern in earlier biblical texts where von Rad found none.[91] Dianne Bergant and Carroll Stuhlmueller distinguished between biblical concern for the creator and that for the material, natural order of creation, asserting the antiquity of the former while acknowledging the later, wisdom-related appearance of the latter.[92] Bernhard Anderson recognized the contributory function of creation faith vis-à-vis Israelite *Heils-*

---

87. Ibid., p. 63; see also Gerhard von Rad, *Wisdom in Israel,* tr. James D. Martin (Nashville, Tenn., 1972), pp. 144–76. The suggestion of a direct link between the wisdom tradition and the primordial blessing appears in Walther Zimmerli, "Ort und Grenze der Weisheit im Rahmen der alttestamentlichen Theologie," in *Les sagesses du Proche-Orient ancien (Colloque de Strassbourg, 17–19 Mai 1962)* (Paris, 1963), pp. 128–29.

88. Douglas A. Knight, "Cosmogony and Order in the Hebrew Tradition," in *Cosmogony and Ethical Order: New Studies in Comparative Ethics,* ed. Robin W. Lovin and Frank E. Reynolds (Chicago, 1985), pp. 133–57; J. W. Rogerson, "The Old Testament View of Nature," in *Instruction and Interpretation: Studies in Hebrew Language, Palestinian Archaeology, and Biblical Exegesis,* by H. A. Brongers et al., Oudtestamentische Studiën 20 (Leiden, 1977), pp. 67–84.

89. H. H. Schmid, "Creation, Righteousness, and Salvation: 'Creation Theology' as the Broad Horizon of Biblical Theology," in *COT,* p. 111.

90. George M. Landes, "Creation and Liberation," *Union Seminary Quarterly Report* 33 (1978), 79–89.

91. Hans-Jürgen Hermission, "Observations on the Creation Theology in Wisdom," in *COT,* pp. 118–34; see also Theodore M. Ludwig, "The Tradition of Establishing the Earth in Deutero-Isaiah," *JBL* 92 (1973), 345–57.

92. Bergant and Stuhlmueller, "Creation," esp. p. 172.

geschichte, but he has argued that one cannot easily separate the two and summarily dismiss one as peripheral and secondary to the other. Anderson explored at some length the central importance of creation faith for historiography, worship, and the concept of covenant in the Bible, and his insightful structural analyses of the first eleven chapters of Genesis bear heavily on any informed appreciation of the primeval history.[93] In the face of such protracted debate, von Rad himself ultimately renounced the unqualified distinction between historically and cosmologically rooted theology.

The controversy over the status of creation faith in the Bible has not abated, but it can facilitate an informed approach to Gen. 1:28 as an expression of such belief. As E. O. James concluded his comparative study of ancient cosmology, "the mystery of creation in the cosmic consciousness becomes an imaginative symbolic interpretation of the sensuous mundane order in relation to transcendent reality."[94] No one, not even the modern scientist, struggles with cosmological questions in a vacuum; any account of cosmic origins invariably mirrors the religious experiences and unique historical situation of the narrator. Hebrew writers thus perceived God's creation of the entire cosmos from within the context of their particular, covenantal, historical relationship with God. Their accounts of creation understandably spoke to their immediate concerns, although this did not demote creation faith to a doctrine of inferior station. Cosmogony in the Bible testifies to the beliefs as well as to the questions of Israelite theology, which posits the salvific election of a single people by a deity whose dominion extends over all. Several years before his death, when he tempered his earlier view of the relative lateness and secondary importance of biblical creation faith, von Rad appropriately linked biblical cosmology to "the relationship between the overall world-view of the Hebrews with its tendency to universalise and their understanding of history tending to particularisation. . . . Israel could not altogether ignore the existence of a very real tension between its views of God's handling of the world as a whole, in which the emphasis tends strongly to universalism, and the equally emphatic tendency to look at the particular case in God's deal-

93. Bernhard W. Anderson, "Mythopoeic and Theological Dimensions of Biblical Creation Faith," in *COT*, pp. 1–24, and *Creation versus Chaos: The Reinterpretation of the Mythical Symbolism in the Bible* (New York, 1967).

94. E. O. James, *Creation and Cosmology: A Historical and Comparative Inquiry,* Studies in the History of Religions (Supplements to *Numen*) 16 (Leiden, 1969), p. 128.

ings with man in history."[95] Biblical creation faith necessarily bespeaks a dialectic between universal and particularistic dimensions of divine providence, and, as we have seen, Gen. 1:28 exemplifies this tension well. If, in the opening chapter of Scripture, the verse conveys divine blessing to all human beings, its distinctive language subsequently denotes God's entry into an exclusive covenantal relationship—first with Noah and his sons, then with the Hebrew patriarchs, and finally with the entire Israelite community. In the world of biblical antiquity, these concerns—not worry over the ecological implications of technology—gave Gen. 1:28 its meaning and significance, a conclusion that is confirmed by centuries of Jewish and Christian commentary on the Bible.

How did the substance of biblical cosmology, and of the opening chapter of Genesis in particular, transmit the singular ideas of the Hebrew religion? For a century and more, scholars have studied the creation stories of other ancient Near Eastern peoples in an attempt to gauge the relationship of those stories to the Bible. Some investigators highlighted the similarities, others highlighted the differences, and still others debated the extent to which one can properly speak of external influences on biblical cosmology. A few deemed Gen. 1 a direct, polemical response to foreign religious influences on the Judeans during their sixth-century exile in Babylonia,[96] although most perceived the opening account of creation as embodying more ancient and traditional material as well. The resulting scholarly literature is massive, and we presently have no need to rehash the weighty contributions of generations of scholars, from Gunkel down to our own day.[97] It is sufficient to

---

95. Von Rad, *Problem*, p. 155. See also Claus Westermann, *Creation*, tr. John J. Scullion (Philadelphia, Pa., 1974), pp. 11ff.; and Steck, *World and Environment*, p. 98.

96. For example, Arvid S. Kapelrud, "The Mythological Features in Gen 1 and the Author's Intentions," *VT* 24 (1974), 178–86, esp. 186, where he comments on the author of Gen. 1: "He wrote for a community which stood in constant danger of being penetrated by Babylonian ideas and religion. In this situation, his fellow countrymen needed a creation story which could not only compete with the Babylonian one, but which was superior intellectually and ideologically." And John J. McKenzie, *The Anchor Bible: Second Isaiah* (Garden City, N.Y., 1968), p. lix: "The creation account of Genesis i is best understood as a piece of anti-mythological polemic; and it is highly probable that this account and Second Isaiah were formed in the same world of thought."

97. Among many others, see Hermann Gunkel, *Schöpfung und Chaos in Urzeit und Endzeit* (Göttingen, 1895); Alexander Heidel, *The Babylonian Genesis: The Story of Creation*, 2nd ed. (1951; repr., Chicago, 1963), esp. pp. 82–140; John J. McKenzie, *Myths and Realities: Studies in Biblical Theology* (Milwaukee, Wis., 1963), chs. 6–7, 9; Speiser, *Genesis*, pp. xliii–lviii; and Luis I. J. Stadelmann, *The Hebrew Conception of the World: A Philological and Literary Study,*

observe that measurements of the extent to which the Hebrews accepted or rejected the beliefs of other Semitic groups often obscure the interdependence of cross-cultural borrowing and polemic. Polemic presupposes familiarity, and specific departures from a prevailing cosmic outlook are instructive only against the background of a general correspondence between realms of religious discourse. Furthermore, the formative role of the ancient Near East in molding the experiences and ideas of biblical Israel, while historically crucial, provides only one of several dimensions to the meaning of Scripture. In considering the political circumstances that might have prompted the composition of a text, the social interaction underlying its form, or the religious tradition that spawned its message, one must recall that the text eventually became a meaningful entity in its own right, no longer bound by the situation or intentions of its authors.

At the beginning of this chapter, we noted that the Bible's elevation of humans over the rest of the natural order itself marks a key departure from the *communis opinio* of other Near Eastern mythologies. Gen. 1:28 depicts God's rationale for creation as the fostering of a distinctively human civilization, maintained with the blessings of divine providence. By contrast, in the Babylonian creation epic *Enuma Elish,* humans assume a less noble function. After defeating his divine opponents in battle, the victorious god Marduk enslaves the survivors but then comes to pity the miserable lot of their servitude; his solution entails the creation of a new species: "Blood will I mass and cause bones to be. I will establish a savage, 'man' shall be his name. Verily, savage-man will I create. He shall be charged with the service of the gods that they might be at ease!"[98] Albeit in a different fashion, the story of Gilgamesh also

---

Analecta biblica 39 (Rome, 1970), esp. pp. 10–37. For insightful considerations of methodology, see S. G. F. Brandon, "The Propaganda Factor in Some Ancient Near Eastern Cosmogonies," in *Promise and Fulfillment: Essays Presented to S. H. Hooke* (Edinburgh, 1963), pp. 20–35; Raffaele Pettazzoni, "Myths of Beginnings and Creation Myths," in his *Essays on the History of Religions,* Studies in the History of Religions (Supplements to *Numen*) 1 (Leiden, 1954), pp. 24–36; and the cautioning essay of W. G. Lambert, "A New Look at the Babylonian Background of Genesis," in *The Bible in Its Literary Milieu: Contemporary Essays,* ed. Vincent L. Tollers and John R. Maier (Grand Rapids, Mich., 1979), pp. 285–97. Helpful summaries of the state of the field include Gerhard F. Hasel, "The Significance of the Cosmology in Gen 1 in Relation to Ancient Near Eastern Parallels," *Andrews University Seminary Studies* 10 (1972), 1–20, and Kapelrud, "Theorie."

98. *Enuma Elish* 6.5–8, in James B. Pritchard, ed., *Ancient Near Eastern Texts Relating to the Old Testament,* 3rd ed. with suppl. (Princeton, N.J., 1969), p. 68.

questions and delimits the enduring value of the human being's sexual, mortal existence.[99]

Yet the most intriguing mythological parallel and contrast to Gen. 1:28 occurs in the Babylonian epic of *Atrahasis*. As in *Enuma Elish*, humans are fashioned from the remains of a slaughtered deity in order to "carry the toil of the gods" and to ease their burden.[100] The maternal goddess ordains for the new human species the institution and sexually reproductive practices of marriage, but as time goes by, the process of procreation appears to get out of hand:

> Twelve hundred years [had not yet passed]
> [When the land extended] and the peoples multiplied.
> The [land] was bellowing [like a bull],
> The god got disturbed with [their uproar].
> [Enlil heard] their noise
> [And addressed] the great gods,
> "The noise of mankind [has become too intense for me],
> [With their uproar] I am deprived of sleep."[101]

Finding the disturbance intolerable, Enlil tries to destroy humankind, first with a plague and then with famine, but he is thwarted by the designs of Enki, patron deity of King Atrahasis. Enlil finally plans a flood, and Enki instructs his client Atrahasis to take refuge in a boat of reeds. After a downpour of seven days, all but Atrahasis and his family have died, and the gods begin to bemoan the destruction; they crave the food and drink that humans had hitherto provided them. When the waters subside, Enlil submits to his fellow deities and agrees to permit human survival, presumably on the condition that his sleep not be disturbed. Despite the lacunae in the cuneiform text, it appears that the curtailment of human fertility and procreation was designed to spare the god discomfort.

---

99. Most recently, see Benjamin Foster, "Gilgamesh: Sex, Love, and the Ascent of Knowledge," in *Love and Death in the Ancient Near East: Essays in Honor of Marvin H. Pope,* ed. John H. Marks and Robert M. Good (Guilford, Conn., 1987), pp. 21–42. See also Alexander Heidel, *The Gilgamesh Epic and Old Testament Parallels,* 2nd ed. (Chicago, 1949), esp. ch. 3.

100. W. G. Lambert and A. R. Millard, eds., *Atra-Hasis: The Babylonian Story of the Flood* (Oxford, 1969), pp. 56–57.

101. Ibid., p. 67.

(Let there be) among the peoples women who bear
    and women who do not bear.
Let there be among the peoples the *Pāšittu*-demon
To snatch the baby from the lap of her who bore it.
Establish *Ugbabtu*-women, *Entu*-women, and *Igiṣītu*-women,
And let them be taboo and so stop childbirth.[102]

Just as in Genesis, the first humans in *Atrahasis* receive divine instructions to reproduce, and excesses in the process of procreation, paralleling the illicit, fruitful union between "divine beings" (*bᵉne ha-'elohim*) and daughters of men (Gen. 6:2, 6:4), set the stage for the flood.[103] Some authorities found the similarities between the texts so compelling that they invoke the one to complete their reading of the other. For Eugene Fisher, the tumult that disturbs Enlil's sleep in *Atrahasis* must correspond to the moral depravity that caused the biblical flood (Gen. 6:5–7, 11–12).[104] Structuralist critic Robert Oden concluded from *Atrahasis* that the flood in Genesis derived not from ethical wrongdoing but from procreation gone haywire, a "violation of the fundamental classificatory scheme [of binary opposites—e.g., divine vs. human] articulated by the cosmology which opens the Hebrew Bible."[105] Carol Meyers attributed the biblical departure from *Atrahasis* to a population shortage in early Israel.[106] But most investigators deem the biblical function of Gen. 1:28 a conscious attack on the value system of *Atrahasis*. From the biblical perspective, only sin and moral decadence—not God's whim or the practical, economic problem of overpopulation—

---

102. Ibid., pp. 102–3; the three kinds of women represent different types of priestesses (cf. pp. 176, 179); on the demon of childbirth, see also Erle Lichty, "Demons and Population Control," *Expedition* 13 (1971), 22–26.

103. A. R. Millard, "A New Babylonian Genesis Story," *Tyndale Bulletin* 18 (1967), 12; Isaac M. Kikawada, "The Literary Convention of the Primeval History," *Annual of the Japanese Biblical Institute* 1 (1975), 11–13; Isaac M. Kikawada and Arthur Quinn, *Before Abraham Was: The Unity of Genesis 1–11* (Nashville, Tenn., 1985). On structural and thematic parallels between *Atrahasis* and the primeval history of Genesis, see also below, p. 61f.

104. Eugene Fisher, "*Gilgamesh* and Genesis: The Flood Story in Context," *CBQ* 32 (1970), 399–400.

105. Robert A. Oden, "Transformations in Near Eastern Myths: Genesis 1–11 and the Old Babylonian Epic of Atrahasis," *Religion* 11 (1981), 34. So too Ronald S. Hendel, "Of Demigods and the Deluge: Toward an Interpretation of Genesis 6:1–4," *JBL* 106 (1987), 13–26.

106. Carol L. Meyers, "Gender and Genesis 3:16 Revisited," in *The Word of the Lord Shall Go Forth: Essays in Honor of David Noel Freedman,* ed. Meyers and M. O'Connor (Winona Lake, Ind., 1983), p. 341. Cf. also Carol L. Meyers, "Procreation, Production, and Protection: Male-Female Balance in Early Israel," *Journal of the American Academy of Religion* 51 (1983), 569–83.

result in divinely wrought affliction. In the wake of the flood, the gods of *Atrahasis* circumscribe human fruitfulness, themselves ordaining barrenness and infant mortality, while the Bible reiterates the blessing of *prh/rbh* three times—first for animals (Gen. 8:17) and then twice for humans (Gen. 9:1, 9:7).[107] Even beyond the question of crime and punishment, the Babylonian epic measures the value of human life in terms of the immediate, physical gratification of the gods. In the Bible, as we have seen, the words of Gen. 1:28 epitomize the blessing of God, investing human life and the means for its perpetuation with a spiritual worth that withstands the evil of Noah's generation and the cataclysm of the flood.

Venturing beyond the parallels between Israelite and Babylonian creation stories, biblical critics have also sought to isolate the socioreligious context (or *Sitz im Leben*) in which a text like Gen. 1 might have taken shape. The important function of cosmogonies in Near Eastern fertility cults has commonly led investigators to identify the opening chapter of Scripture as a liturgy for the primal Sabbath or new year festival, when ancient Semites strove to maintain the natural order by relating and reliving its primal victory over the forces of chaos. As Phyllis Bird explained: "In the mythopoeic world that was Israel's cradle, accounts of origins did not simply explain what happened in the beginning; they were statements about the nature of things as they 'are' (or as they should be). In the recitation or reenactment of the myth the original drama of creation was repeated and the present order maintained through re-creation."[108] The formulaic repetitions of Gen. 1—

---

107. Among others, see W. L. Moran, "Atrahasis: The Babylonian Story of the Flood," *Biblica* 52 (1971), 51–61; Rainer Alberz, "Die Kulturarbeit im Atramhasis im Vergleich zur biblischen Urgeschichte," in *Werden und Wirken des Alten Testaments: Festschrift für Claus Westermann zum 70. Geburtstag,* ed. Rainer Alberz et al. (Göttingen, 1980), pp. 38–57; Anne Dreffkorn Kilmer, "The Mesopotamian Concept of Overpopulation and Its Solution as Reflected in Mythology," *Orientalia* 41 (1972), 160–77; Tikva Frymer-Kensky, "The Atrahasis Epic and Its Significance for Our Understanding of Genesis 1–9," *Biblical Archeologist* 40 (1977), 147–55; idem, "What the Babylonian Flood Stories Can and Cannot Teach Us about the Genesis Flood," *Biblical Archaeology Review* 4,4 (1978), 32–41; and Kikawada and Quinn, *Before Abraham.*

108. Phyllis A. Bird, "Images of Women in the Old Testament," in *Religion and Sexism: Images of Women in the Jewish and Christian Traditions,* ed. Rosemary Radford Ruether (New York, 1974), p. 71. Among many others, see also Theodor H. Gaster, *Thespis: Ritual, Myth, and Drama in the Ancient Near East,* rev. ed. (1961; repr., New York, 1966); Paul Humbert, "La relation de Genèse 1 et du Psaume 104 avec la liturgie du Nouvel-An israélite," *Revue d'histoire et de philosophie religieuses* 15 (1935), 1–27; and Geo Widengren, "Early Hebrew Myths and Their Interpretations," in *Myth, Ritual, and Kingship: Essays on the Theory and Practice of Kingship in the Ancient Near East and in Israel,* ed. S. H. Hooke (Oxford, 1958), pp. 149–203.

"and it was so," "and God saw that this was good," and "there was evening and there was morning . . ."—do suggest the milieu of such an organized worship service,[109] which, given the Near Eastern tradition likening the construction of cultic shrines to the divine creation of the world,[110] may well have befitted the Israelite temple in Jerusalem.[111] Although a Hebrew equivalent of the Babylonian new year or *akitu* festival proposed by Sigmund Mowinckel still remains in the realm of the hypothetical, a liturgical setting for the composition of the biblical cosmogony would bear directly on the message of Gen. 1:28. The ritualized enthronement of the king, often accompanied by the rites of sacred marriage, typically dominated these ancient celebrations of the new year; the king, representing the deity and modeled after the primordial man, guaranteed fertility and prosperity on a day-to-day basis.[112] The Bible could hardly incorporate this contemporary practice in its entirety. In its assignment of marital duties to humans *and not to God,* as well as in its call to subdue "mother" earth, Gen. 1:28 itself entails a deliberate rejection of the fertility cult and its ritualized sex and pantheistic mythology. In addition, the verse radically transforms the Near Eastern pattern of royal investiture, as it democratically confers fertility and dominion on humanity as a corporate whole.[113] Rather than extol a particular human monarch, the Hebrew cosmogony pays tribute above

109. Contrast, however, McEvenue, *Narrative Style,* pp. 12ff., on "the relation between priestly style and children's literature."

110. See Jean Battero, "Antiquités assyro-babyloniennes," *Annuaire de l'Ecole pratique des hautes études—IVe Section: Sciences historiques et philologiques* 3 (1978–79), 100–219. Battero's entire essay (pp. 85–135) provides a helpful overview of recent developments in the study of Mesopotamian cosmogonies.

111. Moshe Weinfeld, "Sabbath, Temple Building, and the Enthronement of the Lord" (Hebrew), *Beth Mikra* 22 (1967), 188–93; Arie Toeg, "Genesis I and the Sabbath" (Hebrew), ibid. 17 (1972), 288–96.

112. Among others, see Sigmund Mowinckel, *The Psalms in Israel's Worship,* tr. D. R. Ap-Thomas, 2 vols. (New York, 1962), esp. chs. 1–2, 5; Geo Widengren, "The King and the Tree of Life in Ancient Near Eastern Religion (King and Saviour, IV)," *Uppsala Universitets Årsskrift* 1951, no. 4; Ivan Engnell, *Studies in Divine Kingship in the Ancient Near East,* 2nd ed. (Oxford, 1967), pp. 174–76; McKenzie, *Myths,* pp. 107–16; Arvid S. Kapelrud, "King and Fertility: A Discussion of II Sam 21:1–14," in *Interpretationes ad Vetus Testamentum pertinentes Sigmundo Mowinckel septuagenario missae* (Oslo, 1955), pp. 113–22; and Kramer, *Sacred Marriage Rite,* esp. ch. 3. Bird, "Images," p. 72, notes that the story of creation comprised a Babylonian midwife's prayer for a good birth; presumably she refers to the lines of the Babylonian *Atrahasis* (1.189–214, ed. Lambert and Millard, pp. 58–59) labeled by Speiser "part of an incantation to facilitate childbirth" in Pritchard, *Ancient Near Eastern Texts,* pp. 99–100. See a similar medieval fertility incantation including Gen. 1:28, below, p. 271.

113. See Anderson, "Human Dominion," pp. 37–43; Schmidt, *Schöpfungsgeschichte,* pp. 130–45; and Samuel E. Loewenstamm, *Comparative Studies in Biblical and Ancient Oriental Literature,* Alter Orient und Altes Testament 204 (Neukirchen, 1980), pp. 48–50.

all to the transcendent kingship of a single, asexual deity, who ante-
ceded the natural order and rules over it. Biblical religion, however,
may well have continued to link creation and the motif of enthronement
in its sabbatical and festival liturgy, exploiting the idiom of the very
cultic ideology against which it polemicized. As Moshe Weinfeld
noted, the levitical recitation of Psalm 93 ("The Lord is king, he is robed
in grandeur . . .") on Friday (the eve of the Sabbath) documents a
nexus between creation and divine enthronement in the worship of
postexilic Israel; referring to the sixth day, the talmudic Rabbi Akiva
explained, "He then completed his work and reigned."[114] Numerous
Psalms (e.g., Pss. 8, 33, 74, 89, 104) offer further evidence of a similar
association, which still pervades the traditional synagogue liturgy, especially on the Sabbath and on the New Year.[115] Despite itself or
deliberately, Gen. 1:28, in which God blesses those just created in his
own image with fertility and dominion, may betray a Near Eastern
liturgical context by hinting at the royal investiture of the first human
beings.

The applications of this interpretation are open to debate.[116] For
Loren Fisher, the liturgical etiology of the biblical cosmogony confirms
its preexilic antiquity.[117] For Joseph Blenkinsopp, Hebrew creation
faith matured at the end of the sixth-century exile, precisely in response
to the Persian king Cyrus' arrogation of Babylonian royal ideology,
which was proclaimed primarily in creation liturgies for the new
year.[118] For Eduard Nielsen, the early, traditional royal imagery of
Gen. 1:22 and Gen. 1:28 accounts for their stylistic incongruity in this
otherwise exilic account of the creation.[119] Nevertheless, the question
of date aside, the presumed cultic origins of Gen. 1:28 and its suggestive
imagery of enthronement reinforce an appreciation of this text as a

---

114. Weinfeld, "Sabbath," which stops short of drawing a connection between the Sabbath
and a festival for the new year; see TB *Rosh ha-Shanah* 31a.

115. See, among others, Aubrey R. Johnson, *Sacral Kingship in Ancient Israel* (Cardiff,
1955); Keith R. Crim, *The Royal Psalms* (Richmond, Va., 1962), with the helpful foreword of
Jacob M. Myers; Loren R. Fisher, "From Creation to Cosmos," *Encounter* 26 (1965), 185ff.;
and John H. Eaton, *Kingship and the Psalms,* 2nd ed., The Biblical Seminar 3 (Sheffield, 1986),
pp. 87–111.

116. Reservations concerning the whole thesis are aired by Schmidt, *Schöpfungsgeschichte*,
p. 73; and Westermann, *Genesis 1–11*, pp. 91–93.

117. Loren R. Fisher, "An Ugaritic Ritual and Genesis I, 1–5," *Ugaritica* 6 (1969), 203–5.

118. Joseph Blenkinsopp, "The Unknown Prophet of the Exile," *Scripture* 14 (1962), 81–
90; cf. also Carroll Stuhlmueller, "The Theology of Creation in Second Isaias," *CBQ* 21
(1959), 429–45.

119. Eduard Nielsen, "Creation and the Fall of Man," *HUCA* 43 (1972), 6–7.

metaphor for divine commitment and covenant. The verse's lasting importance would have resided not in the primeval event that it recounted but in its function as liturgical formula: *repeatedly* to reassure ancient Israel of God's promises.[120] If elements of the *akitu* festival underlie the blessing of Gen. 1:28, they too did not prevent the Bible from using its Near Eastern heritage to enunciate its own singular values.

The Kerygma of P

Virtually without exception, source critics of the Bible ascribe Gen. 1 and all subsequent pentateuchal instances of the *prh/rbh* hendiadys to the Priestly document. With this consensus, however, general agreement comes to an end. Hard-pressed to explain why Scripture compressed God's eight creative works into six days and why God created sometimes by fiat and sometimes by deed, scholars of the first half of the twentieth century commonly maintained that the Priestly writer of the Genesis cosmogony fused at least two earlier sources. Many differentiated between a *Wortbericht,* which portrayed the process of creation as a series of divine commands, and a *Tatbericht,* which related God's execution of a series of creative acts. Considerable contention remained about which account preceded the other, while some rejected the bifurcation altogether. Recently, W. H. Schmidt posed a formidable challenge to the assumption of two parallel cosmogonies, contending instead that the extant text of Gen. 1 resulted from a prolonged Priestly reinterpretation of a traditional and more mythological creation story.[121] Schmidt identified Gen. 1:28 as a product of the Priestly reinterpretation instead of the underlying cosmogonic tradition,[122] and although some investigators have continued to speak of an execution-report and a command-report in Gen. 1, most acknowledge that in its present form and context Gen. 1:28 bespeaks the distinctive theological ideas of its Priestly author/editor.[123] Consequently, our present interest in pen-

---

120. Cf. Arvid S. Kapelrud, "The Date of the Priestly Code (P)," *Annual of the Swedish Theological Institute* 3 (1964), 58–64; and Walter Brueggemann, *The Land: Place as Gift, Promise, and Challenge in Biblical Faith,* Overtures to Biblical Theology 1 (Philadelphia, Pa., 1977), p. 146.

121. Helpful summaries of the pertinent scholarly literature appear in Schmidt, *Schöpfungsgeschichte,* pp. 9–20; and Westermann, *Genesis 1–11,* pp. 80–90.

122. Schmidt, *Schöpfungsgeschichte,* esp. pp. 127–49.

123. Westermann, *Genesis 1–11,* pp. 80–90; L. Monsengivo Pasinya, "Le cadre littéraire de

tateuchal source criticism will lie not with the textual evolution of Gen. 1 but with scholarly analysis of the ideology of P in general and with Gen. 1:28 as an expression of this outlook in particular.

Julius Wellhausen himself proposed the view that Priestly historiography advanced from one covenant to another in the divine scheme for Israel's salvation; the covenants of Adam, Noah, Abraham, and Moses each demarcated a new phase in the movement from creation toward redemption. Wellhausen understood Gen. 1:28 as initiating God's covenant with Adam and as providing the substantive and terminological basis for God's subsequent pact with Noah. Various investigators have rejected the claim that Gen. 1:28 itself constituted a covenant, but most have upheld Wellhausen's identification of an essentially covenantal theology that characterizes the Priestly narrative.[124] This in turn defines the Priestly interest in creation: to depict the materialization of the divine election of Israel in an unfolding series of orderings, classifications, and regulations that commenced at the very beginning of time and climaxed in the construction of the sanctuary and the myriad of cultic observances associated with it. In the words of George Coats:

> The primeval saga establishes a context for the patriarchs. Its intention, however, is not simply to place the patriarchs in a world scene, but more precisely to depict a typical state of affairs for people and to suggest that the patriarchs are a part of that state. . . . Moreover, whatever stability might have been offered by the perpetual repetition of a creation in a cultic act, controlled by the king or the priest or even the prophet, is here denied. Stability (and thus the power of royal man) comes only through the events God established with his people once, long ago and far away. . . . For P, these intentions can be accomplished

---

Genèse 1," *Biblica* 57 (1976), 225–41; P. A. H. de Boer, *Fatherhood and Motherhood in Israelite Piety* (Leiden, 1974), pp. 49ff.; Bird, "Male and Female"; but contra Nielsen, "Creation."

124. Wellhausen, *Prolegomena*, pp. 338–41. Among many others, see Frank Moore Cross, *Canaanite Myth and Hebrew Epic: Essays in the History of the Religion of Israel* (Cambridge, Mass., 1973), pp. 295–300; Eichrodt, *Theology*, 1:56ff.; Delbert R. Hillers, *Covenant: The History of a Biblical Idea* (Baltimore, Md., 1969), p. 158; Joseph Blenkinsopp, "The Structure of P," *CBQ* 38 (1976), 275–92; Anderson, "Mythopoeic and Theological Dimensions," pp. 14ff.; and Norman K. Gottwald, *The Hebrew Bible: A Socio-Literary Introduction* (Philadelphia, Pa., 1985), pp. 471–77. It is interesting that Wellhausen's reading of Gen. 1:28 as a covenant with Adam finds support among those who reject his Documentary Hypothesis: Cassuto, *Commentary*, 2:130–31; Aaron Soviv, "The Confirmation of Noah's Blessing," *Dor le-Dor* 9 (1981), 144–47; and H. Hirsch Cohen, *The Drunkenness of Noah* (University, Ala., 1974), p. 63.

only through the covenantal relationships established in the flood as a prefiguration for relationships established with Abraham. The concern for proper order . . . hangs on obedience as a sign of righteousness.[125]

The writer of P, Coats asserted, has denied the significance of his cosmogony's presumed cultic roots and has subordinated them to the covenantal framework of Israelite *Heilsgeschichte*. Such a perspective explains the penchant of Gen. 1 for division and taxonomic categorization, and it is in accord with the pentateuchal series of *prh/rbh* blessings discussed earlier in this chapter. Even if it derived from a traditional cosmogony that he inherited, the Priestly writer transformed the substance of Gen. 1:28 into a formulaic guarantee of divine providence and election, a central component of each successive covenant. Thus, concluded Westermann, "the formula serves P as a link between parts of his work: the blessing of living beings at the creation, the promise of increase to the patriarchs, the beginning of the story of the people," and ultimately the covenantal demand for the people's obedience.[126]

Why did the hendiadys of *prh/rbh,* along with the promise of land and dominion, epitomize the Priestly notion of election and covenant? The answer to this question depends on the historical and political circumstances surrounding the composition of P, on which scholarly opinion divides into two main schools of thought. According to Wellhausen, the Priestly document was the last of the four pentateuchal sources and originated during (and after) the Babylonian captivity when the Judean priesthood "reduced to writing and to a system what they had formerly practised in the way of their calling. After the temple was restored this theoretical zeal still continued to work, and the ritual when renewed was still further developed by the action and reaction on each other of theory and practice: the priests who had stayed in Babylon took as great a part, from a distance, in the sacred services, as their brothers at Jerusalem who had actually to conduct them." Only in the second half of the fifth century did Ezra formally publish and introduce "the Priestly Code, worked into the Pentateuch as the standard legislative

125. Coats, *Genesis,* p. 39; on the Priestly cosmogony as deliberate antimythological (and anti-Yahwist) polemic, see also John Sandys-Wunsch, "Before Adam and Eve—or What the Censor Saw," *Studies in Religion* 11 (1982), 23–28.

126. Westermann, *Genesis 1–11,* pp. 140–41; in addition to sources cited above, n. 120, see P. Buis, "Comment au septième siècle envisageait-on l'avenir de l'alliance? Etude de Lv. 26,3–45," in *Questions disputées d'Ancien Testament: Methode et théologique,* ed. C. Brekelmans, Bibliotheca ephemeridum theologicarum lovaniensium 33 (Louvain, 1974), pp. 131–40.

element in it, [and it] became the definite 'Mosaic law.'"[127] Subsequent
investigators have differentiated between several distinct strata in P,
have debated whether or not the Priestly opus also entailed the redaction of the Pentateuch, and have acknowledged P's preservation of
preexilic material. But the essence of Wellhausen's thesis still prevails:
The origins of P were both exilic and postexilic. Confronted with the
trauma of the destruction of the Jerusalem temple and the understandably resultant crisis of faith, P expounded a "theology forged in a time
of despair."[128] It reaffirmed God's promises of progeny, the land, and
the covenant to Israel; it stressed God's control of human history,
beginning with the creation and the congenital orderliness of the cosmos; and it asserted the election of Israel by depicting the order of
creation as institutionalized in the cult of the sanctuary. God had not
abandoned his people in exile. His providence extended beyond the
geographical boundaries of Palestine; and as he had delivered Abraham,
who at the end of the primeval history still resided on foreign soil, from
his idolatrous Mesopotamian milieu, he soon would return Israel to its
land and to its temple—all according to schedule.[129]

Cosmogony figured prominently in the expression of the Priestly
message. We have noted how the story of God's creation may have
resisted the threatening influences of Babylonian mythology on the
Judean exiles. And responding at last to the needs of the despondent
Israelites, "the creative power of God would once again form them into
a faithful people, assuming responsibility for the rest of the created
world."[130] The meticulous taxonomy of creation—every species fashioned distinctively, with a peculiar purpose, each according to its own
kind—mirrored God's painstaking direction of human affairs toward
the end of Israel's salvation as well as the corresponding obsession for

127. Wellhausen, *Prolegomena*, pp. 404–9.

128. Terence E. Fretheim, "The Theology of the Major Traditions in Genesis-Numbers,"
Review and Expositor 74 (1977), 314–19; among others, see also Martin Noth, *A History of
Pentateuchal Traditions*, tr. Bernhard W. Anderson (Englewood Cliffs, N.J., 1972), pp. 243ff.;
Robert Polzin, *Late Biblical Hebrew: Toward a Typology of Biblical Hebrew Prose*, Harvard
Semitic Monographs 12 (Missoula, Mont., 1976), ch. 3; Sue Boorer, "The Kerygmatic
Intention of the Priestly Document," *Australian Biblical Review* 25 (1977), 12–20; Leo Laberge,
"Ministères et esprit dans les communautés postexiliques," *Eglise et théologie* 9 (1978), 379–
411; and Ralph W. Klein, "The Message of P," in *Die Botschaft und die Boten: Festschrift für Hans
Walter Wolff zum 70. Geburtstag*, ed. Jörg Jeremias and Lothar Perlitt (Neukirchen, 1981),
pp. 57–66.

129. David J. A. Clines, "'Theme' in Genesis 1–11," *CBQ* 38 (1976), 483–507.

130. Bergant and Stuhlmueller, "Creation," pp. 159–62. See also Stadelmann, *Hebrew
Conception*, p. 10; and Klein, *Israel*, ch. 6.

order in the priestly dominated sanctuary and temple cult. It is not insignificant that P concludes God's detailed instructions for building the tent of meeting with an injunction to observe the Sabbath (Ex. 31:12–17), in whose institution the heptameral cosmogony also reaches its climax. The sanctuary was appropriately completed on the first day of the new year (Ex. 40:17), and the lengthy acount of the construction ends (Ex. 40:33) "when Moses had finished (*wa-yᵉkhal*) the work (*mᵉla'-khah*)," employing exactly the same words used to explain God's rest on the original Sabbath day (Gen. 2:2).[131] Centuries later, the Talmud rationalized the prohibition of thirty-nine categories of work (also *mᵉla'khah*) on the Sabbath as "corresponding to the labors of the sanctuary."[132] And just as the seventh day of creation exemplified the harmonious relationship between God and his creation, so P labels the Sabbath a perpetual sign (*'ot*) and covenant (*bᵉrit*) between God and the children of Israel (Ex. 31:13, 16–17).

Most proponents of the Wellhausen thesis discern an instructive connection between the Priestly cosmogony and the impassioned sermons of Second Isaiah.[133] Creation faith assumed unprecedented significance for this exilic prophet, who used the motif of God as creator to counter the presumptuous aspirations of Babylonian and Persian monarchs to omnipotence and who thereby incorporated contemporary events into an all-encompassing divine plan for the restoration of Israel. Reflecting both the universal and particularistic dimensions of divine providence, creation served P and Second Isaiah in a like manner, and scholars have typically pointed to their similar usage of technical terms denoting God's primeval victory over the forces of chaos—for instance, in Isaiah 45:18: "For thus said the Lord, the Creator of heaven who alone is God, who formed the earth and made it, who alone established it—he did not create it a waste (*lo' tohu bᵉra'ah*), but formed it for habitation: I am the Lord, and there is none else." John McKenzie commented on this passage: "In some ways this poem represents a peak both of theology and of poetic intensity in the discourses of Second

---

131. See Martin Buber, *Die Schrift und ihre Verdeutschung* (Berlin, 1936), pp. 39ff., cited by Fishbane, *Text*, p. 12.

132. TB *Sab.* 49b; cf. TJ *Sab.* 7.2, 9b.

133. Eichrodt, *Theology*, 1:61–63; Stuhlmueller, "Theology"; Blenkinsopp, "Unknown Prophet"; Kapelrud, "Date"; P. B. Harner, "Creation Faith in Deutero-Isaiah," *VT* 17 (1967), 298–306; Andreas Eitz, "Studien zum Verhältnis von Priesterschrift und Deutero-jesaja" (Th.D. Dissertation, Ruprecht-Karl Universität, Heidelberg, 1969); Klein, *Israel*, pp. 114–16.

Isaiah. It brings together the themes of the absolute unique divinity of Yahweh and of the unity of mankind under the sovereignty of Yahweh." Westermann added: "Deutero-Isaiah here displays the same universalistic attitude as also determines what is said of God in the primaeval history."[134]

As Israel beheld her exilic experience mirrored in the memories of creation, God's blessing of the first parents should have struck an especially responsive note. The words of Gen. 1:28, repeated for Noah in the wake of destruction and for the patriarchs in moments of crisis, promised progeny, land, and dominion to a people deprived of all three. References to the past fulfillment of these promises in Egypt (Gen. 47:27, Ex. 1:7) affirmed that the divine covenant could withstand Israel's dislocation from Palestine. As Joseph Blenkinsopp observed, the injunction to master (*kbš*) the earth looked forward to an imminent reoccupation of the land and reconstruction of the Temple, envisaged through memories of the initial conquest and sanctuary in the days of Joshua (18:1): "The whole community of the Israelite people assembled at Shiloh, and set up the Tent of Meeting there. The land was now under their control (*weha-'areẓ nikhbeshah lifnehem*)." Not by coincidence did Joshua conclude his conquest with the same verb (*klh*, Josh. 19:51) that marked the end of creation, the institution of the Sabbath, and, as we have noted, the completion of the sanctuary.[135] Exilic law code (Lev. 26:9) and prophecy (Jer. 3:16, 23:3;[136] Ezek. 36:11) alike used the formula of *prh/rbh* to portray the blissful prosperity of an impending restoration. No wonder Walter Brueggemann deemed the blessing of Gen. 1:28 the core of the kerygma of P,

> the central message in the faith of the Priestly circle. . . . The "blessing" is a bold and overpowering affirmation in which the sovereign's intent is clear. While the verbs are expressed as imperatives, they are not so much commands as authorizations by which the people are empowered to believe and act toward the future. Thus the five verbs assert God's radical intention to promote well-being and prosperity. And that intent

134. McKenzie, *Second Isaiah*, pp. 82–83; Claus Westermann, *Isaiah 40–66: A Commentary*, tr. David M. G. Stalker (Philadelphia, Pa., 1969), pp. 172–73. And see also H. Wheeler Robinson, *Inspiration and Revelation in the Old Testament* (1946; repr., Oxford, 1960), p. 19; and Norman C. Habel, "'Yahweh, Maker of Heaven and Earth': A Study in Tradition Criticism," *JBL* 91 (1972), 332–35.

135. Blenkinsopp, "Structure," p. 290.

136. The exilic dating of P goes hand in hand with the opinion that a later exilic writer, and not Jeremiah himself, authored the two passages in question.

cannot be frustrated by any circumstance, not even such a circumstance as the traditionist's context of exile. God's claim to sovereignty (according to the text) is over the creation which he has just called into being out of *chaos*. Historically his claim refers to the *exilic situation* of poverty, defeat, and despair which he now transforms into a situation of joy and shalom. These five assertions complete the creation of humankind, affirming its primacy and ordaining it as the agent of order in his world which he now wills to be fertile and productive.[137]

Although the exilic dating of the Priestly document was not universally accepted even in Wellhausen's Germany, a second school of thought on the issue, consisting mostly of Jewish investigators in Israel and in the United States, traces its lineage to the scholarly opus of Yehezkel Kaufmann. In the first of his eight-volume study *The History of the Israelite Religion,* published some fifty years ago, Kaufman argued vigorously that P preceded the Deuteronomic source as well as the Babylonian captivity. Introducing his monumental study, Kaufmann proposed:

> [The claim] that the priestly stratum of the Torah was composed in the Babylonian exile, and that the literature of the Torah was still being written and revised in and after the Exile[,] is untenable. The Torah—it will be shown—is the literary product of the earliest stage of Israelite religion, the stage prior to literary prophecy. Although its compilation and canonization took place later, its sources are demonstrably ancient—not in part, not in their general content, but in their entirety, even to their language and formulation.[138]

As Kaufmann's words suggest, the question of the date of P bore directly on the doctrinal originality and prestige of the Mosaic law. Just as his work manifests an element of apologetic, so too did the ideologi-

137. Brueggemann, "Kerygma," pp. 103–4 (italics Brueggemann's); see also idem, *Land,* pp. 144–46. Cf. the supporting arguments of Peter Weimar, "Struktur und Komposition der priesterschriftlichen Geschichtsdarstellung," *Biblische Notizen* 23 (1984), esp. 86ff., where the formula of *prh/rbh* actually defines the textual boundaries of P. But see also the reservations of Klein, "Message," p. 59; and the outright disagreement of Norbert Lohfink, "Die Priesterschrift und die Geschichte," in *Congress Volume: Göttingen, 1977,* Supplements to *VT* 29 (Leiden, 1978), pp. 218–21.

138. Yehezkel Kaufmann, *Tol^edot ha-'Emunah ha-Yisra'elit, m-Yme Qedem 'ad Sof Bayit Sheni,* 8 pts. in 4 vols. (1937–56; repr., Jerusalem, 1972), 1:6, translation in idem, *The Religion of Israel, from Its Beginnings to the Babylonian Exile,* abr. and tr. Moshe Greenberg (Chicago, 1960), pp. 1–2; and see *Tol^edot,* 1:113–42, translation in *Religion,* pp. 175–200: "The Antiquity of the Priestly Code."

cal agenda of the Wellhausen school contribute to the disfavor and obscurity in which the preexilic dating of P languished for years, outside of its small group of advocates. But during the last two decades a growing number of investigators have leveled potent criticisms at the methodology and conclusions of the Wellhausen school, arguing on linguistic, terminological, and conceptual grounds that the literary formulation of P must have preceded the destruction of Solomon's temple in 587 B.C.E.[139] Moshe Weinfeld and Michael Fishbane lent additional support to this interpretation by deeming the creation faith of Second Isaiah a direct polemical rejoinder to the Priestly cosmogony, instead of its affirmation or its source. From their perspective, the aforecited prophetic description of God's creation (45:18), that "he did not create it a waste (*lo᾽ tohu bᵉra᾽ah*)," actually denies the picture in Gen. 1:2 of "the earth being unformed (*tohu*) and void."[140] Most recently, Richard Friedman attempted to pinpoint the composition of P in the court of King Hezekiah at the end of the eighth century. In the wake of the Assyrian conquest of Israel, Friedman argued, Aaronid priests in Judea produced their Torah in response to the doctrinal implications of the earlier JE compilation, imported by refugees from the north, with which they had little sympathy.[141]

Widely respected advocacy of the Kaufmann thesis is still a recent,

139. E. A. Speiser, "Leviticus and the Critics," in *Yehezkel Kaufmann Jubilee Volume: Studies in Bible and Jewish Religion Presented to Yehezkel Kaufmann on the Occasion of His Seventieth Birthday,* ed. Menahem Haran (Jerusalem, 1960), pp. 29–45; Moshe Weinfeld, *Deuteronomy and the Deuteronomic School* (Oxford, 1972), pp. 179–89, and *Getting at the Roots of Wellhausen's Understanding of the Law of Israel on the 100th Anniversary of the "Prolegomena"* (Jerusalem, 1981); Avi Hurvitz, "The Evidence of Language in Dating the Priestly Code," *Revue biblique* 81 (1974), 24–56, and *A Linguistic Study of the Relationship between the Priestly Source and the Book of Ezekiel: A New Approach to an Old Problem,* Cahiers de la *Revue Biblique* 20 (Paris 1982); the papers of Jacob Milgrom collected in his *Studies in Cultic Theology and Terminology,* Studies in Judaism in Late Antiquity 36 (Leiden, 1983), pp. 1–66; Menahem Haran, *Temples and Temple-Service in Ancient Israel: An Inquiry into the Character of Cult Phenomena and the Historical Setting of the Priestly School* (Oxford, 1978), and "Behind the Scenes of History: Determining the Date of the Priestly Source," *JBL* 100 (1981), 321–33; Ziony Zevit, "Converging Lines of Evidence Bearing on the Date of P," *ZAW* 94 (1982), 481–511; and Gary A. Rendsburg, *The Redaction of Genesis* (Winona Lake, Ind., 1986), pp. 107–20. Several additional advocates of a preexilic date for P are cited by J. G. Vink, "The Date and Origin of the Priestly Code in the Old Testament," in *The Priestly Code and Seven Other Studies,* by J. G. Vink et al., Oudtestamentische Studiën 15 (Leiden, 1969), pp. 10–11. It is interesting that Vink himself argues against the Wellhausen thesis for a later, postexilic (ca. early fourth century) date, but for our purposes his theory may be subsumed under the first school of thought considered above.

140. Moshe Weinfeld, "God the Creator in Gen. I and in the Prophecy of Second Isaiah" (Hebrew), *Tarbiẓ* 37 (1968), 105–32; Fishbane, *Biblical Interpretation,* pp. 325–26.

141. Friedman, *Who Wrote the Bible?* chs. 10–13.

maturing phenomenon, and its implications for our appreciation of the Priestly narrative have yet to crystallize. Kaufmann himself paid minimal attention to the primeval history in Genesis,[142] and his more recent followers have based their arguments almost exclusively on the legal sections of P. A preexilic origin notwithstanding, P still placed great emphasis on the covenant between God and his elect and on the ritualized and cultic representations of the covenantal relationship in the Sabbath, circumcision, the priesthood, and the sanctuary. Focusing specifically on circumcision, Michael Fox maintained that the Priestly narrative reworked earlier, oracular traditions of divine promise to all Abrahamitic tribes so as to limit the purview of God's covenant to Israel alone. Fox relies on the divine guarantees to both Abraham (Gen. 17) and Jacob (Gen. 35), which embody the ancient oracles of *'El Shaddai,* indicate that the patriarch in question would have multiple lines of descendants, and convey the commitments of God with the blessing of *prh/rbh.* The language of Gen. 1:28 thus contributed directly to the Priestly assertion of exclusiveness in the covenant between Israel and God, and itself explains the significance of circumcision as a marriage and fertility rite that bespoke that relationship. "Circumcision is a cognition sign—like the other *'otôt* in P—whose function is to remind God to keep his promise of posterity." In Fox's view, only modesty restrained the Priestly writer from explaining, "God will see the Israelite's circumcised penis during or before sexual congress and will remember to keep his covenant by making the union a fruitful one."[143]

Yet can the historical situation of the Priestly writer as conceived by the Kaufmann school account for the prominence that P accorded to the instructions of Gen. 1:28? A provocative essay by David Biale,[144] coupled with the admittedly extreme, pre-Josianic dating of P by Friedman, offers the basis for a suggestive, albeit highly speculative, reply.

---

142. Kaufmann, *Tol°dot,* 2:404–15, 433–40, translated in part in *Religion,* pp. 292–98.

143. Michael Fox, "The Sign of the Covenant: Circumcision in the Light of the Priestly *'ot* Etiologies," *Revue biblique* 81 (1974), 557–96, esp. 559 (and n. 4), 588–94 (quotations on 595). The reservation of Klein, "Message," p. 64, who "would prefer to see circumcision as a mnemonic cognition sign for the Israelites, which would constantly remind them of their status as covenanted people or, like the sign of the Sabbath, remind them to carry out God's commands," does not depreciate the Priestly association of the organ of procreation with the notion of exclusive covenant. On the importance of circumcision in P, see also Kapelrud, "Mythological," p. 185.

144. David Biale, "The God with Breasts: El Shaddai in the Bible," *History of Religions* 21 (1982), 240–56; and cf. the intriguing comments of Trible, *God,* ch. 3, which preceded Biale's essay by several years.

Of the six references to *'El Shaddai* in Genesis (17:1, 28:3, 35:11, 43:14, 48:3, 49:25), all but one (43:14) appear in fertility blessings, all but one (49:25) belong to the Priestly document, and, of these five Priestly passages, four appear in tandem with the hendiadys of *prh/rbh*.[145] Biale concludes that the antiquity of the non-Priestly exception (49:25),[146] the mention of kings in two of the Priestly blessings (17:6, 35:11),[147] and Jacob's transmission of the *prh/rbh* blessing to Ephraim and Manasseh in a third (48:3) all hint at a northern monarchic provenance of the *'El Shaddai* oracles, which ultimately derive from popular belief in a Canaanite fertility goddess with breasts (*shadayim*).[148] According to Biale, P neutralized the polytheistic myth by investing the powers of fertility in the God of Israel, who explicitly identified himself as *'El Shaddai* of the Hebrew patriarchs (Ex. 6:2–4): "I am the Lord. I appeared to Abraham, Isaac, and Jacob as *'El Shaddai,* but I did not make myself known to them by My name YHWH. I also established (*haqimoti*) my covenant (*bᵉriti*) with them, to give them the land of Canaan." In so doing, the Priestly document appropriated the motif of a procreator deity in order to fuel its covenantal theology. As Biale suggested,

> It may well be that this author possessed an authentic tradition according to which the patriarchs worshipped a God named *'El Shaddai,* whom he wishes to associate with Yahweh. But more importantly, his use of a special divine name in conjunction with fertility blessings for

145. Biale, "God," p. 247, proposes that because the sole Priestly mention of the name in Genesis (43:14) without the *prh/rbh* formula occurs in the context of a prayer for *rahamim* (mercy), it may allude to the word *rehem* (womb) and hence to fertility as well.

146. On the reading of *'El Shaddai* in this verse, see Claus Westermann, *Genesis 37–50: A Commentary,* tr. John J. Scullion (Minneapolis, Minn., 1986), pp. 219–20.

147. Cf. Gen. 17:20.

148. Gen. 49:25 concludes with "blessings of the breast (*shadayim*) and womb (*raham*)." Cf. also the possibility of phonetic allusions to *'El Shaddai* in Is. 32:12: "Lament upon the breasts (*'al-shadayim*), for the pleasant fields, for the spreading (*poriyyah*) grapevines"; and in Ps. 22:10–11: "You drew me from the womb, made me secure at my mother's breast (*'al shᵉde 'immi*). I became Your charge at birth (*me-rahem*); from my mother's womb You have been my God (*'eli*)." On *'El* and *Shaddai,* and their associations with procreation, sexuality, and fertility in particular, see Marvin H. Pope, *El in the Ugaritic Texts,* Supplements to *VT* 2 (Leiden, 1955), esp. pp. 35–42, 49–54; Ulf Oldenburg, *The Conflict between El and Ba'al in Canaanite Religion,* Supplementa ad *Numen,* Altera series, Dissertationes ad historiam religionum pertinentes 3 (Leiden, 1969), esp. pp. 164–68; Cross, *Canaanite Myth,* pp. 46–60; Klaus Koch, "Saddaj," *VT* 26 (1976), 299–332; Johannes C. de Moor, "El, the Creator," in *The Bible World: Essays in Honor of Cyrus Gordon,* ed. Gary Rendsburg et al. (New York, 1980), pp. 171–87; Patrick Miller, Jr., "El, the Creator of Earth," *Bulletin of the American Schools of Oriental Research* 239 (1980), 43–46; and Claus Westermann, *Genesis 12–36: A Commentary,* tr. John J. Scullion (Minneapolis, Minn., 1985), pp. 257–58.

the patriarchs is a result of his view of the patriarchal legends. . . . The repeated emphasis in Genesis on the miraculous birth of sons and the unnatural preference of the younger son . . . suggest the necessity of God's intervention in the process of reproduction to guarantee the future of the Israelite nation. Nowhere else in the Bible is fertility such a persistent focus of concern; nowhere is it so central to the theological and historical message of the text. The purpose of the Genesis stories for P . . . is to demonstrate that the covenant between God and his people is the consequence of the deity's active intervention in the family affairs of the patriarchs.[149]

Friedman's dating of P in the aftermath of Assyria's conquest of Israel, and his view that P proffered an Aaronid alternative to unpalatable northern beliefs that then made their way south, and that may have been tinged with the mythology of the Canaanite fertility cult, proffer an attractive corollary to Biale's thesis: Repeated Priestly allusion to the blessing of Gen. 1:28 stemmed from a perceived need to reaffirm divine election in the wake of destruction and to promote the partisan ideology of the Judean priesthood. These arguments remain highly conjectural, but they suggest that for the Wellhausen and Kaufmann schools alike the Priestly origins of Gen. 1:28 have similar bearing on the covenantal meaning and function of the verse.

The Primeval History from Within

Instead of concentrating on the religious traditions underlying a biblical passage or on the sociohistorical circumstances of its composition, a third school of modern Bible criticism seeks the meaning of Scripture through the literary analysis of its final, received text. Regardless of any particular ideas or events that may originally have given rise to a text, that text quickly became independent, capable of transmitting to subsequent listeners, editors, and readers a message—or messages—that may never have occurred to the author. In a recent book, whose title has inspired the name for this unit in our study, Meir Weiss pleaded for a totalistic approach to Scripture (as opposed to a disintegrating one), a mode of criticism that appreciates the text of the Bible as a literary entity unto itself, whose meaning derives primarily from the interaction be-

149. Biale, "God," pp. 251–52.

tween what is *in* the text and its interpreter.[150] Rightly construed in a
broad sense, such an "internal" approach to biblical study need not
entail the extreme deconstructionist premise that a text has no essential
meaning, or the refusal to acknowledge the role of intended stylistic
devices and structural patterns in determining such meaning. Nor need
this type of analysis negate the value of the "external" approaches we
have already considered. Weiss himself conceded the need for both
analytic directions and explains: "First, . . . historical criticism *as prac-
ticed* is not truly critical because of its unbalanced ideas about the relationship between literature and history. Second, the method of Total
Interpretation, far from seeking to supplant historical criticism aims to
redress that imbalance."[151] Indeed, an increasing number of investigators, some of whose historical studies have been cited above, have
recognized this complementary relationship and have moved to strike
the appropriate balance within their own critical scholarship.

Perhaps because of their prominence at the beginning of Scripture
and the relative ease with which they can be isolated in the text, both the
story of creation in seven days and the primeval history as a whole[152]
have constituted frequent objects for such "structural" or "rhetorical"
criticism.[153] Inasmuch as we have already discussed the function of
Gen. 1:28 in the heptameral cosmogony earlier in this chapter, we here
turn to the thematic significance of God's initial blessing of the first
parents within the larger context of Gen. 1–11. Additional occurrences

150. Meir Weiss, *The Bible from Within: The Method of Total Interpretation* (Jerusalem, 1984),
pp. 1–73, provides an extremely clear and helpful survey of important trends in the last
century of biblical and literary criticism.

151. Ibid., p. 65 (italics Weiss').

152. Obvious as they may appear, even the limits of these literary units have been open to
debate. On the creation story, see, among others, Bernhard W. Anderson, "A Stylistic Study
of the Priestly Creation Story," in *Canon and Authority: Essays in Old Testament Religion and
Theology,* ed. George W. Coats and Burke O. Long (Philadelphia, Pa., 1977), pp. 159–61, and
M. H. Woudstra, "The *Toledot* of the Book of Genesis and Their Redemptive-Historical
Significance," *Calvin Theological Journal* 5 (1970), 184–89; on the primeval history, see
W. Malcolm Clark, "The Flood and the Structure of the Pre-Patriarchal History," *ZAW* 83
(1971), 204–11, Clines, " 'Theme' in Genesis 1–11," pp. 502–3, and Warren Austin Gage, *The
Gospel of Genesis: Studies in Protology and Eschatology* (Winona Lake, Ind., 1984).

153. Noteworthy examples include, on the heptameral cosmogony, Kenneth R. R. Gros
Louis, "Genesis I–II," in *Literary Interpretations of Biblical Narratives,* ed. Kenneth R. R. Gros
Louis et al. (Nashville, Tenn., 1974), pp. 41–46, Anderson, "Stylistic Study," and John
Sailhamer, "Exegetical Notes: Genesis 1:1—2:4a," *Trinity Journal* 5 (1984), 73–82; and on the
entire primeval history, Bernhard W. Anderson, "From Analysis to Synthesis: The Interpretation of Genesis 1–11," *JBL* 97 (1978), 23–39; Sasson, " 'Tower' "; Westermann, *Genesis
1–11,* esp. pp. 600–606; and Kikawada and Quinn, *Before Abraham.*

of *prh/rbh* indicate that this importance extended into the remainder of the Pentateuch too, but the primeval context will suit us well.[154] Inquiries into the overall theme of the primeval history have yielded several interrelated alternatives.[155] Some have stressed the pattern of divine creation, ordering, and blessing, their subversion by human rebelliousness, and the eventual result of divinely wrought punishment.[156] Others have emphasized the groundwork laid for the course of Israelite salvation history that follows, expressed not only in the covenantal framework for divine-human relations but also in the failure of Abraham's predecessors to uphold such a relationship.[157] Still others have drawn attention especially to the sexual dimension of the violence and sinfulness that undermine the ideal created order.[158]

Gen. 1:28 comports well with such observations and may in fact serve to integrate them into a more coherent understanding of the primeval history. Fishbane and Coats both saw the motif of dominion—that is, the conferral and abuse of power—as a prominent concern of Scripture from creation until the appearance of Abraham. In Fishbane's words,

> The very hierarchy of the divine dominion described in the opening lines of Genesis, particularly with respect to Elohim's lordship over man, implies a world of boundaries and subservience. And more: the blessing to man in Genesis 1:28ff. regarding his dominion over the

154. The extended thematic significance of Gen. 1:28 is hinted at by David J. A. Clines, *The Theme of the Pentateuch, JSOT* Supplement Series 10 (1978; repr., Sheffield, 1982), p. 29 (italics Clines'): "*The theme of the Pentateuch is the partial fulfillment—which implies also the partial nonfulfillment—of the promise to or blessing of the patriarchs.* . . . The promise has three elements: posterity, divine-human relationship, and land."

155. The range of possibilities is described by Clark, "The Flood," pp. 204ff., Clines, "'Theme' in Genesis 1–11," and Fishbane, *Text*, pp. 38–39.

156. Von Rad, *Genesis*, pp. 152–55; Dennis J. McCarthey, "'Creation' Motifs in Ancient Hebrew Poetry," in *COT*, pp. 76–77; Coats, "God of Death"; Westermann, "Der Mensch."

157. J. B. Bauer, "Israels Schau in die Vorgeschichte (Gen. 1–11)," in *Wort und Botschaft: Probleme des Alten Testaments,* ed. J. Schreiner (Würzburg, 1967), pp. 74–87; P. E. S. Thompson, "The Yahwist Creation Story," *VT* 21 (1971), 197–208; J. P. Fokkelman, *Narrative Art in Genesis: Specimens of Stylistic and Structural Analysis,* Studia semitica neerlandica 17 (Assen, 1975), ch. 1; Gage, *Gospel;* Dumbrell, *Covenant and Creation,* ch. 1. On the covenantal theme of Gen. 2–3 in particular, see also Walter Brueggemann, "Of the Same Flesh and Blood (Gn 2,23a)," *CBQ* 32 (1970), 539–42, and Luis Alonso-Schöckel, "Sapiential and Covenant Themes in Gen 2–3," in *Studies in Ancient Israelite Wisdom,* ed. James L. Crenshaw (New York, 1976), pp. 468–80.

158. For example, H. H. Cohen, *Drunkenness,* esp. pp. 33–48; Bird, "Male and Female," pp. 158–59; Edmund Leach, "Genesis as Myth," in *The Bible in Its Literary Milieu: Contemporary Essays,* ed. Vincent L. Tollers and John R. Maier (Grand Rapids, Mich., 1979), pp. 411–22; and Luk de Vos, "Entwürfe von Universumssystemen: Entstehungsmythen und Ideologie," *Linguistica biblica* 50 (1982), 41–111.

earthly realm implies that man is a creature with a will. . . . When God informs man of the fixed hierarchies between creator and creature, and so sets limits to human will, He provokes a cognitive paradox. It is precisely the imposition of this prohibition that stimulates man as a willful autonomous agent.[159]

Westermann highlighted the unfolding development of a distinctively human civilization, replete with technological discovery and artistic refinement, which begins with the divine commission of Gen. 1:28, results in the agricultural control of Eden (Gen. 2:15), moves on to the respective cultural achievements of Cain and his family (Gen. 4:17–26), and at last leads to the presumptuous architectural blueprints for a tower that will reach into heaven (Gen. 11:1–9).[160]

In several ways, the motif of procreation and filling the earth also pervades the dramatic episodes in these first chapters of Genesis. Despite its Yahwistic origins, Westermann and W. J. Dumbrell viewed the story of Adam and Eve in its present biblical context as a narrative elaboration of Gen. 1:28. The marriage of the first parents and their occupation of the Garden of Eden reflect their proper relationship with God; when they undermine that relationship, they forfeit both their domestic tranquility (including the ability to bear and support children with ease) and their paradisiacal residence.[161] Commenting on the sixth day of creation, Edmund Leach noted: "The whole system of living creatures is instructed to 'be fruitful and multiply,' but the problems of Life versus Death and Incest versus Procreation are not faced at all." On the basis of his structuralist analysis, Leach maintains that Gen. 2–4 expands on Gen. 1:28 as it responds to such questions: As a result of the Fall, "monosexual existence in Paradise may be exchanged for fertile heterosexual existence in reality."[162] According to Ivan Engnell and Joel Rosenberg, only the fall, which demands that humans confront their sexuality and mortality, leads Adam and Eve to have children.[163] In any event, Cain and Abel are the first fruits of postlapsarian repro-

159. Fishbane, *Text,* pp. 9, 18; see also Coats, "God of Death."
160. Westermann, *Creation,* p. 25.
161. Westermann, "Der Mensch," pp. 237–38, and Dumbrell, *Covenant and Creation,* pp. 35–37.
162. Leach, "Genesis," pp. 415ff.
163. Ivan Engnell, " 'Knowledge' and 'Life' in the Creation Story," in *Wisdom in Israel and in the Ancient Near East (Presented to Professor Harold Henry Rowley),* ed. Martin Noth and D. Winton Thomas, Supplements to *VT* 3 (Leiden, 1955), pp. 115–16; Joel W. Rosenberg, "The Garden Story Forward and Backward: The Non-Narrative Dimension of Gen. 2–3," *Prooftexts* 1 (1981), esp. 13–15.

duction, and their story appropriately begins by recording the initial procreative act (Gen. 4:1). As Cain wanders in exile, he and his descendants fill the earth, and the union between "divine beings" and daughters of men, perhaps indicating that the process of procreation has gone awry, sets the stage for Noah and the flood. As the waters eventually clear, having destroyed the products of all animate fertility, God instructs Noah and his sons to procreate and fill the earth yet again—but once more proper compliance with this duty is thwarted, this time by the builders of the Tower of Babel, who strive to construct their edifice (Gen. 11:4), "else we shall be scattered all over the world."[164] A sexual interpretation of the tree of knowledge,[165] the murder of Abel,[166] the evil that precipitated the flood,[167] and the crime of Ham and Canaan[168] would afford additional testimony to the centrality of procreation as a theme of the primeval history. And numerous scholars agree that the lengthy genealogies of Gen. 4–5 and 10–11 unify the narrative of the primeval history by demonstrating the realization of God's initial promise of fertility.[169]

164. For such a reading of the Tower of Babel story, see Isaac M. Kikawada, "The Shape of Genesis 11:1–9," in *Rhetorical Criticism: Essays in Honor of James Muilenburg,* ed. Jared J. Jackson and Martin Kessler (Pittsburgh, Pa., 1974), pp. 18–32; Bernhard W. Anderson, "Babel: Unity and Diversity in God's Creation," *Currents in Theology and Mission* 5 (1978), 69–81; Sacks, "The Lion and the Ass," *Interpretation* 9 (1980), 3; Allen P. Ross, "The Dispersion of the Nations in Genesis 11:1–9," *Bibliotheca sacra* 138 (1981), 119–38; Donald E. Gowan, *When Man Becomes God: Humanism and "Hybris" in the Old Testament,* Pittsburgh Theological Monograph Series 6 (Pittsburgh, Pa., 1975); Sarna, *Understanding Genesis,* pp. 65–66; and A. Frisch, "Lᵉ-Verur Ḥeṭ Dor ha-Haflagah," *Bi-Sdeh Ḥemed* 14 (1971), 440, who lists the rabbinic commentators who have subscribed to this interpretation. See also below, p. 78f.

165. Among others, see J. Coppens, *La connaissance du bien et du mal et le péché du Paradis: Contribution à l'interpretation de Gen., II–III,* Analecta lovaniensia biblica et orientalia 2,3 (Gembloux, 1948); McKenzie, *Myths,* pp. 164ff.; Engnell, "'Knowledge,'" pp. 114ff.; Robert Gordis, "The Knowledge of Good and Evil in the Old Testament and the Qumran Scrolls," *JBL* 76 (1957), 123–38; Collins, *Christian Morality,* pp. 160–61; and Rosenberg, "Garden Story." Critics of this controversial interpretation include Paul Humbert, *Etudes sur le récit du Paradis et de la chute dans la Genèse,* Mémoires de l'Université de Neuchâtel 14 (Neuchâtel, 1940), pp. 97–101; John A. Bailey, "Initiation and the Primal Woman in Gilgamesh and Genesis 2–3," *JBL* 89 (1970), 144–47; J. Alberto Soggin, *Old Testament and Oriental Studies,* Biblica et orientalia 29 (Rome, 1975), pp. 88–111, esp. pp. 101–2 (with nn. 34–35); and Howard N. Wallace, *The Eden Narrative,* Harvard Semitic Monographs 32 (Atlanta, Ga., 1985), ch. 4.

166. Leach, "Genesis," p. 15.

167. H. H. Cohen, *Drunkenness,* esp. pp. 33–48.

168. For example, ibid.; S. Gevirtz, "A Father's Curse [in the Literatures of Ugarit, Israel, and Greece]," *Mosaic: Literature and History* 2,3 (1969), 58–59; Frederick W. Bassett, "Noah's Nakedness and the Curse of Canaan: A Case of Incest?" *VT* 21 (1971), 232–37; Collins, *Christian Morality,* p. 173.

169. For example, Daniélou, *In the Beginning,* p. 77; von Rad, *Genesis,* p. 144; Wilson, *Genealogy,* p. 164; and Westermann, *Genesis 1–11,* p. 17.

If the ideas of Gen. 1:28 permeate so much of the primeval history, how should we evaluate the thematic significance of the verse? As it first defines the status of human beings in the order of God's creation, and as it dictates the background and framework for divine-human interaction in the generations that follow, we suggest that Gen. 1:28 encapsulates the basic covenantal message that investigators have attributed to the opening chapters of Scripture. Isaac Kikawada and Arthur Quinn recently proposed that Gen. 1–11 be treated as a literary unity modeled after the *Atrahasis* epic in both structure and theme, even though it bespeaks a markedly different system of values:

> Atrahasis offers population control as the solution to overcrowding; Genesis offers dispersion, the nomadic way of life. Population growth is from the very beginning of the Genesis primeval history presented as an unqualified blessing. The blessing of Genesis 1:28 finds fulfillment in the dispersion "upon the face of the whole earth," which concludes the primeval history. Genesis 1–11 then constitutes a rejection of Babel and Babylon—of civilization itself, if its continuance requires human existence to be treated as a contingent good. For Genesis the existence of a new human was always good.[170]

For Kikawada and Quinn the unyielding movement of the primeval history from creation to dispersion implements the injunctions of Gen. 1:28, affirming the ultimate value of human life in God's world and setting the historical and theological stage for his relationship with Israel. In sum, "Genesis 1–2:3 tells how the cosmic divisions found their fulfillment in God's command to be fruitful, multiply, and fill the earth. Genesis 11 tells why God decided that to make men obey his command, he had to create divisions within them."[171]

Many would object that such a reading of the primeval history overlooks the glaring incongruities of its various documentary components. Reviewing the book by Kikawada and Quinn, Jacob Milgrom contended that the Yahwist story of human origins in Gen. 2–3, which confines Adam and Eve in their unfallen state to the Garden of Eden, effectively contradicts the Priestly cosmogony, which orders the first humans to disperse throughout the earth.[172] Nevertheless, the redacted

---

170. Kikawada and Quinn, *Before Abraham*, p. 51.

171. Ibid., 71; cf. also Oden, "Transformations," who on the basis of a structuralist analysis asserts the equivalence of the messages of *Atrahasis* and Gen. 1–11.

172. Jacob Milgrom, Review of *Before Abraham Was: The Unity of Genesis 1–11*, by Isaac M. Kikawada and Arthur Quinn, *Judaism* 35 (1986), 372.

text of the primeval history, when confronted as a single unit, cannot resist a structural analysis that highlights the message of Gen. 1:28. As the list below suggests, the primeval history conveniently divided into two periods of ten generations each, beginning with Adam and Noah, respectively. Adapting the critical approach already undertaken by Jack Sasson and Gary Rendsburg,[173] one might further argue that each of these two "acts" contains three dramatic scenes, genealogical lists, and a brief narrative epilogue to pave the way for the era that follows.

From Adam to Noah (Gen. 1:1—6:4)	*From Noah to Abraham (6:5—11:32)*
Scene 1: Creation (1:1—2:3)	Scene 1: The Flood (6:5—9:17)
Scene 2: Adam and Eve (2:4—3:24)	Scene 2: Noah and His Sons (9:18—10:32)
Scene 3: Cain and Abel (4:1—4:26)	Scene 3: The Tower of Babel (11:1–9)
Genealogy (5:1–32)	Genealogy (11:10–26)
Epilogue: "divine beings" and daughters of men (6:1–4)	Epilogue: The Appearance of Abraham (11:26–32)

While Gen. 10 consists entirely of family records, we have followed Gary Smith in deeming it (much like the concluding verses of Gen. 4) "a table of nations instead of a classical genealogy . . . , the fulfilment of God's blessing to Noah that he and his seed should 'fill the earth' "[174] and therefore part of the narrative concerning Noah and his sons. In the resulting symmetrical pattern, the first episode of each primeval period depicts the establishment of a natural order whose superior, human constituents receive the divine promises of fertility and dominion and the divine command to procreate. The formula of *prh/rbh* thus defines the matrix of relationships between God, human beings, and the world that all must strive to maintain. The second and third scenes of each act offer a complex elaboration of this theme, illustrating human survival and expansion in spite of the tragedies of fall and flood—hence the fulfillment of God's blessing—on the one hand, and the sinful subversion of the program of Gen. 1:28, on the other hand. A sexual inter-

---

173. Sasson, " 'Tower' "; Rendsburg, *Redaction,* pp. 8–25.
174. Gary V. Smith, "Structure and Purpose in Genesis 1–11," *Journal of the Evangelical Theological Society* 20 (1977), 312; see also Allen P. Ross, "The Table of Nations in Genesis 10—Its Structure," *Bibliotheca sacra* 137 (1980), 340–53, and "The Table of Nations in Genesis 10—Its Content," ibid. 138 (1981), 22–34, who discerns the significance of Gen. 10 in its emphasis on those nations of geopolitical importance to Israel.

pretation of the crimes of Adam and Eve, Cain, Noah's contemporaries, and Ham (and/or Canaan) would dictate that they rebel against God precisely in terms of the reproductive process ordained by Gen. 1:28, just as the engineers of Babel defy their responsibility to disperse. It is appropriate that the punishments allotted to Adam and Eve (Gen. 3:16–19), Cain (Gen. 4:10–12), and the inhabitants of Babel (Gen. 11:8) affect their ability to bear children, their control over the physical environment, and their duty to scatter over the face of the earth.[175] Would the divine mandate for human civilization endure? Although human beings forsake their allegiance to God in each half of the primeval history, the genealogies demonstrate that the blessing of *prh/rbh* remained intact. Yet the epilogue or conclusion to each primeval period, depicting still another development in the chain of procreation, indicates that in response to human failure God does limit the focus of his covenant—first to Noah and his progeny, then to Abraham and the Hebrews.[176] Reflecting on this correspondence of theme and structure in the primeval history, Smith dubbed Gen. 1:28 "the key theological focal point in the two parallel sections of Genesis 1–11."[177]

GEN. 1:28 AND THE BIBLICAL COVENANT

Within the framework of the heptameral cosmogony, Gen. 1:28 encapsulates much that was singular in the anthropology of the Hebrew Bible. Endowing the first parents with the power to perpetuate their species and to harness the forces of nature, the divine blessing defines the peculiar status of men and women in terms of three spheres of human relations: with other human beings, with the rest of the natural world, and with God. The opening words of Gen. 1:28 first call upon man and woman to forge a sexual bond between themselves and thus to maintain the work of creation inaugurated by their maker. In this task humans may resemble other creatures, but the ensuing conferral of

175. Eugene Combs, "The Political Teaching of Genesis I–XI," *Studia biblica 1978*, 1, JSOT Supplement Series 11 (Sheffield, 1979), p. 109, argued that the absence of *prh/rbh* at the end of Gen. 9, describing the dispersion of Noah's sons with the negative term *nfz*, derives from their violent subversion of our verse's mandate for procreative sex.

176. Sasson, "'Tower,'" p. 218.

177. Smith, "Structure," p. 311. Cf. the similar conclusions of Robert L. Cohn, "Narrative Structure and Canonical Perspective in Genesis," *JSOT* 25 (1983), 4–5, and Coppens, *Connaissance*, p. 27.

dominion belongs to them alone. Hence the mandate for a second genre of relationship: If the divine rationale for the man and the woman begins with their participation in the most natural and universal activity of reproduction, it also extends to their primacy in the order of creation. Scholars may disagree about the precise limits and prerogatives that the blessing of dominion entails, but the superiority of humans and their determinative function in relating to other species are beyond question. Mastering the earth and ruling over the animals, man and woman fashion a distinctively human civilization, the affirmation of whose intrinsic value sets the Bible apart from other ancient Near Eastern religions and cultures. These responsibilities bespeak a third realm of relationship—namely, with God himself. Alone of all his works, God fashions humans in his own image, which they in turn must exemplify by meeting the charges of Gen. 1:28.

The substance of our verse therefore highlights the dual character of human beings as creatures and as agents of the creator—an anomaly to which the language and structure of Gen. 1 testify as well. Humans comprise the last, and greatest, of God's creative endeavors, and the verb of their creation (*br'*) differentiates them from other animals. But never do they play the part of grammatical subject in the cosmogony, and they have no stated role in the culmination of the first week, the divinely instituted Sabbath. Replete with the imagery of enthronement, Gen. 1:28 follows immediately upon the creation of the first parents in the image of God, but the verse gives way to the ostensive limitation of their power, in an apparent ban on consuming the very creatures just subjected to their rule. Man and woman are indeed the sole addressees of direct divine discourse in Gen. 1. Their blessing, however, is only one of three; the beneficent words of *prh/rbh* liken them to the fish and the birds (Gen. 1:22), integrating them into the totality of nature that revels in the ultimate blessing of the Sabbath (Gen. 2:3).

In all, the words of Gen. 1:28 define the status of men and women in relation to both God and the world. Yet if such is their immediate function in the story of creation, we have endeavored to demonstrate that their message within the biblical text and for the biblical community extended considerably further. Scripture includes—and begins with—the story of creation not out of an interest in natural history but because of the theological message of that story for Israelites living long after the events it records. Applying the narrational model of Hugh White cited at the beginning of this chapter, one may conclude that the event and discourse recorded by Gen. 1:28 derived their greatest significance from the evolving interpretation of the text inside the community for whom it was written, for in the Bible

> the narrative does not climax with the situation of the narrator narrating[,] because the process of word reception, such as is normally the exclusive experience of the narrator or author of stories, is now a constitutive element of the social life of the nation whose actions he is recounting. Through the words which are brought to it chiefly by the prophets, the nation is constituted as an open subject which then engages in writing the story of its own life in the actions which it takes collectively (or through representative persons) in response to these words. . . . You might say that the story writes itself in life and the narrator is formally (not actually) consigned to the position of the faceless recorder of the process. The narrator is then in the strange position of not being able to conclude the story. It is beyond his control since the words come from a source outside of himself. The story can end only when the words cease to come to the nation.[178]

As White explained, the biblical text reflects one stage, though neither the first nor the last stage, in the process whereby the words of Israel's God assumed meaning for his people. Seeking to exploit the Bible's ability to illuminate this phenomenon in its various dimensions, we have accordingly focused not only on Gen. 1:28 in its immediate context, but also on what Paul Ricoeur dubbed the "travail d'interprétation inscrit dans le texte lui-même."[179] We examined the subsequent allusions to Gen. 1:28 in the Pentateuch and the books of the prophets, the theological basis of Israelite creation faith underlying the cosmogony, the liturgical milieu in which our verse originally may have functioned, the historical setting and the ideology of its Priestly author, and its role in the redacted text of the primeval history. The recurring motif that binds all these facets of the verse's career is that of election, the guarantee of divine providence, and an enduring relationship between God and the recipients of his blessing—in a word, the motif of covenant. Granted that many have rejected Wellhausen's identification of Gen. 1:28 as a *bᵉrit* between God and Adam; in the story of creation the verse in fact does not display the formal, technical trappings of a

---

178. H. C. White, "Word Reception," p. 71.
179. Paul Ricoeur, "Sur l'exégèse de Genèse 1,1–2,4a," in *Exégèse et herméneutique*, by Roland Barthes et al. (Paris, 1971), p. 84.

binding, contractual arrangement.[180] Still, the blessings of our verse do take on a formulaic role in the divine covenants with Noah, the patriarchs, and the Hebrew nation. And, although perhaps in a nontechnical sense, the covenantal message of Gen. 1:28 explains the function of the verse in the ritualized celebration of the creation, its frequent appearance in P, and its thematic centrality in the first eleven chapters of Genesis. What begins as a general description of the human condition in the order of God's creation eventually serves as a metaphor for the peculiar station of Israel among the other nations of the world.

The key to the "original" meaning of Gen. 1:28 lies not in its alleged license of environmental irresponsibility, nor for that matter in any more praiseworthy ecological lesson. Rather, the career of Gen. 1:28 begins in the midrashic process itself, whereby the Bible appropriates God's blessing of all humankind with fertility and dominion in order to define an exclusive relationship between God and his chosen people. Such was the meaning of our biblical verse when it was first confronted by postbiblical writers, and such were the questions it continued to provoke: how to resolve this seeming contradiction in human nature, between animal-like sexuality and God-like rulership, and how to interpret this universal blessing in the wake of God's covenant with his people, Israel.

---

180. On the language, idea, and definition of covenant in the biblical world, see, among others, Dennis J. McCarthey, *Treaty and Covenant: A Study in Form in the Ancient Oriental Documents and in the Old Testament,* Analecta biblica 21 (Rome, 1963), *Old Testament Covenant: A Survey of Current Opinions* (Richmond, Va., 1972), and "Covenant-Relationships," in *Questions disputées d'Ancien Testament: Methode et théologique,* ed. C. Brekelmans, Bibliotheca ephemeridum theologicarum lovaniensium 33 (Louvain, 1974), pp. 91–103; Ernst Kutsch, *Verheissung und Gesetz: Untersuchungen zum sogennanten "Bund" im Alten Testament,* Beihefte zur *ZAW* 131 (Berlin, 1973); Klaus Baltzer, *The Covenant Formulary in Old Testament, Jewish, and Early Christian Writings,* tr. David E. Green (Philadelphia, Pa., 1971), pt. 1; and Jonathan Bishop, *The Covenant: A Reading* (Springfield, Ill., 1983). Cf. above, n. 124.

CHAPTER 2

Defining a Cosmic Frontier:
Genesis 1:28 in the Aggadah

T HE biblical understanding of Gen. 1:28 laid the groundwork for both Jewish and Christian contributions to the history of its interpretation. For two thousand years and more, our verse commanded the attention of preachers, theologians, mystics, lawyers, and poets both within and on the periphery of the synagogue and the church, and we propose to follow the noteworthy developments in that lengthy career into whatever genre of literature such an inquiry might lead. Yet in turning to reflections on Gen. 1:28 in the texts of classical rabbinic Judaism, we must acknowledge that the division of this book into chapters on Judaism and Christianity is not without its risks. First, although postbiblical Jewish reflection on the Bible began before the birth of Christianity, and was responsible for that birth, the Jewish religious teachers and texts considered in this chapter and its two successors did not necessarily antedate their Christian counterparts, the subjects of Chapters 5 and 6. Many of the church fathers mentioned in Chapter 5 actually lived before rabbis cited in this chapter and the next, and the instruction attributed to these patristic scholars can usually be verified as theirs with greater certainty than that of the talmudic sages. Second, not only did the rabbinic ideas under discussion below often postdate patristic interpretations of Gen. 1:28, but the Jewish exegesis cannot always be said to comprise a logically prior stage in our verse's unfolding career. And third, a rigid bifurcation between Jewish and

Christian interpretation history might tend to obscure the repeated intersection of the two.

While not even the social boundaries between Jewish and Christian communities were fixed in the first centuries of the common era, we have nevertheless elected to deal with the understanding of Gen. 1:28 first in the Jewish tradition and only then in Christianity. Constant alternation between one tradition and the other would obscure the most consequential influences on a given writer and the primary continuity or discontinuity to which his work contributed: those within his own religious circle. No less important, the literature of each tradition had its own technical terminology, distinct theological premises, and particular sociopolitical objectives. While Jews and Christians could, and often did, share any or many of these, the singular characteristics of each religious system constitute an indispensable focus in the evaluation of exegetical literature. We therefore confront the literature of rabbinic Judaism and that of premodern Christianity in turn, drawing attention to cross-cultural parallels and interdependence in both text and notes, when and wherever possible.

In the single most impressive development in the postbiblical interpretation of Gen. 1:28, the rabbis of the Talmud construed God's blessing of the first parents as a Mosaic commandment, a legal obligation of the Torah binding upon every free, adult, Jewish male. Chapter 3 is devoted to this recasting of divine promise as statutory law. Yet much of the significance of such reformulation in the encounter between rabbinic Jew and biblical text would remain hidden without a prior appreciation of the nonlegal and less pragmatic theological implications of our verse. Gen. 1:28 in the Aggadah is therefore our immediate concern.

INTERTESTAMENTAL BACKGROUND

With their pervasive interest in the Genesis cosmogony and its multifarious ramifications, Jewish writers of the Hellenistic period anticipated much of the subsequent interpretation that comprises our story. Numerous works from the later years of the second Jewish commonwealth and its immediate aftermath offer embellished accounts of the creation in six days, giving birth to the genre of the hexameron commentary, in which patristic and medieval theologians typically conveyed their midrashic reflections on Gen. 1:28. As David Jobling has shown, the idea of human dominion over nature figured prominently in the intertestamental literature, bearing directly on various dimensions of ancient Jewish cosmology, anthropology, and eschatology.[1] Readers of the Bible began to focus on the enduring significance of God's blessing to the first parents, and their comments attest to the thematic importance of our verse in early postbiblical theology. The Book of the Watchers in 1 Enoch (chs. 6–8, 15), expanding on the similar motif in Gen. 6:1–4, depicts reproductive sexual relations with women as effecting the fall of the rebellious angels from heaven.[2] Several centuries later, Josephus Flavius explained that the architects of the Tower of Babel had rejected the divine command to "cultivate much of the earth and enjoy an abundance of its fruits" and therefore incurred the wrath of God.[3] But despite the many substantive parallels between such early midrash and the subsequent homilies of rabbinic and patristic writers, the definitive intertestamental allusions to Gen. 1:28 are strikingly few indeed, and those presently deserving of our attention are fewer still. We consider here the reflections of three early exegetes on our verse.

Early in the second pre-Christian century, Ben Sira (17:1–12) wrote of the wondrous accomplishments of God:[4]

> The Lord created man out of earth, and turned him back to it again. [2] He gave to men few days, a limited time, but granted them authority over the things upon the earth. [3] He endowed them with strength like his own, and made them in his own image. [4] He placed the fear of them in all living beings, and granted them dominion[5] over beasts and

1. Jobl., diss. Jobling's study is organized topically rather than chronologically or by genre of literature. Jobling cites a possible allusion to Gen. 1:28 in Ovid, *Metamorphoses* 1.77, ed. Frank Justus Miller, LCL, 2 vols. (1916; repr., Cambridge, Mass., 1984), 1:6–7, which explains that man was born "quod dominari in cetera posset"; and the more certain references in *Corpus hermeticum* 1.18, 3.3, ed. A. D. Nock and A.-J. Festugière, 6th ed., 4 vols. (Paris, 1983), 1:13, 45. C. H. Dodd, *The Bible and the Greeks* (1935; repr., London, 1954), esp. chs. 7, 10, has ventured further than most in asserting the dependence of the pagan *Corpus* on biblical ideas of creation.

2. On the midrashic function of these chapters in 1 Enoch, and on the motif of sexual reproduction gone awry as characteristic of "rebellion-in-heaven" myths, see Paul D. Hanson, "Rebellion in Heaven: Azazel and Euhemeristic Heroes in Enoch 6–11," *JBL* 96 (1977), esp. 204ff., and cf. below, nn. 68–69.

3. Josephus, *Antiquitates iudaicae* 1.110, in *Works,* ed. H. St. J. Thackeray et al., LCL, 9 vols. (Cambridge, Mass., 1926–65), 4:52–53.

4. RSV. W. O. E. Oesterley in *APOT,* 1:375n., deems v. 5 a scribal emendation based on Stoic notions of the constitution of the human soul. See below, nn. 102–3.

5. Greek *katakyrieúein;* cf. LXX's *kaì katakyrieúsate autês* for Hebrew *wᵉ-khivshuha* (Gen. 1:28) and putative *u-rᵉdu vah* (Gen. 9:1).

birds. [5] [They obtained the use of the five operations of the Lord; as sixth he distributed to them the gift of mind, and as seventh reason, the interpreter of his operations.] [6] He made for them tongue and eyes; he gave them ears and a mind for thinking. [7] He filled them with knowledge and understanding, and showed them good and evil. . . . [12] He established with them an eternal covenant, and showed them his judgments.

Ben Sira's paraphrase of the biblical account of human origins returns us to several key features of the Genesis cosmogony discussed in the preceding chapter. Although the Hebrew original of this passage has still not been recovered, it is evident that God grants the first parents divine-like qualities (as in Gen. 1:26), creating them in his own image (as in Gen. 1:26–27) and according them dominion (as in Gen. 1:28) over birds and beasts. Ben Sira thus acknowledged the link between creation in the divine image and the blessings of Gen. 1:28, underscoring the covenantal significance of those blessings in no uncertain terms. On the other hand, Ben Sira modified the biblical story in several respects. His paraphrase of Gen. 1:28 makes no mention of woman, procreation, the blessing of human fertility, or human dominion over the fish.[6] Through various means, he sought to minimize the effects of the fall from paradise on human superiority in the created order. The words that in Genesis bring God's reproof of the sinful Adam to its climax (Gen. 3:19)—"from it [the earth] you were taken, for dust you are, and to dust you shall return"—here underlie the original divine plan for the creation of human beings. This apocryphal text appears to contest the view that human control over nature diminished in the wake of the flood,[7] for it describes the dominion of Adam and Eve by alluding to God's postdiluvian blessing of Noah (Gen. 9:2), in which the animals' fear of humans substituted for the mention of human rule over them in Gen. 1. Unlike the author of Genesis, Ben Sira specified that the first humans were created for "a few days, a limited time"—that is, in a state of mortality—their divine image and their dominion over nature notwithstanding. The sin of Adam and Eve did not alter human nature, nor did it detract from their privileged status in the animal kingdom.

6. See the comment of Robert Gordis, "The Social Background of Wisdom Literature," *HUCA* 18 (1944), 111, that Ben Sira "goes considerably further than any Biblical writer in making woman the cause of evil and death in the world."

7. See above, Chapter 1, nn. 65–68.

Instead, the blessing of Gen. 1:28 appears to inform Ben Sira's conception of the distinctive status of all human beings, superior to that of other creatures but nonetheless unquestionably mortal.

Later in the same century,[8] the author of Jubilees also recounted God's formation of the first humans (2:14) in his summary of the hexameral creation: On the sixth day,

> after all of this, he made man—male and female he made them—and he gave him dominion over everything which was upon the earth and which was in the seas and over everything which flies, and over beasts and cattle and everything which moves upon the earth or above the whole earth. And over all this he gave him dominion.[9]

While Jubilees evidently restored fish to the list of creatures subject to human rule, Michel Testuz maintained that the inclusion of woman in the intitial creation of human beings derives from a scribal emendation intent on harmonizing this passage with Gen. 1:27.[10] As in Ben Sira, dominion is bestowed exclusively on the male, and Jubilees similarly omits the divine instructions to reproduce and fill the earth. The blessing of procreation awaits the aftermath of the flood, when God addresses Noah (6:1–11) in language borrowed directly from Gen. 8 and 9.

> [1] And on the first of the third month, he went out of the ark, and he built an altar on that mountain. . . . [4] And the Lord smelled the sweet aroma, and he made a covenant with him so that there might not be floodwaters which would destroy the earth. . . . [5] "But as for you, increase and be multiplied on the earth and become many upon it, and become a blessing upon it. Fear and terror of you I will set upon everything which is on the land or in the sea. . . . [9] And as for you, increase and become many in the land." [10] And Noah and his sons swore that they would not eat any blood which was in any flesh. And he made a covenant before the Lord God forever in all of the generations of the earth in that month. [11] Therefore he spoke to you so that you also

---

8. On the date of Jubilees, see James C. VanderKam, *Textual and Historical Studies in the Book of Jubilees,* Harvard Semitic Monographs 14 (Missoula, Mont., 1977), ch. 3.

9. *OTP,* 2:57.

10. Michel Testuz, *Les idées religieuses du Livre des Jubilés* (Geneva, 1960), p. 45. On the exegetical/theological issue of whether God had created woman in his image in early postbiblical sources, see also Horowitz, "The Image of God."

might make a covenant with the children of Israel with an oath in this month upon the mountain.[11]

As in Genesis (9:1 and 9:7), the mandate to reproduce is stated twice,[12] within the context of a ritualized covenant ceremony, which in its date and in its focus on blood clearly prefigures God's subsequent covenant with Israel.[13] For their own reasons, the conservative Ben Sira and the priestly writer of Jubilees perhaps wanted to avoid any reference to sexuality in their descriptions of God's initial plan for a perfect world. Jubilees itself indicates (3:34) that Adam and Eve did not engage in sexual relations until after their expulsion from Eden, a view later echoed by 2 Baruch (56:6) and various other Jewish and Christian documents.[14]

Like Ben Sira and the author of Jubilees, Philo the Jew expressed considerably more interest in the dominion of the first humans over nature than in their reproductive fertility, and this with a minimum of direct reference to Gen. 1:28. The clearest allusion to the blessing of dominion in our verse occurs as Philo concluded his description of the works of the six days of creation. Asserting that the creation of man *after* all other beings comports well with his function as ruler, exemplified by man's superiority over the animals and by drivers and pilots who ride behind their subordinates, Philo remarked: "So the creator made man after all things, as a sort of driver and pilot, to drive and steer the things on earth, and charged him with the care of animals and plants, like a governor subordinate (*hýparchos*) to the chief and great king."[15] The juxtaposition of plants and animals reveals that Philo understood Gen. 1:29, with its grant of fruits and vegetables to humans for their consumption, as an elaboration of the dominion bestowed in Gen. 1:28, which makes mention only of animals. Moreover, the portrayal of dominion as an administrative responsibility of management on behalf of a superior officer construes Gen. 1:28b as mandate or commandment as least as much as blessing. The blatant anthropocentrism of Philo's

11. *OTP*, 2:66–67.

12. Yet the order of the biblical instructions appears to be reversed. Charles, *APOT*, 2:21n., maintains that "become a blessing upon it" replaces the second *u-rᵉvu-vah* of Gen. 9:7.

13. The covenant at Mount Sinai was struck in the third month (Ex. 19:1), as was, according to Jubilees (14:1), the covenant with Abraham.

14. *LOJ*, 5:134 n. 4, and see below, n. 88.

15. Philo, *De opificio mundi* 83–88, in *Works*, ed. F. H. Colson et al., LCL, 10 vols. and 2 suppl. vols. (Cambridge, Mass., 1929–53), 1:66–73 (quotation in 88, pp. 72–73).

world view notwithstanding,[16] the Jew of Alexandria did not read our verse as a license to exploit the physical world, nor did he perceive its bequest as gratuitous, demanding nothing in return. Notice of Gen. 1:28a, with its call for fertility and procreation, is still absent in the Philonic cosmogony. Only in his *Quaestiones et solutiones in Genesim* did Philo confront our verse directly and in its entirety, advancing several lines of interpretation that would retain their popularity for centuries after him. Struck by the reiteration of the blessings of Gen. 1:28 in the aftermath of the flood, Philo questioned why God blessed Noah with the call to procreation, fertility, and dominion and with the promise that the animals would fear him.

> This prayer was granted to the man (made) in the image (of God) even at the beginning of creation on the sixth day. For (Scripture) says. . . . [Philo quotes Gen. 1:27–28, slightly abbreviating the language of each verse.] But has it not indeed been clearly shown through these words that he considers Noah, who became, as it were, the beginning of a second genesis of man, of equal honor with him who was first made in (his) image? And so he granted rule over earthly creatures in equal measure to the former and the latter. And it should be carefully noted that (Scripture) shows him who in the flood was made righteous king of earthly creatures to have been equal in honor not with the moulded and earthy man but with him who was (made) in the form and likeness of the truly incorporeal being; and to him (Noah) he also gives authority, appointing as king not the moulded man but him who was (made) in the likeness and form (of God), who is incorporeal. . . . And so, by the literal meaning (of Scripture) it has been shown how the beginning of the second genesis of the human race was worthy of the same kingship as the man (made) in the likeness and form (of God).[17]

Philo explained the repetition of our verse in Gen. 9 as an indication of the structural symmetry of the primeval history, which divides neatly into two halves, much as we proposed toward the end of Chapter 1. The respective careers of Adam and Noah each mark the creation by

16. David Jobling, " 'And Have Dominion . . .': The Interpretation of Genesis 1,28 in Philo Judaeus," *Journal for the Study of Judaism in the Persian, Hellenistic, and Roman Period* 8 (1977), 50–82; and see also Charles Kannengiesser, "Philon et les Pères sur la double création de l'homme," in *Philon d'Alexandrie: Lyon, 11–15 Septembre 1966*, Colloques nationaux du Centre national de la recherche scientifique (Paris, 1967), pp. 277–96.

17. Philo, *Quaestiones et solutiones in Genesim* 2.56, suppl. 1:140–42; here and in subsequent quotations from this work parenthetical insertions are those of the translator, those in brackets are my own.

God of a world order in which humans serve a key administrative and monarchic function, one that the blessing of Gen. 1:28 defines. The blessing thus constitutes an essential component of both first and second geneses, and its omission after the flood would detract from the parity between Adam and Noah that Scripture wanted to communicate. Following the lead of the compilers of the Septuagint, who themselves had added *wᵉ-khivshuha (katakyrieùsate autês)* from Gen. 1:28 to the Noachide blessing of Gen. 9:1 (reading "increase and multiply and fill the earth and dominate it"), Philo concluded that the dominion vested in Noah differed not at all from that granted to Adam. For Philo, who thereby conformed to the pattern set by his apocryphal predecessors above, the key to the divine commission of Adam and Noah was their dominion over nature rather than their call to reproduce and fill the earth. Sexuality and procreation receive no attention in the passage before us, apart from Philo's quotations from Genesis. In his other works, he refers disparagingly to the first woman as "the beginning of blameworthy life" for man,[18] and he interprets the marital union described in Gen. 2:24, for the sake of which God created Eve, as the mind's abandonment of God in order to satisfy the sensual passions.[19] I have encountered only one passage where Philo acknowledged the desirability of sexual relations, explaining that God divided the human being into male and female so that they might comply with "nature's urgent purpose, the reproduction of themselves in a third person."[20] As for human kingship in the natural order, it derives from the creation of the first man and of Noah in the image of God. Noah therefore ranks in the Philonic species of the heavenly man, created by God in Gen. 1:26–27, as opposed to that of the earthy man, whose formation is recorded in Gen. 2:7. Although, as Thomas Tobin argued, Philo failed to distinguish consistently between these two men and their respective creations and realms,[21] this text in his *Quaestiones et solutiones in Genesim* demonstrates that the commission of the first man and of Noah with the blessings of Gen. 1:28 pertained to the noble, spiritual human creature worthy of enthronement because each "was (made) in the form and likeness of the truly incorporeal being."

18. Philo, *De opificio mundi*, 53.151–53, 1:118–21.
19. Philo, *Legum allegoria* 2.14.49–52, 1:254–57.
20. Philo, *Quis rerum divinarum heres sit* 33.164, 4:364–65.
21. Thomas H. Tobin, *The Creation of Man: Philo and the History of Interpretation*, CBQ Monograph Series 14 (Washington, D.C., 1983), chs. 2–5.

With this reasoning, Philo claimed to have used the "literal" or more apparent sense of Gen. 1:28 to explain why the divine commission of the first man is again given to Noah. Nevertheless, his answer that "the beginning of the second genesis of the human race was worthy of the same kingship as the man (made) in the likeness and form (of God)" naturally directed Philo toward a more spiritual, allegorical interpretation of our verse. He thus continued:

> As for the deeper meaning, it is to be interpreted as follows. He [God] desires that the souls of intelligent men increase in greatness and multitude (and) in the form of virtues, and fill the mind with its form, as though it were the earth, leaving no part empty and void for follies; and that they should dominate and rule over the earthy body and its senses, and strike terror and fear into beasts, which is the exercise of the will against evil, for evil is untamed and savage. And (he wishes that they should rule) over the birds, (that is) those who are lightly lifted up in thought, those who are (filled) with vain and empty arrogance, (and) having been previously armed, cause great harm, not being restrained by fear. Moreover, (he wishes that they should rule over) the reptiles, which are a symbol of poisonous passions; for through every soul sense-pleasures and desire and grief and fear creep, stabbing and piercing and wounding. And by the fish I understand those who eagerly welcome a moist and fluid life but not one that is continent, healthy and lasting.[22]

Philo here integrated Gen. 1:28 into his extensive allegory of the soul, in which, as Tobin summarized, "the text of Genesis is taken to refer not to events of the external world but to conflicting elements within the individual human being, especially to the soul."[23] Our verse thus served Philo's general exegetical objective of reconciling Mosaic and Platonic cosmologies, a critical approach to Scripture inspired by earlier works of Hellenistic scholarship, both Jewish and Gentile. The particulars of Philo's allegorical midrash on Gen. 1:28 require little additional explanation at present, and the substance of his cosmology and the methods of his exegesis have repeatedly been subject to scholarly scrutiny.[24] It is sufficient to note here that this Philonic allegory became the

---

22. Philo, *Quaestiones et solutiones in Genesim* 2.56, suppl. 1:142–43.
23. Tobin, *Creation of Man*, p. 178. See also Richard A. Baer, Jr., *Philo's Use of the Categories Male and Female*, Arbeiten zur Literatur und Geschichte des hellenistisches Judentums 3 (Leiden, 1970).
24. Among many others, see Harry Austryn Wolfson, *Philo: Foundations of Religious Philosophy in Judaism, Christianity, and Islam*, 2 vols. (Cambridge, Mass., 1947), chs. 1–5;

paradigm for the figurative reading of Gen. 1:28 advanced by numerous Christian scholars, in Alexandria and elsewhere, even when their exegesis derived from different and sometimes opposing theological principles. At the same time, however, Philo's interpretation of Gen. 1:28 never forsook the verse's literal meaning in order to propound the allegorical. Both levels of exegesis operated simultaneously and often even in tandem, perhaps resulting at times in confusion and inconsistency but bespeaking Philo's intensely Jewish commitment to the immediate and necessarily practical relevance of the Torah of Moses.

RABBINIC MIDRASH

Turning to the literature of *midrash 'aggadah,* the texts of nonlegal rabbinic homilies, one finds that allusions to Gen. 1:28 abound and that the rabbinic interest in our verse hinges primarily on its opening charge to "be fertile and increase" rather than on its investiture of human beings with dominion over animals. In traditional rabbinic parlance, the very term for procreation was *p^eriyyah u-r^eviyyah* (or *piryah w^e-rivyah*), a nominalized form of the verbal biblical hendiadys *prh/rbh.*[25] Therefore virtually any rabbinic reference to sexual reproduction would draw attention to the opening imperatives of Gen. 1:28, *p^eru u-r^evu*—a terminological association accentuating the importance the rabbis attributed to our verse and to its mandates.[26]

Several rabbinic homilies attest to the centrality of Gen. 1:28 in the

---

Ursula Früchtel, *Die kosmologischen Vorstellungen bei Philo von Alexandrien,* Arbeiten zur Literatur und Geschichte des hellenistisches Judentums 2 (Leiden, 1968); V. Nikiprowetzky, *Le commentaire de l'Ecriture chez Philon d'Alexandrie,* Arbeiten zur Literatur und Geschichte des hellenistisches Judentums 11 (Leiden, 1977); Tobin, *Creation of Man,* chs. 1, 6; and David T. Runia, *Philo of Alexandria and the "Timaeus" of Plato,* Philosophia antiqua 44 (Leiden, 1986).

25. While the first form is grammatically correct and therefore employed consistently herein, the second form (spelled *pyryh wryvyh*) is attested in numerous rabbinic texts; see M. H. Segal, *A Grammar of Mishnaic Hebrew* (1927; repr., Oxford, 1970), p. 104, and Eliezer Ben-Yehudah, *A Complete Dictionary of Ancient and Modern Hebrew* (Hebrew), 16 vols. (Tel Aviv, 1948–59), 10:5173 and n. 1.

26. In the Palestinian Targum ad Num. 24:25, the expression even appears as a euphemism for prostitution. See *Neofiti 1: Targum palestinense ms de la Biblioteca vaticana,* ed. Alejandro Díez Macho, 6 vols. (Madrid, 1968–79), 4:243: *"w^e-'af Balaq hazar l^e'atreh w^e-'aqem b^enateh 'al prh/rbh,"* meaning (p. 600), "and Balak also returned to his place and set up his daughters as prostitutes"—evidently an explanation of the connection between Num. 24:25b ("and Balak also went his way") and 25:1 ("While Israel was staying at Shittim, the people profaned themselves by whoring with the Moabite women"). On the ancient antecedents of this interpretation, see Geza Vermes, *Scripture and Tradition in Judaism* (Leiden, 1963), pp. 162–64, 169.

biblical cosmogony by affirming that God created the world expressly
for the purpose of human procreation. As we shall see, such a judgment
had halakhic (i.e., legal) as well as homiletical ramifications, but within
the realm of the Aggadah it typically informed rabbinic recollections of
ancient biblical personages, especially those of the primeval history and
the patriarchal period. The late midrashic work *Genesis Rabbati,* attributed to R. Moses the Preacher of eleventh-century Narbonne, explains that the Torah commences with the letter *bet,* (whose numerical
value is 2 and) which corresponds to masculine and feminine genders,
"to teach you that God, blessed be he, did not create his world but that
humans should engage in procreation (*p^eriyyah u-r^eviyyah*), as Scripture
states (Is. 45:18), 'He did not create it a waste, but formed it for
habitation.'"[27] In a similar vein, *Deuteronomy Rabbah* records in the
name of R. Simon what happened when Adam, despondent over the
wretched fate of both Abel and Cain, abstained from sexual relations
with Eve for 130 years.

> What did the holy one, blessed be he, do? He increased his [Adam's]
> desire so that he engaged in sexual relations with Eve and begot Seth.
> Said the holy one, blessed be he, for no reason did I create my world but
> for that of procreation (*p^eriyyah u-r^eviyyah*), as Scripture states (Is.
> 45:18), "He did not create it a waste"; and thus it states (Gen. 1:28),
> "God said to them, 'Be fertile and increase.'" Thus from the outset did
> the holy one, blessed be he, create Adam and Eve in order to procreate
> (*lifrot w^e-lirbot*). Why? For such is the glory of the holy one, blessed be
> he.[28]

Several traditions in *Genesis Rabbah* relate that after a prolonged period
of sexual abstinence Adam reassumed his procreative duties in response
to the admonition of Eve,[29] to the reproof of Lemekh and his wives,[30]
or to his own vision of Israel's future acceptance of the Torah.[31]

27. *MBR,* p. 9; cf. *MAgg,* p. 2, and the similar sentiments expressed in *NumR* 12.4. (For
the pun on 'apiryon, cf. *TB Ket.* 10b.

28. *DtR,* pp. 10–11. *Yalquṭ ha-Makhiri,* ad Prov. 14:28, in L. Grünhut, ed., *Sefer ha-
Liqquṭim,* 6 vols. (1898–1903; repr., Jerusalem, 1967), 6:15a adds: "when the Jews are fertile
and increase, as it is written (ibid.), 'a numerous people is the glory of a king.'" Elements of
the same tradition in the name of R. Simon appear in *GenR* 20.11 (ad 3:20), 1:195–96, and 24.6
(ad 5:1), 1:236; and in *TanB* (*B^ereshit* 26), 2:10b, without a direct quotation of Gen. 1:28 but
with the phrase *p^eriyyah u-r^eviyyah* and with reference to Is. 45:18.

29. *GenR* 19.5 (ad 3:6), 1:174 (with n. 7, citing a ms. commentary that interprets *hitlis*
[from Greek *atelés*], as *baṭel b^e-lo' p^eriyyah u-r^eviyyah*), and 20:8 (ad 3:17), 1:191, both with
references to Is. 45:18.

30. Ibid. 23.4 (ad 4:23–25), 1:225.

31. Ibid. 21.9 (ad 3:24), 1:204.

According to a number of rabbinic homilies, Noah's contemporaries incurred the punishment of the flood because of their sexual misbehavior in general and their refusal to fulfill the procreative mandate of Gen. 1:28a in particular.[32] Some traditions assert that these men also mixed diverse species of animals with one another and with humans,[33] or that the animals themselves exercised no sexual restraint.[34] Distressed by the destruction of his generation, Noah also postponed fathering children until the age of 500, at which time he recalled the words of Gen. 1:28 and begot his three sons.[35] During the flood, sexual relations (lit., procreation, *p͏eriyyah u-r͏eviyyah*) were forbidden to Noah but once again were enjoined upon him when he disembarked from the ark.[36] Fearing that another catastrophe would consume his descendants, however, Noah hesitated to return to his sexual duties until God swore he would never again destroy the world;[37] the sages debated whether Noah thereby spurned the divine command (and was consequently shamed by his progeny), or whether he thus displayed more pious behavior (for which he merited the divine covenant of Gen. 9).[38] Like Josephus,[39] two later midrashic sources charge the builders of the Tower of Babel with subverting the divine injunction to procreate, either by reproduc-

---

32. Ibid. 23.2 (ad 4:19), 1:222, according to which the men of the generation of the flood each kept two wives, one for sexual gratification who drank a sterilizing potion, dined on delicacies, and was constantly adorned like a bride, and another for *p͏eriyyah u-r͏eviyyah,* who was neglected like a widow; cf. TJ *Yev.* 6.5, 7c (alluding to Lemekh's two wives, but without explicit mention of *p͏eriyyah u-r͏eviyyah*) and the more detailed elaboration of the *GenR* tradition in *Lekach-Tob (Pesikta-Sutarta)* (Hebrew), ed. Solomon Buber, 2 vols. (Vilna, 1884), 2:15b–16a. In *PDRE,* ch. 22, 9:147, Noah's contemporaries explicitly inform him that they refrain from *p͏eriyyah u-r͏eviyyah,* spilling their semen on the ground to avoid fathering children. For additional references, see *LOJ,* 5:173–74 n. 17; 178 n. 26.

33. TB *San.* 108a.

34. *GenR* 28.8 (ad 6:7), 1:266; cf. *TanB (Noah* 18), 2:23a, *Tan. (Noah* 12), p. 6a.

35. *TanB (B͏ereshit* 39), 2:13ab.

36. *GenR* 31.12 (ad 6:18), 1:286, 34.7 ad (8:16), 1:316; cf. also TJ *Taan.* 1.6, 64d, and TB *San.* 108b (which substitute *tashmish ha-miṭṭah* for *p͏eriyyah u-r͏eviyyah*), as well as *PDRE,* ch. 23, 9:152. On the reason for the prohibition, see *TanB (Noah* 17), 2:22a, and *Tan. (Noah* 11), p. 6a, where God forbids Noah to build the world while he himself is destroying it; see also the additional suggestions adduced by M. M. Kasher, *Torah Shelemah: Talmudic-Midrashic Encyclopedia of the Pentateuch* (Hebrew), 39 vols. to date (Jerusalem and New York, 1927–85), 2:408 n. 200: that all unnecessary pleasures were inappropriate during a time of calamity, that sex would have violated the sanctity of the ark, and that the excessive humidity made sexual activity physically dangerous.

37. *GenR* 34.6 (ad 8:16), 1:315–16.

38. *GenR* 35.1 (ad 9:8–9), 1:328; in 34.12 (ad 9:1), 1:323, God's reiteration of the primordial blessings to Noah is linked to the sacrifices offered by the latter.

39. See above, n. 3.

ing recklessly[40] or by neglecting procreation and thereby failing to fill the earth.[41]

Aggadic texts further suggest that the divine instructions of Gen. 1:28 figured significantly in the covenantal relationship between God and the Hebrew patriarchs. Abraham and Isaac are said to have heeded the duty of procreation zealously, taking special care to find wives for their sons.[42] The blessing of fertility is deemed the epitome of God's promises to the patriarchs[43]—one text terms it the distinctive "lot of the righteous (*'inyan ha-ẓaddiqim*)"[44]—which the rapid increase of their descendants in Egypt (reported in Ex. 1:7) eventually realized. The *Sifra'* strengthens the connection between Lev. 26:9 and Gen. 1:28 drawn in the preceding chapter, asserting that the reward of the pious will include not only fertility but dominion as well.[45] As a blessing, procreation constituted the reward for punishing a murderer,[46] and as a duty it was an important agenda item in one's interrogation on judgment day.[47] Conversely, the refusal of a single Jew to fulfill the mandates of Gen. 1:28 could cause the divine presence to leave the community of Israel,[48] and various sources report that important Jewish leaders suffered because they neglected the commandment. Nadav and Avihu, the sons of Aaron, may have been killed because they had no children;[49] Joshua, according to one opinion, had no heir because he prevented marital relations among the Israelites on a single night;[50] and Hezekiah took gravely ill because he too did not fulfill his obligation.[51] The Talmud berates R. Eleazar b. Simeon, whose police duties on behalf of Rome

40. *PDRE*, ch. 24, 9:155.

41. Samuel b. Nissim, *Midrash Bᵉreshit Zuṭa'*, ed. Mordekhai ha-Kohen (Jerusalem, 1962), p. 32.

42. *TanB* (*Noaḥ* 18), 2:23a.

43. *GenR* 39.11 (ad 12:2), 1:374–75, 47.5 (ad 17:19–20), 1:473–74; TB *Ḥul.* 92a; *PesR* 11, p. 45a; *NumR* 2.14; *Agadath Bereschith* (Hebrew) 5.1, ed. Solomon Buber (Krakow, 1902), p. 11; *MBR*, p. 74.

44. *MBR*, p. 153.

45. *Sifra'* (*Bᵉ-ḥuqqotai* 2.6) (1545; repr., Jerusalem, 1970), p. 56b; see above, p. 31.

46. *MAgg*, p. 22.

47. TB *Sab.* 31a.

48. TB *Yev.* 64a; cf. *BQ* 83a (without explicit mention of *pᵉriyyah u-rᵉviyyah*).

49. TB *Yev.* 64a; *PRK*, 2:395; *LevR*, 2:463–64. See also Avigdor Shinan, "The Sin of Nadab and Abihu in Rabbinic Literature" (Hebrew), *Tarbiẓ* 48 (1979), 209–10; and Robert Kirschner, "The Rabbinic and Philonic Exegeses of the Nadab and Abihu Incident (Lev. 10:1–6)," *JQR*, n.s. 73 (1983), 375–93.

50. TB *Eruv.* 63b.

51. TB *Ber.* 10a. See also Fred Rosner, "The Illness of King Hezekiah and the 'Book of Remedies' Which He Hid," *Koroth* 9 (1985), 193–97.

prevented him from serving as a rabbinic judge; thus distracted, he neglected the opportunity to permit wives with questions concerning ritual impurity to return to their husbands.[52] The Jewish man without wife and children numbers among those banned from the heavenly congregation (*m^{e}nudin la-shammayim*),[53] and the Jew without children, like the blind, the poor, and the leper, is no better off than dead.[54] Commenting on the trimonthly rotation of the laborers whom Solomon sent to Lebanon in order to bring cedar and cypress wood for the construction of the Temple (1 Kings 6:26), R. Avin reportedly concluded: "The holy one, blessed be he, preferred marital relations (*p^{e}riyyah u-r^{e}viyyah*) to the Temple. How so? [Scripture states: "they would spend] one month in Lebanon and two months at home.""[55]

This assortment of rabbinic homilies may testify to the high valuation of marriage and the family in the ethos of the classical Jewish sages, and it may in fact demonstrate the role of Gen. 1:28 as a valuable scriptural proof-text for legitimating that judgment. Yet it also highlights a constellation of methodological problems in the scholarly analysis of rabbinic texts in general, and specifically in the topical and diachronic orientation of the present study. The sources cited in the preceding paragraphs belong to varying genres of literature—midrashic anthologies of different species, the two Talmuds, and the Palestinian Targum—each of which imposed structural and functional constraints on the material they included. These books date from a period that was at least eight hundred years long, from the fourth through the twelfth centuries, although the traditions they collect are typically ascribed, with varying degrees of reliability, to rabbis who lived even centuries earlier. The compilers of these books lived in Babylonia, in Palestine and other lands of the eastern Mediterranean, or in western Europe, where social, economic, and political conditions fluctuated widely over time and over regional boundaries, as did the religious needs of the

---

52. TB *BM* 84b.
53. TB *Pes.* 113b.
54. TB *AZ* 5a.
55. TJ *Ket.* 5.8, 30b. *TanB* (*Naso'* 16), 5:16b–17a, compares Solomon's bed (Song 3:7) to the Temple and a forest: "For his bed represents the Temple. And why is the Temple compared to a bed? Just as a bed is not but for procreation (*p^{e}riyyah u-r^{e}viyyah*), so too everything in the Temple was fertile and increased (*hayu parin w^e-ravin*), . . . for it bore fruit, and thus Scripture says (1 Kings 7:2), 'He built the Lebanon forest house.' Why was it compared to a forest? Just as a forest is fertile and increases (*pareh w^e-raveh*), so too everything in the Temple was fertile and increased."

Jewish communities that books and writers sought to address. Each work accordingly possessed a distinctive character and agenda, which its contents presumably served. The editorial and transmissional factors that affected differing renditions of a given homiletic tradition were numerous indeed, and all too often one can pinpoint that tradition's origins and track its subsequent history only with great difficulty and much conjecture. Attempts to characterize *the* rabbinic view or stance on a specific theological issue pose similar hazards, especially in the realm of the Aggadah (more than in that of the Halakhah), where an issue's lack of practical consequences allowed for considerable ideological latitude, even concerning fundamental theological questions. While the preceding collection of aggadic pronouncements hints that the preponderance of rabbinic interest in Gen. 1:28 lay in its call for procreation rather than in its grant of dominion, simply amassing such texts does little to explicate the exegetical and theological considerations that facilitated the significance of our verse in the thought of the rabbis.

The accompanying risks notwithstanding, we propose to proceed on the following basis. We reiterate that our point of departure is the rabbinic encounter with the text of Gen. 1:28, not any theme or message that the verse enunciates to its modern readers. The ensuing analysis therefore derives primarily from citations of Gen. 1:28 or from clear allusions to it—for example, the *prh/rbh* hendiadys—in talmudic, midrashic, and targumic literature. (Secondarily, and to a very limited extent, our data will include citations of and allusions to other biblical passages, discussed in Chapter 1, that themselves constitute allusions to Gen. 1:28.) Because no one can deny that the editors and personae of these rabbinic works had the biblical texts before them, the factor determining the relevance or irrelevance of a rabbinic tradition to our own discussion is not anachronistic. And neither is it an artificial thematic construct retrojected onto the rabbinic texts, nor does it hinge on the ultimately elusive or indeterminable—for instance, the corpus of teachings of a particular talmudic sage or school. Scrutiny of the data themselves has resulted in the thematic rubrics that divide our analysis, but these themes did not control the selection of the data. I believe that I have found and studied nearly all allusions to Gen. 1:28 in published texts of the Mishnah, Tosefta, Talmuds, midrashim, and Targums. All cannot receive equal attention here, but a majority are at least cited in the footnotes to this chapter and the next. The susceptibility or ripeness of specific traditions for extended discussion is admittedly a subjective variable, but we have sought to ground our own editorial prerogative of selection in the quality and quantity of their contributions to the interpretation-history of our biblical verse.

Viewed collectively, these contributions display an impressive semblance of unity. To appreciate that unity properly, one must surely have a sensitivity to the chronology, the geographical provenance, and what Jacob Neusner termed the "integrity" of the works containing our data.[56] But these, along with the credibility of attributions to individual rabbinic personae, will bear only irregularly on our central conclusions. Most of the homiletic instructions we examine "traveled" from one rabbinic compilation to the next, failing to betray the basic objectives for which a specific work may have been written. With the possible exception of *Genesis Rabbah,* no single rabbinic document contains enough references to our verse to figure in an analysis of that entire work, and the verse does not appear repeatedly in the traditions ascribed to any specific talmudic sage in a way that reflects meaningfully on him (or on his assumed opus). An illustrative example concerns one of the few pertinent aggadic traditions extant in a Tannaitic source.[57] This discussion of the importance of procreation among several sages of Yavneh appears in the Tosefta, in *Genesis Rabbah,* and in the Babylonian Talmud, in addition to some subsequent compilations. The names of the Yavnean rabbis vary, as does the context in which the pericope is adduced, but its exegetical import is identical in every case. Moreover, while a Yavnean origin for this pericope would manifest a rather precise correspondence between rabbinic and contemporary Stoic thought, it is hardly essential in order to suggest the possibility of cross-cultural exchange, or at least an instructive parallel between Jewish and Greco-Roman intellectual history. Because no comparable Yavnean discussion of Gen 1:28 remains, even this pericope would not facilitate an estimation of a distinctively Yavnean approach to its ramifications. Despite numerous unanswered questions, which must be asked and considered, the knowledge that here survives a popular Tannaitic midrash will nevertheless be of help in charting the singular career of a biblical idea.

56. Among his many recent publications on the subject, see Jacob Neusner, *The Integrity of "Leviticus Rabbah": The Problem of the Autonomy of a Rabbinic Document,* Brown Judaic Studies 93 (Chico, Calif., 1985), and *Comparative Midrash: The Plan and Program of "Genesis Rabbah" and "Leviticus Rabbah,"* Brown Judaic Studies 111 (Atlanta, Ga., 1986).

57. See below, p. 110.

Defining Human Nature

In the biblical cosmogony, Gen. 1:28 serves to situate the first human beings with the array of creatures that precede them. On the one hand, the injunction to "be fertile and increase" likens humans to other animate creatures, at least some of which received a similar blessing from God at the end of the fifth day of creation. On the other hand, procreation directed toward filling, mastering, and ruling over the earth sets humans apart, with powers and responsibilities shared by no other species. The aggadic imagination of the rabbis developed this dual purpose of our verse in various directions, yielding the first group of traditions which we shall consider at length.

Sexuality and the Natural Order. In the Aggadah, as in Scripture, sexual reproduction incorporates human beings into the rest of the natural order, epitomizing the creative powers God implanted in the cosmos. *Genesis Rabbah* quotes R. Levi:[58]

> The upper waters are male and the lower waters female. And the former say to the latter, "Take us, for you are the creation of the holy one, blessed be he, and we are his messengers"; and at once they receive them. Thus Scripture states (Is. 45:8): "Let the earth open up," like a female when she opens for a male; "and triumph sprout (*we-yifru yesha'*)," for they are fertile (*parim*) and increase (*we-ravim*);[59] "let vindication spring up"—this is the falling of the rains; "I the Lord have created it"—for this reason did I create it, for the settlement of the world and its perfection (*le-tiqqun ha-'olam ule-yishuvo*).

From the days of the *Enuma Elish* epic, water had consistently played a major role in ancient Near Eastern cosmogonies, which regularly characterized different types or bodies of water as masculine or feminine forces. This motif appears in a Jewish work of the early Hellenistic period,[60] and *Genesis Rabbah* integrates it into an extensive series of reflections on the importance of water and rain in the secrets of cre-

---

58. *GenR* 13.13 (ad 2:6), 1:122–23. Cf. parallels in TJ *Ber.* 9.3, 14a, *Taan.* 1.3, 64b; and on the resemblance of creation and procreation, see also *Tan.* (*Pequde* 3), p. 49a.
59. Parallels in TJ read "this is procreation (*zo periyyah u-reviyyah*)."
60. 1 Enoch 54:8, *OTP* 1:38.

ation.[61] Emphasizing the analogous and essential functions of water and sexuality in the primal, natural order, *Midrash ha-Gadol* subsequently commented on this differentiation between upper and lower waters: "Just as the world cannot exist without male and female, so the world cannot exist without rain."[62] According to *Genesis Rabbah,* the same R. Levi explained that God appropriately punished the contemporaries of Noah with water because of their unnatural sexual practices.[63] Carefully read, however, the text of *Genesis Rabbah* suggests that the sexuality mandated and sanctified by Gen. 1:28 not only belongs to the untamed world of nature but also pertains to the distinctively human, and therefore "meta-natural," purpose in the divine plan. God created the world so that it could be settled and civilized, processes whereby humans harness and overcome the forces of nature, and not for it to remain in its pristine, natural state. The juxtaposition of *yifru* (from *prh*) and *yesha'* (triumph or salvation) in Is. 45:8 might hint that sexuality must aim toward the ultimate goal of life in the world and does not merely betray its primal origins. The Babylonian Talmud draws this inference in the name of R. Oshaya: "Great is the day on which the rains fall, for on it even salvation (*yeshu'ah*) increases greatly (*parah w^e-ravah*), as Scripture states, 'Let the earth open up and triumph sprout (*w^e-yifru yesha'*).'"[64] And *Midrash T^{e}hillim* records the homily of R. Levi anonymously but with the expanded gloss, "'and triumph sprout (*w^e-yifru yesha'*),' for they are fertile (*parim*) and increase (*w^e-ravim*) and bring on salvation (*y^{e}shu'ah*)."[65] The link between procreation and this prophetic text contrasts against its more frequent association with another verse (Is. 45:18) in the same chapter: "He did not create it a waste, but formed it for habitation." The implications of these differing midrashic associations fueled rabbinic debate over the very purpose of Gen. 1:28, a dispute with legal as well as theological consequences. Does the commandment of procreation aim to develop God's creation of this world,

---

61. *GenR* 2.4 (ad 1:2), 1:17 (with notes); 5.4 (ad 1:9), 1:34–35; and 13.9–17 (ad 2:6), 1:118–26. See the additional references in *LOJ*, 5:17–18 nn. 50, 52, 53; pp. 27–28 n. 74.

62. *MHG*, 1:27. Cf. also *PDRE*, ch. 4, 8:96–97 (ch. 5 in standard eds.), where different varieties of rain are likened to proper and improper patterns of sexual reproduction, and ch. 23, 9:151, where, in order to destroy the world during the primeval flood, the upper, masculine waters conjoin with the lower, feminine waters.

63. *GenR* 32.7 (ad 7:11), 1:294; cf. TB *San.* 108a. On the "measure for measure" quality of the punishment, see also *LOJ*, 5:182–83 nn. 39, 42.

64. TB *Taan.* 7b.

65. *MTeh* 42.5 (ad 42:8), p. 134a; cf. *Midrash Zuṭa* ad Eccl. 1:5, ed. Solomon Buber (Berlin, 1894), p. 57a.

or does it prepare for messianic salvation and thus an end to worldly existence as we now know it? We shall return to this question more than once, but for the moment we proceed to explore the ambiguous significance of sexuality in the human constitution, or precisely where Gen. 1:28 situated man and woman in the hierarchy of the divine creation.

The Human as a Cosmic Frontier. The idea that human beings straddle the colloquial fence dividing heavenly (spiritual) and earthly (material) worlds, blending characteristics of both and somehow marking the point of transition between them, enjoyed considerable popularity in ancient and medieval thought. The idea was present among the Stoics, it appears in the works of Philo, and it eventually entered the anthropology of patristic and rabbinic scholars.[66] The history of this notion per se lies beyond the purview of the present study, but the intersection of that history with the career of Gen. 1:28 is both fascinating and relevant. One might well argue that Ps. 8, discussed in Chapter 1, constitutes a noteworthy precedent in this regard. Dominion places humans slightly below the heavenly realm but above all other creatures on earth.[67] And in the Book of the Watchers in 1 Enoch, procreation serves as the line of demarcation between mortal and immortal beings; thus God addresses the fallen angels (15:4–7):

> But you were holy, spirits that live forever, yet you defiled yourselves with the blood of women, and have begotten (children) by the blood of flesh; and you lusted after the daughters of men and have produced flesh and blood, just as they do who die and perish. It was for this reason I gave them females that they might impregnate them and thus produce children by them, that pregnancy should never fail them upon the earth. But as for you, you formerly were spirits that live for ever and do not die for all generations for ever. And for this reason I did not provide wives for you, because for celestial spirits heaven is their dwelling-place.[68]

In a word, sexual reproduction and immortality are mutually exclusive. As Bernhard Lang noted, the Book of the Watchers depicts even the "eternal life" promised the righteous as a finite, albeit lengthy, period of

---

66. Jobling, pp. 117ff.; *LOJ*, 5:64–66 nn. 4, 6.
67. See above, p. 34f.
68. *The Book of Enoch or 1 Enoch: A New English Edition*, ed. Matthew Black, Studia in Veteris Testamenti Pseudepigrapha 7 (Leiden, 1985), p. 34.

time (10:10) in which they will have many children and live out their days in peace (10:17–22).[69]

This passage from 1 Enoch may not allude to Gen. 1:28, but it sheds light on pertinent rabbinic traditions that do. Once again our tale begins with *Genesis Rabbah,* in its glosses on Gen. 1:27:

> R. Tifdai said in the name of R. Aha: The creatures of the upper world were created in the divine image and likeness and do not engage in procreation (*'enam parim we-ravim*), while the creatures of the lower world engage in procreation and were not created in the divine image and likeness. The holy one, blessed be he, said, "I shall hereby create him [man] in the divine image and likeness like the creatures of the upper world, and as one who engages in procreation (*pareh we-raveh*) like the creatures of the lower world."
>
> R. Tifdai said in the name of R. Aha: The holy one, blessed be he, said, "If I create him like the creatures of the upper world, he will live and never die; and if [I create him] like the creatures of the lower world, he will die and not live. Rather, I shall hereby create him like creatures of the upper world and like creatures of the lower world. If he sins, he will die; and if he does not sin, he will live."[70]

The homilies attributed to the otherwise unknown R. Tifdai (some manuscripts read Tifrai) follow immediately upon a list of the characteristics—four in each case—humans share with angels (erect stature, speech, understanding, and sight) and with beasts (the consumption of food and drink, procreation, defecation, and death). For R. Tifdai, however, the dialectic between the angelic and beastly traits of human beings boils down to that between the divine image in which God created man and woman, and their sexuality. Such is his understanding of Gen. 1:27, which reports that God created humans in his image, actualizing the divine intention pronounced in Gen. 1:26, and which

---

69. Bernhard Lang, "No Sex in Heaven: The Logic of Procreation, Death, and Eternal Life in the Judaeo-Christian Tradition," in *Mélanges bibliques et orientaux en l'honneur de M. Mathias Delcor,* ed. A. Caquot et al., Alter Orient und Altes Testament 215 (Neukirchen-Vluyn, 1985), pp. 238–39.

70. GenR 8.11, 1:65; the same homilies appear in 14.3 (ad 2.7), 1:128, subsequent to the remark that God "created [Adam] (*wa-yizer,* written *wyyzr,* and therefore meaning) two creations, from [the realm of] the creatures of the upper world and [the realm of] the creatures of the lower world." In this later occurrence of this tradition, as well as in several manuscript variants of the first, Tifdai concludes his second homily "If he sins, he will die; and if he dies, he will live," meaning that if he destroys his selfish, material passions, he will merit divine reward. See J. Theodor's notes, ad loca, and cf. David b. Joseph Kimhi, *Perushe RaDa"Q 'al ha-Torah,* ed. Moshe Kamelhar (Jerusalem, 1970), p. 21.

concludes, "male and female he created them," anticipating the mandate of procreation in Gen. 1:28.[71] Yet if the Book of the Watchers implies the utter incompatibility of angelic immortality and human sexuality, R. Tifdai suggests that the anomalous, sexual, God-like human being defies the ostensive logic of this polar opposition. Tifdai's second homily indicates that, unlike the angel and the beast, humans can determine their own destiny; their merits will yield for them the deserts of the upper world or those of the lower, epitomized in life and death, respectively. Within such a framework, sexual reproduction denotes not only an attribute of the lower world, but also—along with the divine image—the essence of the singular perfection that allows humans, and humans alone, to choose between life and death. The ensuing discussion in *Genesis Rabbah* confirms this impression:

> "And rule the fish of the sea (Gen. 1:28)." R. Hanina said: If he has been meritorious, "and rule (*u-r*e*du*, Gen. 1:28)" [applies]; and if he has not been meritorious, "they will descend (*yer*e*du*, Gen. 1:26)" [applies]. R. Jacob of Kfar Hanan said: "And rule (*u-r*e*du*)" [applies] to him who is in our image and likeness, "they will descend (*yer*e*du*)" [applies] to him who is not in our image and likeness.[72]

Vocalizing the consonants of the verb *yrdw* in Gen. 1:26 to mean "they will descend (*yer*e*du*)"—or, perhaps, "they will be ruled (*yeradu*)"[73]—rather than "they shall rule (*yirdu*)" as in Scripture, R. Hanina and R. Jacob both instruct that humans can merit either reward or punishment, to be expressed in the fulfillment or nonfulfillment of the blessing of dominion in Gen. 1:28. Yet why has the editor of *Genesis Rabbah* skipped from Gen. 1:27 to Gen. 1:28b, commenting on human dominion over the animals, before taking note of Gen. 1:28a, "Be fertile and increase . . ."? In addition to reiterating the message of Tifdai's second homily, the pun on *yrdw* strengthens the intrinsic connection between Gen. 1:26, announcing the creation of humans in God's image, and Gen. 1:28, mandating their procreative function. Once this connection has been established, *Genesis Rabbah* then proceeds to consider "be

71. Contra Gary G. Porton, *Understanding Rabbinic Midrash: Text and Commentary* (Hoboken, N.J., 1985), p. 184, who insists that this midrash ignores the substance of the biblical text it glosses.

72. *GenR* 8.12, 1:65; and see Samuel b. Isaac Jaffe, *Y*e*feh To'ar* (Fürth, 1692), p. 59b.

73. See Michael Sokoloff, ed., *The Geniza Fragments of Bereshit Rabba* (Hebrew) (Jerusalem, 1982), p. 97.

fertile and increase," for as R. Tifdai would have it, sexuality and the divine image are the defining characteristics of the human being, and their proper expression leads directly to the exercise of dominion. As a proximate homily in *Genesis Rabbah* ascribed to R. Yohanan instructs, the human situation on this "cosmic frontier" affords a unique opportunity; "if a man is deserving, he consumes [the rewards of] two worlds."[74]

Numerous aggadic traditions reflect on the various considerations in this train of thought. None retraces precisely the same steps as the text in *Genesis Rabbah* that we quoted, but they all illuminate the logic that may have motivated R. Tifdai and/or his midrashic editor. The notion that humans combine the spiritual qualities of heavenly beings with the physical traits of earthly creatures recurs in early and in late aggadic sources, in some instances rationalized by the symmetry of the hexameral creation, whose works prior to the formation of humans divided equally between heavenly and earthly realms.[75] Other texts offer an alternative list of the angelic and animal characteristics embodied by human beings, with procreation consistently numbering among the animal traits.[76] An interesting variant of this motif reconstructs the impassioned prayer of the childless Hannah, commencing with the hitherto unprecedented biblical epithet "O Lord of hosts (1 Sam. 1:11)."[77]

What is the significance of "O Lord of hosts"? R. Judah the son of R. Simon said: Hannah said to the holy one, blessed be he: "Master of the universe, there is a host above and there is a host below. The host above do not eat, do not drink, do not procreate, and do not die, but they live forever; and the host below eat, drink, procreate, and die. Yet I do not know of which host I am, whether of the one above or of the one below. If I am of the host above, I should not be eating, drinking, bearing children, or dying, but I should live forever, just as they [of the host above] live for ever. But if I am of the host below, then I should be eating and drinking, bearing children, and dying, just as they [of the

74. *GenR* 8.1 (ad 1:26), 1:54–55, *LevR* 14.1 (ad 12:2), 2:295, *MTeh*, p. 264b (ad 139:5). See also the similar conclusion attributed to R. Simai in *SifD* 306, pp. 340–41.

75. *SifD*, loc. cit., *GenR* 12.8 (ad 2:4), 1:106, *LevR* 9.9 (ad 7:11), 1:193—all citing later parallels in their respective notes. See also *LOJ*, 5:65–66 n. 6.

76. TB *Hag.* 16a; *ARNA* 37, p. 55a, with additional parallels cited there by Schechter.

77. *PesR* 43, p. 179b, with shorter parallels in *Baraita' de-32 Middot* 16, in *The Mishnah of Rabbi Eliezer* (Hebrew), ed. H. G. Enelow (New York, 1933), p. 29, and in *Midrash Shemu'el* 2.4, ed. Solomon Buber (Krakow, 1893), p. 24b.

host below] eat and drink, procreate, and die." This is the significance of "O Lord of hosts."

From the barren Hannah's perspective, procreation obviously outweighed her other earthly characteristics in importance, for without it she felt deprived of her identity as a mortal creature—a conclusion that the end of this pericope leaves unquestionable. Because God is lord of both heavenly and earthly hosts, and because Hannah was of the latter, her request to the deity was appropriate.

In Hannah's entreaty before God, procreation constitutes the hallmark of mortality; as in the Book of the Watchers—but not the sermons of R. Tifdai—there is here no suggestion that sexuality, albeit a trait of the lower world, figures in the distinctively human capability of meriting divine reward. Without alluding to our verse, *Genesis Rabbah* elsewhere records the teaching that immortality and bearing children simply do not mix.[78] This view of procreation emerges as well from the following description of Adam in *Pirqe d^e-R. 'Eli^ezer:*

> He was strolling in the Garden of Eden like one of the ministering angels. Said the holy one, blessed be he: "I am unique in my world, and this man is unique in his. Procreation (*p^eriyyah u-r^eviyyah*) is not within my realm of existence (lit., before me), nor is procreation within his realm of existence. In the future all the creatures will say: Because he does not procreate, he is our creator. [Therefore] it is not good for man to be alone; I will make a fitting helper for him (Gen. 2:18)."[79]

Just as an asexual existence characterizes the supernatural realm of God, procreation in this homily defines Adam as a mortal creature, preventing confusion between him and God the creator on the part of other creatures. As such, the divine institution of marriage and procreation resembles the slumber imposed on Adam by God in *Genesis Rabbah*, in a tradition attributed to R. Hoshaya.[80]

---

78. *GenR* 12.7 (ad 2:4), 1:106.

79. *PDRE*, ch. 11, 9:101–2 (ch. 12 in standard eds.); cf. *MHG* 1:84. According to David Luria in his comments on *Pirqe Rabbi 'Eli^ezer* ad loc. (Warsaw, 1852), p. 29b, this homily addresses the biblical specification that it is detrimental that man be alone (*lo' ṭov heyot ha-'adam l^evado*) and not that it is to man's detriment to be alone (*lo' ṭov la-'adam lihyot l^evado*). Cf. ch. 10, 9:97 (ch. 11 in standard eds.), where the animals do mistake Adam for their maker.

80. *GenR* 8.5 (ad 1:26), 1:63–64 (cf. Sokoloff, *Geniza Fragments*, p. 96). This tradition subsequently reappeared in several medieval works. See *Midrash Zuṭa* ad Eccl. 6:10, p. 66b; *Yalqut Shim^oni: N^evi'im u-Kh^etuvim* 394, 2 vols. (1521; repr., Jerusalem, 1973), 1:63b; and Makhir b. Abba Mari, *The Yalkut on Isaiah* (Hebrew) 2.22, ed. J. Spira (Berlin, 1894), p. 25.

When the holy one, blessed be he, created Adam, the ministering angels mistook him [as divine] and sought to declare "Holy!" before him.[81] To what is this similar? To a king and his governor that were placed in a chariot, and their subjects sought to cry *Domine!* before the king but did not know which was he. What did the king do? He pushed and ejected him [his lieutenant] from the chariot, and they knew [who was] the king. So too when the holy one, blessed be he, created Adam and the angels mistook him, what did the holy one, blessed be he, do? He made slumber fall upon him [Adam], and all knew that he was human.

Scholarly opinion has recently divided concerning such rabbinic portrayals of the primordial Adam. Alexander Altmann[82] has grouped R. Hoshaya's homily together with other aggadic traditions in which Adam himself corrects the angels' mistake[83] or in which God reduces Adam in size[84] to demonstrate his humanity. (Curiously, in *Sefer Ḥasidim* the latter version of the story follows immediately upon a halakhic reference to procreation.)[85] Together, Altmann maintained, they represent the polemical response of the rabbis to a threatening Gnostic mythology, which the sages sought to neutralize by incorporating its motif of the reduction of Adam into a biblical framework— that is, as divine punishment for human sin. Other investigators have challenged the Gnostic background of these homilies, arguing that they derive from tendencies endemic to the thinking of the rabbis themselves.[86] In either case, ejection from the divine chariot, sleep, and sexuality all epitomize human entanglement in the material world. The institution of marriage—along with its result, procreation—in *Pirqe de-R. 'Eli'ezer* serves exactly the same purpose as sleep in *Genesis Rabbah:*

81. Presumably as in Is. 6:3.

82. Alexander Altmann, "The Gnostic Background of the Rabbinic Adam Legends," in *Essays in Jewish Intellectual History* (Hanover, N.H., 1981), pp. 6ff. (quotations on pp. 11–12). Cf. *LOJ,* 5:80 n. 25.

83. *PDRE,* ch. 10, 9:97 (ch. 11 in standard eds.).

84. *'Ottiyot de-R. 'Aqiva',* ed. Shlomo Aharon Wertheimer and Abraham Joseph Wertheimer, in *Batei Midrashot* (Hebrew), 2nd ed., 2 vols. (1950–53; repr., Jerusalem, 1968), 2:412; *Yalquṭ Shim'oni 'al ha-Torah* 20, ed. Dov Hyman et al., 7 vols. in 4 pts. to date (Jerusalem, 1973–86), 1,1:66. On Adam's physical enormity, see also *LOJ,* 5:79 n. 22, and the references cited below, n. 121.

85. *SHP* 1145, p. 290.

86. Above all, see Susan Niditch, "The Cosmic Adam: Man as Mediator in Rabbinic Literature," *Journal of Jewish Studies* 34 (1983), 137–46; and Moshe Idel, "Enoch Is Metatron" (Hebrew), *Jerusalem Studies in Jewish Thought* 6,1–2 (1987), 151–70. For the identification of God's ejected subordinate, see Saul Lieberman, "Metatron, the Meaning of His Name and His Functions," in *Apocalyptic and Merkavah Mysticism,* by Ithamar Gruenwald, Arbeiten zur Geschichte des antiken Judentums und des Urchristentums 14 (Leiden, 1980), pp. 239–40.

to make Adam mortal. This would suggest that procreation, the obverse of human mortality, characterized human beings only after their
fall from paradise; it serves as a form of punishment, or at least a direct
result of their sin. While other Palestinian and Babylonian rabbis reportedly shared R. Tifdai's antidualistic outlook that marital relations and
procreation reflected God's original intentions for human beings,[87] the
equation of sex and sin, manifest in such intertestamental texts as
Jubilees (3:34), here resurfaced in this later aggadic work.[88] Additional
evidence for such a divergent tradition might be present in the midrashic gloss of the Palestinian Targum on Gen. 3:22, which recounts the
expulsion from Eden in the wake of human sin; in almost exactly the
same words as *Pirqe d^e-R. 'Eli'ezer,* God introduces the sentence of exile:
"Adam is unique on earth just as I am unique in heaven."[89]

The substance of Hannah's plea for a child, however, also relates to a
more positive, optimistic aggadic approach to human sexuality and
procreation, and this too has roots in the literature of the intertestamental period. In an earlier, talmudic version of her petition[90] (as well as in a
similar prayer later ascribed to the barren matriarch Rebekah),[91] the
female supplicant declares that because God created all human organs

---

87. *GenR* 18.6 (ad 2:25), 1:168–69 (Joshua b. Korhah); 19.3 (ad 3:2), 1:171–72 (Abba
Halfon b. Kuriyah); 22.2 (ad 4:1), 1:205 (Eleazar b. Azariah); TB *San.* 38b (Yohanan b.
Hanina); *ARNA* 1, p. 3a; and cf. RaSh"I ad Gen. 4:1, p. 9. See also the variant in *PRK,* 2:334
(and parallels cited in *GenR,* 1:168nn.), which makes no mention of coupling or childbirth,
perhaps under the influence of the popular tradition we are describing here. On the anti-
Gnostic motives of R. Tifdai's viewpoint, see Jacob Neusner, "*Genesis Rabbah* as Polemic: An
Introductory Account," *Hebrew Annual Review* 9 (1985), esp. 257–58.

88. See also the comments ad Gen. 4:1 of Abraham b. Meir ibn Ezra, *Perushe ha-Torah,* ed.
Asher Weizer, 3 vols. (Jerusalem, 1976) 1:31, and Bahya b. Asher, *Be'ur 'al ha-Torah,* ed. C. B.
Chavel, 3 vols. (Jerusalem, 1966–68), 1:88. On the association of Gnostic opposition to
marital sex and the legends of Cain in *PDRE,* see A. Goldberg, "Kain: Sohn des Menschen
oder Sohn der Schlange," *Judaica* 25 (1969), 202–21, and Louis Ginzberg, *Die Haggada bei den
Kirchenvätern und in der apokryphischen Litteratur* (Berlin, 1900), pp. 56–60. PDRE, ch. 10, 9:96
(ch. 11 in standard eds.), includes the conflicting aggadah regarding the twelve hours of the
day on which the first parents were created, which David Luria explains as the interpolation of
a copyist seeking accordance with the talmudic tradition.

89. Pseudo-Jonathan, *Targum Jonathan b. Uziel on the Pentateuch* (Hebrew), ed. David
Rieder (Jerusalem, 1974), p. 5; *Neofiti 1,* 1:19; *The Fragment-Targums of the Pentateuch According
to Their Extant Sources,* ed. Michael L. Klein, Analecta biblica 76, 2 vols. (Rome, 1980), 1:46,
127; for the idea that human mortality resulted from—and did not precede—human transgression, see the opinions cited in *GenR* 21.5 (ad 3:22), 1:200–201, *PesR* suppl. 1, p. 192ab, and
the additional references cited by Etan Levine in his appendix to *Neofiti 1,* 2:546 (ad 3:22). On
the term "unique" (*yahid*), see the excursus of Fritzleo Lentzen-Deis, *Die Taufe Jesu nach den
Synoptikern: Literarkritische und gattungsgeschichtliche Untersuchungen,* Frankfurter theologische
Studien 4 (Frankfurt a.M., 1970), pp. 228–40.

90. TB *Ber.* 31b.

91. *MHG,* 1:435.

(eyes, ears, nose, mouth, hands, legs, and breasts) for a purpose, she who has breasts deserves a child to nurse. The suggestive comment of Samuel Eliezer Edels[92] that Hannah mentioned "those organs employed by the five senses" brings to mind a singular midrashic allusion to Gen. 1:28 in *Midrash Tadshe*:[93]

> To every [human] faculty (*le-khol hargashah we-hargashah*) the holy one, blessed be he, gave instruction (*torah*) what to do and what not to do. To the heart, "do not follow [your heart . . . in your lustful urge] (Num. 15:39)." To the eyes, "[do not follow] your eyes (ibid.)." To the ears, "you must not carry false rumors (Ex. 23:1)." To the mouth, "you shall not eat anything abhorrent (Deut. 14:3)." To the tongue, "you shall not swear [falsely] by the name of the Lord, etc. (Ex. 20:7)"; "you shall not swear [falsely by my name] (Lev. 19:12)"; "you shall not deal falsely (Lev. 19:11)"; [and] you shall not bear [false witness] (Ex. 20:13)." To the hands, "you must not join hands with the guilty (Ex. 23:1)." To the genitals ('*erwah*), "you shall not commit adultery (Ex. 20:13)"; [and] "do not fall into harlotry (Lev. 19:29)."[94] [To the] legs, "do not follow other gods (Deut. 6:14)."[95] These are the proscriptive precepts, and thus Solomon said (Prov. 6:12–19): "A scoundrel, etc., winking his eyes, etc., duplicity is in his heart[, etc.]. Therefore [calamity will come upon him] without warning, etc. Six things the Lord hates; seven are an abomination to him: a haughty bearing ('*enayim ramot*), a lying tongue,[96] hands that shed innocent blood, etc., [and one who incites] brothers [to quarrel]."[97] And what does he instruct [them]

92. *Hiddushe 'Aggadot* ad *Ber.* 31b, s.v. *lo' bara'ta.*

93. *MTad* 9, pp. 152–53. Cf. the similar instruction regarding the five senses in Bahya b. Asher, *Kad ha-Qemah,* in *Kitve Rabbenu Bahya,* ed. C. B. Chavel (Jerusalem, 1969), pp. 164–69.

94. *MTad* has distorted Scripture's *lo' tizneh ha-'arez,* reading *tizneh* in the second—rather than the third—person.

95. *MTad* reads *telekhu* for Deut.'s *telekhun.*

96. *MTad* reads *u-leshon* for Prov.'s *leshon.*

97. Vv. 12–14 list six hateful activities; five are related to bodily organs (mouth, eyes, legs, fingers, heart), the sixth pertains to inciting quarrels (*midyanim* [written *mdnym*] *yeshalleah*). Vv. 17–19 list seven such activities, five relating to organs (eyes, tongue, hands, heart, legs), and the remaining two to false testimony and inciting quarrels. *MTad* lists eight proscriptive precepts and seven prescriptive ones, omitting the mouth in the list of prescriptions. *MTad*'s reading of Prov. 6, understanding v. 16 as referring both to vv. 12–15 and to vv. 17–19, is echoed by Saadya b. Joseph, *Mishle: Tirgum u-Ferush,* ed. Joseph Kafah (n.p., 1976), pp. 61–62. Yet most commentators, medieval and modern, construe v. 16 simply as an introduction to the following vv. See, for example, the comments of Rashi and Levi Gersonides ad loc.; Menahem b. Solomon ha-Me'iri, *Perush 'al Sefer Mishle,* ed. Menahem Mendel Meshi-Zahav (Jerusalem, 1969), pp. 60–62; Crawford H. Toy, *A Critical and Exegetical Commentary on the Book of Proverbs,* ICC (New York, 1904), pp. 125–29, 132; and William McKane, *Proverbs: A New Approach* (Philadelphia, Pa., 1970), pp. 325–26.

to do? To the heart, "impress these my words upon your heart (Deut. 11:18)." To the eyes, "[watch yourselves scrupulously,] so that you do not forget the things that you saw with your own eyes (Deut. 4:9)." To the ears, "hear, O Israel, etc. (Deut. 6:4)." To the tongue, "impress (*wᵉ-shinnantam*) [them upon your children] (Deut. 6:7)." To the hands, "you must open your hand (Deut. 15:8)." To the genitals, "be fertile and increase (Gen. 1:28)";[98] and he said, "take wives and beget sons (Jer. 29:6)." To the legs, "follow only the path that the Lord your God has enjoined upon you (Deut. 5:30)." Just as the holy one, blessed be he, decreed to the creatures (*ha-bᵉriyyot*—perhaps humans, or else the creatures of the upper world) and the creatures of the lower world (*wᵉha-taḥtonim*)[99] what to do, so he prescribed to all the faculties of human organs (*lᵉ-khol hargashot ha-ʾevarim shel ʾadam*) what to do.

Midrash Tadsheʾ dates from the end of the first Christian millennium, but the Jewish idea that the theological categories of divine service and of sin extend to all of one's faculties originated in biblical antiquity, as this homily itself testifies. Many earlier rabbinic sources convey the same lesson, and the pseudepigraphic Testament of Naphtali (2:8–10) exemplifies much of the rabbinic instruction that succeeded it when it proclaims that "God made all things good in their order," mentions "the five senses in the head," lists thirteen additional limbs and organs, and finally concludes: "Thus my children you exist in accord with order for a good purpose in fear of God; do nothing in a disorderly manner, arrogantly, or at an inappropriate time. If you tell the eye to hear, it cannot; so you are unable to perform the works of light while you are in darkness."[100] Although our pericope in *Midrash Tadsheʾ* does not em-

---

98. *Yalquṭ Shimʿoni: Nᵉviʾim u-Khᵉtuvim* 42, 1:12a, and *Sefer Raziʾel ha-Malʾakh* (Amsterdam, 1701), pp. 8b–9a, read *wᵉ-ʾattem pᵉru u-rᵉvu*, referring to Gen. 9:7.

99. The phrase *ha-bᵉriyyot wᵉha-taḥtonim*, suggesting two different sets of creatures, is perplexing, because one would generally consider *ha-taḥtonim* to be a subset of the more inclusive *ha-bᵉriyyot*. Moreover, the analogy between *kol hargashot ha-ʾevarim shel ʾadam* and both of these two sets suggests that *ha-bᵉriyyot* cannot denote human creatures either, and the supernal creatures constitute the only remaining alternative. Cf. *ExR* 23.13, where Adam is identified as *geʾeh shebba-bᵉriyyot*—in contrast to the eagle, ox, and lion, the proudest of birds, livestock, and beasts, respectively—also indicating a higher class of creatures. In *MTad* 7, p. 150, *ha-bᵉriyyot* appears to signify human beings.

100. *OTP* 1:811. See also the interpolation recorded in Ben Sira 17:5, above, n. 4. Cf. 2 Enoch 30:8–9; TB *Ber.* 61ab; the prayers of Hannah and Rebekah cited above; and the lists of organs elaborating on the theme of human being as microcosm in *ARNA* 31, p. 46ab, and in *EcclR* 1.4, ed. Marc G. Hirshman, "Midrash Qohelet Rabbah, Chapters 1–4: Commentary (Ch. 1) and Introduction" (Ph.D. Dissertation, Jewish Theological Seminary of America, New York, 1982), 3:43–45 (and 2:33nn.). In *ʾOtiyyot de-R. ʿAqivaʾ*, ed. Wertheimer, *Batei Midrashot*, 2:386–87, the divinely intended purpose of the *ʾevar qaṭan* is "to urinate and to

ploy the designation of the five senses, and its list of bodily functions does not include smell, the term *hargashah* certainly denotes a sense or bodily faculty of precisely the same genre.[101] For the Stoics, the power of generation numbered among the essential faculties of the human body alongside speech, understanding, and the five senses we traditionally count;[102] and its sole justification was procreation within the context of marriage.[103] Philo incorporated this schema into his own conception of the human being,[104] and he certainly anticipated *Midrash Tadshe'* in the following exposition:

> It is a cruel thing that the inlets of the senses should be opened wide for the torrent of the objects of sense to be poured, like a river in spate, into

---

implant semen." On the theme of the human being as microcosm, see *LOJ*, 5:64–65, the literature cited below in Chapter 6, and, on the fundamental importance of the theme in *MTad*, see the comments of Epstein, *Mi-Qadmoniyyot ha-Yᵉhudim*, pp. 130ff.

101. Both *MTad* 10, p. 155, and *NumR* 14.24, explain that each of the tribal chieftains offered five he-goats and five yearling lambs when celebrating the dedication of the sanctuary (Num. 7), corresponding to "five senses (*hargashot*) and five sensations (*murgashot*)." On the respective relationships of these two midrashic works with the school of Moses the Preacher, see Epstein's introduction to *MTad*, pp. 139–40, and Albeck's introduction to *MBR*, pp. ix–xviii. Joseph b. Isaac Kimhi, *Sefer ha-Galuy*, ed. Henry J. Mathews (Berlin, 1887), p. 1, equated the five *hargashot shebba-'adam* with the five *ḥushim*, proceeding to list the organs of hearing, sight, smell, taste, and touch. See also Judah ibn Tibbon's translation of Judah b. Samuel ha-Levi, *Kuzari* 5.12, in *Das Buch al-Chazari* (Hebrew), ed. Hartwig Hirschfeld (Leipzig, 1887), p. 313, with the commentary *Qol Yᵉhudah* of Judah b. Joseph Moscato (sixteenth century), in ha-Levi's *Sefer ha-Kuzari*, 5 pts. in 1 vol. (1880; repr., Tel Aviv, 1959), 5.19b, which makes the same identification of *hargashot* with the five *ḥushim;* and see Abraham ibn Ezra, *Perushe ha-Torah*, 1:117 (ad Gen. 42:1), 2:45 (ad Ex. 5:21), and 2:140 (ad Ex. 20:15). The term *hargashot* also denotes a set of five senses whose membership varied—in the comments of Abraham Ibn Ezra ad Ps. 115:6 (with speech substituting for touch), and David b. Joseph Kimhi, *Ha-Perush ha-Shalem 'al Tᵉhillim*, ed. Abraham Darom (Jerusalem, 1967), p. 259 (ad 115:5–7, with speech evidently substituting for taste).

102. Aëtius, *Placita* 4.4, in Hermannus Diels, ed., *Doxographi graeci*, rev. ed. (Berlin, 1929), p. 390, and in Hans von Arnim, ed., *Stoicorum veterum fragmenta*, 2 (Leipzig, 1922), 226; and Diogenes Laërtius, *Lives of Eminent Philosophers*, 7.110, ed. R. D. Hicks, LCL, 2 vols. (London, 1925), 2:214–17. Diels, p. 1, notes that the pseudo-Plutarchean *De placitis* is first attested in the *De providentia* attributed to Philo. *Hargashah*, meaning (1) sense or faculty, (2) the organ of such sense, and (3) sensation, corresponds well to the Greek *aísthesis*, which shares the same three meanings; see G. W. H. Lampe, *A Patristic Greek Lexicon* (Oxford, 1961), p. 52, with numerous citations. See also Richard Broxton Onians, *The Origins of European Thought about the Body, the Mind, the Soul, the World, Time, and Fate* (Cambridge, 1954), ch. 4.

103. See John T. Noonan, Jr., *Contraception: A History of Its Treatment by the Catholic Theologians and Canonists*, enlarged ed. (Cambridge, Mass., 1986), pp. 46–49, and the representative texts cited there.

104. Philo mentions the seven faculties of the irrational soul, including the five senses (*aisthéseis*), speech, and begetting, which together with reason constitute the human spirit, in *De opificio mundi* 40.117, *Works*, 1:94–95, *Legum allegoria* 1.4.1, 1:152–53, *Quod deterius potiori insidiari soleat* 46.168, 2:312–33, *De agricultura* 7.30, 3:122–23, *Quis rerum divinarum heres* 48.232, 4:398–99, *De mutatione nominum* 19.110, 5:198–99, and *Quaestiones et solutiones in Genesim* 1.75, suppl. 1:44.

their gaping orifices, with nothing to stay their violent rush. For then the mind, swallowed up by the huge inpouring, is found at the bottom, unable so much as to rise to the surface and look out. We ought to employ each one of these faculties, not on all that it is capable of doing but rather on the objects of greatest value. The eye is capable of seeing all colors and forms, but let it see those that are meet for light not for darkness. The ear too is capable of apprehending all uttered words, but some let it refuse to hear, for countless things that are said are disgraceful. And because nature has given you taste, as she has to us all, do not, O senseless one, be like a cormorant and greedily devour all things. . . . And because, with a view to the persistence of the race, you were endowed with generative organs, do not run after rapes and adulteries and other unhallowed forms of intercourse, but only those which are the lawful means of propagating the human race. And because a tongue and a mouth and organs of speech have been allotted to you, do not blurt out all things. . . . So let us make it our earnest endeavor to bind up each of the openings which we have mentioned with the adamantine chains of self-control.[105]

With its penchant for reliance on Philonic and other intertestamental texts, noted and discussed by Abraham Epstein and Samuel Belkin,[106] *Midrash Tadshe'* has thus reformulated Stoic anthropology, but in a decisively rabbinic manner. For unlike *Pirqe dᵉ-R. 'Eliᶜezer,* which expressed a negative view of human sexuality inherited from Greco-Roman times as its own, *Midrash Tadshe'* discarded the Philonic discomfort with matters sexual and physical, and came to view the entire human anatomy in a more positive light. No distinction is drawn between the seat of human intelligence—namely, the heart—and those organs with physical, nonrational functions.[107] Each *hargashah* or sense

105. *Quod deterius potiori insidiari soleat* 27.100–103, 2:268–71, cited by Samuel Belkin, "Midrash Tadshe', 'o Midrash dᶜ-R. Pinḥas b. Ya'ir: Midrash Hellenisti Qadmon," *Horeb* 11 (1951), p. 32.

106. Belkin, loc. cit., pp. 1–52; Epstein's comments on *MTad,* pp. 133–39, and "Le livre des Jubilés, Philon, et le Midrasch Tadsche," *REJ* 21 (1890), 80–97; 22 (1891), 1–25. On the reclamation of intertestamental texts in medieval aggadic works, see Martha Himmelfarb, "R. Moses the Preacher and the Testaments of the Twelve Patriarchs," *AJS Review* 9 (1984), 55–78. On pp. 73ff. Himmelfarb considers the possibility that midrashic compilers like Moses found access to their intertestamental sources in the books of their Christian neighbors. On the transmission of Stoic ideas on the components of the human soul to the church fathers, see Diels, *Doxographi graeci,* pp. 5, 389ff., and von Arnim, *Stoicorum veterum fragmenta,* pp. 225–26. And on the Christian appropriation of Stoic views on procreation (cf. above n. 102), see Noonan, *Contraception,* pts. 1–2.

107. On the function of the heart in the human anatomy, see the aforecited (n. 100) list of organs and limbs in *'Otiyyot de-R. ᶜAqiva': lev lᵉ-havin binah;* Rebekah's aforecited prayer (n. 91) in *MHG;* and the sources cited in Moshe Perlmann, *Midrash ha-Rᵉfu'ah,* 3 vols. (Tel Aviv, 1926–34), 1:20–21.

constitutes the object of specific divine commandments, prescriptions as well as prohibitions, whose fulfillment allows human beings to assume their distinctive station in the order of creation, midway between the creatures of the lower world and those of the upper world. Not only does our text include sexuality in its list of human senses, but mention of the generative organs and the subjection of sexual passion to the rule of divine law actually gives *Midrash Tadshe'* its entrée into the discussion. Considering the various tribal origins of ancient Israelite leaders, the previous paragraph explains that only the tribe of Simeon "produced neither king nor judge on account of the sin of licentiousness. The covenant of circumcision was therefore placed on the genitals (*'erwah*), so that the fear of God would restrain them from sin."[108] The covenantal importance of sexuality, bespoken by the anatomical locus of circumcision, prompts the enumeration of the Mosaic precepts pertaining to all of the key human organs, and the commandment of procreation in Gen. 1:28, along with the subsequent biblical ban on adultery, elaborates the proper expression of human sexual desire. Our verse emerges yet again as defining the distinctively human role in the divine economy of creation.[109]

Other later midrashim joined *Midrash Tadshe'* in upholding the opinion ascribed by *Genesis Rabbah* to R. Tifdai, that procreation—its evidence of mortality and an animal nature notwithstanding—contributed to a human condition that bridged two worlds and was therefore uniquely valuable. According to *Midrash T^ehillim* in its comments on Ps. 8, when the angels protested the divine intention to give the Torah to human beings, asserting that they themselves were more worthy, God responded that they were incapable of performing its commandments. Suggesting a correspondence between Mosaic precepts and the organs of the human body, this midrash likens the angelic petition to a father's desire that his son who lacked a finger learn how to weave. "Thus the holy one, blessed be he, said: 'The Torah cannot be upheld among you; for there is not procreation (*p^eriyyah u-r^eviyyah*) among you, nor impurity, nor death and sickness, but you are entirely holy.'"[110] A late

---

108. *MTad* 8, p. 152; the allusion is to the fornication of Zimri, a notable in the tribe of Simeon, recounted in Num. 25.

109. Similar associations of procreation, circumcision, and the covenant at Sinai appear below in Chapters 3 and 4.

110. *MTeh* 8.2, pp. 37b–38a; cf. the variant of the parable, without reference to procreation in *PesR* 25, p. 128a.

aggadic fragment copied by Solomon Buber from a manuscript of the *Tanḥuma'* amplifies the underlying message of this parable, specifying that the perfection of the Torah befits (and even requires) the imperfection of its human subjects. In this text, God airs his frustration after "the angels were created on the fourth day and the beasts were created on the fifth [*sic!*] day":

> Said the holy one, blessed be he: "I have no satisfaction from these creatures. It is nothing significant if the angels do my will, since they have no evil inclination; and I am not obliged to reward them, since they have only a good inclination. . . . From the beasts too I derive no satisfaction, since they have only an evil inclination and therefore cannot be punished. I shall create a creature, so that both evil and good inclinations will enter him and will struggle against one another. If the good will control the evil, it will be well for him; if the evil will control the good, it will be ill for him."[111]

Finally, Buber's surmise that this pericope derives from the school of Moses the Preacher of Narbonne leads us to *Genesis Rabbati*'s expansion of the homily of R. Tifdai, with which we began.[112]

> R. Yohanan said: Adam was born circumcised, as Scripture states (Gen. 1:27): "And God created man in his image, in the image of God he created him." But why did he not create him in the divine likeness? R. Yohanan said in the name of R. Aha: God, blessed be he, said: "The creatures of the upper world were created in the divine image and likeness, and live eternally, and do not engage in procreation; and creatures of the lower world were not created in the divine image and likeness, and procreate, and die. If I create him like the creatures of the upper world in the divine image and likeness, he will live eternally and not procreate, and I did not create the world except for the purpose of procreation, as Scripture states (Is. 45:18): 'He did not create it a waste, etc.' And if I create him neither in the divine image nor in the divine likeness, [he will engage in procreation and die.][113] Rather, I shall not create him in the likeness of the creatures of the upper world, in order that he will engage in procreation. Yet I shall create him in the image of the creatures of the upper world, so that if he dies, he will live, and if he lives, he will die."[114]

---

111. Parma ms. de Rossi 261, cited by Buber in *TanB*, 1:lxxvib (see also lxxviib); and cf. *SHP* 1957, p. 478. On the superiority of humans over angels, see *LOJ*, 5:66 n. 6.

112. *MBR*, pp. 54–55.

113. Albeck's emendation.

114. For the meaning of this concluding phrase, see above, n. 70.

The similarities and differences between this later pericope and its forerunner in *Genesis Rabbah* are equally instructive. Like the earlier tradition, *Genesis Rabbati* adduces its thoughts on the bridging of two worlds in response to Gen. 1:27. And like R. Tifdai, R. Yohanan attributes his answer to R. Aha, blending the themes of both of Tifdai's homilies in *Genesis Rabbah*—the oxymoronic combination of the divine image and procreation in human beings, and the singular human capacity to merit either reward (life) or punishment (death). In *Genesis Rabbati*, however, the biblical stimulus is not the juxtaposition of the divine image and sexuality in humans, but the verse's ostensive specification that God created man only in his image and not in his likeness.[115] Responding to his own exegetical question, R. Yohanan ascribes to R. Aha the consideration that no creature embodying both the image and the likeness of God could bear children. Because God undertook his creation for the sake of procreation, he therefore formed Adam in his image but not in his likeness, so that humans might both procreate and merit eternal life. R. Yohanan also introduces his gloss on Gen. 1:27 with the assertion that Adam was born without a foreskin, which testified to the divine image within him; this tradition appears in several earlier aggadic texts, in two of which the godliness bespoken by circumcision was reflected in exemplary sexual behavior.[116]

The qualitative distinction between divine image and likeness, as well as that between angelic immortality and the immortality of the first parents, may well manifest Christian influences on the school of Moses the Preacher. Presently, however, our text from *Genesis Rabbati* offers an appropriate summation to this unit in our discussion. Conceding that angelic immortality and human sexuality are physically and metaphysically incompatible, *Genesis Rabbati* still echoes the sentiments of R. Tifdai in *Genesis Rabbah*, opposing the quasi-Gnostic message implicit in *Pirqe de-R. 'Eli'ezer*. As in *Midrash Tadshe'*, the proper channeling of sexual energies epitomizes the covenant between God and Israel, appropriately signified by the generative organ itself. The procreation enjoined in Gen. 1:28 here emerges in a markedly positive light, providing all of God's creation with its rationale and combining with the image of God to determine the essence of human nature and of human potential.

---

115. Contra Gen. 5:1, cited in *MBR*, p. 57.

116. In *ARNA*, ch. 2, p. 6b, Job's sexual morality testifies to his unusual congenital state; and in *Tan.* (*Noah* 5), p. 5a, the same condition accords with Noah's steadfast refusal to participate in the perversions of his contemporaries. See also *MTeh* 9.7, pp. 42b–43a.

Power and Dominion. Beyond its instructions to bear children and fill the earth, Gen. 1:28 also contributed to rabbinic perceptions of human nature with its enthronement of the first parents over the rest of the animal kingdom. While modern Jewish writers have strenuously denied that their classical rabbinic predecessors construed this dominion as a license to exploit the natural environment selfishly and irresponsibly,[117] the midrashic elaborations on the precise meaning of the divine bequest in Gen. 1:28b are few. Most ancient and medieval religious thinkers concurred that God had fashioned the world expressly for human use and sustenance,[118] and the second half of our verse evidently required much less homiletic interpretation than the first. According to one manuscript tradition of *Genesis Rabbah,* when Gen. 2:19 reports God's creation (using the term *wa-yiẓer*) of the animals for the second time, it refers to their subjection to Adam's rule; in the terminology of Gen. 1:28 the midrash concludes: "Above [the Torah reported (Gen. 1:24) their] creation, and here [it reports their] domination (*kibbush*)."[119] Embellishing an Amoraic tradition, *Midrash Tᵉhillim* records that the lion, ox, and eagle rule proudly over wild beasts, livestock, and birds, respectively. "And who takes pride in his rule over them all? Man, as Scripture states (Gen. 1:26): 'They shall rule the fish of the sea, the birds of the sky. . . .'"[120] Citing Gen. 1:28 and 9:2, *Midrash Tan-*

---

117. Among others, see Robert Gordis, "Ecology in the Jewish Tradition," *Midstream* 31 (October 1985), 19–23; Norman Lamm, *Faith and Doubt: Studies in Traditional Jewish Thought* (New York, 1971), pp. 162–85; Norman H. Bronsnick, "From the Language of the Talmud to That of the Bible" (Hebrew), *Beth Mikra* 29 (1983), 37–41; and Eric G. Freudenstein, "Ecology and the Jewish Tradition," *Judaism* 19 (1970), 406–14.

118. See Jobl., diss., esp. ch. 1; and *LOJ,* 5:67–68 n. 8. Among many similar rabbinic statements, see *GenR* 8.6 (ad 1:26), 1:60–61, and *MHG,* 1:26. The anthropocentric view of the cosmos was maintained by Saadya b. Joseph, *Sefer ha-Nivḥar ba-'Emunot wᵉha-Deʿot (Ha-'Emunot wᵉha-Deʿot)* 4.intr., ed. Joseph Kafaḥ (Jerusalem, 1970), pp. 150–51, and Bahya b. Joseph ibn Paquda, *Sefer Torat Ḥovot ha-Lᵉvavot* 2.5, 3.9, ed. Joseph Kafaḥ (Jerusalem, 1973), pp. 107, 176, but it found opposition in the works of Moses ben Maimon, *Guide of the Perplexed* 3.13–14, tr. Shlomo Pines (Chicago, 1963), pp. 448–59, and of Abraham ibn Ezra, *Perushe ha-Torah,* 1:7–8.

119. *GenR* 17.4 (ad 2:19), 1:155 and n. 8. Cf. RaSh"I ad Gen. 2:19, p. 6, who explains why this homily sees fit to cite Deut. 20:19: "creation (*yeẓirah*) is a term for domination (*ridduy*) and subjugation (*kibbush*), as in 'when in your war against a city you have to besiege (*taẓur*) it a long time in order to capture it.'" In connection with Adam's naming of the animals in Gen. 2:19–20, some explained that the Bible mentioned only animals and birds but not fish, because the latter did not fall under human dominion (contra Gen. 1:28); see the interesting discussion of Kasher, 2:239 n. 265. On naming the animals as an expression of dominion, see Jobl., diss., pp. 167–68, 182–83.

120. *MTeh* 103.16, p. 219a. See parallels in *Lekach-Tob,* 1:8a; and in TB *Ḥag.* 13b, *SSR* 3.19 (ad 3:10), p. 96, *TanB (Bᵉ-Shallaḥ* 14), 3:31a, *ExR* 23.13 (without the quotation from Gen. 1), and *Yalquṭ Shimʿoni ʿal ha-Torah* 243, 2,1:314.

ḥuma' similarly rationalizes human dominion with an earlier aggadah on how the prelapsarian Adam filled the entire world.[121] The Palestinian Targum of Pseudo-Jonathan translates "and master it (*wᵉ-khivshuha*)" as "and rule over it with possessions (*u-tᵉqufu ʿalah bᵉ-nikhsin*)," hinting that dominion over the earth involves its development with the tools and fruits of human creativity.[122] And *Midrash 'Aggadah* explains that human dominion over nature derived from the intellectual capability to acknowledge God; "therefore he [God] gave him [man] the ability to govern his creatures."[123] On the other hand, several aggadic sources do relate that Adam had to labor even before his fall from Eden,[124] and the Babylonian Gemara rejects an earlier opinion that Gen. 1:28b entitled human beings to kill other creatures for food.[125]

Several rabbinic homilies maintain that God linked his grant of dominion in Gen. 1:28 to the good and obedient behavior of its human recipients. In a passage from *Genesis Rabbah* quoted above, R. Hanina proclaims that while a meritorious human would rule the animals, the sinful human would be ruled; R. Jacob of Kfar Hanan proceeds to define the qualification for dominion as conformity to the divine image.[126] Attesting to the creation of humans on the borderline between the upper and lower worlds, as well as to their singular ability to deserve a heavenly reward, numerous traditions conclude that the truly righteous need have no fear of harmful creatures. For instance, "a noxious animal does not rule over a man unless he appears to it like a beast";[127] and, by

---

121. *TanB* (*Tazriaʿ* 10), 4:19a, *Tan.* (*Tazriaʿ* 8), p. 59b; for the earlier descriptions of Adam's global dimensions, see TB *Hag.* 12a, *San.* 38ab, *GenR* 8.1 (ad 1:26), 1:55–56, and *LevR* 18.2 (ad 15:2), 2:400–401.

122. *Targum Jonathan b. Uziel*, p. 2. Cf. *Targum du Pentateuque*, tr. Roger le Déaut, 5 vols., Sources chrétiennes 245, 256, 261, 271, 282 (Paris, 1978–81), 1:83: "devenez-y puissants en possessions." Pointing to Pseudo-Jonathan's translation (*Targum Jonathan b. Uziel*, p. 38) of Gen. 26:16 (*ʿazamta mimmennu*), Bronsnick, "From the Language," p. 39, paraphrases: *lᵉ-hishtaleṭ ʿaleha bᵉ-haʿasharat ha-'areẓ bᵉ-ribbuy nᵉkhasim*." Etan Levine, in his appendix to *Neofiti 1*, 2:544, asserts that this marks a polemical response to the Christian antimaterialism of the kind addressed in Mt. 6:19–20.

123. *MAgg*, p. 7.

124. E.g., *ARNA* 11, p. 23a; *ARNB* 21, p. 22b; *SifD* 41, p. 87; *GenR* 16.5 (ad 2:15), 1:149; and the references cited by Etan Levine in his appendix to *Neofiti 1*, 2:545 (ad 2:15).

125. TB *San.* 59b. On the question of whether antediluvian humans were permitted to eat meat at all—our verse notwithstanding—see the citations and lengthy analysis in Kasher, 1:169–72 nn. 808–11.

126. *GenR* 8.12 (ad 1:28), 1:65; see above, nn. 72–74, with the additional references cited there.

127. TB *San.* 38b; and *Sab.* 151b, with the comments of Samuel Edels, *Ḥiddushe 'Aggadot* ad loc., s.v. *nimshal*.

the same token, the animals will pay homage to the image of God in you "when you observe the precepts of the Torah."[128] According to *Midrash Tanḥuma'*, God stipulated very clearly to Adam himself: "If you are meritorious, I shall make you king over the creatures of the lower world just as I am king over the creatures of the upper world."[129]

Somewhat more complicated is the question of whether Adam and Eve, in the wake of their fall from paradise, lost the blessings granted them by God in Gen. 1:28. Rabbinic opinion tended to resist the post-biblical notion, evident in Jewish texts of the intertestamental period as well as in Christian sources, that the disobedience of the first parents in paradise irrevocably corrupted the human condition, leading to a sinful nature and mortality that otherwise would not have been.[130] Still, the aggadic imagination could not resist setting to work on the condemnation and punishment of Adam and Eve in Gen. 3:16–19. The resulting midrashic traditions seldom quote Gen. 1:28, but like the divine decrees in Gen. 3 they interpret the punishments imposed on the first parents as bearing directly on both components of our verse's instruction: the bearing of children, and the control of the natural environment.[131] Of the two recurring types of homilies we shall cite, one departed from the word *tolᵉdot* (meaning annals or progeny, here spelled *twldwt*) in Gen. 2:4:[132]

Every time *tolᵉdot* appears in Scripture, it is written defectively (*tldwt*), with two exceptions: "This is the line (*tolᵉdot*) of Perez (Ruth 4:18),"

---

128. *DtR*, p. 93, the roots of whose lesson are already evident in the pseudepigraphic Apocalypse of Moses 10:1–3, *OTP*, 2:273. Cf. also *SifD* 50, p. 115; *Neofiti 1* ad Gen. 3:15, 1:17, with the parallels cited by Etan Levine, 2:545–46; *PRK*, 1:84; *Agadath Bereschith* 15.1, pp. 32–33. Many parallels in Jewish, Greco-Roman, and Christian sources are cited and discussed by Jobl., diss., ch. 3; and by Ginzberg, in *LOJ*, 5:119–20 n. 113, and *Haggada*, pp. 80–81.

129. *TanB* (*Bᵉ-ḥuqqotai 5*), 4:55b. On the philosophical ramifications of the notion that the truly righteous wield dominion over nature, see Aviezer Ravitsky, "The Anthropological Theory of Miracles in Medieval Jewish Philosophy," in *Studies in Medieval Jewish History and Literature*, ed. Isadore Twersky, 2 (Cambridge, Mass., 1984), 231–72.

130. Among many studies pertinent to this complex issue, see Samuel S. Cohon, "Original Sin," *HUCA* 21 (1948), 275–330, and Jeremy Cohen, "Original Sin as the Evil Inclination—A Polemicist's Appreciation of Human Nature," *HTR* 73 (1980), 495–520, together with the numerous sources cited in the notes therein.

131. See above, nn. 87–88, for the sources debating whether sexual intercourse actually occurred in paradise. For the view that it did not, the mandate of procreation—i.e., the blessing of Gen. 1:28—became relevant only after the fall!

132. *GenR* 12.6 (ad 2:4), 1:101–2, 104; cf. the many parallels and variants listed in the notes ad loc. and in Kasher, 2:195–96 n. 69.

and this one. And why are they spelled defectively (*ḥaserin*)? R. Yudan
[said] in the name of R. Avun: [They are missing, i.e., *ḥaserin*] six (the
numerical value of the missing *w*), corresponding to six things taken
from Adam [upon his fall]: his radiance, his immortality, his stature,
the fruit of the ground, the fruit of the tree, and the [light of the]
heavenly luminaries. . . . R. Berekhiah [said] in the name of Samuel:
Even though the following were created[133] in their full perfection (*'al
mᵉle'atan*), when Adam sinned they were corrupted, and will not return
to their full perfection until the descendant of Perez (i.e., the messiah)
arrives—his radiance, his immortality, his stature, the fruit of the
ground, the fruit of the tree, and the [light of the] heavenly luminaries.
[Scripture states:] "This is the line [*tolᵉdot*] of Perez (Ruth 4:18)," with
tolᵉdot in its full [spelling] (*male'*).

A second type of homily lists the decrees of God against Adam and Eve,
grouped in numerically equivalent sets:

On that very day [of creation and fall] three decrees were imposed on
Adam, as Scripture states (Gen. 3:17–18): "To Adam he said: 'Because
you did as your wife said, etc., cursed be the ground because of you, by
toil shall you eat of it, etc., thorns and thistles shall it sprout for you. But
your food shall be the grasses of the field.'" When Adam heard that the
holy one, blessed be he, told him, "but your food shall be the grasses of
the field," his limbs were overcome with fright. He said to him: "Master of the universe, shall I and my beast eat of the same trough?" The
holy one, blessed be he, said to him: "Because your limbs were overcome with fright, 'by the sweat of your brow shall you get bread to eat'
(Gen. 3:19)." And just as three decrees were imposed on Adam, so three
decrees were imposed on Eve. "And to the woman he said: 'I will make
most severe (*harbah 'arbeh*) your pangs in childbearing; in pain shall you
bear children. Yet your urge shall be for your husband, and he shall rule
over you' (Gen. 3:16)." *harbah*—When a woman starts to bleed at the
beginning of her period, it is difficult for her. *'arbeh*—When a woman
engages in sexual intercourse, the beginning of coitus is difficult for her.
"Your pangs in childbearing"—When a woman is pregnant her face is
ugly and pale for all of the first three months.[134]

The numbers and particulars of the punishments inflicted on the first
parents vary from source to source, and each decree could provide the

133. Heb. *she-ne'emru dᵉvarim,* explained by Theodor as the divine commands of the
cosmogony.
134. *ARNA* 1, pp. 3b–4a.

basis for extensive discussion.[135] Yet these homilies and their parallels in other texts share a basic message: Owing to sin, Adam forfeited the human attributes that contributed to his primacy in the natural order as well as to the responsiveness of that natural order to his needs and desires. Instead of ruling the animals, Adam descended to their status,[136] and he now was subjected to their domination and power.[137] For Eve, the sexual process of reproduction was no longer an unmitigated blessing but a source of anguish and pain.[138]

Like the fathers of the Christian church, many classical rabbis maintained that the punishments that accompanied the fall would be lifted with the onset of messianic salvation—witness the first pericope quoted in the preceding paragraph. Nevertheless, several noteworthy aggadic themes serve to differentiate rabbinic views on the postlapsarian validity of Gen. 1:28 and its blessings from the predominant sentiments of patristic writers. For the rabbis, the punishments inflicted upon Adam and Eve did not make the event of their fall from a blessed state *sui generis*, but the sins of subsequent generations also worsened various aspects of the human condition, some of which must await the messianic era for their repair.[139] Moreover, rabbinic teaching allowed for the possibility that postlapsarian humans might enjoy various dimensions of the primordial state in which God had created the first parents. Inferring from Gen. 9:1 that God restored the blessing of "be fertile and increase" to Noah, *Genesis Rabbah* next deduces from Gen. 9:2: " 'The fear and dread of you, etc.' Fear and dread returned, but dominion (*rᵉdayyah*) did not return. When did it return? In the days of Solomon,

135. See Kasher, 2:279 n. 151, and *LOJ*, 5:100–103 nn. 83–92. In some sources (*ARNB* 42, p. 59a; *PDRE*, ch. 14, 9:110), even the serpent and the earth receive equal numbers of decrees.

136. For the motif of Adam and the beast eating of the same trough, see also *Neofiti 1* ad Gen. 3:18, 1:17, TB *Pes.* 118a, *GenR* 20.10 (ad 3:18), 1:194, *MHG* 1:107–108, and the additional parallels cited by Theodor in the notes ad *GenR* loc. cit. In *ARN*, *Neofiti 1*, and *MHG*, God's substitution of toil for the decree of eating grass is construed as a consolation, but TB *Pes.* and *GenR* deem it a more severe punishment.

137. E.g., *ARNB* 42, p. 59a; *SSR*, p. 70; *MBR*, p. 51; *MHG* 1:98; and numerous other parallels, including intertestamental and Christian sources, cited in *LOJ*, 5:119–20 n. 113. On this point, however, early rabbinic opinion also included the view that animals will still fear any living human, however small or defenseless; see T *Sab.* 17(18).19, ed. Saul Lieberman, 4 vols. (New York, 1955–73), 2:84, *GenR* 34.12 (ad 9:2), 1:323–24, and Kasher, 2:459 n. 6.

138. An additional list of Eve's (ten) curses appears in TB *Eruv.* 100b. The standard editions of *Pirqe dᵉ-R. 'Eliᶜezer*, ch. 14, record that Adam was reduced in strength and stature as a result of his sexual impurity (but not the edition of Higger, 9:111, which simply lists sexual impurity among Adam's punishments); cf. *MHG*, 1:106.

139. *LOJ*, 5:113–14 n. 105. With regard to the blessings of Gen. 1:28 in particular, see the texts cited below in this paragraph.

'for he controlled (*rodeh*) the whole region west of the Euphrates (1 Kings 5:4).'"[140] Finally, some rabbis maintained that the primordial blessing of Gen. 1:28 was simply the first in a series of divine benedictions, without which the world and its economy of salvation could not have been maintained. Drawing on earlier sources, *Midrash ha-Gadol* records the following homily to elaborate on Gen. 25:11, "God blessed his son Isaac":[141]

> Why did he bless him? For at the time when the holy one, blessed be he, created his world and created man within it, he [man] said: "The world cannot survive without a blessing." The holy one, blessed be he, revealed himself to him and blessed him, as Scripture states (Gen. 1:28), "And God blessed them." And the world was maintained by that blessing until the generation of the flood came and behaved perversely, and the blessing was taken from them and they were wiped out. And when Noah and his sons left the ark the holy one, blessed be he, restored the blessing to them, as Scripture states (Gen. 9:1), "God blessed Noah and his sons." And the entire world was maintained by that blessing until the generation of the Tower of Babel[142] came and, standing defiantly, sought to ascend into heaven, when the blessing was removed from them and [God] scattered their council in every direction. Then said the holy one, blessed be he: "It is pointless for me to bless my world by myself; for from within the framework of my blessing, they rebel and remove the yoke of heaven from upon themselves. Rather, I hereby transfer the blessing to Abraham and his progeny; him whom blessing befits they shall bless, and him whom imprecation befits they shall curse, and I agree on their behalf, as Scripture states: 'I will bless those who bless you and curse him who curses you.'" When it came time for Abraham to depart from the world, he said: "My son Isaac is worthy of blessing, but I cannot bless him lest Ishmael be jealous of him. Rather, I shall leave the matter unresolved, and the holy one, blessed be he, will bless him whom he deems worthy." When Abraham died, the holy one, blessed be he, revealed himself to Isaac and blessed him, as Scripture states (Gen. 25:11): "God blessed Isaac." He thereby

---

140. *GenR* 34.12 (ad 9:1–2), 1:323; cf. *PRK*, 1:84: "so long as Solomon did not sin, he ruled (*hayah rodeh*) over male and female demons."

141. *MHG*, 1:422–23. The earliest extant version of this aggadah appears in *PRK*, which cites Gen. 5:2, although some mss. do cite Gen. 1:28, as do *TanB* (B^erakhah 1), 6:27a—cf. also (*Lekh L^ekha* 5), 2:32a—and *Tan.* (B^erakhah 1), p. 104ab—cf. also (*Lekh l^ekha* 4), p. 7b, (*Naso'* 9), p. 74b. Without reference to Gen. 1:28, *TanB* (Q^edoshim 7), 4:38ab, depicts the willingness of the earth to bear fruit as having vacillated repeatedly since the creation, depending on the spiritual merits of its inhabitants.

142. Heb., *dor haflagah*.

restored the blessing to its rightful place. And Isaac blessed Jacob . . . , and Jacob blessed his sons . . . , and the blessing remained with them permanently."

Just as it did in Scripture, Gen. 1:28 here defines the human condition, and without its blessing the natural order could not endure. Yet in the reiteration of this blessing first to Noah and then exclusively to the Hebrew patriarchs, in its denial to Ishmael, and in the relegation of its conferral to Abraham as the exemplar of divine election, our verse also epitomizes God's covenant with his chosen people. In this homily as in many others, Gen. 1:28 endows human beings with fertility and power, but it also directs them toward that end for which God created and maintains his world.

Between Human and God

As an expression of covenant, Gen. 1:28 entails both divine commitment and human responsibility. Rabbinic homilists therefore approached the verse as a window to both dimensions of the bilateral relationship between God and his human creatures. The verse defines human nature, as we have seen, but it revealed to preachers the charitable manner in which God had endowed the first parents with their singular assets. Furthermore, it dictated the means whereby human beings might fulfill their divinely ordained role in the order of creation, ultimately entitling them to the final reward of salvation.

Divine Blessing and Grace. In addition to the themes of procreation and dominion in Gen. 1:28, the rabbis focused their attention on our verse's narrative introduction, "God blessed them," which elicited aggadic discussion on a number of subjects. According to one tradition, these words rationalize the Mishnaic prescription that a widow remarry on Thursday (or Thursday evening); she would first join with her husband that night—technically already Friday—in the hope that the primordial blessing of the sixth day of creation would become theirs.[143] Substituting Gen. 1:28 for a prophetic verse, *Midrash T'hillim* reformulates an old Amoraic adage: "Anyone who has no wife lives without blessing, as Scripture states, 'God blessed them'—'them' [meaning]

---

143. M *Ket.* 1.1; TJ ibid., 24d; TB ibid., 5a; *GenR* 8.12 (ad 1:28), 1:66 (with notes).

when they are a couple."[144] *Midrash Tadshe'* questions why Scripture singles out certain creatures for blessing—fish, birds, and humans—while omitting others. "Why was a blessing not stated for the land animals as one was stated for the creatures of the sea? Because of the future evil of the serpent [for which] he would be worthy of imprecation—had the holy one, blessed be he, blessed him, he then could not have cursed him."[145] Particularly intriguing, however, is the reflection of *Genesis Rabbah* on the divine blessing of the first parents:

> R. Avahu said: The holy one, blessed be he, took a cup of blessing (*kos shel berakhah*) and blessed them. R. Judah the son of R. Simon said: Michael and Gabriel were Adam's groomsmen. R. Simlai said: We find that the holy one, blessed be he, blesses bridegrooms, adorns brides, visits sick persons, buries dead people, and offers the blessing for mourners. He blesses bridegrooms, as it is written, "God blessed them. . . ." R. Samuel b. Nahman said: He even appears to the mourner, as it is written (Gen. 35:9, following the death of Rebekah's nurse Deborah), "God appeared again to Jacob on his arrival from Paddan-Aram, and he blessed him." What blessing did he offer him? The blessing for mourners.[146]

The opening clause of Gen. 1:28 here evokes an image of God performing exemplary acts of piety and charity (*gemilut ḥasadim*), especially in the celebration of the primordial wedding, presumably in order to inspire humans to the same mode of behavior. Taking the cup of blessing, which in rabbinic terminology refers to the nuptial blessings most infrequently,[147] here in *Genesis Rabbah* clearly denotes *birkat ḥatanim*, the benedictions recited at the wedding banquet. One manuscript of *Genesis Rabbah* adds to R. Avahu's statement that God blessed them with "seven benedictions in the verse, and the sages proceeded to ordain [the seven benedictions of the nuptial feast] on the basis of their example."[148] This interpolation is perhaps based on a tradition recorded

144. *MTeh* 59.2, p. 151ab; TB *Yev.* 62b, *GenR* 17.2 (ad 2:18), 1:151–52, and *EcclR* 9.7 quote Ezek. 44:30 instead of Gen. 1:28. See also Samson Itzchaky et al., "Fertility in Jewish Tradition (Ethno-Medical and Folkloric Aspects)," *Koroth* 9 (1985), 122–35.

145. *MTad* 1, p. 144. The question is also posed: "Why did Scripture not include [the blessing of] "be fertile and increase" in the creation of the heavenly luminaries? For they do not need to procreate like mortal creatures, but they remain just as they were created; they do not diminish nor do they increase." Cf. also *MAgg*, pp. 3–4.

146. *GenR* 8.13 (ad 1:28), 1:66–67.

147. *ET*, 18:181, s.v. *kos shel berakhah*.

148. *GenR*, 1:66–67nn.

in *Midrash Tadshe'*, which reckons in Gen. 1:28 seven of the ten blessings given by God to Adam upon his creation.[149] Although this evidence for a stated link between our verse and the sevenfold nuptial
liturgy undoubtedly postdates the institution of the "seven benedictions," the understanding of Gen. 1:28 as prefiguring the nuptial rite
appears in the minor tractate *Kallah Rabbati:*[150]

> How are the nuptial benedictions (*birkat hatanim*) derived from Scrip-
> ture? Scripture states (Gen. 24:60): "And they blessed Rebekah." But
> did they bless her over a cup of wine? This is only supporting evidence
> (*'asmakhta'*, i.e., but not conclusive proof).[151] R. Yohanan said: It is
> derived from "God blessed them and God said to them, 'Be fertile and
> increase (Gen. 1:28).'" How, then, can one explain that it is also written
> concerning the animals, "God blessed them (Gen. 1:22)." Rather, it is
> because it is written (Gen. 2:22), "and the Lord God fashioned (*wa-
> yiven*, from *bnh*) the rib [. . . and he brought her to the man]"; for it has
> been taught that in the coastal towns they call *q^eli^cata'* (from *ql^c*, to
> adorn) *binyata'* (veils).

Although Gen. 2 makes no explicit mention of a blessing recited over
wine, the creation of a wife for Adam, complete with its rationalization
of matrimony (Gen. 2:18–24), evidently demonstrated that God had
ordained the wedding ceremony in his own primordial actions. Ante-
dating the late Amoraic or early geonic *Kallah Rabbati*, the midrashic
understanding of *bnh* as bedecking the bride appears with varying
attributions in both Talmuds and in various midrashic works, sometimes with enumerations of the many wedding canopies fashioned by
God for the first parents. In two instances, the Babylonian Talmud
interprets Gen. 2:22 to demonstrate also that "the holy one, blessed be
he, served as a groomsman to Adam," and this in turn leads the Talmud
to the presumed message of our text in *Genesis Rabbah:* "Here the Torah
teaches proper behavior, that the greater man should minister to the
lesser man as a groomsman, and it should not vex him."[152] While the

149. *MTad* 5, pp. 147–48. Cf. *MBR*, p. 55, which counts eight blessings in Gen. 1:28 and
two in Gen. 1:29–30.

150. *Kallah Rabbati* 1.2, in *Masekhtot Kallah*, ed. Michael Higger (Brooklyn, N.Y., 1936),
p. 173. See Nahman Neta Coronil, "Hitnazlut," *Ha-Maggid* 9:31 (August 9, 1865), 246.

151. The absence of a cup notwithstanding, the example of Rebekah lived on as the
scriptural foundation for *birkat hatanim*. Within several centuries, cantorial formality and even
a cup of wine had entered aggadic descriptions of Rebekah's wedding; see *PDRE*, ch. 16,
9:116, and the ms. cited by Kasher, 4:987 n. 244.

152. TB *Ber.* 61a, *Eruv.* 18b. The same midrash on *ql^c/bnh* appears in TJ *Sab.* 10.7, 12c, TB

talmudic pericope does not refer to Gen. 1:28, it does make clear that the adornment of Eve entailed God's formation of her body to facilitate the birth of children. R. Simlai's aforecited list of charitable deeds exemplified in the actions of God also appears in the Palestinian Targum, which interprets God's blessing of Jacob (Gen. 35:9) after Deborah's death as the blessing of mourners and which in several manuscripts includes a citation of Gen. 1:28.[153] Interweaving many of these earlier motifs, *Pirqe d^e-R. 'Eli^cezer* eventually offers the most elaborate description of the primordial wedding:[154]

> The holy one, blessed be he, made ten wedding canopies for Adam in the Garden of Eden, all of precious stones, pearls, and gold. Even though for a normal groom there is merely one wedding canopy, and for a king there are three wedding canopies, to confer honor on Adam the holy one, blessed be he, made him ten wedding canopies in the Garden of Eden, as Scripture states (Ezek. 28:13): "You were in Eden, the garden of God; every precious stone [was your adornment: carnelian, chrysolite, and amethyst; beryl, lapis lazuli, and jasper; sapphire, turquoise, and emerald; and gold], etc."—these are ten wedding canopies. And the angels (*ha-mal'akhim*) were beating on drums (*tuppim*) and dancing like maidens (*n^eqevot*),[155] [as Scripture states (ibid.)]: "the workmanship (*m^ele'khet*) of your settings (*tuppekha*) and sockets (*n^e-qavekha*) was in you."[156] And this was on the day that Adam was created, as Scripture states (ibid.): "prepared the day you were created." The holy one, blessed be he, said to the ministering angels: "Come and let us render kindness to Adam and his spouse; for on the basis of rendering kindness (*g^emilut ḥasadim*) the world survives." Said the holy one, blessed be he: "Rendering kindness is more pleasing than the sacrifices and burnt offerings which the Jews will in the future offer to me on the altar, as Scripture states (Hos. 6:6): "For I desire goodness, not sacrifice." And the ministering angels were parading like grooms-

Nid. 45b, TB *Sab.* 95a, and *GenR* 18.1 (ad 2:22), 1:160–61. Other parallels and explanations of the various reckonings of wedding canopies, which derived from different interpretations of Ezek. 28:13, are cited and discussed in the notes to *GenR* ad loc. On the significance of multiple wedding canopies, see Adolph Büchler, "Das Ausgiessen von Wein und Öl als Ehrung bei den Juden," *MGWJ* 49 (1905), 18–19.

153. *Neofiti 1*, 1:235; *Fragment-Targums*, 1:59–60, 148. See also the comments of Mordechai Akiva Friedman, *Jewish Marriage in Palestine: A Cairo Genizah Study*, 2 vols. (Tel Aviv, 1980–81), 1:90.

154. *PDRE*, ch. 11, 9:103–104 (ch. 12 in standard eds.); cf. also ch. 16, 9:114. I have followed those ms. variants adhering most closely to the printed text; exceptions, as well as instances where variants involve substantive changes, are noted.

155. Following printed versions and David Luria (vs. *b^e-niqvim* in Higger's ms.).

156. On basis of OJPS; NJPS does not allow for midrashic puns in *PDRE*.

men[157] tending (*ha-m*ᵉ*shamm*ᵉ*rim*) to the wedding canopies, as Scripture states (Ps. 91:11): "For he will order his angels to guard you (*lishmorkha*) wherever you go (*b*ᵉ-*khol d*ᵉ*rakhekha;* lit., all of your paths)." And "your paths (*d*ᵉ*rakhekha*)" cannot but mean the way of bridegrooms. [And the holy one, blessed be he,][158] was like a cantor;[159] just as a cantor tends to stand and bless the bride under her wedding canopy, so the holy one, blessed be he, stood and blessed Adam and his spouse, as Scripture states (Gen. 1:28): "God blessed them."

Gen. 1:28 brings this portrait of the primordial wedding feast to its climax. Having erected numerous and resplendent wedding canopies, God and his angels extend themselves to the first parents in the ultimate expression of gratuitous kindness—ministering to their subordinates as bridesmaids and groomsmen. The ceremony does not conclude until God himself raises the cup of blessing and like a cantor pronounces the nuptial benedictions. Our verse thus embodies the divine blessing par excellence. But in alluding to the sacrificial cult, this aggadic text makes explicit what R. Avahu, R. Judah the son of R. Simon, and R. Simlai reportedly implied above. Acknowledging the bounteous grace bestowed on their progenitors, human beings must in turn contribute to the maintenance and perfection of the divine creation. This too the rabbis perceived within the message of Gen. 1:28.

Promoting the Image of God. In one of the oldest rabbinic traditions that has relevance to our discussion, the Tannaitic sages of Yavneh, presumably at the beginning of the second century, exchange their views on the relative importance of two Mosaic precepts: the mandate for procreation, and the ban on murder. While the conversation admittedly derives from issues of a halakhic nature, the views expressed have no legal consequences per se, and their primary concern is the theological lesson of Scripture in its juxtaposition of several key verses. We therefore include the tradition in this chapter on the Aggadah, and we quote its earliest attestable version, following Saul Lieberman's reconstruction of the text of the Tosefta.[160]

---

157. Following printed versions and David Luria (vs. *ro'im* in Higger's ms.).

158. Following David Luria, who emends on the basis of *Menorat ha-Ma'or* and *Yalqut ha-Makhiri.*

159. Some mss. read *ḥatan*, bridegroom, but since this character is compared to God blessing Adam as well as Eve, *ḥazzan* is more likely correct; cf. *PDRE*'s similar analogy with reference to the betrothal of Rebekah, ch. 16, 9:116, where all mss. read *ḥazzan.*

160. T *Yev.* 8.7, ed. Lieberman, 3:26.

(A) R. Akiva says: Anyone who commits murder nullifies the image of God (d*e*mut), as Scripture states (Gen. 9:6), "Whoever sheds the blood of man, by man shall his blood be shed[; for in his image (*z*elem) did God make man]." (B) R. Eleazar b. Azariah says: Anyone who does not engage in procreation[161] nullifies the image of God, as Scripture states (ibid.), "for in his image did God make man"; and it is written (Gen. 9:7), "Be fertile, then, and increase." (C) Ben Azzai says: Anyone who does not engage in procreation commits murder and nullifies the image of God, as Scripture states (ibid.), "[Whoever sheds the blood of man, by man shall his blood be shed;] for in his image did God make man"; and it is written (Gen. 9:7), "Be fertile, then, and increase." (D) R. Eleazar b. Azariah said to him: "Ben Azzai, instruction is edifying when preached by those who practice it; some, however, preach well but do not act properly, while others act properly but do not preach well.[162] Ben Azzai preaches well but does not act properly." (E) Ben Azzai said to him: "What shall I do? My soul craves the Torah; so let the world endure through the efforts of others."

The Palestinian *Genesis Rabbah* recounts this conversation with only minor variations.[163] Babylonian records of the same discussion replace R. Akiva's opening statement (A) with R. Eliezer's view (A'): "Anyone who does not engage in procreation commits murder, as Scripture states: 'Whoever sheds the blood of man, by man shall his blood be shed'; and it is written (Gen. 9:7), 'Be fertile, then, and increase.'"[164] The Babylonian texts also attribute Eleazar's reproof of Ben Azzai (D) to both of the latter's interlocutors, and some attribute to R. Akiva the equation of the failure to procreate and diminishing the divine image (B).[165] Later medieval texts blended elements of Palestinian and Babylonian traditions.[166]

The Yavnean provenance of all the discussants makes it plausible that such an exchange of views did occur during the Yavnean period,[167] that

---

161. Omitting "commits murder and," dittography from R. Akiva's statement above or Ben Azzai's below; see Lieberman's nn. 31–32, and the comments in his *Tosefta ki-Fshutah: A Comprehensive Commentary on the Tosefta* (Hebrew), 8 vols. (New York, 1955–73), 6:75.

162. Cf. TB *Hag.* 14b, where the Yavnean R. Yohanan b. Zakkai adduces this maxim in praise of his disciple R. Eleazar b. Arakh, who evidently did act and preach properly.

163. *GenR* 34.14 (ad 9:6), 1:326–27.

164. TB *Yev.* 63b (which records two versions of this *baraita*'); Sh*e*'iltot 5, ed. Mirsky, 1:35–36. See also *Yalquṭ Shim'oni 'al ha-Torah* 61, 1,1:212, which follows the Babylonian tradition.

165. Sh*e*'iltot, ed. Mirsky, loc. cit., and cf. *Yalquṭ*, loc. cit.; the first version of the *baraita*' in TB *Yev.* 63b ascribes this view to R. Jacob (an Ushan Tanna)—probably a scribal error, reading y'qb for 'qyb'.

166. *MHG*, 1:184–85; Samuel b. Nissim, *Midrash B*e*reshit Zuṭa*', pp. 35–36.

167. Cf. Mirsky's observation in Sh*e*'iltot, 1:35–36n.

the sages involved agreed on the fundamental importance of procreation as a religious duty, and that they disagreed merely on the exegetical basis for that importance. The analogy between the failure to procreate and the commission of murder, attributed (C) to Ben Azzai—and in the Babylonian tradition (A') to R. Eliezer as well—reasons that in remaining childless an individual deprives others of life that is rightfully theirs. The notion of nullifying (or diminishing) the image of God is related and is best explained by another Tannaitic homily in the M^ekhilta' of R. Ishmael:[168]

> How were the Ten Commandments given? Five on one tablet and five on the other. Inasmuch as it is written (Ex. 20:2) "I am the Lord your God," and opposite it (Ex. 20:13), "you shall not commit murder," Scripture teaches that anyone who commits murder is deemed as if he has diminished the image of the [divine] king. A parable: A human king entered a city and set up portraits ('*iqonot*), erected statues, and minted coins. Subsequently, they overturned his portraits, shattered his statues, and defaced his coins, thereby diminishing the image of the king. So too, anyone who commits murder is deemed as if he has diminished the image of the [divine] king.

If murder diminishes the image of God because it destroys one who embodies or represents that image, so too does the failure to procreate detract from the divine image because it prevents the representation of that image. From the vantage point of the Yavnean sages, God created the human species to embody his image, and sexual reproduction transmits that image from one generation to the next. As we noted earlier in our discussion of the human being as bridging two worlds, procreation hardly ranks as an activity merely characteristic of beasts, but it rates as a distinctively human responsibility. Without it—just as without a ban on murder—civilization, for the sake of which God created humans in his image and offered them the blessings of Gen. 1:28, cannot endure.

The citation of Gen. 9:6, recalling the creation of man in the divine image (*ʒelem*) to validate analogies to diminishing the divine likeness (*d^emut*), suggests that the masters of Yavneh drew no distinction be-

---

168. *Mechilta d'Rabbi Ismael* (Hebrew), ed. H. S. Horowitz and I. A. Rabin, 2nd ed. (Jerusalem, 1960), p. 233. Cf. the same homiletical message conveyed in the liturgical poem of Simeon b. Avun, *Sh^evuyat Marom Luqq^eḥah k^eha-Yom*, in *Sefer Q^erovot, Hu' Maḥzor l^e-Ḥag ha-Shavu'ot*, ed. Wolf Heindheim and Isaac Berlin (Hannover, 1839), p. 225. See also Israel Davidson, *Thesaurus of Medieval Hebrew Poetry* (Hebrew), 4 vols. (1924–33; repr., New York, 1970), 3:411.

tween these two terms, which appear side by side in the biblical cosmogony (Gen. 1:26). This tendency is also manifest in the Septuagint, which translates both *ẓelem* (in Gen. 1:26, 5:3, 9:6) and *dᵉmut* (in Gen. 5:1) as *eikón* (precisely the term for a material representation of the king in the *Mᵉkhilta's* parable), and in the Targum of Pseudo-Jonathan, which reads *dᵉyoqan*, a derivative of the same word, for both *ẓelem* (Gen. 1:27, 9:6) and *dᵉmut* (Gen. 1:26, 5:1). The Yavnean sages do not indicate that they located the divine image/likeness exclusively in the human intellect or soul, and their interchange does not manifest any perceived difference between the divine image in Adam and that in his descendants. These ideas, all of which appear in the writings of Philo, enter rabbinic thought only in later periods, and only then did they pose exegetical problems in the Tannaitic texts we have quoted.[169] Rather, as Ephraim Urbach and Morton Smith maintained, early rabbinic sages construed the divine likeness in a human being as the whole person, and, perhaps influenced by the statue-cult of Hellenistic rulers, they employed the concept to promote respect for God and his human creatures.[170]

Hellenistic influences are also evident in our pericope's concluding exchange between Ben Azzai and his colleagues. R. Eleazar b. Azariah (D) implies that Ben Azzai, as the Talmud states elsewhere,[171] never married, or at least that he had no children. Ben Azzai's response (E), which later became the focus of halakhic discussions on dispensation from the duty to father children,[172] echoes the sentiments of his Stoic contemporary Epictetus. Decrying in graphic terms the lot of the married Cynic, the exemplary holy man, Epictetus complains:[173]

169. Menahem b. Solomon ha-Me'iri, *Bet ha-Bᵉḥirah ʿal Masekhet Yᵉvamot*, ed. Samuel Dickmann (Jerusalem, 1962), p. 233; the comments of Samuel Edels, *Ḥiddushe 'Aggadot ad Yev.* 63b, s.v. *kᵉ-'illu*; and Jaffe, *Yᵉfeh To'ar*, pp. 217b–219a.

170. Ephraim E. Urbach, *The Sages: Their Concepts and Beliefs*, tr. Israel Abrahams, 2 vols. (Jerusalem, 1975), 1:226ff.; Morton Smith, "The Image of God: Notes on the Hellenization of Judaism, with Especial Reference to Goodenough's Work on Jewish Symbols," *BJRL* 40 (1958), 473–512. See also Alexander Altmann, "*Homo imago Dei* in Jewish and Christian Theology," *Journal of Religion* 48 (1968), 235–59; Jacob Jervell, *Imago Dei: Gen 1,26f. im Spätjudentum, in der Gnosis und in den paulinischen Briefen* (Göttingen, 1960), esp. pp. 52ff., 71ff.; and Wolfson, *Philo*, esp. chs. 6–7.

171. TJ *Soṭah* 1.2, 16c, TB *Soṭah* 4b; but cf. TB *Ket.* 63a, with the comments of Tosafot, s.v. *bᵉrateh*, and Tosafot ad *Yev.* 63b, s.v. *she-yitqayyem*.

172. See below, Chapter 3.

173. Epictetus, *The Discourses* 3.22.69–72, ed. W. A. Oldfather, LCL, 2 vols. (1925–28; repr., Cambridge, Mass., 1978–79), 2:154–55.

In such an order of things as the present, which is like that of a battle-field, it is a question, perhaps, if the Cynic ought not to be free from distraction, wholly devoted to the service of God, free to go about among men, not tied down by the private duties of men, nor involved in relationships which he cannot violate and still maintain his role as a good and excellent man, whereas, on the other hand, if he observes them, he will destroy the messenger, the scout, the herald of the gods, that he is. For see, he must show certain services to his father-in-law, to the rest of his wife's relatives, to his wife herself; finally he is driven from his profession, to act as a nurse in his own family and to provide for them. To make a long story short, he must get a kettle to heat water for the baby, for washing it in a bath-tub; wool for his wife when she has had a child, oil, a cot, a cup (the vessels get more and more numerous); not to speak of the rest of his business, and his distraction. Where, I beseech you, is left now our king, the man who has leisure for the public interest, "who hath charge of the folk and for many a thing must be watchful (*Iliad* 2.25)."

Appended to a midrashic analysis of Gen. 9, Ben Azzai's exclamation that his soul craves the Torah (i.e., the study of Torah) may also hint at yet another matter at stake in our Yavnean *baraita'*. The focus of the Yavnean sages on God's postdiluvian pact with Noah—the biblical source for the Noachide commandments, which in the rabbinic perspective obligated Jew and Gentile alike—suggests the universal applicability of the mandate to procreate and its centrality in God's relationship with all humanity.[174] Ben Azzai's stated preference for God's covenant with Israel bespeaks a tension between universal and particularist dimensions of rabbinic theology, an issue that creation in the divine image and the blessings of Gen. 1:28 brought to the fore. Such a dialectic assumed much greater prominence in the halakhic analysis of our verse, to be considered below, and it may also underlie the statements attributed to R. Akiva in *Pirqe 'Avot*:[175] "Beloved is man (*'adam*) in that he was created in the divine image. . . . Beloved are Israel in that they are called the children of God. . . . Beloved is Israel in that the precious instrument [with which the world was created] was given to them." Samuel Loewenstamm noted that epithets of divine image and sonship function in documents of the ancient Assyrian monarchy to

---

174. Cf., however, the questionable argument of Jervell, *Imago Dei*, pp. 71–96, that the rabbis identified the human image of God as residing exclusively in the Jewish community.
175. M *'Avot* 3.14.

express a special connection between ruler and deity.[176] *Pirqe 'Avot* juxtaposes them, ranks them in an ascending order, and adds God's revelation of the Torah to Israel as a still greater manifestation of his love. Itself suggestive of royal enthronement and expressive of the divine image in human beings, Gen. 1:28 with its call for procreation may have symbolized for Ben Azzai a divine compact with all people, which he believed the Sinaitic covenant had superseded. Yet not all rabbinic sages agreed. Some, like R. Eleazar b. Azariah, continued to stress the fundamental significance of procreation for everyone, perhaps as a polemical rejoinder to his contemporaries who advocated celibacy.[177] Others, who may have shared Ben Azzai's concern, proceeded

---

176. Samuel E. Loewenstamm, "Man as the Image and Son of God" (Hebrew), *Tarbiẓ* 27 (1957), 1–2. Cf. also *Sayings of the Jewish Fathers,* ed. Charles Taylor (1897; repr., New York, 1970), pp. 56–59 nn. 36–37.

177. A polemical motive of these Yanvean midrashim on Gen. 9 might also explain the ostensively incongruous enthusiasm with which Ben Azzai participated in the discussion, offering the most extreme deprecation of him who fathers no children and yet at the same time defending his own bachelorhood. The intended direction of such a polemic (Jews, Gnostics, or Christians), however, remains obscure. The most likely possibility is the Jews themselves, who in the wake of the destruction of the Temple and faced with the Hadrianic persecutions may have advocated sexual abstinence. T *Soṭah* 15.11, ed. Lieberman, 4:243, attributes ascetic tendencies to various Pharisees (*mishe-ḥarav ha-bayit ha-'aḥaron ravu ha-pᵉrushin bᵉ-Yisra'el*), having just recorded (15.10) the words attributed to a colleague of our Yavnean interlocutors. "R. Ishmael b. Elisha said: From the day the Temple was destroyed, we ought in principle not to eat meat and not to drink wine, but a court may not impose a decree on the community which the community cannot uphold. And he used to say: Because they uproot the Torah from amongst us, it has been decreed that the world should be desolate—i.e., that we ought not to marry, not to beget children, and not to maintain the practice of circumcision (*shevu'a ben;* lit., the week of the son, after which circumcision took place), until the seed of Abraham would be depleted of its own accord. They said to him: It is better for the community that people err unintentionally, and that they not violate the law on purpose." Despite a similar contemporary pessimism with regard to the state of Jewish life, an adamant persistence in childbearing is advocated by Moses' father, Amram, in Pseudo-Philo, *Liber antiquitatum biblicarum* 9.3–5, ed. Guido Kisch, University of Notre Dame Publications in Mediaeval Studies 10 (Notre Dame, Ind., 1949), p. 137 (cf. TB *Soṭah* 12a). On the probable composition of the *Biblical Antiquities* during the Yavnean period, see Louis H. Feldman's prolegomenon to Pseudo-Philo, *The Biblical Antiquities of Philo,* tr. M. R. James (1917; repr., New York, 1971), pp. xxviii–xxxi; and on the question of Jewish and Pharisaic celibacy, see Steven D. Fraade, "Ascetical Aspects of Ancient Judaism," in *JS,* pp. 271ff. Regardless of the original intent of Akiva, Eleazar, and Ben Azzai, Jews later attacked Christian clergy for ignoring this the first biblical commandment; in addition to the citations of Eusebius and Aphrahat below, Chapter 5, see, for example, *The Jewish-Christian Debate in the High Middle Ages: A Critical Edition of the "Niẓẓaḥon Vetus"* 209, ed. David Berger, Judaica: Texts and Translations 4 (Philadelphia, Pa., 1979), Heb. p. 144, trans. p. 205. Christians eventually did construe their exchange as an attack on clerical celibacy, and Christian censors accordingly inserted the word *Yᵉhudi,* reading "any Jew who does not engage in procreation . . . ," into the editions of TB *Yev.* printed in 1579 in Basel and in 1737 in Prague. Beside their emendations of the talmudic text, the censors also inserted the marginal gloss, *ha' 'al derekh ha-ṭeva' lᵉ-qayyem 'et ha-'olam.* This

to reevaluate procreation as the bedrock of God's exclusive relationship with his chosen people.

Preparing for the Messiah. Conveying the ultimate expression of divine blessing and grace, and illustrating the means whereby human beings should maintain their unique status in the natural order, Gen. 1:28 also struck the aggadic imagination as bearing on the salvation that God had long promised his people. For rabbis in the talmudic period, procreation constituted a necessary preparation for the eschaton; in later aggadic works, the divine instructions in our verse symbolized key characteristics of the messianic era itself.

The Babylonian Talmud repeatedly adduces the assertion of the Palestinian Amora R. Assi,[178] to the effect that "the Son of David will not come until the *guf* (a storehouse for preexistent souls) has been depleted of all its souls, as Scripture states (Is. 57:16):[179] '[For I will not contend for ever, neither will I always be wroth;] for the spirit (*ruaḥ*) that enwraps itself (*ya-ʿaṭof*) is from me, and the souls which I have made.'"[180] Medieval commentators disagreed about whether *ruaḥ* denotes the messiah[181] or the souls whose birth would precede his arrival,[182] but most accepted the eschatological setting of the prophecy,[183] construing *ya-ʿaṭof* as an indication of delay, as in Jacob's allotment of the "late-breeding" animals (*ha-ʿaṭufim*) to Laban (Gen. 30:42). R. Assi's assertion reflects the ancient Jewish beliefs that a cosmic way-station or storage

---

reading, to my knowledge unattested in any cataloged ms. of TB *Yev.*, was before Naftali Z. Y. Berlin while composing his *Haʿameq Sheʾelah* on the *Sheʾiltot* (1861–67), 1:27–30; Berlin accepted it as genuine, employing it as evidence for a more enlightened, universalistic attitude on the part of the *Sheʾiltot*, which retains the original reading, as in our present text of TB *Yev.* See Raphael N. N. Rabbinovicz, *History of the Printing of the Talmud* (Hebrew), ed. A. M. Habermann, Jakob Michel Library: Translations and Collections in Jewish Studies 12 (Jerusalem, 1965), pp. 76–79, esp. nn. 6, 10, pp. 112–15. In the absence of a critical apparatus on TB *Yev.*, I am grateful to Jacob Zussmann and Haym Soloveitchik for their assistance in locating the appropriate ms. fragments. The vagaries of censorship, whereby Christians in this instance excluded themselves from any share in the rewards of procreation, are explored further in Ephraim E. Urbach's study of a distinct but nevertheless somewhat related Tannaitic tradition: "'Kol Ha-meqayyem Nefesh Aḥat . . .': Development of the Version, Vicissitudes of Censorship, and Business Manipulations of Printers" (Hebrew), *Tarbiz* 40 (1971), 268–84.

178. Following Wilhelm Bacher, *ʾAggadat ʾAmoraʾe ʾEreẓ-Yisraʾel*, tr. A. S. Rabinovitz, 3 vols. in 7 pts. (Tel Aviv, 1925–38), 2,1:160 and n.3, and Urbach, *Sages*, 2:792 n. 79.

179. Following OJPS to allow for midrashic interpretation at work.

180. TB *Yev.* 62a, 63b, *AZ* 5a, *Nid.* 13b; see also *Kallah Rabbati* 2.4, ed. Higger, p. 196.

181. Tosafot ad *AZ* 5a, s.v. ki.

182. Rashi ad *Nid.* 13b, s.v. *ki ruaḥ*.

183. Cf. also the comments of David Kimhi ad Is. 57:16.

depot existed for human souls and that a predetermined, secret number of souls had to be born into bodies before the final redemption might occur.[184] At times pseudepigraphic texts understand the souls in question to be those of the righteous,[185] and, with reference to Is. 57:16, the Babylonian Talmud also juxtaposes the souls of the righteous and preexistent souls in an Amoraic list of those things located in heaven.[186] The particular concept informing R. Assai's homily is expressed most clearly in 2 Bar. 23:4–5:[187]

> For when Adam sinned and death was decreed against those who were to be born, the multitude of those who would be born was numbered. And for that number a place was prepared where the living ones might live and where the dead might be preserved. No creature will live again unless the number that has been appointed is completed. For my spirit creates the living, and the realm of death receives the dead.

Frank Chamberlin Porter, Urbach, and Lieberman agreed that the *guf* in our talmudic homily is not the *'oẓar,* or promptuary, for the souls of the dead mentioned in pseudepigraphic, Tannaitic, and early Christian texts, and they also held[188] that R. Assi does not hereby subscribe to the dualistic opposition of body and soul essential to Platonic cosmology. But contrary to Urbach's denial that R. Assi implies the prior, presumably simultaneous, creation of all human souls,[189] both Porter and Lieberman have argued convincingly that according to this Amora "a fixed number of souls were created from the beginning of time."[190] As

184. A. Marmorstein, "Ideas of Resurrection in the Aggadah of the Amoraim" (Hebrew), *Metsudah* 2 (1943), 94–105.

185. 4 Ezra 4:33–43, 5:36; 2 Bar. 30:2, 75:6; and cf. Rev. 6:11.

186. TB *Hag.* 12b.

187. *OTP*, 1:629.

188. Contra Yitzhak Baer, "On the Problem of Eschatological Doctrine during the Period of the Second Temple" (Hebrew), *Zion,* n.s. 23–24 (1957–59), 3–34.

189. Urbach, *Sages,* 1:236–42.

190. Frank Chamberlin Porter, "The Pre-existence of the Soul in the Book of Wisdom and in the Rabbinical Writings," in *Old Testament and Semitic Studies in Memory of William Rainey Harper,* ed. Robert Francis Harper et al. (Chicago, 1908), pp. 205–69; Saul Lieberman, "Some Aspects of Afterlife in Early Rabbinic Literature," in *Harry Austryn Wolfson Jubilee Volume,* ed. Saul Lieberman et al., 3 vols. (Jerusalem, 1965), 2:495–532, esp. 501–502 n. 41. This is the view of *The Mishnah of Rabbi Eliezer,* p. 374, *Tan.* (P^equde 3), pp. 49a–50b (cf. *Seder Y^eẓirat ha-Walad,* ed. Adolph Jellinek, in *Beth ha-Midrasch* [Hebrew], 3rd ed., 6 pts. in 2 vols. [Jerusalem, 1967], 1,1:153–58), and Rashi ad *AZ* 5a, s.v. *'ad she-yikhlu;* and see Raymond Martini, *Pugio fidei adversus Mauros et Judaeos* 2.13.4 (1687; repr., Farnborough, 1967), p. 441, who, alluding to Rashi, decries "hanc . . . insaniam, videlicet quod omnes animae sint simul creatae." See also Hermann L. Strack and Paul Billerbeck, *Kommentar zum neuen Testament aus Talmud und*

such, *Genesis Rabbah* takes issue with the Babylonian tradition when, with reference to the same verse in Isaiah, it records in R. Tanhum's name: "The messianic king will never come until all those souls intended for creation have been created."[191]

On two occasions in the Talmud, R. Assi's homily has halakhic implications: to rationalize the commandment of procreation in support of R. Huna's view that a man whose children predecease him has fulfilled his obligations,[192] and to explain why "those who sport with young girls (*ha-mᵉsaḥaqin bᵉ-tinnoqot*)," meaning those who marry maidens too young to bear children, delay the coming of the messiah.[193] In a third instance, the statement successfully challenges the aggadic assertion that without the sin of the golden calf the Israelites who left Egypt would never have died and thus would have had no need to beget children.[194] Yet the midrash of R. Assi must first stand independent of its editorially perceived implications, numbering among other similarly constructed statements ("the son of David will not come until . . ." or "the son of David will not come except in a generation which . . .") which typify the Babylonian Talmud's outlook on the prerequisites for the messianic era. Many of these propositions describe the cessation or interruption of physical, social, and political processes that characterized contemporary Jewish life, and it is curious that most of them share a distinctive phonetic allusion to the exhaustion or completion of worldly activities as we now know them.[195] They clearly reflect a growing despondency and pessimism in the generations following the abortive Bar Kokhba rebellion, which led in rabbinic thought to what Urbach termed a "complete abandonment of the realistic elements surrounding the redemption and its absolute integration into supernatural processes built on the ruins of existing history and actualities." Particularly as the glorious end of the Tannaitic age

---

Midrasch, 6 vols. in 7 pts. (Munich, 1922–61), 2:341–52; Robert Hammerton-Kelly, "The Idea of Preexistence in Early Judaism" (Ph.D. Dissertation, Union Theological Seminary, New York, 1966); and the sources cited in *LOJ,* 5:75 n. 19.

191. *GenR* 24.14 (ad 5:1), 1:233, with notes; and cf. *LevR* 15.1 (ad 13:2), 2:321nn. Variant in Sokoloff, *Geniza Fragments,* p. 112, reads *she-yavo'u* for *she-yibbarᵉ'u.*

192. TB *Yev.* 62ab.

193. TB *Nid.* 13b.

194. TB *AZ* 5a.

195. Of statements beginning "'*en ben David* (or *melekh ha-mashiaḥ*) *ba*' . . ." that I found in the Talmuds and midrashim, approximately half contain forms of the verb *klh,* most of the remainder contain forms of *kol* (e.g., *kol, kulo*), and several include the consonantal pairs *kl* and *hl* in other words (e.g., *kelev, ḥoleh*).

(the administration of R. Judah the Patriarch) gave way to the period of the Amora'im, "a Utopian trend prevailed in the vision of redemption. This was undoubtedly due to the decline of the Roman Empire, the wars it waged against the Persians, the degeneration in the economic position, and also the criticism levelled against the administrative institutions, the Patriarchate, and the courts. There actually exists a kind of competition in depicting anarchy and upheaval as indications of the advent of the son of David."[196] Joseph Klausner's view of R. Assi's statement as a plea for procreation in spite of the Hadrianic persecutions—and thus as a direct rejoinder to the aforecited hopelessness of sages like Ishmael b. Elisha[197]—depends upon its attribution to the Tannaitic R. Yosi b. Halafta and is therefore highly doubtful.[198] Moreover, it would seem that R. Assi's statement intended primarily to contrast this world and the next, highlighting the posthistoric character of the messianic era, which will arrive only when the natural processes implanted in the order of creation have played themselves out to completion. One might infer that R. Assi would have agreed with the assertion ascribed to Rav, that sexual reproduction (*p^eriyyah u-r^eviyyah*) will not be part of life in the world to come.[199]

Yet however utopian and pessimistic our homilist may have been, his words fortified a perceived connection between the duty of procreation in the present and the commencement of the redemption in the future. Procreation for the talmudic rabbis, David Feldman noted, "in the face of a precarious future, was essentially an act of faith."[200] This inference motivated the talmudic editors to adduce his words in a more optimistic, upbeat vein in order to explain the critical importance of childbearing in the active preparation of the world for its messianic redemption. Unlike the oft-quoted rationalization for procreation in Is. 45:18—that

196. Urbach, *Sages,* 1:676, 678.
197. Quoted above, n. 177.
198. Joseph Klausner, *The Messianic Idea in Israel,* 3rd ed., tr. W. F. Stinespring (New York, 1955), pp. 430ff. See the note of Wilhelm Bousset, *Die Religion des Judentums in späthellinistischen Zeitalter,* 3rd ed., ed. Hugo Gressmann, Handbuch zum Neuen Testament 21 (Tübingen, 1966), p. 248 n. 2, that Klausner's "zeitgeschichtliche Erklärung dieser Stellen ist falsch"; and Klausner's response (3rd ed., p. 432 n. 26) that "these passages can hardly be explained in any other way."
199. TB *Ber.* 17a.
200. David M. Feldman, *Birth Control in Jewish Law: Marital Relations, Contraception, and Abortion as Set Forth in the Classic Texts of Jewish Law* (New York, 1964), p. 52. On the duty of Israel to prepare for the messiah expressed by such homilies as that of R. Assi, see also Jacob Neusner, *Messiah in Context: Israel's History and Destiny in Formative Judaism,* Foundations of Judaism: Method, Teleology, Doctrine 2 (Philadelphia, Pa., 1984), ch. 4.

God "did not create it [the world] a waste, but formed it for habitation"—such an evaluation of the commandment places it squarely within God's covenant with Israel, for Israel must work actively to deserve the coming of the messiah, and Israel will be the principal beneficiary of his efforts. Accordingly, the mandate of Gen. 1:28 derived from the beginning of time and from God's covenant with humanity at large, but it looked forward to the end, when God's chosen people would be saved. One suspects that those for whom procreation bespoke redemption, instead of promoting the opinion of Rav, would have championed the prediction attributed to R. Gamaliel of Yavneh: "In the future, a woman will give birth every day."[201]

Centuries after the redaction of the Talmud, a European aggadic work interpreted the blessings of Gen. 1:28 as prefiguring the triumph of Israel during the messianic age itself. After relating God's blessing of the fish and birds on the fifth day of creation (Gen. 1:22) to Isaac's blessing of Esau—and by extension to the wicked rule of the Gentiles in this world—*Genesis Rabbati* perceives the sixth day of the cosmogony as referring to the redemption. The dominion intended by God for humans in Gen. 1:26 corresponds to the future rule of Israel over heavenly and earthly realms, which Gen. 1:28 elaborates in detail.[202]

> "God blessed them." In that time God, blessed be he, will bless Israel that they should be fertile and increase and fill the earth, in the manner that Scripture states (Is. 44:4): "And they shall sprout like grass." And it is written (Is. 49:21): "Who bore these for me?" Therefore Scripture states: "Be fertile and increase." "And master it," for [Israel] will in the future conquer the entire world, as it is written (Zech. 9:10): "And his rule shall extend from sea to sea." "And rule the fish of the sea"—these are Israel. "The birds of the sky"—these are the angels. "And all the living things that creep"—these are the nations of the world.

For the writer of this midrash, the primordial blessings of the first parents, much like the messianic prophecies of Isaiah, will be realized only upon the future liberation of Israel from Gentile rule. Gen. 1:28 here evokes the alienation of medieval Jews under Christian rule, a longing for the presently unavailable political evidence of divine elec-

---

201. TB *Sab.* 30b. The implied difference in outlook is noted by Tosafot ad *AZ* 5a, s.v. *'en*, which also explains that the redemption-inducing procreation is specifically that of the Jews, "since the souls of Israel and of Gentiles are not in the same *guf*."
202. *MBR*, p. 19.

tion that such Jews perceived as rightfully their own. To my knowledge, it is the first extant example of a Jewish typological interpretation of our verse, and one of many cross-cultural exchanges in the history of its interpretation.[203] The figurative exegesis of Gen. 1:28 was prevalent in the Christian milieu of *Genesis Rabbati,* and it is ironic but nonetheless instructive that its rabbinic author yearned for freedom in the idiom and under the influence of his oppressor's hermeneutic.[204]

FROM THE BIBLE TO POSTBIBLICAL JUDAISM

As we noted at the beginning of this chapter, the statutory ramifications of the primordial blessing have monopolized much of the postbiblical Jewish interaction with our verse, and any meaningful evaluation of the significance of Gen. 1:28 in classical rabbinic Judaism must await the ensuing analysis of its function as Mosaic commandment. However, the extant aggadic allusions to Gen. 1:28 do manifest related areas of concern that this biblical passage was understood to have addressed. If, in large measure because of the methodological difficulties discussed above, one cannot succinctly formulate the precise "meaning of Gen. 1:28 in rabbinic Judaism," these concerns still underlie the verse's career as *mizwah* and point to the theological tenets that the commandment was believed to concretize.

The documents reviewed above reveal that alternative interpretations of Gen. 1:28 presented themselves to its postbiblical readers, that the Bible's own understanding of the primordial blessing hardly stifled further discussion of its enduring relevance. Writers of the intertestamental period shied away from the verse's endorsement of human sexuality, harping instead on the dominion and the generic superiority that derived from the creation of humans in the image of God. This exclusion of sexual reproduction from the sphere of fundamentally

203. On messianic typology in rabbinic exegesis, see the recent studies of Amos Funkenstein, "Nachmanides' Typological Reading of History" (Hebrew), *Zion,* n.s. 45 (1980), 35–59, and David Berger, "Three Typological Themes in Early Jewish Messianism: Messiah Son of Joseph, Rabbinic Calculations, and the Figure of Armilus," *AJS Review* 10 (1985), 141–64. Cf. also below, Chapter 5, at n. 8 and elsewhere.

204. On the school of Moses the Preacher and its opus, see Abraham Epstein, *R. Mosheh ha-Darshan mi-Narbonah* (Vienna, 1891; repr. in *Kitve R. 'Avraham 'Epshtein,* ed. A. M. Habermann, I [Jerusalem, 1950], 213–44), and Albeck's introduction to *MBR.*

important human activities undoubtedly resulted from the prevailing philosophical and religious climate of the Hellenistic period, which promoted ascetic tendencies among pagans, among Jews, and eventually among Christians. Within such a cultural framework, sexual activity epitomized a physical, material, animal existence, one that human souls should seek to transcend. Little aggadic material concerning Gen. 1:28 survives from the Tannaitic period, but various Amoraic sages restored Gen. 1:28a to center stage in their instruction, alluding repeatedly to the cosmic importance of procreation and paying relatively little attention to the enthronement of human beings over the rest of the natural order in Gen. 1:28b. Logic might quickly lead to the conclusion that Gen. 1:28 figured in rabbinic polemics against Jewish, Christian, and/or Gnostic groups that disparaged marriage and childbearing among their constituencies.[205] Our numerous citations of *Genesis Rabbah,* a work often viewed as replete with rejoinders to Gnostic and Christian ideas, might strengthen this impression.[206] But it is regrettable that the available evidence rarely allows for the correlation of the aggadic texts considered here to particular incidences of polemical exchange between talmudic rabbis and their ideological opponents. Despite the attribution of most of the homilies cited in this chapter to Amoraic sages, and despite the continuous reappearance of *Genesis Rabbah* and the Palestinian Talmud (the magna opera of the Palestinian Amoraic academies) in our footnotes, one cannot safely generalize about the geographical, chronological, or sociopolitical background of the motifs we have studied. Traditions first attested in medieval works may well have derived from earlier, perhaps even intertestamental, sources. Furthermore, rabbinic views on our subject were themselves not monolithic even within individual works, and as one school of thought has proposed, a blatantly Gnostic mythology may have left its mark in the occasional Jewish statement that sexual reproduction among humans resulted from their primeval sin and fall.

205. See above, n. 177.
206. The most recent attempts to identify the targets of *GenR*'s polemic are those of Jacob Neusner; see his "*Genesis Rabbah* as Polemic," *Genesis and Judaism: The Perspective of "Genesis Rabbah"*—*An Analytical Anthology,* Brown Judaic Studies 108 (Atlanta, Ga., 1985), and *Comparative Midrash.* Cf., however, the well-argued reservations of Ithamar Gruenwald, "The Problem of the Anti-Gnostic Polemic in Rabbinic Literature," in *Studies in Gnosticism and Hellenistic Religions Presented to Gilles Quispel on the Occasion of His 65th Birthday,* ed. R. Van Den Broeck and M. J. Vermaseren, Etudes préliminaires aux religions orientales dans l'Empire romain 91 (Leiden, 1981), pp. 171–89.

Granted that one cannot substantiate the adversarial intentions of specific aggadic homilies, these occasional Jewish expressions, along with Gnostic ideas and the patristic attitudes surveyed below in Chapter 5, do offer valuable points of contrast against which to take stock of the preponderance of rabbinic opinion. Many of the aggadic traditions anaylzed above approach the anthropological implications of Gen. 1:28 as a key to rationalizing the cosmogony. God fashioned his world so as to facilitate human life and civilization. God conceived of human activity in terms of procreation, settlement, and dominion. The elements of Gen. 1:28 therefore define human nature, and they also comprise the means for human fulfillment of God's cosmic plan. At once they denote privilege and responsibility, which are inextricably linked, for in the rabbinic perspective, responsibility leads directly to reward. Hence the repeated assertions that God created the world expressly for the purpose of procreation (*p^eriyyah u-r^eviyyah*), that the biblical forefathers of the Jews performed the duties and thus enjoyed the bounties of Gen. 1:28, and that the fulfillment or neglect of these duties weighs heavily in the divine assessment of human merit.

Probing further, we note that in the aggadic imagination Gen. 1:28 suggested a series of polar oppositions that contributed to the singular status and character of human beings.[207] Sexuality did not alienate humans from the natural rhythm of God's creation; it enabled them to work *within* that world toward its transformation according to an *otherworldly* model (*l^e-tiqqun ha-'olam ul^e-yishuvo*). Albeit a characteristic of animals, procreation joined with the image of God in yielding a human creature that bridged two worlds and was thereby uniquely capable of deserving divine reward, unlike the angel and unlike the beast. Only human sexuality could defy the logical contradiction between supernal and terrestrial forms of life. One who engaged in procreation had marshaled his potentially basest impulses in the service of God. One who neglected his procreative duties undermined the godly dimension to his nature, qualitatively and quantitatively detracting from human civilization. Thus conveying divine promise conditional upon compliance, our verse evoked the rabbinic belief in the covenant, and another polar opposition that such belief entailed: that between Gentile and Jew. Gen. 1:28 expressed divine providence in a universal

207. Susan Niditch, "The Cosmic Adam," offered a similar observation with regard to *GenR* 8, which we have quoted frequently.

sense; God did not create his world "a waste, but formed it for habitation." Yet the goal of that civilization was its messianic redemption—in particular, the fulfillment of God's promises to Israel. Recognizing this tension, Ben Azzai reportedly told his Yavnean colleagues that for him the exclusive covenant of the Torah took precedence. Subsequent generations of sages endeavored to resolve the tension by recasting procreation as prerequisite to the arrival of the son of David—that is, to the liberation and salvation of God's elect. Just as it did in Scripture, in rabbinic Judaism Gen. 1:28 related directly to the issue of divine covenant, that with all the descendants of Adam and Noah and that with Israel alone. Only against this aggadic background can one appreciate the rabbinic career of our verse as ordaining the first precept in the Torah: "Be fertile and increase."

CHAPTER 3

Transformation in the Halakhah

REFLECTING on the ability of medieval Jews to maintain a distinct cultural identity in spite of their prolonged dispersion and subjugation by a series of foreign powers, Salo Wittmayer Baron observed: "Notwithstanding unceasing sectarian clashes and the growing organizational dissolution into provincial and local communal groups, the main body of the Jewish people preserved its world unity primarily through the unbroken continuity of its legal structure."[1] The Aggadah expressed the complexity and the depth of rabbinic theology, but rabbinic law, or Halakhah, systematized the fundamental principles of talmudic Judaism into a comprehensive regimen for daily life. Construed as the substance of the covenant at Sinai, the law substituted for prince and cultic shrine in its demand for allegiance, and the sociocultural cohesiveness it generated among medieval Jews helped counterbalance the centrifugal forces of assimilation from the end of the talmudic period until the onset of modernity.

Within the framework of rabbinic law, the Jewish career of Gen. 1:28 came to maturity in the reformulation of the primordial blessing as legal statute. Our goal in this chapter is to assess our verse's significance as commandment or *mizwah,* a function that both medieval and modern

---

1. Salo Wittmayer Baron, *A Social and Religious History of the Jews,* 2nd ed., 18 vols. to date (New York, 1952–83), 6:3.

rabbinic authorities conceded it did not have in the biblical text.[2] How did the rabbis translate God's instructions to the first parents into concrete, enforceable, legal obligations? Whom did the law include in its demands, and whom did it exclude? What theological issues motivated ongoing debate over seemingly trivial points of law, matters that may still remain unresolved? As we grapple with this agenda, we shall not direct our analysis toward the resolution of specific legal questions, as David Feldman did in his important study entitled *Birth Control in Jewish Law*. Nor is our purpose to apply the halakhic approach to sexuality, marriage, and procreation to the concerns and circumstances of the contemporary Jewish community.[3] Rather, our primary interest lies with the rabbinic interpretation of the Bible, and the significance of this hermeneutical process for the historian of religion and ideas. Once again, the relevant data is presented under broad, topical rubrics, yet in this instance the legal nature of the material facilitates more precise definition of the subject at hand in particular texts, and the evolving nature of the Halakhah will require greater sensitivity to chronological sequence. Where appropriate, we pursue the halakhic issues raised in the Talmud into the Middle Ages, considering their treatment by rabbinic authorities as late as the publication of Joseph Karo's *Shulḥan 'Arukh* (1567). Questions that first arose after the talmudic period will concern us in the next chapter, as will the practical application of talmudic law in the literature of medieval responsa.

THE DUTY OF PROCREATION

The Tannaitic compilations of the Mishnah and the Tosefta include the legal obligation to reproduce in tractate *Yevamot*: "A man may not desist from procreation (*periyyah u-reviyyah*) unless he has children."[4] Because the Mishnah was redacted soon after 200 C.E., this statement establishes the early third century as a *terminus ante quem* for the legal

---

2. See the Genesis commentaries of Abraham ibn Ezra, David Kimhi, Joseph b. Eliezer Bonfils, and Isaac Karo, cited below in Chapter 4, nn. 92–93. Most recently, see David S. Shapiro, "Be Fruitful and Multiply," *Tradition* 13:4–14:1 (1973), 47: "The Oral Tradition has declared procreation a religious duty."

3. Among others, see Robert Gordis, "'Be Fruitful and Multiply': Biography of a Mitzvah," *Midstream* 28 (August–September 1982), 21–29; and Reuven P. Bulka, *Jewish Marriage: A Halakhic Ethic*, Library of Jewish Law and Ethics 12 (New York, 1986).

4. M *Yev.* 6.6; T *Yev.* 8.4, ed. Lieberman, 3:24–25.

interpretation of "be fertile and increase." But ensuing discussion of the precept and its various implications indicates that the rabbis may have deemed Gen. 1:28 a Mosaic commandment at least several generations earlier.

The Minimum of Compliance

Following immediately upon this opening declaration, the Mishnah reports a dispute among the Pharisaic houses of Hillel and Shammai over the number of children that fulfills the responsibility of procreation. The House of Shammai stipulated two sons, while the House of Hillel required a son and a daughter, in keeping with the divine example "male and female he created them (Gen. 5:2)."[5] The Tosefta, however, recounts that R. Nathan and R. Jonathan, both sages of the second century, proposed conflicting versions of the earlier Pharisaic dispute. Nathan repeated the statement of the Mishnah but added a rationale for the Shammaitic ruling: The judgment of two sons as sufficient followed the precedent set by Moses, as Scripture states (1 Chr. 23:15), "and the sons of Moses: Gershom and Eliezer." Jonathan reported a different tradition altogether: The House of Shammai had mandated one male child and one female child, the House of Hillel one or the other.[6] Although such attributions of talmudic traditions to particular sages are open to serious question and doubt, this discussion may suggest that rabbinic authorities considered procreation a commandment one generation before R. Judah the Patriarch edited the Mishnah. Disagreement over the wording of an early Pharisaic debate, on whose occurrence two Ushan sages reportedly agreed and which does not question the duty of procreation but only its quantitative extent, raises the possibility that the tradition interpreting Gen. 1:28 as law was itself considerably older. On the other hand, the Mishnaic statement may also date from the aftermath of the Bar Kokhba rebellion, when rabbinic leaders had to vie against a spirit of pessimism that stifled a desire for progeny. One must

5. On the Mishnaic view of procreation as *imitatio Dei*, see Howard Eilberg-Schwartz, *The Human Will in Judaism: The Mishnah's Philosophy of Intention*, Brown Judaic Studies 103 (Atlanta, Ga., 1986), p. 105.
6. The name Jonathan may represent a scribal confusion for Nathan, whose name appears instead of Jonathan in two manuscripts of the Tosefta (ed. Lieberman, 3:25nn.); in that case, the Tosefta would be reporting differing versions of the tradition concerning the houses attributed to Nathan. Cf. Lieberman, *Tosefta ki-Fshutah*, 6:70.

consider the possibility that the Ushan masters then ascribed their own legislation to the earlier Pharisaic houses so as to enhance its urgency and credibility.[7]

The Mishnah does not regularly cite Scripture to substantiate a halakhic position;[8] perhaps the citation here resulted from the rabbis' own sensitivity to the absence of a biblical law requiring procreation. In this case the Mishnaic text is curious also because the Shammaites receive no scriptural support for their point of view; evidence for their opinion appears first in the Tosefta. The Palestinian Talmud cites these proof-texts and then concludes that according to the Hillelites *even* one male child and one female satisfy the obligation, although the two sons required by the Shammaites would certainly suffice.[9] Otherwise, a Hillelite view requiring a male and a female would appear more stringent than the position of the Shammaites and as such would appear to merit inclusion in the Mishnaic list of Hillelite stringencies, which it does not receive.[10] The Babylonian Talmud, on the other hand, espouses the stricter understanding of the Hillelite ruling (a male and a female, but not two males), justifying its stance with an analysis of the various biblical testimonies. Turning first to the dispute of the Pharisaic houses as reported by the Mishnah, the Babylonian Gemara explains the Shammaites' refusal to draw their inference from the example of Adam and Eve, because in those primordial circumstances the human species could not have survived without God's creation of a female. (Now,

---

7. See above, Chapter 2, n. 177. Skepticism with regard to attributions of rabbinic traditions has emerged most prominently in the scholarly opus of Jacob Neusner. Among his numerous works bearing on the issue, see *The Rabbinic Traditions about the Pharisees before 70*, 3 vols. (Leiden, 1971), and *Judaism: The Evidence of the Mishnah* (Chicago, 1981), pp. 307ff. Neusner has grown increasingly more doubtful of attributions. In the earlier *Rabbinic Traditions*, 2:198, he observed that this Mishnaic pericope is remarkable, for it "tells us that Pharisees wished to abstain from sexual relations and . . . [that] within Pharisaism were ascetics who preferred the solitary life." He thus assumed that the Shammaite-Hillelite dispute did indeed antedate the destruction of the Temple.

8. See Jacob Neusner, "Scripture and Tradition in Judaism, with Special Reference to the Mishnah," in *Approaches to Ancient Judaism: Volume II*, ed. William Scott Green, Brown Judaic Studies 9 (Chico, Calif., 1980), pp. 173–91; and David Weiss Halivni, *Midrash, Mishnah, and Gemara: The Jewish Predilection for Justified Law* (Cambridge, Mass., 1986), ch. 3, esp. pp. 55–58.

9. TJ *Yev.* 6.6, 7c. Evidently, this view was followed by Saadya b. Joseph, *Commentary on Genesis* (Arabic with Hebrew trans.), ed. Moshe Zucker (New York, 1984), pp. 94, 321–22 with Zucker's n. 148; and cf. Mubashir b. Nissi ha-Levi, *A Critique against the Writings of R. Saadya Gaon* (Arabic with Hebrew trans.), ed. Moshe Zucker (New York, 1955), pp. 28, 81–82 with Zucker's n. 80.

10. M *'Eduyot*, ch. 4.

however, one household's failure to produce female offspring would hardly have such a macrocosmic effect.) The Hillelites refused to follow the example of Moses, reasoned the Talmud, inasmuch as this matter was one of several in which Moses received special dispensation to depart from God's original instructions. In view of Moses' need for a dispensation, he would not otherwise have met his procreative responsibilities by fathering two sons.[11] The Babylonian Gemara also attributes to R. Nathan yet additional permutations of the Shammaite-Hillelite debate, again adducing the midrashic evidence for each position. According to one report, the Shammaites held that a person is obligated to produce two sons and two daughters,[12] the Hillelites one and one; according to another report, the Shammaites stipulated one son and one daughter, the Hillelites one or the other.[13] Among most medi-

---

11. TB *Yev.* 62a, which quotes the anonymous *baraita'* (cited also in TB *Sab.* 87a), "Moses did three things of his own accord, and his design comported with that of God. He abstained from sexual relations [after he had already fathered two sons], he broke the tablets, and he added one day [to the two days of sexual abstinence prescribed by God for the Israelites (Ex. 19:10) prior to the revelation at Sinai]." Rashi, in his comments ad loc., s.v. *mi-d^e'ateh,* explained "of his own accord" in terms of his unique inspiration by God (*mi-shum sh^{e}khinah*), and that the House of Hillel therefore held that others may not emulate his example. This argument is problematic on two counts. First, the *Sh^e'iltot* 184 (165), ed. Mirsky, 5:71, adduces the same *baraita'* (attributed to the Tannaitic school of R. Ishmael) in support of the Shammaitic position—to demonstrate that Moses abstained from marital relations entirely of his own accord, implying that with the birth of his two sons he must have fulfilled the commandment to procreate. Otherwise, how could he have presumed to neglect his duties? This reading of the *baraita'* corresponds to the aforecited inference of TJ, that the House of Hillel certainly accepted two sons as meeting the biblical injunction to procreate. And second, although Rashi's (Hillelite) understanding of the *baraita'* is supported in *ARNA*, ch. 2, p. 5b, and *SifN* 103, p. 101, the logic of the *baraita'* itself demands that Moses acted without divine instruction. See Tosafot ad *Yev.* 62a, s.v. *di-khtiv;* Moses b. Nahman, *Ḥiddushe ha-RaMba"N . . . 'al Masekhtot ha-Sha"S,* ed. Moshe Hershler et al., 4 vols. to date (Jerusalem, 1970–87), 2:301 (ad *Sab.*); Menahem Me'iri, *Bet ha-B^{e}ḥirah . . . Y^{e}vamot,* p. 228; Yom Tov b. Abraham Ishbili, *Ḥiddushe ha-RITb"A,* 6 vols. (Jerusalem, 1967), 1,1:71–72; and the lengthy comments of N. Z. Y. Berlin, *Ha'ameq Sh^e'elah,* in *Sh^e'iltot* (1861–67), 3:280–81. According to the medieval Yemenite Nathaniel b. Isaiah, *Sefer Ma'or ha-'Afelah,* ed. and tr. Joseph Kafah (Jerusalem, 1959), p. 67, the requirement of one son and one daughter derives from Gen. 9:7, whose repetition of "be fertile" denotes a male child, while that of "and increase" signifies a female.

12. The otherwise meaningless accusative particle *'et* in Gen. 4:1–2 is interpreted to imply that Eve bore daughters as twins to each of her sons; Eve's statement in Gen. 4:25, that God gave her Seth to substitute for the murdered Abel, yields the inference that without this additional son Adam and Eve would not have fulfilled the mandate of Gen. 1:28. On the twin sisters of Cain and Abel, see also *GenR* 22.2–3 (ad 4:1–2), 1:205–6; for the linkage of the Shammaitic position to the example of Cain and Abel, see also *TanB* (*B^{e}reshit* 26), 2:10a, and *DtR* 12, p. 10.

13. Rava links this position to "He did not create it a waste, but formed it for habitation (*shevet,* Is. 45:18), explaining, "*w^e-ha' 'avad lah shevet*"; cf. Rava's similar rationalization of the obligation to bear children below, n. 23. For the use of the plural term "children" to denote even a single son or daughter in other ancient legal texts, see Boaz Cohen, *Jewish and Roman Law: A Comparative Study,* 2 vols. (New York, 1966), 1:390 n. 58.

eval codifiers, the Hillelite position as understood by the Babylonian Gemara—one son and one daughter, but not two sons—prevailed as the law.[14]

The biblical evidence marshaled by the Mishnah and the Tosefta in the support of the respective houses' opinions links the commandment of procreation to the revelation at Sinai (and the example of Moses) or to the creation of the world. As such, the dispute between the houses as perceived by the rabbis may reflect a tension between God's exclusive covenant with Israel, on the one hand, and his providence for all humanity, on the other. This contrast appears to underlie the Amoraic dispute reported by the Babylonian Gemara under the rubric of the same Mishnaic passage:[15]

> If a man had children and they died—R. Huna ruled that he has fulfilled the duty of procreation: R. Yohanan ruled that he has not fulfilled it. R. Huna ruled that he has fulfilled it because of R. Assi's teaching; for R. Assi said: The son of David will not come until the *guf* has been depleted of all its souls. . . . R. Yohanan ruled that he has not fulfilled the duty of procreation because we require [the fulfillment of the text (Is. 45:18)] "he formed it for habitation," which is not the case here.

The connection between procreation and the salvation of Israel, which the talmudic rabbis inferred from R. Assi's assertion, was discussed at length in the previous chapter. Yet the reported dispute between R. Huna and R. Yohanan indicates that from the perspective of this rabbinic text the theological rationale for the mandate of procreation necessarily informed its statutory applications. According to the Talmud, R. Huna ruled that a person predeceased by his children has

---

14. *MT, 'Ishut* 15.4, *Tur, EH* 1, *ShA, EH* 1.5. Solomon b. Abraham ibn Adret, *Sefer Ḥiddushe ha-RaShb"A 'al Ḥamesh-'esreh Shiṭṭot*, 3 pts. in 1 vol. (Warsaw, 1922), 2:15b (ad *Yev.* 61b), responded to the argument of TJ, claiming that since the Shammaites require two sons (and not simply two children, at least of whom a son—as the text of Rashi's talmudic commentary before him suggests) and the Hillelites at least one son and one daughter, neither opinion is more stringent then the other. Abraham of Montpellier, *Commentary on the Tractate Yevamoth* (Hebrew), ed. M. Y. Blau (New York, 1962), p. 145, also referred to this version of Rashi, which opinion Menahem Me'iri, *Bet ha-Beḥirah . . . Yevamot*, p. 227, attributed to *gedole ha-rabbanim*. Me'iri adhered to the position of TB, but he mentioned *gedole ha-dorot*, who ruled with TJ, perhaps referring to Isaiah b. Mali of Trani, in *Piskei HaRid, Piskei HaRiaz* (Hebrew), ed. Abraham Joseph Wertheimer and Abraham Liess, 8 vols. (Jerusalem, 1964–82), 4,1:139, or to Meshullam b. Judah of Béziers, *Sefer ha-Hashlamah*, ed. Abraham Haputa, 10 vols. (Tel Aviv, 1961–75), 4:68–69. Unlike his grandfather, Isaiah b. Elijah of Trani, ibid., 4,2:48, conformed to the Babylonian tradition.

15. TB *Yev.* 62ab.

fulfilled the commandment of procreation. In this view, reproduction serves to exhaust the workings of nature and thus to prepare for the next world and the redemption of God's chosen. Yet R. Yohanan interpreted the law to require that one produce children who survive him. Like the Tannaitic Eleazar b. Azariah in his reported repartee with Ben Azzai, Yohanan's position implies that the Jew cannot neglect his citizenship in the macrocosm, but must strive to maintain the present world order. Quoting the Tosefta[16] to the effect that grandchildren may substitute for deceased children in allowing an individual to meet his obligation, so long as they outlive him and are in turn capable of reproducing, a later hand discredits Huna and sides with Yohanan.[17] The survival of offspring who themselves can reproduce is the object of our precept. This presumption would support the conclusion attributed by the Palestinian Talmud to R. Avin, that even an illegitimate child, a *mamzer,* numbers among those who meet their father's procreative obligations.[18] Although the act leading to his conception transgressed God's law, and although the Torah prohibited his marriage within the Jewish community, sanctioning that all his children born to a Jewish spouse would inherit his illegitimacy, the *mamzer* was still physiologically equipped to produce children. Paradoxically, the birth of a *mamzer* did serve to fulfill the Mosaic commandment of "be fertile and increase," a ruling with which numerous subsequent rabbis were uncomfortable indeed. While Moses Nahmanides, Solomon ibn Adret, Yom Tov b. Abraham Ishbili, and Menahem Me'iri all recorded the ruling of the Palestinian Talmud as law,[19] Isaac al-Fasi, Moses Maimonides, and Asher b. Yehiel omit it entirely from their codes. *Sefer Ḥasidim* states emphatically: "One who begets a *mamzer* has not fulfilled the duty of procreation.[20] And convinced that the talmudic R. Avin was merely posing a question rather than formulating an answer, the late medieval David b. Solomon ibn Zimra declared to a correspondent that those

---

16. Loc. cit.

17. Cf. *Sheʾiltot* 184 (165), ed. Mirsky, 5:72 (with n.), where the Tosefta is adduced first to challenge R. Yohanan. The Tosefta specifically excludes a male who becomes incapable of impregnation (*saris*); TJ *Yev.* 6.6, 7c, adds the *'ailonit* and others unable to bear children, hence *MT, 'Ishut* 15.4.

18. TJ *Yev.* 2.6, 3d.

19. Moses b. Nahman, *Ḥiddushe ha-RaMba"N,* 4,1:64; Solomon ibn Adret, *Sefer Ḥiddushe ha-RaShb"A,* 2:6a; Menahem Me'iri, *Bet ha-Bᵉḥirah . . . Yᵉvamot,* p. 92; Yom Tov Ishbili, *Ḥiddushe ha-RITb"A,* 3,1:31–32.

20. SHP 1145, p. 290.

illegitimate children, "with whom one thinks he has performed the commandment of procreation, lower him to the grave and remove him from that existence which is the very rationale for the commandment."[21]

How many grandchildren of each gender suffice to meet one's obligation? All opinions require at least two: one born to one's son and one born to one's daughter. The Palestinian Talmud stipulates that one's son must produce a male child and one's daughter a female in order to yield the minimum complement of grandson and granddaughter.[22] In the Babylonian Talmud, the Amora Abbayye maintains that "a male [grandchild] may count for a male [child], a female may count for a female, and how much the more so may a male count for a female, but a female may not count for a male." His contemporary Rava retorts, "We require [fulfillment of] 'he formed it for habitation,' which is the case" even when a granddaughter counts for a son.[23] In other words, since the commandment of procreation was ordained to perpetuate human settlement of the earth, the gender of one's grandchildren "substituting" for his deceased children matters little. The language of this talmudic dispute suggests that the same theoretical issue was again at stake. Did the commandment of procreation pertain to the Jews' exclusive relationship with God, leading Abbayye to prefer male progeny who would actively perform more religious duties? Or did reproduction serve the needs of the world at large, in which case a male or female might contribute equally to the perpetuation of human civilization? Medieval rabbis generally sided with Rava.[24]

---

21. David b. Solomon ibn Zimra, *Shu"T* 7.2, 7 pts. in 2 vols. (Jerusalem, 1967), 7:3a. On the ongoing debate among postmedieval halakhists, which does little to illuminate their appreciation of the biblical commandment, see *ShA, EH* 1:6 with glosses (where Moses Isserles ruled that a *mamzer*, a deafmute, and a deranged child all fulfill the duty of procreation), and Hayyim Joseph David Azulai, *Sefer Birke Yosef* ad *EH* (1.6) 1.12, 4 vols. (Vienna, 1859), 3:1b; the notes of Reuben Margaliot to *SHB* 500, pp. 335–36; and the comments of Joseph Babad, *Sefer Minḥat Ḥinnukh*, 2 vols. (New York, 1966), 1:1a. With regard to a deafmute and/or deranged child, see Jacob b. Moses ha-Levi Molin, *Responsa of . . . Maharil* (Hebrew) 196, ed. Yitzchok Satz (Jerusalem, 1979), p. 312, who reasoned that such children were no less significant than the Gentile offspring of a convert (see below, at n. 77) and that they contributed to either goal of the commandment of procreation—settling the world or preparing for the messiah.

22. Loc. cit.

23. TB *Yev.* 62b.

24. Yet here too room remained for disagreement. According to *MT, 'Ishut* 15.5 (and thus *ShA, EH* 1.6), one's deceased son and daughter must each have left him a grandchild, one male and one female (although not necessarily respectively); so too Abraham of Montpellier, *Commentary on the Tractate Yevamoth*, p. 147. Menahem Me'iri, *Bet ha-Bᵉḥirah . . . Yᵉvamot*,

The Mishnah implies that once one has produced the required number of children he may desist from procreation, as the Babylonian Gemara immediately notes.[25] Nevertheless, the same Gemara subsequently notes a divergence of opinion between this Mishnah and the instruction of R. Joshua recorded in a *baraita*:

> Though a man married in his youth, he should marry in his old age; though he had children in his youth, he should have children in his old age. As Scripture states (Eccl. 11:6), "Sow your seed in the morning, and don't hold back your hand in the evening (*wela-'erev 'al tannaḥ yadekha*), since you don't know which is going to succeed, the one or the other, or if both are equally good."

The Talmud then quotes R. Matna to the effect that the opinion of R. Joshua is binding[26]—so that childbearing is obligatory even after the Mishnaic complement of children has been produced. R. Matna's ruling attests to the importance the rabbis attributed to procreation as a religious duty; its value and urgency were not subject to numerical limitation. Because some children predecease their parents, R. Joshua's counsel would ensure more instances of ultimate compliance with the obligation to reproduce; as the biblical preacher would have it, one simply does not know if one's first children will live to bear reproductive children of their own. On the other hand, the eventual codification of the principle of la-'erev ("in the evening," following the text of Ecclesiastes) as law effectively nullified the Mishnaic dispensation for abstaining from reproductive activity once the required number of children have been born. Notably, medieval rabbis did retain a distinction between *la-'erev*, which they usually classified a rabbinic ordinance (*mide-rabbanan*), and the law of the Mishnah, which they labeled as grounded in Scripture (*mide-'oraita*).[27] Yet once again they differed as to

---

p. 229, and Isaiah b. Elijah of Trani, *Piskei HaRid, Piskei HaRiaz,* 4,2:49, held that the deceased son and daughter must each have left him one grandchild of either gender—so that two granddaughters ultimately fulfill the commandment. Cf. Israel b. Petahiah Isserlein, *Shu"T Terumat ha-Deshen* 262 (Warsaw, 1882), pp. 47b–48a, and David ibn Zimra, *Shu"T* 5.36, 5:8a, who endeavored to prove that Rava actually intended the ruling later codified by Maimonides.

25. TB *Yev.* 61b.

26. Ibid. 62b.

27. Isaac b. Jacob al-Fasi, *Hilkhot Rav 'Alfas,* ed. Nissan Zacks, 2 vols. (Jerusalem, 1969), 2:29, omitted the statement of TB that the Mishnah is in dispute with the opinion of R. Joshua, and added that R. Matna's definition of the law as following R. Joshua applies to a rabbinic ordinance (*mide-rabbanan*), while the Hillelite prescription of a son and a daughter comprises the scriptural commandment (*mide-'oraita*). *MT, 'Ishut* 15.16, follows suit. Asher b. Yehiel, in

the theoretical basis for the law. While most of his colleagues assumed a link between the additional obligation of *la-ʿerev* and the promotion of human civilization at large (*shevet*), Maimonides advanced a more particularistic rationale for *la-ʿerev*, obsering that "one who adds a single soul to the community of Israel rates as if he has built an entire world."[28] In any event, so sure were medieval halakhists that the Torah had prescribed the duty of procreation, they could contrast the biblical precept to supplementary regulations of an admittedly postbiblical origin.

Marital Priorities

The obligation to reproduce bore heavily on the order and substance of key decisions that an individual would make in the course of his

---

his commentary ad *Yev.* 6.8, explained that the statement omitted by al-Fasi has implications for the circumstances under which one may sell a Torah scroll for the sake of procreation (see below at n. 33): If one deems the Mishnah and R. Joshua in dispute, then R. Matna's ruling requires one to sell a Torah scroll even if he already has children; omitting reference to a dispute between Mishnah and *baraita'*, al-Fasi can hold that once one fulfills the Mishnaic quota he is obligated to father more children but need not sell a Torah scroll to do so. So also Menahem Meʾiri, *Bet ha-Bᵉḥirah . . . Yᵉvamot*, p. 227. The implication of TB *Yev.* 61b is that the Torah scroll can be sold only to fulfill the Mosaic ordinance of procreation as defined by the Mishnah. In contrast to this view, however, *Shᵉʾiltot* 5, ed. Mirsky, 1:37–38, rules on the basis of R. Joshua's opinion that one may still sell a Torah scroll to marry a wife capable of bearing children even after the minimal obligation has been met; so too *OHG* ad *Yev.* 329–31, 7:142. Questioning the failure of the Meʾiri to cite the *Shᵉʾiltot*, Mirsky suggests that he (along with other medieval authorities) relied on Moses b. Nahman, *Milḥamot ha-Shem* (ad al-Fasi, loc. cit.), who responded to the objection of Zerahiah b. Isaac ha-Levi Gerondi, *Ha-Maʾor ha-Gadol*, ad loc., that al-Fasi simply ignored the contradiction between the Mishnah and R. Joshua. Asserting that the Mishnah and the ensuing Gemara would make little sense were the ruling of R. Joshua *midᵉ-ʾoraita'*, Nahmanides adduced the *Shᵉʾiltot* to argue that even after meeting the requirements of the Mishnah one may still rely on R. Joshua's rabbinic ordinance to sell a Torah scroll in order to marry for the sake of procreation, since one thereby continues to fulfill the duty of *shevet*—i.e., promoting the habitation of God's creation (as in Is. 45:18). So too Abraham of Montpellier, *Commentary on the Tractate Yevamoth*, pp. 147–48, and the authorities cited in Feldman, p. 50 n. 26. (See also Mirsky's long notes ad loc., explaining how the original text of the *Shᵉʾiltot* was later dismembered, with portions of this chapter relocated to 184 [165], 5:69–74.) According to N. Z. Y. Berlin, *Haʿameq Shᵉʾelah* ad loc., in *Shᵉʾiltot* (1861–67), 3:279, the *Shᵉʾiltot* construes the duty of *la-ʿerev* as a possible scriptural requirement (*sᵉfeq dᵉvar Torah*) and expressly for that reason permits one with children to sell a Torah scroll in order to father more. This view is also advanced in Hayyim Hezekiah Medini, *Rabbinical Encyclopedia "Sede Chemed"* (Hebrew), rev. ed., 10 vols. (Brooklyn, N.Y., 1949–53), 1:128b–129b. (On the sale of the Torah and its importance, see below, n. 33.) At the other end of the spectrum of opinion, Isaiah b. Elijah of Trani, in *Piskei HaRid, Piskei HaRiaz*, 4,2:49, took issue with the majority (citing *MT*) and concluded that one may blamelessly choose not to have more children than those stipulated in the Mishnah.

28. Loc. cit.

lifetime. We noted in Chapter 2 how vehemently the sages of Yavneh reportedly frowned upon celibacy. To their mind, it subverted the foundations of human civilization precisely because it prevented compliance with the biblical injunction to procreate. Following the biblical norm, the rabbis of the Talmud understandably treated marriage as an indispensable component of the childbearing process. To the Mishnaic ordinance that one may not neglect the duty of procreation until he has already had children, the Tosefta appended the ruling "A man is not permitted to dwell without a wife."[29] And drawing on any of several talmudic dicta, Maimonides posed the question "When does a man become obligated by this commandment [of procreation]? From the age of seventeen. And if his twentieth year has passed and he still has not married, he transgresses and nullifies a positive commandment."[30] The urgency of the obligation is reflected in one Amoraic rationale for the Mishnaic prohibition of marriage during the intermediate days of a festival: In order to avoid the expense of a separate wedding feast by combining it with the celebration of the festival, an individual might otherwise postpone his reproductive activity.[31] Palestinian and Babylonian Amora'im debated whether one might legitimately defer marriage in order to study the Torah,[32] but even when sanctioned such a postponement could only be temporary. Because of the fundamental importance of procreation, some sages ranked marriage alongside Torah study itself. Citing Is. 45:18 as the reason, the Babylonian Talmud reports: "R. Yohanan said in the name of R. Meir: One may not sell a Torah scroll except in order to study the Torah or to marry."[33] The

29. T *Yev.* 8.4, p. 25.

30. *MT*, 3 (Jerusalem, 1977), 135 (*'Ishut* 15.2). Different ms. variants read sixteen and eighteen instead of seventeen. Vidal Yom Tov, in his *Maggid Mishneh*, ad loc., links the age of seventeen to the counsel of R. Judah b. Tema in M *'Avot* 5.21: "an eighteen-year-old boy is ready for the marital canopy"—i.e., after seventeen full years have passed. A reading of eighteen in *MT* would accord more easily with the same Mishnah. That of sixteen, along with the terminus of the twentieth year, would probably derive from TB *Qid.* 29b–30a.

31. M *MQ* 1.7; TJ, ad loc., 80d offers this as the first of three explanations, TB 8b as one of several. On the questionable logic of this explanation, see Tosafot ad loc., s.v. *mippᵉne biṭṭul pᵉriyyah u-rᵉviyyah*, and *Shishah Sidre Mishnah*, ed. C. Albeck, 6 vols. (Jerusalem, 1958–59), 2:507n.

32. TB *Qid.* 29b. Cf. the recasting of the problem in *Shᵉ'iltot* 5, ed. Mirsky, 1:36–37: What if one has the financial means either to study or to marry but not both—which responsibility takes precedence?

33. TB *Meg.* 27a. On the theological implications of this ruling—specifically, for determining the relative importance of different commandments—see N. Z. Y. Berlin, *Haʿameq Shᵉ'elah*, in *Shᵉ'iltot* (1861–67), 1:28–29, and the suggestion of Tosafot ad *Git.* 41b, s.v. *loʾ tohu bᵉraʾah*, BB 13a, s.v. *she-ne'emar*, Hag. 2b, s.v. *loʾ tohu bᵉraʾah*. Also with reference to Is. 45:18, *Shᵉ'iltot* 3, ed. Mirsky, 1:28–29 (with long note on problematic reading), rules that the obligation to dower a bride takes precedence over burying the dead.

Gemara relates several incidents of rabbis rebuking their peers for neglecting their marital and procreative responsibilities.[34] The case of the Yavnean Simeon b. Azzai, who acknowledged the theological significance of procreation but refused to have children for fear they would divert him from his studies, caused noteworthy discomfort in the ensuing halakhic tradition. Ben Azzai exemplified diligence and dedication among the sages of his generation,[35] but in the eyes of his colleagues his celibacy left him incomplete, lacking the perfection of one who practices what he preaches.[36] Maimonides, followed by Jacob b. Asher and Joseph Karo, ruled that one who emulates Ben Azzai in this regard does not sin, so long as sexual desire does not distract him from study.[37] Other medieval authorities, however, deemed Ben Azzai a sole instance from which one could not generalize. Isaac Al-Fasi failed to mention Ben Azzai's plea for dispensation in his code; Asher b. Yehiel deemed Ben Azzai the colloquial exception that proves the rule;[38] and Yom Tov b. Abraham Ishbili cited the Tosafists to the effect that no one in the post-talmudic era would qualify for Ben Azzai's exemption.[39]

But marriage per se did not suffice to comply with the biblical precept. One had to marry a woman who was ostensibly capable of bearing children. In the paragraph preceding its prescription of procreation, the Mishnah rules that a priest may not marry an 'ailonit, a woman visibly lacking the physiological capacity to bear children, unless he already has a wife and children.[40] The Babylonian Gemara at once clarifies that this regulation derives from the duty of procreation (p^{e}riyyah u-r^{e}viyyah), that it therefore binds all Jews, and that the Mishnah specifies a priest only to introduce R. Judah's more stringent opinion that a priest may never marry an 'ailonit.[41] Within this category of

34. TB *Yev.* 62b, 64b; *Qid.* 29b.
35. M *Soṭah* 9.15.
36. See above, Chapter 2, n. 160.
37. *MT*, *'Ishut* 15.3; *Tur*, *EH* 1; *ShA*, *EH* 1.4. See also Abraham of Montpellier, *Commentary on the Tractate Yevamoth*, p. 149, and Menahem Me'iri, *Bet ha-B^{e}ḥirah . . . Y^{e}vamot*, p. 233.
38. Commentary ad *Qid.* 1.42.
39. Yom Tov Ishbili, *Ḥiddushe ha-RITb"A*, 3, 1:93. See also Joseph Karo, *Shu"T Bet Yosef* 14, p. 159: The incidence of one who dedicates himself exclusively to Torah study like Ben Azzai "is exceptional, occurring only once in several generations, and we have not heard that there was ever another such instance."
40. M *Yev.* 6.5.
41. Elsewhere, the Mishnah itself lends support to this inference, for it includes the 'ailonit among those women who may not undergo the cleansing ordeal imposed by the Torah (Num. 5:11–31) on a woman suspected of adultery (*Soṭah* 4.3). Because these women should never have been married in the first place, they must leave their husbands in any event, without the compensation stipulated in their marriage contracts. R. Eliezer's dissenting opinion, that the 'ailonit accused of adultery may undergo the ordeal because her husband

women, the Tosefta includes the barren, those too old or too young for childbearing, and those unfit for any other reason.[42]

Once married, a man is forbidden by the same passage in the Tosefta from drinking a sterilizing potion, and the rabbis repeatedly frowned on any sexual practice that did not aim toward conception. Yet did the rabbis relate this ban on "the needless emission of semen" (*hoza'at zera' le-vattalah*) to the biblical mandate of "be fertile and increase"? The talmudic masters drew no explicit connection between the two, but several classical rabbinic texts did facilitate extensive discussion on the subject among subsequent halakhic authorities. Under the rubric of a mishnaic pericope that condemns autoerotic activity, the Babylonian Germara records the notably hyperbolic comments of several Palestinian Amora'im. "R. Yohanan said: Anyone who needlessly emits semen deserves capital punishment, as Scripture states (Gen. 38:10): 'What he did was displeasing to the Lord, and he took his life also.' " R. Isaac and R. Ammi said: "It is as if he commits murder. . . . R. Assi said: It is as if he practices idolatry."[43] R. Yohanan's allusion to the biblical story of Er and Onan, who refused to impregnate the wife of their deceased brother, suggests that prohibiting needless ejaculation is indeed the obverse of mandating procreation. For these sages, impeding the natural reproductive process clearly undermines the basis for a healthy society,[44] just as the bearing of children reinforces it. But in reporting an exchange attributed to the sages of Yavneh, the Gemara complicates the issue.[45]

> (A) For all of the twenty-four months [that his wife is nursing an infant child], one threshes inside and winnows outside [a euphemism for *coitus interruptus*]—according to R. Eliezer. (B) They said to him: This is certainly like the deed of Er and Onan. (C) It is like the deed of Er and

---

"could take another wife and have children (lit., be fertile and increase, *lifrot we-lirbot*) from her," suggests the underlying Mishnaic concern: Because of the duty to procreate, one may not marry a woman unfit to bear children.

42. Loc. cit.

43. TB *Nid.* 13a. On Christian associations of Gen. 1:28 with the avoidance of idolatry, see Jobl. diss., pp. 137–39.

44. The analogy to idolatry is particularly illuminating. See the statement of R. Ammi, ibid. 13b, that one who engages in autoerotic activity "is called a sinner, for such is the handiwork of the evil inclination. Today it tells him, 'Do this.' The next day it tells him, 'Do that.' And the following day it tells him, 'Go and worship idols,' and he goes and worships." The same parable reinforces the comparison of idolatry and the needless destruction of any object in TB *Sab.* 105b.

45. TB *Yev.* 34b.

Onan and yet unlike the deed of Er and Onan. It is like the deed of Er and Onan, as it is written (Gen. 38:9), "Whenever he joined with his brother's wife, he let [his seed] go to waste." And yet it is unlike the deed of Er and Onan, for while in their instance the coition was unnatural [i.e., not vaginal intercourse] (*she-lo' ke-darkah*), in this it is natural (*ke-darkah*).

The Gemara's resolution (C) of the two conflicting, Tannaitic opinions (A, B) posits a key distinction between him who engages in *coitus interruptus* with his nursing wife and the infamous Onan. Not only did the sinful brother-in-law of Tamar let his seed go to waste, but his sexual practices allegedly stood entirely outside the arena of reproductive activity. One who withdraws prematurely from a nursing woman, on the other hand, merely ends the normal reproductive act early, and he presumably does so to safeguard a newborn child—whose mother might cease to lactate if she conceived again—and not to interfere with the process of procreation. This text would appear to strengthen the premise that concern for procreation underlies the rabbinic reading of the story of Er and Onan: Acts normally leading to procreation are permitted even if one occasionally obviates conception; sexual activity of a type that does not facilitate the bearing and rearing of children is condemnable. Nevertheless, in a third talmudic text, the same R. Yohanan who reportedly likened "the needless emission of semen" to a capital crime quoted his predecessors to the effect that a man may engage in any sexual practice with his wife.[46]

Confronted with these sources, medieval rabbis generally espoused one of two approaches to the issue. According to one interpretation,[47] the ejaculation of semen in any instance but that of completed, "natural," vaginal intercourse is forbidden; the guilt of Er and Onan lay in their *act* of spilling seed in a nonreproductive manner, just as the challengers[48] of the Yavnean R. Eliezer proposed.[48] Menahem Kasher[49] has suggested that this school of thought considered their behavior murderous, inasmuch as they deprived putative, unborn souls of an opportunity for life. Thus construed, the prohibition of "the needless emis-

46. TB *Ned.* 20b.
47. Tosafot ad *Yev.* 34b, s.v. *welo' ke-ma'aseh 'Er we-'Onan*, the first opinion of R. Isaac (b. Samuel); *MT*, *'Issure Bi'ah* 21.9; Menahem Me'iri, *Bet ha-Beḥirah . . . Yevamot*, p. 142, rules that it is forbidden to follow R. Eliezer's opinion.
48. So too *GenR* 85.4 (ad 38:7), 2:1037; *MHG*, 1:644.
49. See his lengthy excursus in Kasher, 6:1454–55 n. 44, which refers to most of the sources cited in this paragraph.

sion of semen" binds women as well as men, therefore leads to a more restrictive stance on the use of contraceptives by women, and applies even after one has fathered the required complement of children.[50] Alternatively, some authorities deemed the *intention* of an individual more important than the form of his sexual act. So long as they are not intended contraceptively, "unnatural" sexual practices (*she-lo' ke-darkah*), even if they result in ejaculation, are permitted occasionally on the grounds that they fulfill sexual desires.[51] When Er and Onan engaged in such activity, they expressly sought to keep Tamar from conceiving, and as such (just as R. Eliezer had reasoned) their "winnowing outside" and their unnatural acts were sinful because they deliberately contravened the precept of "be fertile and increase." Proscription derives from prescription; it therefore applies only to those bound by Mosaic law to procreate,[52] and it results in a more permissive posture with regard to female contraceptives. Paradoxically, even proponents of this latter, liberal position on contraceptives eventually came to disregard its theoretical basis. Finding the countenance of any "unnatural" sexual behavior repulsive, they freed the ban on "the needless emission of semen" from its dependence on mandate for procreation.[53]

Several talmudic rulings permit one who has not yet fathered children to marry and engage in sexual activity even during famine, a period of mourning, or some national calamity when conjugal relations would otherwise be prohibited.[54] Moreover, should a couple remain childless for ten years, the Mishnah and the Tosefta require that the husband divorce his wife and then remarry. Because the husband may have been

---

50. This is the view of Rashi according to Tosafot ad *Nid.* 13a, s.v. *nashim, Yev.* 12b, s.v. *shalosh,* and *Ket.* 39a, s.v. *shalosh;* and the view shared by Rashi and Hananel b. Hushiel according to Asher b. Yehiel, *Tosefe ha-RO"sh* ad *Nid.* 13a, s.v. *nashim.* In agreement are also Moses b. Nahman, *Ḥiddushe ha-RaMba"N,* 3,2:54–55; Solomon b. Abraham ibn Adret, *Ḥiddushe ha-RaShb"A 'al Masekhet Niddah,* ed. Isaac Meir Ben-Menahem (Jerusalem, 1938), pp. 20–21; Nissim B. Reuben Gerondi, *Ḥiddushe ha-Ra"N 'al Masekhet Niddah* (Jerusalem, 1973), p. 15; Yom Tov b. Abraham Ishbili, *Ḥiddushe ha-RITb"A: Masekhet Niddah,* ed. David Metzger (Jerusalem, 1978), cols. 69–71.

51. Tosafot ad *Yev.* 34b, s.v. *we-lo' ke-ma'aseh 'Er we-'Onan,* the second opinion of Isaac (b. Samuel); Isaiah b. Mali of Trani, *Tosefot RI"D: Masekhet Yevamot* (Jerusalem, 1931), p. 2b.

52. Thus the view of Tosafot ad *San.* 59b, s.v. *we-ha' periyyah u-reviyyah;* and that of Jacob b. Meir Tam, cited in Tosafot ad *Nid.* 13a, s.v. *nashim, Yev.* 12b, s.v. *shalosh,* and *Ket.* 39a, s.v. *shalosh.*

53. See Feldman, esp. pp. 112–13.

54. TJ *Taan.* 1.6, 64d; TB ibid., 11a; TB *MQ* 23a. *MT, Taan.* 3.8. A tradition forbidding sexual activity even to a childless husband in times of famine survives in *Tan.* (*Noaḥ* 11), p. 6a, reasoning that "the holy one, blessed be he, should not be occupied in the destruction of the world and he [the husband] be building it." As Kasher, 7:1559–60, clarifies, however, the Halakhah has consistently allowed childless couples to have conjugal relations even during disastrous times. Cf. the sources cited above, Chapter 2, nn. 177, 200.

the infertile one, his wife too may marry again, but after her second (or third) childless marriage she may only marry a man who already has a wife and children, since otherwise her marriage would be legally improper (*nissu'e ṭa'ut*).[55] The Tosefta elaborates further that periods during which the husband is absent, ill, or too old to father children do not count toward the ten-year limit, and much discussion ensued, both in the Talmuds and among later authorities, as to diverse contingencies arising from all of these situations. Most of this discussion relates only marginally to the rabbinic exegesis of Gen. 1:28 and therefore will not concern us at present.[56] One might note, however, that in considering whether a childless woman may marry a still childless man once or twice more after her first divorce, both Talmuds draw an analogy between infertile marriages and circumcisions resulting in death.[57] Once again an association between procreation and God's covenant with Israel has practical ramifications within the realm of Halakhah.

The subordination of marriage and conjugal relations to the priority of procreation confirms the statutory authority that the talmudic sages attributed to the mandate of Gen. 1:28, and it comports with the rationalization for marriage among much of the Greco-Roman intelligentsia at the dawn of the common era. Philo repeatedly justified marriage as the means to procreation, asserting that "the end we seek in wedlock is not pleasure but the begetting of lawful children." He wrote that Moses accordingly chose to forgo all sexual activity "save for the lawful begetting of children," and that just as the Torah forbade sexual contact with a menstruant, so too was it unlawful to marry a barren woman.[58] Such sentiments prevailed particularly among the Stoics,[59] and even Plato had called for female officials appointed by the state to

---

55. M *Yev.* 6.6, T ibid., 8.5–6.

56. Particularly interesting is the question of whether the Tosefta's exclusion (from the ten-year limit) of time spent in the Diaspora now applies to Jews who live their whole lives outside Palestine; see below, Chapter 4, nn. 8–9.

57. TJ *Yev.* 6.6, 7d; TB ibid., 64b. The rabbis disputed whether the circumcision-induced deaths of two or three brothers excused their father from circumcising his subsequent children.

58. Philo, *De Iosepho* 9.43, LCL 6:162–65; *De vita Moysis* 1.28, 6:290–91; *De specialibus legibus* 3.6.32–36, 7:494–97. Cf. also *Quod deterius potiori insidiari soleat* 27.102, 2:270–71. On Philo's attitudes toward sexuality and on their relation to Hellenistic and rabbinic ideas, see Isaak Heinemann, *Philons griechische und jüdische Bildung: Kulturvergleichende Untersuchungen zu Philons Darstellung der jüdischen Gesetze* (Hildesheim, 1962), pp. 261–92.

59. Max Pohlenz, *Die Stoa: Geschichte einer geistigen Bewegung*, 4th ed., 2 vols. (Göttingen, 1970–72), 1:140, 2:76; Marcia L. Colish, *The Stoic Tradition from Antiquity to the Early Middle Ages*, 2 vols., Studies in the History of Christian Thought 34–35 (Leiden, 1985), 1:39–41, 270–72; and Noonan, *Contraception*, pp. 46–49.

supervise conjugal relations, like the Mishnah ensuring that no childless couple would remain married for longer than ten years.[60]

Yet while the rabbis of the Talmud concurred that matrimony must facilitate reproduction, in their view marriage also possesses a distinct, independent value of its own. After a man has met his procreative obligations, the Talmud still orders him to be married,[61] and in its discussion of the Mishnaic law of procreation the Babylonian Gemara records numerous homilies on the importance and rewards of marriage.[62] "Any man who has no wife is not a man," quipped R. Eleazar, and according to his contemporary R. Hanilai, as quoted by R. Tanhum, "any man who has no wife lives without happiness, without blessing, and without goodness." Maimonides eventually codified the obligation to be married as a rabbinic ordinance (*mizwat ḥakhamim*) clearly separate from "be fertile and increase."[63] As we shall see in Chapter 4, medieval rabbinic halakhists worked strenuously to define the line of demarcation between the responsibility to marry and the commandment of procreation.

IDENTIFYING THE DUTY-BOUND

Having endeavored to conclude exactly what responsibilities the commandment of procreation entailed, the Talmud also struggles to determine whom the biblical precept of "be fertile and increase" obligates to have children. In the text of the Bible, God addresses these words to both of the first parents, to man and to woman; but in construing the primordial blessing as Mosaic law, the rabbis defined a religious duty for the Jewish community alone, and not even for all Jews at that. This contrast between the seemingly blatant meaning of Scripture and the narrow application of the law deriving therefrom left a clear mark in rabbinic literature. While rabbinic law translated a universally applicable biblical text into a statute binding upon a care-

---

60. Plato, *Laws* 6.783E–784D, ed. R. G. Bury, LCL, 2 vols. (Cambridge, Mass., 1926), 1:496–99. For additional parallels in Greek, Roman, and even Hindu cultures, see B. Cohen, *Jewish and Roman Law*, 1:389–93; and cf. Eva C. Keuls, *The Reign of the Phallus* (New York, 1985), esp. ch. 4.

61. TB *Yev.* 61b.

62. Ibid., 62b–63b.

63. *MT*, *'Ishut* 15.16.

fully circumscribed class of individuals, some rabbis, from the talmudic period until the present day, have resisted that process, questioning its logic and desirability. The issues we shall soon consider, though almost entirely devoid of practical, juridical consequences, have never been satisfactorily resolved, and precisely for that reason they comprise most illuminating data for the present study.

Women

Coupled with the biblical narrative, the basic facts of life render noteworthy the rabbinic discussion of whether God included women in his mandate for procreation. The basic patriarchal orientation of ancient Judaism does not suffice as a satisfactory explanation. Although the bearing of children is not a legal duty that must be performed at a specific time and from which women would thus normally be exempt,[64] the Mishnah appends the following qualification to its law of procreation: "A man is bound by the duty of procreation but not a woman. R. Yohanan b. Broka says: With regard to them both Scripture states, 'God blessed them and [God] said to them, "Be fertile and increase."'"[65]

While the editor of the Mishnah listed Yohanan b. Broka's opinion as a dissenting opinion, the logic of his inclusive position did strike other rabbis as compelling. Expanding on the Mishnaic law of procreation, several manuscript versions of the Tosefta reflect and develop Yohanan's ruling by including women in the bans on (1) remaining unmarried, (2) drinking a sterilizing potion, and (3) marrying a person unfit to have children.[66] Palestinian texts of the Amoraic period state

---

64. M *Qid.* 1.7, and see TB ibid., 34b–35a.

65. M *Yev.* 6.6.

66. The immediate juxtaposition (T *Yev.* 8.4, ed. Lieberman, 3:24–25) of R. Judah's view that "one who severs the reproductive organs of males is culpable but [one who severs the reproductive organs of] females is not culpable" indicates that the Tosefta viewed the duty of procreation as the obverse of the ban on castration. R. Judah's dissenting, permissive view regarding the sterilization of females may therefore imply that the opposing, anonymous rulings of this *baraita'*, as recorded in the manuscripts we have mentioned, derive from Yohanan b. Broka's position. Even if the original version of this *baraita'* did not include women in the three bans listed, the Tosefta elsewhere (*Mak.* 5.6) adduces R. Judah's view permitting the sterilization of females as a single, dissenting voice; see *Tosephta* (Hebrew), ed. M. S. Zuckermandel, new ed. (Jerusalem, 1970), p. 444. This again would suggest a preference for the stricter position of Yohanan b. Broka, who included women in the commandment of Gen. 1:28 and therefore, according to the Babylonian Gemara (TB *Sab.* 111a), forbade their sterilization. See the analysis of Lieberman, *Tosefta ki-Fshutah*, 6:67–70, who, relying on

that the Halakhah adheres to this position, a view evidently espoused as late as the tenth century by Saadya b. Joseph, the Gaon of the Babylonian academy of Sura.[67] The Babylonian Gemara cites a dispute between two Palestinian Amora'im on the subject, but it eventually follows the anonymous and evidently preferred opinion in the Mishnah. Seeking to rationalize this position, both Talmuds adduce an Amoraic midrash on "fill the earth and master it," that "it is the manner of a man to master (*likhbosh*) but it is not the manner of a woman to master"; if God directed "and master it" exclusively to men, "be fertile and increase" must apply to them alone as well.[68] To the objection that the Torah's verb "and master it" (*we-khivshuha*) is plural and must refer to both man and woman, R. Nahman b. Isaac argued that *we-khivshuha* is spelled defectively (*wkbsh*) and may therefore be read as a singular form (*we-khovsheha*). Perhaps aware of the response from the "camp" of Yohanan b. Broka, that the singular *we-khovsheha* might be a command for the husband to master his wife (rather than the land) and thus have no delimiting impact on the preceding instructions to reproduce,[69] the Gemara offers the alternative explanation of R. Joseph: The commandment to procreate binds men only because it derives from the unquestionably singular verbs in God's blessing of Jacob (Gen. 35:11), "be fertile (*pereh*) and increase (*u-reveh*)." Although it does not consider a woman bound by Gen. 1:28, the Babylonian Gemara reasons that she

---

MT, *'Ishut* 15.16, and *'Issure Bi'ah* 16.12, 21.26, argued that the correct reading might forbid women to (1) remain unmarried, but permit them (2) to drink a sterilizing potion and (3) to marry a sterile man. On the essential correspondence of the biblical prescription of procreation and prohibition of sterilization, cf. TB *San.* 57a, which records the view that the Noachide ban on castration derived from Gen. 9:7: "[be fertile, then, and increase;] abound on the earth and increase on it." And see the medieval authorities cited by Lieberman, *Tosefta ki-Fshutah*, 6:70 n. 24.

67. TJ *Yev.* 6.6, 7d; *GenR* 8.12, as cited in n. 69 below; and Saadya, *Commentary on Genesis*, pp. 94, 321–22, with Zucker's note 146; and cf. the objection of Mubashir b. Nissi ha-Levi, *A Critique against the Writings of R. Saadya Gaon*, pp. 28, 81–82, with Zucker's note 83.

68. TB *Yev.* 65b; cf. TJ ibid., 7d: "Whose manner is it to master? The man and not the woman." The logic of this midrash is explained by Rashi in his commentary ad TB *Qid.* 35a, s.v. *darko likhbosh:* "It is his manner to master the land in war and not her manner. And since we do not apply *we-khivshuha* to her, we do not apply *peru u-revu* to her."

69. *GenR* 8.12 (ad 1:28), 1:66. The assertion of Porton, *Understanding Rabbinic Midrash*, p. 181, that according to the Babylonian Gemara's interpretation of *we-khovsheha* a husband "may force his wife to have intercourse with him in order to fulfill his obligation to produce children" (and that according to *GenR* he may control her activities short of forcing her to bed) is incorrect. See Nahum Rakover, "Yahase 'Ishut bi-Khfiyyah ben Ba'al le-'Ishto," *Shenaton ha-Mishpat ha-'Ivri* 6–7 (1979–80), 295–317. I am grateful to Mordechai Friedman for calling this reference to my attention.

can still sue for divorce to free her from a childless marriage on the grounds that she needs offspring to care for her in her old age.

As usual, the Babylonian tradition ultimately prevailed among medieval rabbinic authorities,[70] but neither the sensibility of Yohanan b. Broka's position nor the exegetical dispute over *wᵉ-khivshuha* was forgotten. Some later midrashic anthologies, regardless of their halakhic opinions, included both interpretations of a singular reading of "and master it" in Gen. 1:28 so as to obscure their original intent.[71] For their part, medieval halakhists often felt impelled to preserve some modicum of obligation for women in the reproductive process, which could not proceed without her. Maimonides forbade a woman voluntarily to forgo conjugal relations with her husband if he has not yet fulfilled his reproductive duties.[72] While earlier rabbis had generally used the concept of *shevet*—the civilized human habitation for whose sake God had reportedly (Is. 45:18) created the world—to rationalize the commandment of procreation and perhaps to extend its fulfillment beyond the minimal complement required by the Mishnah, Tosafists like Isaac b. Mordecai construed it as a broader category of obligation: "Be fertile and increase" binds men alone; *shevet* includes women as well.[73] Several other halakhists grappled with the talmudic statement that though a woman may accept betrothal through an agent she better fulfills her

70. *Shᵉ'iltot* 18, ed. Mirsky, 1:121; *OHG* ad *Yev.* 359, 7:156; Isaac al-Fasi, *Hilkhot Rav 'Alfas*, 2:31; *MT*, *'Ishut* 15.2, 15.10; Asher b. Yehiel, commentary ad *Yev.*, 6.19.

71. Evidently ruling with TJ and Yohanan b. Broka that the law of Gen. 1:28 does include women, *Tan.* (*Noah* 12), p. 6a, reasons from the defective spelling of *wᵉ-khivshuha* that "a man masters the land and a woman does not master the land" and therefore that "a man is commanded concerning procreation more than a woman"; cf. *Tan.* (*Wa-yishlah* 5), p. 16b (with a change in typeface suggesting an interpolation in the ms.), which includes both interpretations of a singular *wᵉ-khovsheha* (*TanB* [*Wa-yishlah* 12], 2:86a, includes only that adduced by *GenR* in favor of Yohanan b. Broka), and see *TanB* (*Noah* 18), 2:22b n. 185. *Yalqut Shim'oni 'al ha-Torah* 16, 1,1:43, on the other hand, asserts that the law does not follow Yohanan b. Broka but at least in one ms. notes that "a man masters his wife." Despite his aforecited (n. 68) assertion that the feminine pronominal suffix of *wᵉ-khivshuha* refers to the land, in his gloss on Gen. 1:28, RaSh"I, p. 4, maintained that the Torah spells the word defectively also "to teach you that the male masters the female." Attempts to resolve the confusion appear in Elijah b. Abraham Mizrahi, *Be'ur lᵉ-Ferush RaSh"I 'al ha-Torah*, in Oẓar Mᵉfarᵉshe ha-Torah, 2 vols. (Jerusalem, 1973), 1:10a, and the *Ḥiddushe 'Aggadot* of Samuel Edels ad *Yev.* 65b, s.v. *'ish*.

72. *MT*, *'Ishut* 15.1.

73. *Tosafot* ad *Git.* 41b, s.v. *lo' tohu bᵉra'ah*, *BB* 13a, s.v. *she-ne'emar*. Cf. the juridical application of this principle in David b. Hayyim ha-Kohen, *Shu"T ha-RaDa"Kh* 2.17 (Salonika, 1803), esp. pp. 61b–62a. Curiously, David b. Hayyim is cited by Elijah b. Hayyim in *Shu"t Mayim 'Amuqim* 2.70 (Berlin, 1778), p. 74b, as ruling "that a woman is bound by the commandment of procreation."

duty if she accepts it herself; of what duty does the Talmud speak? Menahem Me'iri responded: "Even though she is not bound by the commandment of procreation (*p^eriyyah u-r^eviyyah*), the commandment is still performed through her agency. Furthermore, even though no definite positive commandment (*'aseh gamur*) applies to her [regarding procreation], she is not removed completely from all obligation."[74] His Spanish successor Nissim b. Reuben Gerondi wrote in a similar vein, in terms that are best compared to the merit that accrues for one who executes an "assist" in an athletic contest: "even though a woman is not bound by the obligation of procreation, she still has a commandment (*yesh lah mizwah*), because she helps her husband fulfill his obligation."[75] More recent authorities have continued to belabor the point. In a technical sense, the Halakhah clearly does not obligate women to bear children, and few still argue that they are included in a commandment of *shevet* deriving from Is. 45:18. But the legacy of R. Yohanan b. Broka lives on, and most jurists have been equally reluctant to read Gen. 1:28 as excluding women altogether.[76]

Gentiles

Genesis relates that twenty generations elapsed between the creation of the world and the life of Abraham, when God first restricted his covenant and directed his providence to one people in particular. The first parents were not Israelites, and neither was Noah, and they received the blessing of "be fertile and increase" precisely because of their role as progenitors of all human beings. The rabbis of the Talmud tacitly acknowledged this when they cited Is. 45:18 to rationalize the commandment of procreation; if God created the world for human

---

74. Menahem b. Solomon ha-Me'iri, *Bet ha-B^ehirah 'al Masekhet Qiddushin*, ed. Abraham Schreiber (Sofer), 4th ed. (Jerusalem, 1971), p. 205 (ad 41a). See also the lengthy discussion in Azulai, *Sefer Birke Yosef* ad EH (1.13) 1.16, 3:2a–2b.

75. Gloss on Isaac al-Fasi's *Halakhot*, ad *Qid.*, beginning of ch. 2 (p. 16b in standard eds. of TB), s.v. *'ikka' d^e-'am^ere*. This judgment is applied in *Teshuvot ha-RaN: Responsa* (Hebrew) 27, ed. Leon A. Feldman (Jerusalem, 1984), p. 103 with notes, and 32, pp. 129–30 with notes, but see also his reiteration in 55, p. 263, that "there is no absolute obligation (*mizwah g^emurah*), since a woman is not bound by the duty of procreation." Cf. the similar rulings of Benjamin b. Mattathias, *Shu"T Binyamin Z^e'ev* 41, 2 vols. (Jerusalem, 1959), 1:160; and Hayyim Kafusi, in David ibn Zimra, *Shu"T*, 3:68b.

76. See, for example, the sources cited by Samuel b. Uri in his *Bet Sh^emu'el* ad ShA, EH 1.2; *OP*, 7:44b (83); and Feldman, pp. 55–56. See also the compelling arguments concerning *shevet* offered by N. Z. Y. Berlin, *Ha'ameq Sh^e'elah*, in *Sh^e'iltot* (1861–67), 3:278.

habitation, the small size of the Jewish population throughout its history suggested that he did not have one specific ethnic group in mind. Still, the Talmud eventually bent over backward to exempt Gentiles from the mandate for procreation, a process that demanded considerable prowess in exegesis and casuistry.

In its discussion of the Mishnaic prescription of procreation, the Babylonian Gemara depicts a dispute between two Palestinian rabbis of the third century:

(A) It was stated: A man had children while a Gentile (lit., one who worships the stars) and then converted to Judaism. R. Yohanan said: He has fulfilled the duty of procreation. And R. Simeon b. Laqish said: He has not fulfilled the duty of procreation. R. Yohanan said he has fulfilled the duty of procreation because he had children. And R. Simeon b. Laqish said he has not fulfilled the duty of procreation, because a proselyte who has converted is considered like a newborn child.

(B) And they were consistent in their views. For it was stated elsewhere: A man had children while a Gentile and then converted to Judaism. R. Yohanan said: He no longer has [i.e., begets after his conversion] a firstborn son with regard to inheritance (b^ekhor nahalah), because he has already had his firstborn (lit., the first fruit of his vigor, cf. Deut. 21:17). And R. Simeon b. Laqish said he [now] does have a firstborn son with regard to inheritance, because a proselyte who has converted is considered like a newborn child. . . .

(C) R. Abba said: All agree in the case of a slave that he has no legally recognized family ties (hayis).[77]

The Gemara then questions why a report of one of the first two recorded disputes between Yohanan and Simeon would not have sufficed, given their similar content and form. Apprised of the first case (A) alone, answers the anonymous voice of the Talmud, one might think that Yohanan considered a converted father already to have met his reproductive obligations, since proselytes were initially bound as Gentiles by the duty of procreation (d^eme-ʿiqqara' name b^ene p^eriyyah u-r^eviyyah ninhu); but regarding inheritance (B), one might suppose that Yohanan would have agreed with his student Simeon since Gentiles are not

77. TB *Yev.* 62a, which reads Rav for R. Abba; see David Weiss Halivni, *Sources and Traditions: A Source Critical Commentary on Seder Nashim* (Hebrew) (Tel Aviv, 1968), p. 70 n. 4, who emends on the basis of the readings of Isaac al-Fasi, Asher b. Yehiel, and the Munich ms.

bound by the Torah's laws of inheritance.[78] Likewise, with only the second case (B), the reader might suppose that only in this instance does Simeon disagree, because of the exclusion of Gentiles from laws of inheritance,[79] and that concerning procreation (A) he would concur with Yohanan. As David Halivni observed, manuscript variants of this talmudic text, along with a parallel version in Tractate B*ekhorot*,[80] raise questions about the authenticity of the explanations supplied by the Gemara for the respective Amoraic positions. The two sages may have debated these points of law, but the rationales for their rulings supplied by the Talmud undoubtedly comprise a later accretion to the tradition of their discussion. Moreover, the statement of Abba (C) appears inappropriate. The Babylonian Gemara elsewhere records universal agreement that non-Jews do have legally recognized kinship;[81] why does Abba, by specifying here that Yohanan and Simeon agreed concerning slaves, imply that they disagreed concerning Gentiles? Halivni has therefore proposed that Abba's statement was mistakenly recorded here by a later editor and originally related to the Palestinian Gemara's opposing account of the exchange between Yohanan and Simeon. The former argued that Gentiles do have legally recognized family ties, the latter that they do not,[82] yet all would agree, added Abba, that slaves do not. The effect of conversion on the proselyte's kinship was not at issue.[83]

This Palestinian account of Yohanan's position may actually clarify the Babylonian explanation of his ruling concerning procreation. In his view, a proselyte who has the sufficient number of children at the time of his conversion has already met the reproductive obligation prescribed by the Torah, because the law always recognized those children as his descendants. Yohanan here conformed to the logic of the aforecited view ascribed to him that one whose children predecease him has

---

78. Tosafot ad *Yev.* 62a, s.v. d*e-law b*ene naḥalah ninhu, qualify that they are not bound by the law of the special inheritance of the firstborn son, but TB *Qid.* 17b does state that according to the Torah a Gentile inherits his father.

79. This inference does not appear in TB *Yev.* but is spelled out in TB *Bekh.* 47a.

80. TB *Bekh.* 47a.

81. TB *BQ* 15a.

82. TJ *Yev.* 2.6, 4a.

83. Halivni, *Sources and Traditions*, pp. 69–70, who prefers the Palestinian version of the dispute because it obviates the "need" for the Amoraic Yohanan to reject the Tannaitic principle (see TB *Yev.* 48b) that "a proselyte who has converted is considered like a newborn child." Cf. the medieval Eliezer b. Nathan, *Sefer 'Even ha-'Ezer*, ed. Shalom Albeck, 2 vols. (Warsaw, 1904), 1:25b–26a, who similarly defended Yohanan's adherence to this principle.

not fulfilled his procreative duties. The Mosaic commandment seeks to promote God's plan for the habitation of the world, and this individual has not made his contribution to that endeavor (*la-shevet y^ezarah* [Is. 45:18] *ba'inan w^e-ha' likka'*).[84] Gentiles, however, do help to realize the divine intention when they have children, and they too are bound by the mandate "be fertile and increase" even before their conversion (*d^eme-'iqqara' name b^ene p^eriyyah u-r^eviyyah ninhu*). The parallel version of our Amoraic dispute in Tractate *B^ekhorot* simply cites Is. 45:18 to explain Yohanan's ruling on procreation and the proselyte, where the text of *Y^evamot* quoted above reasons, "because he had children." From the perspective attributed to Yohanan, the two arguments are in fact equivalent! Simeon, in applying the logic of his stance that Gentiles have no legally recognized family ties, restricted the commandment of procreation to Jews. His ruling would suggest that the commandment pertained not to the civilization of the world at large but to the relationship between God and Israel in particular.

As they usually did in instances of dispute between Yohanan and Simeon b. Laqish, medieval rabbis followed the opinion of the former sage with regard to a proselyte.[85] Yet Maimonides, in the spirit of his view that "one who adds a single soul to the community of Israel rates as if he has built an entire world,"[86] added the stipulation—completely extraneous to the talmudic discussion—that the proselyte's offspring must also convert to count toward their father's required complement of children, and numerous other authorities subsequently followed suit. The late medieval Vidal Yom Tov eloquently explained the rationale for this stipulation in his gloss *Maggid Mishneh* on Maimonides' code: "Our master [Maimonides] understood that the children have converted too. This is correct, since otherwise he would have to marry so that he would have Jewish children; for R. Yohanan would not have said that Gentile children were sufficient for him."[87] In other words,

---

84. TB *Yev.* 62a; see above, p. 129.

85. Isaac al-Fasi, *Hilkhot Rav 'Alfas*, 2:29; Isaiah b. Mali of Trani, in *Piskei HaRid, Piskei HaRiaz*, 4,1:141; Moses b. Jacob of Coucy, *Sefer Mizwot Gadol*, 2 vols. (1547; repr., Jerusalem, 1961), 2:128b–129a; Moses b. Nahman, *Hilkhot B^ekhorot* (appendix to standard eds. of TB *Bekh.*), p. 55a; Asher b. Yehiel, commentary ad *Bekh.*, 8.1; Isaiah b. Elijah of Trani, in *Piskei HaRid, Piskei HaRiaz* 4,2:49.

86. See above, n. 28.

87. *MT*, *'Ishut* 15.6, with *Maggid Mishneh*, ad loc. See also Asher b. Yehiel, commentary ad *Yev.* 6.8 (cf. Nathaniel b. Naftali Weil, *Qorban N^etan'el* ad loc., who inferred this stipulation from the Asheri's rewording of the talmudic text, "a man had children and they converted");

while the law was ostensibly in accord with Yohanan's view that Gentiles have legally recognized descendants, the exclusivist interpretation of the biblical mandate for procreation implied by Simeon's position ultimately prevailed. Jewish children, rather than the settlement of the macrocosm, constituted the goal of "be fertile and increase." The Babylonian Talmud itself fueled this perplexing development in its analysis of a *baraita'* enumerating the Noachide precepts, those laws ordained by God for Gentiles as well as for Jews.[88] We quote it at length to demonstrate the pains taken by talmudic rabbis in excluding Gentiles from the commandment of procreation:

(A) R. Yosi b. R. Hanina said: (1) Every commandment uttered to the Noachides and repeated [to the Israelites] at Sinai was given to both groups; (2) [every commandment uttered] to the Noachides and not repeated [to the Israelites] at Sinai was given to Israel and not to the Noachides. (3) The only law falling into the latter category is a [ban on eating] the thigh muscle, and that according to the [minority] view of R. Judah [that this ban was given to the sons of Jacob before the revelation at Sinai. . . .[89]

(B) And yet the commandment of circumcision, which (1) was uttered to the Noachides—as it is written (Gen. 17:9), "you shall keep my covenant"—and which (2) was repeated at Sinai—[as it is written (Lev. 12:3)], "on the eighth day he shall be circumcised"—(3) was given to Israel and not to the Noachides. The latter text came specifically (4) to permit circumcision on the Sabbath—"on the [eighth] *day*," meaning even on the Sabbath—[and cannot be considered a repetition of the commandment at Sinai. Therefore Gentiles were not given the commandment.]

(C) And yet the commandment of procreation, which (1) was uttered to the Noachides—as it is written (Gen. 9:7), "be fertile, then, and increase"—and which (2) was repeated at Sinai—[as it is written (Deut. 5:27)], "go, say to them, 'return to your tents [to resume the conjugal relations suspended prior to the utterance of the Ten Commandments]'"—(3) was given to Israel and not to the Noachides. The latter

---

Menahem Me'iri, *Bet ha-Beḥirah . . . Yevamot*, p. 228; *Tur, EH* 1; David ibn Zimra, *Shu"T* 7.2, 7:3a; *ShA, EH* 1.7; *OP*, 1:6b (44). Yet for the opinion that the children need not have converted with their father, see Jacob Molin, *Responsa* 196, p. 312. In his *Be'ur* on *ShA*, ad loc., Elijah b. Solomon of Vilna argued at length that in TB *Yev.* (as opposed to TB *Bekh.*) the language and logic of the text mandate the Maimonidean stipulation, but Elijah ultimately conceded that the weight of the evidence militates against its validity.

88. TB *San.* 59ab.
89. See M *Ḥul.* 7.6.

text came specifically to teach that (4) anything forbidden by a judicial authority requires a dispensation from a judicial authority to permit it. [Because the latter text therefore cannot be considered a repetition of the commandment at Sinai, Gentiles were not given the commandment.]

(D) If this is so, can we not conclude that (1) each Noachide commandment was reiterated for a particular purpose [and therefore cannot be considered as actually repeated at Sinai]? (2) Why else should an entire prohibition be repeated [as opposed to a particular detail (as in the cases of circumcision and procreation), except to include both Noachides and Israelites]?

(E) "The only law [uttered to the Noachides and not repeated at Sinai is a ban on eating] the thigh muscle, and that according to the [minority] view of R. Judah." (1) Were not these [commandments of circumcision and procreation] also not repeated? (2) These were repeated for a particular reason, whereas the other [i.e., ban on the thigh muscle] was not repeated at all. (3) There are those who offer an alternative answer: Abraham was the one initially commanded by God (Gen. 17:9), "as for you, you and your offspring to come throughout the ages shall keep my covenant." This means you and your offspring, but no one else.

This talmudic text is rather intricate and technical in its argumentation and therefore requires careful review and paraphrase. In order to explain why the Noachide law banning the consumption of limbs severed from a live animal was reiterated among the commandments revealed at Sinai, the Talmud cites the paradoxical hermeneutical principle of R. Yosi: (A1) If the Torah repeats a Noachide law—that is, a law revealed to all people before the Sinaitic covenant—as part of the Sinaitic covenant, the law applies to Jews and Gentiles alike. (A2) If, however, the Torah does not so repeat a Noachide law at the time of the Sinaitic revelation, that law applies henceforth to Jews alone. The tradition reporting Yosi's generalization also includes the observation (A3) that only the ban on consuming an animal's thigh muscle falls into the second category (A2), and that law only according to the minority opinion of a single Tannaitic sage. The Talmud then subjects Yosi's principle to extensive scrutiny. In the passage for which we have substituted the ellipsis at the end of the first paragraph (A), Yosi's assertion is twice challenged on the basis of its internal logic and defended on the basis of external considerations: Would not one normally expect that a law once given to all people and subsequently repeated exclusively to the Israelites now applies to the Israelites alone? Maybe so, but because the ban on idolatry once legislated for Gentiles was reiterated for the

Jews at Sinai, and because Gentiles were punished after Sinai for their crimes of idolatry, such a law must still bind them. Conversely, would not one presume that a law once given to Gentiles and never given to the Jews would still bind Gentiles alone? Again, perhaps; but it is inconceivable that a divine law would forbid something to the Gentiles and permit it to the Jews.

Next, the Gemara challenges Yosi's rule with two commandments first uttered in the pre-Sinaitic era and then included in the Sinaitic legislation, yet which now are binding on Jews alone. In the case of circumcision (B), the Talmud offers the defense (B4) that when prescribing the ritual at Sinai (B2), the Torah intended not to repeat the pre-Sinaitic law but solely to permit an otherwise forbidden procedure on the Sabbath.[90] In the absence of outright repetition, the law should not, according to Yosi's rule, apply to Gentiles. With regard to procreation (C), the argument defending Yosi's rule is similar, albeit more difficult to follow. The challenge derives from Deut. 5:27: Why would the Torah have ordered the Jews at Sinai to engage in conjugal relations at Sinai if not for procreative purposes? And if (C2) the instruction of "return to your tents" actually prescribed the duty of procreation, thereby repeating (C1) the earlier, primeval legislation of "be fertile and increase," why does the commandment now apply exclusively to Jews? Again, the Talmud replies that the Sinaitic mandate did not constitute a repetition of the earlier precept so as to extend it to Jews and Gentiles according to Yosi's principle (A1). Rather, one must recall that three days prior to the revelation at Sinai, Moses had instructed the Israelites not to engage in sexual activity for the next three days (Ex. 19:15). One would assume that the passage of three days should automatically permit the resumption of marital relations. Yet in ordering the Jews "Return to your tents," the Torah intends not to reiterate the commandment of procreation but (C4) to dispel this assumption. The passage of an explicitly stipulated period of time notwithstanding, the prohibitive decree of a duly constituted judicial authority does not expire automatically but requires formal annulment on the part of another legitimate authority.[91]

---

90. This halakhic midrash on *ba-yom* of Lev. 12:3 appears also in TB *Sab.* 132b.

91. This is the simple understanding of the text at hand, comporting with the commentary of Rashi ad loc. See, however, the suggestion of Tosafot, s.v. *le-khol davar shebbe-minyan,* Jonah b. Abraham Gerondi, *Ḥiddushe Rabbenu Yonah 'al Masekhet Sanhedrin* (1705; repr., Jerusalem,

This response, however, does not put the matter to rest. The Gemara logically suggests that (D1) one might similarly discern a particular nuance in the Sinaitic repetition of every Noachide law, effectively obviating the post-Sinaitic application of all such legislation to Gentiles. (This would leave the first half of Yosi's rule with no practical application, and the second half with but one questionable example.) While specific *prescriptive* ordinances given at Sinai might be interpreted thus, answers the Talmud (D2), the reiteration of basic prohibitions can be explained only with Yosi's generalization (A1). The Gemara's anonymous questioner now rallies with one final query (E): Yosi's twofold hermeneutical principle includes the stipulation (A3) that in its second category of commandments (A2)—those uttered to the Noachides and not repeated to the Israelites at Sinai—there is only the ban on eating the thigh muscle. But in defense of Yosi's rule, the Gemara has argued (B4, C4) that circumcision and procreation were likewise uttered to the Noachides and not repeated to the Israelites at Sinai (and therefore now binding upon Jews alone)! According to the rather feeble ensuing reply (E2), the limitation of Yosi's second category of laws to the ban on the thigh muscle alone means that this commandment was not reiterated at all at Sinai, while the precepts of circumcision and procreation were repeated, albeit for particular reasons (and not to apply to non-Jews). Alternatively, some would reply (E3) that the commandment of circumcision does not fall into Yosi's second category (A2) because it was initially uttered (B1) to Abraham and his descendants alone, not to the Noachides.

This exercise in rabbinic argumentation leads to several important observations. First, in juxtaposing the biblical precepts of procreation and circumcision, the Talmud again attests to the covenantal associations of the primordial blessing. Second, the Gemara manifests a work-

---

1968), p. 40b, and Nissim b. Reuben Gerondi, *Ḥiddushe ha-Ra"N ʿal Masekhet Sanhedrin* (Jerusalem, 1973), p. 121, that if a precise time limit had been set for the original decree, no subsequent dispensation would have been required; in this case, though, the original decree— "be ready for the third day: do not go near a woman"—never stipulated its own expiration. Cf. also TB *Beẓah* 5ab, with Tosafot s.v. *kol davar shebbᵉ-minyan.* . . . Nathan b. Isaiah, *Sefer Maʾor ha-Afelah,* p. 67, held that repetition of "be fertile and increase" at Sinai would have resulted in uncontrolled, excessive population growth; his compatriot Zechariah b. Solomon the Physician, *Midrash ha-Ḥefeẓ,* ed. Meir Havazelet (Jerusalem, 1981), p. 109, deemed such repetition unnecessary because recognition of the need to reproduce had been sufficiently ingrained in human nature. By contrast, Levi b. Gerson insisted that the commandment of procreation was not revealed before the covenant at Sinai; see his *Perush ʿal ha-Torah Derekh Beʾur,* 2 vols. (Venice, 1547), 1:12ab.

ing assumption (C3) that the commandment of "be fertile and increase" once did apply to Gentiles but in the post-Sinaitic era does not. Third, the Gemara has considerable difficulty defending this position. The logic of R. Yosi's hermeneutical rule appears to dictate that the commandments of procreation and circumcision do include Gentiles, an inference deemed untenable because the Tannaitic enumeration of the Noachide laws that precedes this talmudic discussion does not list them.[92] Yet denying their status as Noachide laws seriously undermines the credibility of Yosi's principle, inasmuch as it repeatedly demands rather farfetched explanations (B4, C4, D2, E2) for seeming exceptions to the rule. Fourth, while the talmudic editors can propose a more compelling alternative solution (E3) in the case of circumcision, their inability to offer a comparable argument regarding procreation amounts to tacit acknowledgment of the weakness of their case. Finally, the premise and (admittedly difficult) conclusion of Tractate *Sanhedrin,* that the commandment of procreation does not obligate Gentiles, contradicts the position that Tractates *Y^evamot* and *B^ekhorot* attribute to R. Yohanan: The Gentile is indeed bound by the commandment of "be fertile and increase," because the law recognizes his offspring as his descendants and he thereby contributes to the settlement of God's creation.

The Talmud here restricts the commandment of procreation to Jews, but the weakness of its position has continued to trouble subsequent rabbinic authorities. Some attempted to resolve the conflict between R. Yohanan and the Gemara in *Sanhedrin* by distinguishing between the obligations of "be fertile and increase (*p^eriyyah u-r^eviyyah*)," deriving from Genesis, and of the settlement of God's creation (*shevet*), deriving from Is. 45:18. The mystically inclined exegete Bahya b. Asher, for instance, reasoned that the former precept bound Jews alone, while the latter fell upon Gentiles as well.

> It is known that marriage has two dimensions. One seeks to maintain and expand the line of descent for the sake of settling the world, in the sense that it is written "He did not create it a waste but formed it for habitation"; and this intention pertains to the nations of the world. The second seeks to direct descendants to the service of the Lord, may he be blessed, and to know him and recognize him, and this intention applies solely to Israel.[93]

92. T *AZ* 8.4–6, ed. Zuckermandel, p. 473, cited in TB *San.* 56ab.
93. Bahya b. Asher, *Kad ha-Qemaḥ,* in *Kitve Rabbenu Bahya,* p. 183. Bahya's view is anticipated in Tosafot ad *Bekh.* 47a, s.v. *w^c-ha' 'avad leh shevet.*

A second, related approach interpreted Yohanan's view to mean that because of his recognized kinship ties a proselyte's Gentile children fulfill his procreative obligations retroactively, but not that Gentiles are themselves bound by "be fertile and increase."[94] Although non-Jews reproduce, they never do so in order to fulfill their obligations to God, observed Jonah Gerondi; and his junior contemporary Yom Tov b. Abraham Ishbili explained that "the holy one, blessed be he, sanctified us more than all other nations with respect to procreation."[95] But following the logic of R. Yohanan's earlier ruling, a third group of halakhists defied the Gemara's ruling in Tractate *Sanhedrin* with an astonishing lack of inhibition. In the words of the Babylonian *Sheʾiltot*, "not only Israelites but even Gentiles are commanded with respect to procreation, as it is written, 'be fertile, then, and increase.' "[96] The gloss of the Tosafists on Tractate *Ḥagigah* likewise asserts that " 'be fertile and increase' is written concerning all non-Jews."[97] Could one justify such a conclusion? The late-medieval *Sefer ha-Qanah* contradicts the Talmud outright when it states: "You should know, my son, that the Gentiles also are commanded with respect to procreation; for the Gentiles too are included in every commandment which was uttered before the revelation of the Torah and was not repeated at Mount Sinai."[98] Relying on the talmudic statement that the Noachides originally accepted thirty commandments upon themselves,[99] another late-medieval work revises the Tannaitic list of the Noachide laws underlying the Gemara in *Sanhedrin* by adding the precept of procreation.[100] Still other, more recent authorities[101] have argued that the inclusion of procreation among the Noachide commandments is in accord with the Tannaitic view of R. Hidka, who added a ban on castration to the basic list of seven Noachide laws.[102] And several commentators found the talmudic argument restricting "be fertile and increase" to Jews so unconvincing

94. Tosafot ad *Yev.* 62a, s.v. *bᵉne pᵉriyyah u-rᵉviyyah ninhu.*

95. Jonah Gerondi, *Ḥiddushe . . . ʿal Masekhet Sanhedrin*, p. 40b; Yom Tov b. Abraham Ishbili, *Ḥiddushe ha-RIṬb"A: Masekhet Kᵉtubot*, ed. Moshe Goldstein (Jerusalem, 1982), col. 49.

96. *Sheʾiltot* 184 (165), ed. Mirsky, 5:70.

97. Ad *Hag.* 2b, s.v. *lo' tohu bᵉra'ah.*

98. *Sefer ha-Qanah* (1894; repr., Jerusalem, 1973), p. 105a.

99. TB *Hul.* 92ab. For various listings of these thirty precepts, see *ET*, 3 (1981), 393–96.

100. Menahem Azariah of Fano, *Sefer ʿAsarah Ma'amarot* (1858; repr., Jerusalem, 1974), p. 108ab, counts "be fertile" and "and increase" as two commandments.

101. Jacob b. Joseph Reischer, *Shᵉvut Yaʿaqov* 2.134, 3 vols. (Lemberg, 1897), 2:22b; Isaiah Berlin, *Sheʾelat Shalom*, in *Sheʾiltot* (1861–67), 3:277.

102. T *AZ* 8.6, ed. Zuckermandel, p. 473; TB *San.* 56b. On the identity of the commandments concerning procreation and castration, see above, n. 66.

that they do not acknowledge it as the Gemara's final word on the subject. According to these readers of the lengthy passage quoted above, the final proposal of an alternative justification for excluding non-Jews from circumcision (E3)—but not from obligatory reproduction—demonstrates a twofold admission (1) that the preceding arguments did not suffice and (2) that the duty of procreation applies to Gentiles as well.[103]

Slaves

According to talmudic law, Gentile men enslaved to Jewish masters must undergo a process of conversion to Judaism, at which point they enjoy an anomalous legal status. Circumcised like Jewish males, they still resemble Gentiles in that they do not share fully in the religious privileges of their masters, and their ritual obligations most closely approximate those of Jewish women.[104] Should the commandment of "be fertile and increase" apply to them?

The Mishnah responds to this question only indirectly, in its report of a curious dispute between the Pharisaic houses of Hillel and Shammai:

> One who is half slave and half freedman—he works for his master one day and for himself the next, according to the House of Hillel. The House of Shammai responded to them: You have set matters right for his master, but you have not set matters right for him. He cannot marry a bondwoman, because he is half freedman; and he cannot marry a free woman, since he is half slave. Should he not marry altogether? And was not the world created specifically for the sake of procreation? As Scrip-

---

103. Menahem b. Solomon, *Sechel Tob: Commentar zum ersten und zweiten Buch Mosis* (Hebrew), ed. Solomon Buber, 2 vols. (Berlin, 1900–1901), 1:176; Judah Loeb b. Simeon, *Yad Yᵉhudah* ad Menahem of Fano, *Sefer ʿAsarah Maʾamarot,* loc. cit.; B. H. Auerbach, *Naḥal ʾEshkol* ad Abraham b. Isaac of Narbonne, *Sefer ha-ʾEshkol,* 3 vols. (Halberstadt, 1867–69), 1:61–62 n. 30 (who points out that Yosi b. Hanina was a disciple of R. Yohanan and therefore held that the commandment of procreation was repeated at Sinai and includes both Jews and Gentiles); Judah Rozanes, *Mishneh la-Melekh* ad *MT, Mᵉlakhim* 10.7; N. Z. Y. Berlin, *Haʿameq Shᵉʾelah,* in *Shᵉʾiltot* (1861–67), 3:277–78.

104. On the rabbinic law of slavery, see Adolph Büchler, "Notes on the Religious Position of the 'Canaanite Slave' a Century before and after the Destruction of the Second Temple" (Hebrew), in *Occident and Orient: Gaster Anniversary Volume,* ed. Bruno Schindler (London, 1936), pp. 549–70; Solomon Zeitlin, "Slavery during the Second Commonwealth and the Tannaitic Period," *JQR,* n.s. 53 (1963), 185–218; B. Cohen, *Jewish and Roman Law,* 1:159–78; and Ephraim E. Urbach, "The Laws Regarding Slavery as a Source for Social History of the Period of the Second Temple, the Mishnah and Talmud," *Papers of the Institute of Jewish Studies, London* 1 (1964), 1–94, esp. 31ff.

ture states, "He did not create it as a waste but formed it for habitation." Rather, for the sake of perfecting the social order (*mipp^ene tiqqun ha-ʿolam*) his master is compelled to manumit him, and he writes [his master] a writ of indebtedness for half his worth. And the House of Hillel changed their ruling to that of the House of Shammai.[105]

Partial enslavement—resulting from the joint purchase of a slave by two partners, one of whom subsequently manumits his "share"—was probably an unusual phenomenon, and modern scholars have appreciated this Mishnaic ruling in diverse fashions. Adolph Büchler deemed it an expression of rabbinic concern over a declining Jewish population in Palestine during the concluding centuries of the Second Commonwealth. Ephraim Urbach wrote that it indeed addressed a recurring social problem,[106] which the house of Shammai did not seek to eliminate; the Pharisees merely undertook to "regularise the position of the male slave who had not fulfilled his religious obligation of procreation."[107] Jacob Neusner, on the other hand, ventured the suggestion that this anomalous personal status was "a legal fabrication, created to explore the ambiguous personal status of someone who may not have existed outside the lawyers' imagination."[108] Whatever the origins of the scenario, in agreeing that the moral fabric of their society demanded that a slave be able to marry, the Pharisaic houses reportedly worked from the incontestable premise that everyone, even a slave, must share in the obligation of childbearing. The Shammaitic assertion that God did not create the world but for the sake of procreation, noted Boaz

105. M *Git.* 4.5, *ʿEduyot* 1.13. TB (*Git.* 38a, 43b, *Yev.* 66a) reports an instance of a partially enslaved Gentile woman whose Jewish master was similarly compelled to manumit her. While the Gemara (*Git.* 43b) prefers the suggestion that this ruling sought to avoid sexual promiscuity (which her status encouraged)—rejecting the inference that Yohanan b. Broka's inclusion of women in the commandment of procreation here prevailed—Büchler, "Notes on the Religious Position," p. 551 n. 5, concludes that the Mishnaic ruling must have applied to bondwomen as well. Cf. the ruling of Zemah b. Isaac, Gaon of Sura, recorded in *Sefer Shaʿare Zedeq: T^eshuvot ha-G^eʾonim* (Jerusalem, 1966), p. 61, that this Mishnah law applied neither to a half-bondwoman nor to a half-enslaved eunuch; the former was not bound by the commandment to procreate, while the latter could not fulfill it.

106. Witness TB *Git.* 41b–42a, *T^emurah* 25a.

107. It is noteworthy that TB *Nid.* 3b quotes Shammai himself as challenging Hillel over excessive halakhic stringency that impeded observance of the commandment of procreation.

108. Büchler, "Notes on the Religious Position," p. 551; Urbach, "Laws Regarding Slavery," pp. 45–46; Neusner, *Rabbinic Traditions,* 2:229. Cf. also Louis Finkelstein's introduction to his edition of *Sifra or Torat Kohanim According to Codex Assemani LXVI* (Hebrew) (New York, 1956), pp. lvi–lvii.

Cohen, constitutes the closest rabbinic equivalent possible to the invocation of natural law (*ius naturale*) as conceived by the Romans.[109]

Questioning whether a slave can marry on the intermediate day of a festival—in view of the concern that he might thereby postpone his reproductive duties—the Palestinian Talmud concluded from this Mishnah that the Mosaic precept of procreation bound him too:[110]

> They asked R. Yassah [R. Assi]: Can a slave marry on the intermediate day of a festival? He said to them: We may conclude from [the Mishnaic pericope] "one who is half slave and half freedman"; and from what R. Simeon b. Abba said in the name of R. Yohanan, [that marriage is forbidden on the intermediate day of a festival] because of the neglect of procreation. The former tradition taught that a slave is bound by the commandment of procreation, and it is forbidden for anyone bound by the commandment of procreation to marry on the intermediate day of a festival.

This text posed problems for later halakhists on several grounds. Why would a slave incur an obligation that bound neither Gentiles, whose status he used to share, nor Jewish women, whose legal responsibilities now determined his own? To be sure, one might argue that R. Assi's judgment conformed to the Amoraic view of R. Yohanan that Gentiles were obligated to have children; and one might also reason that R. Assi shared the Palestinian Talmud's preference for the Tannaitic opinion of R. Yohanan b. Broka, that the mandate of "be fertile and increase" obligated women as well. In either case, such a surmise has much to commend itself. But R. Yohanan's inclusion of Gentiles in the commandment derived from the law's formal recognition of their kinship ties, and all talmudic authorities concurred that the familial relationships of slaves enjoyed no such recognition.[111] Furthermore, although the minority position of R. Yohanan b. Broka may have prevailed in Palestine,[112] Babylonian and post-talmudic authorities, who did not

---

109. *Jewish and Roman Law*, 1:28 and n. 97; cf. *Digest* 1.1.1.3, in *Corpus iuris civilis*, ed. Paulus Krueger et al., 3 vols. (1954–67; repr., Berlin, 1973) 1,2:29: "Ius naturale est, quod natura omnia animalia docuit: nam ius istud non humani generis proprium, sed omnium animalium, quae in terra, quae in mari nascuntur, avium quoque commune est. hinc descendit maris atque feminae coniunctio, quam nos matrimonium appellamus, hinc liberorum procreatio, hinc educatio."

110. TJ *MQ* 1.7, 80d; *Git.* 4.5, 46a. See above, n. 31.

111. TJ *Yev.* 2.6, 4a, TB ibid., 62a; and see *GenR* 56.2 (ad 22:5), 2:595–96 with notes, as well as the ruling of R. Hisda in TB *San.* 58b.

112. See above, n. 67.

share it, still had to reckon with the unchallenged, presumably authoritative of R. Assi in the Palestinian Gemara.

The Mishnaic law of "one who is half slave and half freedman" is cited several times in the Babylonian Gemara, and the medieval Tosafists addressed these issues more than once. Between their various comments, three alternative approaches to the problem emerged. According to Isaac b. Mordecai, the Mishnah quoted the prophetic mandate for *shevet* rather than the instructions of Genesis to "be fertile and increase," because the former obligates slaves and the latter applies only to free people. If a male slave could marry a bondwoman, his master would not have to free him because their children would contribute to the settlement of God's creation. When the Palestinian Gemara considers the marriage of a slave, it rules that all who are "bound by the commandment of procreation" because of *shevet* may not marry during a festival.[113] Isaac b. Samuel also distinguished between the duties of *shevet* and *p^eriyyah u-r^eviyyah*, but in his view the law's release of a slave from the latter and not from the former testifies to the priority and urgency of *shevet*, not to its expression of a minimal but less than optimal degree of compliance with "be fertile and increase."[114] A third approach accepted the clear sense of both Mishnah and Palestinian Gemara that the commandment of procreation is binding upon slaves. When God addressed the words "be fertile and increase" to the Noachides, he included them all—even Noah's grandson Canaan, the prototypical slave (Gen. 9:26–27). And while a slave admittedly does not have legally recognized kinship ties, these are a necessary component of a free Jew's fulfillment of the commandment, not the compliance of a slave.[115] Because it included Gentiles in the mandate for procreation, this interpretation raised the eyebrows of numerous later halakhists, who struggled hard to overcome its incompatibility with prevalent halakhic opinion as well as with the previously mentioned statements of the Tosafists themselves.[116]

---

113. Tosafot ad *Git.* 41b, s.v. *lo' tohu b^era'ah; BB* 13a, s.v. *she-ne'emar;* and cf. also Tosafot ad *Yev.* 62a, s.v. *ha-kol modim.*

114. Tosafot ad *BB* 13a, s.v. *she-ne'emar.*

115. Tosafot ad *Hag.* 2b, s.v. *lo' tohu bera'ah.*

116. See Edels, *Ḥiddushe Halakhot* ad *Hag.* 2b, s.v. *lo' tohu bera'ah;* Judah Rozanes, *Mishneh la-Melekh* ad *MT, M^elakhim* 10.7; Aryeh Leib ha-Kohen, *Sefer Ṭure 'Even* (Vienna, 1875) ad *Hag.,* pp. 1b–2a, and Aryeh Leib b. Joseph ha-Kohen Heller, *Sefer 'Avne Millu'im* (Jerusalem, 1976), pp. 1a–1b; and Babad, *Minḥat Ḥinnukh,* 1:1b–2a.

RABBINIC LAW AND BIBLICAL THEOLOGY

Although the call of Gen. 1:28b for humans to master the earth and assume dominion over other living creatures had no halakhic ramifications, the rabbis of the talmudic age deemed the divine injunction to "be fertile and increase" a Mosaic law of cardinal importance. It dictated the urgency of marriage, one's choice of a spouse, the terms under which a marriage might properly be maintained, and the nature of the sexual activities appropriate within marriage. Fulfillment of one's reproductive duties constituted one of two legitimate reasons for selling a Torah scroll, the sacred physical repository of God's covenant with Israel, and it ultimately took precedence over the other: the pursuit of Torah study. The neglect of procreation, on the other hand, was likened to a transgression tantamount to murder; in the eyes of various sages, it diminished the image of God, impeded the messianic redemption, and led an individual to the pitfalls of idolatry. As time ensued, the Halakhah further acknowledged the significance of the biblical mandate by adding to it: The human habitation, or *shevet,* for whose sake Is. 45:18 reported that God had created the world and which rationalized the commandment of procreation for the Tannaitic and early Amoraic masters, later came to denote a broader category of obligation. While "be fertile and increase" applied to free Jewish males alone, demanding that they father a specific, minimal number of children, some authorities extended the more general duty of *shevet* to women, Gentiles, and slaves. And referring to the counsel of *la-'erev* in Eccl. 11:6, "Sow your seed in the morning, and don't hold back your hand in the evening," most halakhists eventually refused to free an individual from the duty of childbearing even after he had complied with the Mosaic precept as defined by the Mishnah.

The talmudic masters evidenced no hesitancy in their understanding of "be fertile and increase" as a commandment; they may well have inherited such an understanding from prior generations. Yet their confidence still should not obscure the novelty in such an interpretation. The Bible understood these words as the divine blessing par excellence, the hallmark of God's commitment, and the assurance of his election and covenant. When did the promises of Gen. 1:28 begin to have legal significance for their Jewish readers, and what effected this translation of the primordial blessing into law? Working answers to these difficult questions depend on the credibility of the attributions in the texts we have discussed. The Mishnah, redacted at the beginning of the third century, clearly construes "be fertile and increase" as an obligation. Twice the Mishnah ascribes such an understanding to the Pharisaic houses of Hillel and Shammai which antedated the destruction of the Temple. Ascribing reports of alternative versions of the Pharisaic dispute to Ushan sages of the second century, the Tosefta raises yet another possibility. And the reported rebuke of the celibate Simeon b. Azzai points to the preceding Yavnean generation. Although the repartee between Simeon and his colleagues does not constitute a legal discussion, the accompanying association of the failure to procreate with murder—along with the Tosefta's transmission of the *baraita'* in an entirely halakhic context—suggests that if the Pharisaic houses themselves did not interpret Gen. 1:28a as law, perhaps their Yavnean successors did.

David Daube proposed that Jews began to consider procreation a religious duty during the reign of the Roman emperor Augustus, under the influence of his decrees that rewarded the prolific and penalized the unmarried and the childless. In Daube's words, "the duty to procreate was adopted together with the machinery of compliance." What motivated the rabbis to emulate the Romans in this regard?

> The import was the result of a combination of factors. Well before Augustus, the Jewish leadership must have paid attention to pagan thought and action in the field of population policy. The communities of the dispersion, in constant danger of being engulfed, would be the first to do so. But urbanisation and allied phenomena imperilled replenishment in Palestine also. Then came the Augustan decrees and the debates surrounding them, which fascinated the entire realm—not only jurists but the educated public at large. Finally, the ruinous war with Rome of 66–70—let alone the rebellion under Hadrian—rendered the situation desperate.[117]

Robert Gordis similarly located the initial Jewish interpretation of Gen. 1:28 as law during the Tannaitic period, and he attributed it to "the institutionalization of Jewish belief and practice in the Halakhah. With

---

117. David Daube, *The Duty of Procreation* (Edinburgh, 1977), esp. pp. 35, 36–37. On the Roman law in question, see also P. A. Brunt, *Italian Manpower, 225 B.C.–A.D. 14* (Oxford, 1971), pp. 558–66; Richard I. Frank, "Augustus' Legislation on Marriage and Children," *California Studies in Classical Antiquity* 8 (1975), 41–52; and Pál Csillag, *The Augustan Laws on Family Relations* (Budapest, 1976), esp. pp. 77–112.

the emergence of the Halakhah as the basic structure of Jewish life, the blessing of procreation was transformed into a mitzvah, an obligation incumbent upon the Jew." Gordis argued, however, that throughout the period of the Mishnah the rabbis did not perceive this obligation as a particularly urgent one—hence the minimal requirement of two children and the application of the law solely to men. Only "during the long period of Galut, when Palestine was no longer the center of Jewish life," did the commandment of procreation assume its full theological and legal importance. For

> medieval Jewish leaders knew very well that the physical survival of the Jewish people was threatened by extraordinary and persistent perils. They decided that the desperate situation required draconian measures, and that the procreation of more and more children was the only means available to them for guaranteeing the Jewish future. Hence the commandment "be fruitful and multiply" had to take precedence over other considerations of health, convenience, or personal desire.

According to Gordis, this national crisis of an endangered population induced halakhic authorities to recognize the obligations of *shevet* and *la-ʿerev,* which added to the minimal requirement of two children stipulated by the Mishnah, and to include women within the obligation of procreation.[118]

The logic of both these interpretations, which link the legal exegesis of "be fertile and increase" to a perceived population shortage resulting from persecution and dispersion (whether during or after the Tannaitic period), is plausible but not compelling. Mishnaic law may have resembled Roman law in penalizing the failure to procreate, but such similarity does not warrant Daube's conclusion that Jews first considered procreation a legal duty as a result of the Augustan decrees. The absence of evidence of such consideration before the first Christian century is a perilous argument from silence at best. Referring to Josephus' description of an Essene group that forbade conjugal relations during pregnancy,[119] Daube himself conceded that "the idea of procreation as a duty must have been around for a good while for such a splinter-group to come into being"; the afterthought that this "corroborates the [Augustan] date given above" hardly follows.[120] The chronology underly-

---

118. " 'Be Fruitful and Multiply,' " esp. pp. 22, 23–24.
119. *Bellum iudaicum* 2.161, LCL 2:384–85.
120. Loc. cit., p. 34.

ing Gordis' argument is equally questionable. During the Tannaitic period, Gordis suggested, the prevalent Halakhic mind-set of the Jews came to construe "be fertile and increase" as commandment; during the Middle Ages, halakhists recognized the emergency of the hour and responded accordingly. What happened to the intervening generations of the Amora'im, the age of the Gemaras? Our own analysis of the extant sources suggests that precisely during this period the juridical significance of "be fertile and increase" was a current issue involving sages in Palestine and Babylonia alike. Furthermore, the Babylonian Gemara ascribes the doctrine of *la-ʿerev* to a Tannaitic master, the Yavnean R. Joshua of the late first century, and it records the opinion of the Amoraic R. Matna that R. Joshua's ruling was already deemed binding.[121] On the issue of women, we have seen how the position of R. Yohanan b. Broka, who included women in the commandment, first prevailed in Amoraic Palestine but then failed to do so in Babylonia and the medieval diaspora—defying the proposition that halakhists added to the commandment as antiquity gave way to the Middle Ages. And as the sources analyzed below in Chapter 4 demonstrate, medieval halakhists gradually ceased to enforce the Mishnah's call for divorce in the case of childless marriages, as well as its rule that a childless man may not marry a woman unfit to bear children. The declining rabbinic willingness to compel adherence to the laws of procreation does not comport with a supposedly growing concern for an imperiled population.[122]

Regrettably, the available evidence does not permit one to identify the circumstances that prompted Jews to understand Gen. 1:28 as a Mosaic commandment and not simply as a blessing. Yet the halakhic texts considered in this chapter reveal a hitherto unnoticed dimension of rabbinic concern with our verse that illuminates the significance of its legal interpretation—and on which the question of attributions bears little. Human reproduction is an incontrovertibly bisexual process. The prescriptive commandment to have children is a law not contingent

---

121. See above, at n. 26.

122. Gordis also points to the Talmud's aversion to child marriage and its liberality with regard to contraception, both of which tendencies he claims medieval halakhists reversed, as additional evidence for his thesis. But because the proposed ban on child marriages pertained only to a girl under the age of twelve, it is not "self-evident that forbidding them would limit the number of child-bearing years for the mother and thus tend to reduce the size of families" (loc. cit., p. 23). As we have seen, medieval halakhists tended not to base their views on contraception on "be fertile and increase," except in the case of those notably permissive in its practice; see above, at nn. 49–53.

upon a particular time and, in the rabbinic perspective, should presumably obligate women and slaves. In addition, Scripture clearly relates that God uttered the call to "be fertile and increase" to both of the first parents (male and female) and to Noah, who were Gentiles, not Jews. We have noted how the mandate of procreation might easily, and certainly logically, have numbered among the primordial Noachide laws that applied to Gentile and Jew alike. In the language of the Mishnah, "was not the world created specifically for the sake of procreation?"[123] Despite these considerations, the rabbis of the Talmud leaned over backward to exclude women, Gentiles, and slaves from the commandment of "be fertile and increase." At the same time as the rabbis augmented the duty of procreation, they narrowed its application, in a way that has recently been termed "morally problematic."[124] Why? Why did the talmudic masters extend themselves so, defying the literal sense of Scripture, perhaps casting doubt on the logic of their judgment, and arousing the vehement objection and resistance of not a few later rabbinic jurists—and all this when the practical, legal consequences of restricting the commandment to Jewish men were negligible?

The answer, I believe, proceeds from the covenantal significance of Gen. 1:28, which underlay its career in Scripture and in the Aggadah and which the Halakhah now sought to reformulate as law. As I have argued consistently, the readers of Gen. 1:28 beheld God's elevation of his human creatures to participate in a unique, mutual relationship with him. We have repeatedly noted how the verse moved its readers to discern a tension between God's primordial commitment to all human beings, on the one hand, and his subsequent election of Israel, on the other. Briefly put, the rabbinic restriction of the law of procreation to free Jewish males bespoke the contention that *they* were the full-fledged partners of God in his divine covenant.

Scholars of religious phenomenology have long studied the recurring dependence of a society's structure and system of classification on its

---

123. See above, at n. 105. On the nature and underlying philosophy of the Noachide laws, see the recent works of W. Zuidema, "Les lois noachiques dans la plus ancienne littérature rabbinique," and A. Guigui, "Les lois noahides dans le Talmud: Etude synthétique," both in *Noé, l'homme universel*, ed. J. Chopineau et al., Publications de l'Institutum iudaicum 3 (Brussels, 1978), pp. 44–71, 77–111; Aaron Lichtenstein, *The Seven Laws of Noah* (New York, 1981); and David Novak, *The Image of the Non-Jew in Judaism: An Historical and Constructive Study of the Noahide Laws*, Toronto Studies in Theology 14 (New York, 1983).

124. Hartman, *A Living Covenant*, p. 307 n. 4.

beliefs concerning the creation; a culture's taxonomy, many have argued, regularly derives from cosmogony. In particular, the allocation of role and status in a community will usually reflect the fundamental aspects of its world view, which in turn are rooted in that community's memories of its origins. Building upon these premises, Howard Eilberg-Schwartz recently proposed that early rabbinic (i.e., Mishnaic) taxonomy revised the older Priestly system of social classification on the basis "of a broader conception of creation" than that proposed by the Priestly school in Gen. 1. Eilberg-Schwartz argued that the theory of classification proposed by the rabbis befitted their distinctive ideals, which prized learning and intellectual achievement—the fruits of human volition and creativity—above all else, rather than the unchanging, congenital qualities of kinship. In the Mishnaic taxonomy the elite status was that of the sage, who even if he were a bastard took precedence over an uneducated high priest.[125]

Accepting the premises and logic of Eilberg-Schwartz's thesis, I suggest that rabbinic taxonomy also stemmed from another criterion for allocating role and status in society. Like Eilberg-Schwartz, I proceed from the perspective elaborated by Ralph Linton in his classic work, *The Study of Man*: Status and role serve to integrate a group of individuals into a collective entity bearing a character and value system of its own.

> Although all statuses and rôles derive from social patterns and are integral parts of patterns, they have an independent function with relation to the individuals who occupy particulars statuses and exercise their rôles. To such individuals, the combined status and rôle represent the minimum of attitudes and behavior which he must assume if he is to participate in the overt expression of the pattern. *Status and rôle serve to reduce the ideal patterns for social life to individual terms.* They become models for organizing the attitudes and behavior of the individual so that these will be congruous with those of the other individuals participating in the expression of that pattern.[126]

And like Eilberg-Schwartz I relate this additional basis for social status to the rabbis' appreciation of their origins, although not in this instance

125. Howard Eilberg-Schwartz, "Creation and Classification in Judaism: From Priestly to Rabbinic Conceptions," *History of Religions* 26 (1987), 357–81, esp. 374.
126. Ralph Linton, *The Study of Man* (New York, 1936), p. 114 (italics added).

merely to the creation of the world. In addition to the creation stories of
Genesis, the rabbis adopted the biblical perspective that a distinctive
Jewish community originated at Mount Sinai, when God revealed the
Torah to Israel and to Israel alone. This covenant set the Jews apart from
all others; it was maintained by the Jews' observance of the commandments and by God's protection of his people. Obligation to observe the
commandments was thus the obverse of divine election, and the rabbis
measured social status in terms of the extent to which one was so
obligated. Free Jewish men, bound by all of the Mosaic commandments, therefore ranked above Jewish women and above slaves, whom
the Halakhah released from all prescriptive ("positive") commandments linked to a particular time, and they in turn ranked above non-
Jews, whom God had bound by the Noachide laws alone.[127]

Recalling the covenantal significance of Gen. 1:28 and the series of
polar oppositions that it evoked in the Aggadah, I suggest that we may
now appreciate the enigmatic treatment of the verse by the Halakhah.
To be sure, the idea that God expected only Jewish men—or, for that
matter, only Jews—to reproduce would have been an absurd deduction
from the text of the Bible's primeval history. Because the verse epitomized the divine-human covenant, however, the restriction of the commandment of procreation to Jewish men made sense.[128] The rabbis of
the Talmud thereby laid claim to an elite status: Not only did they enjoy
the divine election signified by an obligation to the laws ordained at
Sinai, but the covenant and election bespoken by God's blessing of the
first parents were now exclusively theirs as well. This interpretation
also facilitates a response to the question of why procreation had to be
legislated in the first place: Why need the Torah have commanded
human beings to engage in sexual reproduction, an activity much like
eating or sleeping in which they—along with the members of every
animal species—would have engaged anyway? To borrow a phrase of
E. P. Sanders, rabbinic Judaism was largely a religion of "covenantal

127. One might extend the same argument to hierarchically ranked subsets of the collective
of free Jewish males: priests, Levites, etc. This in turn might help to explain why the Pharisaic
and rabbinic sages undertook to uphold a more stringent set of responsibilities than the Mosaic
precepts contained in Scripture, simply understood.

128. We therefore differ with the judgment of Prudence Allen that the rabbinic interpretation of Gen. 1:28 proceeded from "a view that the female contribution to generation is not
considered to be significant"; see her *Concept of Woman: The Aristotelian Revolution, 750 B.C.–
A.D. 1250* (Montreal, 1985), p. 357. Evidently unaware of the intricate legal history involved,
Allen cited only the record of the Mishnaic ruling in Maimonides' *MT*.

nomism"; humans related to God primarily through the performance of his law.[129] By interpreting the primordial blessing as legal statute, rabbinic texts may have altered the meaning of Scripture in no small measure. Yet in so doing the rabbis incorporated the essentially covenantal significance of Gen. 1:28 into the Halakhah, correctly evaluating the biblical message of "be fertile and increase" and extending its career in the idiom of their own community.

129. E. P. Sanders, *Paul and Palestinian Judaism: A Comparison of Patterns of Religion* (Philadelphia, Pa., 1977), esp. pp. 419–28.

CHAPTER 4

Medieval Rabbinic Applications: Jurisprudence, Exegesis, and Mysticism

Jews of the Middle Ages inherited and treasured the rabbinic texts discussed in the two preceding chapters, and the classical aggadic and halakhic understanding of Gen. 1:28 continued to find expression throughout the remaining centuries of concern in this book. Because a comprehensive review of medieval Jewish citations of our verse would prove onerously repetitive as well as impractical, this chapter takes an avowedly eclectic approach. Turning to distinctively post-talmudic genres of rabbinic literature, it seeks to highlight the most interesting applications and interpretations of Gen. 1:28 by Jews living in the world of medieval Islam and Christianity. How did they adapt the scriptural passage and its postbiblical appreciation to the pressing issues of their age? How and why did the verse figure in new varieties of socioreligious and cultural expression? And, inasmuch as the present chapter will bring our discussion of Jewish intellectual history to a close, how did these exegetical developments refine the Judaic contribution to the evolving career of our verse? My focus is on three types of evidence: the practical application of rabbinic law in the literature of medieval responsa, the exegesis of medieval biblical commentaries, and the esoteric doctrines of medieval Kabbalah.

RABBINIC RESPONSA: IMPLEMENTING THE LAWS OF PROCREATION

Medieval halakhists, cited repeatedly in the previous chapter, compiled the laws of *p^eriyyah u-r^eviyyah* much as they would have dealt with any other subject. Yet collections of "novellae" on various tractates of the Talmud or codifications of the Halakhah reveal what scholars believed the law should be, not necessarily how the law affected individuals on a daily basis. Implementing and enforcing legislation were another matter, and in the case of reproductive responsibility the gap between theory and practice was prone to widen considerably. The intimacy and sanctity of the marital relationship, the intensity of the emotions accompanying all human efforts, successful or otherwise, to have children, and the truly universal character of the desire to reproduce bore directly on the ability of rabbinic legislation to control behavior. In view of the unifying function served by the Halakhah for a physically dispersed and politically subjugated Jewry, medieval rabbinic jurists appreciated the challenge before them. Especially with regard to procreation, a matter so vital both to Judaism as a religious system and to the individuals comprising its constituency, the law could not remain out of touch with reality. Neither could the Halakhah afford to forgo compliance, nor would Jews submit to legislation that did not provide for their basic human needs.

While extant documentary sources attest to the high valuation of childbearing in medieval Jewish communities,[1] the data that might quantify the observance of rabbinic legislation on the subject do not exist. Still, the literature of medieval rabbinic responsa—namely, the texts of correspondence in which legal scholars answered specific questions and requests for instruction—opens a window to the problems that commonly arose and to the priorities dictating the proposed solu-

---

1. See S. D. Goitein, *A Mediterranean Society,* 5 vols. (Berkeley, Calif., 1967–88), 3:223–29. Research on the history of the medieval European Jewish family is itself in its infancy, and the studies that do exist rarely explore the religious ideals and legal values that might underlie the statistical data at hand. A recent and important step toward this desideratum is Kenneth R. Stow, "The Jewish Family in the Rhineland in the High Middle Ages: Form and Function," *American Historical Review* 92 (1987), 1085–1110. Yet while Stow has judiciously characterized the relations of husbands and wives alongside his calculations of the average size of Jewish families in several German communities, his essay does not consider the halakhic duty of procreation. At the very least, the responsa discussed below confirm that Western Jews shared most of the sentiments attributed by Goitein to their Oriental counterparts.

tions. Diverse methodological considerations complicate the use of any particular responsum as historical evidence. Some responsa, reacting to the ostensibly theoretical, academic interests of the questioner, intend no practical consequences whatsoever. While some provide judicial rulings directly to the petitioners involved in a dispute, whose background we may or may not understand, others communicate guidelines to local rabbinic judges who had turned to more competent authorities for advice. Many responsa therefore employ hypothetical language, referring to the *dramatis personae* simply as Reuben, Simeon, Rachel, and Leah—equivalents for the proverbial John Doe and Robin Roe. Not infrequently, the surviving texts omit the question that prompted the responsum, or they paraphrase it in the language of the scholarly respondent. The nearly two hundred medieval responsa touching upon the commandment of procreation which I have located appear in several dozen published collections and date from eight or nine centuries, hardly the basis for extensive statistical tabulation. I have therefore confronted the responsa collectively, hoping to isolate several key areas of concern to their authors and to demonstrate by example how Gen. 1:28 functioned in practice as law. Furthermore, the halakhic applications of "be fertile and increase" can themselves shed light on the textual genre of the responsum and its role in the socioreligious history of medieval Jewry. In contrast to the more academic legal works considered in the previous chapter, Jacob Bazak noted that "the literature of the responsa is alive and vibrant, full of matters actual and real."[2] And as Salo Baron rightly observed, the responsum militated against "the possible 'petrification' of Jewish law at a particular stage in its evolution," preserving the vitality of a historical tradition shared by Jews throughout most of the civilized world.[3] Again, one must approach the question of the effectiveness of any one responsum with caution. The application of the laws of procreation, however, did yield noteworthy and unexpected results, extending the career of the primordial blessing into yet another facet of Jewish religious history.

Some of the responsa discuss theoretical dimensions of the laws of procreation considered elsewhere in this chapter and the preceding one: the biblical source of the commandment, its relation to other respon-

2. Jacob Bazak, ed. *Jewish Law—Selected Responsa* (Hebrew), 2 vols. (Tel Aviv, 1971–75), 1:11.
3. Baron, *A Social and Religious History*, 6:109.

sibilities and prohibitions deriving from the Torah, the characteristics of the children and/or grandchildren who fulfill a parent's obligation, and the like.[4] Yet most of the pertinent correspondence grapples with the extent to which a Jew's procreative responsibilities affect the performance of other religious duties and bear upon various aspects of his or her personal life. Such texts usually address the judges and claimants in litigation that had already commenced, and nearly one-third concern protracted marital conflicts in which one spouse, usually the husband, sought a lenient divorce settlement or some other dispensation on the grounds that the responsibility of "be fertile and increase" had still not been met. Not uncommon was the scenario in which a childless husband petitioned not to incur the financial penalties he had once agreed to bear should he remarry during his wife's lifetime and without her consent.[5] In many such instances, the factors determining the ruling of the responsum do not reveal any particular interpretation of the biblical mandate to "be fertile and increase." But two related issues do address our concerns directly: the problematic nature of enforcement in this area of the Halakhah, and the precedence that this commandment takes over other obligations of law and equity.

A Reluctance to Enforce the Law

Inasmuch as they record the efforts of rabbis to preserve the integrity of the Halakhah through the complexities and vagaries of everyday life, medieval responsa help to illuminate an important dimension of the legal career of Gen. 1:28 that other documents reflect as well: The same rabbinic tradition that transposed the primordial blessing into commandment, testifying to its importance in legal and nonlegal idioms, refrained from enforcing this law in practice. The Mishnah, we recall, orders that those who remain childless for ten years be divorced so that the husband might marry again. This too falls under the rubric of the basic injunction that "a man may not desist from procreation unless he

---

4. I have cited these in the footnotes to Chapter 3 where appropriate.

5. On the standard nature of this commitment, see Mordechai Akiva Friedman, "Polygamy in the Documents of the Genizah" (Hebrew), *Tarbiz* 40 (1971), 320–59; "The Monogamy Clause in Jewish Marriage Contracts," *Perspectives in Jewish Learning* 4 (1972), 20–40; "Polygyny in Jewish Tradition and Practice: New Sources from the Cairo Geniza," *Proceedings of the American Academy for Jewish Research* 49 (1982), esp. 46ff., 54ff.; and *Jewish Polygyny in the Middle Ages: New Documents from the Cairo Genizah* (Hebrew) (Jerusalem, 1986), esp. pp. 44–45.

has children."[6] But almost as soon as the talmudic rabbis mandated divorce for childless couples, the Halakhah started to decrease the compulsion that would be brought to bear. The Babylonian Gemara records the opinion of R. Nahman that only verbal pressure, not physical compulsion, is exerted in such an instance.[7] Having reiterated the Mishnaic limit of ten childless years, the Tosefta adds that the years when one spouse is ill or physically separated from the other, as well as years spent by the couple outside of Palestine, do not count in this computation.[8] While some later halakhists held that this exclusion was no longer valid or that it applied exclusively to couples who themselves left Palestine for the Diaspora, the Tosefta's stipulation could effectively neutralize the Mishnaic requirement for childless couples in the Diaspora. The thirteenth-century Isaac b. Moses of Vienna thus concluded: "Even among us who accept the decree of our master Gershom . . . that a man may not take a second wife, we do not force a man to divorce [his childless wife], since we ascribe [their infertility] to the sin of living in the Diaspora."[9]

In strict adherence to the Mishnah, Babylonian rabbis of the geonic period insisted that a husband divorce his childless wife if he would marry another woman in any event;[10] they evidently reasoned that a man would not devote himself to reproductive activity with his second wife were he still married to his first. As early as the twelfth century, however, the Spanish Joseph b. Meir ha-Levi ibn Migash allowed such a husband to forgo the required divorce, so long as he would marry and have children with a second wife.[11] Two centuries later, Isaac b. Sheshet Perfet openly stated his willingness to dispense with the enforcement of

---

6. M *Yev.* 6.6.

7. TB *Ket.* 77a.

8. T *Yev.* 8.5–6, ed. Lieberman, 3:25–26; and so too TJ, 6.6, 7c.

9. Isaac b. Moses of Vienna, *Sefer 'Or Zarua'* 653.5, 2 vols. (1862; repr., B'nei B'rak, 1958), 1:91a. The different views are cited by Lieberman, *Tosefta ki-Fshutah*, 6:71–72 with n. 33, and in *She'iltot*, ed. Mirsky, 1:119–20n.

10. *OHG* ad *Yev.* 334, 7:142–43. The same posture is reflected in *She'iltot* 18, ed. Mirsky, loc. cit.; *Sefer Halakhot Gedolot* (Hebrew), ed. Ezriel Hildesheimer, 2 vols. (Jerusalem, 1971–80), 2:239–40; *Sefer Halakhot Pesuqot 'o Hilkhot Re'u*, ed. S. Z. H. Halberstam (Versailles, 1886), p. 87.

11. Joseph b. Meir ha-Levi ibn Migash, *Shu"T* 150 (Jerusalem, 1959), pp. 24b–25b. Cf. the similar views of Rashi, ad TB *Yev.* 64a, s.v. 'eno rashai libbatel; MT, 'Ishut 15.7; and Joseph Haviva, *Nimmuqe Yosef* ad TB, loc. cit. Isaac al-Fasi, *Hilkhot Rav 'Alfas*, 2:101, and MT, loc. cit., codified the talmudic suggestion (TB *Ket.* 77b) that if a childless couple takes a vow of celibacy the husband still must be compelled to divorce his wife or take a second wife; the concern is clearly his procreative responsibility and not the futility of marital relations with a barren woman.

obligations pertaining to procreation. He received an inquiry from a distant locale, where a childless man sought to marry a wealthy widow ninety years old simply for her fortune, and the Jewish community refused to permit the marriage. The aspiring husband had appealed to the Gentile ruler of the city:

> These Jews have prevented me from marrying. I have no knowledge of why—simply that they held that because she is old she may not marry. And this is not of the law of God, may he be blessed, and not of the law of our Torah. Rather, anyone who so desires may take the opportunity that presents itself: a young boy [may marry] an old lady and an old man a young girl. Such is our custom in every community.

The Jewish authorities had responded to the ruler that "such may not be done in the Jewish community until one has fulfilled the commandment of procreation, and this man still refrains from doing so." Both Jewish and Gentile authorities agreed to let Isaac arbitrate. After reviewing the relevant talmudic law, which clearly forbade the behavior of the man in question, Isaac reflected on the divergence of theory and practice:

> All this is the letter of the law according to the Gemara. But as for what is practiced, we have not encountered in our own day nor heard for several generations of a court that took it upon itself to compel the divorce of a woman who lived with her husband for ten years and did not give birth or who was elderly—even if the husband were childless.

In theory, the court should force the man in question to divorce his wife or to take another wife, just as it should intervene in many marriages that the Talmud deems undesirable. Nevertheless,

> if the courts took it upon themselves to enforce the letter of the law and exert compulsion in the selection of mates, they would have to exert compulsion in all such instances. And most wives nowadays would be divorced and would collect their dowries and the settlements stipulated in their marrige contracts. And since there is no such settlement which would go undisputed, strife and dissension would abound. For this reason, the sages of past generations have closed their eyes in matters of selecting one's mate—not to prevent couples from marrying, and, it goes without saying, not to separate them after marriage—as long as both partners are agreed and there is no forbidden kinship between them or other sacred prohibition. And it suffices the courts to judge according to the law when there is a dispute between a man and his wife.

Isaac therefore acknowledged that if the man and his intended elderly bride themselves had no objection, his petitioners had permission to "close their eyes, just as they have done in many fine communities full of sages and men of accomplishment."[12]

At the end of his responsum, Isaac recognized that local practice varied considerably with regard to childless marriages—and the husband's obligation to "be fertile and increase" that remained unmet as a result—and it is certain that not all agreed with him. The Mishnah itself had prescribed divorce in such a case, and its mandate was not easily forgotten. Extant responsa composed after Isaac b. Sheshet continued to cite this law without reservation, as a given and not as a point of contention.[13] The few documents of the European Middle Ages that squarely confront the question of whether or not to compel divorce do indicate that change was transpiring. Jurists might enforce the Mishnaic statute selectively, so as to achieve a result having little to do with reproduction. The same Isaac b. Moses of Vienna, who ruled that no childless couples in the Diaspora had to separate after ten years, advised a rabbinical court to invoke this law and to compel the divorce of a betrothed woman who regretted her marriage before its consummation and who otherwise might have remained abandoned by her husband "until her head should turn white."[14] A contemporary of Isaac's therefore could argue that the Mishnaic injunction "'he must divorce her' does not mean under compulsion except in a case where he behaves improperly with his wife, but in that context where the Mishnah states 'he must divorce her' to avoid neglect of the commandment of procreation, it does not mean that they compel him."[15] Citing Isaac b. Moses' responsum, the sixteenth-century Eliezer b. Elijah Ashkenazi rendered a similar judgment, compelling a Jewish criminal to divorce his abandoned wife, ostensibly so that *he* might fulfill the commandment of

---

12. Isaac b. Sheshet Perfet, *Shu"T* 15 (Vilna, 1879), pp. 4b–5a. One should note that Isaac also gave his petitioners the right to be strict and to forbid the marriage, especially because the man in question "spoke rebelliously to the judge." In a different responsum, ibid. 91, p. 17a, Isaac also acknowledged that while the law requires a childless couple to separate after ten years of marriage "the courts overlook such matters." Louis Jacobs, *A Tree of Life: Diversity, Flexibility, and Creativity in Jewish Law* (Oxford, 1984), pp. 140–41, who identifies the community of the first responsum as Tunis, has adduced Isaac's ruling as an example of medieval rabbinic responsiveness to changing social conditions and needs.

13. For example, David ibn Zimra, *Shu"T* 1.440, 1:73b; Benjamin b. Mattathias, *Shu"T Binyamin Ze'ev* 158, 1:432; and even Isaac b. Sheshet himself, *Shu"T* 127, p. 26b.

14. *Hagahot Maimuniyyot* 34 (ad *MT, Gerushin*), in *MT*, 3:437.

15. *Tosafot* ad *Ket.* 77a, s.v. *litne.*

procreation. As such, the duty of procreation could serve to rationalize, after the fact, a judicial decision based on considerations of equity.[16] But at the end of our period, Moses Isserles of Krakow clearly echoed Isaac b. Sheshet, when he glossed the ruling of Joseph Karo's *Shulḥan ʿArukh* that a man twenty years old should be compelled to marry.

> In this age the custom is not to exert compulsion in such matters. Therefore, if one who has not fulfilled the commandment of procreation seeks to marry a woman unfit to bear children—like a barren woman, an elderly woman, or a young girl—because he desires her or because of her wealth, even though by law he should be restrained, for several generations the practice has been not to be rigorous in matters of selecting a mate. Likewise, if one has married and lived with his wife for ten years, the custom is not to compel him to divorce her, even though he has not fulfilled the commandment of procreation. Such is the practice with other particulars for selecting a mate, provided that she not be prohibited to him.[17]

While many of the responsa touching on the duty of procreation engaged in protracted halakhic excurses having little relation to Gen. 1:28 and its meaning, collectively they illustrate the realism of medieval rabbinic jurists. No law can compel individuals to have children against their will, nor can the law guarantee that couples who want to have children will be able to do so. If "be fertile and increase" now entailed religious obligation, perhaps rabbinic authorities came to acknowledge that procreation still depended on the blessing of God.

A Willingness to Relax the Law

As if to compensate for the unenforceability of the laws of procreation, medieval rabbis evidenced considerable flexibility vis-à-vis other areas of Halakhah in order to enable Jews to have children. The extant

16. As in Moses Isserles, *Shu"T ha-RaM"A* 96, ed. Asher Ziv (Jerusalem, 1970), pp. 420–24.

17. Ad *ShA, EH* 1.3. Cf. the suggestion of Isaac S. Horwitz, *Yad ha-Levi*, in Moses b. Maimon, *Sefer ha-Miẓwot* (Jerusalem, 1926), pp. 156b–157a, that the inappropriateness of procreation in the wake of the Temple's destruction (see above, Chapter 2, n. 177) motivated medieval halakhic authorities to choose not to exert compulsion in this regard. Joseph Karo, *Shu"T Bet Yosef* 14 (Jerusalem, 1960), p. 159, cites this point of view, only to reject it on the grounds that the talmudic sages themselves articulated the commandment of *pᵉriyyah u-rᵉviyyah* after the destruction of the Temple.

responsa frequently permit individuals in mourning to marry sooner than they otherwise might, if they have not yet performed their reproductive duties or if they have small children who require the care of a stepmother. Reflecting on the responsa of Jacob b. Meir Tam, Mordecai b. Hillel ha-Kohen wrote that the great rabbi of twelfth-century Troyes permitted a childless mourner to consummate his marriage within the first thirty days of mourning, "because the marriage itself would not be permitted at all but for the sake of procreation, and what is the point of the marriage within the thirty days if he will not be able to engage in sexual relations? Nevertheless, during the seven days of mourning it is not permitted." Mordecai also took note of a more radical dispensation (*wᵉ-ʿod gᵉdolah mi-zot*) on the part of Jacob Tam, when the latter permitted a woman whose brother had just died to proceed with a scheduled marriage, because postponement would result "in the neglect of procreation on the husband's part, since it was known that he would not marry another—even though she was not bound by the commandment of procreation."[18] Other restrictions on the time for transacting marriage also gave way before the urgency of the commandment of procreation, and the responsa record dispensations to marry on Purim,[19] during the seven weeks between Passover and Pentecost,[20] and even on the Sabbath. In this last instance, Moses Isserles allowed the betrothal of an impoverished orphan bride on Friday night because the groom, who had refused to marry at the appointed hour on Friday when he did not receive the dowry once promised him by his fiancée's father, suddenly acquiesced and agreed to betrothe. Isserles cited the opinion of Jacob Tam, who had inferred from the talmudic ban on Sabbath be-

18. Mordecai b. Hillel ha-Kohen, commentary ad TB, *MQ* 890. In his *Sefer ha-Yashar: Ḥeleq ha-Shᵉʾelot wᵉha-Tᵉshuvot* 23, ed. S. P. Rosenthal (Berlin, 1898), pp. 38–39, Jacob b. Meir Tam ruled that if one has not yet fulfilled the commandment of procreation he may betroth immediately after the first seven days of mourning and consummate his marriage after the first thirty days. If he already has children, he can still marry after thirty days for sake of *la-ʿerev*. Eliezer b. Joel ha-Levi, *Sefer ha-RAvYa"H* 909, ed. Victor Aptowitzer, 2nd ed. (vols. 1–3), 4 vols. (Jerusalem, 1964–65), 4:207–11, handed down a similar ruling, as did Moses Maimonides, *MT, 'Evel* 6.5, and Asher b. Yehiel, *Shu"T* 27.1, 27.5 (Vilna, 1881), pp. 28a, 28b. Yom Tov b. Abraham Ishbili, *Shu"T,* ed. Joseph Kafah (Jerusalem, 1959), p. 171, held that despite the lenient views of his predecessors one should properly wait thirty days in any event. Also cf. the dispensations of Moses b. Jacob of Trani, *Shu"T Mabbiṭ* 2.99, 3 vols. (Lemberg, 1861), 2:26b; and Elijah b. Ḥayyim, *Shu"T Mayim ʿAmuqim* 2.4 (Berlin, 1778), p. 31b.

19. Solomon b. Abraham ibn Adret, *Shu"T* 3.276, 3 vols. (Jerusalem and B'nei B'rak, 1958–65), 3:164.

20. David ibn Zimra, *Shu"T* 687, 2:17b: "We do not worry about the custom [of not marrying during this period] when he has not fulfilled the commandment of procreation."

trothals that it did not restrict one who had not fulfilled the commandment of procreation.[21] He then noted other dispensations to contract
marriage on the Sabbath in extenuating circumstances and proceeded to
defend himself against his critics.

> For it was an emergency, and the maiden, having immersed in the ritual
> bath, would have been ashamed to wait with her wedding canopy until
> after the Sabbath. Moreover, it is not the practice of [our] communities
> to don the veil (*henuma'*) after the Sabbath and to make the wedding on
> Sunday, since this is the practice of the Gentiles who make their wed-
> dings on their holy day. . . . And there are no circumstances more
> extenuating than these, since a grown orphan girl would have been
> embarrassed, and it would have been a disgrace for her throughout her
> life, almost to distinguish her permanently from the other maidens. If
> human dignity is a sufficient factor to set aside a Mosaic prohibi-
> tion . . . , in this matter it is only a rabbinic restriction. . . . Besides
> which, we here had to take care that the engagement should not be
> broken completely and the couple separated as a result of the quarrels
> and disputes between them, so that owing to the arguments they would
> want to remove the veil on the head of the bride. For great is the value of
> peace between a man and his wife.[22]

The precept of *p^eriyyah u-r^eviyyah* might outweigh the need to settle in
the land of Israel,[23] as well as the duty to honor one's parents by settling
in their city.[24] In circumstances that impeded a wife's timely immersion
in the ritual bath following her menstrual period, some jurists bent
specific rules to facilitate the immediate resumption of conjugal rela-

21. Tosafot ad TB, *Be ̣zah* 36b, s.v. *w^e-ha' mi ̣zwah qa' 'avid;* Jacob Tam, *Sefer ha-Yashar*
48.10, p. 101. Cf. the additional references in Mordecai b. Hillel ha-Kohen, *Sefer Mord^ekhai ha-
Shalem 'al Masekhet Be ̣zah,* ed. Joshua Horowitz and Isaac Kleinman (Jerusalem, 1983),
pp. 117–18nn.
22. Moses Isserles, *Shu"T ha-RaM"A* 125, pp. 488–95 (quotation on 491).
23. See the responsum of an unnamed Ashkenazic pietist in I. Ta-Shema, "Eretz-Israel
Studies" (Hebrew), *Shalem* 1 (1974), 81–82. On the halakhic issues in medieval rabbinic
discussions of migration to Palestine, see also Ephraim Kanarfogel, "The 'Aliyah of 'Three
Hundred Rabbis' in 1211: Tosafist Attitudes toward Settling in the Land of Israel," *JQR,* n.s.
76 (1986), 191–215.
24. Solomon b. Abraham ibn Adret, *Sefer T^eshuvot ha-M^eyuhasot l^eha-RaMba"N* 272 (Tel
Aviv, 1959), pp. 226–27, reasoned that because according to TB *Meg.* 27a the commandment
of Torah study outweighs that of honoring one's parents, and because the obligations of
procreation and Torah study alone justify the sale of a Torah scroll, procreation too takes
precedence over honoring one's parents. See also Benjamin b. Mattathias, *Shu"T Binyamin
Z^e'ev* 281, 2:162–63.

tions and the conception of offspring.[25] The importance of procreation justified leniency in permitting the marriage of a Jewish man to a Karaite woman[26] or that of an apostate's son to a Jewish woman.[27] Invoking the principle that one may not swear to violate a commandment,[28] halakhic authorities tended to absolve individuals from commitments that obviated procreation. They extended this dispensation even to widows (who had sworn to their husbands that they would never remarry), arguing that in some general or secondary way women too are bound by the law of "be fertile and increase."[29] On the other hand, good faith and the honesty of one's intentions also entered into the equation. Jurists refused to absolve a husband from an oath never to remarry if he knew at the time of betrothal that his wife could not bear children. Asher b. Yehiel thus rejected the petition of a man who had married an older widow for her money, only to discover that none of her fortune would be his.

> He swore he would not marry another woman during her lifetime; and he stipulated no contingency in his oath but swore outright. And who is the sage who will take it upon himself to release him from his oath, which he swore with her understanding that she would therefore marry him? There is no sage who will release him! As we say (TB *Ned.* 65a): "You took your vow in Midian; go and be released from your vow in Midian [i.e., before the person who obliged you to take it]." As for his desire to marry another woman to fulfill the commandment of procreation—he should not break his serious oath, because the whole world would thereby be shaken, inasmuch as Scripture states (Ex. 20:7), "[The Lord] will not clear [one who swears falsely by his name]" on

---

25. Jacob b. Moses ha-Levi Molin, *New Responsa of . . . Maharil* (Hebrew) 96, ed. Yitzchok Satz (Jerusalem, 1977), pp. 100–102; Joseph b. Solomon Colon, *Shu"T* 56 (1884; repr., New York, 1968), pp. 31b–33a; Benjamin b. Mattathias, *Shu"T Binyamin Ze'ev* 158, 1:417–23; Joseph b. Efraim Karo, *Sefer 'Avqat Rokhel* 61 (Leipzig, 1859), pp. 53b–55a. It is curious that the concern of these responsa is that Jewish women (daughters of Israel) are neglecting the duty of procreation; see TB *Nid.* 3b and the statement of Shammai to Hillel. On the other hand, Simeon b. Zemah Duran, *Sefer ha-Tashbaẕ* 1.46, 4 vols. (Lemberg, 1891), 1:18a, ruled that a wife who could not tolerate the cold water of the ritual bath had to be divorced immediately so that her husband not neglect his procreative duties.

26. David ibn Zimra, *Shu"T* 1.73, 1:12b.

27. Levi b. Jacob ibn Habib, *Shu"T MahaRLba"Ḥ* 42 (Lemberg, 1865), pp. 30b–31a.

28. M *Ned.* 2.2, *Shev.* 3.8.

29. See the responsa of Nissim Gerondi, David b. Hayyim ha-Kohen, Benjamin b. Mattathias, and David ibn Zimra cited above, Chapter 3, nn. 73–75. Yom Tov Ishbili, *Shu"T* 43, p. 45, struggled earlier with a similar question but found no cause for releasing a woman from her oath on the basis of her inclusion in the precepts of "be fertile and increase" and "he formed it for habitation (*shevet*)."

account of the commandment of procreation. And if she had given him money as he desired, he would have no concern for the commandment of procreation. I therefore see no reason whatsoever to release him from his oath.[30]

For the sake of procreation, some rabbinic jurists relaxed the Ashkenazic ban on polygamy, along with the correlative prohibition of divorcing a woman against her will. Monogamy evidently prevailed in practice already during talmudic times, but the law permitted a husband to take more than one wife if he had adequate financial means. In medieval France and Germany, however, no doubt under the influence of a Christian environment whose religious leadership vehemently decried polygamy, Jewish authorities banned it as well, and they further sought to protect a wife from the resulting possibility of an unwanted divorce. What makes this development particularly interesting is that its historical origins and the extent of its technical validity remain obscure. Subsequent generations attributed these decrees to Gershom b. Judah of Mainz (ca. 960–1028), remembered by posterity as "the light of the exile (*Me'or ha-Golah*)," but no document older than the twelfth century testifies to their observance; the earliest evidence makes no mention of Gershom, and the bans apparently were first conceived as applying to a limited geographical area for a finite period of time.[31] It is striking, then, that Ashkenazic Jewry quickly came to view the ordinances as sacred and of permanent, fundamental importance. A late twelfth- or early thirteenth-century source considers the epitome of uncivilized and unethical behavior to be that of "a man who has married two wives and has violated the ordinance of Rabbenu Gershom. Everyone remarks:

30. Asher b. Yehiel, *Shu"T* 8.8, p. 12b. Cf. the similar ruling in Isaac b. Sheshet, *Shu"T* 98, p. 18b, where one could not deem the husband's behavior ethically reprehensible.

31. On the origins of and attestations to the "ban of Rabbenu Gershom," see Louis Finkelstein, *Jewish Self-government in the Middle Ages* (1924; repr., New York, 1964), pp. 23–30, 142–43 n. 2; Louis M. Epstein, *Marriage Laws in the Bible and the Talmud*, Harvard Semitic Series 12 (1942; repr., New York, 1968), ch. 1; S. Lowy, "The Extent of Jewish Polygamy in Talmudic Times," *Journal of Jewish Studies* 9 (1958), 115–38; Peretz Tishby, "Concerning the Enactments (*Taqqanot*) of Rabbenu Gershom Me'or Haggolah: Was the Prohibition against Polygamy Enacted by Rabbenu Gershom?" (Hebrew), *Tarbiẓ* 34 (1965), 49–55; the astute rejoinders of S. Eidelberg, "A Comment to the Article of Peretz Tishby" (Hebrew), ibid., pp. 287–88, and Ze'ev W. Falk, "Concerning the Enactments of Rabbenu Gershom" (Hebrew), ibid., 35 (1965), 193; idem, *Jewish Matrimonial Law in the Middle Ages*, Scripta judaica 6 (Oxford, 1966), ch. 1; and the insightful, nuanced discussion in Avraham Grossman, *The Early Sages of Ashkenaz: Their Lives, Leadership, and Works (900–1096)* (Hebrew) (Jerusalem, 1981), pp. 132–49.

'How impudent is that man! It is fitting to banish and excommunicate him.' "[32]

Yet as much as bigamy—and compulsory divorce—may have offended the sensitivities of medieval Jews, their prohibition could easily impede the pursuit of a similarly valued priority: compliance with the commandment of "be fertile and increase." The Mishnah had prescribed the dissolution of a marriage that remained childless for ten years, but we have noted that medieval rabbis increasingly refrained from enforcing this law against the wishes of the individuals involved. The decrees ascribed to Gershom now forbade a man from contracting multiple marriages in the hope that at least one would be fruitful, and they also ostensibly prevented the divorce of a childless woman against her will. Faced with this quandary, a few medieval halakhists refused to violate the new ordinances. One responsum of the twelfth century describes how a council of Ashkenazic communities did not dispense with the antibigamy decree for the sake of procreation, reasoning that "it is better to sacrifice a single soul than to set a destructive precedent for subsequent generations."[33] Others preferred compulsory divorce to bigamy as the appropriate means of dealing with a childless couple, perhaps because it was mandated by the Talmud.[34] Nevertheless, several rabbis who responded to questions on this matter agreed that "the master [Gershom] of blessed memory never intended to enact an ordinance in order to overturn rabbinic law."[35] Even some late medieval Ashkenazic halakhists numbered among those who ruled that a childless husband could take a second wife in order to meet his reproductive responsibilities, and procreation also provided the rationale for permitting bigamy or compulsory divorce in the case of a "rebellious" wife (who refused to perform her marital obligations).[36] Curiously, the

---

32. *SHB* 49, p. 109.

33. A responsum of Eliezer b. Joel ha-Levi and Efraim b. Jacob of Bonn, appearing in Victor Aptowitzer, *Introductio ad Sefer Rabiah* (Hebrew) (Jerusalem, 1938), p. 201. See also the sharply worded responsum of Judah b. Eliezer Mintz in his and Meir b. Isaac Katzenellenbogen of Padua's *Sefer Shu"T* (Krakow, 1882), pp. 16b–19a.

34. For example, Benjamin b. Mattathias, *Shu"T Binyamin Z^eʿev* 64, 1:202; and cf. the ruling of Gershom himself as quoted by Mordecai b. Hillel and interpreted by Falk, n. 37 below.

35. Estori b. Moses ha-Parhi, *Kaftor wa-Feraḥ*, 2 vols. (New York, 1958–64), 1:322; and cf. Joseph b. Solomon Colon, *Shu"T* 101, pp. 57ab. *Kaftor wa-Feraḥ* refers to the duty of procreation as rabbinic law (*divre soferim*), perhaps reflecting the acknowledgment of several medieval exegetes that the rabbis, and not Scripture, had first construed "be fertile and increase" as a commandment. See below, nn. 92–93.

36. Numerous opinions on all sides of this question are cited in *OP*, 1:14a; Solomon Zalman Havlin, "Taqqanot Rabbenu Gershom Meʿor ha-Golah beʿ-Inyʿene 'Ishut bi-Thume

evidence that Gershom (and his students) sanctioned bigamy in such circumstances may actually antedate that for the promulgation of the ban on polygamy.[37] In other words, Ashkenazic rabbis may have asserted the propriety of bigamy for procreative purposes even before they formalized their general objection to bigamy. And Gershom's authority was itself invoked to take exception to the rule that bears his name. The precedence taken by the commandment of procreation over the sanctity of monogamy is also ironic from an exegetical perspective. While Scripture never formulated the blessing of "be fertile and increase" as law, its account of human origins depicts a blissfully (at least before the fall) monogamous union between the first parents, and it validates the institution of marriage with an ode of praise (Gen. 2:23–24) for a seemingly monogamous relationship: "A man leaves his father and mother and clings to his wife (singular), so that they become one flesh."

The responsa we have discussed invariably impress a reader with their flexibility, their sensitivity, and their realism. In the final analysis, the laws of procreation were unenforceable. But medieval rabbis did not resign themselves to this truth passively, effectively abandoning the mandate bequeathed them by their talmudic forebears. When the latter construed "be fertile and increase" as Mosaic law, they affirmed the importance of God's primordial design for humankind in the distinctive mission of Israel. If subsequent halakhists determined that they could not impose this law on those unwilling or unable to comply, they nevertheless persisted in applying it strenuously. Expressive of the

---

Sefarad u-Frovans," *Shenaton ha-Mishpaṭ ha-ʿIvri* 2 (1975), 200–257; and *ET*, 17:411–15. Much controversy has focused on the posture of Solomon ibn Adret, whom Colon and others subsequently cited to defend their respective positions. See the meticulous reconstruction of the textual tradition in Havlin, loc. cit.; the conflicting opinion of Yom-Tov Assis, "The 'Ordinance of Rabbenu Gershom' and Polygamous Marriages in Spain" (Hebrew), *Zion*, n.s. 46 (1981), 251–77; and the rejoinder of Havlin, "Berurim Ḥadashim be-ʿInyene Taqqanot RaGMa"H, Yiḥusan, Teḥulatan, we-Hitpashṭutan," *Shenaton ha-Mishpaṭ ha-ʿIvri* 11–12 (1986), 317–36.

37. See Gershom b. Judah, *The Responsa of Rabbenu Gershom Meor Hagolah* (Hebrew) 42, ed. Shlomo Eidelberg (New York, 1955), pp. 113–14 (with notes ad loc. and on p. 19); and the responsum of Rashi appearing in Joel Mueller, ed., *Teshuvot Ḥakhme Zarefat we-Lotir* 28 (Vienna, 1881), pp. 14b–15a. Contra Falk, *Jewish Matrimonial Law*, p. 15, I would espouse the position of *OP*, 1:14a, that Gershom's prescription of compulsory divorce for a childless couple recorded in Mordecai b. Hillel's gloss ad TB *Yev.* 113 (and in Gershom, *Responsa* 44, p. 115) does not necessarily contradict his position sanctioning bigamy. Rather, it might derive from the talmudic logic that this man would not remarry as long as his first wife remains with him; nonetheless, one might infer that, were it not for this consideration, Gershom would permit bigamy as we know he did elsewhere.

foundations of biblical and rabbinic theology, the divine call for procreation in Gen. 1:28 now became a tool of the jurist, a category of legal
priority to which much else had to defer. Discerning the process of
procreation in the basic rhythms of the natural order, the aggadic
homilist had portrayed God as undertaking the creation "for the settlement of the world and its civilization (*le-tiqqun ha-ʿolam ule-yishuvo*)."[38]
For the sake of perfecting the social order (*mippene tiqqun ha-ʿolam*), the
Mishnah had also invoked the teleological importance of procreation.[39]
In some sense, it was not inappropriate that medieval halakhists used
the legal urgency of procreation to heal wounds in their own communities, setting matters aright between husband and wife, parent and
child, individual and community. As much as a legal interpretation of
Gen. 1:28 *ipso facto* signified a departure from the intended meaning of
Scripture, it did not forsake that meaning. The authors of our responsa
themselves read the Bible, and, like us, they too endeavored to recover
its "literal" sense.

A RETURN TO THE TEXT OF THE BIBLE

Diverse factors contributed to the resurgence of biblical scholarship
in the medieval Jewish community. Especially in the world of Islam,
critical science and philosophy impelled rabbinic leaders to justify the
precepts of their faith in rational terms. The success or failure of such an
endeavor depended in large measure on a defense of the Torah of
Moses, which provided not only the theological and historical foundations for belief in Judaism, but also the basic legal ordinances that
comprised its observance. Similar motives had undoubtedly inspired
Philo of Alexandria centuries earlier, but his writings were largely
forgotten by rabbinic Jews and exerted their immediate influence on the
Greek fathers of the Christian church. Ruled by Muslims and Christians
who themselves laid claim to the inheritance of the biblical covenant,
and particularly so in Christendom, Jews employed exegesis to cope
with their subordinate, minority status. Rabbis strove to promote and
validate their own interpretation of Scripture—both to respond directly
to the polemic of the majority and to strengthen the resolve of their own

38. Above, Chapter 2, at n. 58.
39. Above, Chapter 3, at n. 105.

constituencies to withstand the hardships of their situation. Reflecting a similar interest among their Christian neighbors, and working from the premise that Jews more than others descended directly from the original Israelite recipients of the Torah, many rabbinic commentators moved increasingly toward a literal exposition of the text, asserting the simple, "historical" sense of the Bible as its authentic, divinely intended meaning. Such a tendency, however, contributed to yet an additional problem that demanded a response from the medieval rabbi. As Karaites and other critics hastened to point out, talmudic Judaism had itself departed significantly from its ancient biblical predecessor; what mandated the rabbi's midrashic interpretation of biblical law and prophecy more than that of his opponent? Nothing less than the integrity and credibility of rabbinic Judaism were at stake, and the treatment of Gen. 1:28 in the resulting exegetical literature exemplifies much of the way that medieval Jews rose to the challenges of their age.

The Verse in Its Biblical Context

A desire to recover the "original" or literal meaning of Scripture led rabbinic exegetes to scrutinize the Genesis cosmogony afresh. To be sure, their commentaries sought an accordance between the biblical text and the teachings of rabbinic tradition that shaped their world view and their lifestyle. Yet if the weight of tradition and the constellation of circumstances motivating the encounter between exegetes and text may thus have set predetermined limits to their interpretations, their questions were subject to less restraint and manifested new dimensions of hermeneutical awareness. One should note with care and reflection how much the questions raised by Jewish and Christian exegetes of late antiquity and the Middle Ages bespeak the concerns of modern biblical scholars, discussed at length in Chapter 1. The range of similarities and differences should not only impress the modern reader with the explicative acuity of our medieval forebears but also, it is hoped, dispel the notion that our own range of concerns constitutes the sole yardstick for measuring critical objectivity.

Like many modern readers of the biblical cosmogony, medieval rabbinic exegetes typically questioned the correspondence of Gen. 1:28 to the similar blessing in Gen. 1:22. This earlier verse, uttered at the end of the fifth day of creation, was directed to fish and fowl, while in Gen. 1:28 God spoke to human beings. Why did the creator fail to include land animals and plants in either blessing of "be fertile and increase"? Plants, some commentators appeared to agree, needed no blessing because they were created in large numbers and reproduced asexually.[40] As for land animals, Rashi explained that like fish and birds they required the blessing of fertility because hunters would otherwise deplete their numbers; but foreseeing the sin of the serpent, God deliberately excluded them.[41] Rashi's grandson Samuel b. Meir held that the blessing of Gen. 1:22 did extend to the animals; Moses Nahmanides agreed, adding that Scripture nevertheless instructed fish and humans to "be fertile and increase," because their food is always readily available and they therefore have more time for procreative activity.[42] A third group of exegetes maintained that fish and birds, whose offspring are born outside their bodies, needed special protection.[43] Still others attributed the exclusion of the animals to the extra threat they posed to humans; empowered with divine blessing, they might subvert the dominion granted man and woman in Gen. 1:28.[44]

Why did humans receive the same blessing of "be fertile and increase" already given to lesser creatures? Noting that Gen. 1:28 specifies, "God blessed them *and God said to them*," while with reference to fish and fowl Scripture simply reports, "God blessed them, *saying*," numerous rabbinic exegetes posited a qualitative difference between the two divine statements. In the case of marine creatures, God merely

---

40. RaMba"N, 1:26; Jacob b. Asher, *Perush ha-Ṭur he-'Arokh 'al ha-Torah* (Jerusalem, 1961), p. 5; Elijah Mizrahi, *Be'ur*, in *'Oẓar Mefareshe ha-Torah*, 1:8a. Saadya, *Commentary on Genesis*, pp. 54–55, 259, explained that God included the plants in the elaboration of his blessing to the first humans (Gen. 1:29–30), as well as in Lev. 25:21 (so too Nahmanides).

41. RaSh"I, p. 7; Eleazar b. Judah of Worms, *Perush ha-Roqeaḥ 'al ha-Torah*, ed. Chaim Konyevsky, 3 vols. (B'nei B'rak, 1978–81), 1:63; Jacob b. Asher, loc. cit.; Zechariah the Physician, *Midrash ha-Ḥefeẓ*, p. 59.

42. Samuel b. Meir, *Commentarium in Pentateuchum* (Hebrew), ed. David Rosin (Breslau, 1881), p. 8; RaMba"N, loc. cit.; so too Elijah Mizrahi, loc. cit. Rashi himself advanced the position that Gen. 1:28a applied to all creatures, while only the blessing of dominion in Gen. 1:28b extended exclusively to humans; see Solomon b. Isaac, *Responsa* (Hebrew) 196, ed. Israel Elfenbein (New York, 1943), p. 220. Cf. Nathaniel b. Isaiah, *Sefer Ma'or ha-'Afelah*, p. 23, and Zechariah the Physician, *Midrash ha-Ḥefeẓ*, loc. cit., who cite the statement in TB *Bekh.* 8a that only among fish and humans do male and female face each other during sexual relations.

43. Levi b. Gerson, *Perush 'al ha-Torah*, 1:12a; Nissim b. Reuben Gerondi, *Commentary on the Bible* (Hebrew), ed. Leon A. Feldman (Jerusalem, 1968), p. 43; Isaac b. Judah Abravanel, *Perush 'al ha-Torah*, 5 pts. in 3 vols. (New York, 1959), 1:27b. Cf. Judah Loew b. Bezalel of Prague, *Gur 'Aryeh*, in *'Oẓar Mefareshe ha-Torah*, 1:8a, who added that God eventually included the beasts in the blessing of "be fertile and increase" given Noah, by which time the serpent had been punished.

44. Hezekiah b. Manoah, *Perushe ha-Ḥizquni 'al ha-Torah*, ed. Charles B. Chavel (Jerusalem, 1981), p. 10; Moses b. Hayyim Alshekh, *Sefer Torat Mosheh*, 5 pts. in 2 vols. (1875–79; repr., Brooklyn, 1960), 1:11a.

endowed their nature with a reproductive faculty, but with man and woman God actually engaged in rational discourse.[45] From this some inferred that God *blessed* the fish with fertility but *commanded* human beings to procreate. Levi Gersonides wrote:[46]

> Man did not need to be blessed so that he would be fertile and would increase, because God, may he be exalted, already had endowed him with a perfect reproductive faculty upon his creation. And thus our sages of blessed memory agreed that what is stated here to man, "and God said to them, be fertile and increase [and] fill the earth," is a positive commandment. And here another reason mandates that this statement was a commandment and not the endowment of a natural reproductive faculty—namely, that this activity, meaning the conjunction of male and female, occurs among humans out of choice. For in man there is the ability to engage in this activity and not to engage in it. And it is possible for him to engage in it so as not to produce offspring, when he threshes inside and winnows outside, as our sages of blessed memory stated concerning Er and Onan . . .[47]—which is not the case with other living creatures. And the determination by God, may he be blessed, that one of two possibilities subject to the [human] will should be willed is necessarily through commandment rather than nature. This being the case, this statement [of Gen. 1:28] is undoubtedly a commandment.

Gersonides' insistence that the call for procreation in Gen. 1:28 constitutes a legal precept and not mere blessing demands an explanation of the verse's opening words: To what does "God blessed them" refer? While most commentators linked these words to procreation and/or dominion, whether or not they characterized what follows as commandment, at least one recalled the aggadic connection between Gen. 1:28 and the seven nuptial benedictions,[48] and several interpreted them independently of the remainder of the verse. The Yemenite Nathaniel b. Isaiah proposed that God "gave them the faculty of perception with

45. Saadya, *Commentary on Genesis*, pp. 45, 244; Abraham b. Moses Maimonides, *Perush ʿal Bᵉreshit u-Shᵉmot*, ed. Efraim Judah Weisenberg (London, 1958), p. 12; David Kimhi, *Perushe RaDa"Q ʿal ha-Torah*, p. 18.

46. Loc. cit. Cf. Jacob Gellis, ed., *Sefer Tosafot Hashalem: Commentary on the Bible* (Hebrew), 1 (Jerusalem, 1982), 56, 68–69. RaMbaʾ"N, 1:27; Isaac b. Moses Arama, *ʿAqedat Yiẓḥaq*, 5 vols. (Pressburg, 1849), 1:334; Joseph b. Hayyim Jabez, *Perush ʿal ha-Torah*, in Y. Gad, ed., *Sefer Ḥamishah Mᵉʾorot Gᵉdolim* (Johannesburg, 1953), p. 50; and Moses b. Jacob al-Balideh, *ʿOlat Tamid* (Venice, 1601), p. 22b.

47. See above, Chapter 3, n. 45.

48. Meyuhas b. Elijah, *Perush ʿal Bᵉreshit*, ed. A. W. Greenup and C. H. Titterton (1909; repr., Jerusalem, 1968), p. 8; and see above, Chapter 2, at nn. 146–148.

which to distinguish between the true and the false and the good and the bad."[49] And Isaac Abravanel denied that the blessing of Gen. 1:28 concerned fertility or dominion. Neither pertained exclusively to human beings; all animals reproduce, and the lion exercises dominion. "Rather, the blessing which the Torah mentioned concerning humans was that they should succeed in their undertakings, produce offspring, live long lives, and all the other good things denoted by the term blessing. For concerning them all he spoke to them in a general sense."[50]

It is significant that Jewish Bible commentators of the Middle Ages began to compensate for the lack of attention paid to Gen. 1:28b in earlier rabbinic sources. For the first time, rabbinic scholars discussed at length the dominion conferred by God on the first parents—its meaning, its limits, and its purpose.[51] Writing in the tenth century, Saadya b. Joseph Gaon anticipated various modern readers of Genesis by defining the divine image in the first human being "in terms of governance and rule, not in terms of the form of his face or his appearance. . . . For God made man in the status of ruler, so that all depends on him, just as he, may he be exalted, is ruler over all."[52] Yet Saadya also brought an unprecedented scientific and technological awareness to bear on the interpretation of Gen. 1, relating the primordial blessing of dominion to the achievements of medieval civilization in a striking excursus well worth quoting:[53]

> The word "they shall rule"[54] includes the entire range of devices with which man rules over the animals: over some with fetters and bridles, over some with ropes and reins, over some with enclosures and chains, over some with weapons of the hunt, over some with cages and towers, and so on—until he [God] instructed him [man] concerning everything. And the word "the fish" includes the stratagems for catching fish from the bottom of the sea and the rivers, the preparation of the permitted species in cooking utensils and their consumption, the extraction of pearls from the shells, and the use of the appropriate portions of skin

49. Nathaniel b. Isaiah, *Sefer Ma'or ha-'Afelah,* p. 12.

50. Isaac Abravanel, *Perush ha-Torah,* 1:30b.

51. Aggadic consideration of human dominion (discussed above in Chapter 2) stressed its dependence on human merit, particularly in the wake of the fall from Eden, and usually related to Gen. 1:28 only indirectly.

52. Saadya, *Commentary on Genesis,* pp. 53, 257; cf. above, Chapter 1, n. 54.

53. Ibid., pp. 53–54, 258–59.

54. Arabic reads thus, according to Gen. 1:26; Zucker translates "and rule" (Gen. 1:28).

and bones and everything associated with this. And he added the word "of the sea" to include man's subjugation of the water as well; for he finds it within the ground and raises it out with pulleys and with . . .[55] or with containers or with a machine utilizing force and pressure. And thus he dams rivers to transfer water from one side to the other, and he uses it to power the mills. As Scripture stated elsewhere (Ps. 8:9), "whatever travels the path of the seas," hinting at the construction of ships and boats and barges with which to cross from shore to shore. He even makes 'al-dra'min, the enormous galleys holding thousands of men with which to traverse the expanses of the seas. . . .[56] And in areas of rocky promontories they make papyrus boats and cross in them so that they should not break. As Isaiah specified (18:2), "in papyrus vessels upon the water." And his word "and the birds" corresponds to the various snares for hunting birds which fly in the sky, the process of taming some in order to hunt others, the preparation from them of foods for his sustenance and potions for medicines and the like. And he added "of the sky" to include the ability of man to understand the heavenly sphere and its composition . . . and to prepare the various instruments for measuring the hours and their components. And with the word "the cattle" he gave him the authority to lead and the power to make use of them all, to eat the flesh of those fit for consumption through various means of cooking and in the different forms of food, to heal from that which is medicinal, to ride on those suited for riding like mules, and to know all their diets, that is, how to feed them. And the words "the whole earth" hint at the talent for building houses, fortresses, and battlements, for plowing the land, for sowing diverse seeds, for planting vegetation, for extracting gold, silver, iron, and copper from the mines, for artfully fashioning utensils and jewels, for refining tools for agricultural work like the blade of the cattle-drawn plow, for making tools of carpentry like saws and axes, for making tools for the weaving of cloth like the weavers' beam . . .[57] and for fashioning writing utensils like pens and inks and the like. . . . And I have been brief [*sic!*] and have not brought scriptural evidence for each one of these. And with the word "and all the creeping things" he hinted at the understanding which he gave man to confine bees in hives to make honey for him and deposit it in a tree.

The treatment of Gen. 1:28 in Saadya's *Tafsir* is exceptional in several respects. Not only did Saadya explore the implications of human do-

---

55. Lacuna in text.
56. Lacuna in text.
57. Lacuna in text.

minion in greater depth than any of his rabbinic predecessors, but he virtually ignored the blessing of fertility in the first half of our verse.[58] Unlike most medieval halakhists, he even failed to include procreation in his enumeration of the 613 Mosaic commandments.[59] For Saadya, the verse bespoke an anthropocentric teleology of creation, which most premodern Jews and Christians probably shared and took for granted[60] but which he felt obliged to elaborate in graphic terms and at great length. Like Ps. 8, which he quoted, the words of Gen. 1:28 struck Saadya as an ode to human inventiveness and technological achievement, the distinctive ability and privilege of humans to overcome and to harness the diverse constituents of the natural environment for their benefit. Saadya perceived in the primordial blessing precisely that mentality which modern writers have decried as ecologically insensitive and destructive. Some of Saadya's successors, including Moses Nahmanides and Obadiah Sforno, also referred to the mechanical devices whereby humans subdued the animals and the earth in their own behalf, as they commented on Gen. 1:28.[61] Others, like David Kimhi, Levi Gersonides, and Isaac Arama, acknowledged the cosmic anthropocentrism implicit in our verse, typically linking the superiority of human beings to their singular powers of reason.[62] The view that God created the entire world expressly for human benefit was not without its rabbinic opponents, and Moses Maimonides openly rejected an overly teleological reading of Gen. 1:28b.[63] Yet most medieval Jewish discus-

---

58. He merely alludes to it in his discussion of Gen. 1:22, pp. 45–46, 244–46. A similar appreciation of Gen. 1:28b is manifest in Saadya's *Sefer ha-Nivḥar ba-'Emunot wᵉha-Deʿot* 4, pp. 150ff.

59. See Saadya b. Joseph, *Sefer ha-Miẓwot*, ed. Yeruham Fischel Perla, 2 vols. (1914–17; repr., New York, 1962), 1:280a–281b, with the troubled comments of the editor ad loc.

60. See the host of ancient references cited in *LOJ*, 5:65–68 nn. 6–8, and Jobling, esp. chs. 1, 6.

61. Moses b. Nahman, *The Commentary of Nahmanides on Genesis Chapters 1–6⁸*, ed. Jacob Newman, Pretoria Oriental Series 4 (Leiden, 1960), p. 57: "He gave them power and governance on the earth to do as they pleased with livestock and insects and all things that crawl in the dust; and to build, to uproot plants, to mine copper from the earth's mountains, and the like"; Obadiah b. Jacob Sforno, *Beʾur ʿal ha-Torah*, ed. Zeʾev Gottlieb and Abraham Darom (Jerusalem, 1980), p. 16: "'and master it'—You should defend yourselves with your reason, so that you prevent the beasts from entering your provinces and so that you should rule them; 'and rule'—with snares and nets to impress them into your service."

62. David Kimhi, *Perushe RaDaʾ'Q ʿal ha-Torah*, p. 20; Levi b. Gerson, *Perush ʿal ha-Torah*, 1:12b; Isaac Arama, *ʿAqedat Yiẓḥaq*, 1:33a. See also Zechariah the Physician, *Midrash ha-Ḥefez*, pp. 63–64; Moses Alshekh, *Sefer Torat Mosheh*, 1:12a; and Abraham b. Jacob Saba, *Sefer Ẓᵉror ha-Mor* (1879; Tel Aviv, 1975), p. 2b.

63. Moses b. Maimon, *The Guide of the Perplexed* 3.13, p. 454. See also the similar sentiments of Abraham ibn Ezra, *Perushe ha-Torah*, 1:7–8, who notes, albeit without reference to Gen. 1:28, that humans have settled only one-twelfth of the earth's surface.

sion of the superior human status and its cosmological ramifications ensued without reference to our verse. No other ancient or medieval writer, Jewish or Christian, interpreted the primordial blessing of dominion to incorporate quite as much as Saadya did. Although the gaon of Sura was the first in a series of Jewish exegetes to redress the traditional rabbinic neglect of that blessing, his extensive comments remained the colloquial exception that proves the rule.

Further anticipating modern critics of the Bible, medieval Jewish commentators debated whether the vegetarian diet prescribed for humans in Gen. 1:29–30 served to limit the power over animals granted them in the previous verse. Many answered in the affirmative,[64] but Saadya Gaon held that Gen. 1 prohibited the human consumption of meat only temporarily, so that the few representatives of each animal species might first assure the survival of their respective kinds.[65] Judah ha-Levi, David Kimhi, and Isaac Abravanel construed the contrast between human and animal diets as confirming human superiority more than as circumscribing human dominion.[66]

Rabbinic exegetes also acknowledged the recurrence of the *prh/rbh* hendiadys in Scripture and deemed it worthy of their comments. The separation of the two verbal roots by other words struck Israel b. Petahiah Isserlein as worthy of homiletic explication.[67] Abraham ibn Ezra and Obadiah b. Abraham of Bertinoro recognized the transmission of the divine blessing from Adam to the Hebrew patriarchs and their enslaved descendants in Egypt signaled by the repetition of *prh/ rbh*.[68] Commenting on Gen. 17, Joseph Bekhor Shor and Eleazar b. Judah of Worms discussed the linkage between the commandment of circumcision, God's covenant with Israel, and the motif of "be fertile and increase."[69] From their mystical perspective, Eleazar and Moses

---

64. For example, RaSh"I, p. 4; Gellis, *Sefer Tosafot Hashalem,* 1:70; RaMba"N, 1:29; Nissim Gerondi, *Commentary,* p. 50; Elijah Mizrahi, *Be'ur,* in *'Oẓar Mᵉfarᵉshe ha-Torah,* 1:10a–11a; Moses Alshekh, *Sefer Torat Mosheh,* 1:12b. Cf. above, Chapter 2, n. 125.

65. Saadya b. Joseph, *Commentary on Genesis,* pp. 54–55, 259–60.

66. Judah ha-Levi, *Das Buch al-Chazari* 5.10, ed. Hirschfeld, pp. 302–303; David Kimhi, *Perushe RaDa"Q 'al ha-Torah,* p. 22; Isaac Abravanel, *Perush 'al ha-Torah,* pp. 30b–31a.

67. Israel b. Petahiah Isserlein, *Sefer Be'ure MahaR"I* (1937; repr., B'nei B'rak, 1963), pp. 19, 40.

68. Abraham ibn Ezra, *Perushe ha-Torah,* 1:103; Obadiah b. Abraham Yare of Bertinoro, *'Amar Nᵉqe'* (Pisa, 1810), p. 20b. Also see *Hadar Zᵉqenim* ad Ex. 1:7, in *'Oẓar Perushim 'al ha-Torah, Miqra'ot Gᵉdolot* 6 (New York, 1950), p. 24ab.

69. Joseph Bekhor Shor, *Perush 'al ha-Torah,* ed. Y. Gad, 3 vols. (Jerusalem, 1956–59), 1:18; according to Eleazar of Worms, *Perush ha-Roqeah,* 1:148, the patriarch Abraham was circumcised and was granted his request for an heir at the age of ninety-nine, because the numerical value (in *gᵉmaṭri'a*) of the letters (*ẓdq ṭyt*) representing that age equals 613, the total number of Mosaic commandments.

Nahmanides also discerned an important connection between the divine name of *'El Shaddai* and the blessing of procreation.[70] And Rashi agreed that procreation (*p[e]riyyah u-r[e]viyyah*) comprised a vital component of God's reward for the observance of his commandments.[71]

As the most blatant allusions to our verse, the two reiterations of "be fertile and increase" to Noah and his sons after the flood (Gen. 9:1, 7) prompted much discussion. For Jews in late antiquity and the Middle Ages, the belief in the divine origin of the Torah dictated that nothing in Scripture was superfluous; ostensibly repetitive words and phrases had to serve a purpose, and much rabbinic interpretation of the Bible endeavored to elucidate precisely what such purposes might be. In this instance, why did God have to repeat himself? Did the divine blessing of the first parents not extend to all of their posterity? Some argued that the divine instruction of Noah to have children constituted the biblical commandment of procreation and that Gen. 1:28 merely recorded the primordial blessing. Such a response, however, did not account for the appearance of the call for procreation twice in God's postdiluvian address to Noah. And most exegetes therefore pointed to some aspect of the flood itself to account for the repetition. If those who perished in the flood had sinned by neglecting their reproductive responsibilities, God may have wished to ensure that the survivors would not incur the same guilt.[72] It is possible that God uttered the blessing of fertility a second time in order to extend it to the land animals omitted in Gen. 1.[73] Earlier midrashic sources understood that God had forbidden sexual relations aboard the ark; upon disembarkation, the call to "be fertile and increase" sanctioned the resumption of sexual activity, and its immediate repetition may have served to mandate it for procreative purposes once again. According to some writers, the devastation wrought by the flood resulted in fear and depression that would have dissuaded Noah and his sons from bringing children into the world were it not for the renewal of the divine injunction otherwise.[74] Perhaps the juxtaposition of the

70. Eleazar of Worms, *Perush ha-Roqeah*, 1:209; RaMba"N, 1:98–99; see also *MBR*, p. 271, and Gellis, *Sefer Tosafot Hashalem*, 1:69. Kabbalistic interpretations of Gen. 1:28 will be considered at length below.

71. RaSh"I, p. 401.

72. Levi b. Gerson, *Perush 'al ha-Torah*, 1:20a; cf. above, Chapter 2, n. 32.

73. Hezekiah b. Manoah, *Perushe ha-Hizquni*, p. 46; cf. Judah Loew of Prague, cited above, n. 43.

74. Isaac Abravanel, *Perush 'al ha-Torah*, 1:71a; Elijah Mizrahi and Judah Loew of Prague, in *'Ozar M[e]far[e]she ha-Torah*, 1:31ab; Isaac b. Joseph Karo, *Tol[e]dot Yizhaq* (1878; repr., Jerusalem, 1959), pp. 14b–15b. Cf. above, Chapter 2, nn. 36–38.

blessing and the prohibition of homicide intended to facilitate the Tannaitic comparison between one who refrains from procreation and the murderer.[75] In a similar vein, it was suggested that the blessing of fertility constituted a reward for enforcing the divine stricture against murder.[76] Most of these propositions derived from doctrinal considerations or from earlier midrashic sources external to the text of Genesis itself. Especially noteworthy, then, are the commentaries that attempt to explain the recurrence of *prh/rbh* in Gen. 9 as resulting from the inner logic and structure of the Bible's primeval history. For example, David Kimhi suggested: "Even though they were already blessed at the beginning of creation, it was now like the beginning of creation for them. For the world was reestablished after it had been unformed and void (*tohu wa-vohu*), inasmuch as the mountains of the earth had been covered with water."[77] Nissim Gerondi likewise argued that "because God reformed the face of the earth, and the situation of Noah and his sons approximated that of Adam, he blessed them just as he had blessed Adam."[78] In the sixteenth century, Moses b. Jacob al-Balideh wrote even more explicitly, pointing out that the animals' fear of human beings promised by God in Gen. 9:2 also reiterated the original grant of dominion in Gen. 1:28b.

> He now returned to bless Noah and his sons and to make the animals afraid of them. For on account of the evil of the generation of the flood, [humans] had reverted to the state of the beasts of the field, and the blessing of Adam had been forfeited. Now, therefore, he again blessed them and increased the fear of them, *suggesting that there was now a new world, as if at that point they began to live in the world.*[79]

In their own terminology and idiom, these medieval commentators asserted the thematic significance of Gen. 1:28 in the first eleven chapters of Scripture, much as we evaluated that function of our verse in the opening chapter of this book. The primordial blessing was an essential component of God's creation, encapsulating its purpose and regulating its order. Because the flood had undone the work of the creation, returning the cosmos to *tohu wa-vohu* by reversing the very processes of

75. RaSh"I, p. 38; Elijah Mizrahi, loc. cit.; Moses Alshekh, *Sefer Torat Mosheh*, 1:33a.
76. Abraham ibn Ezra, *Perushe ha-Torah*, 1:184.
77. David Kimhi, *Perushe RaDa"Q 'al ha-Torah*, p. 65.
78. Nissim Gerondi, *Commentary*, p. 115.
79. Moses al-Balideh, *'Olat Tamid*, p. 52b.

separation so crucial to the cosmogony, the reinstitution of form and direction in the world demanded that God reiterate the substance of Gen. 1:28.[80]

Identifying the Commandment of Procreation

The tradition that God revealed 613 commandments to Moses at Mount Sinai extended back to talmudic times, but the systematic enumeration, categorization, and location of these biblical precepts remained a task for medieval Jewish scholars.[81] Although rabbinic efforts along these lines resulted in entire treatises that listed and at times explained the commandments and their classification, we have elected to consider them together with scriptural commentaries under the broad rubric of biblical exegesis. Their interest in legal codification notwithstanding, such "books of the commandments" also proceeded from a new reading of Scripture. They manifest a desire to determine the precise contents and limits of Mosaic law, to defend the rationality and necessity of biblical statutes, and to assert the integrity of the Halakhah as a whole by elaborating the correspondence between the "written Torah" of the Pentateuch and the "oral Torah" of rabbinic tradition. The efforts of medieval rabbis to pinpoint the scriptural basis for the commandment of procreation readily offer evidence of these motives, but they reflect other considerations as well. As indicated above, the availability of several alternative verses with which to identify the precept demanded that each serve a distinct purpose; presumably only one could prescribe the *miẓwah* itself. On the other hand, the Bible never conveyed its call to "be fertile and increase" in legal terms or within a statutory context. The talmudic reformulation of the primordial blessing as a legal ordinance might easily evoke question and doubt in the careful reader of the Torah, and, as we noted repeatedly in Chapter 3, the definition of the statute as binding free Jewish males

---

80. Isaac Abravanel, *Perush ha-Torah,* 1:70a (cited by L. Feldman in Nissim Gerondi, *Commentary,* p. 115 n. 191), objected that if the blessing of "be fertile and increase" was reiterated after the flood owing to a new creation of the world, it should also have been given to Abraham. Abravanel's objection itself expresses the idea of three successive creations in Gen. 1–12 (as proposed above, Chapter 1); yet on 1:65b Abravanel did deem Noah "the second beginning of the human race."

81. On the origins and early history of the tradition that the Torah includes 613 commandments, see B. Halper's introduction to his edition of Hefez b. Yazliah, *A Volume of the Book of Precepts* (Arabic with Hebrew transl.) (Philadelphia, Pa., 1915), pp. 1–8.

alone—when the first parents were neither Jewish nor of the same gender—only compounded the problem.

Complicating the issue still further was the talmudic identification of the commandment with several biblical texts, in instances that suggest that the choice of one scriptural verse or another might lead to different halakhic consequences. The Mishnaic pericope that limits the duty of procreation to men relates the dissenting, more inclusive opinion of R. Yohanan b. Broka to his reading of Gen. 1:28: "With regard to both of them Scripture states, 'God blessed them and [God] said to them, "Be fertile and increase." ' " The Babylonian Gemara then considers the plural form of "[fill the earth] and master it (*we-khivshuha*)" and records R. Nahman b. Isaac's assertion that the defective spelling of *we-khiv-shuha* (*wkbsh,* allowing for the vocalization of a masculine singular imperative, *we-khovsheha*) indicates its application to males only. Although the Gemara also adduces R. Joseph's suggestion that the commandment originated with God's words to Jacob (Gen. 35:11), "be fertile and increase"—in the masculine singular—the limiting interpretation of the defective *we-khivshuha* remained the preferred, seemingly decisive argument against R. Yohanan b. Broka's view in most subsequent sources. One can therefore infer that the Mishnah, the ensuing Gemara, and many of their post-talmudic readers accepted Yohanan b. Broka's attribution of the commandment to Gen. 1:28; had anyone objected, an alternative proof-text might have clinched the argument more easily.[82] Nevertheless, the Yavnean Tanna'im who reportedly acclaimed the duty of parenting, comparing it in importance to the Noachide law against homicide, deduced their conclusions from Gen. 9:7, the second utterance of "be fertile and increase" to Noah.[83] On two other occasions, including the cumbersome argument that excludes Gentiles from the obligation to bear children, the Babylonian Gemara also cites Gen. 9:7 as the source of the commandment.[84] And in yet another instance the Gemara terms Gen. 1:28 a blessing given on the sixth day of creation, concluding that it is most auspicious for a widow to remarry on Friday.[85]

---

82. These sources are cited above, Chapter 3, at nn. 64–71. See also the citation of Yohanan's reading of Gen. 1:28 in TB *Qid.* 34b–35a; and cf. the opinion recorded in TB *San.* 57a that Gen. 9:7, the most popular alternative to Gen. 1:28 as the source of the commandment, was intended "simply as blessing."

83. Above, Chapter 2, at n. 160.

84. TB *San.* 59ab (cited above, Chapter 3, n. 88), *AZ* 5a.

85. Above, Chapter 2, n. 143.

Faced with these conflicting signals, medieval Jewish exegetes and enumerators of the 613 commandments offered divergent responses. Some simply avoided the question. The introduction to the geonic *Sefer Halakhot Gᵉdolot* lists procreation (*pᵉriyyah u-rᵉviyyah*) as a commandment but links it to no biblical text, while Saadya Gaon did not even mention it in his enumeration of the commandments.[86] The Tosafists Eliezer b. Samuel of Metz and Moses b. Jacob of Coucy, on the other hand, indicated that four times in the course of its primeval history the Torah refers to the commandment of procreation.[87] Yet as the Middle Ages wore on, most felt compelled to commit themselves to one biblical verse or another. Rashi and Moses Nahmanides linked the commandment to Gen. 9:7, the only primeval utterance of "be fertile and increase" to human beings not preceded by the words "God blessed."[88] Perhaps the talmudic specification that the words of this verse now applied only to Jews, as well as the Yavnean sages' famous reference to it, also contributed to their choice. Locating the commandment of procreation in the weekly Pentateuchal portion of *Noah*, *before* the prohibition against eating a limb severed from a live animal (*ʾevar min ha-ḥai*) in Gen. 9:4, the *Shᵉʾiltot* may imply that the precept derived from God's first blessing of Noah and his sons in Gen. 9:1.[89] Several later authorities espoused this view, but it remained the least popular opinion.[90] Beginning in the fourteenth century, most rabbinic exegetes

86. *Sefer Halakhot Gᵉdolot* (1874; repr., Tel Aviv, 1962), p. 5a.

87. See Eliezer b. Samuel of Metz, *Sefer Yᵉreʾim* 413, ed. Israel Isser Goldblum and Abraham Abba Schiff, 2 vols. (1892–1902; repr., Jerusalem, 1973), 2:231b, who quoted Gen. 1:28 and 9:17, presumably including Gen. 8:17 and 9:1 as well; Moses of Coucy, *Sefer Miẓwot Gadol* 49 (positive), 2:128b. This opinion was also espoused by Benjamin b. Mattathias, *ShuʾʾT Binyamin Zᵉʾev* 281, 2:163.

88. RaShʾʾI, p. 38; RaMbaʾʾN, 1:63. The position of Moses Maimonides is difficult to determine. The evidence of his *MT*, *ʾIshut* 15.1, and *Sefer ha-Miẓwot* 212 (positive), ed. Joseph Kafah (Jerusalem, 1971), pp. 166–67, is inconclusive, but it appears that he too linked the commandment to Gen. 9:7. (Thus concludes Kafah, in his notes ad loc., but in his edition of *Mishnah ʿim Perush Rabbenu Moshe b. Maimon*, 6 pts. in 7 vols. [Jerusalem, 1963–68], 4:451–52 n. 1, Kafah had reached the opposite conclusion.) Maimonides' son Abraham, *Perush ʿal Bᵉreshit u-Shᵉmot*, p. 12, construed Gen. 1:28 entirely as blessing; and Moses Nahmanides posed no critique of Maimonides when espousing this position. *Sefer ha-Ḥinnukh*, ed. Charles B. Chavel (Jerusalem, 1952), p. 55, however, links the commandment to Gen. 1:28. But see the conclusion of Hayyim Heller in his edition to Moses b. Maimon, *Sefer ha-Miẓwot* (1946; repr., Jerusalem, 1980), p. 88 n. 6, that the Maimonidean view is in this instance impossible to determine.

89. *Shᵉʾiltot* 5, ed. Mirsky, 1:35, with note; cf. also 165, 5:70, which cites Gen. 9:7.

90. See Abraham b. David of Posquierres, *Baʿale ha-Nefesh*, ed. Joseph Kafah (Jerusalem, 1964), p. 116; *Lekach-Tob*, 1:24a; Nathaniel b. Isaiah, *Sefer Maʾor ha-ʾAfelah*, p. 67; and cf. the gloss of Rashi ad TB *Yev*. 62a, s.v. *bᵉne Noaḥ*.

identified Gen. 1:28 as the source of a Jew's religious obligation to reproduce.[91] Of all the proposed alternatives, that which displays the best appreciation of the verse and its career appears in the gloss of Abraham ibn Ezra on Gen. 1:28: "The reference to procreation with regard to man is a blessing, just as it was for the creatures of the sea. Our ancestors of blessed memory, however, transmitted the interpretation (*heʿetiquha*) that it is a commandment, and they used this verse as a reminder (*zekher la-davar*)."[92] David Kimhi and Isaac Karo echoed these sentiments, but Joseph b. Eliezer Bonfils expressed their logic most forcefully in his supercommentary on Ibn Ezra's aforecited gloss:

> "Our ancestors [. . .], however, transmitted the interpretation (*heʿetiquha*) that it is a commandment"—meaning, our forefathers learned this from Moses by word of mouth. "And they used this verse as a reminder"—meaning, for those of meager faith. If they should say that this is not a commandment grounded in the Torah, they [i.e., the rabbis] would respond that here is the proof. However, he who is knowledgeable will understand of his own accord that it would be necessary to perpetuate the species even if it were not written in the Torah, and he will believe their interpretation without need of [scriptural] evidence.[93]

The critically spirited Bonfils confronted the intention of our biblical verse as straightforwardly as a medieval rabbi could. Any intelligent human being will acknowledge that the need to procreate is self-evident. As Scripture itself reports, God's initial utterance to the first parents consisted of words of blessing. The Jew's religious obligation to have children truly has no biblical source, but it derives from a law that God must have revealed orally to Moses; it falls into the category of *halakhah lᵉ-Mosheh mi-Sinai*.

Rabbinic exegetes and enumerators of the biblical commandments did not confine their discussion of the Mosaic precept of procreation to the textual locus of its origin. They debated over the boundaries be-

91. Nissim Gerondi, *Commentary*, p. 49; Isaac Arama, ʿ*Aqedat Yiẓḥaq*, 1:33a; Isaac Abravanel, *Perush ha-Torah*, 1:30b; Elijah Mizrachi, in ʾ*Oẓar Mᵉfarᵉshe ha-Torah*, 1:31ab; and Moses al-Balideh, ʿ*Olat Tamid*, p. 22b.

92. Abraham ibn Ezra, *Perushe ha-Torah*, 1:19.

93. Joseph b. Eliezer Bonfils, *Ẕafᵉnat Paʿneaḥ*, ed. David Herzog (Krakow, 1912), 1:48. Cf. David Kimhi, *Perushe RaDaʾQ ʿal ha-Torah*, p. 22: "Even though [procreation] is a blessing, as we interpreted it concerning fish, our sages of blessed memory relied on the tradition that it is a commandment to human beings"; and Isaac Karo, *Tolᵉdot Yiẓḥaq*, p. 15b.

tween the obligation to reproduce and other, related laws of the Torah. The author of the *Sheʾiltot* and Moses Maimonides, for example, held that the duty of procreation entailed a prior, albeit distinct, responsibility to marry;[94] Asher b. Yehiel, on the other hand, argued that a Jew could meet his reproductive responsibilities through his relationship with a concubine just as well as through marriage.[95] Consideration of this issue often extended to the liturgical benedictions recited upon betrothal and at the nuptial feast, which, according to some earlier rabbinic sources, somehow derived from the blessing of Gen. 1:28; some halakhists questioned why, upon contracting marriage, the groom did not recite a blessing of the genre specifying that he was about to fulfill a religious obligation.[96] Medieval authorities continued to dispute whether the commandment of procreation was the obverse of the Mosaic ban on castration[97] or that on the needless emission of semen,[98] matters which did affect the practical application of these laws, as noted above in Chapter 3. And Solomon ibn Adret asserted that the purpose of the commandments concerning levirate marriage was fulfillment of the duty of procreation.[99]

Finally, medieval Jewish scholars also explored the rationale for the commandment to reproduce. Talmudic sources, we recall, harped on the tension between universalistic and particularist foundations of the precept, the desire to realize the divine wish to settle the world versus the urge to expedite the messianic redemption of Israel. While the Halakhah had by now excluded Gentiles from the law of "be fertile and

---

94. *Sheʾiltot* 5, ed. Mirsky, 1:35; Moses b. Maimon, *Sefer ha-Miẓwot* 213 (positive), ed. Kafah, pp. 166–67. See the defense of Maimonides' position in Abraham b. Moses Maimonides, *Shu"T Birkat ʾAvraham* 44 (1860; repr., Jerusalem, 1960), p. 62.

95. Asher b. Yehiel, commentary ad TB *Ket.* 1.12; see also the comments of Yom Tov Ishbili cited above, Chapter 3, n. 95. Several centuries later, Issachar Baer Eilenburg, *Sefer Beʾer Shevaʿ* 212 (1890; repr., Jerusalem, 1969), p. 106b, asked of Asher b. Yehiel, "Why did he mortgage his soul to take issue with Maimonides?"

96. Asher b. Yehiel, and Yom Tov Ishbili, as cited in the previous note. Simeon b. Zemah Duran, *Sefer ha-Tashbaẓ* 2.74, 2:13b, records the tradition that Yehiel b. Joseph of Paris did prescribe such a blessing. The issue of whether marriage constitutes a commandment independent of procreation leads to the additional matter of what actually completes the performance of the commandment of procreation. *Tosafot*, ad *Hag.* 2b, s.v. *li-ssaʾ shifḥah ʾeno yakhol*, and ad *BB* 13a, s.v. *kofin ʾet rabbo*, make the problematic proposal of the completion of the act of sexual intercourse; see the critique of Babad, *Minḥat Ḥinnukh*, 1:1b.

97. See Eliezer of Metz, *Sefer Yeʾreʾim* 342, 2:191a; *Sefer ha-Ḥinnukh*, p. 291; Levi Gersonides, *Perush ʿal ha-Torah*, 1:13a; ShA, *EH* 5.15–16.

98. *Tosafot* ad *San.* 59b, s.v. *weʾha periyyah u-reviyyah*; Jacob b. Meir Tam, cited above, Chapter 3, at n. 52; Meyuhas b. Elijah, *Perush ʿal Bereshit*, p. 29.

99. Solomon ibn Adret, *Shu"T* 1.18, 1:9.

increase," medieval codifiers and commentators usually wrote of the need to perpetuate the human species in broad, nonexclusive language. In his list of the Mosaic precepts, Maimonides included "the ordinance whereby we were commanded to reproduce and to intend to maintain the human species; this is the commandment of procreation, as he, may he be exalted, pronounced it, 'Be fertile and increase.'"[100] A century later, the author of *Sefer ha-Hinnukh* elaborated further:

> The rationale for this commandment is that the world should be settled, because God, may he be blessed, desires its settlement, as it is written, "He did not create it a waste but formed it for habitation." And this is a great commandment for whose sake there exist all of the other commandments, for they were given to human beings and not to the ministering angels. . . . And he who does not fulfill it annuls a positive commandment; and his punishment is very great, because he himself demonstrates that he does not wish to fulfill God's desire to settle his world.[101]

Gen. 1:28 thus continued to bespeak the distinctively human role in completing the divine creation, for which purpose God had originally fashioned man and woman, choosing people over angels to receive his Torah. Bahya b. Asher specified emphatically that precisely this spiritual motivation distinguishes the sexual activity of Israel from that of the Gentiles,[102] but most of his successors did not follow suit. The need for human beings to integrate both their divine image and their sexuality into a single life of service to God, a theme that underlay much of the aggadic midrash on our verse, is expressed most eloquently in the gloss of Isaac Abravanel.[103]

> The reason for the commandment is that man is created in the image of God and his purpose is to try and achieve human perfection and not [merely] to preserve the species like the other animals—to the extent that for this reason Scripture did not state "according to their kinds"[104]

---

100. Moses Maimonides, *Sefer ha-Miẓwot* 212 (positive), ed. Kafah, pp. 166–67.

101. *Sefer ha-Hinnukh*, p. 55.

102. Bahya b. Asher, *Be'ur ʿal ha-Torah*, 1:48–49; see also his *Kad ha-Qemaḥ*, cited above, Chapter 3, n. 93.

103. Isaac Abravanel, *Perush ha-Torah*, 1:30b; cf. also the earlier comments of Eleazar of Worms, *Perush ha-Roqeaḥ*, 1:66, who explained the juxtaposition of *'Elohim* and *pᵉru* in Gen. 1:28 as a mandate that sexual reproduction derive from a desire to serve God.

104. RSV.

in the account of his creation as in the account of theirs. And because from the perspective of intellectual perfection the procreative faculty is detrimental, inasmuch as it is an animal function harmful to the intellect, maybe man will think that it is therefore proper to forgo its exercise completely. For this reason Adam and his wife were obligated by the commandment of procreation, as if to say: "Even though I created you in the image of God, do not be drawn so much by the intellectual that you abstain from the material altogether. For in this way reproduction would cease and the world would be destroyed. Such is not my intention; it is rather that you should be fertile and increase and fill the earth."

Such "nonpartisan" explanations for the commandment of procreation are particularly striking because medieval rabbis lived as aliens amid an unsympathetic Gentile majority and were prone to sense the unredeemed nature of their situation at least as acutely as their talmudic forebears. Maimonides, Joseph Bonfils, and Isaac Abravanel all uprooted themselves and their families repeatedly, traveling from one corner of the Diaspora to another, often in flight from physical persecution. As they sought to explain the laws of Moses the rationalist temperaments of these particular writers may have outweighed their sense of alienation from the Gentile world. For some of their mystically inclined contemporaries like Bahya, however, that alienation loomed so large that it could not conceive of God's discourse with the first parents as addressing anyone but the Jew.

THE EARLY KABBALAH

In the theosophical Kabbalah of the late thirteenth century, an array of the biblical, aggadic, and halakhic motifs we have already discussed converged to give Gen. 1:28 new meaning and unprecedented significance. Recent scholarship has devoted much attention to the origins and development of the Kabbalah in the twelfth and thirteenth centuries—subjects too vast and complex for extensive consideration in this study, though they do bear upon it. In and of itself, even the distinctive kabbalistic interest in sexuality in both human and divine realms, what Gershom Scholem has termed "the syzygy of the masculine and the feminine,"[105] lies beyond our purview. We must restrict our concern to the manner in which Gen. 1:28 underlies and informs the esoteric doctrines of the Kabbalah, particularly those of the *Zohar*, a phenomenon that modern scholars have acknowledged but largely failed to elucidate.

Nonetheless, a few introductory thoughts might help the uninitiated appreciate what follows. Adapting ancient patterns of belief, perhaps some of them Gnostic and Neoplatonic, kabbalists conceived of the deity as embodying ten dimensions or *sᵉfirot*, whose configuration they typically envisaged in the form of a tree or a primordial human being. Each *sᵉfirah* represented a different component of the divine personality, as it were, and interrelated with the others according to its distinctive character—male or female, merciful or stern, and the like. When the *sᵉfirot* interacted harmoniously, they integrated the godhead so that its creative goodness might overflow, extending ultimately into the realm of the terrestrial and there providing for the needs of its creatures. By the same token, when the mystic conformed to the divine will with the proper intention, he effected the appropriate connections in the sefirotic realm on high. A direct correspondence therefore existed between (1) proper or improper behavior on earth, (2) integration or alienation of the *sᵉfirot*, and (3) the divine promotion of human spiritual welfare. An important case in point[106] was the conjunction of the sixth (and central) *sᵉfirah*, the masculine *Tifʾeret*, with the tenth *sᵉfirah*, the feminine *Malkhut* or *Shᵉkhinah*, a sort of conduit or vessel through which the remainder of the godhead might transmit its goodness to the worlds below; the ninth (in the earliest texts, seventh) *sᵉfirah*, the masculine *Yᵉsod*, often depicted as a river linking various elements of the godhead or with other blatantly phallic imagery, frequently played an instrumental role in facilitating this union. The proper human observance of any divine commandment brings these *sᵉfirot* together; neglect of the commandments causes disharmony in their relationship and alienates

105. Gershom Scholem, *Origins of the Kabbalah*, ed. R. J. Z. Werblowsky, tr. Alan Arkush (Philadelphia, Pa., 1986), pp. 151ff. The most recent studies of sexual themes in the Kabbalah are Moshe Idel, "Métaphores et pratiques sexuelles dans la Cabale," in *La lettre sur la sainteté*, ed. Charles Mopsik (Paris, 1986), pp. 327–58, and Mopsik's own introduction, pp. 45–219, whose notes review previous scholarship on the subject. I am indebted to Moshe Idel for allowing me to read his essay prior to its publication.

106. But by no means the only such sefirotic conjunction; see, for example, the comments of Mopsik in *Lettre sur la sainteté*, pp. 163ff.

them from humans as well. But owing to the sexual nature of this sefirotic attraction, conjugal relations, when undertaken by a kabbalist and his wife with the correct mystical objectives in mind, work especially well to seal a harmonious union between *Tif'eret* and *Malkhut*. Conveying the bounty of divine creativity and providence, *Malkhut* in turn becomes accessible to the kabbalist, helping the latter to overcome the alienating separation from his maker. The triangular nature of this correspondence is essential to any valid understanding of sexual imagery in kabbalistic texts. As Karen Guberman has correctly emphasized in her analysis of a kabbalistic marriage manual, "these three levels of exegesis . . . exist concurrently in the language of the text as mutually explicative interpretations. One is neither more nor less important. . . . The physical love between husband and wife resembles the soul's cleaving to the divine world, both of these resemble the balancing of the sefirotic pairs, and vice versa."[107] It is noteworthy that the sanctity and significance the Kabbalah attributes to sexual love stand independent of the biblical injunction to "be fertile and increase." The production of offspring does rank high among the intentions expected of a kabbalist when engaging in marital relations. But it is not the only one. The duty of *p*ᵉ*riyyah u-r*ᵉ*viyyah* receives only minimal attention in kabbalistic texts that preceded the *Zohar,* although these works did lay the groundwork for our verse's treatment by Moses de León in several important respects.

One final word of caution: As they reflected on biblical and rabbinic literature, kabbalists intentionally disguised their esoteric doctrines in ostensibly straightforward and simple language. The code they employed, however, is neither consistent nor scientifically logical; numerous epithets denote the same *s*ᵉ*firah,* and the same epithet can at different times signify multiple *s*ᵉ*firot.* The fact that a text's superficial, literal sense does serve to convey one of its intended meanings, so that one cannot always know whether to search for hidden allusions or not, only complicates matters further. If we stressed at the beginning of this book how Scripture is not univocal, the same can be said more emphatically of the writings of medieval Kabbalah. Frank Talmage's com-

---

107. Karen Guberman, "The Language of Love in Spanish Kabbalah: An Examination of the *'Iggeret ha-Kodesh,*" in *Approaches to Judaism in Medieval Times: Volume I,* ed. David R. Blumenthal, Brown Judaic Studies 54 (Chico, Calif., 1984), pp. 92–93.

parison of symbolic exegesis to the glorious palace of the Alhambra is instructive indeed:

> Here one finds not tedious and monotonous corridors but dramatically arranged courts and chambers, so placed that one beckons to the other or, more properly, the others, for there is generally an option. A passage will lead now to the right, now to the left, now to a cul-de-sac, now to another passage where the whole march begins anew. It is a maze and a labyrinth—not one that discourages but one that entices, as the archways lead one to another, at first perhaps to disappointment, but finally, with persistence, to the princess or the [metaphorical] golden apple [i.e., the goal of allegorical interpretation].[108]

Pre-Zoharic Foundations

Scholem has located the origins of the Kabbalah in the appearance of *Sefer ha-Bahir* and in the illuminating experiences of certain mystically inclined rabbinic leaders, which occurred contemporaneously in twelfth-century Provence. *Sefer ha-Bahir,* which collects and reformulates fragments of older Gnostic and mystical traditions, offers the first display of the sefirotic system that we can term kabbalistic in a technical sense.[109] Several passages concerning the nature and activities of the seventh *sefirah* undoubtedly fueled the subsequent interpretation of Gen. 1:28 by Moses de León, and they simultaneously highlight by contrast the latter's distinctive contribution to our story. We therefore quote them at some length.

Although the seventh *sefirah* in the doctrine of *Sefer ha-Bahir* became the ninth *sefirah, Yesod,* in the Kabbalah of the thirteenth century, its primary characteristics and functions in the supernal realm underwent

---

108. Frank Talmage, "Apples of Gold: The Inner Meaning of Sacred Texts in Medieval Judaism," in *JS,* p. 317. On the kabbalistic conception of language, see also Moshe Idel, "Infinities of Torah in Kabbalah," and Betty Roitman, "Sacred Language and Open Text," both in *Midrash and Literature,* ed. Geoffrey H. Hartman and Sanford Budick (New Haven, Conn., 1986), pp. 141–57 and 159–75 (respectively).

109. Scholem's assertion of the Gnostic roots of the Kabbalah has recently undergone extensive criticism in the works of Moshe Idel (see Idel, "Métaphores et pratiques sexuelles dans la Cabale," pp. 353ff.; "The Problem of the Sources of the *Bahir*" [Hebrew], *Jerusalem Studies in Jewish Thought* 6.3–4 [1987], 55–72; and *Kabbalah: New Perspectives* [New Haven, Conn., 1988], pp. 112–28). The question has yet to be decided conclusively and ultimately bears only marginally on our present concern.

relatively little change. In a passage that reworks a well-known tal-mudic homily, *Sefer ha-Bahir* likens this dimension of the godhead to[110]

> a column (*'ammud*) which extends from the earth to the heaven whose name is Righteous (*Zaddiq*), after the righteous people. If there are righteous people in the world he grows strong (*mitgabber*), and if not he grows weak (*mithallesh*). He supports the entire world, as it is written (Prov. 10:25), "the righteous (*zaddiq*) is the foundation (*y^esod*) of the world";[111] and if he is weak, the world cannot survive.

The phallic imagery with which this *s^efirah* is portrayed is unmistakable, and the interdependence of terrestrial and supernal existence is equally apparent. One must note further that the nature of this divine-human interaction is itself sexual: The sexual potency or impotence of the *s^efirah* derives from behavior on earth, and it in turn, like an upright column, supports the entire cosmos by linking earth and heaven. As Scholem pointed out,[112] the terms "earth" and "heaven" in this text can readily symbolize the tenth (feminine) and sixth (masculine) *s^efirot*, respectively, in which case the erect column results in their conjunction.

Matching the first seven *s^efirot* and the seven days of creation, *Sefer ha-Bahir* elsewhere explores the affinity between the seventh *s^efirah* and the Sabbath, amplifying the illustration of its unifying, nourishing function in the godhead with a parable.[113]

> Each day of the hexameron has a word [*ma'amar*, i.e., a *s^efirah*] that is its master, not because it was created with it, but because through it it performs that task entrusted to it. When they all have performed their tasks and completed their activity, the seventh day comes and performs its task, and all rejoice, even the holy one, blessed be he; furthermore, it [i.e., the activity of the seventh day] enlarges their soul, as it is written (Ex. 31:17), "On the seventh day he ceased from work and was re-freshed [*wa-yinnafash*, suggesting *nefesh*, or soul]." What is this cessa-tion that entailed not work but rest, as it is written, "He ceased from work"? It may be compared to a king who had seven gardens and in the

---

110. *Sefer ha-Bahir* 102, ed. Reuben Margaliot (1951; repr., Jerusalem, 1978), p. 44; cf. *Das Buch Bahir: Ein Schriftdenkmal aus der Frühzeit der Kabbalah* 71, ed. and tr. Gershom Scholem, Qabbalah: Quellen und Forschungen der jüdischen Mystik 1 (Leipzig, 1923), p. 74.

111. My translation, to accord with the homily intended by the text.

112. Scholem, *Origins*, pp. 152–54. See also the comments of Y. Liebes, "Ha-Mashiaḥ shel ha-*Zohar*," in *Ha-Ra'ayon ha-M^eshiḥi b^e-Yisra'el* (Jerusalem, 1982), pp. 120ff.

113. *Sefer ha-Bahir* 159, p. 69.

central one—with three to its right and three to its left—a spring deriving from the source of life.[114] As soon as it performs its task and grows full, all rejoice, because they say, "it grows full for our sake"; and it waters them and enlarges them.

In the realm of the supernal, the seventh *sefirah* irrigates, providing vitality and nourishment with its flow that originates in the source of life. It is not coincidental that this fructifying activity occurs on—or at least is identified with—the Sabbath, which in rabbinic tradition presented the ideal time for marital sex.[115]

By metonymy, however, the column also evokes the image of the entire sefirotic tree, whose creativity bears fruit in the birth of new souls that maintain the realm of the mundane; this *sefirah* thereby assumes the role of progenitor of human souls. How does such production occur? With unusually difficult language, *Sefer ha-Bahir* elaborates:[116]

> Just as the tree produces fruit by means of water, so the holy one, blessed be he, increases the powers of the tree by means of water. What is the water of the holy one, blessed be he? It is wisdom. And they [i.e., the fruits of God's tree] are the souls of the righteous,[117] which sprout from the source to the great channel, and it[118] rises and clings to the tree. And what makes it flower? The people of Israel. When they are good and righteous, the divine presence (*Shekhinah*) abides in their midst and, owing to their deeds, they reside (or, it—the *Shekhinah*—resides)[119] in the bosom of the holy one, blessed be he, and he causes them to be fertile (*mafreh 'otam*) and increase (*u-marbeh 'otam*).

Now the seventh *sefirah* appears as "the great channel," which first begets human souls by conveying them from the supernal source of life and then enables them to ascend to the sefirotic tree. Once more we

---

114. Following Margaliot; Scholem, *Das Buch Bahir* 105, p. 113, translated the earlier printed version: "a beautiful, bubbling spring [lit., source] from a well of running water irrigates the three to its right and the three to its left."

115. For extensive discussion of this theme, see Elliot Kiba Ginsburg, "The Sabbath in the Classical Kabbalah" (Ph.D. Dissertation, University of Pennsylvania, Philadelphia, Pa., 1984), pp. 130–45, 187–90.

116. *Sefer ha-Bahir* 119, p. 53.

117. Following Gershom Scholem, *Ursprung und Anfänge der Kabbala*, Studia judaica 3 (Berlin, 1962), p. 66.

118. Scholem, *Das Buch Bahir*, p. 92 n. 3, understood this to be the channel; in *Ursprung und Anfänge der Kabbala*, p. 66, he offered the alternatives of the fruit or the souls; *Origins*, p. 75, indicates the fruit. The singular verb "it rises" (*we-'oleh*) would appear to rule out the souls.

119. See Scholem, *Das Buch Bahir*, p. 92 n. 6.

encounter this *sᵉfirah* both as activating the proper, fruitful conjunctions within the godhead and as bridging the gap between deity and creature. And again the behavior of righteous human beings, whom *Sefer ha-Bahir* openly identifies here as Jews, effects the integration within the godhead and its accessibility to them. *Sefer ha-Bahir* itself compares each *sᵉfirah* to a linguistic entity (*ma'amar*); and like the "mutually explicative" interpretations of kabbalistic language, the various levels on which a *sᵉfirah* might function are not mutually exclusive. They too illustrate the triangular correspondence of heavenly and earthly spheres of life and of the intermediate plane on which they interact.

Finally, *Sefer ha-Bahir* attributes to the seventh *sᵉfirah* a central role in metempsychosis (*gilgul nᵉfashot*), the transmigration of human souls, a process that the book links to procreation only implicitly in its citation of a talmudic homily analyzed above in Chapter 2.[120]

> In his control is the storehouse (*'oẓar*) of all the souls. When the people of Israel are good, the souls are entitled to depart and to enter the terrestrial world; and if they are not good, they will not depart. This is as we say, "The son of David will not come until the *guf* has been depleted of all of its souls." What are all of the souls of the *guf*? These are all the souls in the human body (*guf ha-'adam*). When the new ones are entitled to depart, then the son of David will come—that is, be entitled to be born—for his new soul will depart amidst the others.

In support of its doctrine of transmigration, unprecedented in rabbinic literature, this text brazenly abandons the traditional understanding of the midrash that it quotes. In the Talmud, *guf* signifies the cosmic storage depot for preexistent souls; here the term refers to the human body itself.[121] *Sefer ha-Bahir* thus proclaims the belief that human souls continue to inhabit one body after another, unless the exemplary behavior of Israel induces the seventh *sᵉfirah,* here called "the life of the worlds (*ḥe ha-'olamim*)," to release unborn souls from their repository; eventually, those released will include the soul of the messiah, who will

---

120. *Sefer ha-Bahir* 184, p. 81; see Scholem's notes to *Das Buch Bahir* 125–26, pp. 134–36. Cf. also above, Chapter 2, n. 180.

121. Cf. Azriel b. Menahem of Gerona, *Commentarius in Aggadot* (Hebrew), ed. Isaiah Tishby (Jerusalem, 1945), p. 12 (with n. 11), where the term *guf* in this homily has come to signify the sixth sefirah, *Tif'eret,* the source of souls in the body of the primordial (i.e., sefirotic) human being.

redeem the world and bring the process of metempsychosis to its end.[122]

We must evaluate these excerpts from *Sefer ha-Bahir* both for what they contain and for what they omit. On the one hand, the book lays the foundations for future kabbalistic interpretation of Gen. 1:28. Describing the seventh (later the ninth) s^{e}firah in phallic imagery, the work allots to sexuality a vital role in the tripartite system of correspondence between terrestrial, supernal, and intermediate spheres of relations. Appropriate human behavior equips the s^{e}firah with the sexual potency necessary for it to effect sexual conjunction within the sefirotic realm. Integration of the divine personality leads to the creation of human souls, which are born into new bodies, freeing existent souls from their transmigration. Ultimately, this will lead to the birth of the messiah and the end of the spiritual alienation signified by the process of metempsychosis. On the other hand, *Sefer ha-Bahir* does not dwell on human sexual activity as particularly significant in this scheme. Given the sexual, procreative role of the seventh s^{e}firah, the completion of its irrigating function on the Sabbath, and the effect of its activity on the production of new human beings, one might expect that the righteous human behavior that facilitates the success of this s^{e}firah would have a major sexual component as well. But the biblical mandate for human reproductive activity is notably absent in the passages we have quoted. God's reward of Israel's righteousness with the dual blessing of *prh/rbh*, along with the maverick interpretation of a midrash that in the Talmud rationalized the commandment of procreation, makes this absence more striking. *Sefer ha-Bahir* had every opportunity to reflect extensively on Gen. 1:28, but it failed to do so.

Several early kabbalists whom we can identify by name anticipated other aspects of the Zoharic treatment of procreation. Abraham b. David of Posquierres stressed the importance of engaging in sexual activity with the proper intentions, and he ranked those that qualify as legitimate; first on his list was the intention "of fulfilling the commandment of procreation, which is the most valid of them all."[123] In a

---

122. See also *Sefer ha-Bahir* 154–56, p. 67; *Das Buch Bahir* 104, pp. 111–12 with notes; and Gershom Scholem, *Elements of the Kabbalah and Its Symbolism* (Hebrew), tr. Joseph Ben-Shlomo (Jerusalem, 1976), pp. 308–16.

123. Abraham b. David, *Ba'ale ha-Nefesh*, pp. 116–18. I hope to consider the roots of the tradition that Abraham here echoed on another occasion.

sermon delivered at a wedding feast, Moses Nahmanides incorporated marriage and procreation (among humans) into the symmetrical correspondence between earthly and heavenly spheres, thereby adumbrating the overall theme of *'Iggeret ha-Qodesh,* which many attributed to him.[124] Along with other mystics of thirteenth-century Gerona, Nahmanides treasured the belief in metempsychosis as a secret unsuited for transmission to the unitiated. He considered this doctrine the basis for the precepts mandating levirate marriage and prohibiting incest, but in his commentary on the Pentateuch he consistently refused to elaborate. Regarding the obligation of Onan to marry the widow of his deceased and childless brother Er (Gen. 38:8), he wrote: "This matter concerning the generation of human beings is one of the greatest secrets of the Torah; it is apparent to the eyes of those who have sight, whom the Lord has given eyes for sight and ears for listening. And the ancient sages who preceded the giving of the Torah knew that there is a great benefit in levirate marriage."[125] Todros b. Joseph ha-Levi Abulafia of Toledo, a junior contemporary of Nahmanides, adduced the aforecited passage from *Sefer ha-Bahir* concerning metempsychosis and did explain the belief under the rubric of the commandment of procreation. Reflecting his tendency to integrate the ideas of the Gerona school and those of a more sefirotically oriented theosophy, Abulafia commented on the Mishnaic ordinance: "A man may not desist (*yibbaṭel*) from procreation":

> Know that this commandment is very great and profound, because he who desists from fulfilling the commandment of procreation thereby detracts (*mᵉvaṭṭel*), as it were, from the ability of the supernal realm to perform its duties. Therefore they [the talmudic sages] admonished that a man must sanctify himself at the time of sexual relations, in order that the supernal powers perform their task in sanctity and purity.[126]

Abulafia finally acknowledged the sefirotic ramifications of human sexuality. (Perhaps taking note of the recurring biblical motif "be fertile

---

124. Moses b. Nahman, *Dᵉrashah lᵉ-Ḥatunah,* in *Kitve RaMba"N,* ed. Charles B. Chavel, 2 vols. (Jerusalem, 1963), 1:133–38.

125. RaMba"N, 1:214–15; cf. his comments ad Gen. 4:1, 46:2, and Lev. 18:6. Perhaps to avoid disclosing his secret, Nahmanides avoided all mention of the esoteric significance of levirate marriage in his gloss on Deut. 25. On the reluctance of the Gerona kabbalists to publicize this doctrine, see Scholem, *Elements,* pp. 316–18.

126. Todros b. Joseph ha-Levi Abulafia, *Sefer 'Oẓar ha-Kavod ha-Shalem* (Warsaw, 1879), p. 25b.

and increase," he proceeded to identify the *sᵉfirah* of *Yᵉsod* with the divine epithet of *'El Shaddai*.)[127] Yet it remained for the author of the *Zohar* in late thirteenth-century Spain to develop this notion to its full potential.

The Kabbalah of Moses de León

Compared with the kabbalistic treatises that preceded it, the *Zohar* of Moses b. Shem Tov de León astounds its reader with the prominence and centrality of its sexual imagery; as Scholem has remarked, the erotic symbolism with which the *Zohar* opens and closes provides glaring rhetorical evidence of a key to the entire work.[128] How did the biblical call to procreation in Gen. 1:28 figure in what became the single most influential text of Jewish mysticism?

The obligation to "be fertile and increase" ranks among the fourteen Mosaic precepts that comprise the foundations of the Torah, which the *Zohar* lists in its introduction.

> The sixth commandment is procreation. Whoever engages in procreation causes that river to flow constantly, and its waters will not be exhausted; the sea fills from all sides, new souls are created and emerge from that tree, and many heavenly powers grow with those souls. Thus it is written, "Let the waters bring forth swarms of living creatures"— this is the sign of the holy covenant. . . . And one who desists from procreation diminishes, as it were, the image that encompasses all images; he causes the waters of that river not to flow, and he despoils the holy covenant in all of its dimensions. Concerning him it is written (Is. 66:24): "They shall go out and gaze on the corpses of the men who have rebelled against me." "Against me"—unquestionably. This [punishment] pertains to the body; the soul may not enter the palace of the king at all, and it is banished from that [supernal] world.[129]

The sefirotic conjunction of the male *Tif'eret* (tree) and the female *Malkhut* (sea, all-encompassing image),[130] implemented by the phallic *Yᵉsod* (river, holy covenant) and resulting in the creation of human

---

127. Ibid., pp. 22b–23a.
128. Scholem, *Elements*, p. 296.
129. *Z*, 1:12b–13a (=*MHZ* 2:628–30). On the significance of these fundamental precepts of the Torah, see Simeon ibn Labi, *Ketem Paz*, 2 vols. (Leghorn, 1795), 1:56a.
130. See *MHZ*, 2:615 n. 63.

souls, corresponds neatly to that described by *Sefer ha-Bahir* and discussed above. But while *Sefer ha-Bahir* identifies the righteous deeds of Israel in general as the human behavior that facilitates this conjunction, the *Zohar* here focuses on procreation as epitomizing such worthy action. This passage touches upon most aspects of the *Zohar's* instruction concerning Gen. 1:28, and it readily serves as a springboard to a more detailed elaboration of that interpretation.

Human Reproduction and Sefirotic Union. The connection drawn in the *Zohar* between human sexual activity and the integration of the divine s^e*firot* clearly did not occur by accident, though neither was it a foregone conclusion. As we have seen, the performance of any commandment might bring about a harmonious union within the godhead. An emphasis on marriage and procreation derived logically, albeit not necessarily, from the idea of mutual correspondence between terrestrial and supernal realities endemic to the Kabbalah. Inasmuch as the seven blessings of the wedding liturgy derive from the blessing of the primordial man in Gen. 1:28, the *Zohar* concludes (1) that a newlywed couple thus blessed conjoin in the manner of the s^e*firot* above and (2) that the terrestrial celebration of marriage serves to effect such sefirotic conjunction.[131] On the one hand, procreative sexual union below, undertaken with the appropriate intentions and sanctity, results in sexual coupling and the birth of souls above.[132] On the other hand, the sefirotic union is logically prior to the marital relations of human beings, serving both as their exemplar and as their final cause. The *Zohar* thus specifies that God endowed human beings with a rational soul and revealed his commandments to them expressly so that they might reproduce the divine image in the world, on the model of and for the benefit of the s^e*firah* Y^e*sod*.[133] Because "this river never desists from procreation (*mi-lifrot w^e-lirbot*) and producing fruit, the other [evil] cosmic power is emasculated and has no appetite for the world, and it does not increase and does not produce fruit. If it would produce fruit, it would destroy the entire

---

131. *Z*, 2:169ab, 3:44b; Moses b. Shem Tov de León, "*Sefer ha-Rimmon:* A Critical Edition [Hebrew] and Introductory Study," ed. Elliot R. Wolfson, 2 vols. (Ph.D. Dissertation, Brandeis University, Waltham, Mass., 1986), 2:227–28.
132. See also *Z*, 1:85b (=*MHZ*, 2:627–28), 1:122a (*Zohar*); and cf. the additional references in *MHZ*, 2:617 nn. 83–86.
133. *Z*, 1:186b.

world."[134] Human procreation thus restores and maintains the unity of the tetragrammaton, symbolic of the multidimensional nature of the godhead, just as it ensures the survival of God's image in the realm of the mundane.[135]

The Rewards of Procreation. For the author of the *Zohar*, sexual reproduction not only follows the divine example but is theurgic as well, introducing God to treat his creatures favorably. Our opening text notes that, in addition to human souls, the sefirotic conjunction gives birth to beneficent heavenly powers, all of which perpetuate terrestrial existence. On an individual level, too, a man's spiritual destiny depends on his procreative record.[136] In the words of Moses de León's *Sefer ha-Rimmon*, the father of children has shown that he loves God as much as himself. The Torah juxtaposes the concluding words of Gen. 1:27 ("male and female he created them") and the opening words of Gen. 1:28 ("God blessed them") to teach that "the Sh*e*khinah rests on the head of the married man. For the heavenly blessing rests only upon male and female who are like one. . . . Therefore, anyone who fears his creator must take a wife in order to beget children from her—so that his image may extend itself and he may enter the [heavenly] palace." Simply put, "every man must strive to fulfill the commandment of procreation, in order that things should go well for him and his children forever."[137] The *Zohar* elaborates that a man who properly maintains conjugal relations with his wife enjoys a "heavenly conjunction" (*ziwwuga' 'ila'ah*) with the Sh*e*khinah, who remains with him even when he is not with his wife precisely on account of that sexual activity.[138] Finally, a

---

134. *Z*, 2:103a (=*MHZ*, 1:348). See the comments of Idel, "Métaphores et pratiques sexuelles dans la Cabale," p. 352, which explain how the erotic symbolism of the Kabbalah qualifies as both "ascending" and "descending": "Cette corrélation entre les différents niveaux du réel a permis aux cabalistes d'appréhender l'union sexuelle d'une part comme une imitatio dei et d'autre part comme un acte théurgique destiné à produire un état d'harmonie entre les entités supérieures."

135. *Z*, 1:264b–65a (*Hashmaṭot*), 3:34a; cf. *TZ* 21, p. 60a.

136. *ZH*, p. 59ab (*Midrash ha-Ne*'*elam, Ki Teze*'). I use the masculine pronoun "his" deliberately and restrictively; the *Zohar* cares little about the spiritual perfection of women. Nevertheless, *Z*, 1:71ab, suggests that the repeated accusative particle *'et* in Gen. 9:1 and the word *w*e*-'attem* in Gen. 9:7 serve to extend the duty of procreation to women.

137. Moses de León, "*Sefer ha-Rimmon*," 2:228. Cf. the remarkably similar language of David b. Judah he-Hasid, *The Book of Mirrors: Sefer Mar'ot ha-Zove'ot* (Hebrew), ed. Daniel C. Matt, Brown Judaic Studies 30 (Chico, Calif., 1982), p. 57.

138. *Z*, 1:49b–50a (=*MHZ*, 2:643–46). It is noteworthy that *Z*, 1:13b, 2:94b—cf. also 2:41b (*Ra'ya' M*e*hemna'*)—relates Gen. 1:28b to the ascent of the righteous individual into the

man's children ensure their father's welfare in the next world as well. The late medieval kabbalist Simeon ibn Labi summarized the Zoharic doctrine in this regard: "Only one who leaves behind progeny in this world will cleave to the divine inheritance, which is the secret of the world above. For in so doing, he resembles his creator, may he be blessed; the latter brings forth souls from the [supernal] 'land of the living,' and he fashions bodies for their respective souls. With these he becomes a partner with his creator, as it were, and he therefore cleaves to the aforementioned divine inheritance."[139] Beyond the merit that accrues from the birth and the upbringing of children, they, still alive, can stand as sureties for him when his soul confronts the heavenly prosecutor on judgment day.[140]

The Sin of Noncompliance. More than any other rabbinic text that I have encountered, the *Zohar* belabors the dire consequences of one's failure to reproduce. Along with one school of halakhic thought, Moses de León equated such failure and the sin of needlessly emitting semen; if having children epitomizes the righteousness that integrates the divine personality, sexual activity devoid of procreative purpose exemplifies the destructive pursuit of evil. "Of all the transgressions from which a man is polluted in this world, this is the transgression from which a man is polluted the most in this world and in the next world—when one spills his seed in vain, needlessly emitting his semen."[141] Alluding to the oft-quoted discussion of Simeon b. Azzai and his Tannaitic colleagues at Yavneh, our opening passage affirms that one who refrains from reproductive activity diminishes the divine image, that image which encompasses all others.[142] But while classical rabbinic traditions usually understood this to mean that one impedes the birth of human beings

---

realm of the supernal; dominion over God's creatures thus signifies the power that accrues from assumption of the divine image and communion with the *Shekhinah*. Like many Christian exegetes (cf. below, Chapter 5), *Z* 3:33b (*Raʿyaʾ Mehemnaʾ*), and *TZ* 21, p. 60a, also liken the dominion conferred in Gen. 1:28b to the control over one's passions. On the question of cross-cultural influence, see Y. Liebes, "Christian Influences on the *Zohar*" (Hebrew), *Jerusalem Studies in Jewish Thought* 2 (1982), 43–74.

139. Simeon ibn Labi, *Ketem Paz*, 1:274b.
140. Moses de León, "*Sefer ha-Rimmon*," 2:228–29; *Z*, 1:115ab (=*MHZ*, 2:651–53).
141. *Z*, 1:188a.
142. Above, n. 129. For intimations that the primordial man embodied the divine image par excellence (i.e., more of the divine likeness than subsequent human beings), see TB *BB* 58a, *MQ* 15b; TJ *MQ* 3.5, 83a; *DtR* 4.4.

who embody the image of God,[143] the *Zohar* discerns the damage as transpiring within the godhead as well. When one fruitlessly expends his semen, likened by the *Zohar* to the brain or the rational soul, he causes the irrigating flow of the *sefirah* *Yesod* to cease and dry up.[144] *Tiferet* no longer unites with *Malkhut*. *Malkhut*, the image that encompasses all others, no longer teems with the fruits of divine fertility. And the supernal creation of human souls comes to a halt.[145] This was the sin of Noah's contemporaries, who thereby precipitated cosmic disaster. Extinguishing the provident light of the *Shekhinah*, they alienated the world from its creator and betrayed it to the demonic force of evil, for which reason the Torah called them evil as well.[146]

Punishment to Fit the Crime. Just as human observance of the commandment to "be fertile and increase" effects harmonious relations both among the *sefirot* and between God and his creatures, so too does one's failure to procreate seal the doom of his soul. The *Zohar* distinguishes the man who, having married, tries in good faith to beget offspring from him who remains childless intentionally, in service of *sitra' 'ahra'*, the force of evil.[147] The latter's crime, the obverse of wasting one's semen, exceeds that of murderers, for "they killed other people, while he killed his own children."[148] The usual modes of repentence will not atone for such wrongdoing. Even murderers will ultimately rise from purgatory, but he will never enter the heavenly palace. As our opening text suggests and as the story of the childless Hezekiah confirms, he will remain without life in this world and the next.[149]

We recall that in *Sefer ha-Bahir* the fruitful syzygy of masculine and feminine *sefirot* decreased the need for metempsychosis, or transmigration, in which most existent human souls participated, by replacing them with new ones; eventually, the newly born soul of the messiah would redeem all souls from their alienation, bringing this process to an

143. See above, Chapter 2, at nn. 160ff.
144. *Z*, 3:254b; cf. 3:244a (*Ra'ya' Mehemna'*), and *TZ* 42, p. 82a.
145. See also, *Z*, 1:264b (*Hashmatot*).
146. *Z*, 1:56b–57a, 62a.
147. *Z*, 1:186b–88a, 2:106a, 112a; cf. Moses b. Shem Tov de León, "*Sefer ha-Mishkal:* Text [Hebrew] and Study," ed. Jochanan H. A. Wijnhoven (Ph.D. Dissertation, Brandeis University, Waltham, Mass., 1964), p. 138.
148. *Z*, 1:219b.
149. *Z*, 1:228b; see above, Chapter 2, n. 51.

end. The author of the *Zohar*, however, reformulated the connection between metempsychosis and the creation of souls within the godhead. His focus on human procreation as the basis for fertile sefirotic union led him to identify transmigration as the penalty for sexual activity that impedes such conjunction.[150] In most instances, only the souls of "those who despoiled their covenant and did not occupy themselves with procreation" are condemned to metempsychosis.[151] These souls, which failed to work for the creation of others, must endure the alienation of a psychic exile, whereby they appear reincarnate in subsequent generations in order to redress their previous failures. Only in exceptional cases can a truly righteous individual merit admission to the next world on the basis of other good deeds. One who in his first life did marry and try to beget children might at least enjoy the company of his first wife in his reincarnation, but his soul too must transmigrate, along with the soul of him who intentionally refrained from procreation. God allows each soul three chances to fulfill his commandment and merit an end to its perigrinations; following the third transmigration, he condemns a childless soul to perpetual banishment.

This doctrine of transmigration prompted the author of the *Zohar* to place an extremely high value on the commandment of levirate marriage. He no longer construed the biblical practice of marrying one's childless brother's widow (Ruth 4:6, 4:10) "to perpetuate the name of the deceased" as intended to leave the dead man an heir.[152] Rather, he believed that the fruit of the levirate union would embody none other than the transmigrating soul of the deceased himself. "Great is the commandment of levirate marriage; for he who fulfills the commandment of levirate marriage for its own sake becomes a partner of the holy one, blessed be he."[153] Like the creative *sefirot* within the deity, the levir secures the release of a soul into the world so that it too might "be fertile and increase."

---

150. On metempsychosis and the resulting evaluation of levirate marriage, see Moses b. Shem Tov de León, "Shu"T . . . bᵉ-ʿInyᵉne ha-Qabbalah," ed. Isaiah Tishby, *Qoveẓ ʿal Yad* 15 (1950), 34–35; idem, "*Sefer ha-Mishkal*," pp. 136ff.; *Z*, 1:187a–88a, 2:105b–106a; *ZH*, pp. 88b–89b (*Midrash Rut*). For an overview of the Zoharic stage in the history of this doctrine, see Scholem, *Elements*, pp. 318–19 and n. 24.

151. *ZH*, p. 89a.

152. Because of the context of *Midrash Rut*, *ZH*, p. 88b, explains the union of Boaz and Ruth with this verse, rather than the Mosaic legislation in Deut. 25:7 ("to establish a name in Israel for his brother").

153. *ZH*, p. 88b.

Reinterpreting Classical Aggadah. The recurring theme of divine-human partnership in the kabbalistic view of procreation returns us to the aggadic appreciation in Gen. 1:28 discussed in Chapter 2. The *Zohar*'s high valuation of human reproductive activity clearly depends on the rabbinic interpretation of "be fertile and increase" as commandment, but within the framework of its esoteric theosophy the *Zohar* reaffirms much of what our verse meant in earlier aggadic texts. We have noted how the nexus between procreation and the maintenance of the divine image, the antireproductive behavior of Noah's contemporaries, the efficacy of procreation in securing salvation for the individual, and the understanding of Gen. 1:28 as the exemplary, quasi-liturgical expression of divine grace all take their place in Zoharic Kabbalah.[154] An additional aggadic motif at work in the *Zohar* warrants specification. Of all terrestrial creatures, only human beings can transcend the chasm that separates earthly and supernal realms; combining soul and body, the traits of angels and animals, they stand at the cosmic frontier. Classical rabbinic homilies viewed this distinctive blend of characteristics not as hopelessly contradictory but as the very rationale for human existence, facilitating the service of God as no other creature can provide it. In this midrashic tradition, the divine call to engage in sexual reproduction epitomized the singular human purpose, that which explained why God could not and did not reveal his Torah to the angels.

Moses de León maintained and developed this notion, testifying to the importance of human sexuality and procreation more emphatically still. Echoing an idea long popular in Christian biblical exegesis, he held that God unquestionably intended the sexual reproduction of Adam and Eve to transpire in Eden; the uncontrollable flame of sexual passion, which awoke in humans only after their fall, would not have pervaded their union. "If Adam had not sinned, he would not have produced offspring in this manner, from the side of the evil inclination, but he would have produced offspring from the side of the holy spirit. Yet now he cannot produce offspring except from the side of the evil inclination."[155] Nevertheless, the benefits of procreation still over-

154. Additional discussion of ancient allusions to this sexual theme appears in Idel, "Métaphores et pratiques sexuelles dans la Cabale."

155. *Z*, 1:60b–61a; see also 3:189a. Variations on this theme appear in RaMba"N, 1:36 (ad Gen. 2:9); *'Iggeret ha-Qodesh*, in *Kitve RaMba"N*, 2:323; and Obadiah Sforno, *Be'ur 'al ha-Torah*, p. 20 (ad Gen. 2:25). On the Christian origins of this tradition, see below, Chapter 5.

shadow the "evil inclination" effecting its sexual process and thus require its perpetuation. "If the evil inclination does not exist, procreation (*p^eriyyah u-r^eviyyah*) cannot exist."[156] Even now a man realizes his human potential and thereby perfects himself spiritually only when he performs his procreative duties as defined by the Talmud. Referring to the design of God in creating human beings, the *Zohar* inquires:[157] "When is a man called complete on the model of the supernal? When he has conjoined with his wife in unity, joy, and affection and has brought forth[158] from himself and his wife a son and a daughter." As the words of Is. 45:18 suggest, precisely for this reason did God create human beings and the world as he did—so that they might populate it, overcoming alienation and void (*tohu*) both above and below and thereby meriting divine reward.[159]

Procreation and Covenant. The author of the *Zohar* amplified on the significance of procreation in a way that the ancient writers and readers of Scripture could never have imagined. In his own kabbalistic idiom, however, he testified to the underlying theological import of Gen. 1:28 in both biblical and classical rabbinic periods. For Moses de León, our verse continued to express the covenant between God and his human creatures, and he formulated this connection more explicitly than any Jewish writer before him. Admittedly, the pressing questions had changed. Departing from a talmudic hermeneutical principle that most scriptural references to 'adam (a man or a person, but also the Hebrew for Adam) applied only to Jews,[160] the author of the *Zohar* excluded Gentiles from this covenantal relationship *a priori*. Unlike many a halakhist, he felt no need to argue the point, but merely stipulated that "there is no one, except for the Jew alone, who is called 'adam." For their part, the spirits of uncircumcised Gentiles were steeped in evil and pollution, and so they do not reckon at all in kabbalistic instruction on service of the deity. The twentieth-century reader cannot but be amazed that kabbalistic discussions of sexuality are directed to men only. Kabbalistic doctrine does not forget that women play an essential role in

156. *Z,* 1:128b. See also my "Original Sin as the Evil Inclination."
157. *Z,* 3:7a.
158. Tishby, *MHZ,* 2:614, translates "there come(s) forth"; I have followed the morphology of Menahem Zevi Kaddari, *The Grammar of the Aramaic of the "Zohar"* (Hebrew) (Jerusalem, 1971), p. 157.
159. *Z,* 1:23a, 187a; cf. *TZ* 19, p. 38a, and 43, p. 86a.
160. TB *BM* 114b; and see the comments of Tosafot ad *AZ* 3a, s.v. *Kohanim,* with the additional references cited there.

reproductive activity and that they too have legitimate sexual needs, yet precisely for these reasons their minimal participation in the mystical repercussions of procreation is additionally surprising.[161] In the *Zohar*, God's blessing of primordial man *and* woman as progenitors of all human beings no longer even hints at an alliance between God and humankind at large. What sort of pact did it entail?

The opening text in our discussion of Zoharic Kabbalah indicates that one who neglects his reproductive duties "despoils the holy covenant in all of its dimensions (*pagim qayyama' qadisha' be-khol sitrin*)." According to the *Zohar*, despoliation of the covenant upsets the harmonious interaction of the *sefirot*, severs the communion between supernal and terrestrial realms, and occurs in reprehensible human activity—for instance, sexual relations with a menstruant woman, sexual relations with a Gentile woman, and forcing one's pregnant wife to abort. "Over these things the holy spirit weeps, and the world is condemned to these judgments. Woe be unto such a man [who engages in such behavior]; it would have been better were he never created." The common denominator of all these transgressions is their sexual impropriety. Each entails the wrongful use of the male genital organ, dubbed the covenant (i.e., of circumcision) by metonymy, as well as damage to the phallic *sefirah* within the godhead—*Yesod*, to whom the epithet "holy covenant" also refers. He who lies with a Gentile woman therefore sins when "he inserts the holy covenant and the sign of the covenant into a foreign domain," an indictment with corresponding physical and sefirotic significance. In polar opposition to such activity, the *Zohar* identifies the meritorious sexual behavior that facilitated the redemption of the Jews from Egypt: "Praiseworthy are the Israelites! Although in exile in Egypt, they refrained from these three [sins] . . . and engaged in procreation . . . , as it is written (Ex. 1:7): 'And the children of Israel were fertile (*paru*), were prolific, and multiplied (*wa-yirbu*).'"[162]

While Moses de León elaborated the importance of circumcision on numerous occasions,[163] his remark on despoiling the covenant "in all of

---

161. Against this background, the application of the precept of "be fertile and increase" to Gentiles and women by the late medieval *Sefer ha-Qanah*, pp. 105ab, is especially curious. See the comments of Michal Kushnir-Oron, "'Ha-Peli'ah' we-'ha-Qanah': Yesodot ha-Qabbalah she-bahem, 'Emdatam ha-Datit Hevratit, we-Derekh 'Izzuvam ha-Sifrutit" (Ph.D. Dissertation, Hebrew University of Jerusalem, 1974), esp. pp. 241ff.

162. *Z*, 2:3a–4a (=*MHZ*, 2:469–72), with slight modification of NJPS.

163. See *MHZ*, 2:618–19 with notes. For an excellent analysis of this theme in the *Zohar*, see Elliot R. Wolfson, "Circumcision, Vision of God, and Textual Interpretation: From Midrashic Trope to Mystical Symbol," *History of Religions* 27 (1987), 189–215.

its dimensions" brings our discussion of Zoharic mysticism full circle and to an appropriate conclusion. The obverse of his assertion is that fulfillment of the commandment of procreation maintains the covenant "in all of its dimensions," suggesting that the covenantal ramifications of Gen. 1:28 extend throughout the entire tripartite scheme of reality at the foundation of his Kabbalah. On a mundane level, procreation constitutes the optimal pursuit of the circumcised male organ; it sanctifies the covenant of Abraham that this organ bears and that gives the Jew his distinctive identity. In the realm of the supernal, human reproduction affords vitality to the masculine *sᵉfirah Yᵉsod*, to whom the *Zohar* ascribes the epithet of "holy covenant," as well as the biblical appellation of *'El Shaddai*.[164] And in causing the infusion of divine creativity, providence, and grace into the terrestrial sphere, procreation facilitates the proper interaction between the Jew—particularly the kabbalist— and the deity. The framework for this divine–human relationship is none other than the Sinaitic covenant, encompassing both written Torah and oral Torah, which represent the masculine *Tif'eret* and the feminine *Malkhut*, respectively.[165] The author of *Tiqqune ha-Zohar*, an early appendage to the *Zohar* of Moses de León, therefore defined the sexual despoliation of the covenant in terms of Isaiah's forecast of doom (19:5), "the river will be parched and dry."[166] The subversion of procreation impeded "that river [*Yᵉsod*] which flows out of Eden and which waters the garden, which is the oral Torah and which is watered from the written Torah."[167] When procreation facilitates the conjunction of the *sᵉfirot* on high, it integrates the components of God's revelation to human beings, perfecting the covenant between the deity and his creatures.

In the Wake of the *Zohar*

Kabbalistic works composed at the same time as the *Zohar* or in the generations thereafter attest to the importance of Moses de León and his school in the career of Gen. 1:28. Offering an extensive description of each of the *sᵉfirot* in his *Sha'are 'Orah*, Joseph b. Abraham Gikatilla failed to discuss *pᵉriyyah u-rᵉviyyah* or our verse in his comments on *Tif'eret*,

---

164. On the phallic role of *Yᵉsod* within the godhead, see Moses de León, "*Sefer ha-Mishkal*," pp. 130–33, and "*Sefer ha-Rimmon*," 2:230.

165. *MHZ*, 2:365–66, 374–75. See also Azriel of Gerona, *Commentarius*, pp. 2–3, 77 n. 5.

166. RSV.

167. *TZ* 42, p. 82a.

Y^esod, or *Malkhut*.[168] Despite Guberman's questionable suggestion that the author of the pseudo-Nahmanidean *'Iggeret ha-Qodesh* consciously alluded to Maimonides' enumeration of the commandment of procreation,[169] this marriage manual, which belabors the supernal consequences of human sexual activity, never refers to the precept or to its scriptural basis. Both these writers were contemporaries of Moses de León; their silence concerning p^e*riyyah u-r^{e}viyyah*, owing either to their ignorance of Moses' ideas or to a reluctance to accept them, confirms the groundbreaking nature of his contribution.

On the other hand, once the ideas of the *Zohar* came to dominate the Kabbalah of the later Middle Ages, little remained for other writers to add to its appreciation of Gen. 1:28. Reviewing numerous reflections of Zoharic influence would serve little purpose here, and we propose simply to illustrate how the doctrine elaborated above functioned in kabbalistic adaptations of two existing genres of rabbinic texts considered earlier in this chapter. Kabbalists, like Moses Nahmanides, had written commentaries on the Torah prior to the career of Moses de León, and they continued to do so after the publication of his works; the students of Nahmanides' own disciples authored the most prominent representatives of this literary genre. It is curious that the Zoharic interpretation of Gen. 1:28 had only occasional impact on these exegetical works. It is notably absent from the commentaries of Shem Tov b. Abraham ibn Gaon, Joshua ibn Shu'ayb (Pseudo-Meir b. Solomon ibn Sahula),[170] Bahya b. Asher, and Menahem b. Benjamin of Recanati— the first two actually mystical supercommentaries on Nahmanides' pentateuchal gloss—which evidently preferred the doctrine of *Sefer ha-Bahir* and the Gerona school to the *Zohar*'s instruction on metempsychosis.[171] Isaac b. Samuel of Acre's *Me'irat 'Enayim*, which Scholem

168. Joseph b. Abraham Gikatila, *Shaare Orah* (Hebrew), ed. Joseph Ben Shlomo, 2 vols. (1971; repr., Jerusalem, 1981).

169. Guberman, "Language of Love," p. 63 and n. 27. Perhaps the problem derives from Guberman's failure to cite Maimonides directly; she refers instead to the article on "Commandments" in the *Encyclopedia Judaica*. For the most recent opinions on the authorship of the *'Iggeret*, see Guberman, p. 101 n. 24; Shraga Avramson, "'*Iggeret ha-Qodesh* ha-M^{c}yuḥeset l^e-RaMba"N," *Sinai* 90 (1982), 232–53; and Mopsik in *Lettre sur la sainteté*, pp. 21–29, 359–62.

170. Following Gershom Scholem, *Kabbalah* (New York, 1974), p. 61.

171. Shem Tov b. Abraham ibn Gaon, *Perush Sodot ha-Torah 'al Pi ha-Qabbalah ha-'Amittit l^{e}ha-RaMba"N Za"L*, in *Ma'or wa-Shemesh*, ed. Judah Koriat (Leghorn, 1819), pp. 31b–32a; Joshua ibn Shu'ayb (Pseudo-Meir b. Solomon ibn Sahula), *Be'ur l^e-Ferush ha-RaMba"N 'al Torah*, in *'Oẓar M^{e}far^{e}she ha-Torah*, 1:9ab; Bahya b. Asher, *Be'ur 'al Torah*, 2:509–11, 3:405–406; and Menahem b. Benjamin of Recanati, *Perush 'al Torah*, in Mordecai Jaffe, *Sefer L^{e}vushe 'Or Y^{e}qarot* (Jerusalem, 1961), pp. 33b–36b, 63a.

dubs "the main storehouse for all the traditions of this school,"[172] provides an exception. Recalling Nadav and Avihu, the childless sons of Aaron, this work relates metempsychosis and the failure to procreate;[173] and with reference to Is. 45:18, it views the fruitful union of man and woman as ensuring the survival of terrestrial and supernal worlds.[174]

In a second textual genre, however, Moses de León's ideas on procreation fared better, coalescing more easily with other strains of kabbalistic thought. While discussion of the reasons for the biblical commandments had pervaded the *Zohar* and many of the kabbalistic works that preceded it, the end of the thirteenth century saw the composition of mystical treatises devoted expressly to this subject, handbooks that blended traditional rabbinic instruction and distinctively mystical doctrine in order to explain the precepts of the Torah.[175] Moses' *Sefer ha-Rimmon* numbers among the earliest of these works, as does a treatise on the commandments traditionally ascribed to the sixteenth-century Isaac ibn Farhi but actually composed by one "Joseph of Shushan," which manifests the Zoharic legacy under the rubric of procreation as well as under that of levirate marriage. In its literal sense, the duty of procreation (which Joseph derived from Gen. 1:28) seeks to realize the divine intention for creating the world. "When one has no children, he is like the destroyer of [entire] worlds. . . . When a man perpetuates the species, it is as if he maintains the entire Torah. . . . Hence, this commandment is that of maintaining the world and maintaining the Torah." The simple, straightforward rationale for levirate marriage is similar. "When a man has no children, he diminishes the image of the [sefirotic] chain," and the soul of a man who dies childless thereby suffers at the hands of demonic powers. The fruitful union of his brother and his widow would make good on his obligation after the fact. "What is the reason for this? Man is [fashioned] on a supernal

172. Scholem, *Kabbalah*, p. 62.

173. Isaac b. Samuel of Acre, "*Meʾirat ʿEnayim*," ed. Amos Goldreich (Ph.D. Dissertation, Hebrew University of Jerusalem, 1981), pp. 35, 159 (with notes on pp. 375–78); on Nadav and Avihu and their failure to procreate, see above, Chapter 2, n. 49.

174. Ibid., p. 21, with Goldreich's discursive notes on pp. 361–66.

175. See the introduction of Menahem Meier to his edition of Pseudo-Isaac ibn Farhi, "*Sefer Taʾamey ha-Mizwoth ('Book of Reasons of the Commandments')*" (Hebrew) (Ph.D. Dissertation, Brandeis University, Waltham, Mass., 1974), pp. 10–16, and E. Wolfson's introduction to Moses de León, "*Sefer ha-Rimmon*," esp. 1:54–67, 101–23, for consideration of kabbalistic use of this textual genre. On kabbalistic understanding of the commandments, see also Daniel C. Matt, "The Mystic and the *Mizwot*," in *JS*, pp. 367–404.

pattern. When anyone produces a son and daughter, it is as if he maintains the heavenly image. One image maintains the other." Moreover, such a man

> assists the holy one, blessed be he, in the work of creation, and it is as though he builds a world unto itself. Therefore, when a man departs from the world having left children, the holy one, blessed be he, says to his soul: "You are worthy to sit with me, and you are my partner. Just as I have created worlds so you have created worlds. Moreover, you have maintained the image of the [sefirotic] chain." Immediately he is admitted to the Garden of Eden, where he is happy.[176]

Although Joseph rationalized the commandment of procreation along blatantly talmudic lines (diminishing the image, begetting a son and a daughter), the notion that human procreation maintains the integrity of the godhead because of a divine-human correspondence is unquestionably Zoharic. Proceeding to the avowedly mystical sense of these commandments, Joseph elaborated on the conjunction of masculine and feminine within the godhead and explained how, by means of levirate marriage, God graciously restores the soul of a childless man to life, releasing it from the banishment that followed upon his death. Apart from the assignment of each commandment to a specific segment of the human anatomy—procreation to the right thigh, levirate marriage to the right testicle, and so forth—there is little new here. One does note with interest that despite his proclaimed distinction between literal and mystical levels of exegesis, Joseph included much that was kabbalistic in the former. The thought of Moses de León had penetrated even the plain, supposedly exterior sense of our biblical verse, allowing for a natural progression, rather than a clear bifurcation, between superficial (*peshaṭ*) and esoteric (*sod*) meaning in Scripture.

Menahem of Recanati, a kabbalist of fourteenth-century Italy, also compiled a treatise on the commandments. As in his commentary on the Pentateuch, Menahem employed the terminology and conclusions of *Sefer ha-Bahir* and Nahmanides regarding metempsychosis in order to explain the duty of levirate marriage.[177] Yet under the rubric of the precept of procreation, Menahem borrowed extensively from the

---

176. Ibid., pp. 250–57, 386–92.
177. Menahem b. Benjamin of Recanati, *Sefer Ṭaʿame ha-Miẓwot ha-Shalem*, ed. S. Lieberman (London, 1962), pp. 72a–73b.

pseudo-Nahmanidean *'Iggeret ha-Qodesh,* offering instruction on the mystical significance, the proper time, and the ideal geographical orientation of sexual activity (*mahut ha-ḥibbur, zᵉman ha-ḥibbur, kiwwun ha-ḥibbur*). While the marriage manual itself had never mentioned Gen. 1:28 or the legal obligation to have children, Menahem employed the *'Iggeret'*s elaboration of the supernal ramifications of marital relations to expound the biblical precept. Moreover, he followed the *'Iggeret*—and the *Baᶜale ha-Nefesh* of Abraham b. David of Posquierres before it—in stressing the mystical impact of thought and motivation at the moment of sexual conjunction more extensively than Moses de León; in matters sexual, "all proceeds according to the intention."[178] The underlying message, that the biblical commandment of procreation seeks to implement the sefirotic union and to facilitate communion between humans and the deity, adheres to Zoharic teaching. It is ironic that in order to propound this Zoharic doctrine, Menahem relied upon a text that noticeably failed to espouse it.

APPLICATIONS OF SCRIPTURE AND TRADITION

The diverse genres of documentary sources considered in this chapter reflect the multifaceted application of Gen. 1:28, as interpreted in classical rabbinic texts, to the needs and concerns of medieval Jewry. The literatures of the responsa, the rabbinic exegesis of the Bible, and the Kabbalah all originated during the Middle Ages, deriving from a constellation of circumstances that did not characterize the talmudic period in Jewish history: a dispersed, decentralized Jewish community; a frequent need to defend Judaism against the critique of rationalist skeptics and non-Jewish heirs to the biblical tradition; and the flowering of a rabbinic species of Gnosticism. The treatment of our verse in each of these textual genres attests to the success of the talmudic translation of the primordial blessing into Mosaic law, just as it manifests the problems and possibilities that such reinterpretation entailed.

While the responsa acknowledge the singular importance of procreation in the life of the pious Jew by relaxing other regulations for its sake, they demonstrate the difficulties of ensuring observance of a commandment to have children. As a statute, "be fertile and increase" was

178. Ibid., pp. 47a–50a.

inherently unenforceable. When medieval rabbis sought to recover and expound the literal sense of the Torah, the need to identify the textual locus of this law posed additional difficulties. The progression of the Genesis cosmogony and primeval history militated against an understanding of "be fertile and increase" as a commandment to the Jews. The enunciation of a similar blessing to the fish and the birds, the nexus between the primordial blessing and creation in God's image, the juxtaposition of the call to fill the earth with the conferral of dominion, both on the sixth day of creation and in the aftermath of the flood, the recurrence of the *prh/rbh* hendiadys five times in the first eleven chapters of Scripture, and the universal focus of the primeval history—all these placed greater demands on the exegete and the enumerator of the commandments intent on defending the talmudic understanding of our verse. No wonder some commentators unabashedly acknowledged the talmudic origins of the commandment of *p^eriyyah u-r^eviyyah*, or explained its rationale as the perpetuation of the entire human species. For its part, the theosophical Kabbalah of Moses de León beheld weighty theological consequences in procreation that the biblical author could not have foreseen in his wildest imagination, enabling us to appreciate the extensive contribution of a single individual to our story.

The novelties of these medieval rabbinic encounters with Gen. 1:28 notwithstanding, all of the texts we have discussed preserved and fortified a definitively rabbinic perspective on the subject. The jurist unable (or unready) to implement talmudic mechanisms of enforcement, the literalist reader of Scripture, and certainly the author of the *Zohar* continued to deem procreation a legal obligation of the first order. While medieval Jewish exegetes did analyze the second half of the primordial blessing in Gen. 1:28b, I have encountered no rabbinic source that construes this too as a Mosaic commandment; procreation continued to overshadow the conferral of dominion as the primary message of the verse. Jewish writers of the Middle Ages drew heavily on classical aggadic midrash, the prominent motifs of whose reactions to Gen. 1:28 underlay its role in the bizarre, esoteric theosophy of Moses de León. Each in its distinctive idiom, the medieval Jewish applications of Gen. 1:28 spoke to the predominantly covenantal message of this biblical text, illustrating by example the evolving dynamics of the Western encounter with Scripture. For the jurist, upholding the biblical covenant entailed the day-to-day implementation of a system of law whose variegated priorities and regulations often dictated mutually exclusive alternatives. For the exegete and for the codifier of the Mosaic precepts, the covenant rested upon the integrity and essential unity of written and oral legal traditions; an accurate reading of Scripture culd not but justify age-old rabbinic instruction, and vice versa. For the kabbalist, covenant could signal mutually explicative, interdependent spheres of discourse and relation between masculine and feminine entities, whose fruitful, harmonious sexual conjunction facilitated its maintenance. In the language of the *Zohar,* the neglect of procreation therefore despoiled the holy covenant, desecrating the circumcision of the sexual organ and impeding the conjunction of *Tif'eret* and *Malkhut.* Moreover, "those who do not protect this covenant of holiness cause a rift between Israel and their heavenly father . . . , because such a person is like one who worships another deity."[179]

Rabbinic writers who followed the medieval period added little to the interpretations of Gen. 1:28 that we have encountered thus far. Reserving some general observations on the Jewish career of this verse for the conclusion to this book, we thus revert our attention to late antiquity and to the classical texts of Christianity.

179. *Z,* 1:189b, 2:26a, cited in *MHZ,* 2:619.

CHAPTER 5

Christian Biblical Commentary

THE career of Gen. 1:28 in late antique and medieval Christianity is no less fascinating than in Jewish tradition, but it yields a markedly shorter story to tell. Although Christian writers of late antiquity and the Middle Ages produced a literature that was much more expansive and voluminous than their rabbinic counterparts, for several reasons they devoted less attention to the primordial blessing. Above all, no New Testament writer quoted or directly alluded to our verse. In addition, christological and trinitarian interests led clerical writers to focus so intently on the creation of humans in God's image (Gen. 1:26–27) that these adjacent verses invariably overshadowed our own in their exegesis.[1] And, quite simply, a mere reference to sexual reproduction or procreation in Greek and Latin did not necessitate the allusion to Gen. 1:28 that it did in rabbinic Hebrew (*periyyah u-reviyyah*), and other biblical verses could readily assume greater prominence in Christian discussions of sex and marriage.[2]

---

1. Some Christian exegetes incorporated Gen. 1:28 into the trinitarian motifs that they discerned in these previous verses, particularly in its contribution to the tripartite process (*dixit* [Gen. 1:26], *fecit* [Gen. 1:27], *benedixit* [Gen. 1:28]) whereby God created human beings. See Justin Martyr, *Dialogue avec Tryphon (Dialogus cum Tryphone Iudaeo)* 62.1–2, ed. G. Archambault, 2 vols. (Paris, 1909), pp. 290–91; Eusebius of Vercelli, *De Trinitate* 1.32ff., CCSL 9:10–11; Faustus of Riez, *De spiritu sancto* 1.6, CSEL 21:109, *Sermo* 30, CSEL 21:341; Pseudo-Eusebius of Emesa, *Sermo* 2.8, CCSL 101B:832; and Caesarius of Arles, *Sermo* 212, CCSL 104:844–45.

2. For example, see Georges Duby, *The Knight, the Lady, and the Priest: The Making of Modern Marriage in Medieval France,* tr. Barbara Bray (New York, 1983), pp. 24ff., where Gen. 1:28 is conspicuously absent.

Where Gen. 1:28 figured significantly in Christian literature, it usually functioned in at least one of three ways. (1) Just as it did for its Jewish readers, God's opening discourse with the first parents offered insight into the singular nature and purpose of the human condition; the contents and context of the verse demanded as much. (2) In so doing, however, Gen. 1:28 also constituted a pressing exegetical and theological problem: How ought one to reconcile this terrestrial orientation of the biblical cosmogony with the otherworldly kerygma of the church? Fundamental issues of Christian biblical interpretation were at stake. (3) As a climax in the Genesis hexameron, the primordial blessing regularly served to evoke an array of doctrinal issues—including the appraisal of human nature (original, fallen, and redeemed), original sin, sexuality, the status of humans in the "great chain of being," and even the value of worldly progress and achievement—which, though related, arose and flourished independently of the verse.[3]

Our story accordingly intersects with many important chapters in the history of Christian theology, although Gen. 1:28 may often have amounted to little more than a window, or perhaps one of several biblical testimonies, to the argument at hand. In such instances, even at the risk of frustration for both author and reader, our primary concern must remain with the career and contributions of the biblical verse, not with the underlying issues of every theological discussion in which it was invoked. The appropriate balance is often difficult to strike. Each subject we have enumerated has its own vast literature of primary and secondary sources; while different readers might draw different lines of demarcation between the central and the peripheral, many questions of interest must remain beyond the purview of this book. Existing studies of patristic and medieval literature pertaining to our subject tend to sacrifice comprehensiveness for the sake of thematic continuity, result-

---

3. On the genre, concerns, and importance of the *Hexaemeron,* a commentary on the Genesis cosmogony, see the valuable studies of Frank Egleston Robbins, *The Hexaemeral Literature: A Study of the Greek and Latin Commentaries on Genesis* (Chicago, 1912); T. Jansma, "L'Hexaméron de Jacques de Sarug," *L'Orient syrien* 4 (1959), 3–42, 129–62, 253–84, 451–521; Yves M.-J. Congar, "Le thème de *Dieu-Créateur* et les explications de l'Hexaméron dans la tradition chrétienne," in *L'homme devant Dieu: Mélanges offerts au Père Henri de Lubac,* 3 vols., Théologie 56–58 (Paris, 1963–64), 1:189–222; Johannes Zahlten, *Creatio mundi: Darstellungen der sechs Schöpfungstage und naturwissenschaftliches Weltbild im Mittelalter,* Stuttgarter Beiträge zur Geschichte und Politik 13 (Stuttgart, 1979); and Alessandra Tarabochia Canavero, *Esegesi biblica e cosmologia: Note sull'interpretazione patristica e medioevale di Genesi 1,2,* Scienze filosofiche 30 (Milan, 1981).

ing in a restricted view of the interpretative potential of Gen. 1:28.[4] Demonstrating the breadth of our verse's implications, which the assortment of its postbiblical contexts corroborates, ranks high among the goals of my book.

Like my treatment of rabbinic sources, the ensuing discussion of Christian literature seeks not only to document the career of Gen. 1:28 but also to analyze its impact on the history of ideas. This chapter examines ancient and medieval biblical commentary, tracking the Greek patristic traditions up until the career of Augustine, and then focusing primarily on the Latin West; in this literature, one can readily review most, if not all, of the pertinent published evidence. Chapter 6 considers the significance of the verse in select medieval discussions of nature and natural law. As we proceed, one must recall that the Christian ideas and texts under discussion date from the same period as the Jewish teachings considered above and that the two traditions shared numerous ideas. In and of themselves, such parallels are instructive for the historian of Western culture. In the case of Gen. 1:28, I shall argue at the end of this volume, they are a key to understanding the legacy of the Bible.

THE GREEK AND SYRIAC FATHERS

The absence of any clear allusion to Gen. 1:28 in the New Testament is noteworthy.[5] The themes of creation, marriage, sexuality, and do-

---

4. Cf. Michael Müller, *Die Lehre des hl. Augustinus von der Paradiesesehe und ihre Auswirkung in der Sexualethik des 12. und 13. Jahrhunderts bis Thomas von Aquin,* Studien zur Geschichte der katholischen Moraltheologie 1 (Regensburg, 1954); Joseph E. Kerns, *The Theology of Marriage: The Historical Development of Christian Attitudes toward Sex and Sanctity in Marriage* (New York, 1964); John Bugge, *Virginitas: An Essay in the History of a Medieval Ideal,* International Archives of the History of Ideas, Series minor 17 (The Hague, 1975), ch. 1; and P. Langa, "Análisis agustiniano de 'crescite et multiplicamini' (Gen 1,28)," *Estudio teológico agustiniano* 18 (1983), 3–38, 147–76—all of which make valuable contributions nonetheless. See also J. M. Evans, *Paradise Lost and the Genesis Tradition* (Oxford, 1968); and M. Gilbert, " 'Soyez féconds et multipliez' (Gn 1,28)," *Nouvelle revue théologique* 106 (1974), 728–42.

5. Jobl., diss., pp. 43ff., 201, rightfully criticizes Jervell, *Imago Dei,* for finding New Testament allusions to Gen. 1:28 and the theme of dominion where none appear; yet even Jobling has overstepped the bounds of credibility, asserting without hesitation (p. 46 n. 74) that "there is a definite reference to Gen 1:28 in James 3:7." One might aptly respond with Jobling's own rejoinder (p. 201) to Jervell's proposed allusions: "The reference to dominion is quite vague and general, and no [convincing] allusion is made to the wording of the Gen 1 dominion texts." On the themes of marriage and human sexuality in the New Testament, see, among others, Robin Scroggs, *The New Testament and Homosexuality: Contextual Background for Contemporary Debate* (Philadelphia, Pa., 1983); A. L. Descamps, "The New Testament

minion all figure significantly in Christian Scripture, and several New Testament texts (I Cor. 15:27, Eph. 1:22, and especially Heb. 2:6–8) definitely refer to Psalm 8 as describing the dominion of Christ, the second Adam. Perhaps the psalm lent itself to christological reinterpretation more easily than our verse in Genesis, because from a Christian perspective human dominion mattered relatively little in the quest for salvation. It pertained to worldly pursuits—those of the "old covenant"—which the spokesmen of the church strove to supplant with those of the "new covenant." Paul's neglect of procreation in his instruction concerning marriage adds credence to this impression. On a practical level, the bearing and rearing of children distracted the true believer from the service of Christ. Morally, procreation was not an issue for Paul; matrimony, not reproduction, obviated the evils of fornication and adultery, which he decried. The expectation of the *parousia*, Bernhard Lang observed, undoubtedly detracted from the urgency of creating succeeding generations; concisely put, "there is no sex in heaven."[6] And as O. Larry Yarbrough recently argued, the Stoic ideal of procreation as a civic responsibility pertained but little to Paul's ministry. "Indeed, Stoics themselves would not have bothered with advising many of Paul's converts to produce children, for their primary concern was with citizens, not with the mass of slaves, tradesmen, and even freedmen who made up the population of a city."[7] It therefore remained for the church fathers who followed the biblical period to extend the career of Gen. 1:28 into Christian tradition.

Gen. 1:28b and Dominion

The oldest patristic reference to Gen. 1:28 focuses on dominion rather than procreation, and we have followed suit in organizing the pertinent comments of the church fathers. Composed late in the first Christian century or early in the second, the *Epistle of Barnabas* proclaims:

> For Scripture is speaking about us when he [God] says to the Son (Gen. 1:26): "Let us make man in accord with our image and likeness, and let

Doctrine on Marriage," in *Contemporary Perspectives on Christian Marriage,* ed. Richard Malone and John R. Connery (Chicago, 1984), pp. 217–73; and O. Larry Yarbrough, *Not Like the Gentiles: Marriage Rules in the Letters of Paul,* Society of Biblical Literature Dissertation Series 80 (Atlanta, Ga., 1985).

   6. Lang, "No Sex in Heaven," pp. 244–51.
   7. Yarbrough, *Not Like the Gentiles,* pp. 107–8, and see also pp. 31–63.

them rule over the beasts of the earth and the birds of heaven and the fish of the sea." And when he saw how well we were formed, the Lord said (Gen. 1:28): "Increase and multiply and fill the earth." These things [he said] to the Son. Again, I will show you how he says to us that he made a second fashioning in the last times. And the Lord says: "Behold, I make the last things like the first." It is for this reason, therefore, that the prophet proclaimed: "Enter into the land flowing with milk and honey, and exercise lordship over it." See, then, we have been fashioned anew! . . . What, then, is the "milk and honey?" Because the infant is initiated into life first by honey, then by milk. Thus also, in a similar way, when we have been initiated into life by faith in the promise and by the word, we will live exercising lordship over the land. But as it was already said above: "And they shall increase, and multiply, and rule over the fish." Who, then, is presently able to rule over beasts or fish or birds of heaven? For we ought to understand that "to rule" implies that one is in control, so that he who gives the orders exercises dominion. If, then, this is not the present situation, he has told us when it will be— when we ourselves have been perfected as heirs of the Lord's covenant.[8]

Writing between the destruction of the Temple in Jerusalem in 70 and Hadrian's defeat of the Bar Kokhba rebellion in 135, a time when one begins to perceive a socioinstitutional rift between Jewish and Christian communities, Pseudo-Barnabas employed Gen. 1:28 polemically to vindicate the beliefs of his co-religionists. God's creation of human beings in his image and in order to rule typifies the "new creation" inaugurated by Jesus. The primordial blessing, originally addressed by God to his son, Jesus, bespeaks the ultimate triumph of the church. Like the promise of the land—an association that led Pseudo-Barnabas to blend the motifs of Canaan flowing with milk and honey and of Israel's rule over it, in what purports to be a quotation from Scripture—Gen. 1:28 signifies election and the assurance of salvation. If current conditions do not yet corroborate this, they soon will, when Christians "have been perfected as heirs of the Lord's covenant," the conferral of whose rewards depend upon compliance with its demands.

This early midrash on our verse sets the tone for much of the patristic exegesis that was to follow. Although subsequent commentators differed widely in their approach to the conferral of dominion, they too

---

8. *Epistula Barnabae* 6.12–19, in *Die apostolischen Väter: Erster Teil*, ed. Francis Xavier Funk and Karl Bihlmeyer, 2nd ed., Sammlung ausgewählter kirchen- und dogmengeschichtlicher Quellenschriften 2,1,1 (Tübingen, 1956), pp. 17–18; I have followed the translation of Robert A. Kraft, *Barnabas and the Didache*, The Apostolic Fathers: A New Translation and Commentary 3 (New York, 1965), pp. 100–101.

related the motif to the distinctive message and circumstances of the church, at the same time as they preserved the teleological and covenantal understanding of the primordial blessing that had characterized the Hebrew Bible itself. Irenaeus of Lyons followed Pseudo-Barnabas in concluding that God had conferred dominion on his son, who transmitted it to human beings for the sake of their spiritual perfection.[9] Many agreed that human preeminence in the natural order thereby expressed and served God's overall purpose in creating the world,[10] a point that responded to the attacks of pagan critics.[11] According to their respective interpretations of "image" (*eikón*) and "likeness" (*homoíosis*) in Gen. 1:26, most discerned some link between the divine resemblance in human beings and their dominion. Either power proceeded from the divine image, which endowed humans with their distinctive rational and spiritual faculties[12] and facilitated control even over creatures with greater physical strength;[13] or humans might use their power to nurture their still unrealized likeness to the deity;[14] or possibly both.[15] Different

9. Irenaeus of Lyons, *Demonstratio praedicationis apostolicae* 97, PO 12,5:728–29; cf. Origen, *Fragmenta e catenis in Matthaeum*, GCS 41,1:15.

10. Origen, *Homélies sur la Genèse (In Genesim homiliae)* 1.12, ed. Henri de Lubac and Louis Doutreleau, rev. ed., SC 7² (Paris, 1976), pp. 54–57; Pseudo-Basil the Great, *Sermones de creatione hominis* 1.8, ed. Hadwiga Hörner, *Gregorii Nysseni opera: Supplementum* (Leiden, 1972), pp. 13–16; Gregory of Nyssa, *De opificio hominis* 8, PG 44:143–46; John Chrysostom, *Homiliae in Genesim* 8.3, PG 53:72; and T. Jansma, "Une homélie anonyme sur la création du monde," *L'Orient syrien* 5 (1960), 390. On the attribution of the *Sermones de creatione hominis* to Basil, cf. the viewpoints of E. Stephanou, "Le sixième jour de l'Hexaeméron de S. Basile," *Echos d'Orient* 31 (1932), 385–98; S. Giet, "S. Basile a-t-il donné une suite à l'Hexaeméron?" *Recherches de science religieuse* 33 (1946), 317–58; Alexis Smets and Michel van Esbroeck, in their edition of Basil, *Sur l'origine de l'homme (De creatione hominis)*, SC 160 (Paris, 1960), pp. 13–26; Emmanuel Amand de Mendietta, "Les deux homélies sur la création de l'homme que les manuscrits attribuent à Basile de Césarée ou à Grégoire de Nysse," in *Zetesis: Album amicorum, door vrienden en collega's aangeboden aan Prof. Dr. E. de Strycker* (Antwerp, 1973), pp. 695–716; and Hadwiga Hörner, ed. cit., pp. vii–ix.

11. Origen, *Contre Celse (Contra Celsum)* 4.23, ed. Marcel Borret, 5 vols., SC 132, 136, 147, 150, 227 (Paris, 1967–76), 2:238–41; John Chrysostom, *Homiliae in Genesim* 9.3, PG 53:78.

12. Pseudo-Clement of Rome, *Recognitiones* 5.2.1, GCS 51:166, *Homiliae* 16.19, 17.7, GCS 42:226f., 232; Basil the Great, *Homiliae in hexaemeron* 9.5, PG 29:199–204; Pseudo-Basil, *Sermones de creatione hominis* 1.6, 1.8, ed. Hörner, pp. 10–16; Severian of Gabala, *In cosmogoniam homiliae* 6.6, PG 56:492; Theodoret of Cyrrhus, *Quaestiones in Genesim* 20, PG 80:103–10.

13. Pseudo-Clement of Rome, *Homiliae* 10.3, GCS 42:143; Didymus the Blind of Alexandria, *Sur la Genèse*, ed. Pierre Nautin and Louis Doutreleau, 2 vols., SC 233, 244 (Paris, 1976–78), 1:152–53; Gregory of Nyssa, *De opificio hominis* 7, PG 44:141–42.

14. Irenaeus of Lyons, *Demonstratio praedicationis apostolicae* 97, PO 12,5:728–29.

15. Among many works on the history of the doctrine of humans' creation in the image of God, see Jervell, *Imago Dei*; Altmann, "*Homo imago Dei*"; Peter Schwanz, *Imago Dei als christologisch-anthropologisches Problem in der Geschichte der alten Kirche von Paulus bis Clemens von Alexandrien* (Halle, 1970); and R. A. Markus, "'Imago' and 'similitudo' in Augustine," *Revue des études augustiniennes* 10 (1965), 125–43.

views on the spiritual state of the first human(s) also resulted in varying thoughts on the essence of the dominion that God bestowed in Gen. 1:28—whether it included all of the beasts,[16] if it extended to the heavenly creatures,[17] and, most significantly, how it was to be implemented in practice. As Pseudo-Barnabas construed it, dominion or rule over the land could serve to validate the salvation of God's faithful, in political as well as spiritual terms. Church fathers who saw a need to develop and achieve perfection in the terrestrial sphere, prior to attaining the ultimate spiritual reward, elaborated on the numerous ways in which humans mastered and subdued the natural environment, agriculturally, technologically, and artistically. Didymus the Blind departed from the allegorical tradition of Alexandria in commenting upon our verse:[18]

"And master it" signifies an extensive power, since one cannot say of him who has a limited power that he has dominion. God has made this gift to the human being . . . in order that land for growing and land for mining, rich in numerous, diverse materials, be under the rule of the human being. Actually, the human being receives bronze, iron, silver, gold, and many other metals from the ground; it is also rendered to him so that he can feed and clothe himself. So great is the dominion the human being has received over the land that he transforms it technologically—when he changes it into glass, pottery, and other similar things. That is in effect what it means for the human being to rule "the whole earth."[19]

Nevertheless, those who adhered more stringently to the Alexandrian traditions of spiritual exegesis followed Origen in construing the animals subjected to human dominion as

either the things which proceed from the inclination of the soul and the thought of the heart, or those which are brought forth from bodily

16. Origen, *Fragmenta in Genesim*, PG 12:97–98, responded in the negative, because Gen. 1:28 made no mention of wild animals.

17. Affirmative responses appear in Irenaeus of Lyons, *Demonstratio praedicationis apostolicae* 12, PO 12,5:668; Pseudo-Clement of Rome, *Homiliae* 3.7, GCS 42:59; Jansma, "Une homélie anonyme," p. 393.

18. Didymus the Blind, *Sur la Genèse*, 1:164–67, following the Nautin/Doutreleau reconstruction of the fragmented text. See also Irenaeus of Lyons, *Demonstratio praedicationis apostolicae* 11, PO 12,5:667–68; Pseudo-Clement of Rome, *Homiliae* 10.3, GCS 42:143 (and cf. 3.36, GCS 42:69–70); Clement of Alexandria, *Stromata* 6.14.115, GCS 52:489–90, *Protrepticus* 10.94, GCS 12³:68–69; John Chrysostom, *Homiliae in Genesim* 9.3, PG 53:78; and Severian of Gabala, *In cosmogoniam homiliae* 6.6–7, PG 56:492.

19. Following LXX in the citation of Gen. 1:28.

desires and the impulses of the flesh. The saints and those who preserve the blessing of God in themselves exercise dominion over these things, guiding the total man by the will of the spirit. But on the other hand, the same things which are brought forth by the voices of the flesh and pleasures of the body hold greater sway over sinners.[20]

Just as it had done for Philo, such an allegorical interpretation of Gen. 1:28 contributed to Origen's doctrine of a completely spiritual primordial man created in the divine image and likeness, thus distinct from the carnal man fashioned in Gen. 2:7 and existing in a blissful state that rivaled that of the final glory.[21]

While the fathers vigorously disputed their interpretations of other Genesis passages on the creation of human beings, they did not deem their resulting, divergent appreciations of Gen. 1:28b to be mutually exclusive. Clement of Alexandria, Didymus the Blind, and John Chrysostom all included both the technological mastery of nature and the subjection of the passions to the will within the dominion vested in the first parents. Boundaries between the Alexandrian, Cappadocian, and Antiochene "schools" of exegetical thought appear to have mattered relatively little in this regard. Furthermore, virtually all of those who commented on the power granted humans in Gen. 1:28 affirmed the covenantal character of its conferral. Like his image in which God had created man and woman,[22] dominion constituted a gift and a reward, conditional upon human loyalty and upon compliance with the divine will. Origen's observation that saints dominate their passions while passions dominate sinners evokes the like-minded rabbinic homily on the verb for exercising rule in Gen. 1:28, *rdh:* The pious will rule (*yirdu*) and the sinful will be ruled (*yeradu,* or will descend, *yer*e*du*).[23] Formalizing this expectation in his ban on the fruit of the tree of knowledge, God

---

20. Origen, *Homélies sur la Genèse* 10.16, pp. 68–69; I have departed slightly from the rendition of Origen, *Homilies on Genesis and Exodus,* tr. Ronald E. Heine, Fathers of the Church 71 (Washington, D.C., 1982), p. 69.

21. Clement of Alexandria, *Stromata* 6.14.115, GCS 52:489–90; Origen, "Ein Bruchstück . . . über Genesis i, 28," ed. Paul Glaue, *Schriften der hessischen Hochschulen, Universität Giessen* 1,11 (1928), 6–12; Didymus the Blind, *Sur la Genèse* 1:154–55; Pseudo-Basil, *Sermones de creatione hominis* 1.8, 1.19, ed. Hörner, pp. 13–16, 36–39; and John Chrysostom, *Homiliae in Genesim* 9.3, PG 53:78. For the views of Philo, see above, Chapter 2, n. 22.

22. On the question of woman's creation in the image of God, see Horowitz, "The Image of God"; and Kari Elisabeth Borresen, "Imago Dei, privilège masculin? Interprétation augustinienne et pseudo-augustinienne de *Gen* 1,27 et *1 Cor* 11,7," *Augustinianum* 25 (1985), 213–34.

23. See above, Chapter 2, at nn. 72–73.

sought to temper the arrogance that rulership might nurture.[24] When Adam and Eve ate from the tree and fell from paradise, they forfeited much of the dominion that once was theirs. Participating in the sinfulness of the first parents and inheriting their punishment, the descendants of Adam and Eve no longer enjoy the power that God intended his human creatures to have, a power that God will restore only with the final redemption.[25] Ephrem Syrus and Severian of Gabala were exceptional in this regard. Noting that humans could neither fill nor master the earth while confined to the Garden of Eden, Ephrem asserted that the blessing of Gen. 1:28b anticipated the fall from paradise, preceding it in time only to avoid the appearance of rewarding sin.[26] More than the other church fathers, who generally admitted that God graciously left postlapsarian humans with some measure of superiority in nature,[27] Severian stressed that the human capacity for the technological and artistic, deriving from the *imago Dei,* truly assumed relevance only after the fall.[28]

Influenced, perhaps, by Jewish traditions of the intertestamental period and by the ideas of Hellenistic philosophers, the Greek fathers paid considerably more attention to the motif of dominion in Gen. 1:28 than the talmudic rabbis did. Still, dominion was rarely a controversial issue for them, a subject with vital theological consequences that prompted extensive discussion and debate. As did the texts of classical rabbinic Judaism, patristic and medieval Christian interest in our verse centered on its call for sexual reproduction, to which the remainder of this volume will be devoted almost entirely.

"Be fertile and increase . . ." (*Auxánesthe kaì plethúnesthe . . .*)

Commenting on the first half of the primordial blessing, the early church fathers had to react to several problems that did not trouble their rabbinic counterparts and that give the classical Christian interpretation of our verse a distinctive and intriguing character. Patristic and medi-

24. For instance, Irenaeus of Lyons, *Demonstratio praedicationis apostolicae* 15, PO 12,5:670.
25. This theme pervaded not only patristic literature, but pseudepigraphic and rabbinic texts as well.
26. Ephrem Syrus, *In Genesim commentarius* 1.30–31, CSCO 152:24–25, 153:18.
27. Cf. John Chrysostom, *Homiliae in Genesim* 9.4, PG 53:78–79.
28. Severian of Gabala, *In cosmogoniam homiliae* 6.6, PG 56:492.

eval exegetes approached the biblical text with a theological commitment to the doctrine of original sin and the resulting fallen state of human nature—ideas that bore not only on the injunction to master the earth but also on the mandate to populate it. Owing to their rebellion in Eden, humans had forfeited an integral part of their original blessedness, including their ability to obey divine law of their own accord. How did postlapsarian procreation measure up to the divine expectation that the primordial blessing conveyed? Moreover, how did the instruction to procreate comport with the Christian idealization of celibacy, or, to be more precise, how did the ideal affect the exegesis of our verse? Understood literally, Gen. 1:28 suggested that God wanted Adam and Eve to engage in sexual intercourse, their presumed spiritual perfection and immortality notwithstanding. Should the Christian therefore interpret this verse allegorically? But did not the church sanctify both marriage and procreation? Or perhaps the instructions in our text applied to postlapsarian humanity. Why then did God prescribe them before the fall? And on a practical level, spokesmen for the church could not overlook the political, ecclesiological implications of their exegesis, for as they polemicized against diverse heresies, they had also to remain sensitive to the attractiveness of specific heretical doctrines for the Christian community. Periodically throughout the ancient and medieval periods, Gnostic and other dualist groups challenged the positive function of the Old Testament in the true God's economy of salvation, denying all value to involvement in the affairs of this world. From such a perspective, the recurrence of which attests to its popularity, how could one justify the life of worldly, sexual pursuits enjoined in Gen. 1:28? The Gnostic *Poimandres,* for example, alludes unmistakably to our verse and comments: "Let the understanding person understand that he himself is immortal and that sexual desire is the cause of death." In this Hermetic text, Robert Segal noted, procreative sexual intercourse represents "the worst form of materiality."[29] On the other hand, for

---

29. *Corpus hermeticum* 1.18, 1:13; Robert A. Segal, *The Poimandres as Myth: Scholarly Theory and Gnostic Meaning,* Religion and Reason 33 (Berlin, 1986), p. 43. Cf. also the allusion to Gen. 1:28 by Justinus Gnosticus, cited by Hippolytus of Rome, *Refutatio omnium haeresium* 5.26, GCS 26: 128. On issues of sexuality in early Christian interpretation of Gen. 1–3, see Elaine H. Pagels, "Exegesis and Exposition of the Genesis Creation Accounts in Selected Texts from Nag Hammadi," in *Nag Hammadi, Gnosticism, and Early Christianity,* ed. Charles W. Hedrick and Robert Hodgson, Jr. (Peabody, Mass., 1986), pp. 257–85, and "Adam and Eve, Christ, and the Church: A Survey of Second Century Controversies Concerning Marriage," in *The New Testament and Gnosis: Essays in Honour of Robert McL. Wilson,* ed. A. H. B. Logan and A. J. M. Wedderburn (Edinburgh, 1983), pp. 146–75.

Pelagian teachers, the commandment to procreate fueled the argument against any congenital guilt inherited from the original sin of the first parents. Monastic asceticism also invited the attacks of Jews, who cited the primordial blessing to demonstrate alleged Christian subversion of God's will.

As in the case of dominion, most Christian expositors of Scripture agreed that the blessing of "be fertile and increase" has survived the fall at least to some degree. The world's large human population testifies to it, and the need to maintain human life on earth in anticipation of the redemption requires it. Not to be misconstrued as sanctioning purpose-less sexual pleasure,[30] Gen. 1:28 reveals that God established sexual reproduction within the natural order that he created, and Irenaeus of Lyons and Clement of Alexandria cited the verse in their defense of marriage against heretical condemnations. In good Stoic tradition, Clement also praised the civic benefits that accrue from marriage, and he argued that compliance with the mandate of Gen. 1:28 allows humans to share in God's role as creator: "He has said, 'increase,' and one must obey; for in this manner one becomes the image of God, inasmuch as one participates, as a human being, in the birth of a human being."[31] Yet all the fathers concurred that in the present, postlapsarian, Christian era the virtues of celibacy—the life that Clement of Alexandria termed angelic—exceed those of marriage and reproduction. God's desire that his earth be settled and inhabited has been fulfilled; the overwhelming consensus held that the biblical obligation to reproduce, which once motivated the Hebrew patriarchs to take several wives, had lapsed.[32] The true virgin, wrote Pseudo-Clement of Rome,[33] renounces all the goods of this world, including the blessings of Gen. 1:28. Even Meth-

---

30. Methodius of Olympus, *Le banquet (Convivium)* 3.11, ed. Herbert Musurillo and Victor-Henry Debidour, SC 95 (Paris, 1963), pp. 114–15.

31. Clement of Alexandria, *Paedagogus* 2.10.83, GCS 12³:208. See also 2.10, passim, pp. 208–26; *Stromata* 2.23, GCS 52:188–94, for Clement's praise of the civic virtues of marriage, and book 3, passim, esp. 3.6.45, pp. 216–17, for his identification of the opponents of marriage as Antichrists. See also Irenaeus of Lyons, *Contre les hérésies (Adversus haereses)* 1.28.1, ed. Adelin Rousseau et al., 5 vols. in 10 pts., SC 100,1–2, 152–53, 210–11, 263–64, 293–94 (Paris, 1965–82), 1,2:354–57; and Athanasius of Alexandria, *Epistula ad Amun*, in *Discipline générale antique (IVe–IXe s.)*, 2, ed. Périclès-Pierre Joannou, Fonti 9 (Rome, 1963), pp. 67–68.

32. For example, H. Fleisch, ed., "Fragments de Clément d'Alexandrie conservés en arabe," *Mélanges de l'Université Saint Joseph* 27 (1947), 68–69; Basil the Great, *Epistula* 160, *Lettres*, ed. Yves Courtonne, 3 vols. (Paris, 1957–66), 2:91; Basil of Ancyra, *De virginitate* 3, 55, PG 30:673–76, 779–80.

33. Pseudo-Clement of Rome, *Epistula 1 ad virgines* 3.6, in *Patres apostolici*, ed. Francis Xavier Funk, 2nd ed., 2 vols. (Tübingen, 1901), 2:3.

odius of Olympus, when presenting the view that some must still comply with this biblical precept in order to maintain the human species, identified procreation as the pursuit of an imperfect community:

> The declaration and commandment of God concerning procreation is avowedly still being fulfilled, as the creator forms humans even now. . . . But once the rivers shall have ceased emptying into the reservoir of the sea and the light shall have been separated completely from the darkness . . . , once the land shall finally have stopped yielding its fruits along with creeping and four-footed creatures, and once the predetermined number of human beings shall have been filled, from then on there will be abstinence from procreation. Yet now it is necessary that humans participate in forming the image of God, while the world is still being fashioned and completed. For it has been commanded, "be fertile and increase." And it is not fitting to detest the commandment of the creator, owing to which we ourselves have come into existence.[34]

Thus interpreted, Gen. 1:28 quickly became a polemical issue, as Jews accused Christianity of forsaking biblical instruction and as Christians insisted that the old had given way to the new. Eusebius of Caesarea paraphrased the hostile question of a Jewish contemporary:

> If we claim that the Gospel teaching of our Savior Christ bids us worship God as did the men of old, and the pre-Mosaic men of God, and that our religion is the same as theirs, and our knowledge of God the same, why were they keenly concerned with marriage and reproduction, while we to some extent disregard it? . . . [Eusebius responded:] The men renowned for piety before Moses are recorded as having lived when human life was first beginning and organizing itself, while we live when it is nearing its end. And so they were anxious for the increase of their descendants, that men might multiply, that the human race might grow (*aúxontos*) and increase (*plethúontos*) at that time, and reach its height. But these things are of little moment to us, who believe the world to be perishing and running down and reaching its last end, since it is expressly said that the gospel teaching will be at the door before the consummation of life, while a new creation and the birth of another age at no distant time is foretold. Such is one reply, and this is a second: The men of old days lived an easier and a freer life, and their care of home and family did not compete with their leisure for religion . . . , but in

---

34. Methodius of Olympus, *Le banquet* 2.1, pp. 68–71.

our days there are many external interests that draw us away, and involve us in uncongenial thoughts, and seduce us from our zeal for the things which please God. . . . And I might give this third reason why the godly men of old were so devoted to the procreation of children. The rest of mankind were increasing in evil . . . , while they themselves, a very scanty remnant, had divorced themselves from the life of the many, and from common association with other men. They were living apart from other nations and in isolation, and were organizing a new kind of polity. They were evolving a life of true wisdom and religion, unmingled with other men. They wished to hand on to posterity the fiery seed of their own religion; they did not intend that their piety should fail and perish when they themselves died, and so they had foresight for production and rearing of children. . . . Hence many prophets and righteous men, indeed, even our Lord and savior himself, with his apostles and disciples, have come from their line.[35]

As Eusebius rationalized the reproductive concerns of the biblical patriarchs and explained why Christians no longer share them, his terminology betrayed Gen. 1:28 lurking in the background. It is curious that Eusebius did not openly group procreation with the Old Testament commandments rendered obsolete by the passion of Christ. Rather, he repeatedly labeled it a noble concern of those who preceded Moses and the formal institution of the Sinaitic covenant. These people formed a distinct, frequently oppressed community of holy individuals, isolated by choice from the godless majority, who rightly desired to perpetuate the "fiery seed" of their religion. Their motives eventually bore fruit in the founders of Christianity.[36] Could Eusebius have been responding tacitly to the talmudic argument discussed above in Chapter 3, that the precept of "be fertile and increase" no longer pertained to the Gentile Noachides but belonged exclusively to the Jews?[37] Eusebius' description of the pre-Sinaitic community—oppressed, isolated, and pious— suggests a perceived typological correspondence between it and the church of his day. While Eusebius had no choice but to answer the charges of his adversary and vindicate the Christian idealization of celibacy, he laid claim to the legacy of the biblical patriarchs instead of

35. Eusebius of Caesarea, *Demonstratio evangelica* 1.9.1–13, GCS 23:40–41; with but slight variation, I have followed Eusebius, *Proof of the Gospel,* tr. W. J. Ferrar, 2 vols. (London, 1920), 1:50–52.

36. Cf. Basil of Ancyra, *De virginitate* 55, PG 30:779–80, on the appropriateness of sexual reproduction in the early biblical period.

37. See above, Chapter 3, at n. 88.

disavowing it, despite their marriage and reproduction. The church had inherited the covenant of Hebrew Scripture, which the blessing of "be fertile and increase" itself expressed, even though circumstances no longer warranted that the pious have children. No wonder that, according to Eusebius, the patriarchs forswore sexual relations after fathering their heirs, and that only then did they truly find favor in the eyes of God.[38] And in the wake of the Incarnation, the primordial blessing was realized completely in the growth of the church. "All who blessed the Christ, glorifying the greatness of their teaching by word and deed, received in return the blessing of God, increasing and multiplying daily, according to the divine commandment, 'Be fertile and increase, and fill the earth.' "[39]

Eusebius' junior contemporary, the fourth-century Iranian monk Aphrahat, also recorded the accusations of at least one Jewish polemicist, who cited Gen. 1:28, 9:1, and 9:7 and other pentateuchal guarantees of fertility and who then exclaimed to the Christians:[40] "But you do a thing which was not commanded by God, for you have received a curse and have multiplied barrenness. You have prohibited procreation, the blessings of righteous men. You do not take wives, and you do not become wives for husbands. You hate procreation, a blessing given by God." Truly incensed, Aphrahat retorted that, the divine promise of fertility to Adam and Noah notwithstanding, procreation did not result in unmitigated bliss for God's creatures. The flood, the destruction of Sodom, the extinction of an entire generation of Hebrews in the desert en route to Canaan, the divine reckoning of idolaters "as if they were nothing"—these and other historical developments proved the ultimate futility of procreation. Perhaps fearful of veering too far from Scripture, Aphrahat then hesitated, trying not to disparage a divine institution. "He created marriage, worldly procreation, and it is very good; but virginity is more excellent than it." God deems compliance with the instructions of Gen. 1:28 of secondary importance, wrote Aphrahat; "one man who does his will is more excellent and distinguished before his majesty than myriads and thousands of those who do evil." Joshua, Elijah, Elisha, and Jeremiah were all celibate, and even Moses himself,

---

38. Eusebius of Caesarea, *Demonstratio evangelica* 1.9.16–21, GCS 23:42–43.
39. Ibid. 9.3.8, GCS 23:410, tr. Ferrar, 2:157.
40. Aphrahat, *Demonstrationes adversus Judaeos* 18.1–8, PS 1,1,2:817–38; my translation follows Jacob Neusner, *Aphrahat and Judaism: The Christian-Jewish Argument in Fourth-Century Iran,* Studia post-biblica 11 (Leiden, 1971), pp. 77–81.

contended the monk, abstained from marriage and sex. Aphrahat's allusion to and adaptation of Jewish aggadic motifs is noteworthy. Rabbinic midrash, we recall, criticized Joshua's prevention of marital relations among the Israelites, reasoning that for this wrongdoing he died without an heir.[41] And the Pharisaic House of Shammai had reportedly stipulated the legal requirements of "be fertile and increase" on the basis of Moses' behavior—his abstinence from conjugal activity after fathering two sons.[42] Considering this tradition in Chapter 3, we suggested that the association of Moses with the commandment of procreation bespoke its covenantal implications; rather than a commitment to the entire human species, "be fertile and increase" signified the election of Israel. Like Eusebius, Aphrahat also sought to identify with the saints of ancient Israel in their attitude toward procreation; who more than Moses embodied the piety that God had legislated in the Old Testament? Although Aphrahat did not apologize for the reproductive activity of the Hebrew patriarchs as Eusebius had done, his reply to his Jewish interlocutor corroborates his linkage of Gen. 1:28 and the biblical covenant.

Arguments such as these did not exhaust the problems that Gen. 1:28 put before the patristic exegete. As we have noted, an assortment of non-Jewish groups also used this passage in their attacks upon the church, and if in answer to the Jews the church fathers generally agreed in their defense of celibacy, the challenges of Gnostics and heretics fomented more serious doctrinal controversy. Ecclesiological considerations aside, the divine call to "be fertile and increase," ostensibly mandating human sexual reproduction in a paradisiacal state of grace, remained a thorny and divisive issue in and of itself. In surveying the extant patristic sources, it is helpful to distinguish between three interpretative tendencies whose origins and careers we can in fact chart, in contrast to the more elusive rabbinic traditions discussed in previous chapters.

First, some patristic exegetes asserted that physical procreation did not befit human life in Eden, and therefore they interpreted the mandate of Gen. 1:28a allegorically. Most insistent in this regard was Origen, who also construed the conferral of dominion in Gen. 1:28b as symbolizing the triumph of the will over the passions and who extended his

---

41. See above, Chapter 2, at n. 50.
42. See above, Chapter 3, esp. at n. 11.

allegorical interpretation of "be fertile and increase" to Gen. 1:22 and 9:1 as well.[43] True to his belief in the incorporeality of the man created by God in Gen. 1, and convinced that differentiation within the human species subverted that primal perfection,[44] Origen seems to have sympathized with the aforecited notion of the Hermetic *Poimandres:* Understood literally, "be fertile and increase" conveyed a message leading to spiritual death rather than to life.[45] Accordingly, Origen maintained that these first words of God to his human creatures actually referred to the virtues of the human soul that derived from the divine image:

> The spirit is said to be male; the soul can be called female. If these have concord and agreement among themselves, they increase and multiply in their conjunction and they produce good inclinations and understandings or useful thoughts for their children, by which they fill the earth and have dominion over it. This means they reorient the inclination of the flesh, which has been subjected to themselves, toward better purposes and have dominion over it.[46]

Alternatively, the blessing of fertility belonged to the community of Christian faithful, just as Pseudo-Barnabas had written concerning dominion. Origen also espoused this interpretation,[47] which even his Christian critic Methodius expressed most eloquently, referring to the salvation and virtue produced in the fruitful marriage of Christ and his church.

> For in this manner the precept of "be fertile and increase" is appropriately fulfilled, as the latter [the church] increases daily in amplitude, beauty, and numbers, owing to the conjunction and union with the Word, which comes down to us even now and ecstasizes in the commemoration of his passion.[48]

43. Origen, *Selecta in Genesim*, PG 12:105–6; *In Lucam homiliae* 11.1, GCS 49:66–67.

44. Origen, *Traité des principes (De principiis)* 3.6.4, ed. Henri Crouzel and Manleo Simonetti, 5 vols., SC 252–53, 268–69, 312 (Paris, 1978–84), 3:242–45—contrast his defense of diversity in the material world, 2.9.5–6, 1:360–67—and *Homiliae in primum Regnorum librum* 4, GCS 33:6. See also Richard A. Norris, *God and World in Early Christian Theology: A Study in Justin Martyr, Irenaeus, Tertullian, and Origen* (London, 1967), esp. pp. 145–49.

45. So concluded Epiphanius of Salamis in a letter to John of Jerusalem written in 394 and subsequently translated into Latin by Jerome, *Epistula* 51.4, CSEL 54:402.

46. Origen, *Homélies sur la Genèse* 1.15, pp. 66–67, with several variations from *Homilies on Genesis*, tr. Heine, p. 68. See also Pseudo-Basil, *Sermones de creatione hominis* 2.5, ed. Hörner, pp. 46–48.

47. Origen, *Contre Celse* 7.21, 4:62–65; and *In Lucam homiliae* 11.1, GCS 49:66–67.

48. Methodius of Olympus, *Le banquet* 3.8, pp. 106–9. See the similar interpretations of Pseudo-Clement of Rome, *Epistula altera ad Corinthios* 14.2, in *Die apostolischen Väter*, ed. Funk

Methodius' association of "be fertile and increase" with the marital and covenantal overtones of the Mass adumbrates the ideas of medieval kabbalists a full millennium before Moses de León, and we shall return to this motif yet again. As for the interpretations of Gen. 1:28 propounded by Origen and Methodius, each manifests a dualistic influence in its adamant exclusion of sexual reproduction from the primal state of grace.[49] According to Origen, the Bible states (Gen. 1:27) that God originally created humans male and female simply to make the allegory of Gen. 1:28 more credible![50]

Second, other church fathers made it clear that while Gen. 1:28a in fact refers to childbearing, the instruction to reproduce sexually was first applicable after the fall. Not only was sexual activity inappropriate in paradise, but it neither occurred nor was supposed to occur before the expulsion from Eden and the conception of Cain.[51] Some specified further that when God created the first parents he consciously provided for their fallen, mortal state, which he then foresaw,[52] while several writers maintained that if Adam and Eve had not sinned God would have had them "be fertile and increase" in some miraculous, asexual manner. Gregory of Nyssa rejected the Origenist view that multiplication detracted from the perfection of humanity. If progeny benefited the first parents and the world, procreation should not have been inconceivable in the absence of sin. He thus disputed with those who

> say that before the sin there is no account of birth, or of travail, or of the desire that tends to procreation, but when they were banished from paradise after their sin, and the woman was condemned by the sentence of travail, Adam thus entered with his consort upon the intercourse of married life, and then took place the beginning of procreation. If, then, marriage did not exist in paradise, nor travail, nor birth, they say that it follows as a necessary conclusion that human souls would not have

---

and Bihlmeyer, p. 77; and Pseudo-Basil, *Sermones de creatione hominis* 2.5, ed. Hörner, pp. 46–48. On the association of "be fertile and increase" with the mass, see below, Chapter 6.

49. In this regard, see the fragment published in Claude Jenkins, "Origen on I Corinthians," *Journal of Theological Studies*, o.s. 9 (1908), 370.

50. Origen, *Homélies sur la Genèse* 1.14, pp. 64–67; cf. also *Comentarii in Matthaeum* 14.16, GCS 40:321–22.

51. In addition to others cited in adjacent footnotes here, see *Book of the Cave of Treasures*, tr. E. A. Wallis Budge (London, 1927), p. 69; and Athanasius of Alexandria, *Expositio in Psalmos* 50.7, PG 27:239–40; and cf. also Robert Graves and Raphael Patai, *Hebrew Myths: The Book of Genesis* (1963; repr., New York, 1983), ch. 15.

52. For example, *Sibylline Oracles* 1:54–55; John Chrysostom, *De virginitate* 17, PG 48:545–46; and Theodoret of Cyrrhus, *Quaestiones in Genesim* 37, PG 80:135–36.

existed in plurality had not the grace of immortality fallen away to mortality, and marriage preserved our race by means of descendants, introducing the offspring of the departing to take their place, so that in a certain way the sin that entered into the world was profitable for the life of man. For the human race would have remained in the pair of the first-formed, had not the fear of death impelled their nature to provide succession.

Arguing from Jesus' description (Gregory quotes Lk. 20:35–36) of the life of the resurrection as angelic, and reasoning that "the resurrection promises us nothing else than the restoration of the fallen to their ancient state," Gregory concluded:

> Yet while, as has been said, there is no marriage among them, the armies of the angels are in countless myriads. . . . So, in the same way, if there had not come upon us as a result of sin a change for the worse, and removal from equality with the angels, neither should we have needed marriage that we might multiply. But whatever the mode of increase in the angelic nature is—unspeakable and inconceivable by human conjectures, except that it assuredly exists—it would have operated also in the case of men, who (Ps. 8:6) were "made a little lower than the angels," to increase mankind to the measure determined by the creator.[53]

With or without this asexual, prelapsarian procreation, the resulting valuation of our verse was the same: Its reproductive mandate epitomized the fallen state of human nature—even if it provided the means for blessing and healing in such a condition—and ranked noticeably below the Christian ideal of celibacy. Like the allegorical interpretation discussed above, with which it was not incompatible, this response to the problem of Gen. 1:28 identified sexual reproduction with human mortality; as one tendency in classical rabbinic thought also maintained, one necessitated the other.[54]

A third approach, which ultimately prevailed in the traditions of the

---

53. Gregory of Nyssa, *De opificio hominis* 17, PG 44:187–90, tr. (with minor variations) in *Gregory of Nyssa, A Select Library of Nicene and Post-Nicene Fathers* 2,5 (1893; repr., New York, 1917), pp. 406–7. While John Chrysostom similarly elaborated on the angelic life of the first parents in paradise, he alone of the major patristic writers denied that God directed the injunction of "be fertile and increase" to them before their fall; see *Homiliae in Genesim* 10.3–4, 15.4, PG 53:85–86, 123–24.

54. See above, Chapter 2, at nn. 77ff.

Western church, began to crystallize in the works of Theophilus of Antioch, Irenaeus of Lyons, and Theodore of Mopsuestia. In contrast to Origen, these church fathers flatly rejected the Philonic notion of a dual creation, whereby God first made a celestial, intellectual human in the divine image (Gen. 1:26) and his angelic subordinates subsequently molded (Gen. 2:7) an earthly man out of matter. Rather, Theophilus and Irenaeus insisted on the creation of a single human being, created in a state of spiritual infancy, as it were, but endowed with lordship over all other creatures and the concomitant ability to realize his innate potential of spiritual perfection. Several additional motifs in the anthropology of these theologians led them to a radically different appreciation of Gen. 1:28a. Above all, they proposed that God created Adam and Eve in an intermediate state, midway between mortality and immortality. Theophilus wrote:

> When God set man, as we have already said, in paradise to work it and guard it . . . , God transferred him out of the earth from which he was made into paradise, giving him an opportunity for progress so that by growing (*auxánon*) and becoming mature, and furthermore having been declared a god, he might also ascend into heaven, possessing immortality. For man was created in an intermediate state, neither entirely mortal nor entirely immortal, but capable of either state; similarly the place paradise—as regards beauty—was created intermediate between the world and heaven.[55]

To achieve immortality, these progenitors of the human species had to increase and to mature, both in number and in perfection, fulfilling the terrestrial vocation ordained by God for their composite nature of body and soul. This distinctive blend of physical and spiritual characteristics reflects the divine image in human beings, suiting the teleology of the creation and explaining why God did not make humans perfect *ab initio*. In the words of Irenaeus,

> God therefore has dominion over all things since he alone is uncreated, is before all things, and is the cause of existence of all things. All else remains subjected to God. . . . Through this system, such arrangement, and this kind of governance, humanity was created according to

---

55. Theophilus of Antioch, *Ad Autolycum* 2.24, ed. Robert M. Grant (Oxford, 1970), pp. 66–67.

the image and established in the likeness of the uncreated God. The Father decided and commanded; the Son molded and shaped; the Spirit nourished and developed. Humanity slowly progresses, approaches perfection, and draws near to the uncreated God. The perfect is the uncreated, God. It was therefore appropriate for humanity first to be made, being made to grow, having grown to be strengthened, being stronger to multiply (*plethynthénai, multiplicari*), having multiplied to grow strong (*enischŷsai, convalescere*), having grown strong to be glorified, and once glorified to see its Lord. God is the one who is going to be seen; the vision of God produces incorruptibility; incorruptibility makes a person approach God.[56]

As Robert Brown demonstrated, Irenaeus did not describe the career intended for postlapsarian humans here, but outlined an optimal program, divinely ordained for the first parents.[57] Reproduction and multiplication figured significantly in this divine scheme, exemplifying the realization of human potential, the passage from infancy to maturity, and the attainment of perfection—not the evil and decay perceived by Origen. For Theophilus and even more certainly for Irenaeus, both of whom alluded to Gen. 1:28 with their use of the Septuagint's verbs for "be fertile and increase" (*auxánon, plethynthénai*), God intended the primordial blessing in its plain, literal sense, referring to the physical procreation of children—hence the need for parental convalescence[58]— on the part of unfallen man and women. As the bishop of Lyons summarized elsewhere, "He fashioned him for growth and increase, inasmuch as Scripture states, 'be fertile and increase.'"[59]

How, then, did human sin and the fall from Eden relate to sexual activity? Antonio Orbe argued at length that for Irenaeus, as for Philo, Theophilus, and Clement of Alexandria, the tree of knowledge of good and evil represented marriage and the sexual activity within it.[60] God

56. Irenaeus of Lyons, *Contre les hérésies* 4.38.3, 4:954–57; I have departed only slightly from the translation of J. Patout Burns, ed., *Theological Anthropology* (Philadelphia, Pa., 1981), pp. 24–25.

57. Robert F. Brown, "On the Necessary Imperfection of Creation: Irenaeus' *Adversus Haereses* IV, 38," *Scottish Journal of Theology* 28 (1975), 17–25; see also Etienne Delaruelle, "La doctrine de la personne humaine, signe de contradiction entre Christianisme et paganisme au IIIᵉ siècle," *Bulletin de littérature ecclésiastique* 53 (1952), 168–70.

58. Brown, loc. cit., specifies that *convalescere* here means to regain one's original strength, not to recover from the illness of sin.

59. Irenaeus of Lyons, *Contre les hérésies* 4.11.1, 4:498–99.

60. My appreciation of Theophilus and Irenaeus owes much to the insightful analysis of Antonio Orbe, *Antropología de San Ireneo*, Biblioteca de autores cristianos 286 (Madrid, 1969),

forbade Adam and Eve the fruit of this tree—that is, he prohibited their sexual conjunction—not because of its inherent evil, but in order to condition the human will to obedience and submission before him. No creature of God, the tree of knowledge included, was evil; in fact, God selected the fruit of this tree as the object of his prohibition precisely because of its value and importance. The ban on sex was only temporary, prescribed to ensure that Adam and Eve would reach the maturity that setting obedience to God ahead of one's physical gratification entailed; when such maturity was achieved, the first parents would have pursued their procreative responsibilities in paradise, until the birth of a predetermined number of humans.[61] The sin of Adam and Eve, like a child's consumption of a food denied the child by his or her parents, was not the essence of their sexual act but its rebellious perpetration before the proper time, against the will of God.[62] In the wake of their fall, the human will remained unsubmissive, and this rebelliousness constitutes the original sin that all have inherited. Relative to other church fathers, however, Theophilus and Irenaeus viewed the fall as somewhat less catastrophic and as bearing only minimally on Gen. 1:28 and its reproductive mandate. Human beings are still in a state of imperfection. Because of their composite nature, physical procreation still contributes to the passage to maturity and perfection. Admittedly, this route now requires the additional element of redemption through Christ (the second Adam), whose self-denial and self-sacrifice, together with those of

esp. chs. 7ff.; and "La definición de hombre en la teología del siglo II°," *Gregorianum* 48 (1967), 522–76. See also Gustav Wingren, *God, Man, and the Incarnation: A Study in the Biblical Theology of Irenaeus* (Philadelphia, Pa., 1959); Schwanz, *Imago Dei*, pp. 117–43; Gregory T. Armstrong, *Die Genesis in der alten Kirche*, Beiträge zur Geschichte der biblischen Hermeneutik 4 (Tübingen, 1962), pp. 67–79; and Barbara Aland, "Fides und Subiectio: Zur Anthropologie des Irenäus," in *Kerygma und Logos: Festschrift für Carl Andresen zum 70. Geburtstag*, ed. A. M. Ritter (Göttingen, 1979), pp. 9–28. On the sexual interpretation of the tree of knowledge in patristic literature, see also the varying positions of J. Coppens, "L'interprétation sexuelle du péché du paradis dans la littérature patristique," *Ephemerides theologicae lovanienses* 24 (1948), 402–8, and *Connaissance;* Félix Asensio, "Tradición sobre un pecado sexual en el Paraíso?" *Gregorianum* 30 (1949), 491–520, 31 (1950), 35–62, 163–91, 362–90; and Orbe, "El pecado original y el matrimonio en la teología del s. II," ibid. 45 (1964), 449–500.
    61. Irenaeus of Lyons, *Contre les hérésies* 2.33.5, 2,2:353–53; cf. a similar motif in the instruction of Methodius of Olympus (above, at n. 34) and Gregory of Nyssa (above, at n. 53).
    62. See Theophilus of Antioch, *Ad Autolycum* 2.25, pp. 66–69; and Clement of Alexandria, *Stromata* 3.14.94, GCS 52:239. On the partial concurrence of Gregory of Nazianzus, who defined the sin of the first parents as partaking prematurely of that which was eventually destined for their consumption, but who interpreted the fruit as intellectual contemplation rather than sexual relations, see Anna-Stina Ellverson, *The Dual Nature of Man: A Study in the Theological Anthropology of Gregory of Nazianzus*, Studia doctrinae christianae upsaliensia 21 (Uppsala, 1981), pp. 52–57.

his virgin mother (the second Eve), have redressed the evil of the lustful rebellion in Eden. Yet the meaning and ramifications of God's call to "be fertile and increase" remain the same.[63]

Nearly two centuries after Theophilus and Irenaeus, Ephrem Syrus wrote that Adam and Eve would have procreated even had they not sinned, despite their immortality.[64] Yet it was Theodore of Mopsuestia who ultimately developed the anthropology of Theophilus and Irenaeus in a controversial manner. God created man and woman mortal, but with the potential of achieving immortality in paradise. Sexual reproduction therefore pertained to their created nature, implying a literal understanding of Gen. 1:28a. As a result, the fall of Adam and Eve notwithstanding, procreative sexual activity neither comprises nor transmits original sin, and each human soul enters the world congenitally untainted by the concupiscence—sexual or otherwise—of its forebears. Although he is not entirely consistent in this regard,[65] Theodore vehemently opposed the doctrine of original sin, which many of his ecclesiastical contemporaries, most notably Augustine, espoused and promulgated. It is regrettable that Theodore's extant writings fail to relate these ideas to Gen. 1:28 directly and explicitly, but his logic is clear: "The distinction between male and female, by which the capacity for producing children was endowed from the beginning, proves that he [God] determined to fashion us as mortals."[66]

The tradition nurtured by Theodore and his second-century predecessors brought patristic views of Gen. 1:28 and sexuality most closely in line with the predominating tendencies in classical rabbinic Judaism. No one is congenitally evil. Every person stands at a cosmic frontier, blending the traits of angels and beasts, of the immortal and the mortal. Despite the dichotomy that it appears would result, humans must integrate their variegated characteristics, marshaling them into the service of God. The primordial blessing went hand in hand with this

---

63. Cf. the comments of Wingren, *God, Man, and the Incarnation*, p. 179 and n. 98.

64. Ephrem Syrus, *In Genesim commentarius* 2.30, CSCO 152:43, 153:33.

65. Among others, see Julius Gross, "Theodor von Mopsuestia, ein Gegner der Erbsündlehre," *Zeitschrift für Kirchengeschichte* 65 (1953), 1–15; Richard A. Norris, *Manhood and Christ: A Study in the Christology of Theodore of Mopsuestia* (Oxford, 1963); William F. Macomber, "The Theological Synthesis of Cyrus of Edessa, an East Syrian Theologian of the Mid-Sixth Century," *Orientalia christiana periodica* 30 (1964), 13–21; and above all the introduction of Phillipe Gignoux to Narsai, *Homélies . . . sur la création*, PO 34,3:449–502.

66. Theodore of Mopsuestia, *Fragmenta in Genesim*, PG 66:641–42; cf. also *Commentarius in Evangelium Iohannis Apostoli*, CSCO 115:55, 78 (Syriac).

singular human condition; when humans heed the instruction to "be fertile and increase," they manifest their creation in the image of God. And when all those destined for human life have been born, the final redemption will ensue. Ironically, the same Augustine who condemned the Eastern denial of original sin adopted this view of procreation, at least as it was intended before the fall, into his own interpretation of Gen. 1:28.

THE LATIN TRADITION

Few of the early Latin church fathers took more than passing notice of human dominion over nature when they commented on Gen. 1:28;[67] instead, those who preceded Augustine directed their attention almost exclusively to the verse's mandate for procreation. Most exerted themselves to defend the divine institution of marriage and procreation, responding to the anti-Catholic doctrines of Marcionites and Manicheans alike. The primordial blessing demonstrates that sexual intercourse, properly transacted, should not be the cause of embarrassment and discomfort, wrote Tertullian, who denigrated Marcion and his god for their hatred of little children. "How much easier it is to believe that affection for little ones should be reckoned an attribute of him who by blessing matrimony for the propagation of the human race has by this blessing made promise also of the fruit of matrimony, which is first concerned with infancy."[68] Despite the potential for misuse of sexual desire, explained Lactantius, one should not obscure the procreative benefits that derive therefrom.[69] The creation of Eve may have led to her commission of sin, elaborated Ambrose, but God still preferred the goods that ultimately were to result from her reproductive activity— the birth of Christ and Christians—to a lone individual (i.e., Adam) free of all error.[70] As in the East, however, general agreement prevailed that the injunction to "be fertile and increase" held sway only tem-

---

67. Notable exceptions include Ambrosiaster, *Quaestiones Veteris et Novi Testamenti* 106.16–17, CSEL 50:242–44; and Prudentius, *Hamartigenia* 673ff., CCSL 126:138–39.

68. Tertullian, *Adversus Marcionem* 4.23.7, ed. Ernest Evans, 2 vols. (Oxford, 1972), 2:386–89; cf. also *De anima* 27.4, 27.9, CCSL 2:823, 824.

69. Lactantius, *De ira Dei* 18, CSEL 27,1:114–17; *Divine institutiones* 6.23, CSEL 19:564–71. See also Jerome, *Epistula* 69, CSEL 54:685; and Philaster, *Diversarum hereseon liber* 120.1, CCSL 9:283.

70. Ambrose of Milan, *De paradiso* 10.46–47, CSEL 32,1:304–5.

porarily and that God now deemed celibacy and virginity more praise-worthy than marriage and reproduction.[71] Particularly outspoken in this regard was Jerome, who held that these latter pursuits, along with the devotion to mammon and observance of the Sabbath, typified the old law of the Jews, now obsolete. Continued literal fulfillment of the precept "be fertile and increase" characterizes Jews, pagans, and here-tics. Virginity, Jerome responded to the heretic Jovinian, epitomizes the new dispensation, which has replaced the old law with its warning (1 Cor. 7:29): "The appointed time has grown very short; from now on let those who have wives live as though they had none."[72] Although Ambrosiaster openly addressed his defense of Gen. 1:28 to Marcion, "[you] who think that the body was fashioned not by God but by the devil," and to the Manichean, "who have subverted marriage as if it were pernicious," he may have here responded to ideas of Jerome as well, rejecting the vilifying dimension to the identification of our verse with Mosaic law.

> When Scripture states, "God made," and "he blessed what he made," who can take issue? Who can doubt? Who can deem accursed that which he hears blessed, unless he be driven by some other spirit? Indeed, if it is said to be a human voice, perhaps it might be thought that there is some deception. But God is said to be speaking and you have doubts? God offers a blessing and you disapprove? Perhaps [you might say] Moses established something wrong in the name of God! Let the signs and miracles worked by Moses in Egypt be enough for you; let the miracles worked in the Red Sea for the liberation of the children of Israel per-suade you. . . . There is a biblical text in which we read of our Lord Christ saying to the Jews (John 5:46), "If you believed Moses you would believe me, for he wrote of me."[73]

71. Tertullian, *De exhortatione castitatis* 6.1–2, CCSL 2:1023, *De anima* 30.4, CCSL 2:827; Cyprian of Carthage, *De habitu virginum* 22–23, CSEL 3.1:202–3; John Cassian, *Conlationes* 17.19.1, CSEL 13:478.

72. Jerome, *De perpetua virginitate b. Mariae liber* 20, PL 23:213. See also *Adversus Jovinianum*, esp. bk. 1, PL 23:221–96; *Epistulae* 22.19, 49.2, 52.10, 66, CSEL 54:168–70, 351–54, 431–33, 650; *In Aggaeum*, ad 1:1, CCSL 76A:714; *In Zachariam*, ad 14:10–11, ibid., pp. 886, 888f. Cf. Philaster, *Diversarum hereseon liber* 57.1–2, CCSL 9:241. On the harshness of Jerome's position, see Elizabeth A. Clark, "Heresy, Asceticism, Adam, and Eve: Interpreta-tions of Genesis 1–3 in the Later Latin Fathers," in idem, *Ascetic Piety and Women's Faith: Essays on Late Ancient Christianity,* Studies in Women and Religion 20 (Lewiston, N.Y., 1986), pp. 358–62. Cf. also David G. Hunter, "Resistance to the Virginal Ideal in Late Fourth-Century Rome: The Case of Jovinian," *Theological Studies* 48 (1987), 45–64.

73. Ambrosiaster, *Quaestiones Veteris et Novi Testamenti* 127.12–13, 17–18, CSEL 50:403–4, 406.

These discussions invariably duplicated many of the arguments of the Eastern fathers concerned with the conceivability and propriety of the command to "be fertile and increase" in the original state of grace. Lactantius, for instance, affirmed that God expected the first parents to merit immortality by achieving spiritual perfection in the course of their terrestrial existence and that the blessing of fertility contributed directly to that effort.[74] Ambrose proclaimed a willingness to interpret different aspects of the Genesis cosmogony allegorically: the distinction between male and female, the nonhuman animals, and even the Garden of Eden itself. He suggested that neither procreation nor physical rule over nature truly befitted the primordial experience.[75] The idea of sex in Eden would have horrified Jerome, as it did his contemporary John Chrysostom.[76] Ambrosiaster, on the other hand, echoed Irenaeus and noted that the punishments accompanying the fall did not destroy the existing female capacity for sexual reproduction.[77] The early Western fathers do not seem to have tackled the issue systematically, and their comments add little new to the often more thoughtful reflections of their Eastern colleagues. Perhaps neither the theological climate nor the heretical challenges to the church warranted more; perhaps some Latin fathers did not appreciate the broad ramifications of the subject at hand. At the very least, biblical interpretation had not yet matured in the West as it had in the East, and maturity bred both nuance and controversy. With Augustine this situation changed. His career provides our story with an important milestone, which will also serve to shift the focus of our analysis from Eastern Christianity to Western Christianity.

Augustine of Hippo

The biblical account of creation never ceased to occupy Augustine's attention, and his comments on the opening chapters of Genesis express the foundations of his theology and anthropology.[78] Within the various Augustinian treatises on the cosmogony, the analysis of Gen. 1:28 regularly intersects with discussion of the divine image in human be-

---

74. Lactantius, *Divinae institutiones* 6.23, 7.5, CSEL 19:564–71, 596–602.
75. Ambrose of Milan, *De paradiso* 11.51, 15.76–77, CSEL 32,1:308, 334–36; cf. Langa, "Análisis," pp. 23–34.
76. See the references cited above at nn. 53, 72; and Langa, "Análisis," pp. 34–35.
77. Ambrosiaster, *Quaestiones Veteris et Novi Testamenti* 127.10, CSEL 50:402–3.
78. Helpful in this regard is Gilles Pelland, *Cinq études d'Augustin sur le début de la Genèse* (Paris, 1972).

ings, the relation of nature and grace, original sin, the soul's entrance into the body, and other complex doctrinal issues. As such, Augustine offered the single most extensive and influential contribution to the Christian career of Gen. 1:28. His thought on the verse and its contents marks a key transition from that of the church fathers who preceded him to that of medieval churchmen who followed. The corpus of his writings enables us to trace the evolution of his thought on the subject and thereby to understand the many and broad implications of our verse for this the greatest of patristic theologians. And the context and substance of the Augustinian exegesis reflect an intricate web of doctrinal and polemical concerns, the resolution of which exerted considerable impact on Western religious ideas throughout the Middle Ages and beyond.

Augustine voiced many of the earlier patristic reactions to our verse. Upon creating man and woman, God repeated the blessing of "be fertile and increase," previously granted other creatures, in order to clarify that human reproduction was not inherently sinful.[79] Humans were created in a condition midway between the angels and the beasts; had they served their creator as required of them, they would have enjoyed the primordial blessings of fertility and dominion.[80] Human dominion derives from creation in the divine image—that is, from the rational faculties of the soul—and therefore diminished when the first parents rebelled against God and undermined their own spiritual abilities.[81] Because the world is now sufficiently populated, one need no longer obey the biblical injunction to procreate, and Christians should ideally choose a life of virginity and celibacy over one of marriage.[82] Yet more than the fathers who preceded him, Augustine emphasized that the primordial blessing survived the sin of Adam and Eve and their fall from Eden, with regard both to procreation and to dominion over nature. In the final book of De civitate Dei, for example, Augustine acknowledged that the wretchedness of the human condition is a just punishment for human sin, but he still proceeded to consider

> how many and what sorts of good things his [God's] providential goodness has infused into all that which he created. First, that blessing

79. DGAL 3.13, CSEL 28.1:78–79.
80. DCD 12.22, CCSL 48:380.
81. DGAL 6.12, 9.14, CSEL 28.1:194–95, 284–86.
82. Augustine of Hippo, De bono conjugali 9.9, 15.17—16.18, CSEL 41:200–201, 209–12. A disparaging association of the Jews with Gen. 1:28 appears in Augustine's Epistula 149.18, CSEL 44:364–65.

which he had conveyed before the sin, stating "Be fertile and increase and fill the earth," he did not wish to withhold even after the sin, and the fecundity thereby granted has remained in the condemned species. The guilt of sin could not remove the wonderful power of the seed— and even more wondrous, the power by which the seed is produced— instilled and somehow ingrained in human bodies. . . . Despite his condemnation, he did not remove all that he had given; otherwise all would cease to exist. Nor did he remove that power from human capability, even when he inflicted a punishment of subjection to the devil, for he did not even exclude the devil himself from human dominion.[83]

Such a positive evaluation of procreation leads to the most radical aspect of the Augustinian commentary on Gen. 1:28: the interpretation of the mandate for the first parents to reproduce while still in a state of grace, before their sin and fall. Augustine's thought on this question changed considerably over time and therefore warrants careful review. His earliest extant comment on our verse appears in *De Genesi contra Manichaeos,* written in 388 and 389, two years after his conversion to Catholicism and two years before his ordination as a priest. As opposed to the negative, material interpretation of the Old Testament propounded by the dualistic Manicheans, among whom Augustine himself had numbered before his conversion, the new Catholic strove to reconcile Mosaic instruction and Christian belief, to demonstrate their common, divine origin. Turning to the creation of human beings, Augustine reiterated the standard patristic opinion that before the fall sexual reproduction was inappropriate:

Most appropriately does one ask how the conjunction of male and female before the [primordial] sin should be understood. And that blessing wherein it is said, "Be fertile and increase, reproduce [*sic!*] and fill the earth"—should it be construed in a physical sense (*carnaliter*) or in a spiritual sense? Indeed, we can rightly understand it in a spiritual sense, so that after the sin it may be thought to have converted to [one of] physical fecundity. For the union of male and female was originally pure, devised for the rule of the former and submission of the latter, with spiritual offspring of intellectual and eternal delights filling the earth—that is, vitalizing the body—and ruling over it—that is, holding it subject so as to suffer no misfortune or disturbance on its account.

83. *DCD* 22.24, CCSL 48:846–47. For Augustine's views on dominion, cf. also *Sermones de Veteri Testamento* 43.3, CCSL 41:508–9; *DGAL* 9.14, CSEL 28,1:284–86; *Quaestiones in Heptateuchum* 1.153, CSEL 28,2:79.

One therefore ought to believe that they were not yet children of this world before they sinned. For children of this world bear children and are born.[84]

In *De Genesi ad litteram imperfectus liber,* a treatise begun in 393 and never finished, Augustine failed to reach Gen. 1:28,[85] but he retained his allegorical understanding of the verse through the end of the fourth century, when he amplified upon it in the *Confessiones,* completed in 401. In the closing chapters of the *Confessiones,* the bishop of Hippo compared human rule over the natural world to the spiritual sovereignty of the Christian church; he interpreted the commandment to procreate as pertaining to the realm of human thought; and he underscored the central importance of our verse in the first chapter of Scripture. Augustine noted the divine benediction of fish, birds, and humans, arguing that the omission of land animals justified a figurative interpretation of "be fertile and increase."

> What sort of mystery is this? You have blessed humans, o Lord, that they might be fertile and increase and fill the earth. Have you not thereby intimated something to us, so that we might understand something in particular? Why did you not bless the light which you called day in this manner, nor the firmament of heaven, nor the heavenly lights, nor the stars, nor the land, nor the sea? I would say that you, o Lord of ours, who created us in your image, I would say that you wished to bestow this gift of blessing exclusively on humans, if you had not blessed fish and whales in precisely this manner, that they be fertile and increase and fill the waters of the sea, and that the birds increase

---

84. Augustine, *De Genesi contra Manichaeos* 1.30, PL 34:187; Augustine's allegorical interpretation of Gen. 1:28b extends into 1.31, cols. 187–88. Langa, "Análisis," p. 150, and P. Agaësse and A. Solignac in their edition *La Genèse au sens littéral (DGAL),* 2 vols., Oeuvres de Saint Augustin 48–49 (Paris, 1972), 2:519, are not convincing in their argument that Augustine does not reject a physical interpretation of procreation here. Augustine's eventual refusal to admit precisely this sort of figurative interpretation (see *DGAL* below) and his ultimate admission of previous error (see *Retractiones* below) testify to such rejection of the literal at this early stage of his career. To Augustine's concluding rationale, that birth and procreation do not pertain to a heavenly existence, cf. the rabbinic homily in *GenR* 12.7 (ad 2:4), 1:106 (cited above, Chapter 2, n. 78): "Anyone who bears children dies and perishes, and is a creature rather than a creator. Yet anyone who does not bear children neither dies nor perishes, and is a creator rather than a creature."

85. Augustine, *De Genesi ad litteram imperfectus liber* 15, CSEL 28,1:494, notes that God's direct discourse to the fish and birds in Gen. 1:22 ceases abruptly in the middle of the verse because these creatures had no rational faculty enabling them to respond: the plants, in turn, received no blessing because they had no intellectual capability whatsoever. The unstated implication for humans in Gen. 1:28 is clear.

above the earth. Likewise, I would say that this blessing applies to those sorts of creatures which are brought into existence by their own species, were I to find it [given to] trees and shrubs and land animals. But in fact "be fertile and increase" was said not to plants, nor to trees, nor to beasts, nor to serpents, even though all these multiply and preserve their species in the same way as fish and birds and humans. . . . If we would consider these words as intended figuratively—which I rather think Scripture intended, since not coincidentally does it extend this blessing solely to the progeny of marine creatures and humans . . .—we would understand the reproduction of marine creatures as referring to objects produced physically, owing to the essential needs of our vast, corporeal being, and human procreation in terms of matters conceived intellectually, on account of the fecundity of reason.[86]

But Augustine did not rest with espousing an Origenist reading of the primordial blessing. He used the primordial blessing to validate the allegorical or spiritual exegesis of Scripture in general!

I perceive in this blessing the capacity and power granted us by you, both to express in numerous ways what we may have understood in a single way, and to understand in numerous ways that which we may have read, expressed only in one obscure fashion.[87]

These lengthy quotations from the end of the *Confessiones* should highlight the exegetical reversal about to occur; within several months, doubts began to surface in Augustine's writings. In *De bono conjugali*, also composed in 401, the bishop enumerated three alternative explanations for the divine commandment of "be fertile and increase" before the commission of sin and the resulting loss of human immortality:[88] God may have intended reproduction to take place in some asexual matter. One might interpret the injunction allegorically. Or, because sexual activity occurs only among mortal beings, perhaps God created Adam and Eve mortal for the express purpose of their procreation, with the expectation that, remaining guiltless, they would receive the gift of immortality before their death. Augustine noted the difficulty of the question, explaining that lack of time presently prevented his opting for one alternative over the others.

---

86. Augustine, *Confessiones* 13.24, CCSL 27:263–64. See John Joseph O'Meara, *The Creation of Man in Augustine's "De Genesi ad litteram"* (Villanova, Pa., 1980), p. 15.
87. Augustine, loc. cit.
88. Augustine, *De bono conjugali* 2.2, CSEL 41:188–90.

Only in *De Genesi ad litteram,* his exegetical magnum opus written in twelve books between 401 and 414, did Augustine distance himself from an allegorical understanding of Gen. 1:28. Gradually and deliberately, he came to interpret "be fertile and increase" in a literal, more "historical" sense. In book three of this work, the Augustinian exegesis tends toward the literal, but it raises the admittedly unproven possibility that procreation might have ensued among immortals without any sexual contact between them.[89] Book six asserts that Adam was in fact created mortal but that God ordained immortality for him on condition that he not sin.[90] The ninth book inquires why God created woman as a "fitting helper" for man (Gen. 2:18, 20):

This purpose was declared in the original creation of the world: "Male and female he created them. God blessed them and God said to them, 'be fertile and increase, fill the earth and master it.'" This reason for creation and union of male and female, as well as this blessing, was not abrogated after the sin and punishment of man. It is by virtue of this blessing that the earth is now filled with human beings who subdue it. Although it was after they were expelled from paradise that they are recorded as having conjoined sexually and begotten children, I still do not see what could have prohibited them from having honorable marriage and the marriage-bed undefiled [see Heb. 13:4] even in paradise. God could have granted them this if they had lived in a faithful and just manner in obedient and holy service to him, so that without the tumultuous ardor of passion and without any labor and pain of childbirth, offspring would be born from their seed. In this case, the purpose would not have been to have children succeeding their parents when they die. Rather, those who produced children would remain in the prime of life and would maintain their physical strength from the tree of life which had been planted in paradise. Those who would be born would develop to the same state, and eventually, when the determined number would be complete, if all lived just and obedient lives, there would be a transformation, so that without any death their natural bodies would receive a new quality, since they obeyed every command of the spirit that ruled them; and with the spirit alone vivifying them, without any help from corporeal nourishment, they would be called spiritual bodies.[91]

---

89. *DGAL* 3.21, CSEL 28,1:88.
90. *DGAL* 6.23–25, CSEL 28,1:196–97.
91. *DGAL* 9.3, CSEL 28,1:271–72; with several variations, I have followed John Hammond Taylor's translation of Augustine, *The Literal Meaning of Genesis,* 2 vols., Ancient Christian Writers 41–42 (New York, 1982), 2:73–74.

It is curious that Augustine buttressed his argument with the same scriptural dictum (Mt. 22:30)—"for in the resurrection they neither marry nor are given in marriage, but are like angels in heaven"—often cited by his predecessors to prove the incompatibility of sexual reproduction and the exalted spiritual state of paradise.[92] For Augustine, the resurrected life will resemble not the primordial situation in paradise but the final glory that the first parents would ultimately have achieved had they not sinned. The fact that sexual reproduction did not occur in Eden, probably because God had not yet ordered it before the fall,[93] hardly means that it could not and would not have occurred in the absence of sin. Yet in observing that God did not actually have the first parents unite sexually in paradise because he foresaw their sin, Augustine once again might have stopped short of spurning all other interpretations.[94] Only toward the end of his commentary, in book eleven, did Augustine proceed with absolute certainty, daring to label as ridiculous (*ridiculum istuc est*) the earlier patristic view that Adam and Eve were not yet ready for sexual activity and in uniting sexually without permission stole from the symbolic fruit of the tree of knowledge.[95] Sharply and without hesitation, Augustine reaffirmed these ideas in at least three of his treatises against the Pelagians.[96] And in *De civitate Dei* he again listed other exegetical options for "be fertile and increase"—that sexual reproduction could never have ensued without the evil of concupiscence, that Gen. 1:28a therefore demanded appreciation as an allegory, and that the divine injunction to procreate took effect only after the expulsion from Eden—but this time he rejected them all with impatience:[97]

> We have no doubt whatsoever that, in accordance with the blessing of God, to be fertile and increase and fill the earth is the gift of marriage,

---

92. *DGAL* 9.6, CSEL 28,1:273–74.

93. *DGAL* 9.4, CSEL 28,1:272–73.

94. P. Agaësse and A. Solignac in Augustine, *La Genèse au sens littéral*, 2:522. Cf. the suggestion of Cornelia W. Wolfsekel, "Some Remarks with Regard to Augustine's Conception of Man as the Image of God," *Vigiliae christianae* 30 (1976), 68: "In the discussion with the Manichaeans it would have been rather out of order to say, what has not been stated explicitly but as a matter of fact *is* the implicated explanation, *viz.*, that God, the supreme Good, anticipated the consequences of the fall, which in fact justified the sexual differences of the bodies."

95. *DGAL* 11.41, CSEL 28,1:376.

96. *De gratia Christi et de peccato originali* 2.35.40, CSEL 42:198–99; *De nuptiis et concupiscentia* 1.5.6, 2.3.9—2.4.13, 2.31.53, CSEL 42:216–18, 260–65, 309–10; *Epistulae ex duobus codicibus* 6.3.3–4, CSEL 88:33.

97. *DCD* 14.22, CCSL 48:444.

which God established originally, prior to human sin, creating male and
female, which sexual quality is indeed evident in the flesh. To this work
of God the blessing itself was in fact linked. For when Scripture stated
(Gen. 1:27), "Male and female he created them," it immediately added,
"God blessed them, saying,[98] 'be fertile and increase, fill the earth and
master it,' " etc. Although all of these things can appropriately be given
a spiritual meaning, masculine and feminine cannot be understood as a
simile for characteristics of the same individual human being, one of
whose attributes being that which rules, another that which is ruled.[99]
And inasmuch as it is most clearly evident in the different sexual characteristics of the body, it would be very absurd to deny that male and
female were created for the purpose of producing offspring, that they
might be fertile and increase and fill the earth.

How should one explain and evaluate these developments in the
thought of Augustine? Soon after his conversion to Catholicism, he
disparaged sexual reproduction, deeming it the result of sin; God's call
in Gen. 1:28 to "be fertile and increase," he argued, should best be
understood figuratively. Yet by 414 at the latest, he denounced this
view, ostensibly contradicting not only himself but the preponderance
of patristic opinion before him. Shortly before his death, Augustine
admitted that during his first years as a Christian he "had not yet seen
that it was possible for immortal creatures to be born of immortal
creatures, even if human nature had not been changed for the worse as a
result of that great sin."[100] Looking back at his *De Genesi contra Manichaeos,* he mentioned his early explanation of our verse, according to
which sexual reproduction could not occur before sin, and unabashedly
concluded, "I do not at all agree."[101] These observations demonstrate
that Augustine himself recognized the development of his interest and
stake in this subject and that he was sensitive to its doctrinal implications. But still, should one properly view Augustine's diverse reactions
to Gen. 1:28 as the results of a single, continuous process in the matura-
tion of his thought? Or should one identify a turning point in Augustine's career, when the bishop of Hippo consciously reversed his
approach to this biblical text?

---

98. Augustine has erred in quoting the opening words of Gen. 1:28, following the
introduction to Gen. 1:22 instead.
99. Cf. the quotation from *De Genesi contra Manichaeos,* above.
100. Augustine, *Retractiones* 1.12.12, CSEL 41:64.
101. Ibid. 1.9.3, pp. 48–49.

I believe that in different respects one can substantiate each of these propositions. On the one hand, Augustine in his later works simply progressed further in the same direction embarked upon in his earlier treatises. In *De Genesi contra Manichaeos*, the newly converted Christian employed allegorical exegesis and Neoplatonic beliefs in order to negate the heresy of dualism. Philosophical monism and the figurative exegesis of Scripture (learned from his teacher Ambrose) enabled Augustine to understand the story of material creation as symbolic of that which transpired in a loftier, spiritual realm. Thus Augustine could argue that only an orthodox form of Christianity, which stressed the identity of the deities in the Old and New Testaments, permits the souls of its faithful to overcome the gap between the transient corporeal life of this world and the eternal, spiritual, divine source on high. When *De Genesi ad litteram* and the books that followed it then depart from allegorical exegesis and to a considerable extent from Neoplatonism, they too emphasize the goodness of all divine works—with regard to the biblical cosmogony in general and to Gen. 1:28 in particular. Contending that God originally intended sexual reproduction to transpire in paradise, Augustine surpassed the antidualistic arguments of his patristic predecessors.[102]

On the other hand, while Augustine continued in his opposition to dualism, he clearly reversed himself in his understanding of Gen. 1:28: The divine commandment and blessing, which he had once interpreted allegorically, he later understood in their literal sense. This undoubtedly reflects a continuous process of encounter with and reflection on the text of the Bible. One should not overlook the possibility of psychological factors. Perhaps the publication of the *Confessiones* in 401 represented an important transition in Augustine's life, a catharsis of sorts, which allowed him once and for all to overcome the sexual appetite that consumed him throughout his youth and to relate calmly and positively to questions of procreation and human sexuality.[103] But I believe that a

---

102. See the instructive comments of Peter Brown, *Augustine and Sexuality*, Center for Hermeneutical Studies in Hellenistic and Modern Culture, Colloquy 46 (Berkeley, Calif., 1983).

103. Among many who have written about the place of the *Confessiones* in Augustine's development, I have here found the following particularly helpful: John Joseph O'Meara, *The Young Augustine: The Growth of St. Augustine's Mind up to His Conversion* (London, 1954); Robert J. O'Connell, *St. Augustine's Early Theory of Man, A.D. 386–391* (Cambridge, Mass., 1968), and *St. Augustine's Confessions: The Odyssey of Soul* (Cambridge, Mass., 1969); and G. R. Evans, *Augustine on Evil* (Cambridge, 1982).

more historically grounded explanation derives from Augustine's constant involvement in the political struggles of his church. As priest, bishop, and theologian, he continually applied abstract doctrine to practical ecclesiological needs and concerns. Augustine was always sensitive to the opponents of the church—to the theoretical dangers of their doctrine and to their day-to-day influence on the Catholic community—and in nearly every written work he polemicized with vigor. Most modern scholars who have dealt with the Augustinian texts considered here appropriately noted their responses to various heretical challenges. Michael Müller, for instance, wrote: "Against the Manicheans he defended the sanctity of marriage; human fecundity is a blessing of God, not the product of an evil principle. Against the Pelagians, however, he stressed the fact of original sin. That concupiscence which presently defiles sexual activity derives not from the work of God's creation but is a defect of the fallen nature."[104]

Müller was undoubtedly correct, but there remains yet another element, distinct and important, to the Augustinian polemic that he and others have failed to identify. Augustine understood that the most effective polemicist exploits the ideas and evidence of his or her opponents to weaken their arguments.[105] And Augustine recognized that the influence of the dualistic Manicheans on the general population stemmed in large measure from their deprecation of worldly pursuits, especially those of marriage and procreation. Consequently, at the same time that Augustine resisted Manichean dualism and defended the unity of the biblical deity, he interpreted Gen. 1:28a as an allegory for intellectual and spiritual fecundity; arguing that marriage did not befit a paradisiacal existence, he in effect devalued sexual reproduction. Soon thereafter, Elizabeth Clark argued, Augustine confronted Jovinian's attack upon Christian asceticism—first in the *De bono conjugali* of 401 and then in his ensuing return to the Genesis cosmogony in *De Genesi ad litteram*. According to Clark, Augustine undercut Jovinian's polemic by asserting the sanctity of marriage no less strenuously than the ultimate superiority of virginity. The new understanding of "be fertile and increase," as intended literally by God *prior to the fall,* supported both halves of Augustine's argument.[106]

---

104. Müller, *Die Lehre,* p. 19.
105. Cf. the polemical strategy enunciated in Augustine, *Adversus Judaeos* 1.2, PL 42:51: "De sanctis ergo Scripturis, quarum et apud eos magna habetur auctoritas, sumenda sunt testimonia, quorum et si nolint oblata utilitate sanari, aperta possint veritate convinci."
106. E. A. Clark, "Heresy, Asceticism, Adam, and Eve."

Rejecting several earlier theories, Clark has therefore concluded that Augustine's exegetical reversal did not derive from his encounter with Pelagianism but antedated it. Yet while Augustine may well have had Jovinian in mind when he began *De Genesi ad litteram,* the Pelagian connection should not be dismissed too hurriedly. As Clark herself admitted, Augustine did not dwell on Gen. 1:28 in his direct rejoinder to Jovinian (i.e., in *De bono conjugali*), but he did do so most forcefully in his subsequent anti-Pelagian treatises. Moreover, Augustine's new focus on our verse—as an expression of the purity of prelapsarian human sexuality—reflects most directly the underlying issues of the Pelagian controversy.[107] Facing the Pelagians' rejection of the doctrine of original sin, Augustine may well have discerned that their popularity proceeded directly from their positive estimation of human nature, even after the fall from Eden. If, as the Pelagians claimed, humans are born with pure, untainted souls, then sexual reproduction does not transmit the guilt of Adam's sin. Augustine still upheld the doctrine that sexual passion, without which procreation no longer occurs, results from and conveys the original sin that we all inherit. Nevertheless, he repudiated his earlier posture and agreed that neither procreation nor sexual relations are inherently evil or impure and that they were destined to transpire in paradise.[108] Augustine complained that the doctrine of original sin and the veneration of celibacy led the Pelagians to dub the Catholics Manicheans. He charged that, in order to deceive the Manicheans, the Pelagians would in the same breath quote Gen. 1:28 and the passage in Mt. 19 where Jesus prohibited divorce, as if Jesus had himself

---

107. Commenting on *De bono conjugali* in his *Retractiones* 2.48.1, CSEL 36:156–58, Augustine may have implied just this when he alluded to his deferral of the issue of procreation to subsequent occasions—"maxime contra novos hereticos Pelagianos diligentius disputavi." On the issues of the Pelagian controversy, see Peter Brown, "Pelagius and His Supporters: Aims and Environment," *Journal of Theological Studies,* n.s. 19 (1968), 93–114, and "Sexuality and Society in the Fifth Century A.D.: Augustine and Julian of Eclanum," in *Tria corda: Scritti in onore di Arnaldo Momigliano,* ed. E. Gabba, Biblioteca di Athenaeum 1 (Como, 1983), pp. 49–70. And among the countless works on the Augustinian doctrine of original sin, see esp. J. Turmel, "Le dogme du péché originel dans Saint Augustin," *Revue d'histoire et de littérature religieuses* 6 (1901), 385–426, 7 (1902), 128–46, 209–30; Hans Staffner, "Die Lehre des Hl. Augustinus über das Wesen der Erbsünde," *Zeitschrift für katholische Theologie* 79 (1957), 385–416; Julius Gross, *Geschichte des Erbsündendogmas,* 4 vols. (Munich, 1960–71), vols. 1–2; A. Sage, "Péché originel: Naissance d'un dogme," *Revue des études augustiniennes* 13 (1967), 211–48; Victorino Capánago, "El hombre-abismo, segun San Agustín," *Augustinus* 20 (1975), 225–52; and Russell de Simone, "Modern Research on the Sources of Saint Augustine's Doctrine of Original Sin," *Augustinian Studies* 11 (1980), 205–27.

108. On the difficulty of Augustine's situation against the Pelagians, see Erich Dinkler, *Die Anthropologie Augustins,* Forschungen zur Kirchen- und Geistesgeschichte 4 (Stuttgart, 1934), pp. 118ff.

cited our verse and required his followers to marry. The extant writings of Julian of Eclanum verify this accusation.[109] Insofar as Catholic doctrine permitted, Augustine was pressured to agree with his Pelagian opponents concerning the sanctity of marriage, to acknowledge that even in paradise sexual desire, while it is subject to the rule of the will, could have played a role in procreation. Can the challenge of Pelagianism offer at least a partial explanation for Augustine's new interpretation of Gen. 1:28? Although Augustine completed his *De Genesi ad litteram* in 414, it is likely—though hardly certain—that he composed his reactions to our verse in book nine before awakening in 412 to the threat of this heresy. Yet the unhesitating declaration at the end of book eleven probably dates from the final months of the work's composition, and the possibility surely remains that the earlier passages in question underwent revision during the biennium prior to publication.[110] At the very least, one can safely assert that Pelagian arguments fueled the gradual Augustinian movement from figurative to literal interpretation of the paradisiacal marriage ordained for the first parents. Augustine's comments dating from after 412 are more incisive, more daring, and avowedly more polemical;[111] had any doubts remained in his mind, he quickly dispelled them. By the time he completed *De civitate Dei* in 426, he not only appreciated the command to "be fertile and increase" in its literal, historical sense but flatly rejected its figurative interpretation as implausible.

Several dimensions of this chapter in the development of Augustinian ideas deserve additional comment. Neoplatonism and allegorical exegesis clearly helped Augustine to overcome the dualistic thought that preoccupied him before his conversion, and he remained cognizant of

---

109. Augustine, *De nuptiis et concupiscentia* 2.4.12–13, CSEL 42:263–65; *Contra duas epistolas Pelagianorum* 4.2.2, 4.5.9, CSEL 60:521, 529–30. The citation of Gen. 1:28 along these lines is attested in Julian of Eclanum, *Epistula ad Rufum Thessalonicum* 19, CCSL 88:339, and *Ad Turbantium* 1.26–27, CCSL 88:347. Clark, "Heresy, Asceticism, Adam, and Eve," p. 359, correctly notes the attribution of similar accusations to Jovinian; for the corresponding citation of Gen. 1:28, see Jerome, *Adversus Jovinianum* 1.5, PL 23:225–26.

110. Augustine's remark in *DGAL* 9.7, CSEL 28,1:276, that he recently (*nuper*, although the word can mean "once" or "formerly") published *De bono conjugali* is suggestive but not conclusive, especially because one observes the progress of Augustinian thought as *DGAL* continues; see Langa, "Análisis," pp. 164–66. P. Agaësse and A. Solignac in Augustine, *La Genèse au sens littéral*, 1:28–31, contend that Augustine probably wrote books 1–9 of *DGAL* by the year 410, and almost certainly by 412; that he composed books 10–12 between 412 and 415; and that he hastily wrote the final chapters of book 11 just prior to the publication of the entire work.

111. See above, at nn. 96ff.

their significance throughout his life. Yet as he advanced from Manichean dualism to the monistic theology of the Bible, Augustine accorded greater value to the historical sense of Scripture and felt impelled to interpret it *ad litteram*. In his notes to *De Genesi ad litteram*, John Hammond Taylor rightly observed that Augustine expressed a definite preference for literal meanings when discussing the biblical account of Adam and Eve in paradise. In a series of comparisons, the bishop of Hippo first contrasted the figurative discourse of Scripture (*locutio figuratarum rerum*) to its exposition in a literal sense (*ad litteram*), then such a figurative exposition (*figurate*) to an appropriate one (*proprie*), and finally the allegorical understanding of the text (*secundum allegoricam locutionem*) to its rightful one (*secundum propriam*).[112] Just as it once underlay Augustine's theory of allegory, Gen. 1:28 now played a part in heightening his regard for the literal interpretation of the Bible.[113]

Noting how the later Augustinian interpretation of "be fertile and increase" rapidly became standard in Western Christian exegesis, modern scholars have tended to emphasize its novelty, as if Augustine innovated in a radical manner.[114] Yet while the bishop of Hippo surely conveyed his views on the issue of prelapsarian marriage and procreation with unprecedented vigor and clarity, one can find all the necessary components of the Augustinian interpretation in the writings of earlier patristic theologians. Understanding the biblical cosmogony primarily in its historical, material sense, Theophilus of Antioch, Irenaeus of Lyons, and Lactantius had maintained that God created human beings in an intermediate state of "tentative immortality"; physically mortal, the first parents had the opportunity to merit eternal life.[115] In this condition, and from such an exegetical perspective, procreation constituted a natural and necessary component of human existence, as

112. *DGAL* 8.1–2, CSEL 28,1:231–33; Taylor in Augustine, *The Literal Meaning of Genesis*, 2:253–54 n. 9.

113. On the nature and influence of Augustine's exegetical method, see, among numerous others, Henri de Lubac, *Exégèse médiévale: Les quatre sens de l'écriture*, 2 vols. in 4 pts., Théologie 41–42, 59 (Paris, 1959–64), vol. 1; Beryl Smalley, *The Study of the Bible in the Middle Ages*, 3rd ed. (Oxford, 1983), pp. 22ff.; Anne-Marie la Bonnardière, *Saint Augustin et la Bible*, Le Bible tous les temps 3 (Paris, 1986); and Bertrand de Margerie, *Introduction à l'histoire de l'exégèse*, 3 vols. (Paris, 1980–83), vol. 3.

114. See Müller, *Die Lehre*; P. Agaësse and A. Solignac in Augustine, *La Genèse au sens littéral*, 2:523; and Langa, "Análisis."

115. On Augustine's formulation of this doctrine, see Gerhart B. Ladner, "St. Augustine's Conception of the Reformation of Man to the Image of God," in Ladner, *Images and Ideas in the Middle Ages: Selected Studies in History and Art*, 2 vols., Storia e letteratura: Raccolta di Studi e testi 155–56 (Rome, 1983), 2:597ff.

Irenaeus acknowledged explicitly. According to Antonio Orbe, Theophilus and Irenaeus believed that Adam and Eve sinned by engaging in sexual relations prematurely but that God intended and wanted their reproductive activity to transpire eventually. Clement of Alexandria also espoused this view, and although Augustine rejected it as "nonsense," it asserted that the divine mandate of "be fertile and increase," understood literally, was applicable in paradise.[116] Behold the essence of Augustine's supposed innovation! Irenaeus and Methodius of Olympus both anticipated the Augustinian contention that God originally planned for the birth of a specific number of individuals. And although he could not reconcile sexual reproduction and the primordial state of grace, Gregory of Nyssa insisted that procreation somehow would have occurred in Eden, for if its inception had depended on the fall from Eden, one might conclude that sin was in fact necessary and beneficial. This reasoning also motivated Augustine, who concluded in *De civitate Dei:*

> Whoever says that they were not destined to unite sexually and to have children without having sinned necessarily states that human sin was required to achieve the proper number of saints. For if without sinning they would have remained alone [without children]—since, as these people think, they could not have children if they had not sinned—sin was assuredly necessary for there to be not merely two righteous human beings, but many human beings. Yet if believing this is absurd, one ought rather to believe that however many saints were necessary to fill that most blessed city would have existed, even if nobody had sinned— as many as are now collected from the multitude of sinners by the grace of God, so long as children of this world bear children and are born.[117]

One cannot accurately gauge the extent to which Augustine read the Greek patristic writings that anticipated his interpretations of Gen. 1:28.[118] Yet certainly among all the church fathers, Augustine first blended the various exegetical motifs just enumerated into a definitive, historical interpretation of "be fertile and increase," an interpretation

---

116. See above, at n. 62.

117. *DCD* 14.23, CCSL 48:444–45.

118. On Augustine's knowledge of the Greek fathers who preceded him, see Langa, "Análisis," pp. 158–62, and the literature cited there; for different scholarly estimations of the Latin translation of Irenaeus' *Adversus haereses*, see Johannes Quasten, *Patrology*, 3 vols. (1950; repr., Westminster, Md., 1986), 1:290–91.

that appreciated the divine mandate for procreation in its plain, literal sense. Evaluating the formative role played by Augustine in developing Western views of human nature, sexuality, and original sin, one should not overlook Augustine's decisive incorporation of marriage and reproduction into the ideal, primordial human condition. This significance of Augustine's contribution to the career of Gen. 1:28 will concern us further below. As we proceed to consider his influence, however, we reiterate that Augustine's exegesis did not create *ex nihilo* with regard to our verse. It crystallized, interwove, refined, and transmitted the ideas of his predecessors.

Augustine's Successors

The Western Christian exegetes who followed Augustine added relatively little that was new to the appreciation of Gen. 1:28 that they inherited. Successive generations of late antique and medieval churchmen continued to echo the oft-repeated motifs of early patristic interpretation. God included all animal creatures in the blessing of "be fertile and increase," first bestowed upon fish and birds, which he then repeated to humans lest anyone disparage human sexuality as inherently evil. As such, our verse demonstrates the divine institution of marriage and procreation, establishing their defense against the condemnations of heretics. Now that the earth is sufficiently populated,[119] however, the injunction of Gen. 1:28a has lost its urgency, and a life of sexual abstinence surpasses that of marriage and childbearing in holiness. Repeated to Noah after the flood to ensure the physical survival of the human race,[120] the mandate of procreation typifies the second of the Samaritan woman's five husbands (Jn. 4:18);[121] like the ceremonial laws of Moses, its time has clearly passed.[122] Human dominion over nature proceeds from the creation in God's image and the rational faculty that resulted therefrom. Since it was conditional upon compliance with the divine will,[123] such dominion has been curtailed but not eliminated in

119. For example, Albertus Magnus, *In 2 Sententiarum* 20.3, in *Opera omnia,* 38 vols. (Paris, 1890–99), 27,1:343–44.

120. Peter Lombard, *Sententiae in IV libris distinctae* 4.26.3, 2 vols. in 3 pts. (Rome, 1971–81), 2:418.

121. Peter the Chanter, cited in Pseudo-Melito of Sardis, *Clavis sanctae scripturae* 10.2, in J. B. Pitra, *Spicilegium solesmense,* 4 vols. (Paris, 1852–58), 3:104.

122. For example, Bede, *In principium Genesis* 1.852ff., CCSL 118A:28–29.

123. Like Irenaeus of Lyons (above, n. 60), Dracontius, *De laudibus Dei* 1.405–15, in

the aftermath of human sin and the fall from paradise. Scattered over the face of the earth, postlapsarian humans actually need it more than the first parents in Eden.[124] The blessing of Gen. 1:28b has resulted in manifold technological achievements, although, as several writers made sure to specify, it did not intend to sanction the rule of one person over another.[125]

More striking is the pervasive influence that the Augustinian reading of the mandate for procreation wielded on Latin exegesis throughout the Middle Ages. The ideas that the blessings of Gen. 1:28 preceded the fall in their relevance as well as their conferral, that human procreation fulfills the original divine plan for human existence in this world, that sexual reproduction, devoid of lust and concupiscence, should have transpired in Eden until the birth of a predetermined number of saints, and that following their reproductive activity the first parents and their progeny should have received the gift of immortality—all these quickly became standard in the traditions of the Roman church. The Augustinian assertion that God originally enabled the first parents to control and to "move the members by which offspring are generated in the same way that one commands his feet when he walks"[126] appeared even in the Pentateuchal commentary of Moses Nahmanides and several other rabbinic works of the later Middle Ages.[127] The spirit of a literal and generally positive reading of the first chapters of Genesis soon infused the works of many Western authors, some of whom allowed it to extend beyond the limits of Augustine's own contributions. Poets of the early Middle Ages idealized the marital bliss of the first parents in

---

Oeuvres, Tome I, ed. Claude Moussy and Colette Camus (Paris, 1985), pp. 171–72, followed by Eugenius of Toledo, *Hexaemeron, Monumenta Germaniae historica,* Auctores antiquissimi 14:45, linked Gen. 1:28 with the prohibition on the fruit of the tree of knowledge.

124. Quodvultdeus, *De symbolo* 1.11, CCSL 60:331; Bede, *In principium Genesis* 1.872ff., CCSL 118A:29; Rabanus Maurus, *In Genesim* 1.7, PL 107:462; *Glossa ordinaria,* in *Biblia sacra cum glossis, interlineari, et ordinaria, Nicolai Lyrani postilla, ac moralitatibus, Burgensis additionibus, et Thoringi replicis,* 6 vols. (Venice, 1588), 1:28FG; and Honorius Augustudensis, *Elucidarium* 1.67, in Yves LeFèvre, *L'"Elucidarium" et les lucidaires,* Bibliothèque des Ecoles françaises d'Athènes et de Rome 180 (Paris, 1954), p. 373.

125. Cf. Augustine, *Quaestiones in Heptateuchum* 1.153, CSEL 28,2:79. See also Ratherius of Verona, *Praeloquia* 1.22, CCCM 46A:22; Andrew of St. Victor, *In Genesim,* CCCM 53:22 (who observed that human slavery derives from the postlapsarian corruption of dominion); [Henry of Ghent?], *Lectura ordinaria super sacram scripturam,* ed. R. Macken, Henrico de Gandavo opera omnia 36 (Louvain, 1980), p. 164.

126. *DGAL* 9.10, CSEL 28,1:278–80; cf. also the citations in n. 96, above, and *DCD* 14.23–24, CCSL 48:444–48.

127. See the citations above in Chapter 4, n. 155.

Eden and affirmed that the fruits of the primordial blessings survived the fall. With graphic imagery calling to mind a Homer or an Ovid, the late fifth-century Dracontius dared to imply that Adam and Eve did have sexual relations in paradise.

> Rejoicing, they passed among the flowers and beds all of roses, amid fragrant fields and verdant forests, innocently as the cattle or the beasts, their bodies without raiment, and their hearts unconscious of shame. Why should any portion of their bodies be considered more to be hidden than the rest? How were they in their inexperience to know what was seemly in moral conduct? In like manner as they regarded their hands and eyes, they also regarded their private parts. Openly and freely they kept mingling kisses with their fond desires, nor was there any sign of a blush, although the reasons for modesty were exposed. They considered nothing whatever forbidden to them, and their belief was justified, since from those for whom he ordained all things for use, only the fruit of a single tree was withheld by his commandment.[128]

Albeit with greater restraint, medieval liturgical texts began to incorporate Gen. 1:28 into the wedding rite, wishing brides and grooms the same fecundity granted Adam and Eve by their creator.[129] Hugh of Amiens suggested that the conception of Cain might have occurred before the fall.[130] Peter Abelard questioned how compliance with the divine command to "be fertile and increase" in the context of marriage could ever entail sin.[131] Under the influence of Aristotelian naturalism, some Scholastic masters of Paris later ventured further still, asserting

---

128. Dracontius, *De laudibus Dei* 1.437–48, ed. Moussy and Camus, pp. 173–74; I have departed only slightly from James Irwin's English translation of Dracontius, *De laudibus Dei, liber I* (Philadelphia, Pa., 1942), p. 47. Colette Camus, in her edition of Dracontius, p. 299n., errs in noting that Dracontius' assertion of prelapsarian sexual union between Adam and Eve follows *DGAL*; in 9.4, CSEL 28, 1:272–73, Augustine stated explicitly that it did not occur. On the hexameral tradition in Latin verse, see Stanislas Gamber, *Le livre de la "Genèse" dans la poesie latine au Ve siècle* (1899; repr., Geneva, 1977).

129. *Praefatio* 948, 1169, CCSL 161C:292, 362; *Benedictio pontificalis* 639, CCSL 162:253, 1798, CCSL 162A:735. Cf. also Honorius Augustudensis, *Speculum ecclesie*, PL 172:867; Alan of Lille, *Summa de arte praedicatoria*, PL 210:193. And for the continuing reappearance of this motif, see the citations and comments of M. Teresa Tavormina, "'Bothe Two Ben Gode': Marriage and Virginity in *Piers Plowman* C. 18.68–100," *Journal of English and Germanic Philology* 81 (1982), 324 and n. 8. These and other references to Gen. 1:28 in liturgical contexts warrant further scrutiny on another occasion.

130. Hugh of Amiens, *Tractatus in hexaemeron* 3.55, in François Lecomte, "Un commentaire scripturaire du XIIe siècle: Le 'Tractatus in hexaemeron' de Hugues d'Amiens (Archevêque de Rouen, 1130–1164)," *Archives d'histoire doctrinale et littéraire du Moyen Age* 25 (1958), 277.

131. Peter Abelard, *Problemata heloissae* 42, PL 178:723–30.

that the sex intended to transpire in Eden would have been pleasurable, perhaps even more so than postlapsarian conjugal relations.[132] Where Augustine had passionately longed for the time when all would willingly remain celibate,[133] Thomas Aquinas, while asserting the greater perfection of virginity for individuals, acknowledged that the human race must still fulfill the injunction of "be fertile and increase" on a collective basis.[134] The Franciscan Duns Scotus seemed to express the rabbinic and kabbalistic idea that procreation hastens the redemption by bringing to life the souls of the pious and repopulating the "commonwealth of heavenly citizens."[135] And as Leo Steinberg recently demonstrated, Renaissance artists unabashedly emphasized the sexual, generative powers of Jesus himself as a means of portraying the ultimate restoration of primordial sinlessness as well as the salvific, life-giving character of the Resurrection. Steinberg argued that modern scholars intentionally overlooked this phenomenon for too long, contributing to a "massive historical retreat from the mythical grounds of Christianity."[136]

Perhaps the most instructive evidence for the victory of Augustine's view of prelapsarian sexuality appears in the medieval European fate of the patristic interpretations that Augustine had rejected. After Augustine's death, the most important proponent of the (now exceptional) allegorical understanding of Gen. 1:28 was Isidore of Seville, who wrote of the first parents: "It was said to them, 'Be fertile and increase'—meaning either in [the multiplication of] languages or in [giving rise to] spiritual degrees of intelligence, so that they might subjugate all unruly bodily passions as if they were senseless creatures."[137] This interpretation of our verse had originated among the ante-Nicene fathers as a means of avoiding the admission of sexual reproduction into the primordial, divinely ordained state of grace. Medieval exegetes who followed Isidore, however, typically reaffirmed the Augustinian con-

132. Albertus Magnus, *In 2 Sententiarum* 2.20.2, *Opera omnia*, 27, 1:342–43; Thomas Aquinas, *ST* 1.98.2, 60 vols. (Cambridge, 1964–76), 13:154–59.

133. Augustine, *De bono conjugali* 10.10, CSEL 41:201–2.

134. See the sources cited below, Chapter 6, nn. 64, 66.

135. Duns Scotus, *In IV Sententiarum (Paris Report)* 28.1.1, *Opera omnia*, 26 vols. (Paris, 1891–95), 24:377. On the relative unpopularity of this view, see Noonan, *Contraception*, pp. 275–76.

136. Leo Steinberg, *The Sexuality of Christ in Renaissance Art and Modern Oblivion* (New York, 1983), p. 108.

137. Isidore of Seville, *Quaestiones in Genesim* 1.15, PL 83:212.

clusion that God had intended Adam and Eve to comply with the mandates of the primordial blessing in their literal sense even before their fall, and they then proceeded to espouse Isidore's figurative reading as well![138] Claudius of Turin, Odo of Cambrai (Tournai), the authors of the *Glossa ordinaria,* Rupert of Deutz, Bruno of Asti, and Thomas Aquinas followed suit, adding that the primordial blessing of fertility is fulfilled in the multiplication of pious Christians and the dissemination of Christianity.[139] The mere mention of all these medieval writers in the same breath reflects on how little their exegesis departed from patristic tradition. To be sure, room still existed for variation. Some espoused the literal, Augustinian interpretation only.[140] Rupert of Deutz warned against employing Gen. 1:28 too strenuously in defense of marriage.[141] Peter Abelard tended in the other direction, responding to the argument that the injunction to "fill the earth" did not comport with the primordial confinement of human life to paradise.

> Nothing requires that the entire multitude of human beings destined to exist would have dwelled in paradise forever had they not sinned.

138. Pseudo-Bede, *Expositio in primum librum Mosis,* PL 91:199–201; Pseudo-Bede, *De sex dierum creatione liber sententiarum ex patribus collectarum,* PL 93:216–17; Rabanus Maurus, *In Genesim* 1.7, 1.10, 1.14, PL 107:458–62, 468, 482; Angelom of Luxeuil, *In Genesim,* PL 115:123; Gilbert of Nogent, *Moralia in Genesim,* PL 156:50–51, 57–58 (who offers only a figurative interpretation of "be fertile and increase"); Arnold of Bonneval, *De operibus sex dierum,* PL 189:1529 (who defends the allegorical interpretation of the Genesis cosmogony in general); Peter Riga, *Aurora,* ed. Paul E. Beichner, 2 vols., University of Notre Dame Publications in Medieval Studies 19 (Notre Dame, Ind., 1965), 1:32, and Albertus Magnus, *In 4 Sententiarum* 31.10, *Opera omnia* 30:238–39.

139. Claudius of Turin (Pseudo-Eucherius of Lyons), *In Genesim,* PL 50:901–2, 908, 934; Odo of Tournai (Cambrai), *De operibus sex dierum,* PL 171:1216; *Glossa ordinaria,* in *Biblia sacra,* 1:68r (interlinear gloss ad Gen. 17:2); Rupert of Deutz, *De sancta Trinitate et operibus eius,* CCCM 21:301, 312, 23:1836–37; Bruno of Asti, *In Genesim,* PL 164:158–59; and Thomas Aquinas, *Summa contra gentiles* 3.136, *Opera omnia* (Rome, 1882–present), 14:412–14. See also Andrew Sunesön, *Hexaemeron* 4.1981–87, ed. Sten Ebbesen and Laurentius Boethius Mortensen, Corpus philosophorum danicorum Medii Aevi 11,1 (Hauniae, 1985), p. 137; and the bull of Eugenius IV, *Exultate Deo,* in J. D. Mansi et al., eds., *Sacrorum conciliorum nova et amplissima collectio,* 53 vols. (Florence and Rome, 1757–1927), 31:1054.

140. Among others: Bede, *In principium Genesis* 1.705ff., 852ff., CCSL 118A:24, 28–29; Wicbod, *Liber quaestionum super librum Genesis ex dictis sanctorum,* PL 96:1132; Joannes Scotus Erigena, *De divisione naturae* 4.14, 4.23, PL 122:806, 846–47; Hugh of Saint Victor, *De sacramentis* 1.6.22–23, 2.11.2–3, PL 176:277, 482–83; Andrew of Saint Victor, *Expositio super Heptateuchum,* CCCM 53:22; Peter Lombard, *Sententiae* 2.20.1, 4.26.2, 1,2:428, 2:417; [Henry of Ghent?], *Lectura ordinaria,* p. 166 (who cited Origen [see above, at n. 50] but reversed his intent, arguing that the truth of the literal interpretation of Gen. 1:28 mandated the specification in Gen. 1:27 that God created male and female); Tolomeo de Lucca, *Exaemeron* 9.6, ed. Pius-Thomas Masetti (Sienna, 1880), pp. 113–15; and Bernadino of Sienna, *De religione christiana* 48.1.1, *Opera omnia,* 9 vols. (Quaracchi, 1950–65), 2:102.

141. Rupert of Deutz, *Commentaria in Evangelium Sancti Iohannis,* CCCM 9:97–98.

Rather, after a while they were supposed to be dispersed throughout the world, just like those disembarking from the ark, without having had any punishment inflicted upon them, and without the earth having been affected by any divine curse on account of sin. Nevertheless we believe that the first humans were originally situated in paradise, where the moderate temperature of the place originally established by God would have produced an abundance of fruits, since neither these nor other fruits had yet been cultivated throughout the world. . . . Then, without doubt, humans would have been able to reign supreme and rule the entire earth, and the other creatures would have served them in multifarious ways, perhaps eventually even as food, just as the Lord entitled Noah after the flood.[142]

A broad, balanced summary of Christian exegesis on Gen. 1:28 appears in the *Hexaemeron* of Robert Grosseteste, bishop of Lincoln, scientist, and theologian in thirteenth-century Oxford, with whom our review of medieval exegesis will draw to a close. Grosseteste echoed the established view that God did not grant his blessing of "be fertile and increase" to plants, which lack sexual differentiation, but that in bestowing it upon fish and birds (Gen. 1:22) did extend it to all land animals; its repetition in Gen. 1:28 seeks to clarify that human sexual reproduction per se entails no sin. In the case of fish and birds, Grosseteste elaborated at length on the figurative, sacramental meaning of the primordial blessing, "since the legislator did not seek to instruct us in the nature of marine creatures as much as in the regulation of the Church and in matters of behavior."[143] Turning to Gen. 1:26, the Oxonian master commented extensively on human dominion over nature. He observed that had they not sinned, humans would eventually have enjoyed this dominion in its entirety; although its conferral by God in Gen. 1:28 clearly anticipated a postlapsarian age, human

---

142. Peter Abelard, "A Critical Edition of . . . *Expositio in hexameron*," ed. Mary Foster Romig (Ph.D. Dissertation, University of Southern California, Los Angeles, 1981), pp. 74–75; noteworthy is Abelard's mention (pp. 75–76) of the view that the blessings of Gen. 1:28 anticipated the fall, which stems from the unwillingness of some to deal in the allegedly frivolous speculation of what would have been had events happened otherwise: "Sunt fortassis quibus huiusmodi questiones frivole esse nec rationabiliter moveri videntur, cum quis videlicet querit de aliquo nunquam eveniente et dicit: 'Quid fieret si ita esset?' Que namque, inquiunt, ratio est querere si ita esset quod nec fieri habet, sicut nec illud esse? Dicunt itaque deum, prescium futurorum, hoc homini concessisse, ut per rationem dominaretur ceteris animantibus, et ea constringere posset atque opprimere, quamvis corpore validiora."

143. Robert Grosseteste, *Hexaëmeron* 6.12.1, ed. Richard C. Dales and Servus Gieben, Auctores britannici Medii Aevi 6 (London, 1982), p. 193.

power actually decreased (*imminuta, viciata et corrupta*) as a result of the fall.[144] One can understand the divine call upon humans to procreate both allegorically, just as Grosseteste interpreted the blessing of fish and birds, and literally. In the latter case, "be fertile and increase" extends to the human race in general and not to each and every individual, because some people remain sterile throughout their lives. Adopting the Augustinian posture that sexual reproduction would have transpired in paradise, Grosseteste observed that, according to Augustine, Gen. 1:28 allowed for human procreation but did not necessitate it.[145] The ensuing divine call to "fill the earth" applies only to humans; even if they have in fact inhabited only one-quarter of the world, the blessing refers to the power of human civilization, or perhaps to the potential for populating the entire world.[146]

THE PATRISTIC LEGACY

This medieval blend of patristic ideas undoubtedly reflected a hermeneutical perspective that countenanced the simultaneous interpretation of a single scriptural text on several distinct levels of meaning. With direct reference to the opening chapters of Genesis, Augustine had himself admitted the legitimacy of such exegesis,[147] but in the particular instance of Gen. 1:28, Augustine denied the possibility of allegory. From his point of view, the literal and figurative readings of "be fertile and increase" were mutually exclusive. Origen, Gregory of Nyssa, John Chrysostom, and other proponents of the earlier consensus—that no sexual relations would have occurred in paradise—undoubtedly agreed. In accepting both exegetical traditions without their common claim to exclusive validity, medieval European writers did not simply salvage the authority of other patristic opinions, older and no less authentic than the works of Augustine. They also effectively neutralized each respective viewpoint vis-à-vis its controversial nature and intent. Within Catholic circles, Augustine had solved the problem of

144. Ibid. 8.13–16, pp. 236–41 (quotation in 8.13.8, p. 239).
145. Ibid. 8.19.1–8.20.2, pp. 244–45.
146. Ibid. 8.23.1, pp. 246–47.
147. DCD 13.21, CCSL 48:404: "Haec et si qua alia commodius dici possunt de intellegendo spiritaliter paradiso nemine prohibente dicantur, dum tamen et illius historiae veritas fidelissima rerum gestarum narratione commendata credatur."

primordial sexuality, and it therefore receded into the background. "Be fertile and increase" continued to serve such medieval writers as Eckbert of Schönau, Peter Comestor, and Andrew Sunesön in the defense of marriage against the attacks of the dualist Cathars.[148] European exegesis continued to presume the supremacy of human beings in the natural order, often referring to their blessing of dominion both as a derivative of and as a means toward their spiritual perfection. But when the same medieval theologians espoused multiple and originally conflicting interpretations of Gen. 1:28, and eventually, when others offered little or no comment on "be fertile and increase,"[149] they demonstrated that the doctrinal issues once raised by our verse burned no longer.

Whether intentionally or not, the medieval churchmen who simultaneously advocated both literal and allegorical interpretations of Gen. 1:28 testified to the covenantal ramifications of this biblical text, previously recognized in Scripture itself, in rabbinic tradition, and among the early fathers. Why should Western theologians have reasserted the figurative reading of our verse in the wake of Augustine's vehement rejection? Why not adopt the instruction of the bishop of Hippo as authoritative, or else discard it for the sake of earlier patristic doctrine? The propensity of many Latin exegetes for reproducing the commentaries of earlier writers, with little explanation or criticism of their own, undoubtedly helped to facilitate their hybrid approach to Gen. 1:28. Yet even more careful and insightful writers opted for this path too. The assertion that the primordial blessings of fertility, increase, and dominion specifically prefigured the triumph of the church and the contemporary experience of Christians and Christianity presupposed the recognition that our verse bespoke divine election and favor. The *Epistle of Barnabas* had reached this conclusion within a century of the birth of Christianity; not only did it underlie the Origenist, allegorical reading of our verse, but it also resounded in many of the rabbinic texts considered above. Christians like Augustine who construed "be fertile and

---

148. Eckbert of Schönau, *Sermones contra Catharos* 5.5–14, PL 195:30–36; Peter Comestor, *Historia scholastica* 1.10, PL 198:1064; Andrew Sunesön, *Hexaemeron,* p. 120: "Crescere praecepit Deus his terramque replere; ad quod praeceptum sequitur coniunctio carnis, quam licitam reddit maiestas summa iubentis, quem praeter licitum nil constat posse iubere; quare coniugium Deus instituisse probatur, et confutatur detestans catharus omnem concubitum, cum coniugium Deus approbet auctor."

149. For instance, Anselm of Canterbury, Nicholas of Lyra, and Meister Eckhart.

increase" strictly in its literal, historical sense forfeited an exclusive claim to the election that it bespoke. How could an advocate and practitioner of virginity purport to uphold the precept of "be fertile and increase?" When Augustine elaborated on the bounteous blessings of our verse, it was his perception that they would be realized in the experiences of all human beings, not Christians in particular.[150] Commentators who interwove both the literal and the figurative, however, could claim (with Augustine) the purity of prelapsarian sexuality as well as the covenantal promise conveyed in the primordial blessing. The violence that this approach inflicted on each of the two ancient interpretations evidently did not disturb medieval exegetes. What mattered was that the church had inherited and had implemented God's primordial covenant with the first parents. In this vein, Rupert of Deutz lashed out at the Jews, who had asserted to Jesus (John 8:33, 39) that they alone, physical descendants of Abraham, enjoyed the election of God:[151]

> Against this presumption the truth presents itself. "He who is of God," he said (John 8:47), "hears the words of God; the reason why you do not hear them is that you are not of God." In other words, not he who is of that excessive overflow of nature, concerning which God said (Gen. 3:16) to Eve, after the sin of the first man, "I will multiply your pangs and your pregnancies."[152] Rather, he who is of that blessing with which God blessed them in paradise before their sin, "be fertile and increase, fill the earth and master it; and rule the fish of the sea, the birds of the sky, and all the living things that creep on earth," . . . such a person "hears the words of God." It is evident that all the saints and elect, who by the grace of Christ are now called, justified, and glorified in various, deserved ways, . . . are of that blessing with which God blessed the first humans before their sin, as has been stated. That indeed is certain, since even if the sin had not been committed, they who are now freed through the grace of Christ would have been born in any event. On the other hand, all those who are now left in perdition are of that curse spoken to the woman, "I will multiply your pangs and your pregnancies"; since if sin had not proceeded from the root of our flesh, nothing would have emerged from that grove which is useful merely for being cut down and thrown into the fire.

150. See above, at n. 83.
151. Rupert of Deutz, *Commentaria in Evangelium Sancti Iohannis*, CCCM 9:477–78.
152. Translating the Latin of the Vulgate literally to facilitate Rupert's homily.

Like their Jewish counterparts, ancient and medieval Christian theologians deemed the mandate to "be fertile and increase" in Gen. 1:28a more provocative than the conferral of dominion in Gen. 1:28b. As they commented on our verse, anticipating both questions and answers of modern textual critics, they frequently dwelled on the subject of dominion at considerable length, unquestionably more so than rabbinic authors of the same period. Perhaps the more direct and expansive influence of Greco-Roman philosophical traditions on Christian exegetes led them to share the classical obsession with anthropology, the unending quest to dissect and to understand the various components of the human being. From the anthropocentric perspective of the pagan, or in a Christian world view that focused on the deity's assumption of human existence, the limits and extent of human capability might sensibly rank high on a list of problems that occupied the intellectual. The fact that from the fourth century onward Christians actually enjoyed dominion in the Greco-Roman world—while Jews never did—invariably added to their interest in the subject.[153] Experience stimulated intellectual inquiry. Nevertheless, when Christian writers did elaborate on the dominion granted humans in Gen. 1:28, they characteristically sought to define its spiritual and rational basis, or to depict the range of its potential applications, or to quantify the extent to which it survived the fall from paradise. Rarely, if ever, did they perceive the primordial blessing as a commandment to conquer and subdue the forces of the physical world, in the manner that the rabbis construed "be fertile and increase" to prescribe that they themselves have children. Christian and Jew alike postulated that God had created the world to facilitate human salvation. Gen. 1:28 confirmed their impression, but the subjugation of nature suggested by the verse did not engross them as a theological or an ethical issue. Christian exegetes might find such an issue in the blessing of dominion by reading it as an allegory of the soul or of Christ and his church. Literally minded Jewish commentators usually found no such issue at all; in the rare instance that they did, one must immediately consider the possibility of Christian influences.[154] Yet among both rabbis and churchmen, the nature that was of doctrinal concern was not that of the physical environment—"the fish of the sea, the birds of the sky, and all the living things that creep on earth"—but

153. Pseudo-Bede, *In primum librum Mosis,* PL 91:200–201, observed that dominion can refer to Christian rule over Jews and pagans, symbolized by the beasts and reptiles of Gen. 1:26, respectively.

154. See *MBR,* cited above, Chapter 2, at n. 202.

that of the human being, standing on the cosmic frontier between the earthly and the heavenly, between the realm of the angel and the realm of the beast.

More than dominion over fish, birds, and animals, sexual reproduction and the divine command to engage in it bore upon human nature as a theological problem. How did the Christian reading of Gen. 1:28 address this issue? For most of Augustine's patristic predecessors and contemporaries, with the probable exception of Theophilus, Irenaeus, and Theodore of Mopsuestia, the answer was clear-cut: "Be fertile and increase" could not withstand a literal interpretation because sexual activity did not comport with the primordial state of grace in which God created the first parents; sexuality befits a fallen human nature. The lasting implications of Augustinian exegesis, however, are difficult to evaluate. In a recent essay, Peter Brown analyzed the debate between the Pelagian heresiarch Julian of Eclanum and Augustine on the issue of sexuality and society. Relying on medical as well as moral and theological texts of the age, Brown demonstrated that for Julian "the reproductive process associated with intercourse was mobilised in obedience to God's command, 'increase and multiply.'" And for many an educated Roman aristocrat,

> Julian's view was coherent and credible. If the *summa voluptas* of orgasm was agreed by all to be necessary for conception. If the emotions associated with this *voluptas* were presented by Augustine as having become inordinately strong, at the expense of the rational mind, as a result of the Fall; and if this Fall was regarded, as Augustine certainly did regard it, as having placed humanity in the power of the Devil: then a contemporary might draw a logical conclusion. Because it was impossible to conceive children in Christian wedlock without a *voluptas*, whose observed strength was presented by Augustine as due to the Fall, it appeared that something of the work of the Devil had entered into the marriage-bed even of a *vir illustris*. It was an unsavory and troubling thought to any married Christian.[155]

As we have seen, the later Augustine's understanding of Gen. 1:28 complemented his doctrine of original sin in response to the Pelagian attack: Human procreation is not the work of the devil; the divine ordinance for male and female to "be fertile and increase" through their sexual conjunction appears in Scripture before the fall because God

---

155. Peter Brown, "Sexuality and Society," pp. 56, 61.

intended such reproduction to occur in paradise. Only after and as a result of the fall, sexual conjunction cannot occur without concupiscence, and this is the work of the devil. By stressing the reality and purity of the primordial sexuality mandated in our verse, Augustine hoped to highlight the contrast between primordial and fallen natures. Marriage and procreation were inherently good before and after the fall. In Eden they entailed no guilt; as a result of human transgression, sexual reproduction now transmits original sin.

Brown concluded that Augustine hereby drove a permanent wedge between sexuality and society. "Julian's presentation of sexuality followed the contours of an ancient, 'civic' model of society. *Politiké paidopoiïa,* 'procreation for the good of the city,' was what the doctors had wished to write about."[156] Such an outlook derived in large measure from a classical world view that identified the natural with the good. But Augustine propounded a new portrait of human nature, as damaged and corrupted in its present condition. Consequently, "the moral arbiter of the struggle to maintain a correct, Christian code of sexual relations within marriage was no longer the doctor, the reassuring expert on the hot pleasures of reproduction, but a bishop whose model of sexuality had been constructed with an exceptional finesse that owed much to the experience of the 'combat of chastity' waged in the desert by the monks."[157]

Its impact notwithstanding, Augustine's proposed definition of the relation between human nature and sexuality did not make the problem go away. Ironically, the bishop of Hippo may ultimately have encouraged others to view even present-day sexuality in a happier light, for when he bequeathed his doctrine of original sin to posterity he buttressed it with his corresponding, literal interpretation of Gen. 1:28. The bliss of marriage and procreation certainly numbered among the natural wonders of the biblical cosmogony, which Augustine himself held in high estimation and understood in their historical sense. Particularly as medieval theologians and poets tended to revive the classical view of nature that Augustine had rejected, or at least significantly modified, the issue of divinely ordained sexuality in postlapsarian human society reared its head once again.

156. Ibid., p. 64.
157. Ibid., p. 69.

CHAPTER 6

The Primordial Blessing and the Law of Nature

A N old Anglo-Saxon charm for curing an infertile or otherwise bewitched field addressed the following instructions to its owner:

> Take then at night, ere it is dawn, four turfs on the four quarters of the land, and mark how they formerly stood. Then take oil and honey and barm and milk of every cattle which is on the land, and part of every kind of tree which is grown on the land except hard beams, and part of every wort known by name except the buckbean only, and add to them holy water, and then drop of it thrice upon the place of the turfs, and then say these words: "Crescite," that is "be fertile"; "et multiplicamini," that is "increase"; "et replete," that is "and fill"; "terram," that is, "this earth." And say the Paternoster as often as the other formula, and after that bear the turfs to church and let a mass priest sing four masses over the turfs.[1]

Centuries later, en route to Canterbury, Geoffrey Chaucer's Wife of Bath also invoked our verse to defend her persistent quest for instinctual gratification:

---

1. Thomas Oswald Cockayne, ed., *Leechdoms, Wortcunning, and Starcraft of Early England,* rev. ed., 3 vols. (London, 1961), 1:398–405. Alternating recitations of Gen. 1:28 and the Paternoster, in multiples of three or nine, reappear in the middle and at the end of this elaborate ritual.

> God bad us for to wexe and multiplye;
> That gentil text kan I wel understonde.[2]

Whether in the realm of agriculture or that of human sexuality, both the Anglo-Saxon farmer and Alison of Bath invoked the primordial blessing in their own behalf, seeking to enjoy the fruits and delights of nature to which they believed they were entitled. The authors of these English texts thereby acknowledged what Jewish and Christian readers of Scripture had long understood: Gen. 1:28 certainly conveys a divine blessing and mandate to the first parents, but it also instructs *de rerum natura,* on the fundamental characteristics and constitutive processes of the natural order that God created. This natural order, often personified in the female character *Natura,* regularly commanded the attention of medieval theologians, jurists, and poets, whose words and ideas on the subject have fueled the investigations of numerous modern scholars. *Natura* commanded attention independently of the Genesis cosmogony, to be sure, and much of her literary career lies beyond the purview of this book. Yet the primordial blessing did figure significantly in medieval consideration of *Natura* and her laws, especially in several instances when the discussion left the clerical academy and entered the realm of secular poetry. Following the career of Gen. 1:28 into new genres of high and late medieval Christian texts, this chapter assesses the perceived relationship between Gen. 1:28 and the law of nature. The kinds of sources reviewed here mandate an occasional brief excursus into literary history, but our focus remains the biblical text and its career. Did the biblical injunction to "be fertile and increase" have the status of natural law? Does it still? Has the essence of natural law changed in the wake of the fall from paradise, weighing in turn on the continued relevance of the primordial blessing? And what might the answers to these questions reveal concerning the medieval encounter with Scripture as well as the appreciation of *Natura* herself?

A TRADITION OF EXCLUSION

The obverse of his doctrine of original sin, Augustine's interpretation of Gen. 1:28 militated against the inclusion of the biblical mandate for

---

2. Geoffrey Chaucer, *Canterbury Tales,* III.28–29, in *The Riverside Chaucer,* ed. Larry D. Benson, 3rd ed. (Boston, Mass., 1987), p. 105.

procreation in the law of nature as it now exists—that is, in the aftermath of the fall from Eden. As noted in Chapter 5, Augustine's insistence that God intended for the first parents to act upon his reproductive mandate in paradise departed from the preponderance of patristic opinion before him. Most of the early church fathers could not conceive of human sexual activity transpiring in a state of grace. But Augustine construed the divine injunction of "be fertile and increase" as applying precisely to that condition: Only then could sexual congress and reproduction have ensued in an optimal fashion, effecting the divine plan for human salvation and rightly constituting the object of the primordial blessing. After the fall, man and woman could not conjoin without the sin of rebellious passion, and Augustine would not admit that the first divine words to Adam and Eve would have referred to such activity, even if God did not entirely revoke the blessings of Gen. 1:28 in the wake of their sin. The law of nature in its present state, however, hardly pertained to the state of primal innocence and grace. Responding to the Pelagians, Augustine proclaimed that when Adam "of his own will committed that great sin, he vitiated, perverted, and defiled human nature in himself."[3] And when Augustine studied the Pauline message (Rom. 5:20) that "law came in, to increase the trespass," he concluded that "we may understand either the natural law, which then appeared among those who could employ their reason, or the written law, which was given by Moses and could not give life or liberate from the law of sin and death passed down from Adam." Like the law of Moses, the law of nature could not save human beings from their wretched state; because of the fall of Adam and Eve, it too only accentuates the sin of concupiscence. "Now that the law given in paradise has been broken, a human being is born of Adam with the law of sin and death, of which it is said (Rom. 7:23), 'I see in my members another law at war with the law of my mind and making me captive to the law of sin which dwells in my members.'"[4] From the perspective of Augustine, the law of nature as we know it is a singularly postlapsarian phenomenon, while the divine mandate to "be fertile and increase" presupposed the primeval bliss of paradise.[5]

---

3. Augustine, *Opus imperfectum contra Julianum* 4.104, PL 45:1401.
4. Augustine, *Epistula* 157.15, CSEL 44:462–63.
5. This takes issue with the argument of Michael William Twomey, "The Anatomy of Sin: Violations of *Kynde* and *Trawthe* in *Cleanness*" (Ph.D. Dissertation, Cornell University, Ithaca, N.Y., 1979), ch. 1, that the reproductive imperative of natural law in the High Middle Ages stemmed directly from Augustinian instruction on nature and sin. Nevertheless, I am

Just as Augustine's literal interpretation of Gen. 1:28 prevailed in Western Christendom for centuries after him, so too did his exclusion of "be fertile and increase" from postlapsarian natural law find general acceptance among Latin writers of the early Middle Ages. When echoing the classic Roman view, preserved for the church by Isidore of Seville, that "the union of man and woman which we call marriage, the procreation of children, and their upbringing" all derive from natural law,[6] Gratian and many of the Decretists drew no connection to Gen. 1:28.[7] Our verse rarely figured in discussions of homosexuality, contraception, clerical celibacy, or even the threefold good of marriage—offspring, fidelity, and symbolic stability—outlined by Augustine,[8] whence derived the test of procreative purpose that justified sexual relations within marriage. One cannot but wonder at how rarely the verse appears in John T. Noonan's monumental study of Christian attitudes toward contraception and in the sources that Noonan cited. As Noonan argued, the reproductive rationale for marriage derived not from Scripture but from classical, most notably Stoic, philosophical tradition.[9]

While the absence of Gen. 1:28 in such contexts as these is itself telling, several theological treatises of the twelfth and thirteenth centuries account more explicitly for its omission. In his *De sacramentis,* Hugh of St. Victor observed that of all the sacraments only marriage was instituted prior to sin. As a result,

> the institution of marriage is twofold: once before sin as a duty, and then after sin as a cure; the first that nature might be multiplied; the second

grateful to Michael Twomey for allowing me to read several of his forthcoming publications that helped inspire the ideas and direction of this chapter. For a review of the history of natural law doctrine, see Felix Flückiger, *Geschichte des Naturrechtes,* 1 (Zurich, 1954).

6. *Digest* 1.1.1.3, in *Corpus iuris civilis* 1,2:29; Isidore of Seville, *Etimologías (Etymologiae)* 5.4, ed. Jose Oroz Reta and Manuel-A. Marcos Casquero, 2 vols., Biblioteca de autores cristianos 433–34 (Madrid, 1982–83), 1:510.

7. Gratian, *Decretum,* D. 1, c. 7, in *Corpus iuris canonici,* ed. Aemilius Friedberg, 2 vols. (1879; repr., Graz, 1959), 1:2.

8. *Proles, fides, sacramentum;* see Augustine, *De bono conjugali* 29.32, CSEL 41:227. For the translation of these terms, see Noonan, *Contraception,* pp. 127–28; on their legal and theological ramifications, see also Müller, *Die Lehre,* and Joseph Freisen, *Geschichte des kanonischen Eherechts bis zum Verfall der Glossenliteratur,* 2nd ed. (1893; repr., Paderborn, 1963).

9. John Boswell, *Christianity, Social Tolerance, and Homosexuality: Gay People in Western Europe from the Beginning of the Christian Era to the Fourteenth Century* (Chicago, 1980), pp. 129–31, objected that Stoic thought did not underlie Christian opposition to homosexual activity. But Boswell is equally insistent in ruling out biblical doctrine as the basis for such opposition; he attributes it instead to prevailing social conditions and popular attitudes in the Roman Empire.

that nature might be supported and vice checked. . . . God himself, the instituter and ordainer, shows why the duty of marriage was first established, when he says: "Be fertile and increase and fill the earth." Now the duty of marriage is this, that the mingling of flesh was established not for the remedy of weakness but for the multiplication of progeny; after sin, blessed Augustine testifies that the very same was conceded as a remedy for weakness.[10]

Marriage might fall within the law of nature both before and after sin, but insofar as it offers a foundation and rationale for the institution, Gen. 1:28 pertains to the duty (*officium*) of marriage prescribed before the fall and not to the cure (*remedium*) for vice conceded to human beings after the fall. Having quoted Hugh at some length, Peter Lombard similarly distinguished between the divine ordinance (*praeceptum*) and the concession (*indulgentia*) of marriage, the former enacted prior to sin with the instruction to "be fertile and increase," and the latter granted in the aftermath of sin.[11] Commenting on Peter's formulation in the next century, Bonaventure made the distinction clearer still: In their obligatory sense, God directed his words of "be fertile and increase" exclusively to human beings and solely before the fall.[12] For these heirs to the Augustinian tradition, Gen. 1:28 expressed the role of procreation in the divine plan for human salvation: facilitating the birth of a predetermined number of saints, who together would achieve immortality and enjoy the final age of glory. As Augustine took pains to specify, in this salvific sense "be fertile and increase" applied specifically to the state of primordial innocence, before the corruption of human nature by sin.

RECONSIDERATION AND INCLUSION

In the twelfth century, however, even as these Scholastic authors reaffirmed their Augustinian heritage, new conceptions of nature and

---

10. Hugh of St. Victor, *De sacramentis* 2.11.3, PL 176:482; with several exceptions, I have followed *On the Sacraments of the Christian Faith*, tr. Roy J. Deferrari (Cambridge, Mass., 1951), p. 325.

11. Peter Lombard, *Sententiae* 4.26.3, 2:418. Peter did note that the *praeceptum* was renewed temporarily in the wake of the flood (Gen. 9) in order to replenish the human race, but now that people have multiplied, marriage "is contracted according to the indulgence, not according to the commandment (*imperium*)." Cf. Walter of Montagne (Ps.-Hugh of St. Victor), *Summa sententiarum* 7.1–3, PL 176:153–56; and Peter of Poitiers, *Sententiarum libri quinque* 5.15, PL 211:1258.

12. Bonaventure, *In 4 Sententiarum* 4.26.1.1–2, *Opera omnia*, 11 vols. (Quaracchi, 1882–1902), 4:661–64.

its laws began to take hold in Western Christendom, ideas that ultimately extended the identification of Gen. 1:28 as natural law into the postlapsarian age. Rather than attempt to review every document that pertains to this process, we approach the evidence selectively, exploring the contexts and issues that yielded this conclusion.

Canon Law

The medieval Christian revival of Roman law complicated the definition of *ius naturale* by blending fine legal distinctions with theological categories inherited from the church fathers. The law of nature, the Roman jurist Ulpian had taught, was universal, antecedent to any act of positive legislation.[13] Yet from a Christian perspective, natural law also had to be of divine origin, because God had fashioned the natural order according to his own specifications. In the opening paragraph of the *Decretum,* Gratian therefore noted: "The law of nature is that recorded in the Law and the Gospel, by which one is ordered to do to another what he desires done to himself, and is forbidden from doing to another what he does not want done to himself."[14] Brian Tierney helpfully described the resulting confusion in Gratian's instruction:

> This further identification (or apparent identification) of natural law with the divine revelation of Scripture is at the root of the problem of terminology that we have to consider. Gratian's own position was more complicated than his opening remark suggested. Natural law, he explained, did not really begin with the divine revelation recorded in the Old and New Testaments, but originated "from the beginning of the rational creature" and remained always immutable. His natural law then corresponded to the Roman category of equitable and just rules that men, as distinct from other creatures, recognized as binding through their inherent rationality. Gratian pointed out that these basic rules of conduct were also defined for Christians in the Scriptures and that accordingly one could say that natural law was divine, but he also indicated that not everything contained in the Scriptures constituted natural law. . . . Natural law and divine law were not then really identical in Gratian's thought; rather the two categories overlapped.[15]

13. *Digest* 1.1.1.3, ed. Krueger et al., 1,2:29.
14. Gratian, *Decretum,* D. 1 (init.), ed. Friedberg, 1:1.
15. Brian Tierney, *"Natura id est Deus:* A Case of Juristic Pantheism?" *Journal of the History of Ideas* 24 (1963), 310–11.

Many canonists who followed Gratian addressed the problematic relationship of divine, natural, and biblical law, but as Tierney has noted, they generally did so not by delimiting the precise meaning of each term but by playing an "academic game" of multiplying alternative definitions.[16] Gratian and many of his colleagues, we have indicated, did not identify the biblical mandate of procreation as a statement of natural law. But Gratian did adduce Isidore of Seville's citation of Justinian's *Digest,* to the effect that the law of nature prescribed "the union of man and woman," and the Decretists felt obliged to consider exactly what this entailed.

Most of the glossators of the *Decretum* avoided mention of our verse and need not concern us at length.[17] Some differentiated between the physical attraction of the sexes and the practice of marriage, tending toward Ulpian's view that natural law characterizes the sexual behavior of all animal creatures; the "union of man and woman" therefore includes any heterosexual relationship, even the extramarital and the incestuous. Others insisted that the law of nature could not be sinful and that the union in question must refer to marriage, perhaps even to its spiritual dimension rather than its sexual one. Several sidestepped the problem altogether, identifying "the union of man and woman" not as a provision of natural law but as its effect. Nevertheless, a few commentators proceeded from Gratian's opening linkage of *ius naturae*[18] to the teaching of the Law and the Gospel, and they deemed Gen. 1:28 a biblical record of natural law. Responding to Isidore's description of natural law as that which antecedes positive legislation, Rufinus specified that Isidore had referred strictly to its priority vis-à-vis human legislation, "for the union of husband and wife derives from the legislation of God, when he himself stated, 'be fertile and increase.'"[19] Johannes Faventius echoed Rufinus in his gloss, as did Odo of Dover, who elaborated slightly:[20] "For the union of man and woman was established by the legislation of God—which is of the highest nature[21]—

16. Idem, *Medieval Poor Law: A Sketch of Its Canonical Theory and Its Application in England* (Berkeley, Calif., 1959), p. 30.
17. See the discussions of Otto Lottin, *Le droit naturel chez Saint Thomas d'Aquin et ses prédécesseurs,* 2nd ed. (Brussels, 1931), pt. 1; and Rudolf Weigand, *Die Naturrechtslehre der Legisten und Dekretisten von Irnerius bis Accursius und von Gratian bis Johannes Teutonicus,* Münchener theologische Studien 3,26 (Munich, 1967), esp. pp. 283–306.
18. Some read *ius naturale;* see Friedberg, *Corpus iuris canonici* 1:1 n. 2.
19. Rufinus of Bologna, *Summa Decretorum,* ed. Heinrich Singer (Paderborn, 1902), p. 8.
20. Cited in Weigand, *Die Naturrechtslehre,* p. 288.
21. On the implications of this phrase, see Tierney, *"Natura id est Deus,"* p. 313.

when he himself stated, 'be fertile and increase.' " Huguccio of Pisa also followed suit, offering the most thorough resolution of legal definition and biblical interpretation. Huguccio concluded that the union of man and woman that derives from natural law is indeed their sexual conjunction, governed by reason so that a man

> should conjoin only with his wife and in a legitimate manner—namely, for the sake of offspring or for the sake of rendering the [marital] debt— since any other sexual union, whether with his wife or with another woman, is not according to natural law but against it. Sexual union among the first parents derived from natural law enacted as a commandment; for it was said to them as a commandment, "Be fertile and increase . . . ," and this commandment was reissued after the flood.[22]

According to these opinions, our verse's mandate of human sexual reproduction amounted to a provision of natural law. And as Huguccio made clear, neither did the fall from Eden alter the status of this ordinance, which God repeated to Noah in the wake of flood, nor have subsequent developments rendered it obsolete. The essentially rational and beneficent natural order reflected in the scriptural blessing of "be fertile and increase" still pertains to the sexual behavior of human beings in the present age, just as it pertained to that of Adam and Eve in their primordial innocence.

It is interesting to note that for canonists like Huguccio who now affirmed the continuing relevance of "be fertile and increase," its status as a commandment derived primarily from its correspondence to the law of nature and only secondarily from its inclusion in Scripture. Most Old Testament precepts had ceased to bind Christians, and the classification of our verse as legislation was itself questionable. Here the accordance of Gen. 1:28 with the teachings of Ulpian mattered more than its primordial pronouncement by God. This affords an instructive contrast to rabbinic legal theory, which has no formal category of natural law. All valid legislation proceeds from God and his duly constituted agents. To the extent that some rabbis challenged the talmudic limitation of God's reproductive mandate to free Jewish males, they generally had to argue on the basis of Scripture and its authoritative traditions of interpretation—although in the final analysis their convic-

---

22. Cited in Weigand, *Die Naturrechtslehre*, p. 291.

tion that "the world was created specifically for the sake of procreation" bordered closely on the notion that all God's creatures reproduce.[23] And precisely this conclusion led Roman jurists and their medieval successors to classify procreation as *ius naturae*.

From Theology to Poetry

At the same time that juridical interests thus led several canonists to identify the procreative mandate of Gen. 1:28 as natural law, the spiritual and philosophical climate of Christian Europe began to move Scholastic theologians in a similar direction. M.-D. Chenu characterized the renaissance of the twelfth century not only in terms of its revival of classical studies and its thirst for new sources of knowledge, but in terms of a preoccupation with the natural world, an interest that pervaded all facets of Western society and culture:

> The discovery of nature: we are not now concerned merely with the feeling for nature which poets of the time evinced here and there in fashionable allegorical constructions, nor are we concerned merely with the plastic representations of nature that sculptors fashioned at the portals and on the capitals of cathedrals. Rather, our concern is with the realization which laid hold upon these men of the twelfth century when they thought of themselves as confronting an external, present, intelligible, and active reality as they might confront a partner . . . whose might and whose decrees called for accommodation or conflict—a realization which struck them at the very moment when, with no less a shock, they reflected that they were themselves caught up within the framework of nature, were themselves also bits of this cosmos they were ready to master.[24]

The physical world became worthy of study for its own sake; Christian interest in the cosmogony increased at an unprecedented rate,[25] and no repository of information or method for retrieving it was disqualified *a priori* from contributing to this endeavor. Yet as Winthrop Wetherbee aptly observed, the burgeoning of scientific concern does not tell the

---

23. See above, Chapter 3, at n. 109.
24. Marie-Dominique Chenu, *Nature, Man, and Society in the Twelfth Century: Essays on New Theological Perspectives in the Latin West*, ed. Jerome Taylor and Lester K. Little (Chicago, 1968), pp. 4–5.
25. See Zahlten, *Creatio mundi*, esp. pp. 90ff., 230ff.

entire story; empirical method and new discoveries were themselves slow to emerge. Perhaps more important was the new disposition underlying the cultural rebirth: "an insistence upon the value of rational investigation, a tendency to elaborate schemata classifying the sciences in terms of their contribution to a single coherent wisdom." These comported well with the regnant Platonic model of "the universe as a single, fully realized, and animate being," whose providential order integrates spiritual and physical realities into a unified, rational whole.[26] Regardless of its source—textual authority, logical argument, or scientific investigation—all truth pertained to this single cosmic order, governed by a nourishing, benevolent world soul that theologians quickly associated with the Holy Spirit itself. In a word, medieval intellectuals came to view nature as divine—not in a pantheistic sense, but inasmuch as the physical world derives from the creativity of the supreme nature, the *Natura naturans* that creates life and maintains it by infusing rational order into the cosmos. Precisely in this vein could Roman and canon lawyers of the age consider *Natura* and God as one and the same (*Natura id est Deus*). A revived, classical notion of natural law thereby challenged the tradition that derived from Augustine: Natural law as an expression of the divine was not limited to the primordial conditions before the fall, but reflects the nature of life as it has always been.[27] This challenge to Augustinian ideas could proceed in several directions, and one finds divergent approaches to the issues of procreation and human sexuality. Some theologians glorified the natural order at the expense of a Christian scheme of salvation history, facilitating the association of "be fertile and increase" with a naturalism of questionable orthodoxy. Yet for theologians who asserted the unity of the salvific and natural realms, the divine mandate for procreation served as valuable biblical testimony.

In the Direction of Heterodoxy. One of the first texts to exemplify the new outlook was the *Cosmographia* of Bernard Silvestris, in which the medieval literary career of *Natura* truly began to flourish. As George D. Economou observed, here

> Natura assumes a central position in the poetic expression of the Chartrian vision of the universe, a vision based on the conviction that man is

26. Bernard Silvestris, *Cosmographia,* tr. Winthrop Wetherbee (New York, 1973), pp. 8, 10.

27. See Tierney, "*Natura id est Deus,*" esp. p. 322.

capable of interpreting and understanding the natural and moral order of a universe which, like its transcendent model, is a single, harmonious whole, a sensible, concrete world that participates in the divine reality which gave it being. The nature of the cosmos reveals the nature of man; to know the macrocosm is to know the microcosm, man, in whom the "immense unity of all things was knotted up together . . . who stands at the paradoxical borderline of matter and spirit."[28]

Albeit without direct reference to Gen. 1:28, the subject of procreation looms prominent in the *Cosmographia,* and Bernard thereby fueled one kind of late medieval appreciation of "be fertile and increase." We therefore must consider his ideas, briefly but with care.

Bernard depicted the cosmogony as proceeding from the intercession of *Natura* between divine providence (personifed as Nous) and the primeval realm of unformed matter (named Silva). As the epic unfolds, Nous infuses a vivifying world soul (Endelechia) into the cosmos to provide for spiritual life and rational order, while *Natura* herself produces bodies for the individual souls created by Endelechia. The harmonious unity of the macrocosm is then recreated in the microcosm of the human being, fashioned "to conform to his two natures, and remain in harmony with the dual principles of his existence."[29] Enlisting the energies of *Natura*'s associates Urania and Physis, Nous directs the former to fashion the human soul, the latter to mold the human body, and *Natura* to execute "the formative uniting of the two, soul and body, through emulation of the order of the heavens."[30] The formation of man brings the cosmogony to a resounding climax, and the epic draws to a close with an ode of praise for "the masterwork of powerful Nature," glorifying the abilities of "the five attendant senses," the heart, and then the liver. In the concluding lines of the poem, attention finally turns to the genitalia and to procreation, echoing the medieval rabbinic association of the senses with the reproductive organs:[31]

> The lower body ends in the wanton loins, and the private parts lie hidden away in this remote region. Their exercise will be enjoyable and profitable, so long as the time, the manner, and the extent are suitable.

28. George D. Economou, *The Goddess Natura in Medieval Literature* (Cambridge, Mass., 1972), p. 58, citing Chenu, *Nature, Man, and Society,* p. 25 (ellipsis Economou's).
29. Bernard Silvestris, *Cosmographia* 2.10, ed. Peter Dronke (Leiden, 1978), pp. 140–41; tr. Wetherbee, p. 113.
30. Ibid. 2.11.1, ed. Dronke, p. 142; tr. Wetherbee, p. 114.
31. See above, Chapter 2, nn. 93ff.

Lest earthly life pass away, and the process of generation be cut off, and material existence, dissolved, return to primordial chaos, propagation was made the charge of two genii, and the act itself assigned to twin brothers. They fight unconquered against death with their life-giving weapons, renew our nature, and perpetuate our kind. They will not allow what is perishable to perish, nor what dies to be wholly owed to death, nor mankind to wither utterly at the root. The phallus wars against Lachesis and carefully rejoins the vital threads severed by the hands of the Fates. Blood sent forth from the seat of the brain flows down to the loins, bearing the image of the shining sperm. Artful Nature molds and shapes the fluid, that in conceiving it may reproduce the forms of the ancestors.[32]

Elements of Platonic as well as biblical cosmology and anthropology clearly permeate Bernard's allegory of the creation, and modern scholars have disputed the relative loyalties of the poet to Athens and Jerusalem. Reacting to the uninhibited adaptation of pagan mythology, Ernst Curtius argued that Bernard departed from the spiritual priorities of the Bible and Plato alike: "The whole is bathed in the atmosphere of a fertility cult, in which religion and sexuality mingle."[33] Yet Etienne Gilson, Theodore Silverstein, and Economou defended Bernard's adherence to a tradition of Christian Platonism.[34] It appears that both views have merit. The Cosmographia may have solved some problems inherent in the quest to integrate earthly and supernal realms into a single chain of being, but it also intensified others. What, precisely, is the relationship of classical Natura with the God of the Bible? Granted that God created her and that she heeds divine instruction as she performs her creative tasks, the reader of Bernard's poem beheld a Natura who functions independently in a realm where God's providence has no active role. The world that Bernard's Natura and her associates fashion and regulate is good because of its original correspondence to a preexistent heavenly model. Bernard's lavish descriptions of both macrocosm

32. Ibid. 2.14, ed. Dronke, p. 154; tr. Wetherbee, p. 126.
33. Ernst Robert Curtius, *European Literature and the Latin Middle Ages,* tr. Willard R. Trask, Bollingen Series 36 (1953; repr., Princeton, N.J., 1967), p. 112.
34. Etienne Gilson, "La cosmogonie de Bernardus Silvestris," *Archives d'histoire doctrinale et littéraire du Moyen Age* 3 (1928), 5–24; Theodore Silverstein, "The Fabulous Cosmogony of Bernardus Silvestris," *Modern Philology* 46 (1948), 92–116; and Economou, *The Goddess Natura,* pp. 58–72. The most balanced and comprehensive treatment of Bernard is Brian Stock, *Myth and Science in the Twelfth Century: A Study of Bernard Silvester* (Princeton, N.J., 1972).

and microcosm extol their intricate orderliness, but not because of any opportunity for spiritual achievement and reward that this order might afford human creatures. In the world of the *Cosmographia,* that which is natural is that which is good *ipso facto;* no higher standard of morality that ought to command the allegiance of its inhabitants is evident. The order of such a world mandates human sexuality simply to provide for its survival; the twin genii appointed to guarantee that "the time, the manner, and the extent [of the sexual act] are suitable" have no apparent concern beyond the production of offspring. But Christianity instructs that human interaction with God over the course of history has had irrevocable effect on the character and value of marriage and reproduction. In their effort to supplant the physical, mundane pursuits of human life with concerns more heavenly and otherworldly, had not the teachings of the church relegated sexual activity to a station less venerable than that accorded it by Bernard?

Such identification of procreation and *Natura,* along with the disjunction of *Natura* and any biblical scheme of salvation history, may help to explain the subsequent linkage of Gen. 1:28 with a naturalistic sort of heterodoxy. In a number of late medieval texts, some critics and some defenders of the church considered Gen. 1:28 the byword of the sexually permissive, who challenged the constraints of a Christian morality. Our verse thus appears in the travelogue of Sir John Mandeville to defend the promiscuity of the inhabitants of the isle of Lamary.

> Thei wedden there no wyfes, for alle the wommen there ben comoun and thei forsake no man. And thei seyn thei synnen yif thei refusen ony man. And so God commanded to Adam and Eue and to alle that comen of him whan He seyde, "Crescite et multiplicamini et replete terram." And therfore may no man in that contree seyn, "This is my wyf," ne no womman may seye, "This is my husbonde."[35]

Although Mandeville probably based his description of Lamary on the *Itinerarium* of Friar Odoric,[36] he himself appears to have accredited the

---

35. *Mandeville's Travels* 20, ed. M. C. Seymour (Oxford, 1967), p. 131. The text proceeds to indicate that these people also held all property in common, an ideal that critics of the church also sought to justify in their interpretation of Gen. 1:28; see, for example, William of Ockham, *Opus nonaginta dierum* 26, in *Opera politica,* ed. J. G. Sikes et al., 3 vols. (Manchester, 1940–63), 2:483–85.

36. Odoric da Pordenone, *Itinerarium,* ed. Carolus Emanuel Aurivillius (Uppsala, 1817), pp. 21–22; and see the note of M. C. Seymour to his edition of *The Bodley Version of Mandeville's Travels* (London, 1963), p. 165.

islanders' behavior with the allusion to Gen. 1:28. Such devotion to the
instinctual demands of nature comports well with Mandeville's concluding praise of all the exotic peoples he encountered:[37]

> Yit is there non of hem alle but that thei han sum resoun within hem and
> vnderstondynge—but yif it be the fewere—and that han certeyn articles
> of oure feith and summe gode poyntes of oure beleeve; and that thei
> beleeven in God that formede alle thing and made the world and clepen
> Him God of Nature, after that the prophete seyth (Ps. 67:8), "Et
> metuent eum omnes fines terre,"[38] and also in another place (Ps. 72:11),
> "Omnes gentes servient ei," that is to seyne, Alle folk schul seruen
> Him.

These people know nothing of the Trinity, we are told, but they are
familiar with books of the Old Testament, especially the book of Genesis. For Mandeville, it would seem, compliance with the rational precepts of natural law, as evidenced in the biblical cosmogony, amounts
to the service of God even in the absence of Christianity.[39]

In the fifteenth century the French author Guillaume Saignet included
Gen. 1:28 in his rendition of Natura's plaint against clerical celibacy.[40]
Across the channel, the English mystic Margery Kempe wrote that she
was detained and interrogated by ecclesiastical authorities who feared
that she came in her white clothes to lead away the wives of English-
men.[41] Soon thereafter another cleric questioned her, "askyng þes
wordys how þei xuld ben vndirstondyn, 'Crescite et multiplicamini.'"
Margery prudently avoided recrimination by responding:

> Ser, þes wordys ben not vndirstondyn only of begetyng of chyldren
> bodily, but also be purchasyng of vertu, whech is frute gostly, as be
> heryng of þe wordys of God, be good exampyl ȝeuyng, be mekenes and

---

37. *Mandeville's Travels* 34, p. 227.

38. "All the ends of the earth shall fear him"—departing from NJPS.

39. Cf. the comments of Morton W. Bloomfield, "Chaucer's Sense of History," *Journal of English and Germanic Philology* 51 (1952), 310–11; and Carlo Ginzburg, *The Cheese and the Worms: The Cosmos of a Sixteenth-Century Miller*, tr. John and Anne Tedeschi (Baltimore, Md., 1980), p. 47. I am grateful to Christian Zacher for calling these references to my attention.

40. Guillaume Saignet, *Lamentacio humane nature adversus nicenam constitutionem*, in Nicole Grévy-Pons, *Célibat et nature: Une controverse médiévale a propos d'un traité du début du XVᵉ siècle*, Centre d'histoire des sciences et des doctrines, Equipe de recherches sur l'humanisme français des XIVᵉ et XVᵉ siècles: Textes et études 1 (Paris, 1975), pp. 146–47.

41. *The Book of Margery Kempe* 48, ed. Sanford Brown Meech and Hope Emily Allen (London, 1940), p. 116.

paciens, charite and chastite, and swech oþer, for pacyens is more
worthy þan myraclys werkyng.[42]

Following the lead of Margery's modern editor,[43] John Mahoney contended that her white clothing caused her beholders to associate Margery with the heresy of the free spirit. Adherents of this heresy disparaged the institution of marriage. They were commonly thought to
participate in ritual orgies, reenacting the primal union of the first
parents in paradise and invoking the text of Gen. 1:28 to validate their
behavior.[44] Robert Lerner wisely doubted the reliability of such tales,
which were probably imaginative embellishments of allusions to Adamite heretics in the works of Augustine and Isidore of Seville.[45] Yet
Augustine and Isidore made no mention of our verse in their descriptions, and the biblical association probably stemmed from a later, medieval outlook, which viewed "be fertile and increase" as expressing
nature's license for human sexuality. The perceived tension between
this natural law and the service of God finds additional recognition in a
fifteenth-century English paraphrase of the Ten Commandments. Discussing the prohibition of adultery, the poet berates the treacherous
machinations of adulterous wives; Gen. 1:28 provides the refrain, as
most stanzas end with a reference to the sexual license and wiles of these
women. For example: "She wil be redy with the twynkelyng of an eie, /
And wyth her lytille whetyng-corne to encrese and multeply."[46]

42. Ibid. 51, p. 121.

43. Ibid., pp. 312, 320–21.

44. John Mahoney, "Alice of Bath: Her 'Secte' and 'Gentil Text,'" *Criticism* 6 (1964), 146–
47, 152–53. See the descriptions of the Adamite heretics in Auguste Jundt, *Histoire du pantheisme populaire au Moyen Age et au seizième siècle* (1875; repr., Frankfurt a.M., 1964), pp. 116–
17; and Norman Cohn, *The Pursuit of the Millennium: Revolutionary Millenarians and Mystical
Anarchists of the Middle Ages*, rev. ed. (New York, 1970), pp. 180, 219–21, 356–56 n. 180, 361–
62 nn. 219–20. On the threatening quality of Margery's white clothes, see also Hope Phyllis
Weissman, "Margery Kempe in Jerusalem: *Hysterica Compassio* in the Late Middle Ages," in
*Acts of Interpretation: The Text in Its Contexts, 700–1600—Essays on Medieval and Renaissance
Literature in Honor of E. Talbot Donaldson*, ed. Mary J. Carruthers and Elizabeth D. Kirk
(Norman, Okla., 1982), p. 216. And for a defense of Margery's orthodoxy, see Clarissa W.
Atkinson, *Mystic and Pilgrim: The "Book" and World of Margery Kempe* (Ithaca, N.Y., 1983),
esp. ch. 4.

45. Robert E. Lerner, *The Heresy of the Free Spirit in the Later Middle Ages* (Berkeley, Calif.,
1972), pp. 25–32, 123–24. See Augustine, *De haeresibus* 31, ed. Liguori G. Müller, Catholic
University of America Patristic Studies 90 (Washington, D.C., 1956), pp. 76–77; and Isidore
of Seville, *Etymologiae* 8.5.14.

46. Thomas Wright and James Orchard Hallwell, eds., *Reliquiae antiquae: Scraps from
Ancient Manuscripts, Illustrating Chiefly Early English Literature and the English Language*, 2 vols.
(1841–43; repr., New York, 1966), 2:27–29.

As a Reaffirmation of Orthodoxy. Writing soon after Bernard Silvestris, Alan of Lille reasserted the primacy of Christian ideals in the world
of *Natura*. Borrowing extensively from the cast and the argument of the
Cosmographia, Alan composed his *De planctu Naturae* to bemoan contemporary abuse of the natural, sensory faculties with which the deity
had endowed human beings. Alone of all God's creatures, humans in
Alan's work stand at the junction of angelic and animal existence,
embodying the complexity of the entire macrocosm within their own
distinctive makeup. Humans thus exemplify the cosmic tension between order and chaos. They are equipped with the divine gift of a
rational will to harness their passionate appetites, microcosmically reflecting the victory of form over matter that underlies the creation and
the survival of the natural order. Nevertheless, the power of choice has
also led human beings to contravene the rational laws of nature as no
other species has done. Alan's *Natura* is most distraught at human
subversion of her primary function, the ensuring of cosmic survival
through the procreative union of opposite sexes. *Natura* herself explains
this reproductive concern:

> When the artisan of the universe had clothed all things in the outward
> aspect befitting their natures and had wed them to one another in the
> relationship of lawful marriage, it was his will that by a mutually related
> circle of birth and death, transitory things should be given stability by
> instability, endlessness by endings, eternity by temporariness, and that
> the series of things should ever be knit by successive renewals of birth.
> He decreed that by the lawful path of derivation by propagation, like
> things, sealed with the stamp of manifest resemblance, should be pro-
> duced from like.
>
> Accordingly he appointed me as his substitute, his vice-regent, the
> mistress of his mint, to put the stamp on the different classes of things so
> that I should mold the images of things, each on its own anvil, not allow
> the product to deviate from the form proper to its anvil but that, by my
> diligence in work, the face of the copy should spring from the counte-
> nance of the exemplar and not be defrauded of any of its natural gifts. I
> obeyed the commander's orders in my work . . . ; yet under the myste-
> rious power of God, I carried out the administration of this office in
> such a way that the right hand of the supreme authority should direct
> my hand in its work, for my writing-reed would go instantly off course
> if it were not guided by the finger of the superintendent on high.[47]

47. Alan of Lille, *De planctu Naturae* 8.208–35, ed. Nikolaus M. Häring, *Studi medievali*,
3rd ser. 19 (1978), 840; *The Plaint of Nature*, tr. James J. Sheridan, Medieval Sources in
Translation 26 (Toronto, 1980), pp. 145–46.

Natura proceeds to describe the violence inflicted upon this harmonious arrangement by her adulterous subordinate Venus, the misdirected excesses of the latter's son Cupid, and the ensuing fall of human beings from their original, virtuous state. At the conclusion of the work, *Natura* appeals to her consort and alter ego Genius,[48] and the two exchange kisses "not corrupted by any poison of lawless Venus, but symbolic of the caresses of epicene attraction and even indicative of the harmony of mystic love."[49] Sharing *Natura*'s grief, Genius dons the vestments of a priest and recites a "prearranged formula of excommunication" against "everyone who blocks the lawful path of Venus."[50]

We have quoted the *De planctu Naturae* at length in order to accentuate some of its departures from the work of Bernard Silvestris, as well as to facilitate our consideration of writers who followed Alan of Lille. By contrast to the *Cosmographia,* Alan's *De planctu Naturae* is "charged with sacramental analogies. The domain of his *Natura* is a church, and Genius is its priest administering the mystical union of the Word with the *materiale verbum* of creation."[51] Alan's *Natura* not only creates in response to divine command but also relies on the direction of God at every step in her endeavors. She unabashedly admits her inferiority and her dependence on the divine. Without divine guidance she simply cannot function, and the providence of God is by implication ever active in her world.[52] As a result, one may not bifurcate between the cosmic order that *Natura* seeks to uphold and the dictates of a divinely revealed morality. Worldly pursuits must serve this higher perfection, and human sexuality, the epitome of *Natura*'s procreative handiwork, above all else. Procreation is not good *ipso facto,* because it promotes the continuation of worldly existence. Rather, its natural good derives from its rational and virtuous conduct, and ultimately from its contribution to God's design for salvation. Sexual activity that varies from these norms appropriately tops a traditionally Christian list of vices that Alan's *Natura* deplores. Such juxtaposition of vices and virtues suggests that *Natura* desires not merely procreative sexual activity, but sexual relations endowed with sacred purpose: "the faithfulness proceeding from the sacrament of matrimony, the peaceful unity of married life,

---

48. Ibid. 16.188, ed. Häring, p. 871: "sibi alteri."
49. Ibid. 18.112–16, ed. Häring, p. 877; tr. Sheridan, p. 219.
50. Ibid. 18.140ff., ed. Häring, pp. 878–79; tr. Sheridan, pp. 220–21.
51. Bernard Silvestris, *Cosmographia,* tr. Wetherbee, p. 56.
52. See G. R. Evans, *Alan of Lille: The Frontiers of Theology in the Later Twelfth Century* (Cambridge, 1983), pp. 148–49.

the inseparable bond of marriage, the indissoluble bond of the wedded parties."[53] No wonder Alan has transformed Bernard's twin genii into a single sacerdotal Genius, who anathematizes the violators of natural law in language that confirms their neglect of commitment to a higher authority:

> Let every such be separated from the kiss of heavenly love as his ingratitude deserves and merits, let him be demoted from Nature's favor, let him be set apart from the harmonious council of the things of Nature. Let him who makes an irregular exception to the rule of Venus be deprived of the seal of Venus.[54]

Where, in all this, is the biblical mandate to "be fertile and increase"? Certainly the attribution of procreation to a primordial decree of God[55] comports well with the substance and context of Gen. 1:28, which Christian theologians had long cited in connection with the divine institution of marriage.[56] One wonders why Alan chose not to link the reproductive imperative of *Natura* to our biblical verse, offering additional evidence for the correspondence of natural law and divine revelation. Although one cannot argue definitively from Alan's silence in this regard, perhaps the allegorical framework of *De planctu Naturae* suggests the basis for an answer; for it was only the ecstatic dream of his protagonist that allowed Alan to see "no contradiction between the formal autonomy of his allegorized natural order and the radical dependency of man on divine Grace. His harking back to the primal harmony of man and Nature is actually an imaginative view of the effect of such Grace, the psychic process involved in the *opus restaurationis*."[57] In the best of all imaginable worlds, sexual activity that is in accord with the dictates of *Natura* serves a sacramental purpose as well, and vice versa. Sexual vice, born of human sin, therefore contravenes natural and divine law alike. The loss of primordial grace is manifest in unnatural human behavior, while the restoration of divine favor will presumably entail renewed concord in the relationship between humans and *Natura*. Yet such neat resolution of the problem that Alan perceived in Ber-

---

53. Alan of Lille, *De planctu Naturae* 16.27–29, ed. Häring, p. 866; tr. Sheridan, p. 197.
54. Ibid. 18.143–51, ed. Häring, p. 878; tr. Sheridan, pp. 220–21.
55. Ibid. 8.222, ed. Häring, p. 840, cited above, n. 47.
56. See above, Chapter 5.
57. Winthrop Wetherbee, "The Literal and the Allegorical: Jean de Meun and the *De planctu Naturae*," *Medieval Studies* 33 (1971), 266.

nard's *Cosmographia* was necessarily allegorical and metahistorical. The real world of contemporary experience is not the ideal world envisioned in *De planctu Naturae,* an unfortunate truth that Alan himself recognized and acknowledged. His character Genius, the link between *Natura* and divine authority who seeks to quell the human rebellion against nature, is truly the priest of *Natura,* not a priest of God.[58] About to excommunicate the rebellious, he temporarily dons a priest's clothing, which he normally does not wear. Even his sentence of excommunication does not arise from his sacerdotal office, but it somehow comprises a stock formula, prepared (perhaps by someone else) some time in advance.[59] Indeed, once one returns from the realm of poetic allegory and sacramental analogy to the world of reality, the problems that the Chartrian synthesis endeavored to overcome return as well. Quite simply, the teachings of *Natura* diverge from those of the Christian God, particularly in matters sexual: While the divine preference for sexual expression changed in the wake of the fall, the procreative imperative of natural law has remained constant. The canonists cited earlier in this chapter struggled with this discrepancy; perhaps Alan, himself a Decretist of note but still unexposed to the Thomistic legitimation of Aristotle, reasoned that to identify Gen. 1:28 as a precept of *Natura* was to highlight the limitations of his own cosmological synthesis. Like Alan's *Natura,* medieval Christian doctrine surely preferred marriage and procreation to sodomy and prostitution as appropriate outlets for human sexuality. *Natura*'s enunciation of "be fertile and increase," however, would have undermined the ascetic ideals of Christianity, and the *De planctu Naturae* would thereby have drawn greater attention to the ultimate futility of its vision.

As the rediscovered teachings of Aristotle began to invade the thought of thirteenth-century Christian theologians, however, noted champions of Christian orthodoxy joined in identifying "be fertile and increase" as natural law even after the fall. In his treatise *De sacramentis,* Albertus Magnus cited Gen. 1:28 to verify the divine institution of marriage according to natural law before sin, and he acknowledged that matrimony still conformed to the law of nature after sin.[60] In his commentary on the *Sentences,* he elaborated further on the duration of

58. Alan of Lille, *De planctu Naturae* 16.175, ed. Häring, p. 871.
59. Ibid. 18.138–40, p. 878.
60. Albertus Magnus, *De sacramentis* 6.1.2.4, 9.1.6, *Opera omnia,* (Aschendorf, 1951–present), 26:79, 159.

the commandment: "If one should ask, when was that commandment repealed, the answer is that it was given for a reason. It therefore was binding as long as that reason existed; it would be binding even now, and it was binding before sin." Albert proceeded to explain that the reason in question was the paucity of human beings. Now that a multitude of people exists, however, those preferring to avoid the evil that accompanies postlapsarian sexual relations are excused from their marital obligations.[61] It is significant that Albert did not follow the pattern of Hugh of St. Victor, Peter Lombard, and Bonaventure and link the biblical commandment of procreation to the state of primal innocence. Although he acknowledged the concupiscence that plagues human sexuality in the aftermath of the fall, he here profferred no distinction between the prelapsarian institution of marriage as duty in Gen. 1:28 and its subsequent reinstitution as a remedy for sexual passion. Owing to an abundance of human beings, those who so desire may now elect a life of virginity over marriage. Yet Albert's indication that they are released (*absolvuntur*) from the injunction of our verse—as opposed to an outright denial of the verse's contemporary applicability—suggests that the expulsion of Adam and Eve from paradise did not remove Gen. 1:28 from its status as natural law.[62]

Thomas Aquinas likewise maintained that "be fertile and increase" is a precept of natural law, "for in it is ordained the act of generation by which nature is preserved and multiplied."[63] Following this rationale to its logical conclusion, Aquinas felt obliged to challenge the Christian ideal of virginity with the charge that it violated the law of nature:[64]

> For everything which is opposed to a precept of natural law is illegal. And just as there is a precept of natural law for the preservation of the individual, which is recorded in Genesis (2:16)—"of every tree in paradise[65] you are free to eat"—so too is there a precept of natural law for

---

61. Idem, *In 2 Sententiarum* 20.C.3, *Opera omnia* (Paris), 27,1:343–44.

62. On matters of sex in Albertus' theology, see Leopold Brandl, *Die Sexualethik des heiligen Albertus Magnus: Eine moralgeschichtliche Untersuchung*, Studien zur Geschichte der katholischen Moraltheologie 2 (Regensburg, 1955).

63. Thomas Aquinas, *Quaestiones quodlibetales* 7.7.1, ed. Raymundus Spiazzi (Torino, 1956), p. 150.

64. Thomas Aquinas, *ST* 2-2.152.2, 43:172–77. Tierney, *Medieval Poor Law*, esp. pp. 28ff., explores the similar attempts of the canonists to resolve the analogous problem of private property: If natural law mandated the common possession of everything, how could the church itself own property?

65. The sense of the Vulgate demands a departure from NJPS.

the preservation of the species which appears in Genesis—"be fertile and increase, and fill the earth." Therefore, just as a person who would abstain from all food would sin insofar as he acts against the good of the individual, so too one who abstains entirely from the reproductive act commits a sin, insofar as he acts against the good of the species.

It is noteworthy that Aquinas in his response made no reference to the traditional bifurcation between the *officium* and *remedium* entailed by conjugal relations. Instead, Thomas rationalized the procreative precept of natural law with greater precision:

> There are many needs of the collective for the fulfillment of which a single individual does not suffice, but they are accomplished by the collective, with one individual doing one thing and another individual doing a different thing. The precept of natural law given to humans concerning eating must be fulfilled by each and every individual; otherwise the individual could not survive. But the precept given concerning procreation pertains to the entire collective of human beings, which must not only increase corporeally but must also progress spiritually. It therefore suffices for the human collective if only certain people meet the needs of bodily reproduction while others abstain, so that they might have the time to contemplate things divine—for the beauty and salvation of the entire human race.[66]

Just as the exclusion of Gen. 1:28 from postlapsarian natural law proceeded from the Augustinian doctrine that the fall of Adam and Eve had vitiated human nature, Aquinas also derived his inclusive position from his understanding of original sin. Yet in the Thomistic view, primordial sin had deprived the first parents of grace but had left their nature essentially intact. "The punishment for original sin," Aquinas asserted, "is principally that human nature is left to itself, deprived of the aid of original justice."[67] Concupiscence does not defy human nature but characterizes it, because the genitals do not by nature submit to the rule

---

66. Aquinas proffered similar answers to the same problem in his *In 4 Sententiarum* 26.1.2, 33.3.2, *Opera omnia*, 7,2:918–19, 977–78.

67. Idem, *ST* 1-2.87.7, 27:34–37. On the Thomistic notion of pure nature—without original justice or original sin—see, among others, J.-B. Kors, *La justice primitive et le péché originel d'après S. Thomas*, Bibliothèque thomiste 2 (Paris, 1930), p. 162; and Charles J. Keating, *The Effects of Original Sin in the Scholastic Tradition from St. Thomas Aquinas to William Ockham*, Catholic University of America Studies in Sacred Theology 2,120 (Washington, D.C., 1959), pp. 52–53.

of reason.[68] Where adherents to the Augustinian tradition had related the marital good of fidelity to the postlapsarian indulgence for rendering the sexual debt to one's spouse, Aquinas linked fidelity to the natural sexual duty (*officium naturae*) that marriage continued to fulfil.[69]

The Thomistic position found support in diverse quarters, including the Augustinian theologian Duns Scotus[70] and the fourteenth-century English poem *Cleanness*, which records the reiteration of the primordial blessing to Noah in his capacity as a second Adam:

> Bot waxez now and wendez forth and worþez to monye,
> Multiplyez on þis molde, and menske yow bytyde. . . .
>
> Þen watz a skylly skyualde, quen scaped alle þe wylde,
> Vche fowle to þe fly3t þat fyþerez my3t serue,
> Vche fysch to þe flod þat fynne couþe nayte,
> Vche beste to þe bent þat bytes on erbez.[71]

Soon thereafter *Cleanness* recounts the divine indictment of the Sodomites, who spurned God by abusing the natural sexuality with which he had endowed them.

> Now haf þay skyfted My skyl and scorned natwre,
> And henttez hem in heþyng an vsage vnclene.
> Hem to smyte for þat smod smartly I þenk,
> Þat wy3ez schal be by hem war, worlde withouten ende.[72]

Michael Twomey argued convincingly that in its repeated use of the word *skyl*, denoting the rational order of nature, *Cleanness* intentionally highlights the contrast between the survivors of the flood and the residents of Sodom: The reproductive mandate of Genesis charges the former to uphold the rational order of nature, while the latter under-

---

68. Thomas Aquinas, *ST* 1-2.17.9 ad 3, 17:206–209. In this regard, see also Marie-Dominique Chenu, "Les passions verteuses: L'anthropologie de Saint Thomas," *Revue philosophique de Louvain* 72 (1974), 11–17; and Otto Lottin, "Le péché originel chez Albert le Grand, Bonaventure et Thomas d'Aquin," *Recherches de théologie ancienne et médiévale* 12 (1940), esp. 314.

69. Josef Fuchs, *Die Sexualethik des heiligen Thomas von Aquin* (Cologne, 1949), p. 69.

70. See Duns Scotus, *In 4 Sententiarum* 28.1.1, *Opera omnia*, 24:377, where the natural human inclination to procreate is identified with the divine mandate to "be fertile and increase," issued "before the fall and after the fall" in Gen. 1 and 9.

71. *Cleanness* 521–22, 529–32, in *The Poems of the Pearl Manuscript*, ed. Malcolm Andrew and Ronald Waldron, rev. ed. (Exeter, 1987), pp. 133–34.

72. Ibid. 709–12, p. 141.

mine that order with their sin.[73] *Cleanness* also moves beyond this straightforward identification of natural and divine law to equate obedience with the sexual imperatives of nature and participation in the divine covenant. From the poem's commencement with the Matthean parable of the wedding feast, the conjugal union of man and woman is compared to the spiritual union of a human being and God achieved through participation in the Eucharist. Charlotte Morse explained the analogy thus:

> The Eucharist dramatically embodies the intimacy of the relationship between God and man in Christianity. . . . Through this sacred meal God provides sustenance to the faithful so that they can continue to keep their covenant with Christ by walking in the way of love. More than that, this feast unites Christ and man, since in eating the Body and Blood the communicant actually makes God a part of his own body, or, to speak in precise and theological language, man becomes part of Christ, incorporated into Christ, literally one body with Christ. This one body was understood to signify a mystic or spiritual reality, the union made in the mystical marriage of Christ and the Church. This spiritual union . . . is thus analogous to human marriage in which two people become one flesh through sexual intercourse. The act of eating becomes a sign of the spiritual union just as sexual intercourse is a sign of the union in human marriage.[74]

Morse appropriately noted precedents for this analogy among various patristic and medieval writers, but an additional motif is at work here. Looking to Gen. 1:28 as the natural, sexual dimension of God's covenant with his faithful, even in the postlapsarian age, *Cleanness* follows the example set by Albertus Magnus and Thomas Aquinas considered above. Under the influence of Aristotle, these Dominican theologians blended the laws of nature into their understanding of divine providence and its scheme for human history, concluding that "be fertile and increase" constitutes a precept of natural law. Each of these Dominican masters further anticipated *Cleanness* by weaving nature's reproductive imperative expressed in Gen. 1:28 into a distinc-

---

73. Twomey, "The Anatomy of Sin," pp. 46–59. See also T. D. Kelly and John T. Irwin, "The Meaning of *Cleanness*: Parable as Effective Sign," *Medieval Studies* 35 (1973), esp. 242–43.

74. Charlotte C. Morse, *The Pattern of Judgment in the "Queste" and "Cleanness"* (Columbia, Mo., 1978), p. 47; similar ideas are advanced in Kelly and Irwin, "The Meaning of *Cleanness*."

tively Christian view of salvation history. Albertus maintained that the divine benediction of the first parents attained its perfect fulfillment in the Virgin Mary, for our verse actually contains a threefold blessing: "fecundity of nature, rule of the land, and dominion over the animals." As natural as well as spiritual mother, in forgoing pleasures of the body (symbolized by the land), and in her superiority vis-à-vis demons, angels, and human beings, Mary realized the intention of the primordial blessing.[75] And in commenting on Jesus' statement to his disciples in Mk. 14:22, "This is my body," Thomas invoked John Chrysostom's association of these words with Gen. 1:28:

> Just as that ordinance which states, "Be fertile and increase and fill the earth," was pronounced only once but its generative effect is perceived for all time in the workings of nature, so this utterance was pronounced only once but establishes the potency in the sacrifice in all masses of the Church, even today and until his final coming.[76]

For Albertus and for Thomas, the primordial blessing assumed salvific importance precisely because it ordained a fundamental law of the natural order. One might draw a similar inference from the constant juxtaposition of Gen. 1:28 and the Paternoster in the Anglo-Saxon charm quoted at the beginning of this chapter. The poet of *Cleanness* carried on in this tradition; for him, Twomey concluded, "the joy of sex . . . is almost paradise."[77]

POETIC REFLECTION AND AMBIVALENCE

Natura procreatrix, nature as parent and guardian of reproductive sexuality, emerged from the twelfth-century renaissance with a distinctive personality and a problematic agenda. As the works of Bernard Silvestris and Alan of Lille suggest in their respective ways, she defied incorporation within a comprehensively Christian cosmology. When subsequent authors pondered *Natura*'s enigmatic role in a biblical world

75. Albertus Magnus, *Mariale* 168, *Opera omnia* (Paris), 37:252–53.

76. Thomas Aquinas, *Catena aurea in quator Evangelia,* ad Mk., 14.6, ed. Angelicus Guarientus, 2 vols. (Torino, 1953), 1:542–43. An earlier patristic association of "be fertile and increase" with the sacrament of the Eucharist appears in the writings of Methodius, cited above, Chapter 5, n. 48.

77. Twomey, "The Anatomy of Sin," p. 30.

view, the very considerations that led Alan to avoid reference to Gen. 1:28 may have induced them to recall it. A biblical precept that deemed reproduction essential for the survival of nature and the natural development of human civilization, our verse expressed much of the complexity in the subject of postlapsarian sexuality. The procreative mandate of God and the sexual imperatives of the goddess put a challenge before the theologian, but their juxtaposition was fertile ground for the rumination of the poet. The works of two late medieval poets suggest that, for them, raising the question rather than advocating any one answer may have assumed higher priority. For so long a proof-text of the jurist and theologian, our verse thus came to epitomize a perennial problem, which in the case of the *Roman de la Rose* and the *Canterbury Tales* continues to defy definitive resolution.

Jean de Meun

The characters of *Natura* and *Genius* reappear in Jean de Meun's *Roman de la Rose,* composed in the second half of the thirteenth century, where they continue to champion the procreative purpose of human sexual activity. As in Alan's *De planctu naturae, Natura* again identifies herself as God's appointee, charged with guaranteeing the ability of his creation to maintain and perpetuate itself. Again *Natura* complains that of all God's creatures humans alone violate the reproductive imperative of her laws. And again, *Natura* calls upon her priest Genius to pardon the sins of those who espouse her cause and to anathematize those who do not. In Jean's *Roman,* however, Genius' proclamation does allude to the primordial blessing in what several modern critics have recognized as a sermonic "elaboration of the counsel of Gen. i. 28, 'increase and multiply.'"[78]

> By the authority of Nature, who has the care of the whole world, as vicar and constable of the eternal emperor, who sits in the sovereign tower of the noble city of the world, of which he made Nature the minister; Nature who administers all good things through the influence of the stars, for they ordain everything according to the imperial justice

---

78. D. W. Robertson, Jr., *A Preface to Chaucer: Studies in Medieval Perspectives* (Princeton, N.J., 1962), pp. 201–202. Cf. John V. Fleming, *The "Roman de la Rose": A Study in Allegory and Iconography* (Princeton, N.J., 1969), p. 210; and Alan M. F. Gunn, *The Mirror of Love: A Reinterpretation of "The Romance of the Rose"* (Lubbock, Tex., 1952), p. 215.

that Nature executes; Nature, who has given birth to all things since this world came into being, who gives them their allotted time for growth and increase . . . by the authority of Nature, let all those disloyal apostates, of high rank or low, who hold in despite the acts by which Nature is supported, be excommunicated and condemned without any delay. And let him who strives with all his force to maintain Nature, who struggles to love well, without any base thought, but with lawful labor, go off to paradise decked with flowers. As long as he makes a good confession, I will take on me all his deeds with such power as I can bring to them, and he will never have to bear the smallest pardon for them.[79]

These opening lines of Genius' lengthy discourse suggest what numerous passages of the *Roman* confirm: that Jean de Meun has removed *Natura* and Genius from the sacramental realm within which Alan of Lille had endeavored to include them.[80] In the *De planctu Naturae*, *Natura* indicts and Genius condemns those guilty of all vice and immorality; procreation, appropriately pursued within the virtuous and sacred context of marriage, takes its place in a comprehensively Christian ethic. Yet in the *Roman*, sexual reproduction constitutes the sole concern of *Natura* and Genius, who grant a blanket pardon for all other sins to those that strive to have children. And where the *De planctu Naturae* questions the sacerdotal authority of Genius by noting his temporary assumption of priestly garb, the *Roman* plays upon this motif to deny him genuine priesthood altogether. Before setting off to pronounce his sentence of excommunication, the *Roman*'s Genius removes the cumbersome accoutrements of his priestly office. Upon commencing his sermon, he must hurriedly borrow some from the God of Love, not from the Christian deity—much to the uncontrollable amusement of Venus.[81] As one reader of the *Roman* has observed, *Natura* and her priest Genius are "servants of an indiscriminate sexual desire";[82] morally

79. Jean de Meun, *Le Roman de la Rose* 19505–42, ed. Ernest Langlois, 5 vols. (Paris, 1914–24), 5:4–6; *The Romance of the Rose,* tr. Charles Dahlberg (1971; repr., Hanover, N.H., 1983), p. 322.

80. See George D. Economou, "The Character Genius in Alan of Lille, Jean de Meun, and John Gower," *Chaucer Review* 4 (1970), 206–8; and Faith Lyons, "Some Notes on the *Roman de la Rose:* The Golden Chain and Other Types in Jean de Meun," in *Studies in Medieval Literature and Languages in Memory of Frederick Whitehead*, ed. W. Rothwell et al. (Manchester, 1973), pp. 201–4.

81. Jean de Meun, *Le Roman de la Rose* 19428–38, ed. Langlois, 4:268–69; Economou, *The Goddess Natura*, pp. 122–23.

82. Michael D. Cherniss, "Irony and Authority: The Ending of the *Roman de la Rose,*" *Modern Language Quarterly* 36 (1975), 229.

neutral, they represent the instinctual, sexual imperative of natural law that all creatures share.

Why does the *Roman*, in stressing the disjunction of divine and natural realms, allude to the procreative mandate of the Bible that Alan of Lille may have omitted purposefully from the *De planctu Naturae?* The answer depends on one's understanding of the allegorical meaning implicit in Jean de Meun's poem, an issue debated vigorously in recent decades of modern scholarship. Without presuming to have discovered Jean's true, elusive message, we shall briefly consider four conflicting interpretations of the *Roman;* significant differences notwithstanding, they all have similar implications for appreciating the function that the poet may have attributed to our verse.

According to one school of thought, which includes Curtius, Gerard Paré, Alan M. F. Gunn, and Norman Cohn among its proponents, *Natura* and Genius enunciate the sentiments of Jean de Meun, just as the character Reason does earlier in the poem.[83] The laws of nature function independently of any divinely revealed moral code; human sexuality makes a valuable contribution to the cosmic order simply because of its procreative results. Comparing this mentality to the more integrated world view of medieval Christian humanism at its zenith, Curtius lamented the message of the *Roman* in terms that resemble the plaint of *Natura* herself.

> The goddess Natura has become the servant of rank promiscuity, her management of the life of love is travestied into obscenity. The un-affected and playful eroticism of Latin Humanism, the stormy attacks of youthful *vagantes* against Christian morality, have sunk to the level of a sexual liberalism which concocts a spicy stew out of erudite tinsel and philistine pruriency. How was this possible? It corresponded with the libertinism of an epoch which had exchanged the heritage of antique beauty for the small coin of academic hair-splitting.

Curtius, Paré, and Cohn have associated this attitude with the Averro-ism condemned at Paris and Oxford in the late 1270s.[84] Gunn has contended that Jean's " 'principle of replenishment' was a dialectical

---

83. Jean de Meun, *Le Roman de la Rose* 4376–88, 4403–21, 4545–56, 5763–94, ed. Lan-glois, 2:216–18, 222–23, 270–71.

84. Curtius, *European Literature*, p. 126; Gerard Paré, *Les idées et les lettres au xiiie siècle: Le "Roman de la Rose"* (Montreal, 1947), pp. 57–58, 86, 313–27; and Norman Cohn, *The World-View of a Thirteenth-Century Parisian Intellectual: Jean de Meun and the "Roman de la Rose"* (Durham [U.K.], 1961), esp. pp. 1, 15–18.

necessity" for the classical philosophy of plenitude and continuity, whose origins and protracted conflict with biblical cosmology comprise the subject of Arthur O. Lovejoy's *Great Chain of Being*.[85] Neither connection is established conclusively. But in each case the disjunction between procreation and morality, along with the concomitant "phenomenon of a thirteenth-century phallicism," arose from a classical view of the natural order, "the influence of which for the nonphilosophic mind must have been reinforced by the Scriptural command to 'multiply and replenish the earth.' "[86] This biblical association is in fact corroborated by the *Summa contra gentiles* of Thomas Aquinas, which reports the citation of Gen. 1:28 by advocates of the heretical principle that "continence is not a virtue."[87]

At the opposite end of the spectrum, other scholars have dissociated the sentiments of *Natura* and Genius from the viewpoint of Jean de Meun. Although *Natura* elicits Jean's respect, *Natura* is unable to curb the violation of her laws, and Genius exemplifies this powerlessness. Genius is clearly a false priest, "a fraud and a buffoon," whose ceremonious excommunication of *Natura*'s foes appear so ridiculous that it verges on the burlesque.[88] He epitomizes the vitiated state of postlapsarian nature, the sinful concupiscence now inherent in procreation, and the futility of seeking salvation in the fulfillment of *Natura*'s laws. From such a perspective, Reason, rather than *Natura* or Genius, speaks for Jean de Meun in the *Roman*. She alone exercises moral judgment in condemning sexual activity that lacks procreative purpose, warning of the vices entailed by the pursuit of physical pleasure for its own sake. Because of the fragmentation of the cosmic order—and its microcosmic reflection in the human being—which has resulted from the fall, she too cannot restrain the wayward Lover who craves gratification from the rose. Nevertheless, John Fleming has asserted, she conveys Jean de Meun's Augustinian view of postlapsarian sexuality: legitimate for the sake of procreation, spiritually troublesome and unfulfilling in any event, but subject at least to the partial control of reason and grace.[89] According to D. W. Robertson, Fleming, and Denise Baker, Genius'

---

85. Gunn, *The Mirror of Love*, chs. 11–12 (quotation on p. 213).
86. Ibid., p. 215.
87. Thomas Aquinas, *Summa contra gentiles* 3.136, *Opera omnia*, 14:412. For the listing of this principle among those condemned by Bishop Stephen Tempier of Paris in 1277, see *Fontes vitae S. Thomae Aquinatis*, 6, ed. M.-H. Laurent (Saint-Maximin, 1937), p. 610.
88. Fleming, *The "Roman de la Rose,"* ch. 4.
89. Idem, *Reason and the Lover* (Princeton, N.J., 1984), esp. pp. 19–22.

allusion to Gen. 1:28 deserves evaluation within this context of Augustinian doctrine, for Genius knows only the literal interpretation of our biblical verse.[90] Although the mandate of "be fertile and increase" was intended literally before the fall, as Augustine had taught, its sexual fulfillment no longer contributes to the spiritual perfection of human beings. Like Genius himself, its identification with the law of nature amounts to mockery.

A third group of critics has objected to this reading of the *Roman*, advocating instead what Fleming has playfully termed "the Ithacan heresy"[91] because its outspoken proponents share an affiliation with Cornell University. While Robertson, Fleming, and all have considered the *Roman* "an iconographic reenactment of the Fall"[92] from a traditional perspective, the Ithacans have viewed Jean de Meun's purpose as the subjection of this perspective to extensive and scathing criticism. Comedy, irony, and cynicism all enable the poem to demonstrate that the age-old Augustinian approach to sexuality simply does not guide human beings to fulfillment in the real world. Reason cannot appreciate the impossibility of her position in the wake of the fall, and her failure to cite Scripture in reflecting on love and sex underscores her lack of theological insight. She too belongs to the world of nature and suffers from its constraints; offering no resolution of the problem at hand, she and her counsel quickly recede into the background as the *Roman* unfolds.[93] Like so much else in human experience, the pressing concern of the *Roman* has no tidy solution. As Thomas Hill has concluded,[94]

> The definition of sexual love which Jean de Meun presents in the course of the *Roman* is a paradoxical one. On the one hand, sexual love can be profoundly destructive, and Jean de Meun does not gloss over this aspect of his theme. Even for the lover, who emerges relatively unscathed from his quest . . . , the love of the rose is the immediate

90. Robertson, *A Preface to Chaucer*, 201–2; Fleming, *The "Roman de la Rose,"* pp. 210–13; Denise N. Baker, "The Priesthood of Genius: A Study of the Medieval Tradition," *Speculum* 51 (1976), 285–86. In basic agreement with this interpretation are also Charles Dahlberg, "Love and the *Roman de la Rose,"* *Speculum* 44 (1969), 568–84; and Economou, *The Goddess Natura*, ch. 4.

91. Fleming, *Reason and the Lover*, pp. 3–4.

92. Idem, *The "Roman de la Rose,"* p. 247.

93. Carol V. Kaske, "Getting around the *Parson's Tale:* An Alternative to Allegory and Irony," in *Chaucer at Albany*, ed. Russell Hope Robbins (New York, 1975), pp. 152–54; Cherniss, "Irony and Authority," p. 230.

94. Thomas D. Hill, "Narcissus, Pygmalion, and the Castration of Saturn: Two Mythological Themes in the *Roman de la Rose,"* *Studies in Philology* 71 (1974), 425–26.

occasion for the heroic folly which he exhibits consistently throughout the poem. And yet his folly and concupiscence are virtually inevitable in the world as we know it . . . ; one wonders how well a courtship conducted on strict Augustinian principles would succeed. And the result of the lover's folly and inordinate desire is a great good.[95] Thus the lover is both an example of lust and folly as Robertson insists, and a man who achieves the good and natural end of sexuality.

From the standpoint of the Ithacans, the *Roman* rejects the Augustinian bifurcation between postlapsarian sexuality and the divinely intended law of nature, and yet it acknowledges the unavoidable contradiction and inconsistency that the Thomistic attempt at synthesis entailed. In the lengthy discourse that dominates the conclusion of the *Roman,* Genius thus emerges as the spokesman of Jean de Meun, "a symbol of all that is best in human nature, with the capabilities and limitations which the fact implies."[96] These shortcomings are severe indeed— hence the biting, satiric irony that the poem eagerly inflicts upon *Natura*'s priest. Yet Genius does describe the garden of the lamb and the good shepherd, implying that a higher, spiritual love does in fact exist.[97] It is Genius, not Reason, who alludes to Scripture. And in echoing the primordial, divine mandate of procreation, Genius asserts that sexuality "is a symptom of the minimal survival of man's original dignity."[98] A precept of natural law, "be fertile and increase" has survived the fall intact, the spiritual inadequacies of postlapsarian human beings notwithstanding.

We merely mention a fourth scholarly interpretation of the *Roman:* that Jean de Meun refrained from proposing any resolution whatsoever. As Rosemund Tuve has argued, he used "his oblique method of long-sustained irony and definition by unacceptable misdefinitions held up to scorn" to demonstrate, rather emphatically, that "the world of the *Roman* is quite loveless."[99] Debate over the *Roman* continues, but a

95. The Ithacans have attributed considerable significance to the *Roman*'s concluding intimation (21730, ed. Langlois, 5:95) that the lover's conquest of the rose resulted in conception and pregnancy.

96. Wetherbee, "The Literal and the Allegorical," p. 284.

97. Jean de Meun, *Le Roman de la Rose* 19931–20000, 5:22–25.

98. Wetherbee, "The Literal and the Allegorical," p. 287; see also Cherniss, "Irony and Authority," pp. 231–33.

99. Rosemund Tuve, *Allegorical Imagery: Some Medieval Books and Their Posterity* (Princeton, N.J., 1966), pp. 260–61; see also C. S. Lewis, *The Allegory of Love: A Study in Medieval Tradition* (1936; repr., London, 1953), esp. pp. 153–54.

particular evaluation of the poem and its intended meaning matters far less to us than the weight of problem posed by Genius in his allusion to Gen. 1:28: how to perceive the relation between biblically mandated sexuality and the sexual imperative of natural law. The issue bore heavily on any attempt to contrast or to reconcile the two axes around which the world of the medieval Christian rotated simultaneously: the world of *Natura* and the world of God. Every effort to find such reconciliation in the *Roman* has had to confront this issue directly, and the alternative solutions discerned by different scholars must grapple with the puzzle of "be fertile and increase."

Geoffrey Chaucer

The lack of resolution that scholars have perceived in the conclusion of the *Roman de la Rose* finds an additional late medieval echo—in the prologue to Chaucer's *Wife of Bath's Tale,* cited at the beginning of this chapter. Adducing the "gentil text" of Gen. 1:28 to justify her opportunistic passage through a series of five successive husbands, Alison of Bath uses our verse to reflect not on the importance of childbearing but on the legitimacy of pursuing her natural sexual desires. As Robert Pratt has noted, Alison has no more of an interest in parenting than the rooster Chauntecleer in *The Nun's Priest's Tale,* who as a servant of Venus "dide al his poweer, / Moore for delit than world to multiplye."[100] Rather, Chaucer's interest lay in the very problem of having to live in two worlds—that of *Natura* and that of the creator God—which had concerned his predecessors. The opening lines of the *Canterbury Tales* manifest such concern with *Natura*'s place in a biblical cosmology;[101] because human sexuality epitomized the tension between these two orders, the Wife of Bath and her prologue convey the poet's response.

Chaucer's debt to numerous theological and literary sources, ranging from Jean de Meun's *Roman* to Jerome's *Adversus Jovinianum* and a

---

100. Chaucer, *Canterbury Tales* VII.3344–45, p. 260; Robert A. Pratt, "Chaucer's 'Natal Jove' and 'Seint Jerome . . . agayn Jovinian,'" *Journal of English and Germanic Philology* 61 (1962), 248.

101. J. C. Nitzche, "Creation in Genesis and Nature in Chaucer's *General Prologue* 1–18," *Papers on Language and Literature* 14 (1978), 459–64; and, on Chaucer's debt to the *Natura* and hexameral traditions, see also David C. Fowler, *The Bible in Middle English Literature* (Seattle, Wash., 1984), ch. 3.

medieval tradition of misogyny that this patristic work had fueled, complicates any attempt to analyze the Wife of Bath.[102] Robertson, among others, has argued that Alison exemplifies a spiritually bankrupt conception of divine teaching. "She is dominated by the senses or the flesh rather than by the understanding or the spirit, by oldness rather than newness. In short, the wife of Bath is a literary personification of rampant 'femininity' or carnality, and her exegesis is, in consequence, rigorously carnal and literal."[103] She therefore cites the procreative mandate of the Old Testament in her defense, unaware of the distinctively Christian, spiritual interpretation of "be fertile and increase." She seeks support in the polygamous examples of Old Testament figures (Lemekh, Abraham, and Jacob), while her allusions to the New Testament are blatantly misguided and self-defeating. Her five husbands liken her to the Samaritan woman of the Gospel (Jn. 4), although she remains impervious to Jesus' counsel to that ancient figure. Instead, she identifies with the five loaves of barley bread that Jesus fed to the multitude at Passover (Jn. 6), whose appearance in the Gospel she misplaces in Mark and which Christians had long understood as symbolic of the old law.[104]

Robertson's appreciation of Alison's "gentil text" as the key to her hopelessly non-Christian carnality is certainly credible, but it is by no means the only interpretation of the Wife of Bath and not necessarily the most convincing. Robertson's opinion hinges on "the fact that Gen. i. 28 is a 'commandment' only under the Old Law; under the new, marriage is still a good, but it is an indulgence rather than a commandment."[105] As illustrated above, this approach to the biblical mandate for procreation in a postlapsarian age stems from the Augustinian reading of our verse and from its contribution to an Augustinian doctrine of corrupted nature and original sin. It is hardly coincidental that Robertson has relied consistently on Augustine to define the exegetical contrast between old and new or between carnal and spiritual. We have seen,

---

102. Charles Muscatine, *Chaucer and the French Tradition: A Study in Style and Meaning* (Berkeley, Calif., 1957), p. 206, has labeled her "the most fully realized character in Chaucer."

103. Robertson, *A Preface to Chaucer,* pp. 317–31 (quotation on p. 321). Because she cites Gen. 1:28, Mahoney, "Alice of Bath," proposed a heretical connection for the Wife of Bath similar to that of Margery Kempe. The suggestion of Daniel S. Silvia, Jr., "The Wife of Bath's Marital State," *Notes and Queries* 212 (1967), 9 and n. 6, that Alison had to burn her husband's misogynist book because this was the punishment specified for heretical writings adds an ironic twist to such a characterization.

104. Chaucer, *Canterbury Tales* III.145–46, p. 107.

105. Robertson, *A Preface to Chaucer,* p. 322.

though, that during the generations prior to Chaucer notable Christian jurists and theologians equated the reproductive imperative of natural law with the mandate of "be fertile and increase" even in the aftermath of the fall. By Chaucer's day, *Natura*, exemplifed above all else by the sexual processes of procreation, had assumed new respect and sanctity. Our verse was not merely a prescription of the old law, but it could denote a precept of the eternal law of nature that still held sway.

For Robertson's picture of a character whom Chaucer scorned and whose world view he repudiated, recent critics have offered a host of alternatives. Not so much the object of the poet's criticism, she conveys his ambivalent reflection on the ethos that she rejects. Armed with our verse, perhaps she personifies rhetoric, challenging the Thomistic synthesis of nature and providence merely to gratify her desires of the moment.[106] Perhaps she is not really a character at all, but deconstructs within the matrix of the conflict between experience and authority. Co-opted by the values of the male-dominated establishment that she defies, perhaps her scriptural citations ironically contribute to its ultimate triumph over her.[107]

On a basic level, I suggest that Alison embodies the difficulties inherent in the medieval attempt to subordinate the maternal goddess *Natura* to the patriarchal God of the Bible. Alison is not merely a recreation of the Old Woman in Jean de Meun's *Roman de la Rose*, who urged women ruthlessly to exploit their sexual charms as the only means to survive in a man's world,[108] for Alison turns to biblical and theological authorities as well as to bitter experience to vindicate her position. Although she and her exegesis might not prevail over their adversaries, Chaucer's General Prologue indicates that she invaded the typically male-dominated activities of commerce and philanthropy:

> Of clooth-makyng she hadde swich an haunt
> She passed hem of Ypres and of Gaunt.
> In al the parisshe wif ne was ther noon
> That to the offrynge bifore hire sholde goon.[109]

---

106. See John A. Alford, "The Wife of Bath versus the Clerk of Oxford: What Their Rivalry Means," *Chaucer Review* 21 (1986), esp. 122–25.

107. See Barbara Gottfried, "Conflict and Relationship, Sovereignty and Survival: Parables of Power in the *Wife of Bath's Prologue*," *Chaucer Review* 19 (1985), 202–24; and David Aers, *Chaucer, Langland, and the Creative Imagination* (London, 1980), pp. 83–89, 147–50.

108. Jean de Meun, *Le Roman de la Rose* 12740–14546, ed. Langlois, 3:255–64, 4:1–66.

109. Chaucer, *Canterbury Tales* I.447–50, p. 30.

She quotes from the old law, to be sure. Yet Hope Phyllis Weissman has shown how Alison's association with the Old Testament enabled Chaucer to parody the virtuous woman of Prov. 31, a traditional Christian figure for the church and for the New Testament woman par excellence, the Virgin Mary herself.[110] Weissman has contended further that in casting Dame Alison as the wife of Bath, Chaucer depicted her as the madam of a bathhouse, an association that only intensified her rejection of the value system imposed upon her. (As we quote from Weissman's compelling argument, recall that in Albertus Magnus' attempt to blend the worlds of God and *Natura* it was the Virgin who truly fulfilled the primordial blessing that is here emblematic of a prostitute.)

> Precisely because the patriarchal establishment resents the Wife's intrusion, her invasion of its sacred precincts must be an invasion that destroys. It was the patriarchy itself which originated the destructiveness by identifying woman with the body's abuses and domiciling her on its borders to suffer a continuing abuse. Now the Wife, in the person of the prostitute with whom she is identified, returns battle-scarred and pox-marked to infect that establishment with its own brand of mortal disease. By her invasion of the patriarchal establishment, the Wife transforms radically the nature of her mission. Instead of simply confirming the stereotype of woman-as-carnality, she announces its origin in patriarchal ideology and in the psychology which ideology overlies. Her marital status symbolizes the fact that aversion to the woman bodily is an aversion to the sexual impulses within. . . . Her merchandizing of religion and marriage as well as woollens forces recognition of the essentially self-aggrandizing, exploitative economy which the medieval patriarchy both created and shamefully defaced. The Wife's portrait and her own autobiographical prologue, taken together, thus serve to dramatize the internal contradictions of later medieval culture. They are indeed, to invoke Marx in an appropriate context, Alison's Eighteenth Brumaire.[111]

Dame Alison overturns the "gentil text" of Scripture both in her theory and in her practice of marriage. We argue that Chaucer linked the Wife of Bath with our verse not in order to condemn her but in order to accentuate her condemnation of medieval Christian values. Her conflict

110. Hope Phyllis Weissman, "Antifeminism and Chaucer's Characterization of Women," in *Geoffrey Chaucer: A Collection of Original Articles,* ed. George D. Economou (New York, 1975), pp. 105ff.

111. Idem, "Why Chaucer's Wife Is from Bath," *Chaucer Review* 15 (1980), 26–27.

addresses the historical need of biblical cultures to envision a super-natural deity, a God who has created, controlled, and sanctified the laws of nature that rule us all.

Over the centuries, Gen. 1:28 evoked conceptions of a revealed cove-nant that found the sexuality of natural law a place within a divine framework for human history. Writers of the later Middle Ages now questioned the very possibility of such comprehensive reconciliation between the heavenly and the mundane,[112] but in so doing they main-tained the covenantal concern that once had canonized our biblical text and that continued to underlie its meaning. How did the universal mandate of *Natura* to "be fertile and increase" contribute to the fulfill-ment of the soul?

112. Many medieval texts that cite or allude to Gen. 1:28 could not be considered here, and some of these undoubtedly warrant further attention.

Conclusion: A Look Forward and Back

As medieval Christianity gave way to the Christianity of the Reformation, the interpretation of Gen. 1:28 underwent few noteworthy developments. Several theologians of the later Middle Ages cited the primordial blessing to buttress their conflicting views of natural rights. Did God's conferral of dominion upon the first parents grant them rights of ownership as individuals, as Pope John XXII argued against the Spiritual Franciscans?[1] Or did God instead intend to grant the right to enjoy and make use of temporal goods to all human beings in common, as William of Ockham replied on behalf of his confreres? Such readings of our verse assumed greater significance in the seventeenth century—beyond the chronological purview of this book—in the opposing theories of Robert Filmer, John Locke, and others on the origins of political power.[2]

Among some early Protestant commentators on the Bible, especially the Lutherans, the exegesis of Gen. 1:28 assumed important polemical

---

1. William of Ockham, *Opus nonaginta dierum* 26, in *Opera politica*, 2:483–85; and cf. also the allusion to Gen. 1:28 in Jean Gerson, *De vita spirituali anime* 3, in *Oeuvres complètes*, ed. Palemon Glorieux, 7 vols. in 8 pts. (Paris, 1960–68), 3:145. I am grateful to Brian Tierney for guiding me to these references.

2. See Robert Filmer, *Patriarcha* 8, in *Patriarcha and Other Political Works*, ed. Peter Laslett (Oxford, 1949), pp. 63–66, and Filmer's preface to *Observations upon Aristotle's Politiques*, ibid., pp. 187–88; and John Locke, *Two Treatises of Government* 1.4, ed. Peter Laslett (Cambridge, 1970), pp. 174–89.

applications. In his commentary on Genesis, Martin Luther followed the Augustinian tradition and extolled the procreative sexual activity that would have transpired in paradise for its purity and sanctity: "For truly in all nature there was no activity more excellent and more admirable than procreation. After the proclamation of the name of God it is the most important activity Adam and Eve in the state of innocence could carry on—as free from sin in doing this as they were in praising God."[3] Yet despite the sin that has plagued humanity since the fall, Luther maintained that the biblical mandate of procreation "is effective to this day."[4] In contrast to the church fathers who had rationalized the reproductive pursuits of the Hebrew patriarchs while defending the ideal of celibacy, Luther attacked Catholics for their disregard of biblical teaching:

> Many are offended by the fact that in this first book Moses relates so much about the procreation of the fathers. But they do not consider the difference in customs in different ages. At that time faith ruled in the fathers, and also faith in this article: "Be fertile and increase." In our age, especially after those papistic monstrosities of celibacy, marriage has been deprived of its prestige and due honor, and true knowledge of the Word and ordinance of God has become extinct. Among the fathers this knowledge was pure and proper. For this reason they had a very high regard for the begetting of children.[5]

In *Vom ehelichen Leben,* Luther fortified his attack with an argument that echoes the natural law theory of the High Middle Ages: Gen. 1:28 is not simply an ordinance of divine legislation, but a divine expression of a characteristic shared by all human beings. "Just as God does not command anyone to be a man or a woman but creates them the way they have to be, so he does not command them to multiply but creates them so they have to multiply."[6] Defiance of the instruction to reproduce not

---

3. Martin Luther, *Vorlesungen über 1. Mose,* ad 2:18, in *Werke: Kritische Gesamtausgabe* (Weimar, 1883–present), 42:89; tr. in *Works,* ed. Jaroslav Pelikan and Helmut T. Lehmann (St. Louis, 1955–86), 1:117–18.

4. Ibid., ad 21:1–3, *Werke,* 43:138; tr. *Works,* 4:4.

5. Ibid., ad 25:1–4, *Werke,* 43:353; tr. *Works,* 4:302–3.

6. Martin Luther, *Vom ehelichen Leben, Werke,* 10,2:276, tr. *Works,* 45:18. Cf. John Chrysostom's comparison of "be fertile and increase" with Jesus' statement "This is my body" along these lines; cited by Thomas Aquinas (see above, Chapter 6, n. 76); it reappears in the *Konkordienformel: Solida declaratio* 7.76, in *Die Bekenntnisschriften der evangelisch-lutherischen Kirche,* 6th ed. (Göttingen, 1967), pp. 998–99.

only contravenes the will of God but subverts the order of God's creation, whose natural imperative our verse bespeaks.

The argument that clerical celibacy nullifies a divine commandment still in force also appears in Philip Melanchthon's *Augsburgische Konfession*.[7] When the Catholics attending the Diet of Augsburg invoked the authority of Jerome to the effect that the commandment no longer holds in a populated world,[8] Melanchthon elaborated in his *Apologie:*

> Since this ordinance of God [Gen. 1:28] cannot be suspended without an extraordinary work of God, it follows that neither regulations nor vows can abolish the right to contract marriage. . . . The Word of God did not form the nature of men to be fruitful only at the beginning of creation, but it still does as long as this physical nature of ours exists. . . . Just as human regulations cannot change the nature of the earth, so neither vows nor human regulations can change the nature of man without an extraordinary act of God. Second, because this creation or divine ordinance in man is a natural right, the jurists have said wisely and correctly that the union of man and woman is by natural right. Now, since natural right is unchangeable, the right to contract marriage must always remain. Where nature does not change, there must remain that ordinance which God has built into nature. . . . So it is ridiculous for our opponents to say that originally marriage was commanded but that it is no longer commanded. . . . Natural right is really divine right, because it is an ordinance divinely stamped on nature.[9]

Melanchthon thus made Luther's allusion to the theory of natural law explicit, adeptly turning the arguments of medieval canon and Roman lawyers against the Church. Commanding the first parents to "be fertile and increase," God expressed an imperative of the natural order he had created. As long as this order persists, such a precept never becomes obsolete, and he who neglects it violates the law of nature and the law of Scripture simultaneously.

In the opening years of the seventeenth century, the Calvinist David Pareus likewise condemned the Catholic clergy for the subversion of God's natural law,[10] and the implication was clear: The primordial

---

7. *Die Bekenntnisschriften*, pp. 86ff.

8. See *Die Confutatio der Confessio augustana vom 3. August 1530*, ed. Herbert Immenkötter (Münster, 1979), p. 153.

9. *Die Bekenntnisschriften*, pp. 334–36; tr. in Theodore G. Tappert, ed., *The Book of Concord* (Philadelphia, Pa., 1959), pp. 240–41.

10. David Pareus, *In Genesin Mosis commentarius*, ad 1:28, in *Opera theologica exegetica*, 2 vols. (Frankfurt a.M., 1647), 1,2:55. Some scholars have also claimed novelty for John

blessing and its fulfillment resided in the community of God's faithful, which the Church of Rome was not. Once again, the interpretation of Gen. 1:28 bore upon the appreciation of the divine covenant, the definition of the truly elect. Ironically, Catholics of the period resorted to an argument that had striking rabbinic overtones: Gen. 1:28 was not a commandment but a blessing—hence the opening words of the verse and its correspondence to God's blessing of birds and fish in Gen. 1:22.[11] But apart from its relevance to the Catholic-Protestant conflict over clerical marriage and celibacy—and even this had been anticipated by earlier writers[12]—exegetes of the Reformation period discerned little new in our verse. They continued to reiterate the sentiments of their patristic and medieval predecessors, upholding their authority and confirming their relevance.

With this observation in mind, we may now consider the pre-modern career of Gen. 1:28 in retrospect. How do the understanding and function of the verse in Jewish and Christian texts shed light on its meaning in the history of Western ideas? Ancient and medieval readers of the Bible did not discount the conferral of dominion in the second half of the primordial blessing, and they often posed numerous questions to define its limits and implications. Yet with a handful of rare and sometimes questionable exceptions, they never construed the divine call to master the earth and rule over its animal population as permission to interfere with the workings of nature—selfishly to exploit the environment or to undermine its pristine integrity.

The words of Gen. 1:28 surely addressed the status of human beings, but in a manner that was more insightful and complex than modern ecological advocates have recognized. Both procreation and dominion defined the purpose for which God had created men and women, who

---

Milton's interpretation of Gen. 1:28, although we have cited numerous precedents for most aspects of his exegesis in earlier chapters. See Milton's *Paradise Lost* 4.748, 10.730, ed. Merritt Y. Hughes (New York, 1962), pp. 105 (with n. 744), 256. The view of Peter A. Fiore, *Milton and Augustine: Patterns of Augustinian Thought in "Paradise Lost"* (University Park, Pa., 1981), p. 31, that Milton broke with tradition in suggesting that Adam and Eve united sexually in Eden before their fall (*Paradise Lost* 8.484ff., ed. Hughes, pp. 197–98), deserves further consideration; cf. the similar assertions of rabbinic commentators cited above, Chapter 2, n. 87.

11. See the Catholic arguments cited by Andrew Willet, *Hexapla in Genesin,* 2 vols. (London, 1608), p. 21; and Cornelius à Lapide, *Commentaria in Pentateuchum Mosis* (Antwerp, 1659), pp. 58–59. These contentions bear a noteworthy resemblance to medieval rabbinic discussion of the status (blessing or commandment) of Gen. 1:28; see above, Chapter 4.

12. See above, Chapter 6, n. 40; and cf. the Jewish attacks on Christian celibacy cited above, Chapter 2, nn. 160, 177, and Chapter 5, nn. 35, 40.

alone of all earthly creatures embodied the divine image. The primordial blessing elaborated on this singularity of the human species, enunciating its *raison d'être* and simultaneously establishing its unique relationship with the creator. Jewish and Christian traditions alike appreciated our verse as a statement of anthropology sooner than ecology: Where did human beings rank in the cosmic scheme of things? What could they expect of their maker to facilitate the realization of their potential? And pondered from such a perspective, the divine mandate for sexual reproduction evoked considerably more interest and comment than the instructions to master and to rule. Perhaps the human desire for progeny generally precedes a concern with superiority over other creatures; perhaps it is more universal. Unquestionably it is more problematic. The logical progression from *imago Dei* to dominion is clear; humans wield a modicum of God's power and share in his creativity because they alone bear his likeness. But if men and women reproduce like all other animals, as the Genesis cosmogony itself reminds us, how does their sexuality comport with their godliness?

"Be fertile and increase" thus dominated Jewish and Christian exegesis of our verse from biblical antiquity until the Reformation. From the early chapters of Genesis, and perhaps even before the final composition of the biblical text, the phrase assumed formulaic significance, expressing God's commitment to blessing and protection, a guarantee of his providence. As the text of Scripture unfolds, the blessing of the first parents is reaffirmed—first to Noah, then to the Hebrew patriarchs, and finally to the Israelite nation. More than an injunction to bear children or a promise of sexual fertility, the biblical hendiadys of *prh/rbh* comes to epitomize the covenant between God and his human creatures. And when the Bible narrows its focus from the primeval experiences of the first men and women to the national history of Israel, it understandably transfers the covenant of "be fertile and increase" from Noah and his sons to the descendants of Abraham, Isaac, and Jacob. In the eyes of the biblical author, the blessing properly belonged to God's chosen people.

Each in its own respective idiom, the various genres of postbiblical texts we have considered repeatedly acknowledge the covenantal significance of Gen. 1:28. In the world view of classical rabbinic society, status and prestige were directly proportional to the degree of one's obligation to the laws of God; the more commandments bound an individual, the greater his or her claim to divine election. Talmudic masters thus reformulated the primordial blessing as a precept of Mosaic law and then limited its application to free Jewish males, excluding slaves, women, and Gentiles. Yet such appropriation of "be fertile and increase" contravened the ostensive intent and context of our biblical passage—conferred by God as a blessing rather than legislated, and spoken to the primeval progenitors of all men and women. Some rabbis rejected an exclusivist interpretation of the Bible's call for procreation, but the preponderance of Jewish legal tradition retained it, refusing to forgo title to the divine guarantees that our verse bespoke. Accordingly, while several medieval rabbinic exegetes willingly admitted that biblical law did not include the duty of procreation, most struggled to isolate its precise scriptural origin. Cognizant of the problems inherent in construing our verse as binding legislation, rabbinic jurists of the Middle Ages typically refrained from trying to enforce it as such, though they too reaffirmed its value by relaxing numerous other regulations to encourage compliance. In Christian circles, an exclusive claim on the primordial blessing posed even greater difficulties: How would God have expressed his providence and election in a call for sexual activity when he and his church idealized virginity and celibacy? Just as some rabbis conceded the broad, universal applicability of our verse, so one school of patristic thought maintained that procreation did not pertain to life in a state of saving grace; they effectively abandoned the particularistic, covenantal interpretation of Gen. 1:28. But most Christian theologians insisted that the primordial blessing belonged to the truly faithful. Either God had intended "be fertile and increase" figuratively, so as to apply to the cultivation of Christian virtue, or he had spoken literally, desiring that humans reproduce in paradise, before their sexual activity entailed the sin of concupiscence.

Sharing a covenantal appreciation of Gen. 1:28, Jewish and Christian texts also manifest an array of common literary motifs and midrashic traditions. The notion that God ordained the procreation of a specific number of human beings, whose birth would facilitate the final redemption, informed both rabbinic and patristic thought; for church fathers like Augustine, it fueled the argument that procreation had its rightful place in God's original plan for human existence. While patristic authors probably inherited this notion from Jewish (rabbinic or pseudepigraphic) sources, they bequeathed to some medieval rabbis the inference that conjugal relations in paradise would have transpired without lust and unbridled passion, because the first parents then controlled their sexual organs much like any other bodily limb. Jews and Christians offered similar explanations of the correspondences and differences between God's primordial blessing of fish and fowl (Gen. 1:22) and the words of Gen. 1:28. Following classical precedent, both religious traditions contain associations of the genital organs with those of the five senses. They both somehow likened "be fertile and increase" to the law of nature,[13] and they periodically linked our verse to their respective rituals symbolizing entry into the divine covenant through a sacrifice of blood: circumcision and the sacrament of the Eucharist. Perhaps it is not mere coincidence that the *Roman de la Rose* and the *Zohar,* both works of the thirteenth century, accord much significance to the biblical mandate for procreation in a man's quest for fulfillment, and they portray the goal of that quest in the erotic symbol of the rose.[14]

Along with numerous others, each of these parallels between the Jewish and Christian careers of Gen. 1:28 suggests the basis for a more narrowly focused essay, and we hope to return to several of these topics on subsequent occasions. For the moment, however, we conclude with reference to one such midrashic theme, which Jews and Christians shared with other classical authors and which dominates much of the history we have reviewed. Our biblical verse depicts human beings both within and above the rest of the animal kingdom. They reproduce like fish, fowl, and beast, but like the astral bodies in heaven (Gen. 1:16) they also wield dominion. Similarly in intertestamental, rabbinic, and Christian texts, sexuality and dominion situate humans on the frontier between earthly and heavenly, with a unique opportunity to cast their lot in one direction or the other. Such was God's implied admonition of Gen. 1:28: "'And rule (*u-r^edu*)' applies to him who is in our image and likeness, 'they will descend (*yer^edu*)' [applies] to him who is not in our image and likeness."[15] Rabbinic tradition took up the challenge by sanctifying sexuality, translating the primordial blessing into a commandment of cardinal importance. Zoharic Kabbalah went further still: Procreation exemplified not only human piety but also the mysterious and harmonious perfection of the deity; by complying with the divine mandate, a human couple replicated *and effected* the integration of the godhead, facilitating their own admission into the realm of the supernal

13. For the rabbinic association, see above, Chapter 3, at n. 109, and Chapter 6, at n. 23.
14. *Z,* 1:1a.
15. See above, Chapter 2, at n. 72.

as well. With its complementary emphases on human sinfulness and on the otherworldly, Christian tradition could not readily bridge the chasm between the sexual and the godly in the realm of human experience. Some churchmen, such as Origen, sought to transcend the conflict by interpreting "be fertile and increase" in a spiritual sense; others, like Augustine, limited the possibility of sex in the service of God alone to a prelapsarian paradise. But the unrelenting human impulsion to resolve the tension between sexual and spiritual and thereby traverse the cosmic frontier persisted. As some Christian writers of the high and later Middle Ages sought to synthesize the orders of *Natura* and the biblical God, others reflected on the complexity and difficulty of the problem—so timeless and fundamental that it has withstood all suggested answers. Throughout, Gen. 1:28 remained central to the discussion, evoking reaction and epitomizing the problem.

Here, we submit, lies the primary meaning of Gen. 1:28 during the period we have studied: an assurance of divine commitment and election, and a corresponding challenge to overcome the ostensive contradiction between the terrestrial and the heavenly inherent in every human being. These are basic and eternal human concerns. They have figured in Western intellectual history no less than other pivotal ideas, such as those grouped by Arthur Lovejoy under the rubric of the Great Chain of Being, to which they are not at all unrelated.[16] In a recent book dealing with another dimension of the idea of divine covenant, Francis Oakley has defended Lovejoy's methodology for studying the history of ideas—that is, "not by focusing on periods, schools, systems, or -isms, all of which involve 'idea-complexes' or compounds, frequently unstable, but by breaking those complexes down, rather in the fashion of an analytical chemist, into their component elements or 'unit-ideas.' "[17] Oakley's platform and his story offer a valuable, welcome reaffirmation of more traditional historiographical concerns, which wide circles of textual critics now deem out of vogue and which underlie much of this book as well. Yet we have here departed consciously from Lovejoy's methodology in two significant respects. First, as Oakley has conceded, "the neuralgic point of Lovejoy's approach

16. Arthur O. Lovejoy, *The Great Chain of Being: A Study of the History of an Idea* (Cambridge, Mass., 1936).
17. Francis Oakley, *Omnipotence, Covenant, and Order: An Excursion in the History of Ideas from Abelard to Leibniz* (Ithaca, N.Y., 1984), pp. 35, 39.

appears to be situated in the degree to which, misled by the analogy he himself had drawn from analytical chemistry, he treated his unit-ideas as if they were things, unchanging atomic particles, incapable themselves of possessing a history." In the case of Gen. 1:28, modern scholars have retrojected contemporary concern with dominion over nature onto Scripture's call to "fill the earth and master it," assuming that here lies the source of Western ecological attitudes that have flourished, more than they have developed, since biblical antiquity. But defining this study around the textual unit instead of around its presumed meaning has revealed otherwise. While the words of our verse have remained fixed for millennia, its message has developed considerably; in antiquity and the Middle Ages this message touched only secondarily on conquering the natural order.

Second, we have argued elsewhere that because of Lovejoy's own philosophical bias—his conviction that all acceptable and consequential beliefs must derive from the logic of reason—he deliberately excluded the legacy of biblical ideas from his magnum opus.[18] Referring to scriptural accounts of divine revelation, he quipped: "Can a proposition about the happening of a particular incident at a certain time in a little corner of the earth really be one of the fundamental verities which every man ought to know and believe for his soul's health?"[19] Lovejoy's plaint may or may not be valid, but his ideology unfairly conditioned his historiography. Before the onset of modernity, Western thinkers considered the legacy of that "little corner of the earth" to be of paramount importance, and it informed their ideas on most "fundamental verities." Having demonstrated the broad, far-reaching ramifications of Gen. 1:28 for its Jewish and Christian readers, this study concludes not only with a plea for a textually oriented approach to the history of ideas but with a call for continuing sensitivity to the legacy of *the* Western text par excellence.

18. Cohen, "The Bible, Man, and Nature," pp. 157–63.
19. Arthur O. Lovejoy, "The Entangling Alliance of Religion and History," *Hibbert Journal* 5 (1907), 269.

Glossary of Names and Terms

All dates are C.E. unless otherwise indicated.

Abbayye   Babylonian talmudic master (Amora); d. ca. 336.

Abraham b. David of Posquierres   Rabbinic jurist and mystic; d. ca. 1198.

Abraham ibn Ezra   Spanish rabbinic exegete; d. 1164.

Aggadah   Nonlegal rabbinic teaching; pl *'aggadot*.

R. Akiva   Talmudic master (Tanna) at Yavneh; fl. early 2nd century.

Alan of Lille   Christian theologian, canonist, and poet; d. 1202.

Albertus Magnus   Dominican theologian and scientist; d. 1280.

Alexandrian school   School of patristic biblical exegesis renowned for its allegorical interpretation.

Ambrose   Italian church father; d. 397.

Ambrosiaster   Latin patristic author; fl. 4th century.

Amora   Talmudic master of period of Gemara, 3rd–5th centuries; pl. Amora'im.

Andrew Suneson   Danish Christian theologian and bishop; fl. early 13th century.

Antiochene school   Patristic school of thought, distinguished by its opposition to excessively allegorical interpretation of Scripture.

Aphrahat   Iranian church father; fl. mid-4th century.

Asher b. Yehiel   Spanish rabbinic jurist and codifier; d. ca. 1327.

R. Assi   Palestinian talmudic master (Amora); fl. ca. 300.

Atrahasis   Babylonian epic of creation and primeval history.

Augustine   West African church father; d. 430.

Bahya b. Asher   Spanish rabbinic exegete and mystic; fl. ca. 1290.

Baraita'   Tannitic legal tradition not contained in the Mishnah.

Bar Kokhba   Messianic pretender; leader of Jewish rebellion against Rome, 132–135.

Ben Sira   Author of apocryphal book Ecclesiasticus; fl. ca. 200 B.C.E.

Bernard Silvestris   Christian poet and cosmographer; fl. mid-12th century.

Bonaventure   Franciscan theologian; d. 1274.

Bruno of Asti   Christian exegete; d. 1123.

Cappadocian school   Basil the Great, Gregory of Nazianzus, and Gregory of Nyssa; church fathers known for blend of allegorical and literal exegesis of Scripture.

Chaucer, Geoffrey   English poet; d. 1400.

Claudius of Turin   Christian exegete; d. ca. 830.

Clement of Alexandria   Egyptian church father; d. ca. 215.

David b. Solomon ibn Zimra   Egyptian/Palestinian rabbinic jurist; d. 1573.

David Kimhi   Narbonnese rabbinic jurist, exegete, and theologian; d. ca. 1235.

Decretists   Commentators on Gratian's compilation of canon law, the *Decretum* (1140).

Deuteronomy Rabbah   Medieval compendium of rabbinic Aggadah; compiled after 800.

Didymus the Blind   Alexandrian church father; d. ca. 398.

Dracontius   North African poet; fl. late 5th century.

Duns Scotus   Franciscan theologian; d. ca. 1308.

Eckbert of Schönau   Christian theologian and preacher; d. 1184.

R. Eleazar b. Azariah   Talmudic master (Tanna) at Yavneh; fl. early 2nd century.

Eleazar b. Judah of Worms   Rabbinic theologian, pietist, and mystic; d. ca. 1230.

R. Eleazar b. Simeon   Palestinian talmudic master (Tanna); fl. 2nd century.

Eliezer b. Elijah Ashkenazi   Rabbinic exegete and physician; d. 1586.

Eliezer b. Samuel of Metz   Talmudic commentator and rabbinic jurist; d. ca. 1198.

Ephrem Syrus   Syrian church father; fl. mid-4th century.

Epictetus   Stoic philosopher; fl. ca. 100.

Eusebius of Caesarea   Palestinian church father; d. ca. 339.

Filmer, Robert English political theorist; d. 1653.

R. Gamaliel of Yavneh Rabbinic patriarch and talmudic master; fl. ca. 100.

Gemara Second stratum of Talmud; compiled in Palestinian and Babylonian recensions, 3rd–6th centuries.

Genesis Rabbah Palestinian compendium of rabbinic Aggadah; compiled 5th century.

Genesis Rabbati Medieval compendium of rabbinic Aggadah, dependent on the work of, and ascribed to, R. Moses the Preacher of Narbonne; compiled ca. 12th century.

geonic period Period of cultural hegemony of rabbinic academies in Babylonia and of their leaders (*geʾonim,* sing. *gaʾon*); ca. 7th–12th centuries.

Gerona school Thirteenth-century circle of Spanish Jewish mystics.

Gershom b. Judah of Mainz Rabbinic jurist; d. 1028.

Gratian Canon lawyer; compiler of *Decretum* (1140).

Gregory of Nyssa Cappadocian church father; d. ca. 396.

Hadrian Roman emperor who quelled Judean Bar Kokhba rebellion; d. 138.

Halakhah Rabbinic law and legal tradition.

hendiadys A term composed of two grammatically equivalent words (e.g., verbs or nouns) that together convey a single idea.

Hermetic Pertaining to the ancient occult literature attributed to Hermes Trismegistus.

Hillel Pharisaic master; contemporary of Jesus.

Huguccio of Pisa Canon lawyer and Decretist; d. 1210.

Hugh of Amiens Christian bishop and exegete; fl. 12th century.

Hugh of St. Victor Christian theologian and exegete; d. 1141.

R. Huna Babylonian talmudic master (Amora); d. ca. 296.

Irenaeus Greek church father, bishop of Lyons; d. ca. 200.

Isaac Abravanel Spanish rabbinic exegete and theologian; d. 1508.

Isaac al-Fasi Moroccan rabbinic jurist and codifier; d. 1103.

Isaac Arama Spanish rabbinic philosopher and exegete; d. 1494.

Isaac b. Joseph Karo Spanish rabbinic exegete and jurist, uncle of Joseph b. Ephraim Karo; fl. ca. 1500.

Isaac b. Mordekhai Franco-German talmudic commentator and rabbinic jurist; fl. 12th century.

Isaac b. Moses of Vienna Talmudic commentator and rabbinic jurist; d. ca. 1250.

Isaac b. Samuel   French talmudic commentator and rabbinic jurist; d. ca. 1189.

Isaac b. Samuel of Acre   Rabbinic mystic in tradition of Moses Nahmonides, fl. ca. 1300.

Isaac b. Sheshet Perfet   Spanish and North African rabbinic jurist; d. 1408.

Ishmael b. Elisha   Talmudic master (Tanna); fl. early 2nd century.

Isidore of Seville   Spanish church father; d. 636.

Israel b. Petahiah Isserlein   German rabbinic jurist; d. 1460.

Jacob b. Meir Tam   French talmudic commentator and rabbinic jurist, grandson of Rashi; 1171.

Jean de Meun   French poet; fl. late 13th century.

Jerome   Latin church father; d. ca. 419 or 420.

John Chrysostom   Antiochene church father; d. 407.

John Mandeville   International traveler and chronicler; fl. 14th century.

John XXII   French pope; d. 1334.

Jonah Gerondi   Spanish rabbinic jurist and theologian; d. ca. 1263.

Joseph Bekhor Shor   French rabbinic exegete; fl. 12th century.

Joseph b. Abraham Gikatilla   Spanish rabbinic mystic; fl. 13th century.

Joseph b. Eliezer Bonfils   Spanish-born rabbinic exegete; fl. late 14th century.

Joseph b. Meir ha-Levi ibn Migash   Spanish rabbinic jurist; d. 1141.

Joseph Karo   Rabbinic jurist, codifier, and mystic; d. 1575.

Josephus Flavius   Palestinian Jewish historian; d. after 100.

R. Joshua   Talmudic master (Tanna) at Yavneh; fl. ca. 100.

Joshua ibn Shu'ayb   Rabbinic mystic in tradition of Moses Nahmonides; fl. 14th century.

Julian of Eclanum   Pelagian heresiarch; d. ca. 455.

Justinian   Byzantine emperor; d. 565.

Kabbalah   Rabbinic mystical tradition.

Karaites   Medieval Jewish opponents of authority of rabbinic/talmudic tradition.

Lactantius   African Latin church father; d. ca. 320/340.

Levi Gersonides   Rabbinic exegete and philosopher; d. 1344.

Locke, John   English philosopher; d. 1704.

Manicheans   Proponents of dualistic belief established by Persian seer Mani.

Marcion   Christian heresiarch, fl. mid-2nd century; proponent of Gnostic dualism.

Margery Kempe   English mystic and autobiographer; fl. 14th century.

Masoretic Text   Canonized text of Hebrew Bible.

M*ᵉ***khilta of R. Ishmael**   Halakhic (legally oriented) midrashic compendium on Exodus.

Melanchthon, Philip   German Lutheran theologian and educator; d. 1560.

Menahem b. Benjamin of Recanati   Italian rabbinic mystic; fl. 14th century.

Menahem Me'iri   Provencal rabbinic jurist and talmudic commentator; d. 1315.

Methodius of Olympus   Greek church father; d. ca. 300/311.

Midrash 'Aggadah   Medieval compendium of rabbinic Aggadah associated with the school of R. Moses the Preacher of Narbonne; compiled ca. 12th century.

Midrash ha-Gadol   Yemenite compendium of rabbinic Midrash; compiled 13th century.

Midrash Tadshe'   Medieval compendium of rabbinic Aggadah; compiled ca. 10th century.

Midrash Tanḥuma'   Medieval compendium of rabbinic Aggadah; compiled ca. 8th–9th centuries.

Midrash Tᵉhillim   Medieval compendium of rabbinic Aggadah; compiled after 900.

Mishnah   Earlier stratum of Talmud; compiled in Palestine 1st–3rd centuries, redacted early 3rd century.

Mordecai b. Hillel ha-Kohen   German rabbinic jurist and talmudic commentator; d. 1298.

Moses b. Jacob al-Balideh   Yemenite rabbinic exegete and theologian; fl. 15th century.

Moses b. Jacob of Coucy   French rabbinic jurist and codifier; fl. 13th century.

Moses de León   Spanish rabbinic mystic and author of *Zohar;* d. ca. 1305.

Moses Isserles   Polish rabbinic jurist and codifier; d. 1572.

Moses Maimonides   Spanish and Egyptian rabbinic jurist, codifier, and theologian; d. 1204.

Moses Nahmanides   Spanish rabbinic exegete, jurist, and mystic; d. 1270.

R. Moses the Preacher   Narbonnese rabbinic aggadist; fl. 11th century.

R. Nathan   Talmudic master (Tanna) of Babylonian origin; fl. 2nd century.

Nathaniel b. Isaiah   Yemenite rabbinic exegete; fl. early 14th century.

Nissim b. Reuben Gerondi   Spanish rabbinic exegete and jurist; d. ca. 1375.

Obadiah b. Abraham of Bertinoro   Italian rabbinic jurist and exegete; fl. ca. 1500.

Obadiah Sforno   Italian rabbinic exegete; d. ca. 1550.

Odo of Cambrai (Tournai)   Christian exegete; d. 1113.

Origen   Alexandrian church father; d. ca. 254.

Pareus, David   Calvinist exegete and theologian; d. 1622.

Pelagians   Christian heretics who rejected the doctrine of original sin.

Peter Abelard   Christian theologian; d. 1142.

Peter Comestor   Christian exegete and theologian; d. ca. 1179/80.

Peter Lombard   Christian theologian, compiler of the *Sententiae;* d. ca. 1160/ 1164.

Philo   Alexandrian Jewish philosopher and exegete; d. ca. 50.

Pirqe ʾAvot   Mishnaic tractate containing theological maxims attributed to Tannaitic masters.

Pirqe dᵉ-R. ʾEliᶜezer   Pseudonymous rabbinic aggadic narrative; compiled ca. 8th century.

Rashi   Solomon b. Isaac of Troyes; leading rabbinic exegete and talmudic commentator of the Middle Ages; d. 1105.

Rav   R. Abba Arikha: Babylonian talmudic master (Amora); d. ca. 247.

Rava   Babylonian talmudic master (Amora); d. ca. 351.

Robert Grosseteste   English bishop, theologian, and scientist; d. 1253.

Rufinus   Canon lawyer and decretist; fl. second half of 12th century.

Rupert of Deutz   German abbot, exegete, and theologian; d. 1129.

Saadya b. Joseph   Gaon (head) of Babylonian academy at Sura; jurist, exegete, and theologian; d. 942.

Samuel b. Meir   French rabbinic exegete, grandson of Rashi; d. ca. 1174.

Samuel Eliezer Edels   Polish rabbinic jurist and talmudic commentator; d. 1631.

Sefer Ḥasidim   Compendium of Ashkenazic Pietism, attributed to Judah b. Samuel (d. 1217).

Severian of Gabala   Antiochene church father; fl. early 5th century.

Shammai   Pharisaic master; contemporary of Jesus.

Shem Tov b. Abraham ibn Gaon   Rabbinic mystic in the tradition of Nahmonides; fl. early 14th century.

Sifraʾ   Halakhic (legally oriented) compendium of Tannaitic midrash on Leviticus.

Simeon b. Azzai   Talmudic master (Tanna) at Yavneh; fl. early 2nd century.

Simeon ibn Labi   Moroccan rabbinic mystic, commentator on *Zohar;* fl. 16th century.

Simeon b. Laqish   Palestinian talmudic master (Amora); fl. 3rd century.

Solomon ibn Adret   Spanish jurist and talmudic commentator; d. ca. 1310.

Tanna   Talmudic master of period of Mishnah, 1st–early 3rd centuries; pl. Tannaʾim.

Targum   Aramaic translation of Hebrew Scripture.

Tertullian   North African church father; d. ca. 220/230.

Theodore of Mopsuestia   Antiochene church father ; d. ca. 428.

Theophilus of Antioch   Church father; d. ca. 181/186.

Thomas Aquinas   Christian theologian; d. 1274.

Todros b. Joseph Ha-Levi Abulafia   Spanish rabbinic mystic; d. 1298.

Tosefta   Collection of primnarily legal teachings of Tanna'im; arranged according to the order of the Mishnah.

Ulpian   Roman jurist; d. 223.

Usha   Galilean seat of rabbinic Sanhedrin, mid-2nd century.

Vidal Yom Tov   Rabbinic jurist; fl. second half of 14th century.

William of Ockham   English Franciscan scholastic philosopher and theologian; d. ca. 1349.

Yavneh   Judean seat of rabbinic Sanhedrin after the fall of Jerusalem, late 1st–early 2nd centuries.

R. Yohanan   Palestinian talmudic master (Amora); d. ca. 287.

R. Yohanan b. Broka   Talmudic master (Tanna); fl. ca. 100.

Yom Tov b. Abraham Ishbili   Spanish rabbinic jurist and talmudic commentator; d. ca. 1330.

Zohar   Magnum opus of medieval Kabbalah; written by Spanish Moses de León, late 14th century.

Works Cited

Primary Sources

Aboth de Rabbi Nathan (Hebrew). Ed. Solomon Schechter. Corr. ed. New York, 1967.

Abraham b. David of Posquierres. *Baʿale ha-Nefesh*. Ed. Joseph Kafah. Jerusalem, 1964.

Abraham b. Isaac of Narbonne. *Sefer ha-ʾEshkol*. 3 vols. Halberstadt, 1867–69.

Abraham b. Jacob Saba. *Sefer Ẓᵉror ha-Mor*. 1879; Tel Aviv, 1975.

Abraham b. Meir ibn Ezra. *Perushe ha-Torah*. Ed. Asher Weizer. 3 vols. Jerusalem, 1976.

Abraham b. Moses Maimonides. *Perush ʿal Bᵉreshit u-Shᵉmot*. Ed. Efraim Judah Weisenberg. London, 1958.

Abraham b. Moses Maimonides. *Shu"T Birkat ʾAvraham*. 1860; repr., Jerusalem, 1960.

Abraham of Montpellier. *Commentary on the Tractate Yevamoth* (Hebrew). Ed. M. Y. Blau. New York, 1962.

Agadath Bereschith (Hebrew). Ed. Solomon Buber. Krakow, 1902.

Alan of Lille. *The Plaint of Nature*. Tr. James J. Sheridan. Medieval Sources in Translation 26. Toronto, 1980.

Alan of Lille. *De planctu Naturae*. Ed. Nikolaus M. Häring. *Studi medievali,* 3rd ser. 19 (1978), 797–879.

Albertus Magnus. *Opera omnia*. 38 vols. Paris, 1890–99.

Albertus Magnus. *Opera omnia*. Aschendorf, 1951–present.

Andrew, Malcolm, and Ronald Waldron, eds. *The Poems of the Pearl Manuscript*. Rev. ed. Exeter, 1987.

Andrew Sunesön. *Hexaemeron*. Ed. Sten Ebbesen and Laurentius Boethius Mortensen. Corpus philosophorum danicorum Medii Aevi 11,1. Hauniae, 1985.

The Apocrypha and Pseudepigrapha of the Old Testament. Ed. R. H. Charles. 2 vols. Oxford, 1913.

Die apostolischen Väter: Erster Teil. Ed. F. X. Funk and Karl Bihlmeyer. 2nd ed. Sammlung ausgewählter kirchen- und dogmengeschichtlicher Quellenschriften 2,1,1. Tübingen, 1956.

Aryeh Leib b. Joseph ha-Kohen Heller. *Sefer 'Avne Millu'im.* Jerusalem, 1976.

Aryeh Leib ha-Kohen. *Sefer Ture 'Even.* Vienna, 1875.

Asher b. Yehiel. *Shu"T.* Vilna, 1881.

Augustine of Hippo. *La Genèse au sens littéral.* Ed. P. Agaësse and A. Solignac, 2 vols. Oeuvres de Saint Augustin 48–49. Paris, 1972.

Augustine of Hippo. *De haeresibus.* Ed. Liguori G. Müller. Catholic University of America Patristic Studies 90. Washington, D.C., 1956.

Augustine of Hippo. *The Literal Meaning of Genesis.* Tr. John Hammond Taylor. 2 vols. Ancient Christian Writers 41–42. New York, 1982.

Azriel b. Menahem of Gerona. *Commentarius in Aggadot* (Hebrew). Ed. Isaiah Tishby. Jerusalem, 1945.

Azulai, Hayyim Joseph David. *Sefer Birke Yosef.* 4 vols. Vienna, 1859.

Babad, Joseph. *Sefer Minhat Hinnukh.* 2 vols. New York, 1966.

Bahya b. Asher. *Be'ur 'al ha-Torah.* Ed. C. B. Chavel. 3 vols. Jerusalem, 1966–68.

Bahya b. Asher. *Kitve Rabbenu Bahya.* Ed. C. B. Chavel. Jerusalem, 1969.

Bahya b. Joseph ibn Paquda. *Sefer Torat Hovot ha-Levavot.* Ed. Joseph Kafah. Jerusalem, 1973.

Barnabas and the Didache. Tr. Robert A. Kraft. The Apostolic Fathers: A New Translation and Commentary 3. New York, 1965.

Basil the Great. *Lettres.* Ed. Yves Courtonne. 3 vols. Paris, 1957–66.

Basil the Great. *Sur l'origine de l'homme (De creatione hominis).* Ed. Alexis Smets and Michel van Esbroeck. SC 160. Paris, 1960.

Pseudo-Basil the Great. *Sermones de creatione hominis.* Ed. Hadwiga Hörner. *Gregorii Nysseni opera: Supplementum.* Leiden, 1972.

Bazak, Jacob, ed. *Jewish Law—Selected Responsa* (Hebrew). 2 vols. Tel Aviv, 1971–75.

Die Bekenntnisschriften der evangelisch-lutherischen Kirche. 6th ed. Göttingen, 1967.

Benjamin b. Mattathias. *Shu"T Binyamin Ze'ev.* 2 vols. Jerusalem, 1959.

Bernadino of Sienna. *Opera omnia.* 9 vols. Quaracchi, 1950–65.

Bernard Silvestris. *Cosmographia.* Ed. Peter Dronke. Leiden, 1978.

Bernard Silvestris. *Cosmographia.* Tr. Winthrop Wetherbee. New York, 1973.

Biblia sacra cum glossis, interlineari, et ordinaria, Nicolai Lyrani postilla, ac moralitatibus, Burgensis additionibus, et Thoringi replicis. 6 vols. Venice, 1588.

Bonaventure. *Opera omnia.* 11 vols. Quaracchi, 1882–1902.

The Book of Enoch or 1 Enoch: A New English Edition. Ed. Matthew Black. Studia in Veteris Testamenti Pseudepigrapha 7. Leiden, 1985.

The Book of Margery Kempe. Ed. Sanford Brown Meech and Hope Emily Allen. London, 1940.

Book of the Cave of Treasures. Tr. E. A. Wallis Budge. London, 1927.

Das Buch Bahir: Ein Schriftdenkmal aus der Frühzeit der Kabbalah. Ed. and tr. Gershom Scholem. Qabbalah: Quellen und Forschungen der jüdischen Mystik 1. Leipzig, 1923.

Burns, J. Patout, ed. *Theological Anthropology.* Philadelphia, Pa., 1981.

Chaucer, Geoffrey. *The Riverside Chaucer*. Ed. Larry D. Benson. 3rd ed. Boston, Mass., 1987.

Cockayne, Thomas Oswald, ed. *Leechdoms, Wortcunning, and Starcraft of Early England*. Rev. ed. 3 vols. London, 1961.

Die Confutatio der Confessio augustana vom 3. August 1530. Ed. Herbert Immenkötter. Münster, 1979.

Corpus hermeticum. Ed. A. D. Nock and A.-J. Festugière. 6th ed. 4 vols. Paris, 1983.

Corpus iuris canonici. Ed. Aemilius Friedberg. 2 vols. 1879; repr., Graz, 1959.

Corpus iuris civilis. Ed. Paulus Krueger et al. 3 vols. 1954–67; repr., Berlin, 1973.

David b. Hayyim ha-Kohen. *Shu"T ha-RaDa"Kh*. Salonika, 1803.

David b. Joseph Kimhi. *Ha-Perush ha-Shalem ʿal Tᵉhillim*. Ed. Abraham Darom. Jerusalem, 1967.

David b. Joseph Kimhi. *Perushe RaDa"Q ʿal ha-Torah*. Ed. Moshe Kamelhar. Jerusalem, 1970.

David b. Judah he-Hasid. *The Book of Mirrors: Sefer Marʾot ha-Zoveʾot* (Hebrew). Ed. Daniel C. Matt. Brown Judaic Studies 30. Chico, Calif., 1982.

Didymus the Blind of Alexandria. *Sur la Genèse*. Ed. Pierre Nautin and Louis Doutreleau. 2 vols. SC 233, 244. Paris, 1976–78.

Diels, Hermannus, ed. *Doxographi graeci*. Rev. ed. Berlin, 1929.

Diogenes Laërtius. *Lives of Eminent Philosophers*. Ed. R. D. Hicks. LCL. 2 vols. London, 1925.

Dracontius. *De laudibus Dei*. Book 1. Tr. James Irwin. Philadelphia, Pa., 1942.

Dracontius. *Oeuvres*. Vol. 1. Ed. Claude Moussy and Colette Camus. Paris, 1985.

Duns Scotus. *Opera omnia*. 26 vols. Paris, 1891–95.

Eleazar b. Judah of Worms. *Perush ha-Roqeah ʿal ha-Torah*. Ed. Chaim Konyevsky. 3 vols. Bʾnei Bʾrak, 1978–81.

Eliezer b. Joel ha-Levi. *Sefer ha-RAvYa"H*. Ed. Victor Aptowitzer. 2nd ed. (vols. 1–3). 4 vols. Jerusalem, 1964–65.

Eliezer b. Nathan. *Sefer ʾEven ha-ʿEzer*. Ed. Shalom Albeck. 2 vols. Warsaw, 1904.

Eliezer b. Samuel of Metz. *Sefer Yᵉreʾim*. Ed. Israel Isser Goldblum and Abraham Abba Schiff. 2 vols. 1892–1902; repr., Jerusalem, 1973.

Elijah b. Abraham Mizrahi. *Shu"T*. Jerusalem, 1938.

Elijah b. Abraham Mizrahi and Elijah b. Hayyim. *Shu"T Mayim ʿAmuqim*. Berlin, 1778.

Epictetus. *The Discourses*. Ed. W. A. Oldfather. LCL. 2 vols. 1925–28; repr., Cambridge, Mass., 1978–79.

Estori b. Moses ha-Parhi. *Kaftor wa-Ferah*. 2 vols. New York, 1958–64.

Eusebius of Caesarea. *Proof of the Gospel*. Tr. W. J. Ferrar. 2 vols. London, 1920.

Filmer, Robert. *Patriarcha and Other Political Works*. Ed. Peter Laslett. Oxford, 1949.

Fleisch, H., ed. "Fragments de Clément d'Alexandrie conservés en arabe." *Mélanges de l'Université Saint Joseph* 27 (1947), 61–71.

Fontes vitae S. Thomae Aquinatis, 6. Ed. M.-H. Laurent. Saint-Maximin, 1937.

The Fragment-Targums of the Pentateuch according to Their Extant Sources. Ed. Michael L. Klein. Analecta biblica 76. 2 vols. Rome, 1980.

Gad, Y., ed. *Sefer Hamishah Mᵉʾorot Gᵉdolim*. Johannesburg, 1953.

Gellis, Jacob, ed. *Sefer Tosafot Hashalem: Commentary on the Bible* (Hebrew), 1. Jerusalem, 1982.

Gershom b. Judah. *The Responsa of Rabbenu Gershom Meor Hagolah* (Hebrew). Ed. Shlomo Eidelberg. New York, 1955.

Gerson, Jean. *Oeuvres complètes*. Ed. Palemon Glorieux. 7 vols. in 8 pts. Paris, 1960–68.

Gregory of Nyssa. A Select Library of Nicene and Post-Nicene Fathers 2,5. 1893; repr., New York, 1917.

Grünhut, Eliezer, ed. *Sefer ha-Liqquṭim.* 6 vols. 1898–1903; repr., Jerusalem, 1967.

Guillaume de Lorris and Jean de Meun. *Le Roman de la Rose.* Ed. Ernest Langlois. 5 vols. Paris, 1914–24.

Guillaume de Lorris and Jean de Meun. *The Romance of the Rose.* Tr. Charles Dahlberg. 1971; repr., Hanover, N.H., 1983.

Hefez b. Yazliah. *A Volume of the Book of Precepts* (Arabic with Hebrew trans.). Ed. B. Halper. Philadelphia, Pa., 1915.

[Henry of Ghent?]. *Lectura ordinaria super sacram scripturam.* Ed. R. Macken. Henrico de Gandavo opera omnia 36. Louvain, 1980.

Hezekiah b. Manoah. *Perushe ha-Ḥizquni ʿal ha-Torah.* Ed. Charles B. Chavel. Jerusalem, 1981.

Hugh of St. Victor. *On the Sacraments of the Christian Faith.* Tr. Roy J. Deferrari. Cambridge, Mass., 1951.

Irenaeus of Lyons. *Contre les hérésies (Adversus haereses).* Ed. Adelin Rousseau et al. 5 vols. in 10 pts. SC 100,1–2, 152–53, 210–11, 263–64, 293–94. Paris, 1965–82.

Isaac b. Jacob al-Fasi. *Hilkhot Rav ʾAlfas.* Ed. Nissan Zacks. 2 vols. Jerusalem, 1969.

Isaac b. Joseph Karo. *Tolᵉdot Yiẓḥaq.* 1878; repr., Jerusalem, 1959.

Isaac b. Judah Abravanel. *Perush ʿal ha-Torah.* 5 pts. in 3 vols. New York, 1959.

Isaac b. Moses Arama. *ʿAqedat Yiẓḥaq.* 5 vols. Pressburg, 1849.

Isaac b. Moses of Vienna. *Sefer ʾOr Zaruaʿ.* 2 vols. 1862; repr., B'nei B'rak, 1958.

Isaac b. Samuel of Acre. *"Mᵉʾirat ʿEnayim."* Ed. Amos Goldreich. Ph.D. Dissertation, Hebrew University of Jerusalem. Jerusalem, 1981.

Isaac b. Sheshet Perfet. *Shu"T.* Vilna, 1879.

Pseudo-Isaac ibn Farhi. *"Sefer Taʾamey ha-Mizwoth (Book of Reasons of the Commandments)"* (Hebrew). Ed. Menahem Meier. Ph.D. Dissertation, Brandeis University. Waltham, Mass., 1974.

Isaiah b. Mali of Trani. *Tosᵉfot RI"D: Masekhet Yᵉvamot.* Jerusalem, 1931.

Isaiah b. Mali of Trani and Isaiah b. Elijah of Trani. *Piskei HaRid, Piskei HaRiaz* (Hebrew). Ed. Abraham Joseph Wertheimer and Abraham Liess. 8 vols. Jerusalem, 1964–82.

Isidore of Seville. *Etimologías (Etymologiae).* Ed. Jose Oroz Reta and Manuel-A. Marcos Casquero. 2 vols. Biblioteca de autores cristianos 433–34. Madrid, 1982–83.

Israel b. Petahiah Isserlein. *Sefer Bᵉʾure MahaR"I.* 1937; repr., B'nei B'rak, 1963.

Israel b. Petahiah Isserlein. *Shu"T Tᵉrumat ha-Deshen.* Warsaw, 1882.

Issachar Baer Eilenburg. *Sefer Bᵉʾer Shevaʿ.* 1890; repr., Jerusalem, 1969.

Jacob b. Asher. *Perush ha-Ṭur he-ʾArokh ʿal ha-Torah.* Jerusalem, 1961.

Jacob b. Joseph Reischer. *Shᵉvut Yaʿaqov.* 3 vols. Lemberg, 1897.

Jacob b. Meir Tam, *Sefer ha-Yashar: Ḥeleq ha-Shᵉʾelot wᵉha-Tᵉshuvot.* Ed. S. P. Rosenthal. Berlin, 1898.

Jacob b. Moses ha-Levi Molin. *New Responsa of . . . Maharil* (Hebrew). Ed. Yitzchok Satz. Jerusalem, 1977.

Jacob b. Moses ha-Levi Molin. *Responsa of . . . Maharil* (Hebrew). Ed. Yitzchok Satz. Jerusalem, 1979.

Jaffe, Mordecai. *Sefer Lᵉvushe 'Or Yᵉqarot.* Jerusalem, 1961.

Jaffe, Samuel b. Isaac. *Yᵉfeh To'ar.* Fürth, 1692.

Jellinek, Adolph, ed. *Beth ha-Midrasch* (Hebrew). 3rd ed. 6 pts. in 2 vols. Jerusalem, 1967.

The Jewish-Christian Debate in the High Middle Ages: A Critical Edition of the "Niẓẓaḥon Vetus." Ed. David Berger. Judaica: Texts and Translations 4. Philadelphia, Pa., 1979.

Joannou, Périclès-Pierre, ed. *Discipline générale antique (IVᵉ–IXᵉ s.),* 2. Fonti 9. Rome, 1963.

Jonah b. Abraham Gerondi. *Ḥiddushe Rabbenu Yonah 'al Masekhet Sanhedrin.* 1705; repr., Jerusalem, 1968.

Pseudo-Jonathan. *Targum Jonathan b. Uziel on the Pentateuch* (Hebrew). Ed. David Rieder. Jerusalem, 1974.

Joseph Bekhor Shor. *Perush 'al ha-Torah.* Ed. Y. Gad. 3 vols. Jerusalem, 1956–59.

Joseph b. Abraham Gikatila. *Shaare Orah* (Hebrew). Ed. Joseph Ben Shlomo. 2 vols. 1971; repr., Jerusalem, 1981.

Joseph b. David ibn Lev. *Shu"T.* Vol. 3. 1726; repr., Jerusalem, 1970.

Joseph b. Efraim Karo. *Sefer 'Avqat Rokhel.* Leipzig, 1859.

Joseph b. Efraim Karo. *Shu"T Bet Yosef.* Jerusalem, 1960.

Joseph b. Eliezer Bonfils. *Ẓafᵉnat Pa'neaḥ.* Ed. David Herzog. Krakow, 1912.

Joseph b. Isaac Kimhi. *Sefer ha-Galuy.* Ed. Henry J. Mathews. Berlin, 1887.

Joseph b. Meir ha-Levi ibn Migash. *Shu"T.* Jerusalem, 1959.

Joseph b. Solomon Colon. *Shu"T.* 1884; repr., New York, 1968.

Josephus. *Works.* Ed. H. St. J. Thackeray et al. LCL. 9 vols. Cambridge, Mass., 1926–65.

Judah b. Asher. *Zikhron Yᵉhudah.* Ed. Judah Rosenberg. Berlin, 1846.

Judah b. Eliezer Mintz and Meir b. Isaac Katzenellenbogen of Padua. *Sefer Shu"T.* Krakow, 1882.

Judah b. Samuel ha-Levi. *Das Buch al-Chazari* (Hebrew). Tr. Judah ibn Tibbon. Ed. Hartwig Hirschfeld. Leipzig, 1887.

Judah b. Samuel ha-Levi. *Sefer ha-Kuzari.* 5 pts. in 1 vol. 1880; repr., Tel Aviv, 1959.

Judah b. Samuel the Pious. *Das Buch der Frommen* (Hebrew). Ed. Jehuda Wistinetzki and J. Freimann. 2nd ed. Frankfurt a.M., 1924.

Judah b. Samuel the Pious. *Sefer Ḥasidim.* Ed. Reuben Margaliot. Jerusalem, 1970.

Justin Martyr. *Dialogue avec Tryphon (Dialogus cum Tryphone Iudaeo).* Ed. G. Archambault. 2 vols. Paris, 1909.

Kempe, Margery. See *The Book of Margery Kempe.*

Koriat, Judah, ed. *Ma'or wa-Shemesh.* Leghorn, 1819.

Lachover, F., and Isaiah Tishby, eds. *The Wisdom of the Book of Splendour* (Hebrew). 2nd ed. (vol. 1 only). 2 vols. Jerusalem, 1957–61.

Lambert, W. G., and A. R. Millard, eds. *Atra-Hasis: The Babylonian Story of the Flood.* Oxford, 1969.

Lapide, Cornelius à. *Commentaria in Pentateuchum Mosis.* Antwerp, 1659.

Lecomte, François, ed. "Un commentaire scripturaire du XIIᵉ siècle: Le 'Tractatus in hexaemeron' de Hugues d'Amiens (Archevêque de Rouen, 1130–1164)." *Archives d'histoire doctrinale et littéraire du Moyen Age* 25 (1958), 227–94.

Lekach-Tob (Pesikta-Sutarta) (Hebrew). Ed. Solomon Buber. 2 vols. Vilna, 1884.

La lettre sur la sainteté. Ed. Charles Mopsik. Paris, 1986.

Levi b. Gerson. *Perush ʿal ha-Torah Derekh Beʾur.* 2 vols. Venice, 1547.

Levi b. Jacob ibn Habib. *Shu"T MahaRLba"H.* Lemberg, 1865.

Lewin, B. M., ed. *Otzar ha-Gaonim: Thesaurus of the Gaonic Responsa and Commentaries* (Hebrew). 15 vols. Haifa and Jerusalem, 1928–43.

Locke, John. *Two Treatises of Government.* Ed. Peter Laslett. Cambridge, 1970.

Luther, Martin. *Werke: Kritische Gesamtausgabe.* Weimar, 1883–present.

Luther, Martin. *Works.* Ed. Jaroslav Pelikan and Helmut T. Lehmann. St. Louis, Mo., 1955–86.

Makhir b. Abba Mari. *The Yalkut on Isaiah* (Hebrew). Ed. J. Spira. Berlin, 1894.

Mandeville's Travels. Ed. M. C. Seymour. Oxford, 1967.

Mansi, J. D., et al., eds. *Sacrorum conciliorum nova et amplissima collectio.* 53 vols. Florence and Rome, 1757–1927.

Masekhtot Kallah. Ed. Michael Higger. Brooklyn, N.Y., 1936.

Mechilta dʾRabbi Ismael (Hebrew). Ed. H. S. Horowitz and I. A. Rabin. 2nd ed. Jerusalem, 1960.

Medini, Hayyim Hezekiah. *Rabbinical Encyclopedia "Sede Chemed"* (Hebrew). Rev. ed. 10 vols. Brooklyn, N.Y., 1949–53.

Meir b. Baruch of Rothenburg. *Shu"T.* Prague, 1608; repr., Budapest, 1895.

Menahem Azariah of Fano. *Sefer ʿAsarah Maʾamarot.* 1858; repr., Jerusalem, 1974.

Menahem b. Benjamin of Recanati. *Sefer Ṭaʿame ha-Miẓwot ha-Shalem.* Ed. S. Lieberman. London, 1962.

Menahem b. Solomon. *Sechel Tob: Commentar zum ersten und zweiten Buch Mosis* (Hebrew). Ed. Solomon Buber. 2 vols. Berlin, 1900–1901.

Menahem b. Solomon ha-Meʾiri. *Bet ha-Bᵉḥirah ʿal Masekhet Qiddushin.* Ed. Abraham Schreiber (Sofer). 4th ed. Jerusalem, 1971.

Menahem b. Solomon ha-Meʾiri. *Bet ha-Bᵉḥirah ʿal Masekhet Yᵉvamot.* Ed. Samuel Dickmann. Jerusalem, 1962.

Menahem b. Solomon ha-Meʾiri. *Perush ʿal Sefer Mishle.* Ed. Menahem Mendel Meshi-Zahav. Jerusalem, 1969.

Meshullam b. Judah of Béziers. *Sefer ha-Hashlamah.* Ed. Abraham Haputa. 10 vols. Tel Aviv, 1961–75.

Methodius of Olympus. *Le banquet (Convivium).* Ed. Herbert Musurillo and Victor-Henry Debidour. SC 95. Paris, 1963.

Meyuhas b. Elijah. *Perush ʿal Bᵉreshit.* Ed. A. W. Greenup and C. H. Titterton. 1909; repr., Jerusalem, 1968.

Midras Beresit Rabbati (Hebrew). Ed. C. Albeck. Jerusalem, 1940.

Midrash ʾAggadah ʿal Ḥamishah Ḥumshe Torah. Ed. Solomon Buber. 1894; repr., Jerusalem, 1972.

Midrash Bereshit Rabba: Critical Edition with Notes and Commentary (Hebrew). Ed. J. Theodor and Ch. Albeck. 3 vols. 1903–36; repr., Jerusalem, 1965.

Midrash Debarim Rabbah (Hebrew). Ed. Saul Lieberman. 3rd ed. Jerusalem, 1974.

Midrash Haggadol on the Pentateuch (Hebrew). Ed. Mordecai Margulies et al. 5 vols. Jerusalem, 1947–75.

"Midrash Qohelet Rabbah, Chapters 1–4: Commentary (Ch. 1) and Introduction." Ed. Marc G. Hirshman. Ph.D. Dissertation, Jewish Theological Seminary of America, New York, 1982.

Midrash Rabbah: Shir ha-Shirim. Ed. Shimshon Dunski. Jerusalem, 1980.

Midrash Sh^emu^ɔel. Ed. Solomon Buber. Krakow, 1893.

Midrash Shir Hashirim (Hebrew). Ed. Eliezer Grünhut and Joseph Chaim Wertheimer. 2nd ed. Jerusalem, 1981.

"*Midrash Tadshe*'." Ed. Abraham Epstein. In *Mi-Qadmoniyyot ha-Y^ehudim: Meḥqarim u-R^eshimot,* pp. 130–75. Ed. A. M. Habermann. Jerusalem, 1957.

Midrash Tanḥuma'. 1563; repr., Jerusalem, 1971.

Midrash Tanḥuma' he-Qadum w^eha-Yashan. Ed. Solomon Buber. 6 pts. in 2 vols. 1885; repr., Jerusalem, 1964.

Midrash T^ehillim. Ed. Solomon Buber. 1891; repr., Jerusalem, 1966.

Midrash Wayyikra Rabbah (Hebrew). Ed. Mordecai Margulies. 5 vols. Jerusalem, 1953–60.

Midrash Zuṭa 'al Shir ha-Shirim, Rut, 'Ekhah w^e-Qohelet. Ed. Solomon Buber. Berlin, 1894.

Milton, John. *Paradise Lost.* Ed. Merritt Y. Hughes. New York, 1962.

Mishnah 'im Perush Rabbenu Moshe b. Maimon. Ed. Joseph Kafah. 6 pts. in 7 vols. Jerusalem, 1963–68.

The Mishnah of Rabbi Eliezer (Hebrew). Ed. H. G. Enelow. New York, 1933.

Mordecai b. Hillel ha-Kohen. *Sefer Mord^ekhai ha-Shalem 'al Masekhet Beẓah.* Ed. Joshua Horowitz and Isaac Kleinman. Jerusalem, 1983.

Moses b. Hayyim Alshekh. *Sefer Torat Mosheh.* 5 pts. in 2 vols. 1875–79; repr., Brooklyn, N.Y., 1960.

Moses b. Jacob al-Balideh. *'Olat Tamid.* Venice, 1601.

Moses b. Jacob of Coucy. *Sefer Miẓwot Gadol.* 2 vols. 1547; repr., Jerusalem, 1961.

Moses b. Jacob of Trani. *Shu"T Mabbiṭ.* 3 vols. Lemberg, 1861.

Moses b. Maimon. *The Guide of the Perplexed.* Tr. Shlomo Pines. Chicago, 1963.

Moses b. Maimon. *Mishneh Torah,* 3. Jerusalem, 1977.

Moses b. Maimon. *Sefer ha-Miẓwot.* Ed. Hayyim Heller. 1946; repr., Jerusalem, 1980.

Moses b. Maimon. *Sefer ha-Miẓwot.* Ed. Joseph Kafah. Jerusalem, 1971.

Moses b. Maimon. *Sefer ha-Miẓwot.* Jerusalem, 1926.

Moses b. Nahman. *The Commentary of Nahmanides on Genesis Chapters 1–6⁸.* Ed. Jacob Newman. Pretoria Oriental Series 4. Leiden, 1960.

Moses b. Nahman. *Ḥiddushe ha-RaMba"N . . . 'al Masekhtot ha-Sha"S.* Ed. Moshe Hershler et al. 4 vols. to date. Jerusalem, 1970–87.

Moses b. Nahman. *Kitve RaMba"N.* Ed. Charles B. Chavel. 2 vols. Jerusalem, 1963.

Moses b. Nahman. *Perush ha-Torah.* Ed. Charles B. Chavel. 2 vols. Jerusalem, 1959–60.

Moses b. Shem Tov de León. "*Sefer ha-Mishkal:* Text [Hebrew] and Study." Ed. Jochanan H. A. Wijnhoven. Ph.D. Dissertation, Brandeis University. Waltham, Mass., 1964.

Moses b. Shem Tov de León. "*Sefer ha-Rimmon:* A Critical Edition [Hebrew] and Introductory Study." Ed. Elliot R. Wolfson. 2 vols. Ph.D. Dissertation, Brandeis University. Waltham, Mass., 1986.

Moses b. Shem Tov de León. "Shu"T . . . b^e-'Iny^ene ha-Qabbalah." Ed. Isaiah Tishby. *Qoveẓ 'al Yad* 15 (1950), 9–38.

Moses Isserles. *Shu"T ha-RaM"A.* Ed. Asher Ziv. Jerusalem, 1970.

Mubashir b. Nissi ha-Levi. *A Critique against the Writings of R. Saadya Gaon* (Arabic with Hebrew trans.). Ed. Moshe Zucker. New York, 1955.

Mueller, Joel, ed. *T^eshuvot Ḥakhme Ẓar^efat w^e-Lotir.* Vienna, 1881.

Nathaniel b. Isaiah. *Sefer Ma'or ha-'Afelah.* Ed. and tr. Joseph Kafah. Jerusalem, 1959.

Neofiti 1: Targum palestinense ms de la Biblioteca vaticana. Ed. Alejandro Díez Macho. 6 vols. Madrid, 1968–79.

Nissim b. Reuben Gerondi. *Commentary on the Bible* (Hebrew). Ed. Leon A. Feldman. Jerusalem, 1968.

Nissim b. Reuben Gerondi. *Ḥiddushe ha-Ra''N 'al Masekhet Niddah.* Jerusalem, 1973.

Nissim b. Reuben Gerondi. *Ḥiddushe ha-Ra''N 'al Masekhet Sanhedrin.* Jerusalem, 1973.

Nissim b. Reuben Gerondi. *Teshuvot ha-RaN: Responsa* (Hebrew). Ed. Leon A. Feldman. Jerusalem, 1984.

Obadiah b. Abraham Yare of Bertinoro. *'Amar N^eqe'.* Pisa, 1810.

Obadiah b. Jacob Sforno. *Be'ur 'al ha-Torah.* Ed. Ze'ev Gottlieb and Abraham Darom. Jerusalem, 1980.

Odoric da Pordenone. *Itinerarium.* Ed. Carolus Emanuel Aurivillius. Uppsala, 1817.

The Old Testament Pseudepigrapha. Ed. James H. Charlesworth. 2 vols. Garden City, N.Y., 1983–85.

Origen. "Ein Bruchstück . . . über Genesis i, 28." Ed. Paul Glaue. *Schriften der hessischen Hochschulen, Universität Giessen* 1,11 (1928), 6–12.

Origen. *Contre Celse (Contra Celsum).* Ed. Marcel Borret. 5 vols. SC 132, 136, 147, 150, 227. Paris, 1967–76.

Origen. *Homélies sur la Genèse (In Genesim homiliae).* Ed. Henri de Lubac and Louis Doutreleau. Rev. ed. SC 7². Paris, 1976.

Origen. *Homilies on Genesis and Exodus.* Tr. Ronald E. Heine. Fathers of the Church 71. Washington, D.C., 1982.

Origen. *Traité des principes (De principiis).* Ed. Henri Crouzel and Manleo Simonetti. 5 vols. SC 252–53, 268–69, 312. Paris, 1978–84.

Otzar Haposkim (Hebrew). Ed. Isaac Halevi Herzog et al. 15 vols. to date. Jerusalem, 1962–87.

Ovid. *Metamorphoses.* Ed. Frank Justus Miller. LCL. 2 vols. Cambridge, Mass., 1916.

'Oẓar M^efar^eshe ha-Torah. 2 vols. Jerusalem, 1973.

'Oẓar Perushim 'al ha-Torah. Miqra'ot G^edolot 6. New York, 1950.

Pareus, David. *Opera theologica exegetica.* 2 vols. Frankfurt a.M., 1647.

Patres apostolici. Ed. Francis Xavier Funk. 2nd ed. 2 vols. Tübingen, 1901.

Perlmann, Moshe, ed. *Midrash ha-R^efu'ah.* 3 vols. Tel Aviv, 1926–34.

Pesikta de Rav Kahana (Hebrew). Ed. Bernard Mandelbaum. 2 vols. New York, 1962.

Pesikta Rabbati: Midrasch für den Fest-Cyclus und die ausgezeichneten Sabbathe (Hebrew). Ed. Meir Friedmann (Ish-Shalom). 1880; repr., Tel Aviv, 1963.

Peter Abelard. "A Critical Edition of . . . *Expositio in hexameron.*" Ed. Mary Foster Romig. Ph.D. Dissertation, University of Southern California, Los Angeles, 1981.

Peter Lombard. *Sententiae in IV libris distinctae.* 2 vols. in 3 pts. Rome, 1971–81.

Peter Riga. *Aurora.* Ed. Paul E. Beichner. 2 vols. University of Notre Dame Publications in Medieval Studies 19. Notre Dame, Ind., 1965.

Philo. *Works.* Ed. F. H. Colson et al. LCL. 10 vols. and 2 suppl. vols. Cambridge, Mass., 1929–53.

Pseudo-Philo. *The Biblical Antiquities of Philo.* Tr. M. R. James. 1917; repr., New York, 1971.

Pseudo-Philo. *Liber antiquitatum biblicarum.* Ed. Guido Kisch. University of Notre Dame Publications in Mediaeval Studies 10. Notre Dame, Ind., 1949.

"*Pirqe dᵉ-Rabbi 'Eliʿezer.*" Ed. Michael Higger. *Horeb* 8 (1944), 82–119; 9 (1946), 94–166; 10 (1948), 185–294.

Pirqe Rabbi 'Eliʿezer. Ed. David Luria. Warsaw, 1852.

Pitra, J. B. *Spicilegium solesmense.* 4 vols. Paris, 1852–58.

Plato. *Laws.* Ed. R. G. Bury. LCL. 2 vols. Cambridge, Mass., 1926.

Pritchard, James B., ed. *Ancient Near Eastern Texts Relating to the Old Testament.* 3rd ed. with suppl. Princeton, N.J., 1969.

Raymond Martini. *Pugio fidei adversus Mauros et Judaeos.* 1687; repr., Farnborough, 1967.

Robert Grosseteste. *Hexaëmeron.* Ed. Richard C. Dales and Servus Gieben. Auctores britannici Medii Aevi 6. London, 1982.

Rufinus of Bologna. *Summa Decretorum.* Ed. Heinrich Singer. Paderborn, 1902.

Saadya b. Joseph. *The Book of Beliefs and Opinions.* Tr. Samuel Rosenblatt. New Haven, Conn., 1948.

Saadya b. Joseph. *Commentary on Genesis* (Arabic with Hebrew trans.). Ed. Moshe Zucker. New York, 1984.

Saadya b. Joseph. *Mishle: Tirgum u-Ferush.* Ed. Joseph Kafah. N.p., 1976.

Saadya b. Joseph. *Sefer ha-Miẓwot.* Ed. Yeruham Fischel Perla. 2 vols. 1914–17; repr., New York, 1962.

Saadya b. Joseph. *Sefer ha-Nivḥar ba-'Emunot wᵉha-Deʿot (Ha-'Emunot wᵉha-Deʿot).* Ed. Joseph Kafah. Jerusalem, 1970.

Samuel b. Meir. *Commentarium in Pentateuchum* (Hebrew). Ed. David Rosin. Breslau, 1881.

Samuel b. Nissim. *Midrash Bᵉreshit Zuṭaʾ.* Ed. Mordekhai ha-Kohen. Jerusalem, 1962.

Sayings of the Jewish Fathers. Ed. Charles Taylor. 1897; repr., New York, 1970.

Sefer ha-Bahir. Ed. Reuben Margaliot. 1951; repr., Jerusalem, 1978.

Sefer ha-Ḥinnukh. Ed. Charles B. Chavel. Jerusalem, 1952.

Sefer Halakhot Gᵉdolot. 1874; repr., Tel Aviv, 1962.

Sefer Halakhot Gedolot (Hebrew). Ed. Ezriel Hildesheimer. 2 vols. Jerusalem, 1971–80.

Sefer Halakhot Pᵉsuqot 'o Hilkhot Rᵉʾu. Ed. S. Z. H. Halberstam. Versailles, 1886.

Sefer ha-Qanah. 1894; repr., Jerusalem, 1973.

Sefer ha-Zohar. Ed. Reuben Margaliot. 3 vols. Jerusalem, 1940–47.

Sefer Qᵉrovot, Huʾ Maḥzor lᵉ-Ḥag ha-Shavuʿot. Ed. Wolf Heindheim and Isaac Berlin. Hannover, 1839.

Sefer Raziʾel ha-Malʾakh. Amsterdam, 1701.

Sefer Shaʿare Ẓedeq: Tᵉshuvot ha-Gᵉʾonim. Jerusalem, 1966.

Sefer Tiqqune ha-Zohar. Ed. Reuben Margaliot. 1948; repr., Jerusalem, 1978 (bound with *Sefer ha-Bahir*).

Septuaginta. Ed. Alfred Rahlfs. 2 vols. Stuttgart, 1935.

Seymour, M. C., ed. *The Bodley Version of Mandeville's Travels*. London, 1963.

Sheeltot de Rab Ahai Gaon (Hebrew). Ed. Samuel K. Mirsky, 5 vols. Jerusalem, 1959–77.

She'iltot. 3 vols. 1861–67; repr., Jerusalem, 1967.

Shishah Sidre Mishnah. Ed. Ch. Albeck. 6 vols. Jerusalem, 1958–59.

Sifra'. 1545; repr., Jerusalem, 1970.

Sifra or Torat Kohanim According to Codex Assemani LXVI (Hebrew). Ed. Louis Finkelstein. New York, 1956.

Sifre on Deuteronomy (Hebrew). Ed. Louis Finkelstein. Corpus tannaiticum 3,3,2. 1939; repr., New York, 1969.

Simeon b. Zemah Duran. *Sefer ha-Tashbaz*. 4 vols. Lemberg, 1891.

Simeon ibn Labi. *Ketem Paz*. 2 vols. Leghorn, 1795.

Siphre ad Numeros adjecto Siphre zutta (Hebrew). Ed. H. S. Horovitz. Corpus tannaiticum 3,3,1. 1917; repr., Jerusalem, 1966.

Sokoloff, Michael, ed. *The Geniza Fragments of Bereshit Rabba* (Hebrew). Jerusalem, 1982.

Solomon b. Abraham ibn Adret. *Ḥiddushe ha-RaShb"A ʿal Masekhet Niddah*. Ed. Isaac Meir Ben-Menahem. Jerusalem, 1938.

Solomon b. Abraham ibn Adret. *Sefer Ḥiddushe ha-RaShb"A ʿal Ḥamesh-ʿesreh Shiṭṭot*. 3 pts. in 1 vol. Warsaw, 1922.

Solomon b. Abraham ibn Adret. *Sefer Tᵉshuvot ha-Mᵉyuḥasot lᵉha-RaMba"N*. Tel Aviv, 1959.

Solomon b. Abraham ibn Adret. *Shu"T*. 3 vols. Jerusalem and B'nei B'rak, 1958–65.

Solomon b. Isaac (Rashi). *RaSh"I ʿal ha-Torah*. Ed. Abraham Berliner and C. B. Chavel. Jerusalem, 1962.

Solomon b. Isaac. *Responsa* (Hebrew). Ed. Israel Elfenbein. New York, 1943.

Tal, Abraham, ed. *The Samaritan Targum of the Pentateuch* (Hebrew). Chaim Rosenberg School of Jewish Studies Texts and Studies in the Hebrew Language and Related Subjects 4. 3 vols. Tel Aviv, 1980–83.

Tappert, Theodore G., ed. *The Book of Concord*. Philadelphia, Pa., 1959.

Targum du Pentateuque. Tr. Roger le Déaut. 5 vols. Sources chrétiennes 245, 256, 261, 271, 282. Paris, 1978–81.

Tertullian. *Adversus Marcionem*. Ed. Ernest Evans. 2 vols. Oxford, 1972.

Theophilus of Antioch. *Ad Autolycum*. Ed. Robert M. Grant. Oxford, 1970.

Thomas Aquinas. *Catena aurea in quator Evangelia*. Ed. Angelicus Guarientus. 2 vols. Torino, 1953.

Thomas Aquinas. *Opera omnia*. Rome, 1882–present.

Thomas Aquinas. *Quaestiones quodlibetales*. Ed. Raymundus Spiazzi. Torino, 1956.

Thomas Aquinas. *Summa theologiae*. 60 vols. Cambridge, 1964–76.

Todros b. Joseph ha-Levi Abulafia. *Sefer 'Oẓar ha-Kavod ha-Shalem*. Warsaw, 1879.

Tolomeo de Lucca. *Exaemeron*. Ed. Pius-Thomas Masetti. Sienna, 1880.

The Tosefta (Hebrew). Ed. Saul Lieberman. 4 vols. New York, 1955–73.

Tosephta (Hebrew). Ed. M. S. Zuckermandel. New ed. Jerusalem, 1970.

Von Arnim, Hans, ed. *Stoicorum veterum fragmenta*, 2. Leipzig, 1922.

Wertheimer, Shlomo Aharon, and Abraham Joseph Wertheimer, eds. *Batei Midrashot* (Hebrew). 2nd ed. 2 vols. 1950–53; repr., Jerusalem, 1968.

Willet, Andrew. *Hexapla in Genesin*. 2 vols. London, 1608.

William of Ockham. *Opera politica.* Ed. J. G. Sikes et al. 3 vols. Manchester, 1940–63.

Wright, Thomas, and James Orchard Hallwell, eds. *Reliquiae antiquae: Scraps from Ancient Manuscripts, Illustrating Chiefly Early English Literature and the English Language.* 2 vols. 1841–43; repr., New York, 1966.

Yalquṭ Shimʿoni ʿal ha-Torah. Ed. Dov Hyman et al. 4 vols. in 7 pts. to date. Jerusalem, 1973–86.

Yalquṭ Shimʿoni: Neviʾim u-Khetuvim. 2 vols. 1521; repr., Jerusalem, 1973.

Yom Tov b. Abraham Ishbili. *Ḥiddushe ha-RIṬb"A.* 6 vols. Jerusalem, 1967.

Yom Tov b. Abraham Ishbili. *Ḥiddushe ha-RIṬb"A: Masekhet Niddah.* Ed. David Metzger. Jerusalem, 1978.

Yom Tov b. Abraham Ishbili. *Ḥiddushe ha-RIṬb"A: Masekhet Ketubot.* Ed. Moshe Goldstein. Jerusalem, 1982.

Yom Tov b. Abraham Ishbili. *Shu"T.* Ed. Joseph Kafah. Jerusalem, 1959.

Zechariah b. Solomon the Physician. *Midrash ha-Ḥefeẓ.* Ed. Meir Havazelet. Jerusalem, 1981.

Zohar Ḥadash. Ed. Reuben Margaliot. 1955; repr., Jerusalem, 1978.

Secondary Sources

Aers, David. *Chaucer, Langland, and the Creative Imagination.* London, 1980.

Aland, Barbara. "Fides und Subiectio: Zur Anthropologie des Irenäus." In *Kerygma und Logos: Festschrift für Carl Andresen zum 70. Geburtstag,* pp. 9–28. Ed. A. M. Ritter. Göttingen, 1979.

Alberz, Rainer. "Die Kulturarbeit im Atramhasis im Vergleich zur biblischen Urgeschichte." In *Werden und Wirken des Alten Testaments: Festschrift für Claus Westermann zum 70. Geburtstag,* pp. 38–57. Ed Rainer Alberz et al. Göttingen, 1980.

Albrektson, Bertil. *History and the Gods: An Essay on the Ideal of Historical Events as Divine Manifestations in the Ancient Near East and in Israel.* Coniectanea biblica: Old Testament Series 1. Lund, 1967.

Alford, John A. "The Wife of Bath versus the Clerk of Oxford: What Their Rivalry Means." *Chaucer Review* 21 (1986), 108–32.

Allen Prudence. *The Concept of Woman: The Aristotelian Revolution, 750 B.C.–A.D. 1250.* Montreal, 1985.

Alonso-Schöckel, Luis, "Sapiential and Covenant Themes in Gen 2–3." In *Studies in Ancient Israelite Wisdom,* pp. 468–80. Ed. James L. Crenshaw. New York, 1976.

Alter, Robert. "The Decline and Fall of Literary Criticism," *Commentary* 77 (March 1984), 50–56.

Altmann, Alexander. "The Gnostic Background of the Rabbinic Adam Legends." In *Essays in Jewish Intellectual History,* pp. 1–16. Hanover, N.H., 1981.

Altmann, Alexander. "*Homo imago Dei* in Jewish and Christian Theology." *Journal of Religion* 48 (1968), 235–59.

Amand de Mendietta, Emmanuel. "Les deux homélies sur la création de l'homme que les manuscrits attribuent à Basile de Césarée ou à Grégoire de Nysse." In

Zetesis: Album amicorum, door vrienden en collega's aangeboden aan Prof. Dr. E. de Strycker, pp. 695–716. Antwerp, 1973.

Andersen, Francis I. *The Sentence in Biblical Hebrew*. Janua linguarum: Studia memoriae Nicolai van Wijk dedicata, Series practica 231. Hague, 1974.

Anderson, Bernhard W. "Babel: Unity and Diversity in God's Creation." *Currents in Theology and Mission* 5 (1978), 69–81.

Anderson, Bernhard W. "Creation and Ecology." In *COT*, pp. 152–71.

Anderson, Bernhard W. *Creation versus Chaos: The Reinterpretation of the Mythical Symbolism in the Bible*. New York, 1967.

Anderson, Bernhard W. "From Analysis to Synthesis: The Interpretation of Genesis 1–11." *JBL* 97 (1978), 23–39.

Anderson, Bernhard W. "Human Dominion over Nature." In *Biblical Studies in Contemporary Thought*, pp. 27–45. Ed. Miriam Ward. Burlington, Vt., 1975.

Anderson, Bernhard W. "Mythopoeic and Theological Dimensions of Biblical Creation Faith." In *COT*, pp. 1–24.

Anderson, Bernhard W. "A Stylistic Study of the Priestly Creation Story." In *Canon and Authority: Essays in Old Testament Religion and Theology*, pp. 148–62. Ed. George W. Coats and Burke O. Long. Philadelphia, Pa., 1977.

Aptowitzer, Victor. *Introductio ad Sefer Rabiah* (Hebrew). Jerusalem, 1938.

Armstrong, Gregory T. *Die Genesis in der alten Kirche*. Beiträge zur Geschichte der biblischen Hermeneutik 4. Tübingen, 1962.

Asensio, Félix. "Tradición sobre un pecado sexual en el Paraíso?" *Gregorianum* 30 (1949), 491–520; 31 (1950), 35–62, 163–91, 362–90.

Asselin, David Tobin. "The Notion of Dominion in Genesis 1–3." *CBQ* 16 (1954), 277–94.

Assis, Yom-Tov. "The 'Ordinance of Rabbenu Gershom' and Polygamous Marriages in Spain" (Hebrew). *Zion*, n.s. 46 (1981), 251–77.

Atkinson, Clarissa W. *Mystic and Pilgrim: The "Book" and World of Margery Kempe*. Ithaca, N.Y., 1983.

Avramson, Shraga. "*'Iggeret ha-Qodesh* ha-Meyuḥeset le-RaMba"N." *Sinai* 90 (1982), 232–53.

Bacher, Wilhelm. *'Aggadat 'Amora'e 'Ereẓ-Yisra'el*. Tr. A. S. Rabinovitz. 3 vols. in 7 pts. Tel Aviv, 1925–38.

Baer, Richard A., Jr. *Philo's Use of the Categories Male and Female*. Arbeiten zur Literatur und Geschichte des hellenistisches Judentums 3. Leiden, 1970.

Baer, Yitzhak. "On the Problem of Eschatological Doctrine during the Period of the Second Temple" (Hebrew). *Zion*, n.s. 23–24 (1957–59), 3–34.

Bailey, John A. "Initiation and the Primal Woman in Gilgamesh and Genesis 2–3." *JBL* 89 (1970), 137–50.

Baker, Denise N. "The Priesthood of Genius: A Study of the Medieval Tradition." *Speculum* 51 (1976), 277–91.

Baltzer, Klaus. *The Covenant Formulary in Old Testament, Jewish, and Early Christian Writings*. Tr. David E. Green. Philadelphia, Pa., 1971.

Baron, Salo Wittmayer. *A Social and Religious History of the Jews*. 2nd ed. 18 vols. to date. New York, 1952–83.

Barr, James. "The Image of God in the Book of Genesis: A Study of Terminology." *Bulletin of the John Rylands Library* 51 (1968), 11–26.

Barr, James. "Man and Nature: The Ecological Controversy and the Old Testament." *Bulletin of the John Rylands Library* 55 (1972), 9–32.

Barré, Lloyd M. "The Poetic Structure of Genesis 9:5." *ZAW* 96 (1984), 101–4.

Barth, Karl. *The Doctrine of Creation.* Church Dogmatics 3,1. Tr. J. W. Edwards et al. Edinburgh, 1958.

Bassett, Frederick W. "Noah's Nakedness and the Curse of Canaan: A Case of Incest?" *VT* 21 (1971), 232–37.

Battero, Jean. "Antiquités assyro-babyloniennes." *Annuaire de l'Ecole practique des hautes études, IVᵉ Section: Sciences historiques et philologiques* 3 (1978–79), 85–135.

Bauer, J. B. "Israels Schau in die Vorgeschichte (Gen. 1–11)." In *Wort und Botschaft: Probleme des Alten Testaments,* pp. 74–87. Ed. J. Schreiner. Würzburg, 1967.

Belkin, Samuel. "Midrash Tadshe', 'o Midrash dᵉ-R. Pinḥas b. Ya'ir: Midrash Hellenisti Qadmon." *Horeb* 11 (1951), 1–52.

Ben-Yehudah, Eliezer. *A Complete Dictionary of Ancient and Modern Hebrew* (Hebrew). 16 vols. Tel Aviv, 1948–59.

Bergant, Dianne, and Carroll Stuhlmueller. "Creation according to the Old Testament." In *Evolution and Creation,* pp. 153–75. Ed. Ernan McMullin. Notre Dame, Ind., 1985.

Berger, David. "Three Typological Themes in Early Jewish Messianism: Messiah Son of Joseph, Rabbinic Calculations, and the Figure of Armilus." *AJS Review* 10 (1985), 141–64.

Berlin, Meyer, and Shlomo Josef Zevin, eds. *Talmudic Encyclopedia* (Hebrew). Jerusalem, 1947–present.

Biale, David. "The God with Breasts: El Shaddai in the Bible." *History of Religions* 21 (1982), 240–56.

Bird, Phyllis A. "Images of Women in the Old Testament." In *Religion and Sexism: Images of Women in the Jewish and Christian Traditions,* pp. 41–88. Ed. Rosemary Radford Ruether. New York, 1974.

Bird, Phyllis A. " 'Male and Female He Created Them': Gen 1:27b in the Context of the Priestly Account of Creation." *HTR* 74 (1981), 129–60.

Bishop, Jonathan. *The Covenant: A Reading.* Springfield, Ill., 1983.

Blenkinsopp, Joseph. "The Structure of P." *CBQ* 38 (1976), 275–92.

Blenkinsopp, Joseph. "The Unknown Prophet of the Exile." *Scripture* 14 (1962), 81–90, 109–18.

Bloomfield, Morton W. "Chaucer's Sense of History." *Journal of English and Germanic Philology* 51 (1952), 301–13.

Boorer, Sue. "The Kerygmatic Intention of the Priestly Document." *Australian Biblical Review* 25 (1977), 12–20.

Borresen, Kari Elisabeth. "Imago Dei, privilège masculin? Interprétation augustinienne et pseudo-augustinienne de *Gen* 1,27 et *1Cor* 11,7." *Augustinianum* 25 (1985), 213–34.

Boswell, John. *Christianity, Social Tolerance, and Homosexuality: Gay People in Western Europe from the Beginning of the Christian Era to the Fourteenth Century.* Chicago, 1980.

Bousset, Wilhelm. *Die Religion des Judentums in späthellinistischen Zeitalter.* 3rd ed. Ed. Hugo Gressmann. Handbuch zum Neuen Testament 21. Tübingen, 1966.

Brandl, Leopold. *Die Sexualethik des heiligen Albertus Magnus: Eine moralgeschichtliche*

Untersuchung. Studien zur Geschichte der katholischen Moraltheologie 2. Regensburg, 1955.

Brandon, S. G. F. "The Propaganda Factor in Some Ancient Near Eastern Cosmogonies." In *Promise and Fulfillment: Essays Presented to S. H. Hooke*, pp. 20–35. Edinburgh, 1963.

Bright, John. *The Anchor Bible: Jeremiah*. Garden City, N.Y., 1965.

Bronsnick, Norman H. "From the Language of the Talmud to That of the Bible" (Hebrew). *Beth Mikra* 29 (1983), 37–46.

Brown, Peter. *Augustine and Sexuality*. Center for Hermeneutical Studies in Hellenistic and Modern Culture, Colloquy 46. Berkeley, Calif., 1983.

Brown, Peter. *The Body and Society: Men, Women, and Sexual Renunciation in Early Christianity*. New York, 1988.

Brown, Peter. "Pelagius and His Supporters: Aims and Environment." *Journal of Theological Studies*, n.s. 19 (1968), 93–114.

Brown, Peter. "Sexuality and Society in the Fifth Century A.D.: Augustine and Julian of Eclanum." In *Tria Corde: Scritti in onore di Arnaldo Momigliano*, pp. 49–70. Ed. E. Gabba. Biblioteca di Athenaeum 1. Como, 1983.

Brown, Robert F. "On the Necessary Imperfection of Creation: Irenaeus' *Adversus Haereses* IV, 38." *Scottish Journal of Theology* 28 (1975), 17–25.

Brueggemann, Walter. *Genesis*. Atlanta, Ga., 1982.

Brueggemann, Walter. "The Kerygma of the Priestly Writers." In *The Vitality of Old Testament Traditions*, pp. 101–13. By Walter Brueggemann and Hans Walter Wolff. 2nd ed. Atlanta, Ga., 1982.

Brueggemann, Walter. *The Land: Place as Gift, Promise, and Challenge in Biblical Faith*. Overtures to Biblical Theology 1. Philadelphia, Pa., 1977.

Brueggemann, Walter. "Of the Same Flesh and Blood (Gn 2,23a)." *CBQ* 32 (1970), 532–42.

Brunt, P. A. *Italian Manpower, 225 B.C.–A.D. 14*. Oxford, 1971.

Buber, Martin. *Die Schrift und ihre Verdeutschung*. Berlin, 1936.

Büchler, Adolph. "Das Ausgiessen von Wein und Öl als Ehrung bei den Juden." *MGWJ* 49 (1905), 12–40.

Büchler, Adolph. "Notes on the Religious Position of the 'Canaanite Slave' a Century before and after the Destruction of the Second Temple" (Hebrew). In *Occident and Orient: Gaster Anniversary Volume*, pp. 549–70. Ed. Bruno Schindler. London, 1936.

Bugge, John. *Virginitas: An Essay in the History of a Medieval Ideal*. International Archives of the History of Ideas, Series minor 17. The Hague, 1975.

Buis, P. "Comment au septième siècle envisageait-on l'avenir de l'alliance? Etude de Lv. 26,3–45." In *Questions disputées d'Ancien Testament: Methode et théologique*, pp. 131–40. Ed. C. Brekelmans. Bibliotheca ephemeridum theologicarum lovaniensium 33. Louvain, 1974.

Bulka, Reuven P. *Jewish Marriage: A Halakhic Ethic*. Library of Jewish Law and Ethics 12. New York, 1986.

Canavero, Alessandra Tarabochia. *Esegesi biblica e cosmologia: Note sull'interpretazione patristica e medioevale di Genesi 1,2*. Scienze filosofiche 30. Milan, 1981.

Capánago, Victorino. "El hombre-abismo, segun San Augustín." *Augustinus* 20 (1975), 225–52.

Carley, Keith W. *The Book of the Prophet Ezekiel*. Cambridge, 1974.

Cassuto, Umberto. *A Commentary on the Book of Genesis.* Tr. Israel Abrahams. 2 vols. Jerusalem, 1961–64.

Chenu, Marie-Dominique. *Nature, Man, and Society in the Twelfth Century: Essays on New Theological Perspectives in the Latin West.* Ed. Jerome Taylor and Lester K. Little. Chicago, 1968.

Chenu, Marie-Dominique. "Les passions verteuses: L'anthropologie de Saint Thomas." *Revue philosophique de Louvain* 72 (1974), 11–17.

Cherniss, Michael D. "Irony and Authority: The Ending of the *Roman de la Rose.*" *Modern Language Quarterly* 36 (1975), 227–38.

Childs, Brevard S. "Psalm 8 in the Context of the Christian Canon." *Interpretation* 23 (1969), 20–31.

Clark, Elizabeth A. "Heresy, Asceticism, Adam, and Eve: Interpretations of Genesis 1–3 in the Later Latin Fathers." In *Ascetic Piety and Women's Faith: Essays on Late Ancient Christianity,* pp. 358–62. Studies in Women and Religion 20. Lewiston, N.Y., 1986.

Clark, W. Malcolm. "The Animal Series in the Primeval History." *Vetus Testamentum* 18 (1968), 433–49.

Clark, W. Malcolm. "The Flood and the Structure of the Pre-Patriarchal History." *ZAW* 83 (1971), 184–211.

Clines, David J. A. "The Image of God in Man." *Tyndale Bulletin* 19 (1968), 53–103.

Clines, David J. A. "'Theme' in Genesis 1–11." *CBQ* 38 (1976), 483–507.

Clines, David J. A. *The Theme of the Pentateuch. JSOT* Supplement Series 10. 1978; repr., Sheffield, 1982.

Coats, George W. *Genesis, with an Introduction to Narrative Literature.* The Forms of the Old Testament Literature 1. Grand Rapids, Mich., 1983.

Coats, George W. "The God of Death: Power and Obedience in the Primeval History." *Interpretation* 29 (1975), 227–39.

Cohen, Boaz. *Jewish and Roman Law: A Comparative Study.* 2 vols. New York, 1966.

Cohen, H. Hirsch. *The Drunkenness of Noah.* University, Ala., 1974.

Cohen, Jeremy. "The Bible, Man, and Nature in the History of Western Thought: A Call for Reassessment." *Journal of Religion* 65 (1985), 155–72.

Cohen, Jeremy. "Original Sin as the Evil Inclination: A Polemicist's Appreciation of Human Nature." *HTR* 73 (1980), 495–520.

Cohn, Norman. *The Pursuit of the Millennium: Revolutionary Millenarians and Mystical Anarchists of the Middle Ages.* Rev. ed. New York, 1970.

Cohn, Norman. *The World-View of a Thirteenth-Century Parisian Intellectual: Jean de Meun and the "Roman de la Rose."* Durham (U.K.), 1961.

Cohn, Robert L. "Narrative Structure and Canonical Perspective in Genesis." *JSOT* 25 (1983), 3–16.

Cohon, Samuel S. "Original Sin." *HUCA* 21 (1948), 275–330.

Colish, Marcia L. *The Stoic Tradition from Antiquity to the Early Middle Ages.* 2 vols. Studies in the History of Christian Thought 34–35. Leiden, 1985.

Collins, Raymond F. *Christian Morality: Biblical Foundations.* Notre Dame, Ind., 1986.

Combs, Eugene. "The Political Teaching of Genesis I–XI." *Studia biblica 1978,* 1:105–110. *JSOT* Supplement Series 11. Sheffield, 1979.

Congar, Yves M.-J. "Le thème de *Dieu-Créateur* et les explications de l'Hexaméron dans la tradition chrétienne." In *L'homme devant Dieu: Mélanges offerts au Père Henri de Lubac,* 1:189–222. 3 vols. Théologie 56–58. Paris, 1963–64.

Cooke, G. A. *A Critical and Exegetical Commentary on the Book of Ezekiel.* International Critical Commentary. Edinburgh, 1951.

Coppens, J. *La connaissance du bien et du mal et le peche du Paradis: Contribution à l'interprétation de Gen., II–III.* Analecta lovaniensia biblica et orientalia 2,3. Gembloux, 1948.

Coppens, J. "L'interprétation sexuelle du péché du paradis dans la littérature patristique." *Ephemerides theologicae lovanienses* 24 (1948), 402–8.

Coronil, Nahman Neta. "Hitnazlut." *Ha-Maggid* 9:31 (August 9, 1865), 245–46.

Crim, Keith R. *The Royal Psalms.* Richmond, Va., 1962.

Cross, Frank Moore. *Canaanite Myth and Hebrew Epic: Essays in the History of the Religion of Israel.* Cambridge, Mass., 1973.

Csillag, Pál. *The Augustan Laws on Family Relations.* Budapest, 1976.

Curtius, Ernst Robert. *European Literature and the Latin Middle Ages.* Tr. Willard R. Trask. Bollingen Series 36. 1953; repr., Princeton, N.J., 1967.

Dahlberg, Charles. "Love and the *Roman de la Rose.*" *Speculum* 44 (1969), 568–84.

Daniélou, Jean. *In the Beginning . . . : Genesis I–III.* Tr. Julien L. Randolf. Baltimore, Md., 1965.

Daube, David. *The Duty of Procreation.* Edinburgh, 1977.

Davidson, Israel. *Thesaurus of Medieval Hebrew Poetry* (Hebrew). 4 vols. 1924–33; repr., New York, 1970.

De Boer, P. A. H. *Fatherhood and Motherhood in Israelite Piety.* Leiden, 1974.

Delaruelle, Etienne. "La doctrine de la personne humaine, signe de contradiction entre Christianisme et paganisme au IIIᵉ siècle." *Bulletin de littérature ecclésiastique* 53 (1952), 161–72.

De Lubac, Henri. *Exégèse médiévale: Les quatre sens de l'écriture.* 2 vols. in 4 pts. Théologie 41–42, 59. Paris, 1959–64.

De Margerie, Bertrand. *Introduction à l'histoire de l'exégèse.* 3 vols. Paris, 1980–83.

De Moor, Johannes C. "El, the Creator." In *The Bible World: Essays in Honor of Cyrus Gordon,* pp. 171–87. Ed. Gary Rendsburg et al. New York, 1980.

Dequeker, L. "L'alliance avec Noé (Gen 9,1–17)." In *Noé, l'homme universel,* pp. 1–17. By J. Chopineau et al. Publications de l'Institutum iudaicum 3. Brussels, 1978.

Dequeker, L. "Green Herbage and Trees Bearing Fruit (Gen 1:28–30, 9:1–3)." *Bijdragen: Tijdschrift voor filosofie en theologie* 38 (1977), 118–27.

Descamps, A. L. "The New Testament Doctrine on Marriage." In *Contemporary Perspectives on Christian Marriage,* pp. 217–73. Ed. Richard Malone and John R. Connery. Chicago, 1984.

De Simone, Russell. "Modern Research on the Sources of Saint Augustine's Doctrine of Original Sin." *Augustinian Studies* 11 (1980), 205–27.

De Vos, Luk. "Entwürfe von Universumssystemen: Entstehungsmythen und Ideologie." *Linguistica biblica* 50 (1982), 41–111.

Dinkler, Erich. *Die Anthropologie Augustins.* Forschungen zur Kirchen- und Geistesgeschichte 4. Stuttgart, 1934.

Dodd, C. H. *The Bible and the Greeks.* 1935; repr., London, 1954.

Duby, Georges. *The Knight, the Lady, and the Priest: The Making of Modern Marriage in Medieval France.* Tr. Barbara Bray. New York, 1983.

Dumbrell, W. J. *Covenant and Creation: An Old Testament Covenantal Theology.* Exeter, 1984.

Dumbrell, W. J. "The Covenant with Noah." *Reformed Theological Review* 38 (1979), 1–9.

Eaton, John H. *Kingship and the Psalms.* 2nd ed. The Biblical Seminar 3. Sheffield, 1986.

Economou, George D. "The Character Genius in Alan of Lille, Jean de Meun, and John Gower." *Chaucer Review* 4 (1970), 203–10.

Economou, George D. *The Goddess Natura in Medieval Literature.* Cambridge, Mass., 1972.

Eichrodt, Walter. *Ezekiel: A Commentary.* Tr. Cosslett Quin. London, 1970.

Eichrodt, Walter. *Man in the Old Testament.* Tr. K. and R. Gregor Smith. Studies in Biblical Theology 4. Chicago, 1951.

Eichrodt, Walter. *Theology of the Old Testament.* Tr. J. A. Baker. 2 vols. Philadelphia, Pa., 1961–67.

Eidelberg, S. "A Comment to the Article of Peretz Tishby" (Hebrew). *Tarbiz* 34 (1965), 287–88.

Eilberg-Schwartz, Howard. "Creation and Classification in Judaism: From Priestly to Rabbinic Conceptions." *History of Religions* 26 (1987), 357–81.

Eilberg-Schwartz, Howard. *The Human Will in Judaism: The Mishnah's Philosophy of Intention.* Brown Judaic Studies 103. Atlanta, Ga., 1986.

Eitz, Andreas. "Studien zum Verhältnis von Priesterschrift und Deuterojesaja." Th.D. Dissertation, Ruprecht-Karl Universität, Heidelberg, 1969.

Elliger, Karl. "Sinn und Ursprung der priesterlichen Geschichterzählung." *Zeitschrift für Theologie und Kirche* 49 (1952), 121–43.

Ellverson, Anna-Stina. *The Dual Nature of Man: A Study in the Theological Anthropology of Gregory of Nazianzus.* Studia doctrinae christianae upsaliensia 21. Uppsala, 1981.

Engnell, Ivan. "'Knowledge' and 'Life' in the Creation Story." In *Wisdom in Israel and in the Ancient Near East (Presented to Professor Harold Henry Rowley),* pp. 103–19. Ed. Martin Noth and D. Winton Thomas. Supplements to *VT* 3. Leiden, 1955.

Engnell, Ivan. *Studies in Divine Kingship in the Ancient Near East.* 2nd ed. Oxford, 1967.

Epstein, Abraham. "Le livre des Jubilés, Philon, et le Midrasch Tadsche." *REJ* 21 (1890), 80–97; 22 (1891), 1–25.

Epstein, Abraham. *R. Mosheh ha-Darshan mi-Narbonah.* Vienna, 1891. Repr. in *Kitve R. 'Avraham 'Epshṭein* 1:213–44. Ed. A. M. Habermann. Jerusalem, 1950.

Epstein, Louis M. *Marriage Laws in the Bible and the Talmud.* Harvard Semitic Series 12. 1942; repr., New York, 1968.

Evans, G. R. *Alan of Lille: The Frontiers of Theology in the Later Twelfth Century.* Cambridge, 1983.

Evans, G. R. *Augustine on Evil.* Cambridge, 1982.

Evans, J. M. *Paradise Lost and the Genesis Tradition.* Oxford, 1968.

Falk, Ze'ev W. "Concerning the Enactments of Rabbenu Gershom" (Hebrew). *Tarbiz* 35 (1965), 193.

Falk, Ze'ev W. *Jewish Matrimonial Law in the Middle Ages.* Scripta judaica 6. Oxford, 1966.

Feldman, David M. *Birth Control in Jewish Law: Marital Relations, Contraception, and Abortion as Set Forth in the Classic Texts of Jewish Law.* New York, 1968.

Finkelstein, Louis. *Jewish Self-government in the Middle Ages.* 1924; repr., New York, 1964.

Fiore, Peter A. *Milton and Augustine: Patterns of Augustinian Thought in "Paradise Lost."* University Park, Pa., 1981.

Fishbane, Michael. *Biblical Interpretation in Ancient Israel.* Oxford, 1985.

Fishbane, Michael. *Text and Texture: Close Readings of Selected Biblical Texts.* New York, 1979.

Fisher, Eugene. "*Gilgamesh* and Genesis: The Flood Story in Context." *CBQ* 32 (1970), 392–403.

Fisher, Loren R. "From Creation to Cosmos." *Encounter* 26 (1965), 183–97.

Fisher, Loren R. "An Ugaritic Ritual and Genesis I, 1–5." *Ugaritica* 6 (1969), 197–205.

Fleming, John V. *Reason and the Lover.* Princeton, N.J., 1984.

Fleming, John V. *The "Roman de la Rose": A Study in Allegory and Iconography.* Princeton, N.J., 1969.

Flückiger, Felix. *Geschichte des Naturrechtes,* 1. Zurich, 1954.

Fohrer, Georg. *Ezechiel.* Handbuch zum Alten Testament 1,13. Tübingen, 1955.

Fokkelman, J. P. *Narrative Art in Genesis: Specimens of Stylistic and Structural Analysis.* Studia semitica neerlandica 17. Assen, 1975.

Foster, Benjamin. "Gilgamesh: Sex, Love, and the Ascent of Knowledge." In *Love and Death in the Ancient Near East: Essays in Honor of Marvin H. Pope,* pp. 21–42. Ed. John H. Marks and Robert M. Good. Guilford, Conn., 1987.

Fowler, David C. *The Bible in Middle English Literature.* Seattle, Wash., 1984.

Fox, Michael. "The Sign of the Covenant: Circumcision in the Light of the Priestly 'ot Etiologies." *Revue biblique* 81 (1974), 557–96.

Fraade, Steven D. "Ascetical Aspects of Ancient Judaism." In *JS,* pp. 253–88.

Frank, Richard I. "Augustus' Legislation on Marriage and Children." *California Studies in Classical Antiquity* 8 (1975), 41–52.

Freisen, Joseph. *Geschichte des kanonischen Eherechts bis zum Verfall der Glossenliteratur.* 2nd ed. 1893; repr., Paderborn, 1963.

Fretheim, Terence E. "The Theology of the Major Traditions in Genesis-Numbers." *Review and Expositor* 74 (1977), 301–20.

Freudenstein, Eric G. "Ecology and the Jewish Tradition." *Judaism* 19 (1970), 406–14.

Friedman, Mordechai Akiva. *Jewish Marriage in Palestine: A Cairo Genizah Study.* 2 vols. Tel Aviv, 1980–81.

Friedman, Mordechai Akiva. *Jewish Polygyny in the Middle Ages: New Documents from the Cairo Genizah* (Hebrew). Jerusalem, 1986.

Friedman, Mordechai Akiva. "The Monogamy Clause in Jewish Marriage Contracts." *Perspectives in Jewish Learning* 4 (1972), 20–40.

Friedman, Mordechai Akiva. "Polygamy in the Documents of the Genizah" (Hebrew). *Tarbiz* 40 (1971) 320–59.

Friedman, Mordechai Akiva. "Polygyny in Jewish Tradition and Practice: New Sources from the Cairo Geniza." *Proceedings of the American Academy for Jewish Research* 49 (1982), 33–68.

Friedman, Richard Elliot. *Who Wrote the Bible?* New York, 1987.

Frisch, A. "Le-Verur Ḥeṭ Dor ha-Haflagah." *Bi-Sdeh Ḥemed* 14 (1971), 440–43.

Froelich, Karlfried. "The Ecology of Creation." *Theology Today* 27 (1971), 263–76.

Früchtel, Ursula. *Die kosmologischen Vorstellungen bei Philo von Alexandrien.* Arbeiten zur Literatur und Geschichte des hellenistisches Judentums 2. Leiden, 1968.

Frymer-Kensky, Tikva. "The Atrahasis Epic and Its Significance for Our Understanding of Genesis 1–9." *Biblical Archeologist* 40 (1977), 147–55.

Frymer-Kensky, Tikva. "What the Babylonian Flood Stories Can and Cannot Teach Us about the Genesis Flood." *Biblical Archaeology Review* 4,4 (1978), 32–41.

Fuchs, Josef. *Die Sexualethik des heiligen Thomas von Aquin.* Cologne, 1949.

Funkenstein, Amos. "Nachmanides' Typological Reading of History" (Hebrew). *Zion,* n.s. 45 (1980), 35–59.

Gage, Warren Austin. *The Gospel of Genesis: Studies in Protology and Eschatology.* Winona Lake, Ind., 1984.

Gamber, Stanislas. *Le livre de la "Genèse" dans la poesie latine au Vᵉ siècle.* 1899; repr., Geneva, 1977.

Gaster, Theodor H. *Thespis: Ritual, Myth, and Drama in the Ancient Near East.* Rev. ed. 1961; repr., New York, 1966.

Gevirtz, S. "A Father's Curse [in the Literatures of Ugarit, Israel and Greece]." *Mosaic: Literature and History* 2,3 (1969), 56–61.

Giesebrecht, F. *Das Buch Jeremia.* 2nd ed. Handkommentar zum Alten Testament 3,2,1. Göttingen, 1907.

Giet, S. "S. Basile a-t-il donné une suite à l'Hexaeméron?" *Recherches de science religieuse* 33 (1946), 317–58.

Gilbert, M. "'Soyez féconds et multipliez' (Gn 1, 28)." *Nouvelle revue théologique* 106 (1974), 728–42.

Gilson, Etienne. "La cosmogonie de Bernardus Silvestris." *Archives d'histoire doctrinale et littéraire du Moyen Age* 3 (1928), 5–24.

Ginsburg, Elliot Kiba. "The Sabbath in the Classical Kabbalah." Ph.D. Dissertation, University of Pennsylvania, Philadelphia, Pa., 1984.

Ginzberg, Louis. *Die Haggada bei den Kirchenvätern und in der apokryphischen Litteratur.* Berlin, 1900.

Ginzberg, Louis. *The Legends of the Jews.* Tr. Henrietta Szold and Paul Radin. 7 vols. Philadelphia, Pa., 1909–38.

Ginzburg, Carlo. *The Cheese and the Worms: The Cosmos of a Sixteenth-Century Miller.* Tr. John and Anne Tedeschi. Baltimore, Md., 1980.

Goitein, S. D. *A Mediterranean Society.* 5 vols. Berkeley, Calif., 1967–88.

Goldberg, A. "Kain: Sohn des Menschen oder Sohn der Schlange." *Judaica* 25 (1969), 202–21.

Gordis, Robert. "'Be Fruitful and Multiply': Biography of a Mitzvah." *Midstream* 28 (August–September 1982), 21–29.

Gordis, Robert. "Ecology in the Jewish Tradition." *Midstream* 31 (October 1985), 19–23.

Gordis, Robert. "The Knowledge of Good and Evil in the Old Testament and the Qumran Scrolls." *JBL* 76 (1957), 123–38.

Gordis, Robert. "The Social Background of Wisdom Literature." *HUCA* 18 (1944), 77–118.

Gottfried, Barbara. "Conflict and Relationship, Sovereignty and Survival: Parables of Power in the *Wife of Bath's Prologue.*" *Chaucer Review* 19 (1985), 202–24.

Gottwald, Norman K. *The Hebrew Bible: A Socio-Literary Introduction.* Philadelphia, Pa., 1985.

Gowan, Donald E. *When Man Becomes God: Humanism and* Hybris *in the Old Testament.* Pittsburgh Theological Monograph Series 6. Pittsburgh, Pa., 1975.

Gowan, Donald E., and Millard Schumaker. *Subduing the Earth: An Exchange of Views.* Kingston, Ont., 1980.

Graves, Robert, and Raphael Patai. *Hebrew Myths: The Book of Genesis.* 1963; repr., New York, 1983.

Grévy-Pons, Nicole. *Célibat et nature: Une controverse médiévale a propos d'un traité du début du XVe siècle.* Centre d'histoire des sciences et des doctrines, Equipe de recherches sur l'humanisme francais des XIVe et XVe siècles: Textes et études 1. Paris, 1975.

Gros Louis, Kenneth R. R. "Genesis I–II." In *Literary Interpretations of Biblical Narratives,* pp. 41–51. Ed. Kenneth R. R. Gros Louis et al. Nashville, Tenn., 1974.

Gross, Julius. *Geschichte des Erbsündendogmas.* 4 vols. Munich, 1960–71.

Gross, Julius. "Theodor von Mopsuestia, ein Gegner der Erbsündlehre." *Zeitschrift für Kirchengeschichte* 65 (1953), 1–15.

Gross, Walter. "Jakob, der Mann des Segens." *Biblica* 49 (1968), 321–44.

Grossman, Avraham. *The Early Sages of Ashkenaz: Their Lives, Leadership, and Works (900–1096)* (Hebrew). Jerusalem, 1981.

Gruenwald, Ithamar. "The Problem of the Anti-Gnostic Polemic in Rabbinic Literature." In *Studies in Gnosticism and Hellenistic Religions Presented to Gilles Quispel on the Occasion of His 65th Birthday,* pp. 171–89. Ed. R. Van Den Broeck and M. J. Vermaseren. Etudes préliminaires aux religions orientales dans l'Empire romain 91. Leiden, 1981.

Guberman, Karen. "The Language of Love in Spanish Kabbalah: An Examination of the '*Iggeret ha-Kodesh.*" In *Approaches to Judaism in Medieval Times: Volume I,* pp. 53–105. Ed. David R. Blumenthal. Brown Judaic Studies 54. Chico, Calif., 1984.

Guigui, A. "Les lois noahides dans le Talmud: Etude synthétique." In *Noé, l'homme universel,* pp. 77–111. Ed. J. Chopineau et al. Publications de l'Institutum iudaicum 3. Brussels, 1978.

Gunkel, Hermann. *Genesis.* Göttinger Handkommentar zum Alten Testament 1,1. 3rd Ed. 1910; repr., Göttingen, 1922.

Gunkel, Hermann. *Schöpfung und Chaos in Urzeit und Endzeit.* Göttingen, 1895.

Gunn, Alan M. F. *The Mirror of Love: A Reinterpretation of "The Romance of the Rose."* Lubbock, Tex., 1952.

Habel, Norman C. "'Yahweh, Maker of Heaven and Earth': A Study in Tradition Criticism." *JBL* 91 (1972), 321–37.

Halivni, David Weiss. *Midrash, Mishnah, and Gemara: The Jewish Predilection for Justified Law.* Cambridge, Mass., 1986.

Halivni, David Weiss. *Sources and Traditions: A Source Critical Commentary on Seder Nashim* (Hebrew). Tel Aviv, 1968.

Hammerton-Kelly, Robert. "The Idea of Pre-existence in Early Judaism." Ph.D. Dissertation, Union Theological Seminary, New York, 1966.

Hand, Carl M. "Religion, Mastery-over-Nature, and Environmental Concern." *Social Forces* 63 (1984), 555–70.

Hanson, Paul D. "Rebellion in Heaven: Azazel and Euhemeristic Heroes in Enoch 6–11." *JBL* 96 (1977), 195–233.

Haran, Menahem. "Behind the Scenes of History: Determining the Date of the Priestly Source." *JBL* 100 (1981), 321–33.

Haran, Menahem. *Temples and Temple-Service in Ancient Israel: An Inquiry into the Character of Cult Phenomena and the Historical Setting of the Priestly School.* Oxford, 1978.

Harner, P.B. "Creation Faith in Deutero-Isaiah." *VT* 17 (1967), 298–306.

Hartman, David. *A Living Covenant: The Innovative Spirit in Traditional Judaism.* New York, 1985.

Hasel, Gerhard F. "The Sabbath in the Pentateuch." In *The Sabbath in Scripture and History*, pp. 21–43. Ed. Kenneth A. Strand. Washington, D.C., 1982.

Hasel, Gerhard F. "The Significance of the Cosmology in Gen 1 in Relation to Ancient Near Eastern Parallels." *Andrews University Seminary Studies* 10 (1972), 1–20.

Havlin, Solomon Zalman. "Berurim Ḥadashim bᵉ-ʿInyᵉne Taqqanot RaGMa"H, Yiḥusan, Tᵉḥulatan, wᵉ-Hitpashṭutan." *Shᵉnaton ha-Mishpaṭ ha-ʿIvri* 11–12 (1986), 317–36.

Havlin, Solomon Zalman. "Taqqanot Rabbenu Gershom Mᵉʾor ha-Golah bᵉ-ʿInyᵉne ʾIshut bi-Thume Sᵉfarad u-Frovans." *Shᵉnaton ha-Mishpaṭ ha-ʿIvri* 2 (1975), 200–57.

Heidel, Alexander. *The Babylonian Genesis: The Story of Creation.* 2nd ed. 1951; repr., Chicago, 1963.

Heidel, Alexander. *The Gilgamesh Epic and Old Testament Parallels.* 2nd ed. Chicago, 1949.

Heinemann, Isaak. *Philons griechische und jüdische Bildung: Kulturvergleichende Untersuchungen zu Philons Darstellung der jüdischen Gesetze.* Hildesheim, 1962.

Hendel, Ronald S. "Of Demigods and the Deluge: Toward an Interpretation of Genesis 6:1–4." *JBL* 106 (1987), 13–26.

Hens-Piazza, Gina. "A Theology of Ecology: God's Image and the Natural World." *Biblical Theology Bulletin* 13 (1983), 107–10.

Hermission, Hans-Jürgen. "Observations on the Creation Theology in Wisdom." In *COT*, pp. 118–34.

Hiers, Richard H. "Ecology, Biblical Theology, and Methodology: Biblical Perspectives on the Environment." *Zygon* 19 (1984), 43–59.

Hill, Thomas D. "Narcissus, Pygmalion, and the Castration of Saturn: Two Mythological Themes in the *Roman de la Rose*." *Studies in Philology* 71 (1974), 404–26.

Hillers, Delbert R. *Covenant: The History of a Biblical Idea.* Baltimore, Md., 1969.

Himmelfarb, Martha. "R. Moses the Preacher and the Testaments of the Twelve Patriarchs." *AJS Review* 9 (1984), 55–78.

Horowitz, Maryanne C. "The Image of God in Man—Is Woman Included?" *HTR* 72 (1979), 175–206.

Hughes, J. Donald. *Ecology in Ancient Civilizations.* Albuquerque, N.M., 1975.

Humbert, Paul. *Etudes sur le récit du Paradis et de la chute dans la Genèse.* Mémoires de l'Université de Neuchâtel 14. Neuchâtel, 1940.

Humbert, Paul. "La relation de Genèse 1 et du Psaume 104 avec la liturgie du Nouvel-An israélite." *Revue d'histoire et de philosophie religieuses* 15 (1935), 1–27.

Humbert, Paul. "Trois notes sur Genèse 1." In *Interpretationes ad Vetus Testamentum pertinentes Sigmundo Mowinckel septuagenario missae,* pp. 85–96. Oslo, 1955.

Hunter, David G. "Resistance to the Virginal Ideal in Late Fourth-Century Rome: The Case of Jovinian." *Theological Studies* 48 (1987), 45–64.

Hurvitz, Avi. "The Evidence of Language in Dating the Priestly Code." *Revue biblique* 81 (1974), 24–56.

Hurvitz, Avi. *A Linguistic Study of the Relationship between the Priestly Source and the Book of Ezekiel: A New Approach to an Old Problem.* Cahiers de la *Revue Biblique* 20. Paris, 1982.

Idel, Moshe. "Enoch Is Metatron" (Hebrew). *Jerusalem Studies in Jewish Thought* 6.1–2 (1987), 151–70.

Idel, Moshe. "Infinities of Torah in Kabbalah." In *Midrash and Literature,* pp. 141–57. Ed. Geoffrey H. Hartman and Sanford Budick. New Haven, Conn., 1986.

Idel, Moshe. *Kabbalah: New Perspectives.* New Haven, Conn., 1988.

Idel, Moshe. "The Problem of the Sources of the *Bahir*" (Hebrew). *Jerusalem Studies in Jewish Thought* 6.3–4 (1987), 55–72.

Itzchaky, Samson, et al. "Fertility in Jewish Tradition (Ethno-Medical and Folk-loric Aspects)." *Koroth* 9 (1985), 122–35.

Jacob, B. *Das erste Buch der Tora: Genesis, übersetzt und erklärt.* Berlin, 1934.

Jacob, B. *The First Book of the Bible: Genesis.* Ed. Ernest I. Jacob and Walter Jacob. New York, 1974.

Jacob, Edmund. *Theology of the Old Testament.* Tr. Arthur W. Heathcote and Philip J. Allcock. London, 1958.

Jacobs, Louis. *A Tree of Life: Diversity, Flexibility, and Creativity in Jewish Law.* Oxford, 1984.

James, E. O. *Creation and Cosmology: A Historical and Comparative Inquiry.* Studies in the History of Religions (Supplements to *Numen*) 16. Leiden, 1969.

Jansma, T. "L'Hexaméron de Jacques de Sarug." *L'Orient syrien* 4 (1959), 3–42, 129–62, 253–84, 451–521.

Jansma, T. "Une homélie anonyme sur la création du monde." *L'Orient syrien* 5 (1960), 385–400.

Jenkins, Claude. "Origen on I Corinthians." *Journal of Theological Studies,* o.s. 9 (1908), 232–47, 353–72, 500–514; 10 (1909), 29–51.

Jervell, Jacob. *Imago Dei: Gen. 1,26f. im Spätjudentum, in der Gnosis, und in den paulinischen Briefen.* Göttingen, 1960.

Jewett, Paul. *Man as Male and Female.* Grand Rapids, Mich., 1975.

Jobling, David. " 'And Have Dominion . . .': The Interpretation of Genesis 1, 28 in Philo Judaeus." *Journal for the Study of Judaism in the Persian, Hellenistic, and Roman Period* 8 (1977), 50–82.

Jobling, David Kenneth. " 'And Have Dominion . . .': The Interpretation of Old Testament Texts Concerning Man's Rule over the Creation (Genesis 1:26, 28, 9:1–2, Psalm 8:7–9) from 200 B.C. to the Time of the Council of Nicea." Th.D. Dissertation, Union Theological Seminary, New York, 1972.

Johnson, Aubrey R. *Sacral Kingship in Ancient Israel.* Cardiff, 1955.

Jundt, Auguste. *Histoire du pantheisme populaire au Moyen Age et au seizième siècle.* 1875; repr., Frankfurt a.M., 1964.

Kaddari, Menahem Zevi. *The Grammar of the Aramaic of the "Zohar"* (Hebrew). Jerusalem, 1971.

Kaiser, Walter C., Jr. *Toward an Old Testament Theology.* Grand Rapids, Mich., 1978.

Kanarfogel, Ephraim. "The ʿAliyah of 'Three Hundred Rabbis' in 1211: Tosafist Attitudes toward Settling in the Land of Israel." *JQR,* n.s. 76 (1986), 191–215.

Kannengiesser, Charles. "Philon et les Pères sur la double création de l'homme." In *Philon d'Alexandrie: Lyon, 11–15 Septembre 1966,* pp. 277–96. Colloques nationaux du Centre national de la recherche scientifique. Paris, 1967.

Kapelrud, Arvid S. "The Date of the Priestly Code (P)." *Annual of the Swedish Theological Institute* 3 (1964), 58–64.

Kapelrud, Arvid S. "King and Fertility: A Discussion of II Sam 21:1–14." In *Interpretationes ad Vetus Testamentum pertinentes Sigmundo Mowinckel septuagenario missae,* pp. 113–22. Oslo, 1955.

Kapelrud, Arvid S. "The Mythological Features in Gen 1 and the Author's Intentions." *VT* 24 (1974), 178–86.

Kapelrud, Arvid S. "Die Theorie der Schöpfung im Alten Testament." *ZAW* 91 (1979), 159–69.

Kasher, M. M. *Torah Shelemah: Talmudic-Midrashic Encyclopedia of the Pentateuch* (Hebrew). 39 vols. to date. Jerusalem and New York, 1927–85. (Vol. 1 in 2nd ed.; Jerusalem, 1936.)

Kaske, Carol V. "Getting around the *Parson's Tale:* An Alternative to Allegory and Irony." In *Chaucer at Albany,* pp. 147–77. Ed. Russell Hope Robbins. New York, 1975.

Kaufmann, Yehezkel. *The Religion of Israel, from Its Beginnings to the Babylonian Exile.* Abr. and tr. Moshe Greenberg. Chicago, 1960.

Kaufmann, Yehezkel. *Toleꞏdot ha-ʾEmunah ha-Yisraʾelit, m-Yme Qedem ʿad Sof Bayit Sheni.* 8 pts. in 4 vols. 1937–56; repr., Jerusalem, 1972.

Keating, Charles J. *The Effects of Original Sin in the Scholastic Tradition from St. Thomas Aquinas to William Ockham.* Catholic University of America Studies in Sacred Theology 2, 120. Washington, D.C., 1959.

Kelly, T. D., and John T. Irwin. "The Meaning of *Cleanness:* Parable as Effective Sign." *Medieval Studies* 35 (1973), 232–60.

Kerns, Joseph E. *The Theology of Marriage: The Historical Development of Christian Attitudes toward Sex and Sanctity in Marriage.* New York, 1964.

Keuls, Eva C. *The Reign of the Phallus.* New York, 1985.

Kikawada, Isaac M. "The Literary Convention of the Primeval History." *Annual of the Japanese Biblical Institute* 1 (1975), 3–21.

Kikawada, Isaac M. "The Shape of Genesis 11:1–9." In *Rhetorical Criticism: Essays in Honor of James Muilenburg,* pp. 18–32. Ed. Jared J. Jackson and Martin Kessler. Pittsburgh, Pa., 1974.

Kikawada, Isaac M., and Arthur Quinn. *Before Abraham Was: The Unity of Genesis 1–11.* Nashville, Tenn., 1985.

Kilmer, Anne Dreffkorn. "The Mesopotamian Concept of Overpopulation and Its Solution as Reflected in Mythology." *Orientalia* 41 (1972), 160–77.

Kirschner, Robert. "The Rabbinic and Philonic Exegeses of the Nadab and Abihu Incident (Lev. 10:1–6)." *JQR,* n.s. 73 (1983), 375–93.

Klausner, Joseph. *The Messianic Idea in Israel.* 3rd ed. Tr. W. F. Stinespring. New York, 1955.

Klein, Ralph W. *Israel in Exile: A Theological Interpretation.* Philadelphia, Pa., 1979.

Klein, Ralph W. "The Message of P." In *Die Botschaft und die Boten: Festschrift für Hans Walter Wolff zum 70. Geburtstag,* pp. 57–66. Ed. Jörg Jeremias and Lothar Perlitt. Neukirchen, 1981.

Knight, Douglas A. "Cosmogony and Order in the Hebrew Tradition." In *Cosmogony and Ethical Order: New Studies in Comparative Ethics,* pp. 133–57. Ed. Robin W. Lovin and Frank E. Reynolds. Chicago, 1985.

Koch, Klaus. "Saddaj." *VT* 26 (1976), 299–332.

Köhler, Ludwig. *Hebrew Man.* Tr. Peter R. Ackroyd. London, 1956.

Kors, J.-B. *La justice primitive et le péché originel d'après S. Thomas.* Bibliothèque thomiste 2. Paris, 1930.

Kramer, Samuel Noah. *The Sacred Marriage Rite: Aspects of Faith, Myth, and Ritual in Ancient Sumer.* Bloomington, Ind., 1969.

Kselman, John S. "The Recovery of Poetic Fragments from the Pentateuchal Priestly Source." *JBL* 97 (1978), 161–73.

Kushnir-Oron, Michal. "'Ha-Peli'ah' we-'ha-Qanah'—Yesodot ha-Qabbalah she-bahem, 'Emdatam ha-Datit Hevratit, we-Derekh 'Izzuvam ha-Sifrutit." Ph.D. Dissertation, Hebrew University of Jerusalem, Jerusalem, 1974.

Kutsch, Ernst. *Verheissung und Gesetz: Untersuchungen zum sogennanten "Bund" im Alten Testament.* Beihefte zur *ZAW* 131. Berlin, 1973.

Laberge, Leo. "Ministères et esprit dans les communautés postexiliques." *Eglise et théologie* 9 (1978), 379–411.

La Bonnardière, Anne-Marie. *Saint Augustin et la Bible.* Le Bible tous les temps 3. Paris, 1986.

Ladner, Gerhart B. *Images and Ideas in the Middle Ages: Selected Studies in History and Art.* 2 vols. Storia e letteratura: Raccolta di *Studi e testi* 155–56. Rome, 1983.

Lambert, W. G. "A New Look at the Babylonian Background of Genesis." In *The Bible in Its Literary Milieu: Contemporary Essays,* pp. 285–97. Ed. Vincent L. Tollers and John R. Maier. Grand Rapids, Mich., 1979.

Lamm, Norman. *Faith and Doubt: Studies in Traditional Jewish Thought.* New York, 1971.

Lampe, G. W. H. *A Patristic Greek Lexicon.* Oxford, 1961.

Landes, George M. "Creation and Liberation." *Union Seminary Quarterly Report* 33 (1978), 79–89.

Lang, Bernhard. "No Sex in Heaven: The Logic of Procreation, Death, and Eternal Life in the Judaeo-Christian Tradition." In *Mélanges bibliques et orientaux en l'honneur de M. Mathias Delcor,* pp. 237–53. Ed. A. Caquot et al. Alter Orient und Altes Testament 215. Neukirchen-Vluyn, 1985.

Langa, P. "Análisis agustiniano de 'crescite et multiplicamini' (Gen 1,28)." *Estudio teológico agustiniano* 18 (1983), 3–38, 147–76.

Leach, Edmund. "Genesis as Myth." In *The Bible in Its Literary Milieu: Contemporary Essays,* pp. 411–22. Ed. Vincent L. Tollers and John R. Maier. Grand Rapids, Mich., 1979.

LeFèvre, Yves. *L' "Elucidarium" et les lucidaires.* Bibliothèque des Ecoles françaises d'Athènes et de Rome 180. Paris, 1954.

Leibowitz, Nehama. *Studies in the Book of Genesis in the Context of Ancient and Modern Jewish Bible Commentary.* Tr. Aryeh Newman. Jerusalem, 1972.

Lentzen-Deis, Fritzleo. *Die Taufe Jesu nach den Synoptikern: Literarkritische und gattungsgeschichtliche Untersuchungen.* Frankfurter theologische Studien 4. Frankfurt a.M., 1970.

Lerner, Robert E. *The Heresy of the Free Spirit in the Later Middle Ages.* Berkeley, Calif., 1972.

Lewis, C. S. *The Allegory of Love: A Study in Medieval Tradition.* 1936; repr., London, 1953.

Lichtenstein, Aaron. *The Seven Laws of Noah.* New York, 1981.

Lichty, Erle. "Demons and Population Control." *Expedition* 13 (1971), 22–26.

Lieberman, Saul. "Metatron, the Meaning of His Name and His Functions." In *Apocalyptic and Merkavah Mysticism,* pp. 235–41. By Ithamar Gruenwald. Arbeiten zur Geschichte des antiken Judentums und des Urchristentums 14. Leiden, 1980.

Lieberman, Saul. "Some Aspects of Afterlife in Early Rabbinic Literature." In *Harry Austryn Wolfson Jubilee Volume,* 2:495–532. Ed. Saul Lieberman et al. 3 vols. Jerusalem, 1965.

Lieberman, Saul. *Tosefta ki-Fshutah: A Comprehensive Commentary on the Tosefta* (Hebrew). 8 vols. New York, 1955–73.

Liebes, Y. "Christian Influences on the *Zohar*" (Hebrew). *Jerusalem Studies in Jewish Thought* 2 (1982), 43–74.

Liebes, Y. "Ha-Mashiaḥ shel ha-*Zohar.*" In *Ha-Ra'ayon ha-Mᵉshiḥi bᵉ-Yisra'el,* pp. 87–236. Jerusalem, 1982.

Linton, Ralph. *The Study of Man.* New York, 1936.

Loewenstamm, Samuel E. *Comparative Studies in Biblical and Ancient Oriental Literature.* Alter Orient und Altes Testament 204. Neukirchen, 1980.

Loewenstamm, Samuel E. "Man as the Image and Son of God" (Hebrew). *Tarbiz* 27 (1957), 1–2.

Lohfink, Norbert. "Die Abänderung der Theologie des priesterlichen Geschichtswerks im Segen des Heiligkeitgesetzes." In *Wort und Geschichte: Festschrift für Karl Elliger zum 70. Geburtstag,* pp. 129–36. Alter Orient und Altes Testament 18. Kevelaer, 1973.

Lohfink, Norbert. "'Macht euch die Erde untertan?'" *Orientierung* 38 (1974), 137–42.

Lohfink, Norbert. "Die Priesterschrift und die Geschichte." In *Congress Volume: Göttingen, 1977,* pp. 189–225. Supplements to *VT* 29. Leiden, 1978.

Loretz, Oswald. *Die Gottenbildlichkeit des Menschen.* Munich, 1967.

Lottin, Otto. *Le droit naturel chez Saint Thomas d'Aquin et ses prédécesseurs.* 2nd ed. Brussels, 1931.

Lottin, Otto. "Le péché originel chez Albert le Grand, Bonaventure et Thomas d'Aquin." *Recherches de théologie ancienne et médiévale* 12 (1940), 235–328.

Louis, Conrad. *The Theology of Psalm VIII: A Study of the Traditions of the Text and the Theological Import.* Catholic University of America Studies in Sacred Theology 99. Washington, D.C., 1946.

Lovejoy, Arthur O. "The Entangling Alliance of Religion and History." *Hibbert Journal* 5 (1907), 258–76.

Lovejoy, Arthur O. *The Great Chain of Being: A Study of the History of an Idea.* Cambridge, Mass., 1936.

Lowy, S. "The Extent of Jewish Polygamy in Talmudic Times." *Journal of Jewish Studies* 9 (1958), 115–38.

Ludwig, Theodore M. "The Tradition of Establishing the Earth in Deutero-Isaiah." *JBL* 92 (1973), 345–57.

Luke, K. "The Biblical Account of Creation and Terrestrial Realities." *Jeevadhara* 8 (1978), 101–20.

Lyons, Faith. "Some Notes on the *Roman de la Rose:* The Golden Chain and Other Types in Jean de Meun." In *Studies in Medieval Literature and Languages in Memory of Frederick Whitehead*, pp. 201–8. Ed. W. Rothwell et al. Manchester, 1973.

Macomber, William F. "The Theological Synthesis of Cyrus of Edessa, an East Syrian Theologian of the Mid-Sixth Century." *Orientalia christiana periodica* 30 (1964), 5–38.

Mahoney, John. "Alice of Bath: Her 'Secte' and 'Gentil Text.'" *Criticism* 6 (1964), 144–55.

Markus, R. A. "'Imago' and 'similitudo' in Augustine." *Revue des études augustiniennes* 10 (1965), 125–43.

Marmorstein, A. "Ideas of Resurrection in the Aggadah of the Amoraim" (Hebrew). *Metsudah* 2 (1943), 94–105.

Marti, Karl. "Die Spuren der sogennanten Grundschrift des Hexateuchs in der vorexilischen Propheten des Alten Testaments." *Jahrbucher für protestantische Theologie* 6 (1880), 127–61, 308–54.

Matt, Daniel C. "The Mystic and the *Mizwot.*" In *JS*, pp. 367–404.

McCarthey, Dennis J. "Covenant-Relationships." In *Questions disputées d'Ancien Testament: Methode et théologique*, pp. 91–103. Ed. C. Brekelmans. Bibliotheca ephemeridum theologicarum lovaniensium 33. Louvain, 1974.

McCarthey, Dennis J. "'Creation' Motifs in Ancient Hebrew Poetry." In *COT*, pp. 74–89.

McCarthey, Dennis J. *Old Testament Covenant: A Survey of Current Opinions.* Richmond, Va., 1972.

McCarthey, Dennis J. *Treaty and Covenant: A Study in Form in the Ancient Oriental Documents and in the Old Testament.* Analecta biblica 21. Rome, 1963.

McEvenue, Sean E. *The Narrative Style of the Priestly Writer.* Analecta biblica 50. Rome, 1971.

McKane, William. *A Critical and Exegetical Commentary on Jeremiah.* International Critical Commentary. Vol. 1. Edinburgh, 1986.

McKane, William. *Proverbs: A New Approach.* Philadelphia, Pa., 1970.

McKenzie, John J. *The Anchor Bible: Second Isaiah.* Garden City, N.Y., 1968.

McKenzie, John J. *Myths and Realities: Studies in Biblical Theology.* Milwaukee, Wis., 1963.

Mendecki, N. "Die Sammlung und die Hineinführung in das Land in Jer. 23,3." *Kairos* 25 (1983), 99–103.

Meyers, Carol L. "Gender and Genesis 3:16 Revisited." In *The Word of the Lord Shall Go Forth: Essays in Honor of David Noel Freedman*, pp. 337–54. Ed. Meyers and M. O'Connor. Winona Lake, Ind., 1983.

Meyers, Carol L. "Procreation, Production, and Protection: Male-Female Balance in Early Israel." *Journal of the American Academy of Religion* 51 (1983), 569–83.

Milgrom, Jacob. "The Biblical Diet Laws as an Ethical System." *Interpretation* 17 (1963), 288–301.

Milgrom, Jacob. Review of *Before Abraham Was: The Unity of Genesis 1–11*, by Isaac M. Kikawada and Arthur Quinn. *Judaism* 35 (1986), 371–74.

Milgrom, Jacob. *Studies in Cultic Theology and Terminology*. Studies in Judaism in Late Antiquity 36. Leiden, 1983.

Millard, A. R. "A New Babylonian Genesis Story." *Tyndale Bulletin* 18 (1967), 3–18.

Miller, J. Maxwell. "In the 'Image' and 'Likeness' of God." *JBL* 91 (1972), 289–304.

Miller, Patrick D., Jr. "El, the Creator of Earth." *Bulletin of the American Schools of Oriental Research* 239 (1980), 43–46.

Miller, Patrick D., Jr. *Genesis 1–11: Studies in Structure and Theme*. JSOT Supplement Series 8. Sheffield, 1978.

Mitchell, Christopher Wright. *The Meaning of "Brk" ("To Bless") in the Old Testament*. Society of Biblical Literature Dissertation Series 95. Atlanta, Ga., 1987.

Monsengivo Pasinya, L. "Le cadre littéraire de Genèse 1." *Biblica* 57 (1976), 225–41.

Moran, W. L. "Atrahasis: The Babylonian Story of the Flood." *Biblica* 52 (1971), 51–61.

Morse, Charlotte C. *The Pattern of Judgment in the "Queste" and "Cleanness."* Columbia, Mo., 1978.

Mowinckel, Sigmund. *The Psalms in Israel's Worship*. Tr. D. R. Ap-Thomas. 2 vols. New York, 1962.

Müller, Michael. *Die Lehre des hl. Augustinus von der Paradiesesehe und ihre Auswirkung in der Sexualethik des 12. und 13. Jahrhunderts bis Thomas von Aquin*. Studien zur Geschichte der katholischen Moraltheologie 1. Regensburg, 1954.

Muscatine, Charles. *Chaucer and the French Tradition: A Study in Style and Meaning*. Berkeley, Calif., 1957.

Napier, B. D. "On Creation-Faith in the Old Testament." *Interpretation* 16 (1962), 21–42.

Neusner, Jacob. *Aphrahat and Judaism: The Christian-Jewish Argument in Fourth-Century Iran*. Studia post-biblica 11. Leiden, 1971.

Neusner, Jacob. *Comparative Midrash: The Plan and Program of "Genesis Rabbah" and "Leviticus Rabbah."* Brown Judaic Studies 111. Atlanta, Ga., 1986.

Neusner, Jacob. *Genesis and Judaism: The Perspective of "Genesis Rabbah"—An Analytical Anthology*. Brown Judaic Studies 108. Atlanta, Ga., 1985.

Neusner, Jacob. "*Genesis Rabbah* as Polemic: An Introductory Account." *Hebrew Annual Review* 9 (1985), 253–65.

Neusner, Jacob. *The Integrity of "Leviticus Rabbah": The Problem of the Autonomy of a Rabbinic Document*. Brown Judaic Studies 93. Chico, Calif., 1985.

Neusner, Jacob. *Judaism: The Evidence of the Mishnah*. Chicago, 1981.

Neusner, Jacob. *Messiah in Context: Israel's History and Destiny in Formative Judaism*. The Foundations of Judaism: Method, Teleology, Doctrine 2. Philadelphia, Pa., 1984.

Neusner, Jacob. *The Rabbinic Traditions about the Pharisees before 70*. 3 vols. Leiden, 1971.

Neusner, Jacob. "Scripture and Tradition in Judaism, with Special Reference to the Mishnah." In *Approaches to Ancient Judaism: Volume II*, pp. 173–91. Ed. William Scott Green. Brown Judaic Studies 9. Chico, Calif., 1980.

Niditch, Susan. "The Cosmic Adam: Man as Mediator in Rabbinic Literature." *Journal of Jewish Studies* 34 (1983), 137–46.

Nielsen, Eduard. "Creation and the Fall of Man." *HUCA* 43 (1972), 1–22.

Nikiprowetzky, V. *Le commentaire de l'Ecriture chez Philon d'Alexandrie.* Arbeiten zur Literatur und Geschichte des hellenistisches Judentums 11. Leiden, 1977.

Nitzche, J. C. "Creation in Genesis and Nature in Chaucer's *General Prologue* 1–18." *Papers on Language and Literature* 14 (1978), 459–64.

Noonan, John T., Jr. *Contraception: A History of Its Treatment by the Catholic Theologians and Canonists.* Enlarged ed. Cambridge, Mass., 1986.

Norris, Richard A. *God and World in Early Christian Theology: A Study in Justin Martyr, Irenaeus, Tertullian, and Origen.* London, 1967.

Norris, Richard A. *Manhood and Christ: A Study in the Christology of Theodore of Mopsuestia.* Oxford, 1963.

Noth, Martin. *A History of Pentateuchal Traditions.* Tr. Bernhard W. Anderson. Englewood Cliffs, N.J., 1972.

Novak, David. *The Image of the Non-Jew in Judaism: An Historical and Constructive Study of the Noahide Laws.* Toronto Studies in Theology 14. New York, 1983.

Oakley, Francis. *Omnipotence, Covenant, and Order: An Excursion in the History of Ideas from Abelard to Leibniz.* Ithaca, N.Y., 1984.

O'Connell, Robert J. *St. Augustine's Confessions: The Odyssey of Soul.* Cambridge, Mass., 1969.

O'Connell, Robert J. *St. Augustine's Early Theory of Man, A.D. 386–391.* Cambridge, Mass., 1968.

O'Connor, Daniel, and Francis Oakley, eds. *Creation: The Impact of an Idea.* New York, 1969.

Oden, Robert A. "Transformations in Near Eastern Myths: Genesis 1–11 and the Old Babylonian Epic of Atrahasis." *Religion* 11 (1981), 21–37.

Oldenburg, Ulf. *The Conflict between El and Ba'al in Canaanite Religion.* Supplementa ad *Numen,* Altera series, Dissertationes ad historiam religionum pertinentes 3. Leiden, 1969.

O'Meara, John Joseph. *The Creation of Man in Augustine's "De Genesi ad litteram."* Villanova, Pa., 1980.

O'Meara, John Joseph. *The Young Augustine: The Growth of St. Augustine's Mind up to His Conversion.* London, 1954.

Onians, Richard Broxton. *The Origins of European Thought about the Body, the Mind, the Soul, the World, Time, and Fate.* Cambridge, 1954.

Orbe, Antonio. *Antropología de San Ireneo.* Biblioteca de autores cristianos 286. Madrid, 1969.

Orbe, Antonio. "La definición de hombre en la teología del siglo II°." *Gregorianum* 48 (1967), 522–76.

Orbe, Antonio. "El pecado original y el matrimonio en la teologia del s. II." *Gregorianum* 45 (1964), 449–500.

Pagels, Elaine H. "Adam and Eve, Christ, and the Church: A Survey of Second-Century Controversies Concerning Marriage." In *The New Testament and Gnosis: Essays in Honour of Robert McL. Wilson,* pp. 146–75. Ed. A. H. B. Logan and A. J. M. Wedderburn. Edinburgh, 1983.

Pagels, Elaine H. *Adam, Eve, and the Serpent.* New York, 1988.

Pagels, Elaine H. "Exegesis and Exposition of the Genesis Creation Accounts in Selected Texts from Nag Hammadi." In *Nag Hammadi, Gnosticism, and Early Christianity,* pp. 257–85. Ed. Charles W. Hedrick and Robert Hodgson, Jr. Peabody, Mass., 1986.

Paré, Gerard. *Les idées et les lettres au xiiie siècle: Le "Roman de la Rose."* Montreal, 1947.

Patai, Raphael. *Sex and Family in the Bible and the Middle East.* Garden City, N.Y., 1959.

Pedersen, Johannes. *Israel: Its Life and Culture.* 2 vols. London, 1926–40.

Pelland, Gilles. *Cinq études d'Augustin sur le début de la Genèse.* Paris, 1972.

Pettazzoni, Raffaele. "Myths of Beginnings and Creation Myths." In *Essays on the History of Religions,* pp. 24–36. By Raffaele Pettazzoni. Studies in the History of Religions (Supplements to *Numen*) 1. Leiden, 1954.

Pohlenz, Max. *Die Stoa: Geschichte einer geistigen Bewegung.* 4th ed. 2 vols. Göttingen, 1970–72.

Polzin, Robert. *Late Biblical Hebrew: Toward a Typology of Biblical Hebrew Prose.* Harvard Semitic Monographs 12. Missoula, Mont., 1976.

Pope, Marvin H. *El in the Ugaritic Texts.* Supplements to *VT* 2. Leiden, 1955.

Porten, Bezalel, and Uriel Rappaport. "Poetic Structure in Gen 9.7." *VT* 21 (1971), 363–69.

Porter, Frank Chamberlin. "The Pre-existence of the Soul in the Book of Wisdom and in the Rabbinical Writings." In *Old Testament and Semitic Studies in Memory of William Rainey Harper,* pp. 205–69. Ed. Robert Francis Harper et al. Chicago, 1908.

Porton, Gary C. *Understanding Rabbinic Midrash: Text and Commentary.* Hoboken, N.J., 1985.

Pratt, Robert A. "Chaucer's 'Natal Jove' and 'Seint Jerome . . . agayn Jovinian.'" *Journal of English and Germanic Philology* 61 (1962), 244–48.

Preus, James S. *From Shadow to Promise: Old Testament Interpretation from Augustine to the Young Luther.* Cambridge, Mass., 1969.

Quasten, Johannes. *Patrology.* 3 vols. 1950; repr., Westminster, Md., 1986.

Rabbinovicz, Raphael N. N. *History of the Printing of the Talmud* (Hebrew). Ed. A. M. Habermann. Jakob Michel Library: Translations and Collections in Jewish Studies 12. Jerusalem, 1965.

Rakover, Nahum. "Yaḥase ʾIshut bi-Khfiyyah ben Baʿal lᵉ-ʾIshto." *Shᵉnaton ha-Mishpaṭ ha-ʿIvri* 6–7 (1979–80), 295–317.

Ravitsky, Aviezer. "The Anthropological Theory of Miracles in Medieval Jewish Philosophy." In *Studies in Medieval Jewish History and Literature,* 2:231–72. Ed. Isadore Twersky. Cambridge, Mass., 1984.

Renckens, Henricus. *Urgeschichte und Heilsgeschichte: Israels Schau in die Vorgangenheit nach Gen. 1–3.* Mainz, 1959.

Rendsburg, Gary A. *The Redaction of Genesis.* Winona Lake, Ind., 1986.

Richardson, Alan. *Genesis I–XI: Introduction and Commentary.* London, 1953.

Ricoeur, Paul. "Sur l'exégèse de Genèse 1,1–2,4a." In *Exégèse et herméneutique,* pp. 67–84. By Roland Barthes et al. Paris, 1971.

Robbins, Frank Egleston. *The Hexaemeral Literature: A Study of the Greek and Latin Commentaries on Genesis.* Chicago, 1912.

Robertson, D. W., Jr. *A Preface to Chaucer: Studies in Medieval Perspectives.* Princeton, N.J., 1962.

Robinson, Gnana. "The Biblical View of Man." *Indian Journal of Theology* 27 (1978), 137–49.

Robinson, H. Wheeler. *Inspiration and Revelation in the Old Testament.* 1946; repr., Oxford, 1960.

Rogerson, J. W. "The Old Testament View of Nature." In *Instruction and Interpretation: Studies in Hebrew Language, Palestinian Archaeology, and Biblical Exegesis,* pp. 67–84. By H. A. Brongers et al. Oudtestamentische Studien 20. Leiden, 1977.

Roitman, Betty. "Sacred Language and Open Text." In *Midrash and Literature,* pp. 159–75. Ed. Geoffrey H. Hartman and Sanford Budick. New Haven, Conn., 1986.

Rondet, Henri. *Original Sin: The Patristic and Theological Background.* Staten Island, N.Y., 1972.

Rordorf, Bernard. "'Dominez la terre' (Gn 1,28)." *Bulletin du Centre protestant d'études* 31 (1979), 5–39.

Rosenberg, Joel W. "The Garden Story Forward and Backward: The Non-Narrative Dimension of Gen. 2–3." *Prooftexts* 1 (1981), 1–27.

Rosner, Fred. "The Illness of King Hezekiah and the 'Book of Remedies' Which He Hid." *Koroth* 9 (1985), 190–97.

Ross, Allen P. "The Dispersion of the Nations in Genesis 11:1–9." *Bibliotheca sacra* 138 (1981), 119–38.

Ross, Allen P. "The Table of Nations in Genesis 10: Its Structure." *Bibliotheca sacra* 137 (1980), 340–53.

Ross, Allen P. "The Table of Nations in Genesis 10: Its Content." *Bibliotheca sacra* 138 (1981), 22–34.

Runia, David T. *Philo of Alexandria and the "Timaeus" of Plato.* Philosophia antiqua 44. Leiden, 1986.

Sacks, Robert. "The Lion and the Ass: A Commentary on the Book of Genesis (Chapters 1–10)." *Interpretation: A Journal of Political Philosophy* 8 (1980), 29–101; 9 (1980), 1–81.

Sage, A. "Péché originel: Naissance d'un dogme." *Revue des études augustiniennes* 13 (1967), 211–48.

Sailhamer, John. "Exegetical Notes: Genesis 1:1–2:4a." *Trinity Journal* 5 (1984), 73–82.

Sanders, E. P. *Paul and Palestinian Judaism: A Comparison of Patterns of Religion.* Philadelphia, Pa., 1977.

Sandys-Wunsch, John. "Before Adam and Eve—or What the Censor Saw." *Studies in Religion* 11 (1982), 23–28.

Sant, C. "The Promise Narratives in Genesis." *Melita theologica* 11 (1959), 1–13; 12 (1960), 14–27.

Sapp, Stephen. *Sexuality, the Bible, and Science.* Philadelphia, Pa., 1977.

Sarna, Nahum M. *Understanding Genesis: The Heritage of Biblical Israel.* 1966; repr., New York, 1970.

Sasson, Jack M. "'Tower of Babel' as a Clue to the Redactional Structuring of the Primeval History [Gen. 1–11:9]." In *The Bible World: Essays in Honor of Cyrus Gordon,* pp. 211–19. Ed. Gary Rendsburg et al. New York, 1980.

Schmid, H. H. "Creation, Righteousness, and Salvation: 'Creation Theology' as the Broad Horizon of Biblical Theology." In *COT,* pp. 102–17.

Schmid, Herbert. "Die 'Mutter Erde' in der Schöpfungsgeschichte der Priesterschrift." *Judaica* 22 (1968), 237–43.

Schmidt, Werner H. *Die Schöpfungsgeschichte der Priesterschrift: Zur Überlieferungsge-schichte von Genesis 1,1–2,4a und 2,4b–3,24*. Wissenschaftliche Monographien zum Alten und Neuen Testament 17. 3rd ed. Neukirchen, 1973.

Scholem, Gershom. *Elements of the Kabbalah and Its Symbolism* (Hebrew). Tr. Joseph Ben-Shlomo. Jerusalem, 1976.

Scholem, Gershom. *Kabbalah*. New York, 1974.

Scholem, Gershom. *Origins of the Kabbalah*. Ed. R. J. Z. Werblowsky. Tr. Alan Arkush. Philadelphia, Pa., 1986.

Scholem, Gershom. *Ursprung und Anfänge der Kabbala*. Studia judaica 3. Berlin, 1962.

Schwanz, Peter. *Imago Dei als christologisch-anthropologisches Problem in der Geschichte der alten Kirche von Paulus bis Clemens von Alexandrien*. Halle, 1970.

Scroggs, Robin. *The New Testament and Homosexuality: Contextual Background for Contemporary Debate*. Philadelphia, Pa., 1983.

Scult, A., et al. "Genesis and Power: An Analysis of the Biblical Story of Creation." *Quarterly Journal of Speech* 72 (1986), 113–31.

Segal, M. H. *A Grammar of Mishnaic Hebrew*. 1927; repr., Oxford, 1970.

Segal, Robert A. *The Poimandres as Myth: Scholarly Theory and Gnostic Meaning*. Religion and Reason 33. Berlin, 1986.

Shapiro, David S. "Be Fruitful and Multiply." *Tradition* 13:4–14:1 (1973), 42–67.

Shinan, Avigdor. "The Sin of Nadab and Abihu in Rabbinic Literature" (Hebrew). *Tarbiz* 48 (1979), 201–14.

Silverstein, Theodore. "The Fabulous Cosmogony of Bernardus Silvestris." *Modern Philology* 46 (1948), 92–116.

Silvia, Daniel S., Jr. "The Wife of Bath's Marital State." *Notes and Queries* 212 (1967), 8–10.

Smalley, Beryl. *The Study of the Bible in the Middle Ages*. 3rd ed. Oxford, 1983.

Smith, Gary V. "Structure and Purpose in Genesis 1–11." *Journal of the Evangelical Theological Society* 20 (1977), 307–19.

Smith, Morton. "The Image of God: Notes on the Hellenization of Judaism, with Especial Reference to Goodenough's Work on Jewish Symbols." *BJRL* 40 (1958), 473–512.

Snell, Bruno. *The Discovery of the Mind: The Greek Origins of European Thought*. Tr. T. G. Rosenmeyer. Oxford, 1953.

Soggin, J. Alberto. *Old Testament and Oriental Studies*. Biblica et orientalia 29. Rome, 1975.

Soviv, Aaron. "The Confirmation of Noah's Blessing." *Dor le-Dor* 9 (1981), 144–47.

Speiser, E. A. *The Anchor Bible: Genesis*. Garden City, N.Y., 1967.

Speiser, E. A. "Leviticus and the Critics." In *Yehezkel Kaufmann Jubilee Volume: Studies in Bible and Jewish Religion Presented to Yehezkel Kaufmann on the Occasion of His Seventieth Birthday*, pp. 29–45. Ed. Menahem Haran. Jerusalem, 1960.

Spring, David, and Eileen Spring, eds. *Ecology and Religion in History*. New York, 1974.

Stadelmann, Luis I. J. *The Hebrew Conception of the World: A Philological and Literary Study*. Analecta biblica 39. Rome, 1970.

Staffner, Hans. "Die Lehre des Hl. Augustinus über das Wesen der Erbsünde." *Zeitschrift für katholische Theologie* 79 (1957), 385–416.

Steck, Odil Hannes. *World and Environment.* Nashville, Tenn., 1980.

Steinberg, Leo. *The Sexuality of Christ in Renaissance Art and Modern Oblivion.* New York, 1983.

Stephanou, E. "Le sixième jour de l'Hexaeméron de S. Basile." *Echos d'Orient* 31 (1932), 385–98.

Stock, Brian. *Myth and Science in the Twelfth Century: A Study of Bernard Silvester.* Princeton, N.J., 1972.

Stow, Kenneth R. "The Jewish Family in the Rhineland in the High Middle Ages: Form and Function." *American Historical Review* 92 (1987), 1085–110.

Strack, Hermann L., and Paul Billerbeck, *Kommentar zum neuen Testament aus Talmud und Midrasch.* 6 vols. in 7 pts. Munich, 1922–61.

Stuhlmueller, Carroll. "The Theology of Creation in Second Isaias." *CBQ* 21 (1959), 429–67.

Talmage, Frank. "Apples of Gold: The Inner Meaning of Sacred Texts in Medieval Judaism." In *JS,* pp. 313–55.

Ta-Shema, I. "Eretz-Israel Studies" (Hebrew). *Shalem* 1 (1974), 81–95.

Tavormina, M. Teresa. " 'Bothe Two Ben Gode': Marriage and Virginity in *Piers Plowman* C. 18.68–100." *Journal of English and Germanic Philology* 81 (1982), 320–30.

Testa, Emmanueli. *Genesi: Versione, introduzione, note.* 4th ed. Rome, 1981.

Testuz, Michel. *Les idées religieuses du Livre des Jubilés.* Geneva, 1960.

Thompson, P. E. S. "The Yahwist Creation Story." *VT* 21 (1971), 197–208.

Tierney, Brian. *Medieval Poor Law: A Sketch of Its Canonical Theory and Its Application in England.* Berkeley, Calif., 1959.

Tierney, Brian. "*Natura id est Deus:* A Case of Juristic Pantheism?" *Journal of the History of Ideas* 24 (1963), 307–22.

Tishby, Peretz. "Concerning the Enactments (*Taqqanot*) of Rabbenu Gershom Me'or Haggolah: Was the Prohibition against Polygamy Enacted by Rabbenu Gershom?" (Hebrew). *Tarbiz* 34 (1965), 49–55.

Tobin, Thomas H. *The Creation of Man: Philo and the History of Interpretation.* CBQ Monograph Series 14. Washington, D.C., 1983.

Toeg, Arie. "Genesis I and the Sabbath" (Hebrew). *Beth Mikra* 17 (1972), 288–96.

Toy, Crawford H. *A Critical and Exegetical Commentary on the Book of Proverbs.* ICC. New York, 1904.

Trible, Phyllis. *God and the Rhetoric of Sexuality.* Overtures to Biblical Theology 2. Philadelphia, Pa., 1978.

Turmel, J. "Le dogme du péché originel dans Saint Augustin." *Revue d'histoire et de littérature religieuses* 6 (1901), 385–426, 7 (1902), 128–46, 209–30.

Tuve, Rosemund. *Allegorical Imagery: Some Medieval Books and Their Posterity.* Princeton, N.J., 1966.

Twomey, Michael William. "The Anatomy of Sin: Violations of *Kynde* and *Trawthe* in *Cleanness.*" Ph.D. Dissertation, Cornell University, Ithaca, N.Y., 1979.

Urbach, Ephraim E. " 'Kol Ha-meqayyem Nefesh Aḥat . . .': Development of the Version, Vicissitudes of Censorship, and Business Manipulations of Printers" (Hebrew). *Tarbiz* 40 (1971), 268–84.

Urbach, Ephraim E. "The Laws Regarding Slavery as a Source for Social History of the Period of the Second Temple, the Mishnah and Talmud." *Papers of the Institute of Jewish Studies, London* 1 (1964), 1–94.

Urbach, Ephraim E. *The Sages: Their Concepts and Beliefs.* Tr. Israel Abrahams. 2 vols. Jerusalem, 1975.

VanderKam, James C. *Textual and Historical Studies in the Book of Jubilees.* Harvard Semitic Monographs 14. Missoula, Mo., 1977.

Van Seters, John. *Abraham in History and Tradition.* New Haven, Conn., 1975.

Vermes, Geza. *Scripture and Tradition in Judaism.* Leiden, 1963.

Vink, J. G. "The Date and Origin of the Priestly Code in the Old Testament." In *The Priestly Code and Seven Other Studies,* pp. 1–144. By J. G. Vink et al. Oudtestamentische Studien 15. Leiden, 1969.

Vogel, Manfred H. "Man and Creation According to the Religious Tradition of Judaism." *Service internationale de documentation judeo-chrétienne* 12 (1979), 5–23.

Von Rad, Gerhard. *Genesis: A Commentary.* Tr. John H. Marks. 9th ed. Philadelphia, Pa., 1972.

Von Rad, Gerhard. *The Problem of the Hexateuch and Other Essays.* Tr. E. W. Trueman Dicken. New York, 1966.

Von Rad, Gerhard. *Wisdom in Israel.* Tr. James D. Martin. Nashville, Tenn., 1972.

Wallace, Howard N. *The Eden Narrative.* Harvard Semitic Monographs 32. Atlanta, Ga., 1985.

Weigand, Rudolf. *Die Naturrechtslehre der Legisten und Dekretisten von Irnerius bis Accursius und von Gratian bis Johannes Teutonicus.* Münchener theologische Studien 3,26. Munich, 1967.

Weimar, Peter. "Struktur und Komposition der priesterschriftlichen Geschichtsdarstellung." *Biblische Notizen* 23 (1984), 81–134.

Weinfeld, Moshe. *Deuteronomy and the Deuteronomic School.* Oxford, 1972.

Weinfeld, Moshe. *Getting at the Roots of Wellhausen's Understanding of the Law of Israel on the 100th Anniversary of the "Prolegomena."* Jerusalem, 1981.

Weinfeld, Moshe. "God the Creator in Gen. I and in the Prophecy of Second Isaiah" (Hebrew). *Tarbiz* 37 (1968), 105–32.

Weinfeld, Moshe. "Jeremiah and the Spiritual Metamorphosis of Israel." *ZAW* 88 (1976), 17–56.

Weinfeld, Moshe. "Sabbath, Temple Building, and the Enthronement of the Lord" (Hebrew). *Beth Mikra* 22 (1967), 188–93.

Weiss, Meir. *The Bible from Within: The Method of Total Interpretation.* Jerusalem, 1984.

Weissman, Hope Phyllis. "Antifeminism and Chaucer's Characterization of Women." In *Geoffrey Chaucer: A Collection of Original Articles,* pp. 93–110. Ed. George D. Economou. New York, 1975.

Weissman, Hope Phyllis. "Margery Kempe in Jerusalem: *Hysterica Compassio* in the Late Middle Ages." In *Acts of Interpretation: The Text in Its Contexts, 700–1600: Essays on Medieval and Renaissance Literature in Honor of E. Talbot Donaldson,* pp. 201–17. Ed. Mary J. Carruthers and Elizabeth D. Kirk. Norman, Okla., 1982.

Weissman, Hope Phyllis. "Why Chaucer's Wife Is from Bath." *Chaucer Review* 15 (1980), 11–36.

Wellhausen, Julius. *Prolegomena to the History of Ancient Israel.* Cleveland, Ohio, 1957.

Westermann, Claus. *Creation.* Tr. John J. Scullion. Philadelphia, Pa., 1974.

Westermann, Claus. *Elements of Old Testament Theology.* Tr. Douglas W. Stott. Atlanta, Ga., 1982.

Westermann, Claus. *Genesis 1–11: A Commentary.* Tr. John J. Scullion. Minneapolis, Minn., 1984.

Westermann, Claus. *Genesis 12–36: A Commentary.* Tr. John J. Scullion. Minneapolis, Minn., 1985.

Westermann, Claus. *Genesis 37–50: A Commentary.* Tr. John J. Scullion. Minneapolis, Minn., 1986.

Westermann, Claus. *Isaiah 40–66: A Commentary.* Tr. David M. G. Stalker. Philadelphia, Pa., 1969.

Westermann, Claus. "Der Mensch im Urgeschehen." *Kerygma und Dogma* 13 (1976), 231–46.

Westermann, Claus. *The Promises to the Fathers: Studies on the Patriarchal Narratives.* Tr. David E. Green. Philadelphia, Pa., 1980.

Wetherbee, Winthrop. "The Literal and the Allegorical: Jean de Meun and the *De planctu Naturae.*" *Medieval Studies* 33 (1971), 264–91.

White, Hugh C. "Word Reception as the Matrix of the Structure of the Genesis Narrative." In *The Biblical Mosaic: Changing Perspectives,* pp. 61–83. Ed. Robert Polzin and Eugene Rothman. Philadelphia, Pa., 1972.

White, Lynn, Jr. "Continuing the Conversation." In *Western Man and Environmental Ethics: Attitudes towards Nature and Technology,* pp. 55–65. Ed. Ian G. Barbour. Reading, Mass., 1973.

White, Lynn, Jr. "The Historic Roots of Our Ecologic Crisis." *Science* 155 (1967), 1203–7.

Whitley, C. F. *The Genius of Ancient Israel: The Distinctive Nature of the Basic Concepts of Israel Studied against the Cultures of the Ancient Near East.* Amsterdam, 1969.

Widengren, Geo. "Early Hebrew Myths and Their Interpretations." In *Myth, Ritual, and Kingship: Essays on the Theory and Practice of Kingship in the Ancient Near East and in Israel,* pp. 149–203. Ed. S. H. Hooke. Oxford, 1958.

Widengren, Geo. "The King and the Tree of Life in Ancient Near Eastern Religion (King and Saviour, IV)." *Uppsala Universitets Årsskrift* 1951, no. 4.

Wilson, Robert R. *Genealogy and History in the Biblical World.* Yale Near Eastern Researches 7. New Haven, Conn., 1977.

Wingren, Gustav. *God, Man, and the Incarnation: A Study in the Biblical Theology of Irenaeus.* Philadelphia, Pa., 1959.

Wolff, Hans Walter. *Anthropology of the Old Testament.* Philadelphia, Pa., 1974.

Wolff, Werner. *Changing Concepts of the Bible: A Psychological Analysis of Its Words, Symbols, and Beliefs.* New York, 1951.

Wolfsekel, Cornelia W. "Some Remarks with Regard to Augustine's Conception of Man as the Image of God." *Vigiliae christianae* 30 (1976), 63–71.

Wolfson, Elliot R. "Circumcision, Vision of God, and Textual Interpretation: From Midrashic Trope to Mystical Symbol." *History of Religions* 27 (1987), 189–215.

Wolfson, Harry Austryn. *Philo: Foundations of Religious Philosophy in Judaism, Christianity, and Islam.* 2 vols. Cambridge, Mass., 1947.

Woudstra, M. H. "The *Toledot* of the Book of Genesis and Their Redemptive-Historical Significance." *Calvin Theological Journal* 5 (1970), 184–89.

Yarbrough, O. Larry. *Not Like the Gentiles: Marriage Rules in the Letters of Paul.* Society of Biblical Literature Dissertation Series 80. Atlanta, Ga., 1985.

Yegerlehner, David Anthony. "'Be Fruitful and Multiply, and Fill the Earth . . .': A History of the Interpretation of Genesis 1:28a and Related Texts in Selected Periods." Ph.D. Dissertation, Boston University, Boston, Mass., 1975.

Zahlten, Johannes. *Creatio mundi: Darstellungen der sechs Schöpfungstage und naturwissenschaftliches Weltbild im Mittelalter.* Stuttgarter Beiträge zur Geschichte und Politik 13. Stuttgart, 1979.

Zeitlin, Solomon. "Slavery during the Second Commonwealth and the Tannaitic Period." *JQR*, n.s. 53 (1963), 185–218.

Zevit, Ziony. "Converging Lines of Evidence Bearing on the Date of P." *ZAW* 94 (1982), 481–511.

Zimmerli, Walther. *1. Mose 1–11: Die Urgeschichte.* 2nd ed. Zurich, 1957.

Zimmerli, Walther. *Ezekiel 2: A Commentary on the Book of the Prophet Ezekiel, Chapters 25–48.* Tr. James D. Martin. Philadelphia, Pa., 1983.

Zimmerli, Walther. *Der Mensch und seine Hoffnung im Alten Testament.* Göttingen, 1968.

Zimmerli, Walther. *The Old Testament and the World.* Tr. John J. Scullion. Atlanta, Ga., 1976.

Zimmerli, Walther. "Ort und Grenze der Weisheit im Rahmen der alttestamentlichen Theologie." In *Les sagesses du Proche-Orient ancien (Colloque de Strasbourg, 17–19 Mai 1962),* pp. 121–36. Paris, 1963.

Zuidema, W. "Les lois noachiques dans la plus ancienne littérature rabbinique." In *Noé, l'homme universel,* pp. 44–71. Ed. J. Chopineau et al. Publications de l'Institutum iudaicum 3. Brussels, 1978.

Index

Library of Congress Cataloging-in-Publication Data

Cohen, Jeremy, 1953–
    Be fertile and increase, fill the earth and master it : the
ancient and medieval career of a Biblical text/Jeremy Cohen.
      p. cm.
    Bibliograph: p.
    Includes index.
    ISBN 0–8014–2307–4 (alk. paper)
    1. Bible.   O.T. Genesis I, 28—Criticism, interpretation, etc.—
History. I. Title.
BS1235.2.C633   1989
222'.1106—dc20   89–7149